THE OXFORD HANDBOOK OF

SPORTS ECONOMICS

VOLUME 2

THE OXFORD HANDBOOK OF

SPORTS ECONOMICS

VOLUME 2: ECONOMICS THROUGH SPORTS

Edited by

STEPHEN SHMANSKE

and

LEO H. KAHANE

OXFORD

UNIVERSITY PRESS

OXFORD
UNIVERSITY PRESS

Oxford University Press, Inc., publishes works that further
Oxford University's objective of excellence
in research, scholarship, and education.

Oxford   New York
Auckland   Cape Town   Dar es Salaam   Hong Kong   Karachi
Kuala Lumpur   Madrid   Melbourne   Mexico City   Nairobi
New Delhi   Shanghai   Taipei   Toronto

With offices in
Argentina   Austria   Brazil   Chile   Czech Republic   France   Greece
Guatemala   Hungary   Italy   Japan   Poland   Portugal   Singapore
South Korea   Switzerland   Thailand   Turkey   Ukraine   Vietnam

Published by Oxford University Press, Inc.
198 Madison Avenue, New York, New York 10016
www.oup.com

Oxford is a registered trademark of Oxford University Press

Library of Congress Cataloging-in-Publication Data
The Oxford handbook of sports economics / edited by Leo H. Kahane and Stephen Shmanske.
p. cm.
Includes bibliographical references and index.
ISBN 987-0-19-538777-3 (cloth : alk. paper) (vol. 1)
ISBN 978-0-19-538778-0 (cloth : alk. paper) (vol. 2)
1. Sports—Economic aspects.   I. Kahane, Leo H.   II. Shmanske, Stephen, 1954–
GV716.O94 2011
796.06'91—dc22
2010036086

1 3 5 7 9 8 6 4 2
Printed in the United States of America
on acid-free paper

CONTENTS

VOLUME 2: ECONOMICS THROUGH SPORTS

PART I   THE ECONOMICS OF DISCRIMINATION

PART II   ILLUSTRATIONS OF PRODUCTION THEORY

PART III   ILLUSTRATIONS OF ECONOMETRIC METHODS

PART IV   ILLUSTRATIONS OF INDUSTRIAL ORGANIZATION

PART V   ILLUSTRATIONS OF FINANCE

PART VI   ILLUSTRATIONS OF PUBLIC FINANCE

PART VII   MISCELLANY

Contributors

Peter von Allmen, Department of Economics and Business, Moravian College

Robert A. Baade, A. B. Dick Professor of Economics, Lake Forest College

David J. Berri, Department of Economics & Finance, Southern Utah University

Michael Bognanno, Department of Economics, Temple University

Richard C. K. Burdekin, Jonathan B. Lovelace Professor of Economics, Claremont McKenna College

Helmut Dietl, Institute for Strategy and Business Economics, University of Zurich

Karl W. Einolf, Department of Business, Accounting and Economics, Mount Saint Mary's University

David Forrest, Centre for the Study of Gambling, University of Salford

Rodney Fort, Department of Sport Management, University of Michigan

Egon Franck, Institute for Strategy and Business Economics, University of Zurich

Harold O. Fried, Department of Economics, Union College

Martin Grossmann, Institute for Strategy and Business Economics, University of Zurich

Bruce K. Johnson, James Graham Brown Professor of Economics, Centre College

Leo H. Kahane, Department of Economics, Providence College

Lawrence M. Kahn, Cornell University, CESifo, IZA, and NCER (Australia)

Anthony C. Krautmann, Department of Economics, DePaul University

Markus Lang, Institute for Strategy and Business Economics, University of Zurich

Young Hoon Lee, Department of Economics, Sogang University

Eva Marikova Leeds, Department of Economics and Business, Moravian College

Michael A. Leeds, Department of Economics, Temple University

Neil Longley, Isenberg School of Management, University of Massachusetts

Joseph P. McGarrity, Economics Department, University of Central Arkansas

Rodney Paul, Department of Finance, St. Bonaventure University

Daniel A. Rascher, Sport Management Program, University of San Francisco

Andrew D. Schwarz, OSKR, LLC

Martin B. Schmidt, Department of Economics, College of William and Mary

Stephen Shmanske, Department of Economics, California State University, East Bay

Loren W. Tauer, Department of Applied Economics and Management, Cornell University

Stephen J. K. Walters, Department of Economics, Loyola University Maryland

Andrew P. Weinbach, Department of Accounting, Finance, and Economics, Coastal Carolina University

John C. Whitehead, Department of Economics, Appalachian State University

Preface to Volume Two:
Economics Through Sports

THIS is the second volume of a two-volume effort to capture the essence and variety of the quickly growing field of sports economics. In arranging these volumes we have divided the field into two thematically separate but often overlapping parts: *The Economics of Sports* (the first volume) and *Economics Through Sports* (this volume). Specifically, in thinking about the field it struck us that many lines of inquiry were essentially economic analyses of certain institutions in sports, like league structure, salary caps, the NCAA, and international labor mobility. Meanwhile, the abundant, high-quality data about salary, performance, competition between teams, and expected and actual outcomes of specific games allow economists to test a variety of propositions that have larger social consequences such as discrimination, antitrust, efficient markets, and managerial efficiency. Admittedly, the separation is not always complete, and many of the chapters in these volumes hit on both themes. Nevertheless, the two-volume approach has helped us to organize our thoughts on sports economics and helped us to organize the research we have received from nearly every important author in the field of sports economics.

In Volume 1, the chapters show how the tools that economists have developed are useful in analyzing the sometimes peculiar aspects of the sports industry. Does competitive balance in leagues increase the social surplus? What do salary caps and luxury taxes do? Is the NCAA a cartel? What are the implications of differences in league structure, playoff structure, or the rules of the game? These are some of the interesting questions addressed there. As such, economic analysis can help guide those responsible for institutional structure in the industry of sports.

The tables are turned in Volume 2. Now it is time for the sports industry to help economists and economics. Both the quality and quantity of data that are available in studying sports provide an exceptional laboratory within which to address, by analogy, larger social or economic issues. Thus, the data from sports allow us to test and illustrate economic theories in specific, relatively well-controlled, settings. This allows economists to present theoretical arguments about the workings of the world at large backed up by some supporting empirical evidence. For example, economists can test theories of discrimination by looking at race in baseball, gender in golf, and national origin in hockey. Economists can test alternative forms of production relationships by looking at how inputs are turned into outputs in individual and team sports. And economists can make similar inroads in testing their theories in the areas of finance, public finance, industrial organization, and econometrics. This volume, divided into seven parts, achieves its goal of looking at economics and economic theories through the lens of sports statistics and institutions because of the remarkable collection of original research by experts in the field of sports economics.

In Part I, the Economics of Discrimination, four chapters address discrimination in four different sports settings. Stephen Walters examines organized baseball's racial record as far back as the 1880s, when segregation took root in baseball, through Branch Rickey's hiring of Jackie Robinson in 1947, up to the present day. Along the way, the models and tests of statistical discrimination are presented and critiqued. Lawrence M. Kahn uses basketball as the laboratory to look at discrimination in pay, hiring, and retention against black NBA players and coaches, and gender discrimination among college coaches. The good news is that the discrimination that was documented in the NBA in the 1980s has declined in the subsequent decades. Stephen Shmanske looks at evidence of gender discrimination in professional golf. Mirroring society at large, males on the PGA Tour consistently earn more than females on the LPGA tour. However, differences in pay are not evidence of discrimination if there are differences in productivity. In industrial society, productivity differences by gender are hard to measure and verify, but not so in professional golf. Males play more and play better, and when controlling for the skills that the golfers bring to the tournament, evidence of gender discrimination disappears. Finally, Neil Longley replicates for hockey what others have done for baseball and basketball, with the interesting exception that alleged discrimination in hockey falls along the lines of language and national origin rather than along racial grounds. Although less so than in earlier years, there may still be some evidence of de facto segregation with fewer French Canadian players on English Canadian teams than might otherwise be expected. As was the case for the chapters on baseball, basketball, and golf, interesting avenues for future research are laid out for hockey as well.

In Part II, Illustrations of Production Theory, five chapters address production theory in five different ways. Anthony Krautmann starts off with an analysis of the baseball production function. Referring to work in earlier studies, Krautmann obtains a list of variables to include in attempting to model a team's number of wins during a season. Thus, along with slugging average, on-base percentage, and earned run average, to capture offense and defense he looks at managerial inputs, league effects, and ballpark-specific effects. David Berri reports on one of his passions, efficiency in production in NBA basketball. He examines several empirical attempts to quantify the productivity of NBA players, and argues that models should be judged both on the consistency of the measures through time and on the correlation with winning percentages. Ad hoc combinations of statistics and incompletely thought through use of plus/minus do not fare as well as the theoretically grounded measure that Berri comes up with. Young Hoon Lee examines another aspect of production theory, namely, the assessment of managerial efficiency using frontier models. Intuitively, teams have skill inputs that managers direct with the goal of producing wins. The better the manager is at obtaining wins relative to the talent level he has, the better is the manager. But this is not a trivial econometric problem to resolve. Lee discusses several methods that have been used to examine managerial efficiency. Harold Fried and Loren Tauer examine a related problem: How well does an individual manage his or her own talent to achieve high performance in an individual sport? Fried and Tauer's setting is LPGA golf. Their methods, in stemming primarily from an operations research setting rather than a statistical regression setting are somewhat different from those which Lee discusses, but the goal is the same, finding out how well a given set of inputs are utilized to produce output. Once the measures of efficiency are calculated, Fried and Tauer examine whether they are affected by age and experience. Finally, in still another variation on a theme, Leo Kahane examines the issue of salary dispersion and its effect on productivity. Kahane examines two competing hypotheses. Earlier models focus on how salary dispersion can provide incentive to work hard thus increasing productivity. Alternatively, more recent theories suggest that too much salary dispersion could negatively impact employee morale and cohesiveness. Kahane uses salary and performance data from the NHL to distinguish between these theoretical alternatives, thus weighing in on an important issue in labor economics and industrial relations.

In Part III, Illustrations of Econometric Methods, three chapters are able to explore and illustrate advances in econometric specification and testing using excellent data sets that are collected in sports settings. Each of the three chapters concentrates on the demand for attendance at sporting events, while seriously considering critiques that are leveled at simple specifications that regress attendance on price and a set of control variables. In the first chapter, David Forrest carefully pursues the insight that the full cost of attending a sporting event includes the ticket price as well as the time costs and travel costs incurred by the fans. Forrest explains the Travel Cost Method (TCM) and applies it using a detailed data set collected in an annual survey of consumers of games sponsored by the FA Premier League in English football. The improved measure of price and quantity that come out of the TCM and the data developed in the sports industry help explain the puzzle/conundrum that other demand studies have run into. Namely, the empirical finding that demand is inelastic, which is inconsistent with simple profit maximization in the uniform price monopoly model, comes from the misspecification in simpler models and disappears in Forrest's work. Martin Schmidt focuses on another problem that comes up in OLS specifications of demand for attendance, namely, the censoring of the data that comes about because of capacity constraints on game-day attendance. Using high-quality data about NFL attendance, Schmidt explains why and shows how a Tobit estimation technique is superior to OLS for testing propositions about price and demand shift variables in the context of the demand to attend sporting events. Generally speaking, the OLS estimates are biased and provide underestimates of several important explanatory variables. The third chapter in this section, by Richard Burdekin, examines several additional concerns about the estimation of an attendance demand function. In particular, Burdekin notes that there are multiple prices and multiple categories of consumer with potentially different demand elasticities to consider in the set of those in attendance at a specific game. Burdekin also notes that price is likely to be endogenous when a longer run perspective is taken. For either of these reasons, a simple OLS model with attendance as a function of only one price variable on the right-hand side, will yield estimates that are biased and misleading.

In Part IV, Illustrations of Industrial Organization, three chapters examine aspects of competition in the sporting world that vividly illustrate theoretical topics in the field. Rodney Fort looks at the history of Major League Baseball (MLB) and examines three cases of competition from rival leagues. In each of the cases the behavior of MLB is best explained as joint venture attempts to exclude entry and eliminate competition in the supply of the highest quality baseball competition. League behaviors like talent raiding and strategic expansion timed to respond to the threat of entry, which would arguably be antitrust targets if pursued in other industries, are carefully documented by Fort. In the second chapter, Robert Baade looks at the market structure of professional sports, focusing on its peculiar uniqueness. What becomes evident is that the interests of the league, on the one hand, and the individual teams, on the other, are in conflict much in the same way that cartel interests diverge from those of individual members. The chapter examines these conflicts for the cases of team relocation and stadium construction, showing how they can be analyzed by simple game theory. Thus, Baade uses the real world sports examples to illustrate theoretical issues in industrial organization and game theory. In the final chapter, Karl W. Einolf also examines the issue of spatial location decisions by leagues. Einolf shows how technical models from management science and industrial engineering that are designed to address the location of a firm's plants or outlets can usefully be employed to study location and entry into sports leagues. One might expect that leagues would locate teams in order to maximize the number of local fans with direct exposure, or equivalently, to minimize a metric of distance between the fans and the teams. However, due to revenue sharing and national media contracts, the local gate revenues may be less important to the league than the ability to negotiate favorable subsidies or tax treatments from local governments. Einolf is able to show discrepancies between "optimal" (based solely on population) location and actual location for each of the major North American sports leagues, and is able to predict where the most beneficial league expansions should occur.

In Part V, Illustrations of Finance, two separate avenues of combining sports-generated data with financial data or financial theory are explored. Eva Marikova Leeds and Michael A. Leeds examine the theory and application of event studies in sports. Event studies correlate movements in asset values to the timing of real world events that might be theoretically expected to affect those asset values. The authors completely explain the methodology and data sources, and they review and critique a number of studies showing the imaginative use to which sports economists have put event analysis. For example, at the micro level, event studies have been used to show whether signing a sports celebrity to an endorsement contract affects the stock value, whether becoming an official sponsor of events like the Olympics, a NASCAR race, the Tour de France, or a tennis tournament affects firm value, or whether buying the naming rights of a new stadium is valuable. At the macro level, event analysis has been used to study the impact on the economy as a whole of events like staging a successful Olympic Games, winning (or losing) a bid to host the Olympics, or even winning or losing an important World Cup Soccer match. Any economist thinking about starting an event study should make the Leeds and Leeds chapter the first stop. The chapter by Rodney J. Paul and Andrew P. Weinbach examines the literature that uses sports gambling markets as an analogy to financial markets. In financial markets, prices capture the relevant available information in the sense that arbitrage assures that no pure profit opportunities are available. In sports gambling markets, point spreads or odds are set in a similar fashion. Paul and Weinbach call into question the usual assumption that sports books attempt to earn riskless profit by acting solely as a middleman by "balancing the book" so that winning bettors are paid with losing bettor's money. They show that for Major League Baseball, the sports books are not "balanced." The authors describe how setting odds as unbiased predictors of the game outcome, instead of balancing the book, is a profitable long-term strategy despite the extra risk inherent in the unbalanced book on each particular line. Consistent with the theme of this volume, the amount and quality of the data once again allow important inferences to be drawn about real world markets.

In Part VI, Illustrations of Public Finance, two chapters use the sports economics setting to theoretically describe and critique important issues in the field. Peter von Allmen examines the multiplier model in the context of the local impact of expenditures on sports infrastructure. The topic, of course, is much wider than sports. Government expenditures on highways, housing, mass transit, museums, parks, golf courses, and even stem cell research are often claimed to bring generalized macroeconomic benefits that are a multiple of the original direct spending. However, there are many theoretical reasons to question the size of the multiplier, if not its very existence. These arguments are explicated in the context of investments in sports stadiums, and the record of such is examined to cast doubt upon the magnitude of the multiplier and the verity of the multiplier argument. Bruce K. Johnson and John C. Whitehead take up the task of using surveys to quantify ex ante the value of a public investment project that offers both an excludable benefit stream and an intangible, subjectively valued benefit stream. The Contingent Valuation Method (CVM) attempts to find out how much a person would be willing to pay, say in increased taxes, to receive the benefits of a public investment project such as a subsidy to a sports stadium. The authors point out several biases that can creep into such calculations. In an examination of the evidence, it appears that the intangible benefit stream is only a fraction of the public cost, and calls into question the wisdom of such public subsidies. The CVM line of research has been most developed in the context of subsidies to sports, but as the authors point out, is potentially useful in many other areas as long as the drawbacks of the technique are recognized and accounted for. Once again, we have an example of research in the sports economics arena having valuable spillover benefits to public finance in general.

Finally, Part VII, Miscellany, includes four chapters that do not fit neatly into any of the other categories. There actually could be many more chapters in this section as a quick review of any recent issue of any of the several journals in the field could attest. The editors apologize for including only those that our limited imaginations could come up with when we put the volumes together. Joseph P. McGarrity uses data on hit batsmen from Major League Baseball to illustrate a mixed-strategy, game theoretic approach to the decisions of the pitcher and the batter. The societal implications come from analogizing from this situation to the real world situation of criminal behavior and optimal, costly, deterrence/ enforcement. In the analogy, the batter is the "criminal" by crowding the plate, and the pitcher is the "police" exerting costly deterrence by throwing inside pitches. The cost of the deterrence to the pitcher is that a hit batsman reaches first base. Meanwhile, the amount of the criminal sanction depends on how hard the pitcher throws. The results indicate that when the criminal penalty increases, as in greater pitch velocity, the costly enforcement effort of the police decreases, as in fewer inside pitches. Daniel A. Rascher and Andrew D. Schwarz use a baseball laboratory in a completely different manner. They examine the ticket pricing behavior of the clubs to illustrate the theory of price discrimination. Our rough count identified at least 37 different kinds of price discrimination in the chapter. Rascher and Schwarz also show that as price discrimination becomes more refined and more profitable, it also opens new opportunities for various subsets of demand and thus amounts to a win-win situation for both the baseball teams and their fans. Helmut Dietl, Egon Franck, Martin Grossman, and Markus Lang examine contest theory in their chapter. The authors show how contest theory has been greatly refined in the sports economics literature to focus attention on issues such as fixed versus flexible talent supply and outcomes such as "overinvestment" in talent. But these issues and outcomes have application in a variety of settings other than sports competition, including: promotion contests, market-share contests, patent race contests, litigation, art competitions, beauty pageants, political campaigns, and military conflicts. Sporting contests are in many ways cleaner, more open, and more easily observable, so that theoretical and empirical study of them provides a useful knowledge framework within which to examine the multitude of examples cited above. Finally, Michael L. Bognanno examines a seven-year period of Professional Bowling Association tournaments to examine the effectiveness of the incentive structure in bringing about effort and performance. The beauty of looking at the bowling data is that the prize structures are not as uniform from tournament to tournament as in other sports. Thus, variation in the prize structure can be used to tease out the incentive effects. The essence of tournament theory is that increased differences in prizes lead to increased effort and performance, a result that is strongly upheld in the bowling data. Outside of the sporting world, institutional salary structures largely depend upon this positive relationship between effort and reward, so it is nice to have empirical verification of the result.

We are sure you will enjoy the chapters in this volume. For those new to the field, the work is invaluable in highlighting and characterizing the existing literature and in pointing the direction to new unanswered questions. For those already familiar with sports economics and with the work of those authors included herein, such as ourselves, there is always something new to learn. We found the organizing and editing of these volumes to be interesting, entertaining, and informative. This job was so enjoyable that we sometimes marvel that we actually get paid to do it. We suspect that you will want to read these volumes from cover to cover.

PART I

....

THE
ECONOMICS OF
DISCRIMINATION

....

CHAPTER 1

PREJUDICE AND PROGRESS IN BASEBALL

LESSONS ON THE ECONOMICS OF RACE AND DISCRIMINATION

STEPHEN J. K. WALTERS

1. INTRODUCTION

ANYONE who doubts that bias is an old and widespread problem need only consult the Book of Leviticus (27:3–4), which reports that the Lord once advised Moses that "a man between twenty and sixty years of age shall be valued at fifty silver shekels ...; a woman shall be valued at thirty shekels."[1]

Perhaps believing the study of prejudice and its consequences to be the domain of psychologists and sociologists (if not theologians), however, economists largely ignored the topic until 1957, when future Nobel Laureate Gary Becker published his doctoral dissertation, *The Economics of Discrimination*. Becker ingeniously modeled prejudice as a "taste for discrimination" in which an individual would be willing to incur costs in order to associate with some persons instead of others; showed how such a taste could have different implications depending on whether it originated with employers, employees, or consumers; and, most provocatively, argued that under perfect competition, prejudiced employers could be driven out of the market in the long run, even absent government strictures against discrimination (Becker, 1971).[2] His thinking spawned an enormous and growing volume of theoretical and empirical work on the nature and effects of discrimination in labor markets and elsewhere.

Professional baseball, it turns out, provides a rich opportunity to test Becker's theories—as well as alternative "statistical discrimination" models in which differential treatment of workers results from uncertainty about an individual's productivity (Phelps, 1972; Aigner and Cain, 1977). As is well known, long before federal legislation made employment discrimination illegal in the United States, baseball was integrated when Branch Rickey hired Jackie Robinson to play for the Brooklyn Dodgers in 1947. Indeed, since Becker was a teenager in Brooklyn at the time and a confessed sports fan (Becker, 1993), it is tempting to speculate that—consciously or not—his observation of Robinson's celebrated achievements in overcoming the prejudices of fellow players, fans, and owners might have contributed to his interest in the topic, if not the development of his theories. In any case, baseball's long and well-documented history, the availability of detailed statistics on the individual productivity of its players (in contrast to other industries, in which performance is often so difficult to measure that researchers must rely on information relating to workers' characteristics rather than their actual output) and even the existence of related markets (e.g., for memorabilia) make it a unique "field laboratory" in which the implications of economists' speculations may be scrutinized.

In what follows, the sport's racial record will be examined in some detail, with two goals in mind. First, it is hoped that readers unfamiliar with the extant economic research on discrimination—in baseball, or more generally—will find this discussion to be a useful and accessible introduction to this topic and summary of what we know about it. Second, those already familiar with this research should find some interesting topics for future inquiry lurking about, for there is obviously a great deal that remains unknown or unresolved.

Though the great preponderance of the literature on the baseball labor market relates to the period after integration, that is not where this discussion begins. The "back story" of Robinson's entry into the National League also contains much illustrative material that can shed light on discrimination's causes and effects; hopefully, providing some historical and institutional information on baseball's segregated era will encourage researchers to devote more attention to this period. Section 2 describes how baseball became segregated; 3 discusses segregation's feedback effects on black players' labor supply decisions; 4 provides data on black-white earning differences prior to re-integration of the sport; 5 considers why re-integration took so long and how it ultimately occurred; 6 discusses Robinson's breakthrough and its immediate aftermath; 7 discusses the empirical literature on the post-integration period; and 8 presents some concluding remarks.

2. THE EVOLUTION OF SEGREGATION

In the years after its Civil War, America was burdened by many prejudices and hatreds, but it was not yet committed to strict racial segregation and ugly intolerance. Surely many—perhaps most—whites considered blacks their intellectual and physical inferiors, and separation of the races was customary in many communities. In some areas, however, more progressive views prevailed. Whether to be fair and just or simply to share in the benefits flowing from the talents of the four million people newly freed from slavery, many sought to integrate African Americans into the country's social and economic mainstream. Of course, those efforts met with considerable resistance and ultimately would end in failure that would take decades to reverse. Baseball, which was evolving into America's "National Pastime" during the same period, would both mirror this conflict and affect its resolution.

Two of the sport's iconic figures of this era typified the competing interests. Cap Anson was one of baseball's greatest hitters and most successful managers in a career that lasted from 1871 to 1897 and won him induction into the sport's Hall of Fame. He was also an unapologetic racist. John Montgomery Ward's career was shorter (1878–1894) but marked by adaptability and innovativeness. A league-leading pitcher, he switched to shortstop after an arm injury and became an accomplished hitter, base-stealer, and manager, also earning induction into the Hall of Fame—and celebrity as the husband of a famous actress of the day and leader of an effort to unionize players and limit their exploitation by team owners.

Anson began a personal but very visible campaign to segregate baseball in August 1883, when he saw a dark-skinned player named Moses Fleetwood Walker warming up for the Toledo club of the Northwestern League prior to an exhibition game against Anson's mighty Chicago White Stockings of the National League. His contemptible response—"Get that nigger off the field!"—has been much written about. Less well known is that, at least that day, Anson's bigotry was confronted and his bluff not to play if Walker did was called: Toledo's manager threatened to cancel the game (thus causing the forfeit of all gate receipts) if Walker didn't play; both he and Anson did so (Zoss and Bowman, 2004, p. 136). But over the next few years, Anson made clear his preference for segregated leagues, and his status as the most famous player of his time doubtless emboldened others to act on their prejudices. Despite many ugly incidents,[3] however, some headway toward integration was being made: in 1884 Walker's Toledo club joined the American Association (the National League's main rival), thus making him the first black player in a recognized major league. By 1887, at least fourteen blacks were playing on a dozen predominantly white teams at various levels (White and Malloy, 1995, p. 163).[4] A popular periodical of the day, *Sporting Life,* would ask "How far will this mania for engaging colored players go? At the present rate of progress the International League [a minor league one step below major-league status] may ere many moons change its name to 'Colored League'" (White and Malloy, 1995, p. xx).

Ward had begun lobbying the president of his New York Giants to acquire a black pitcher named George Stovey in 1886, motivated largely by the desire to catch Anson's White Stockings in the National League standings. In this endeavor, he presaged Rickey, whose interest in Robinson sixty years later was also, at least in part, a product of his desire to enable his Brooklyn Dodgers to compete more effectively for fans against the two other teams in New York—the Giants and the Yankees. Ward's efforts got a boost during an April 1887 exhibition game against Newark of the International League in which Stovey outpitched the Giants' top hurler and catcher Fleet Walker threw out Ward—who would that year set a National League record for steals that endured until 1974—trying to swipe second base (Stevens, 1998, p. 53). Clearly, this "colored battery" could help the Giants contend for the league pennant, and a trade for both players was rumored to be in place until "a brawl was heard from Chicago to New York" (White and Malloy, 1995, p. 76). Anson asserted that "there's a law against that" (Zoss and Bowman, 2004, p. 138), and the deal collapsed. In truth, there was no such law, but custom was on Anson's side—and he soon made clear that violating tradition might involve costs. Prior to a scheduled July, 1887, exhibition game against Newark, Anson announced that he and his White Stockings would not take the field if Stovey or Walker did. This time his threat succeeded: Newark kept both players on the bench that day. The episode heightened club owners' fears that similar showdowns could mean the loss of considerable gate receipts. The next day, International League owners voted—its six segregated teams outpolling its four integrated ones—not to sign any more black players (though those already in the league could continue). The National League adopted no formal resolution preventing the acquisition of blacks, but its customary whites-only policy was now established as a "gentleman's agreement." There would be no more African American players in the major leagues until Robinson's arrival in 1947; their numbers in the minors dwindled steadily until, by 1900, none remained.

This crucial period illustrates at least two key elements of Becker's theory—but also raises some interesting questions. First, it appears to provide a straightforward illustration of the consequences of employee prejudice. Though press accounts during this era contain evidence of racial bias among some fans (in the form of occasionally boorish behavior toward black players or teams) and the "gentleman's agreement" in the National League shows that some team owners shared this prejudice, it seems clear that white players—in effect, the Ansons, who likely outnumbered or outshouted the Wards—most actively sought a segregated workplace. Their occasional threats not to take the field against black opponents (and forfeit wages) signaled their willingness to "pay something ... in the form of a reduced income" (Becker, 1971, p. 14) to avoid playing with or against blacks. Further, the ultimate result—all-white teams in all-white leagues—was as Becker predicted: given the white workers' obvious tastes, putting together integrated workplaces would not have been profit-maximizing even for unbiased employers, since doing so would necessarily require paying white workers in such circumstances more than whites in segregated firms (Becker, 1971, p. 56).[5]

Second, conduct like Ward's and various teams' and leagues' interest in hiring blacks—unmistakably "perfect substitutes in production" for whites[6]—is quite consistent with Becker's predictions about how competitive conduct and heterogeneous tastes for discrimination among employers should play out over time (Becker, 1971, pp. 44–45). Baseball was still reasonably competitive in those days (i.e., league entry and exit conditions were far more liberal than they would ultimately become), market pressures were leading blacks to be hired by the least-prejudiced employers in the industry, and these firms evidently were growing relative to more-prejudiced ones (as seen by the ascendance of teams such as Toledo to major status). It would have been very interesting to see how baseball—and perhaps American racial history—might have evolved differently had players' biases not been so important and had this competitive dynamic been allowed to play out more fully.

The players' success in having their preferences served raises some interesting issues for future research. Becker understood that unions could implement workers' biases (Becker, 1971, pp. 62–63), but there were no players' unions involved in this affair—and when one did form it was run by Ward and aimed entirely at ending owners' use of the monopsonistic "reserve clause" that bound players to teams forever (Stevens, 1998). How workers might pursue collectively utility- or income-maximizing objectives absent some formal (union) governance structure appears to be under-studied. Another question in this case is whether Anson's followers truly shared his prejudices (at least to such a strong extent) or whether they sensed pecuniary gain if owners could be persuaded to limit or bar entry by substitute workers. In Becker's model, employer discrimination against blacks reduces the return to white capital but raises the return to white labor (Becker, 1971, pp. 21–22). In other words, white players might have had an incentive to represent to owners that they were strongly biased against blacks even if they weren't.[7]

3. ENDOGENOUS LABOR SUPPLY

One of the most troubling and noteworthy outcomes of baseball's U-turn toward full segregation in the late 1880s is its effect on the labor supply decisions of black athletes. Though the evidence here is anecdotal and fragmentary, it appears that the quantity and quality of African American ballplayers declined (for at least a while) after 1890. Sol White was black baseball's first historian and played professionally in 1887–1909 (five seasons on integrated teams, 18 on all-black ones); his assessments on the matter must be accorded great weight. He described the years 1885–1890 as "the money period" during which "colored base ball flourished," while "[1891] marked the decline of colored base ball in the

East for several years" (White and Malloy, 1995, p. 20). Indeed, there was only a single black professional team in the United States in 1892–1894 (Peterson, 1970, p. 49). White wrote in 1907 that "when [the colored professional] looks into the future he sees no place ... even were he superior to Lajoie or Wagner, Waddell or Mathewson. ... Consequently, he loses interest. He knows that, so far shall I go, and no farther, and, as it is with the profession, so it is with his ability" (White and Malloy, 1995, p. 118).

The effect of unequal opportunities on workers' initial skill levels appears to be another under-studied topic. Lundberg and Startz (1983) provided a model in which human capital investment decisions are affected by discrimination, Neal and Johnson (1996) noted the importance of "premarket factors" (e.g., the quantity or quality of schooling acquired by minority groups) in explaining existing wage gaps, and Loury (1998) argued that past discrimination can result in "patterns of behavior among poor blacks which lead to seemingly self-imposed limits on their acquisition of skills" (p. 121). Nevertheless, there appears to be little empirical research assessing whether or how much beliefs about future discrimination affect individuals' decisions to make investments that can affect their ability to compete in the labor force—though see Goldin, Katz, and Kuziemko (2006) for some evidence that the removal of obstacles to female advancement in certain sectors (along with other factors) has had dramatic effects on the proportion of women choosing to attend college.

African Americans who did seek careers in professional baseball were, until 1920, generally limited to playing on all-black teams in non-league settings that involved "barnstorming" from place to place. The absence of leagues' competitive structures and rewards—and of minor league systems where apprenticeships could be served—could not have helped black players enhance their baseball-specific skills. As well, many barnstorming teams incorporated various entertainment elements into their games in order to attract fans. One, for example, promoted its appearances by having its players ride bicycles about town in full-dress suits with silk umbrellas, offering to play local teams thus attired (Zoss and Bowman, 2004, p. 139). This was a way to make a living, but also diverted energy from the types of developmental activities that might help players "climb the ladder" and earn a job in the big leagues—except, of course, such jobs were now clearly unavailable anyway. As well, on-field clowning reinforced some negative stereotypes held by many whites, likely contributing—over decades of segregated ball—to the kinds of presumptions about ability that economists would ultimately describe in statistical models of discrimination (in which, e.g., employers base hiring decisions on what they believe to be valid inferences about productivity or risk). One reporter for a New York daily, for example, would write in 1934 that "a Negro ball game is not a staid and stolid demonstration of fielding and hitting. It embodies comic relief impossible in white games because no Caucasian can play baseball with the rhythmic quality inherent in the black race" (Lanctot, 2004, p. 227).

4. WAGE GAPS

It wasn't until 1920 that eight of the more successful Midwestern barnstorming teams formed a somewhat stable black league; in 1923 six Eastern teams formed a rival league. Both were under-capitalized and struggled financially, and it wasn't until the mid-1930s that successor leagues were on reasonably firm financial ground. By the early 1940s the Negro Leagues might have been the largest black-dominated industry in the United States (though there were a few white owners); average annual gross revenues were a little over $100,000 per team (Peterson, 1970, p. 93), though variance was high, with a few high-profile teams dominating league standings and banking much higher profits than marginal teams. Given the smaller average crowds at Negro League games and the lower incomes of black attendees, it is no surprise that white major league clubs grossed about $700,000 per team per year over the same period (Fort, 2009).

Equally unsurprising, therefore, is the large and persistent observed wage gap between players in the white and black major leagues. Sol White estimated in 1907 that white major leaguers earned average annual salaries about 4.3 times those of black professionals of the day (White and Malloy, 1995, p. 67). Subsequent individual salary data are hard to find, but Michael Haupert (2007; 2009) dug financial data for selected black and white teams out of their archives and found even greater wage gaps later in the segregated era. For example, in 1927 the Birmingham Black Barons were an elite team, narrowly losing the Negro National League pennant to the Chicago American Giants but featuring the most famous black pitcher of the day, Satchel Paige. The average salary of the players on the best white major league team in 1927, the New York Yankees, was 17 times that of the average Barons player, and even six times Paige's salary. There is evidence in Haupert's data, however, that the wage gap was closing as the Negro Leagues became better established: by 1942, average salaries on the Yankees were about eight times those on the Newark Eagles, a perennial contender in the reconstituted Negro National League, and by 1946 the Yankees:Eagles wage ratio was 4:1.

Though far more time-series data on the white:black wage ratio in the years leading up to integration is needed to confirm whether this apparent trend toward rising relative black incomes was real, the available information points to another interesting (and under-studied) issue: though cut off from (white) Organized Baseball, black players may have benefited from a far more competitive labor market *within* the Negro Leagues. In part this may have been because of the informality of those leagues and a general tendency for clubs not to rely on formal contracts with their players; alternatively, this informality may have been a by-product of the fact that Negro League clubs were not governed by white baseball's National Agreement, in which teams agreed to respect others' contracts—especially the "reserve clause," which bound a player to a particular team in perpetuity (unless his team sold, traded, or released him). The net result was that Negro League clubs frequently raided their rivals for top talent—and, presumably, bid these players' salaries closer to their marginal revenue products (though that was much lower than it would have been in an integrated setting). Teams in Organized Baseball never engaged in such raids during this era; Scully (1974) estimated that, as a result, the exploitation ratio (the amount of a player's marginal revenue product retained by owners under the reserve clause) was 79 to 88 percent for hitters and 80 to 90 percent for pitchers. No one has attempted to assess whether freer player movement within the Negro Leagues led to lower (league-specific) exploitation ratios, or whether the effective absence of a reserve clause in this setting affected competitive balance or other characteristics of the industry.

5. LEAST-PREJUDICED EMPLOYER(S)

Even if the white:black wage ratio was falling over time, it was generally sizable enough—and the industry competitive enough—for entrepreneurially minded white baseball executives and owners to consider disturbing the segregated equilibrium. In 1901, the greatest field manager of the era, John McGraw, tried to sign a black second baseman named Charlie Grant to play for his Baltimore Orioles of the American League by changing his name to Charlie Tokohama and presenting him as a Native American. In 1915, the manager of Portland in the Pacific Coast League (one step below the majors) tried to sign non-white players (including one of Chinese-Hawaiian parentage) until his players rebelled. It was rumored in 1929 that Connie Mack, owner-manager of the Philadelphia Athletics of the American League, sought to integrate his team, and Bill Veeck reportedly planned to buy the Philadelphia Phillies of the National League in 1943 and stock the club with the top stars of the Negro Leagues (Peterson, 1970, pp. 55–57, 171–174, 180). Again, even this segregated era appears consistent with Becker's model of heterogeneous tastes for discrimination amid competitive pressures.

A key question is why it took so long for these pressures to result in the demise of baseball's color line. It is likely that America's level of racial bias rose at various times during this era both in the South (where Jim Crow laws flourished) and North (where race riots were tragically common with the beginning of the Great Migration of blacks northward after 1915). Defenders of baseball's "gentleman's agreement" commonly argued that, though they personally were not biased, the intolerance of players (about a third of whom were from Southern states) or fans made integration impractical. But this begs the question. There were managers and owners willing to put such assertions to a market test, so why didn't they get the chance? Becker's model implies that it is not the tastes of the most prejudiced or even the average employer that determine relative wages and employment rates of favored and disfavored groups, but those of the marginal employer (Becker, 1971, pp. 43–47). Is baseball's long embrace of segregation—even as the growth and prominence of the Negro Leagues made clear that there were many highly productive black players available at low cost—contrary to this prediction?

The answer might be found in baseball's peculiar governance structure and an accident of history. After some corrupt Chicago White Sox players "fixed" the 1919 World Series, major league owners tried to control the damage arising from this scandal by hiring a commissioner with broad powers to act in "the best interests of the game." The man selected, federal judge Kenesaw [sic] Mountain Landis, would rule the sport with an iron hand until his death in 1944. The problem, according to one baseball historian, is that "[Landis] was not only a bigot but also a hypocrite, making public statements that 'no regulations' barred Negroes from Organized Baseball while making it clear that any club trying to hire one would have to deal with him" (Koppett, 2004, p. 222). In effect, the authority that owners vested in the commissioner's office made the marginal competitor's tastes for discrimination far less relevant than Landis's, who may have felt—quite apart from any personal racial animus (or lack thereof)—that his job entailed enforcing the average owner's preferences, which most certainly favored the segregated status quo. Luckily, Landis's successor—a former Kentucky governor named Happy Chandler—did not stand in Branch Rickey's way when the latter signed Jackie Robinson for the Dodgers. Chandler later explained that he "didn't want to meet his maker one day having made the wrong decision on such an important issue" (McNary, 2006, p. 38).

6. ROBINSON AND BEYOND: THE PACE AND EFFECTS OF INTEGRATION

Rickey's motives in signing Robinson have been the subject of considerable speculation; some argue that he was guided by moral principles and religious belief, others by simple greed. Support for the latter view comes from Rickey's determination not to pay Robinson's former employer, the Kansas City Monarchs of the Negro American League, to assign his contract to the Dodgers. Under the National Agreement, minor-league clubs that uncovered or developed talented players routinely received $25,000 to $100,000 to sell them to big-league teams, costs that Rickey sought to avoid by inventing the sport's "farm system" developmental approach years earlier, when he ran the St. Louis Cardinals. In this case, he insisted that the Negro Leagues were not governed by the Agreement, insultingly called them "a racket" with no formal contracts he needed to respect, and ignored Robinson's verbal agreement with the Monarchs. That deal had paid Robinson a mere $400 monthly, and Rickey offered $600 plus a modest signing bonus (Peterson, 1970, p. 190). Since the major league average salary at the time was a little over $1,000 monthly (Fort, 2009), Rickey got a wonderful bargain.

And the Dodgers' executive had done his homework and chosen exactly the right player. Robinson was college-educated (UCLA), a veteran, a teetotaler, and, though fiercely competitive, so perfectly self-controlled as to withstand the incredible volume of insults and even physical assaults he would have to endure as the man who would break baseball's color line.[8] The literature on his monumental triumph is vast and deservedly adulatory, and his on-field performance and off-field character were of such stellar quality that other teams soon began to imitate the Dodgers—though some dragged their feet, and the Boston Red Sox (owned by a Southern "sportsman" named Tom Yawkey, who on this record must qualify as the owner having the greatest "taste for discrimination") would remain all-white until 1959.

In one of the first empirical assessments of the pace and consequences of integration in baseball, Gwartney and Haworth (1974) found that "low discriminators" obtained a competitive advantage over their rivals in the 1950s, winning more games (after adjusting for initial team quality) via the substitution of highly productive black stars for the marginal whites who had previously occupied their positions. They also found no evidence of customer discrimination during this era, with each black player on a team's roster increasing its annual attendance by roughly 2.8 percent of the average team's annual figure during this period (Fort, 2009) after controlling for the team's improved record.[9] Indeed, given the significant on-field and financial benefits accruing to low discriminators, the authors conclude that the only surprise was baseball's slow pace of integration: five years after Robinson's breakthrough, less than half of big-league teams were desegregated.[10]

Goff, McCormick, and Tollison (2002) modeled racial integration as an innovative process, and found support in baseball's hiring record over 1947–1971 for a "managerial alertness hypothesis" in which teams that were simply better managed—that is, winners—were the leaders in desegregating the sport, in contrast to an "external incentive hypothesis" in which poorer teams might innovate sooner because the potential rewards of doing so were proportionately greater. They also concluded that it took roughly twenty to twenty-five years for baseball to reach an integrated equilibrium in which marginal white and black players were of equal productivity—a period corresponding roughly to the interval necessary for all the owners and managers from the segregated era to exit the industry. Hanssen and Meehan (2009), however, have argued that the model used by Goff et al. is misspecified and that the evidence on their alternative hypotheses is inconclusive, while Coyne et al. (2007) have argued that the innovators were those who judged that their teams could profit by contending more successfully even if some fans held a taste for discrimination. More study of this period and the process of integration appears warranted.

7. Evidence on Post-Integration Discrimination

Even with a desegregated workplace, of course, it is still possible that the baseball labor market was and/or is afflicted with discrimination in the form of (1) unequal pay for equal work, (2) unequal hiring standards, and/or (3) positional segregation, in which blacks might be channeled to certain field positions and away from others based on negative stereotypes about their abilities or a presumption that white players would balk if blacks took leadership roles on teams.

The earliest investigations of such issues have been ably reviewed by Kahn (1991; 1992), who concluded they showed "little evidence of salary or hiring discrimination by major league baseball" by the late 1960s and 1970s, but did contain some evidence of "racial differences in career length [suggesting blacks faced some retention barriers relative to whites] and persistent, though slowly falling, segregation by position" (1991, p. 414). Kahn noted, however, that many of these early studies are based on relatively small samples (often due to incomplete salary data for the period studied).

Studies of pay inequality and hiring barriers in baseball have become rare in recent years, perhaps because researchers consider these to be settled questions.[11] Note, however, that the earlier studies controlled for the *amount* of a player's on-field output but not its *value*. Burger and Walters (2003) have shown, and Brown and Link (2008) have confirmed, that a player's marginal revenue product (MRP) varies positively with the size of the market in which he plays—that is, a given level of performance generates more revenue (in the form of gate and concession proceeds, broadcast rights fees, and merchandise sales) the greater the population in a particular team's market area. Jackie Robinson's MRP, for example, was far greater for the Dodgers, who in the 1940s and 1950s shared a market containing almost eight million potential fans with two other teams, than it would have been in, say, Cincinnati, the population of which was barely a half-million. The unanswered question is how omitting consideration of this fact might affect researchers' tests for salary or hiring discrimination. In a different context, Burger and Walters (2008) showed that when wage regressions control for physical productivity but not its value, mistaken inferences (e.g., about wage fairness) can result. Here, it is conceivable that the existence of variation in the value of a given amount of output across markets might generate evidence of discrimination when bias is not present, or mask it when it is. For example, in an unbiased market in which all players receive wages equal to their MRPs but large-market teams pay higher average wages for a given level of physical productivity, a given cohort of black players might receive lower average wages and appear to be discriminated against if they are (randomly) assigned more frequently to small-market teams. Alternatively, if all employers are similarly biased—that is, pay blacks a smaller fraction of their MRPs than they are willing to pay whites—average black wages may look comparable to those of whites if they are (randomly) assigned more frequently to large-market teams. Clearly, the effect of considering this previously omitted variable will depend on many factors, including the distribution of tastes for discrimination (if any) across markets; revisiting the early evidence on the pattern of wages and hiring thus might be warranted.[12]

Recent studies have generally focused on areas that appeared less settled, or on assessing whether forms of discrimination documented earlier have persisted. For example, Groothuis and Hill (2008) updated the finding by Jiobu (1988) that, *ceteris paribus*, blacks' careers were shorter than whites' over 1971–1985, and found no evidence that race affected career duration of hitters over 1990–2004, a finding consistent with Becker's model of market competition diminishing discriminatory behavior over time. Marburger (1996) also found no evidence of contract-length discrimination against non-whites over 1990–1993. And Medoff (2004) revisited the issue of positional segregation, finding that over 1980–2000 blacks increasingly occupied "central" (i.e., high-skill or leadership) positions, indicating either that discrimination had declined or that blacks' rising socioeconomic status over this period had reduced their costs of acquiring the skills requisite for those positions.

Since the effects of customer discrimination are generally not mitigated by competitive forces, a good deal of the recent literature has been aimed at gauging its existence and persistence. For example, Hanssen and Andersen (1999) found evidence of fan bias against African American players in the voting for baseball's annual All-Star game in the early 1970s, but concluded that vote differentials declined sharply over time as discriminatory attitudes diminished; Depken and Ford (2006) found that minority players were actually preferred by voters during the early 1990s. By contrast, Findlay and Reid (1997), Desser, Monks, and Robinson (1999), and Jewell, Brown, and Miles (2002) found some evidence of bias against nonwhites among the sportswriters who elect players to the sport's Hall of Fame.

The existence of an active market for baseball memorabilia has enabled researchers to test for fan bias in the form of a willingness to pay more (less) for products featuring white (black) players, *ceteris paribus*. The evidence is mixed, though perhaps consistent with diminishing bias over time. Nardinelli and Simon (1990) and Andersen and LaCroix (1991) found evidence of some consumer discrimination in 1980s card prices, but Gabriel, Johnson, and Stanton (1995) found none for rookie cards over 1984–1990, and McGarrity, Palmer, and Poitras (1999) found none in 1994 card prices. Fort and Gill (2000) revisited the issue using 1987 prices, a more continuous measure of market participants' impressions about race/ethnicity, and a control variable for the market size of players' teams, and found evidence of discrimination against black and Hispanic hitters and black pitchers, but not against Hispanic pitchers.

There is not much literature on the issue of bias in the market for managers in baseball or in the conduct of the sport's officials, but it is unsettling. Though Singell (1991) modeled a player's chances of becoming a coach or manager and obtained a statistically insignificant coefficient on a race dummy variable, Volz (2009a; 2009b) found that black players are significantly less likely than comparable white players to become managers (who have far greater visibility and responsibility than coaches) and tend to survive longer once hired (a result that is consistent with the existence of a barrier in hiring, as those who surmount it prove to be of above-average quality over time). Fizel (1996) and Burger and Walters (2005) found some evidence of bias against minorities in the decisions of arbitrators hired to resolve contract disputes. Finally, Parsons et al. (2007) found evidence of umpire partiality, with strikes more likely to be called, *ceteris paribus,* if the umpire and pitcher match race/ethnicity, improving such pitchers' performance and their teams' chances of winning.

8. Concluding Remarks

This examination of the baseball labor market has identified many occasions where the behavior of market participants and the consequences of that behavior have coincided nicely with the predictions of various economic models of discrimination, especially Becker's (1971). The brief period in the sport's early history when heterogeneous tastes for discrimination among employers and competitive forces led many predominantly white teams to hire blacks is particularly instructive—but so is the ability of the employee bias so widespread at the time that it ultimately generated segregated teams and leagues, even absent a structure for collective action (such as a union).

Indeed, baseball's experience with race and prejudice must serve as a cautionary tale to those who believe that competition must inevitably eliminate wage inequality or hiring barriers—or that it will do so quickly. The segregation that took root in baseball in the late 1880s lasted over six decades. In part, this was due to the sport's unique governance structure, in which an all-powerful commissioner could overrule the interests of its least-prejudiced employers in integrating the sport. But this slow rate of progress may also have been a by-product of the (endogenous) labor supply decisions of black athletes as segregation became a feature of baseball life; as fewer blacks invested in the skills necessary to compete on the diamond with whites and as fewer black professional teams provided them with the opportunity to do so, the costs to white employers of ignoring the pool of black playing talent appeared low. Eventually, of course, as black professional leagues began and flourished, the availability of high-quality, low-cost black players proved irresistible to at least some big-league teams, and baseball integrated. Nevertheless, the pace was slow, and signs of wage inequality and hiring did not disappear until essentially all the owners and executives from the sport's segregated era had passed from the scene—and there remained some evidence of consumer discrimination and other manifestations of bias even longer than that.

Clearly, then, baseball has taught us a great deal about how complicated and persistent are racial bias's effects, and about the short- and long-term economic consequences of discrimination. But given the large number of questions that remain unsettled or under-studied, only a few of which have been identified here, it has the capacity to teach us much more.

NOTES

The author is grateful to John Burger, Fred Derrick, Jeremy S. Schwartz, Charles Scott, and Norman Sedgley for helpful comments, and to John J. Walters for capable research assistance.

1   The Lord was advising Moses what to tell anyone who "vows the value of a person to Yahweh and wishes to discharge the vow" (Leviticus 27:2). I am grateful to Kaufman and Hotchkiss (2003) for bringing this provocative passage to my attention; they note that female/male wage ratios of 60 percent endured for some time, but, blessedly, have recently been improving.

2   Many subsequent researchers have pointed out that employer prejudice can depress the earnings of disfavored groups even in the long run in the presence of imperfect competition, non-convexities, or imperfect information (see, e.g., Arrow, 1972). More recently, Charles and Guryan (2008) presented an interesting argument that wage gaps can persist even under perfect competition in a Becker-type model.

3   Even on integrated teams, it was not uncommon for white players to make intentional errors when a black teammate pitched and to refuse to sit for team portraits that included blacks (White and Malloy, 1995, p. xx). Frank Grant, a black second baseman regarded as one of the best players in the International League, has been credited with the invention of shin guards because whites sharpened their spikes and tried to injure him when sliding into second—and a few fancifully said that the "feet-first slide" was invented in this context (Peterson, 1970, p. 43).

4   Another promising sign was that in 1887 the League of Colored Base Ball Clubs was officially sanctioned as a minor league (and, thus, a potential training ground and supplier of black talent to major league clubs) under the National Agreement, the guiding document for Organized Baseball. Under-capitalized, however, the league soon folded.

5   Alternatively, an unbiased owner could field an all-black team in a predominantly white league—which occurred in 1889, 1890, 1891, and 1898 in various lower-level minor leagues (White and Malloy, 1995, pp. 164–166).

6   There is little reason to suppose that statistical theories of discrimination (Phelps, 1972; Aigner and Cain, 1977) or that ignorance about black players' abilities would have much explanatory power in this era. All-black teams that played against all-white teams generally acquitted themselves well, as did the black players who joined predominantly white teams. A telling quote comes from one of Fleet Walker's teammates, a pitcher named Tony Mullane, who confessed "he was the best catcher I ever worked with, but I disliked a Negro and whenever I had to pitch to him I used to pitch anything I wanted without looking at his signals," sometimes causing injury to Walker (Heaphy, 2003, p. 14).

7 Even Anson's motives have been the subject of speculation. Like Ward (Penn State) and Walker (Oberlin), he was a college man (Notre Dame), had grown up in the North, and played in a city with a reputation for (relative) racial progressiveness. After he retired as a player, he umpired at least one game between all-white and all-black teams and his behavior was "impartial ... clean, honest, and good-natured." Zoss and Bowman (2004) suggest that "[i]t is possible to conclude that his animosity toward blacks had a significant economic basis, for once they were excluded from his profession ... he didn't much seem to care who or what they played" (p. 138).

8 Evidence of continued co-worker bias is seen in reports that one Dodger asked to be traded so he would not have to play alongside Robinson (a request that was granted) and that the St. Louis Cardinals threatened to strike rather than play against him (Kahn, 1991, p. 397).

9 Scully (1974), on the other hand, found that attendance was lower at games started by black pitchers; later, Sommers and Quinton (1982) found no statistically significant relationship between attendance and the number of African American players on a team.

10 Hanssen (1998) largely confirmed the findings of Gwartney and Haworth (1974) and offered evidence that the American League lagged in integration because of bias by its fans. Foley and Smith (2007) also found evidence of fan bias in several cities, and as recently as 1992.

11 Exceptions are Palmer and King (2006), who found some remaining discrimination against blacks and Hispanics at the margins of a team's roster, among its benchwarmers (where indulging a taste for discrimination might have the least cost).

12 It is also worth noting that many of the control variables used in the early wage and hiring studies are incomplete or misleading indicators of players' overall contributions to team success. Students of the game (dubbed "sabermetricians," after the Society for American Baseball Research or SABR) recently have made great strides in identifying which measures of performance are most meaningful, how they must be adjusted for different historic or geographic context, and how they might be aggregated to yield more reliable measures of total player productivity (see, e.g., James and Henzler, 2002); in combination with recently available data on team finances, such measures can be used to value individual players' output very precisely and make more meaningful judgments about wage inequality and hiring discrimination.

References

Aigner, Dennis J., and Glenn G. Cain (1977). Statistical theories of discrimination in labor markets. *Industrial and Labor Relations Review,* 30: 175–187.

Andersen, Torben, and Sumner J. LaCroix (1991). Customer racial discrimination in Major League Baseball. *Economic Inquiry,* 29: 665–677.

Arrow, Kenneth (1972). Some mathematical models of race in the labor market, in A.H. Pascal (ed.), *Racial discrimination in economic life.* Lexington, MA: Lexington Books.

Becker, Gary (1971). *The economics of discrimination* (2nd ed.). Chicago: University of Chicago Press.

Becker, Gary (1993). Autobiography, in Tore Frängsmyr (ed.), *The Nobel Prizes 1992.* Stockholm: Nobel Foundation.

Brown, Daniel, and Charles R. Link (2008). Population and bandwagon effects on local team revenues in Major League Baseball. *Journal of Sports Economics,* 9: 470–487.

Burger, John D., and Stephen J. K. Walters (2003). Market size, pay, and performance: A general model and application to Major League Baseball. *Journal of Sports Economics,* 4: 108–125.

Burger, John D., and Stephen J. K. Walters (2005). Arbitrator bias and self-interest: Lessons from the baseball labor market. *Journal of Labor Research,* 26: 267–280.

Burger, John D., and Stephen J. K. Walters (2008). Testing fair wage theory. *Journal of Labor Research,* 29: 318–332.

Charles, Kerwin Kofi, and Jonathan Guryan (2008). Prejudice and wages: An empirical assessment of Becker's *The Economics of Discrimination. Journal of Political Economy,* 116: 773–809.

Coyne, Christopher J., Justin P. Isaacs, Jeremy T. Schwartz, and Anthony M. Carilli (2007). Put me in, Coach, I'm ready to play. *Review of Austrian Economics,* 20: 237–246.

Depken, Craig A., and Jon M. Ford (2006). Customer-based discrimination against Major League Baseball players: Additional evidence from All-Star ballots. *Journal of Socio-Economics,* 35: 1061–1077.

Desser, Arna, James Monks, and Michael Robinson (1999). Baseball Hall of Fame voting: A test of the customer discrimination hypothesis. *Social Science Quarterly,* 80: 591–603.

Findlay, David W., and Clifford E. Reid (1997). Voting behavior, discrimination and the National Baseball Hall of Fame. *Economic Inquiry,* 35: 562–578.

Fizel, John (1996). Bias in salary arbitration: The case of Major League Baseball. *Applied Economics,* 28: 255–265.

Foley, Mark, and Fred H. Smith (2007). Consumer discrimination in professional sports: New evidence from Major League Baseball. *Applied Economics Letters,* 14: 951–55.

Fort, Rodney (2009). Sports business data pages. http://www.rodneyfort.com/, accessed August 20.

Fort, Rodney, and Andrew Gill (2000). Race and ethnicity assessment in baseball card markets. *Journal of Sports Economics,* 1: 21–38.

Gabriel, Paul E., Curtis Johnson, and Timothy J. Stanton (1995). An examination of customer racial discrimination in the market for baseball memorabilia. *Journal of Business,* 68: 215–230.

Goff, Brian L., Robert E. McCormick, and Robert D. Tollison (2002). Racial integration as an innovation: Empirical evidence from sports leagues. *American Economic Review,* 92: 16–26.

Goldin, Claudia, Lawrence F. Katz, and Ilyana Kuziemko (2006). The homecoming of American college women: The reversal of the college gender gap. *Journal of Economic Perspectives,* 20: 133–156.

Groothuis, Peter A., and James Richard Hill (2008). Exit discrimination in Major League Baseball: 1990–2004. *Southern Economic Journal,* 75: 574–590.

Gwartney, James, and Charles Haworth (1974). Employer costs and discrimination: The case of baseball. *Journal of Political Economy,* 82: 873–881.

Hanssen, Andrew (1998). The cost of discrimination: A study of Major League Baseball. *Southern Economic Journal,* 64: 603–627.

Hanssen, F. Andrew, and Torben Andersen (1999). Has discrimination lessened over time? A test using baseball's All-Star vote. *Economic Inquiry,* 37: 326–352.

Hanssen, F. Andrew, and James W. Meehan (2009). Who integrated Major League Baseball faster—winning teams or losing teams? *Journal of Sports Economics,* 10: 141–154.

Haupert, Michael J. (2007). Fair pay for fair play: A preliminary analysis of race-based wages in MLB and the Negro Leagues. *Outside the Lines,* 12: 1–6.

Haupert, Michael J. (2009). Pay, performance, and race during the integration era. *Black Ball: A Negro Leagues Journal,* 2: 37–51.

Heaphy, Leslie A. (2003). *The Negro Leagues, 1869–1960.* Jefferson, NC: McFarland.

James, Bill, and Jim Henzler (2002). *Win shares.* Morton Grove, IL: STATS, Inc.

Jewell, R. Todd, Robert W. Brown, and Scott E. Miles (2002). Measuring discrimination in Major League Baseball. *Applied Economics,* 34: 167–177.

Jiobu, Robert M. (1988). Racial inequality in a public arena: The case of professional baseball. *Social Forces,* 67: 524–534.

Kahn, Lawrence M. (1991). Discrimination in professional sports: A survey of the literature. *Industrial and Labor Relations Review,* 44: 395–418.

Kahn, Lawrence M. (1992). Discrimination in baseball, in Paul M. Sommers (ed.), *Diamonds are forever: The business of baseball.* Washington, DC: The Brookings Institution.

Kaufman, Bruce E., and Julie L. Hotchkiss (2003). *The economics of labor markets* (6th ed.). Mason, OH: Thomson South-Western.

Koppett, Leonard (2004). *Koppett's concise history of Major League Baseball.* New York: Carroll & Graf Publishers.

Lanctot, Neil (2004). *Negro League Baseball: The rise and ruin of a black institution.* Philadelphia: Univ. of Pennsylvania Press.

Loury, Glenn C. (1998). Discrimination in the post-civil rights era: Beyond market interactions. *Journal of Economic Perspectives,* 12: 117–126.

Lundberg, Shelly J., and Richard Startz (1983). Private discrimination and social intervention in competitive labor markets. *American Economic Review,* 73: 340–347.

McGarrity, Joseph, Harvey D. Palmer, and Marc Poitras (1999). Consumer racial discrimination: A reassessment of the market for baseball cards. *Journal of Labor Research,* 20: 247–258.

McNary, Kyle (2006). *Black baseball: A history of African-Americans and the national game.* New York: Sterling Publishing.

Marburger, Daniel R. (1996). Racial discrimination and long-term contracts in Major League Baseball. *Review of Black Political Economy,* 25: 83–94.

Medoff, Marshall H. (2004). Revisiting the economic hypothesis and positional segregation. *Review of Black Political Economy,* 32: 83–95.

Nardinelli, Clark, and Curtis Simon (1990). Customer racial discrimination in the market for memorabilia: The case of baseball. *Quarterly Journal of Economics,* 105: 575–595.

Neal, Derek A. and William R. Johnson (1996). The role of premarket factors in black-white wage differences. *Journal of Political Economy,* 104: 869–895.

Palmer, Matthew C., and Randall H. King (2006). Has salary discrimination really disappeared from Major League Baseball? *Eastern Economic Journal,* 32: 285–297.

Parsons, Christopher A., Johan Sulaeman, Michael C. Yates, and Daniel S. Hamermesh (2007). Strike three: Umpires' demand for discrimination. National Bureau of Economic Research Working Paper 13665, 38 pp.

Peterson, Robert (1970). *Only the ball was white.* Englewood Cliffs, NJ: Prentice-Hall.

Phelps, Edmund S. (1972). The statistical theory of racism and sexism. *American Economic Review,* 62: 659–661.

Scully, Gerald W. (1974). Pay and performance in Major League Baseball. *American Economic Review,* 64: 915–930.

Singell, Larry D., Jr. (1991). Baseball-specific human capital: Why good but not great players are more likely to coach in the Major Leagues. *Southern Economic Journal,* 58: 77–86.

Sommers, Paul M., and Noel Quinton (1982). Pay and performance in Major League Baseball: The case of the first family of free agents. *Journal of Human Resources,* 17: 426–436.

Stevens, David (1998). *Baseball's radical for all seasons: A biography of John Montgomery Ward.* Lanham, MD: Scarecrow Press.

Volz, Brian (2009a). Race and the likelihood of managing in Major League Baseball. University of Connecticut Working Paper, 32 pp.

Volz, Brian (2009b). Minority status and managerial survival in Major League Baseball. *Journal of Sports Economics,* 20: 522–542.

White, Sol, and Jerry Malloy (ed.) (1995). *Sol White's history of colored baseball, with other documents on the early black game, 1886–1936.* Lincoln: Univ. of Nebraska Press.

Zoss, Joel, and John Stewart Bowman (2004). *Diamonds in the rough: The untold history of baseball.* Lincoln, NE: Univ. of Nebraska Press.

## CHAPTER 2

THE ECONOMICS OF DISCRIMINATION

EVIDENCE FROM BASKETBALL

LAWRENCE M. KAHN

1. INTRODUCTION

SINCE the publication of Gary Becker's *The Economics of Discrimination* (1957), economists have devoted considerable attention to the theory and empirical analysis of labor market discrimination. While a common definition of labor market discrimination would be "unequal treatment of equally qualified workers," it is very difficult to test whether it exists and if so, what its extent is.[1] This is the case because in most data sets one can use to analyze this question, such as the Census or the Current Population Survey (CPS), our measures of qualifications or productivity are very crude. For example, in the very commonly used March CPS, the only qualifications-related information we have are a worker's age, type of degree obtained in school (if any), and crude measures of industry and occupation. The CPS doesn't provide any information about workers' performance levels, the quality of their schooling, their work histories, or which employer they work for. Thus, while Census or CPS data can identify race or gender differences in pay for workers with similar measured characteristics, these data don't allow for a strong conclusion about the extent of labor market discrimination. In addition, since earnings in such data bases are self-reported, they can suffer from considerable measurement error as well.

In contrast to these deficiencies in the Census or the CPS, the sports business is an excellent setting in which to test theories of labor market discrimination. Unlike the Census or the CPS (or, indeed, longitudinal data such as the Michigan Panel Study of Income Dynamics or the National Longitudinal Surveys), in sports we have detailed information on each production worker's performance at every time during his or her career. We know exactly which firm each worker is employed by, and we also have information on the identity and performance of each athlete's co-workers (teammates) and immediate supervisor (i.e., the coach or manager). In many cases, we have detailed information about each player's compensation package (contract), often supplied by the league or a players' association. These administrative sources of compensation data are likely to be more accurate than self-reports of earnings and have the advantage that they "often contain the actual information used to make economic decisions" (Angrist and Krueger, 1999, p. 1338). In professional sports settings, we know how each player was selected for employment, and in many cases we also know the circumstances surrounding a player's exit from the team, allowing for a study of hiring and retention discrimination.

In this chapter, I review evidence on the extent of discrimination in basketball. This is an especially interesting sport in which to study racial discrimination, for several reasons.[2] The National Basketball Association (NBA) is seen by many as an oasis of economic opportunity for highly skilled African American athletes. Roughly 80 percent of the league's players are black. Of the 42 players who as of the 2001–2002 season had signed contracts with annual salaries of more than $10 million (the top decile of the league's 415 players), fully 37 (88 percent) were black (these figures are taken from data used in Kahn and Shah 2005). Of the 50 players who had ever been on an NBA All-Star team before signing their current contracts (as of the 2001–2002 season), only four were white. Black success has even progressed to the coaching ranks, where as of the beginning of the 2008–2009 season, 11 of the NBA's 30 coaches were black (www.espn.com, accessed October 14, 2008), representing a higher percentage than in football or baseball.[3]

Despite this clear evidence of black success in the NBA, the question of discrimination against African Americans remains a salient one. It has been reported, for example, that black players look with suspicion at specific, marginal white players' generous contracts as possible evidence of discrimination (Platt 2000). The 1998 NBA lockout, involving a league of white team owners and an 80 percent black union, was seen by many players as a racial confrontation (Shropshire, 2000). And sports league punishments imposed on players who commit acts of violence are seen by some as biased against black players (Shropshire, 2000). Whether these perceptions are accurate in the individual cases involved, and whether, assuming they are accurate, they represent the pattern and practice of the NBA, the fact that they are held at all is reason enough to explore the issue of race in the NBA, in addition to the econometric advantages of sports data.

This chapter reviews evidence on discrimination in basketball. I first discuss the economics of discrimination, focusing on Becker's (1957) analysis of the possible sources of discrimination in labor markets (firms, coworkers and customers). A key feature of this discussion will be the persistence of various types of discrimination in competitive labor markets. Any of these sources can lead to various manifestations of discrimination, including pay, access to jobs, and susceptibility to layoff or discharge. I then review evidence on each of these possible forms of discrimination in basketball, including both a discussion of methodological issues as well as substantive findings. While there is a variety of results in the literature, in general, racial discrimination in professional basketball seemed more prevalent in the 1980s than is the case today.

2. THE ECONOMICS OF DISCRIMINATION: THEORETICAL CONSIDERATIONS

Gary Becker (1957), in his seminal work on the economics of discrimination, identified three sources of discrimination: employers, coworkers (including supervisors and supervisees as well as lateral coworkers), and customers. With constant returns to scale, free entry, and the existence of some profit-maximizing firms, discriminating employers will be driven out of business by the nondiscriminator(s), and coworker discrimination will lead to equally competitive segregated firms with equal pay for equal work. However, customer discrimination is different from these forms of prejudice, because an employer that pays more money to the types of workers whom customers prefer is likely to be rewarded by the market. Conversely, those workers who are not preferred by customers, but have a personal comparative advantage in the affected job, will either need to accept lower pay, if they remain in the customer sector, or else move to the noncustomer sector, where their comparative advantage is lost (Kahn 1991a). This argument suggests that competitive forces are less likely to eliminate customer-based discrimination than that based on employer or coworker prejudice. With heterogeneous consumer preferences, we may observe segregation and equal wages, if consumers have equal income and access to capital. Thus, the persistence of wage differences based on customer discrimination will be an empirical question. Of course, the sports industry is a customer-based service sector. Further, sports leagues as monopolies may not face the kind of free entry that might serve to discipline discriminating employers, although stockholders of publicly traded companies that own sports franchises may exert pressure on management to maximize profits.

If most employers have a taste for discrimination, then a nondiscriminating employer can either win more games, or reduce expenses, or both, by hiring the most productive workers at the lowest cost possible. This argument has been tested formally and upheld in the context of college basketball. Specifically, Goff, McCormick, and Tollison (2002) studied the integration of black men's basketball players into teams in the Atlantic Coast Conference in the 1960s through 1981. The authors found that the teams that integrated earlier did better on the court than those integrating later, other things equal. Further, the Boston Celtics' early dominance and its early deployment of many black stars in the late 1950s and early 1960s, such as Bill Russell, Sam Jones, K. C. Jones, and Tom Sanders, may be considered anecdotal evidence for this view.

As noted, black players today comprise about 80 percent of NBA rosters, so the type of coworker prejudice and demands by some white players to be traded rather than have black teammates, as in the early days of baseball integration (Kahn, 1991b), may not be so relevant to today's NBA. However, the effects of customer prejudice can be felt even if owners and white players are not prejudiced. Suppose, for example, that fans prefer to see white players, and also suppose that a black and a white NBA player of equal ability each become free agents at the same time. If fans are prejudiced, the white player is more likely to have a large fan club and a highly rated television or radio show in his current locality than an equally accomplished black player. The white player's agent is likely to present this information to alternative teams in negotiating for a new contract. Even if the teams aren't thinking about the player's race, they will be thinking about the player's ability to draw fans. Under these circumstances, we expect the white player to obtain a better offer than the black player.

As I will discuss in more detail below, players with less than roughly three to four years of NBA experience are not allowed to be free agents (at least until they are released by their current team) and must either deal with the team that owns their contract or leave the industry. Thus these players are subject to the monopsony power of their team. If black and white players have different labor supply elasticities to the team, then even in the absence of racial prejudice by teams, players, or fans, we would expect unequal wages for equally qualified black and white players. This reasoning has been used by Robinson (1969) and Madden (1973) to explain sex differences in pay (on the assumption that women have lower labor supply elasticities to the firm than men do), and, more relevant to the current review, by McCormick and Tollison (2001) to explain the black salary shortfall in the NBA in the 1980s. Along the same lines, in a Nash bargain, the player with lower status quo income will end up with the lower salary level (Binmore, Rubinstein, and Wolinsky, 1986). Thus, if black non-free agents have lower family incomes than whites do (as is likely), then these bargaining considerations could also lead to lower salary levels for black than white players of equal ability (Kahn and Shah 2005). Free agents, in contrast, are expected to receive their market value, which may of course include the impact of customer prejudice (as would the salaries of the non-free agents through the Nash bargaining process).

3. Research on Salary Discrimination in Basketball

Most studies of salary discrimination in basketball, analyzing NBA players, use as a basic empirical model the following type of wage regression referring to a given season:

$$\ln Salary_i = B'X_i + a*WHITE_i + u_i, \tag{1}$$

where for each player i, Salary is the annual salary, X is a vector of player and team characteristics to be discussed below, WHITE is a dummy variable for white players, and u is a disturbance summarizing unmeasured influences on salary.

The dependent variable in most studies is the log of current year's salary, although in many cases, players (or coaches) sign long-term guaranteed contracts that include signing bonuses and deferred payments. An accurate accounting of compensation should take into account these non-salary payments. Even so, it is not obvious what the dependent variable should be. On the one hand, we would like a measure of the price of labor, and the player's annual compensation (including the annualized bonuses and deferred payments) fits this bill. On the other hand, for many players, a three-year $18 million contract does not yield the same utility as a one-year $6 million contract, for instance, even though the annual price of labor is the same. It is therefore also possible that using as an additional dependent variable the log of total compensation guaranteed in the contract yields additional information beyond a model using only the log of average annual compensation. In addition, it is important to know when a player signed his current contract in order to collect information about his playing record or negotiation rights that was known as of the signing. For example, a player during the 2007–2008 season may have signed his contract in 2003, when he wasn't a free agent, even if under the rules, he would have been eligible for free agency had he negotiated in 2007. These issues are explored in Kahn and Shah's (2005) study of NBA players and Kahn's (2006) analysis of NBA coaches.

The list of control variables X usually contains player performance variables such as scoring, rebounding, steals, and blocked shots, as well as NBA experience, one's place in the order of drafted players (if drafted), NBA awards and All-Star team participation, and team and market factors. These market factors can include the income and population levels of the team's location as well as its racial composition. While these variables are straightforward to interpret, as noted earlier, they comprise a much more comprehensive list of performance and qualifications measures than we can obtain from sources such as the Census or the CPS. For example, the 2008 CPS uses the 2002 Census Codes for industry and occupation. In the CPS, an NBA first round draft pick who, say, attended one year of college, would be observationally equivalent to a player of the same race and age who dropped out of college after one year, was not drafted and is currently playing minor league basketball in a venue such as the NBA Developmental League.[4]

The explanatory variable of most interest in equation (1) for analyzing discrimination is the race indicator (WHITE). The equation forces the *ceteris paribus* racial pay differential to be the same regardless of performance level, although some authors have investigated whether there are interaction effects between a player's race and some explanatory variables such as playing experience (Kahn and Sherer, 1988) or the racial makeup of the community (Kahn and Sherer, 1988; Bodvarsson and Partridge, 2001; Kahn and Shah, 2005).

While we are tempted to conclude that the coefficient on WHITE is an estimate of the extent of discrimination against black players, we still need to be cautious in this regard, although as mentioned, the set of controls here is much more extensive than in other non-sport settings. First, the race variable may be correlated with unmeasured factors such as teamwork that affect productivity and pay, even controlling for the X variables. The sign of such correlations is uncertain; if black players have higher levels of unmeasured productivity, then the WHITE coefficient will understate the extent of salary discrimination, while if white players are more productive in ways we can't measure, then the opposite will be true. Below I will present some suggestive evidence on this question. Second, some of the explanatory variables may themselves be the result of discrimination, implying that the WHITE coefficient may understate the full effects of discrimination on pay. For example, if coaches give white players more playing time (possibly in response to fan preferences), then they will have better performance statistics than otherwise. In addition, it has recently been suggested that on average, referees may make calls more favorable to white players, again inflating their performance statistics (Price and Wolfers, 2010).

With these preliminaries in mind, let us turn to the evidence on wage discrimination in basketball. Table 2.1 summarizes results from several studies of race and NBA salaries (players or coaches) and one of gender and college basketball coaches' salaries.[5] Using data from the mid-1980s, several authors found apparently discriminatory wage differentials favoring white players in the NBA. Controlling for a variety of performance and market-related statistics, there were statistically significant black salary shortfalls of 11–25 percent, depending on sample and specification (Kahn and Sherer, 1988; Koch and Vander Hill, 1988; Wallace, 1988; and Brown, Spiro, and Keenan, 1991). The apparent discrimination was especially noteworthy since for the 1985–1986 season, black players on average earned $407,000, while whites earned $397,000; however, controlling for performance and market related variables, the *ceteris paribus* white effect was 21–25 percent and was highly statistically significant (Kahn and Sherer, 1988). This combination of results shows how important it can be to control for productivity, which in this case was higher for black players, in assessing the extent of discrimination.

As noted earlier, there may still be omitted variables that could have explained the *ceteris paribus* white salary advantage; however, reverse regression tests can under some restricted circumstances take account of such problems (Goldberger 1984). These tests involve using the productivity factors as dependent variables in regressions with log salary as the explanatory variable. In the 1985–1986 NBA data, they showed even larger apparent discrimination coefficients against black players

Table 2.1 Summary of Studies of Wage Discrimination in Basketball

Study	Setting	Results
Kahn and Sherer (1988)	NBA players 1985–1986	21–25% salary premium for white players, statistically significant.
Koch and Vander Hill (1988)	NBA players 1984–1985	12% premium for white players, marginally significant.
Wallace (1988)	NBA players 1984–1985	18% premium for white players, marginally significant.
Brown, Spiro, and Keenan (1991)	NBA players 1984–1985	14–16% premium for white players, the reported 16% effect is significant.
Bodvarsson and Brastow (1998)	NBA players 1990–1991	No evidence of salary discrimination.
Hamilton (1997)	NBA players 1994–1995	No average white premium; 19% white premium at upper end of distribution, marginally significant.
Dey (1997)	NBA players 1987–1993	No evidence of salary discrimination.
Gius and Johnson (1998)	NBA players 1996–1997	No evidence of salary discrimination.
Eschker, Perez, and Siegler (2004)	NBA players 1996–2002	No significant race salary differences in 5 of 6 seasons; in 1998–1999, significant 14–20% white premium.
Kahn and Shah (2005)	NBA players 2001–2002	No significant race differences in annual salary overall; significantly longer contracts and higher total contractwide compensation for whites overall; for non-free agent players who are not on rookie scale contracts, a significant white premium in annual salary, contract duration and total contractwide compensation.
Kahn (2006)	NBA coaches 1997–2004	No evidence of salary discrimination against black coaches.
Humphreys (2000)	College Coaches 1990–1991	No significant gender salary gap, controlling for type of program, performance and experience.

than the usual direct regression of log salary on X and WHITE did (Kahn and Sherer 1988). These tests therefore imply that black players in the mid-1980s had better unmeasured productivity characteristics than white players with the same Xs. This may not be surprising, since black players had more favorable measured productivity as well.

By the 1990s, there appeared to be much less evidence of salary discrimination against black NBA players. Table 2.1 shows that studies of the 1990–1991 (Bodvarsson and Brastow, 1998), 1994–1995 (Hamilton, 1997), 1987–1993 (Dey, 1997), and 1996–1997 (Gius and Johnson, 1998) seasons all showed no significant racial salary differentials on average, all else equal. Moreover, Eschker, Perez, and Piegler (2004) found insignificant racial salary gaps in 5 of 6 seasons between 1996 and 2002, with only 1998–1999 showing a significant white premium (14–20 percent). However, Hamilton (1997) did find evidence of unexplained black salary shortfalls among the elite players in the NBA. To examine discrimination across the distribution of playing talent, he used quantile regressions and found no significant racial salary differentials at the 10th, 25th, and 50th percentiles but positive and significant (at the 5.6 percent and 12 percent levels on two-tailed tests) white pay effects at the 75th and 90th percentiles amounting to 0.18 to 0.19 log points.[6] These results suggest that while there was no significant unexplained black salary shortfall on average in the NBA in the 1994–1995 season, for star players (i.e., those at the 75th percentile and above in the conditional wage distribution), there may have been substantial discrimination in favor of whites.

A recent study of the 2001–2002 NBA season found that for the league as a whole, there were small to moderate and generally statistically insignificant annual salary differentials favoring white players, all else equal (Kahn and Shah 2005). However, there were larger and usually statistically significant racial differentials in total compensation favoring white players, and whites overall also had statistically significantly longer contract duration (Table 2.1). An important feature of this study was its disaggregation of the sample into three groups according to their negotiation rights: (1) veterans with less than three years of service, plus rookies not drafted on the first round, as well as rookies who entered the NBA before 1995, when a rookie salary scale was put in place—players who are not free agents and are subject to their individual teams' monopsony power; (2) first round draft picks who entered since 1995—that is, those whose salary is set in the collective bargaining agreement; and (3) free agents (who need to have at least 3–4 years of NBA experience). The authors found large, statistically significant racial effects favoring whites in annual salary (.30–.50 log points), total contractwide compensation (.7–.9 log points), and contract duration (1.3–1.5 more years of guaranteed money) only among group (1)—players subject to individual teams' monopsony power. But for the other groups—players under the rookie salary scale, as well as veteran free agents, there were only very small and statistically insignificant racial effects for each of these dependent variables. Thus, the results appear to support the discriminating monopsony model (McCormick and Tollison, 2001) or models of Nash bargaining where black players have lower status quo income than whites. For group (2)—players on the rookie salary scale—salary is exogenous once we know one's position in the draft order, and for group (3)—free agents—the market is competitive, so the discriminating monopsony/Nash bilateral monopoly model is less relevant for them.

It is interesting to note that in Kahn and Shah's (2005) study, there were two situations in which racial pay differentials for similarly qualified players were absent: (1) players under the rookie salary scale; and (2) free agents. The rookie salary schedule is a union pay scale, and the absence of racial salary differences once one controls for draft position is analogous to the small racial pay differences one would expect to observe under union standard rate schemes (Ashenfelter, 1972; Freeman, 1982). The nonwhite free agents are protected by employer competition, at least in the seeming absence of customer discrimination (as also found by Kahn and Shah, 2005), as predicted by Becker's (1957) model of discrimination. Thus, union pay scales and competition are both potential mechanisms that can reduce racial pay differences.

As noted earlier, these studies of race and pay in basketball may understate discrimination if some of the explanatory variables are themselves caused by discrimination. In a recent study, Price and Wolfers (2010) have found evidence consistent with this outcome. Specifically, the authors studied NBA games between 1991 and 2004 and found that players were assessed by as many as 4 percent fewer fouls and scored 2½ percent more points during games in which their race matched that of the refereeing crew. The study was notable for the extensive list of controls including player fixed effects, referee fixed effects, and game fixed effects. Since most referees are white, this matching effect is more likely to benefit white players than black players. The authors' results imply that replacing an all-white refereeing crew with an all-black crew will raise black players' scoring average by about 2.5 percent, or by 0.26 points per game among experienced black players in the 2001–2002 season, according to data used by Kahn and Shah (2005). Using these data for the 2001–2002 season, one finds that among experienced players, raising one's points per game scoring average by one point leads to a statistically significant 0.056 log point salary increase, controlling for experience, rebounding, assists, blocked shots, race, position and market characteristics. Thus, replacing all-white refereeing crews by all-black crews would raise an individual black player's salary by 0.015 log points (i.e., 0.26 more points per game times 0.056 log points of salary); an individual white player's salary would be lowered also by 0.015 log points.[7] The refereeing crews during Price and Wolfers' (2010) sample period were 68 percent white, in contrast to the 20 percent white representation among players. If refereeing crews' racial composition were the same as that of the players, then white representation among referees would decline by 48 percentage points. We would therefore predict a rise in black player salaries due to scoring by 0.007 log points, and an equal fall in white player salaries. Therefore, average white relative salaries would fall by 1.4 percentage points, a modest change. Of course, other aspects of playing such as playing time and style may also be affected by refereeing. But overall, biased refereeing does not appear to be responsible for a large decline in black players' relative pay.

All of the studies of salary discrimination mentioned so far have focused on race and NBA players. There have been two studies of discrimination in coaches' salaries. First, Kahn (2006) found that in 1997–2004, there were small and statistically insignificant salary racial salary differentials, all else equal, between white and black NBA head coaches. Second, Humphreys (2000) studied male and female college basketball coaches for the 1990–1991 season. While on average, men earned more than women, this difference disappeared once the author controlled for revenues, whether the team was a women's or a men's team, type of school, and the coach's experience and performance. Thus, Humphreys (2000) did not find evidence of unequal pay for equal work. However, as discussed above, some of the controls themselves may be subject to discrimination, implying that the regressions may have understated the extent of salary discrimination. A Federal sex discrimination suit filed by the female former coach of the University of Southern California women's basketball team made precisely this allegation (*Stanley v. USC*, 9th Circuit Court of Appeals, 1999).[8] The program paid the male men's coach more than the women's coach, partly on the grounds that the men's program brought in more revenue than the women's program. The plaintiff had argued that the men's team revenues were higher than the women's team revenues due to discriminatory access to marketing resources. In the end, the Appeals Court did not need to rule on the question of whether the higher men's team revenues were tainted by discrimination. Rather, the Court noted that the men's coach had more experience and a more successful coaching career than the women's coach; in addition, the Court noted that, unlike the women's coach, the men's coach was a recognized authority on basketball coaching, as shown by noting the books he had authored. Therefore, the issue of whether a gender difference in revenue produced is a legitimate factor upon which to base a gender difference in coaching salaries is an open question from the legal point of view.

4. RESEARCH ON DISCRIMINATION IN HIRING AND RETENTION IN BASKETBALL

Even if there were equal pay for equal work in basketball, it is still possible that black players (or coaches) face barriers to entry or lower probabilities of being retained than equally performing white players (or coaches). Several studies have examined these issues in basketball (Table 2.2). Straightforward analyses of entry barriers for players include studies of the player draft, where the determinants of one's place in the order of drafted players are estimated as a function of college (if any) performance and race. Analyses of the 1985–1986 (Kahn and Sherer, 1988), 1987–1992 (Dey, 1997), and 2001–2002 seasons (Kahn and Shah, 2005) all fail to find racial effects on draft position, all else equal. There thus doesn't appear to be direct entry discrimination into the NBA on the basis of race, although it is still possible that there are racial barriers to entry into college basketball. In particular, college entrance exam requirements by the NCAA may have racially disparate effects on entry, given the likely racial gap in the quality of high schools. These studies of the draft also don't estimate the probability of being drafted in the first place, presumably because such an analysis would require data on all college and high school players eligible for the draft.

Table 2.2 Summary of Studies of Hiring or Retention Discrimination in Basketball

Study	Setting	Results
Kahn and Sherer (1988)	NBA players 1985–1986	No evidence of racial discrimination in player draft, controlling for college performance.
Dey (1997)	NBA players 1987–1992	No evidence of discrimination in player draft, controlling for college performance.
Brown, Spiro, and Keenan (1991)	NBA players 1984–1985	Black benchwarmers generally do not perform significantly better than white benchwarmers.
Kahn (2006)	NBA coaches 1997–2003	No evidence of racial discrimination in discharges; also no significant differences between performance of marginal black and marginal white coaches.
Hoang and Rascher (1999)	NBA players 1980–1991	White players have 36% lower risk of being cut than black players, marginally significant.
Groothuis and Hill (2004)	NBA players 1989–1999	No evidence of racial exit discrimination.
Kahn and Shah (2005)	NBA players 2001–2002	No evidence of racial discrimination in player draft, controlling for college performance.

An alternative take on the question of entry discrimination is to compare the performance of black and white incumbents, as some authors have done. The idea behind such analyses is that if, for example, black players or coaches face racial entry barriers, then the performance of black incumbents should be greater than that of white incumbents. The most valid of these studies focus on performance differences of *marginal*, rather than *average*, incumbents, as the following two examples will illustrate. In both cases, suppose that there are two black and two white players and that we can measure their quality on a cardinal scale. In the first case, let the two white players have quality levels of q and 2q (q > 0), and let the two black players have quality levels of q and 3q. And let q be the minimum league standard for hiring a player, which in this example is the same for black and white candidates. In this case, the average white player will have quality 1.5q, and the average black player quality is 2.0q. Using average performance differentials would suggest hiring discrimination against black players. However, such a conclusion would be incorrect if q is the minimum hiring standard of quality the league accepts regardless of race, as assumed in this example. At the margin, where the hiring decision is made, whites and blacks are equally qualified in this example.[9]

In the second example, let the white players' quality be q and 3q and the black players' quality be 2q and 2q. In this case, black and white players have the same average quality, and an analysis based on average quality will conclude that there is no hiring discrimination. However, if the minimum quality white and black players are both at the margin of entry, then the league in this case has a tougher standard for black than for white candidates. Thus, in this example, focusing on average quality or performance may cause us to incorrectly conclude that there is no hiring discrimination. In both of these examples, focusing on the marginal players allows us to make the correct inference.

Table 2.2 shows the results of two analyses of racial differences in the performance of marginal workers. First, Brown, Spiro, and Keenan (1991) found that there were few performance differentials between black and white benchwarmers in the NBA during 1984–1985, suggesting the absence of hiring discrimination. Interestingly, for the average player, blacks generally outperformed whites, a finding that might have led one to erroneously conclude that there was entry discrimination against black players. Second, Kahn (2006) found that among NBA coaches who were at the margin of being in the league, there were no statistically significant racial performance differences. He used quantile regressions of winning percentage, focusing on the 10th percentile of the conditional distribution as an indicator of being at the margin.

An additional form of quantity-based discrimination is differential treatment with respect to layoffs or discharges. Two studies of exit discrimination against black NBA players come to opposite conclusions. On the one hand, using a hazard function analysis, Hoang and Rascher (1999) found that during the 1980–1991 period, white players had a 36 percent lower risk of being cut than comparable black players, an effect that was marginally significant. On the other hand, also using a hazard function approach, Groothuis and Hill (2004) found no evidence of exit discrimination during the 1989–1999 period.[10] Moreover, for the 1997–2003 period, Kahn (2006) found no racial differences among NBA coaches' quit, discharge, or overall exit (i.e., quits and discharges aggregated) hazards, all else equal. These latter two studies suggest the absence of retention discrimination against either black players or coaches in the 1990s and early 2000s.

5. Research on Customer Discrimination in Basketball

The previous two sections have found some evidence, especially for the 1980s, of both salary and retention discrimination against black players in the NBA. By the 1990s, there much less evidence of these kinds of discrimination. As discussed earlier, when there is customer discrimination, free entry and profit maximization may not eliminate or even reduce discriminatory differentials in employment outcomes. In fact, markets will generally reward firms that bestow higher rewards on the kinds of workers their customers want to be served by. Accordingly, I now review evidence on the extent of customer discrimination in basketball.

Table 2.3 summarizes results from a variety of studies of customer discrimination in basketball. And there is indeed evidence from the 1980s consistent with the existence of such preferences. For example, Kahn and Sherer (1988) found that, all else equal, during the 1980–1986 period each white player on average generated 5,700 to 13,000 additional fans per year. The dollar value of this extra attendance was estimated to be more than the white salary premium they found (see Table 2.1). Hoang and Rascher (1999) also examined NBA attendance during the 1980–1991 period and found that, other things equal, larger values of (percent white on the team/percent white in the city) were significantly positively associated with attendance. This finding is consistent with the idea of customer preferences for white players. Consistent with these studies of NBA attendance, Brown and Jewell (1994) found that, all else equal, a higher share of white players raised college basketball programs' revenues during the 1988–1989 season: on average, a white player generated slightly over $100,000 more annual gate revenue than an identically productive black player.

Further evidence on customer discrimination during this period comes from studies that found a close match between the racial makeup of NBA teams in the 1980s and of the areas where they were located, again suggesting the importance of customer preferences (Brown, Spiro, and Keenan 1991; Burdekin and Idson, 1991; Hoang and Rascher, 1999; Bodvarsson and Partridge, 2001). I note that player preferences could also have produced a similar result, if black players, for example, prefer to play in areas with a larger relative black population. In this regard, Bodvarsson and Partridge (2001) found that black population share interacted with team black share had significantly positive effects on black salaries in 1985–1986 and 1990–1991, although the authors point out that team racial composition is likely to be endogenous. But if this result is indeed causal, it does suggest customer discrimination, since in its absence we would expect black players to make less in the areas they want to live in (through the usual compensating differentials mechanism).

While most of the evidence from the 1980s does suggest the existence of customer preferences for white players, McCormick and Tollison (2001) found no overall statistical relationship between team racial composition and home attendance for the 1980–1987 period, although among the quartile of metropolitan area locations with the largest black population shares, more white players actually reduced attendance, all else equal. And Brown, Spiro, and Keenan (1991) found that the percent of black playing time in the NBA did not affect attendance in the 1983–1984 season.

The evidence for customer discrimination in the NBA in the 1990s and 2000s seems weaker than it was during the 1980s. Dey (1997), for example, found that all else equal, white players added a statistically insignificant and economically relatively unimportant 60 fans apiece per season during the 1987–1993 period.

Table 2.3 Summary of Studies of Customer Discrimination in Basketball

Study	Setting	Results
Kahn and Sherer (1988)	NBA 1980–1986	White players significantly raise attendance by 5,700–13,000 per year per white player.
Brown, Spiro, and Keenan (1991)	NBA 1988 and 1983–1984	Racial makeup of team is significantly positively related to racial makeup of the area (1988); percent of time played by blacks does not significantly affect attendance (1983–1984).
Burdekin and Idson (1991)	NBA 1980–1986	Racial makeup of team is significantly positively related to racial makeup of the area; closeness of racial match between team and SMSA significantly positively affects attendance.
McCormick and Tollison (2001)	NBA 1980–1988	Team racial composition on average has no effect on attendance; in the MSA's with highest black relative population, black players raise attendance.
Hoang and Rascher (1999)	NBA 1980–1991	Racial makeup of team is significantly positively related to racial makeup of the area. Higher values of white representation on the team relative to white representation in the population raise attendance.
Bodvarsson and Partridge (2001)	NBA 1985–1986 and 1990–1991	Black population share interacts positively with black team share in salary determination.
Dey (1997)	NBA 1987–1993	No significant effect of team racial composition on attendance.
Stone and Warren (1999)	NBA trading cards 1993	No significant racial effect on pricing of NBA trading cards.
Kanazawa and Funk (2001)	NBA 1996–1997	White players significantly raise Nielsen television ratings.
Burdekin, Hossfeld, and Smith (2005)	NBA 1990–1999	Racial makeup of team is significantly positively related to racial makeup of the area; closeness of racial match between team and SMSA significantly positively affects attendance.
Kahn and Shah (2005)	NBA 1996–2001	No significant effect of team racial composition on attendance.
Coleman, DuMond, and Lynch (2008)	NBA 1995–2005	No evidence of racial discrimination in NBA Most Valuable Player award voting by writers and broadcasters.
Brown and Jewell (1994)	College basketball 1988–1989	Higher share of black players significantly lowers gate revenue.

Moreover, Stone and Warren (1999) studied 1993 basketball trading card prices, an indicator of fan preferences, and found no racial differences in prices, controlling for player performance. Kahn and Shah (2005) found no evidence of any impact of team racial composition on fan attendance in the NBA during the 1996–2001 seasons. And Coleman, DuMond, and Lynch (2008) found no evidence of racial discrimination in NBA Most Valuable Player voting by writers and sportscasters during the 1995–2005 period. On the other hand, Kanazawa and Funk (2001) found that, other things equal, more white players had a significantly positive effect on Nielsen ratings of televised NBA games during the 1996–1997 season. And Burdekin, Hossfeld, and Smith (2005) found for the 1990–1999 NBA seasons that the closeness of the racial match between the team and its metropolitan area raised attendance. This comparison of the evidence on customer discrimination in basketball during the 1980s versus the post-1980s period decades is consistent with the evidence that suggested a decline in salary and retention discrimination in the NBA during this period.

6. Conclusions

In this chapter, I have reviewed evidence on salary, hiring and retention, and customer discrimination in basketball. There was much evidence for each of these forms of discrimination against black NBA players in the 1980s. However, there appears to be less evidence of racial compensation, hiring and retention discrimination in the 1990s and early 2000s than the 1980s, and the apparent decline in customer discrimination since the 1980s is consistent with these changes. It is interesting to note that analyses of racial pay gaps in football and baseball generally do not find large or statistically significant nonwhite salary shortfalls, *ceteris paribus* (Kahn 2000). It is perhaps noteworthy that the sport with the most evidence consistent with racial salary discrimination, basketball, has historically had the largest black representation: as of the mid-1990s, it was 80 percent, in contrast to baseball's 30 percent and football's 65 percent.[11] These differences in racial representation suggest that customer preferences may have something to do with the racial pay gap we observed in basketball in the 1980s.

Notes

1   There are of course other potential forms of discrimination, such as discrimination in access to qualifications or differential standards for hiring, promotion, or retention. I will explore evidence on these in the context of basketball, as well as the more familiar form of discrimination, unequal treatment of equally qualified workers.

2 While most of my review will center on race, I will also discuss some evidence on discrimination against female college basketball coaches.

3 For example, in Major League Baseball in 2008, only 7 of 30 managers were black or Hispanic, and in the NFL, only 6 of 32 coaches in 2008 were black (www.espn.com, and www.nfl.com, both accessed October 14, 2008).

4 They would both be in the same detailed industry (Census Code 8560: "Independent artists, performing arts, spectator sports, and related industries") and the same detailed occupation (Census Code 2720: "Athletes, coaches, umpires, and related workers"). See www.nber.org for this documentation. Further pursuing the comparison between the CPS and NBA data, note that the 2008 March CPS earnings data are topcoded at $200,000, while the minimum NBA salary for the 2008–2009 season was $442,114 (see the 2005 NBA Collective Bargaining Agreement at www. nbpa.com). Thus, players on at least an annual NBA contract would be topcoded in the CPS, making it impossible to determine their individual salaries.

5 Of the studies of NBA players, Table 2.1 only includes those using data from 1984 onward and covering most or all players. There were a number of earlier studies using small samples (28 or fewer) from 1970–1981, and these are summarized in Kahn (1991b).

6 The effect on log salary of being white for the lower percentiles was: -.184 (asymptotic standard error .291) for the 10th percentile, -.209 (.183) for the 25th percentile, and -.005 (.152) for the 50th percentile.

7 While the overall effect on average salary levels of such a change in the composition of referees cannot be determined, the logic of this example implies that black relative salaries would rise by 0.03 log points.

8 The Appeals Court decision can be found at: http://laws.findlaw.com/9th/9555466.html.

9 This point about the conceptual difficulties in using racial differences in average performance levels as an indicator of discrimination in hiring was first made in the sports context in Pascal and Rapping's (1972) study of baseball players.

10 Since pro basketball is likely to be players' best earnings opportunity by far, it is reasonable to suppose that most exits from the league are due to injury or being cut, rather than due to locating a better job in another sector.

11 These figures were very similar in the 1980s as well. See Kahn (1991b) and Staudohar (1996).

REFERENCES

Angrist, J. D, and Krueger, A. B. 1999. Empirical strategies in labor economics, in O. Ashenfelter and D. Card (eds.), *Handbook of labor economics*, vol. IIIA. Amsterdam: North-Holland, 1277–1366.

Ashenfelter, O. 1972. Racial discrimination and trade unionism. *Journal of Political Economy*, 80(3): 435–464.

Becker, G. S. 1957. *The economics of discrimination*. Chicago: University of Chicago Press.

Binmore, K., Rubinstein, A., and Wolinsky, A. 1986. The Nash bargaining solution in economic modelling. *Rand Journal of Economics*, 17(2): 176–188.

Bodvarsson, Ö., and Brastow, R. T. 1998. Do employers pay for consistent performance? Evidence from the NBA. *Economic Inquiry*, 36(1): 145–160.

Bodvarsson, Ö., and Partridge, M. D. 2001. A supply and demand model of co-worker, employer and customer discrimination. *Labour Economics*, 8(2): 389–416.

Brown, E., Spiro, R., and Keenan, D. 1991. Wage and nonwage discrimination in professional basketball: Do fans affect it? *American Journal of Economics and Sociology*, 50(3): 333–345.

Brown, R. W., and Jewell, R. T. 1994. Is there customer discrimination in college basketball? The premium fans pay for white players. *Social Science Quarterly*, 75(2): 401–413.

Burdekin, R. C. K., Hossfeld, R. T., and Smith, J. K. 2005. Are NBA fans becoming indifferent to race? *Journal of Sports Economics*, 6(2): 144–159.

Burdekin, R. C. K., and Idson, T. L. 1991. Customer preferences, attendance and the racial structure of professional basketball teams. *Applied Economics*, 23(1), Part B: 179–186.

Coleman, B. J., DuMond, J. M., and Lynch, A. K. 2008. An examination of NBA MVP voting behavior: Does race matter? *Journal of Sports Economics*, 9(6): 606–627.

Dey, M. S. 1997. Racial differences in National Basketball Association players' salaries: Another look. *The American Economist*, 41(2): 84–90.

Eschker, E., Perez, S. J., and Siegler, M. V. 2004. The NBA and the influx of international players. *Applied Economics*, 6(10): 1009–1020.

Freeman, R. B. 1982. Union wage practices and wage dispersion within establishments. *Industrial & Labor Relations Review*, 36(1): 3–21.

Gius, M., and Johnson, D. 1998. An empirical investigation of wage discrimination in professional basketball. *Applied Economics Letters*, 5(11): 703–705.

Goff, B. L., McCormick, R. E., and Tollison, R. D. 2002. Racial integration as an innovation: Empirical evidence from sports leagues. *American Economic Review*, 92(1): 16–26.

Goldberger, A. S. 1984. Reverse regression and salary discrimination. *Journal of Human Resources*, 19(3): 293–318.

Groothuis, P. A., and Hill, J. R. 2004. Exit discrimination in the NBA: A duration analysis of career length. *Economic Inquiry*, 42(2): 341–349.

Hamilton, B. H. 1997. Racial discrimination and professional basketball salaries in the 1990s. *Applied Economics*, 29(3): 287–296.

Hoang, H., and Rascher, D. 1999. The NBA, exit discrimination, and career earnings. *Industrial Relations*, 38(1): 69–91.

Humphreys. B. R. 2000. Equal pay on the hardwood: The earnings gap between male and female NCAA Division I basketball coaches. *Journal of Sports Economics*, 1(3): 299–307.

Kahn, L. M. 1991a. Customer discrimination and affirmative action. *Economic Inquiry*, 29(3): 555–571.

Kahn, L. M. 1991b. Discrimination in professional sports: A survey of the literature, *Industrial & Labor Relations Review*, 44(3): 395–418.

Kahn, L. M. 2000. The sports business as a labor market laboratory. *Journal of Economic Perspectives*, 14(3): 75–94.

Kahn, L. M. 2006. Race, performance, pay, and retention among National Basketball Association head coaches. *Journal of Sports Economics*, 7(2): 119–149.

Kahn, L. M. and Shah, M. 2005. Race, compensation and contract length in the NBA: 2001–2002. *Industrial Relations*, 44(3): 444–462.

Kahn, L. M., and Sherer, P.D. 1988. Racial differences in professional basketball players' compensation. *Journal of Labor Economics*, 6(1): 40–61.

Kanazawa, M. T., and Funk, J. P. 2001. Racial discrimination in professional basketball: Evidence from Nielsen Ratings. *Economic Inquiry*, 39(4): 599–608.

Koch, J. V., and Vander Hill, C. W. 1988. Is there discrimination in the "black man's game"? *Social Science Quarterly*, 69(1): 83–94.

Madden, J. F. 1973. *The economics of sex discrimination*. Lexington, MA: Lexington Books.

McCormick, R. E., and Tollison, R. D. 2001. Why do black basketball players work more for less money? *Journal of Economic Behavior & Organization*, 44(2): 201–219.

NBA Collective Bargaining Agreement 2005.

Pascal, A. H., and Rapping, L. A. 1972. The economics of racial discrimination in organized baseball, in A. H. Pascal (ed.), *Racial discrimination in economic life*. Lexington, MA.: DC Heath, 119–156.

Platt, L. 2000. The white shadow, in T. Boyd and K. L. Shropshire (eds.), *Basketball Jones*. New York: New York University Press, 68–74.

Price, J., and Wolfers, J. 2010. Racial discrimination among NBA referees. *Quarterly Journal of Economics*, 125(4): 1859–1887.

Robinson, J. 1969. *The economics of imperfect competition*, 2nd ed. London: Macmillan.

Shropshire, K. L. 2000. Deconstructing the NBA, in T. Boyd and K. L. Shropshire (eds.), *Basketball Jones*. New York: New York University Press, 75–89.

Staudohar, P. D. 1996. *Playing for dollars: Labor relations and the sports business*. Ithaca, NY: Cornell University Press.

Stone, E. W., and Warren, Jr., R.S. 1999. Customer discrimination in professional basketball: Evidence from the trading-card market. *Applied Economics*, 31(6): 679–685.

Wallace, M. 1988.Labor market structure and salary determination among professional basketball players. *Work and Occupations*, 15(3): 294–312.

CHAPTER 3

GENDER AND DISCRIMINATION IN PROFESSIONAL GOLF

STEPHEN SHMANSKE

IF one group of people earns less than another, it may be because they are less productive, or because they are discriminated against, or both. In most industrial settings it is not possible to accurately measure all of the relevant dimensions of productivity, so it is impossible to determine the extent of discrimination that may exist. The benefit of pursuing "economics through sports" is that the existence of high-quality data on individual productivity allows one to untangle the productivity effect from the discrimination effect.

Shmanske (2000, 2004) used the high quality data collected by the PGA Tour and the Ladies Professional Golf Association (LPGA) during the 1998 seasons to examine the issue of gender discrimination in the earnings of professional golfers. Even though the men on the PGA Tour earn more in total and more per tournament than the women on the LPGA, their extra earnings are justified because the men play more tournaments, play longer tournaments, and exhibit more skill. If anything, there is a bias in favor of the women who play in tournaments that are closed to men, whereas the PGA Tour events are open to all who can qualify regardless of gender. Indeed, a handful of women, including Babe Zaharias, Annika Sorenstam, and Michelle Wie, have competed in PGA Tour events.

This chapter will update the analysis of gender discrimination in professional golf by using 2008 data to recreate the previous study. There may have been changes in the extent of discrimination in the past ten years, and by comparing recent data to those of 1998, the changes can be highlighted. For example, the National Committee on Pay Equity calculates a "wage gap," which is a raw measure of how much less women earn than men. According to their web site, the gap narrowed by approximately 20 percent from 1999 to 2007, as women's earnings climbed from 72.2 cents to 77.8 cents for each dollar of men's earnings.[1] These calculations indicate that the wage gap is narrowing but still exists. But since these calculations do not control for productivity, education, or experience, they could be misleading. By using the sports data, we can control for productivity and get a better picture of what has been happening to gender earnings differences over the past ten years.

The next section of the chapter explains the methodology used to examine the earnings gap. Explanations of the golf production function follow. Then comes the description of the data, including summary comparisons between men and women for the years 1998 and 2008. The results follow and a brief summary concludes the chapter.

METHODOLOGY

This chapter will use regression analysis to measure the effect of each of the skills used by professional golfers to win prize money in tournaments. The specific skills and their measurements are described in the next section. The first set of regressions will use 2008 earnings per tournament as the dependent variable. The regressions will be run for men and women separately:

$$Y_M = B_M X_M \text{ and } Y_W = B_W X_W \tag{1}$$

and pooled with an intercept-shifting dummy variable:

$$Y = BX \tag{2}$$

In equations (1) and (2), Y stands for income per tournament, X is a vector of relevant golf skills, and B is a vector of unknown coefficients interpretable as the price or value of each skill. In equation (1), the M and W subscripts refer to the split sample of men and women estimated separately. In equation (2) a dummy variable for women is added to the skill vector. These regressions will be compared to the same specifications from 1998. The sign and significance of the dummy variable will be the first indication of the extent of and change in gender discrimination.

It is well known in earnings regressions on levels that heteroskedasticity usually exists. By transforming the dependent variable to natural logarithms, this problem is avoided and a new (better) set of estimates can be obtained. Again, these regressions will be run on men and women separately and pooled, and the results compared to 1998.

The examination of discrimination based on the dummy variable in the above pooled regressions can be supplemented with a decomposition of the earnings gap following the method of Oaxaca (1973). The equations in (1) can be combined to yield:

$$Y_M - Y_W = (B_M - B_W) X_W + B_M (X_M - X_W) \tag{3}$$

Since the regression lines go through the means of the data, equation (3) can be interpreted to mean that the difference between mean earnings for men and women can be broken down into two terms. The first term on the right-hand side is the discrimination term. It is the difference in prices (B's) paid to men and women, and weighted by the average skill level of the women. The second term is not discrimination; it is due to the differences in skills as weighted by the men's coefficients. The payoff to this earnings gap decomposition is that the total gap, $Y_M - Y_W$, is separated into its component parts, so much for each separate dimension of the skill vector, X, so much due to different implicit prices paid to men and women, and a general component associated with the constant term.

The Oaxaca decomposition is not without ambiguities. First, the weights in equation (3) could be reversed as (3) can be rewritten as:

$$Y_M - Y_W = (B_M - B_W) X_M + B_W (X_M - X_W) \tag{3a}$$

As Oaxaca notes, this is essentially an index number problem. Results for the decomposition in (3) are reported in Tables 3.6 and 3.7, but see the notes accompanying the tables for the alternate weighting in (3a).

Second, as Oaxaca and Ransom (1999) point out, the calculations are sensitive to the measurement of the independent variables in equation (1). The overall amount of discrimination is not affected, but its breakdown among the individual skill dimensions and the constant term is. Furthermore, the interpretation of the results is not straightforward when some of the skills have negative prices.[2] For this reason, each of the skill variables is transformed linearly (for the purposes of the earnings decomposition, but not for the original regressions), so that zero measures the lowest level of each skill by anyone in the data, and all skills are measured positively. Thus, a higher measure indicates a higher skill and all prices will be positive. These linear transformations do not change the statistical properties of the regression equation or the size of the coefficients except for the constant term.

Ultimately, these ambiguities are not as troublesome as they might ordinarily be because the exact same methodology is used to assess the 1998 data as the 2008 data. Although no specific bias is expected, if some bias is present in both years, then its effect will cancel out and the trend in gender discrimination can still be discerned.

THE GOLF PRODUCTION FUNCTION

Professional golfers use a variety of skills to hit a small ball into a small hole in the ground that is sometimes over a quarter of a mile away. A round of golf consists of eighteen holes, and a typical tournament consists of four rounds over four consecutive days. The object is to complete the tournament in the fewest number of strokes, thereby winning monetary prizes that vary decidedly nonlinearly based on rank order performance. The basic skills can be enumerated in the explanation of play over a particular hole (called a par four) designed to take four strokes.

A player's first stroke on each hole is called the drive and the object is to hit the ball as far as possible down a closely mowed area of the course called the fairway. There are two measures of this skill. DRIVDIST is the length in yards of the drive, and DRIVACC is the percentage of a player's drives that end up in the fairway. See Table 3.1 for the summary statistics for these variables for both years and both genders. The next shot is typically played to the green, which is an even more closely mowed and smoothed area of grass where the hole is located. If the second shot on a par four hole is on the green, then the player is said to have reached the green in regulation. GIR is the percentage of times that the golfer achieves this, and thus measures the degree of this skill that the player exhibits. Once on the green in regulation, a player can take two putts to achieve par for the hole, but of course, the player is attempting to take only one putt. PUTTPER measures the average number of putts taken by a golfer to finish a hole on which the green was reached in regulation. PUTTPER is negatively related to the skill of putting since the object is to take as few strokes as possible. If a player does not reach the green in regulation, the ball sometimes ends up in a sandy area known as a bunker from which another special skill is required to extract the ball from the sandy area. This skill, called SANDSAVE, is the percentage of times that the player hits from a greenside bunker and sinks the next shot to finish the hole. These five skills are tracked by the PGA Tour and the LPGA and form the basis of all of the statistical work on the relationship between skills and earnings in professional golf.

Economists have been analyzing the relationship between golfer's skills and earnings since Shmanske (1992), who regressed earnings per tournament on these five skills. With minor variations in the list of control variables or the year or golfers for which the data was collected, others (Moy and Liaw, 1998; Nero, 2001; Shmanske, 2000; Rishe, 2001; Alexander and Kern, 2005) have followed this lead. These studies are typically reduced-form models in which earnings, earnings per tournament, or their logarithmic transformations are regressed on a vector of the skill variables. PUTTPER and GIR are always statistically and economically significant in these studies. Most of the time DRIVDIST is significant, and DRIVACC and SANDSAVE are often statistically significant in the theorized direction.

Notwithstanding the robustness of the reduced-form studies, Scully (2002), among others, has suggested that a multistage structural model should be examined. For example, Callan and Thomas (2007) have estimated a three-stage model in which skills produce scores which produce tournament ranks which produce earnings. Callan and Thomas (2007) derive slightly different parameter values but change none of the basic inferences about the skills and achieve a modest improvement in adjusted r-squared to the 0.73 range.

The above studies have all used the year-end averages of the skills measures as the explanatory variables. Shmanske (2008) has extended the analysis by using tournament by tournament data to calculate the variance and skewness of the skills along with the means in a structural model in which the distributions of skills produce distributions of scores which, in turn, produce earnings. The inferences do not change much in this approach, although the measurement of the skills does improve.

More recently, Kahane (2010) has used quantile regression techniques to confirm once again the strong relationships between the skills introduced above and earnings. The magnitudes of the coefficients are influenced by the quantile ranking of the golfer, but each of the skills does retain its significance in the regressions.

DATA

The 1998 data are taken directly from Shmanske (2000), where the description of the sources and calculations is documented. In this chapter we shall reprint the appropriate statistics from the tables therein. The 2008 data are taken from the web sites of the PGA Tour and the LPGA.[3]

There are four separate sets of data, two genders in each of two years. Each of the four sets has a different number of golfers for whom all of the statistics on skills and earnings were retrievable: for the PGA Tour, 130 top golfers in 1998 and 197 in 2008; for the LPGA, 178 top golfers in 1998 and 159 in 2008. The regressions below use all of the available data. However, for the purposes of comparing the summary statistics, the clearest comparison comes from considering the same number of top golfers from each data set. Therefore, in each part of Table 3.1, only the top 130 money earners are included.

The table shows that the biggest changes occurring over the ten-year period are in the dollar amounts, which jump dramatically for both the men and the women even after controlling for inflation. Men's average earnings, average earnings per event, and the earnings of the money leader all more than double. The women's earnings also increased, but did not quite keep up with the men's. The leading money winner's earnings almost doubled, as did the average earnings per event, but the average earnings for the top 130 women increased by "only" 62 percent in real terms.

When it comes to assessing the changes in skills over the past ten years, the obvious difference is a marked and statistically significant increase in driving distance of over 16 yards for the men on the PGA Tour. This is coupled with a large, statistically significant decrease in driving accuracy. There are also decreases in the measures of the other skills, although the magnitudes of the decreases suggest that the changes are of lesser importance.

Table 3.1 Summary Statistics PGA Tour

Panel A: 1998 Top 130 Money Winners				
Variable	Mean	Standard Deviation	Minimum	Maximum
DRIVDIST	271.25	7.800	249	299.4
DRIVACC	69.77	4.931	52.4	80.4
GIR	65.62	2.679	55.5	71.3
PUTTPER	1.778	0.0223	1.724	1.865
SANDSAVE	52.46	5.749	36.2	69.8
EVENTS	26.15	4.357	15	35
Y1998 nominal	623,400	500,330	10,870	2,591,031
(constant $2008)	823,511			
YPEREVENT	25,123	22,065	374.7	112,700
(constant $2008)	33,187			
LNYPEREVENT	9.808	0.831	5.926	11.632

Panel B: 2008 Top 130 Money Winners				
Variable	Mean	Standard Deviation	Minimum	Maximum
DRIVDIST	287.99	8.612	261.4	315
DRIVACC	63.41	5.154	51.1	74.0
GIR	64.91	2.633	58.0	71.1
PUTTPER	1.783	0.0227	1.718	1.842
SANDSAVE	49.92	5.628	36.8	63.7
EVENTS	26.26	4.464	15	36
Y2008	1,752,418	1,034,401	775,899	6,601,094
YPEREVENT	71,323	51,495	23,026	287,570
LNYPEREVENT	10.995	0.564	10.044	12.569

Summary Statistics LPGA

Panel C: 1998 Top 130 Money Winners				
Variable	Mean	Standard Deviation	Minimum	Maximum
DRIVDIST	238.00	8.834	215.1	260.4
DRIVACC	70.00	5.697	56.3	83.2
GIR	65.79	3.862	55.6	78.1
PUTTPER*	1.815	0.0258	1.734	1.870
SANDSAVE	39.75	7.200	21.9	62.2

(Continued)

Table 3.1 (*Continued*)

Variable	Mean	Standard Deviation	Minimum	Maximum
EVENTS	23.34	3.989	13	32
Y1998 nominal	186,010	195,630	27,720	1,092,748
(constant $2008)	245,719			
YPEREVENT	7,751	8,033	1,517	52,040
(constant $2008)	10,239			
LNYPEREVENT	8.576	0.835	7.325	10.860

Panel D: 2008 Top 130 Money Winners				
Variable	Mean	Standard Deviation	Minimum	Maximum
DRIVDIST	248.08	8.605	224.8	269.3
DRIVACC	67.79	5.266	50.3	79.9
GIR	63.69	3.226	54.7	71.6
PUTTPER	1.820	0.0280	1.736	1.918
SANDSAVE	38.08	8.228	14.29	60.0
EVENTS	21.84	4.517	10	30
Y2008	398,871	439,304	57,015	2,763,193
YPEREVENT 71,323	19,299	21,672	2,441	110,528
LNYPEREVENT	9.351	1.013	7.800	11.613

Notes: The 1998 data come from Shmanske [2000]. The 2008 data come from the web sites of the PGA Tour and the LPGA. DRIVDIST is measured in yards. DRIVACC, GIR, and SANDSAVE are measured in percentages times 100. PUTTPER is measured in putts per green.

* In 1998 the LPGA did not keep the PUTTPER statistic. The values used are estimates of what PUTTPER would have been given the other statistics. See Shmanske (2000) for details.

The changes on the LPGA mimic the men's results very closely. For driving, there is a large and statistically significant increase in driving distance (about 10 yards) and a decrease in driving accuracy. Additionally, there are decreases in the other three skills. The main difference between the men and the women is that the decrease in GIR for the women at just over two percentage points is of a magnitude that would seem to make an important difference.

Distance has improved for golfers at all levels of the game, including top level professionals, senior professionals, serious amateur competitors, and casual weekend golfers. There is no question that major sources of the increased distance are the technology improvements in the design and materials used in golf balls and golf clubs. As a matter of pure geometry, the farther one hits a ball, the farther (in feet) it strays from its intended direction for any given positive deflection (in degrees) from its intended direction. Therefore, a natural outcome of hitting the ball farther is the decrease in driving accuracy noted in the statistics. Of course, since both distance and accuracy are desirable, golfers attempt to manage the trade-off. There is room for more research on this one micro trade-off involved in golf, but it is beyond the scope of this chapter.

RESULTS

This section will compare results from 1998 to those of 2008. There are three sets of tests, taken in the following order. First, the section presents regressions of earnings per tournament, measured in levels where the coefficients are interpreted as the prices of each particular skill. The test for discrimination is in the dummy variable in the combined regressions. Following this come the regressions of earnings per tournament, measured in natural logarithms where the coefficients are interpreted as percentage changes in earnings due to each particular skill. Again, the test for discrimination focuses on the coefficient of FEMALE. Finally, a decomposition of the earnings gap based on the better-fitting logarithmic model is presented.

Consider Tables 3.2 and 3.3. Table 3.2 shows the regressions on levels for men and women separately, and combined with a dummy variable for women in 1998, as reprinted from the earlier study. To summarize, for the men, all the skills except SANDSAVE are significant in the theoretically predicted direction, and the estimates are of an economically meaningful magnitude. For the women, only GIR and PUTTPER are significant, and their values are less than those for the men. In the combined regression, DRIVDIST, DRIVACC, and PUTTPER are significant, and the dummy variable for the women indicates a bias *in favor* of the women of over $9,000 per tournament.

In 2008 there are some changes indicated in Table 3.3. For the men, all of the skills except DRIVACC are significant and of relevant magnitudes. In fact, the magnitudes of the significant coefficients all increase, which is to be expected given the roughly 32 percent accumulated inflation over the period and the increase in the inflation-adjusted prize levels. SANDSAVE is now significant but accuracy with tee shots seems to be unimportant. The decrease in the player's accuracy with tee shots that was noted in the summary statistics is consistent with a rational response of golfers to the waning importance of this skill.

For the women, putting and hitting greens in regulation are still significantly related to earnings per tournament and SANDSAVE is added to the list of significant skills. Furthermore, the magnitudes of the coefficients increase markedly, almost tripling for the case of GIR.

Table 3.2 Regressions of Earnings per Tournament (Levels) on Skills, 1998
(t-statistics in parentheses)

Dependent variable	Men only YPEREVENT	Women only YPEREVENT	Combined YPEREVENT
Constant	334,476*	117,193***	102,461
	(1.809)	(4.000)	(1.516)
FEMALE			9,136.14*
			(1.777)
DRIVDIST	980.499***	47.1722	527.503***
	(3.560)	(0.724)	(4.004)
DRIVACC	832.748*	42.8813	501.202***
	(1.729)	(0.489)	(2.611)
GIR	1381.27*	656.092***	232.120
	(1.673)	(5.069)	(0.812)
SANDSAVE	31.1046	35.3340	139.199
	(0.106)	(0.663)	(1.179)
PUTTPER	−408,078***	−92,432***	−156,287***
	(−4.704)	(−7.100)	(−5.246)
adjusted R2	0.334	0.547	0.443
n	130	178	308

Source: Shmanske (2000). *, **, *** indicate significance at the .10, .05, .01 levels, respectively.

In the combined regression, GIR, SANDSAVE, and, PUTTPER are significant, and their coefficients increase by an average of over 400 percent from the 1998 figures. Interestingly, however, driving distance and accuracy are no longer important in the combined regression. Also losing its significance is the dummy variable for women. This equation no longer supports the claim that the LPGA is discriminating in favor of women in their tournament setups, prize funds, and exclusion of male competitors.

Overall, the 2008 regressions on levels of earnings per tournament are estimated with less precision than those from 1998. The levels regressions are easily interpretable; however, they suffer from heteroskedascity that is corrected by the logarithmic transformation we now move to.

Consider Tables 3.4 and 3.5. Table 3.4 recaps the 1998 results. In all three regressions, all of the coefficients have the expected sign and all are statistically significant except SANDSAVE for the men. An increase in a yard of driving distance can increase earnings by between 1 percent and 3 percent. An increase of a percentage

Table 3.3 Regressions of Earnings per Tournament (Levels) on Skills, 2008
(t-statistics in parentheses)

Dependent variable	Men only YPEREVENT	Women only YPEREVENT	Combined YPEREVENT
Constant	490,196	88,856	304,015*
	(1.506)	(0.800)	(1.763)
FEMALE			9,257.93
			(0.708)
DRIVDIST	1032.29*	238.62	438.28
	(1.704)	(1.011)	(1.277)
DRIVACC	−1000.20	−230.27	−838.01
	(−1.045)	(−0.655)	(−1.571)
GIR	2792.49*	1861.02***	1718.77**
	(1.740)	(3.424)	(2.044)
SANDSAVE	1994.33***	300.09*	858.23***
	(3.093)	(1.836)	(2.992)
PUTTPER	−531,893***	−133,760**	−267,581***
	(−3.504)	(−2.987)	(−3.731)
adjusted R2	0.167	0.296	0.279
n	197	159	356

*, **, *** indicate significance at the .10, .05, .01 levels, respectively.

point in DRIVACC or SANDSAVE can also increase earnings by a few percent. GIR is especially important in that an increase by one percentage point in this skill can increase earnings by 7 percent to 12 percent. Intuitively grasping the magnitude of the coefficient of PUTTPER involves a little computation on the side. The coefficient measures the effect of a decrease of one putt per green reached in regulation. Consider the effect of one more made putt per tournament. Since tournaments typically have 72 holes with roughly 65 percent of them reached in regulation, we must divide the coefficient of PUTTPER by $0.65 \times 72 = 46.8$ to get the effect. For the combined sample the effect of a decrease of one putt is about a 42 percent increase in earnings per tournament. This figure is reasonable. For the leaders in a tournament, moving up one place in rank order can almost double one's payoff. Meanwhile, in the middle of the pack, a one-stroke improvement could increase one's rank from a ten-way tie for fortieth place into a ten-way tie for thirtieth place, with a commensurate increase in earnings. The bottom line for

Table 3.4 Regressions of Earnings per Tournament (Logarithms) on Skills, 1998 (t-statistics in parentheses)

	Men only	Women only	Combined
Dependent variable	LNYPEREVENT	LNYPEREVENT	LNYPEREVENT
Constant	23.8913***	31.0894***	28.6281***
	(4.024)	(9.637)	(10.09)
FEMALE			0.2859
			(1.324)
DRIVDIST	0.03624***	0.01574**	0.02327***
	(4.099)	(2.195)	(4.205)
DRIVACC	0.05112***	0.01683*	0.02715***
	(3.307)	(1.743)	(3.367)
GIR	0.07519***	0.12225***	0.11012***
	(2.836)	(8.578)	(9.172)
SANDSAVE	0.00398	0.01585***	0.01203**
	(0.422)	(2.700)	(2.427)
PUTTPER	−18.3444***	−19.9488***	−19.6158***
	(−6.588)	(−13.92)	(−15.68)
adjusted R2	0.516	0.814	0.844
n	130	178	308

Source: Shmanske (2000). *, **, *** indicate significance at the .10, .05, .01 levels, respectively.

the 1998 equations is that the FEMALE dummy was insignificant, again, failing to show discrimination against women in professional golf.

Now, moving up to 2008 and Table 3.5, we see that, as in 1998, the best fitting model is the combined equation with no evidence of a discrimination for or against women. The magnitudes of the coefficient estimates are very similar to those of 1998 for all of the variables except DRIVACC which is decidedly insignificant in all three equations. Each yard of driving distance can add about 1.7 percent to earnings. A percentage point increase in GIR leads to about a 9 percent increase. A percentage point increase in SANDSAVE adds between 1 percent and 2 percent. Finally, earnings are once again extremely sensitive to putting. Like 1998, there is no evidence showing discrimination against female professional golfers once skill levels are taken into account.

Based on the logarithmic models the unadjusted earnings gap at the mean of the data is 1.8216 log points in 1998 and 1.5485 in 2008. The change represents a decrease in the gap of 15 percent, a figure comparable to the 20 percent reduction in the gap

Table 3.5 Regressions of Earnings per Tournament (Logarithms) on Skills, 2008 (t-statistics in parentheses)

	Men only	Women only	Combined
Dependent variable	LNYPEREVENT	LNYPEREVENT	LNYPEREVENT
Constant	28.1582***	23.153***	26.6406***
	(4.819)	(3.701)	(6.405)
FEMALE			0.1293
			(0.410)
DRIVDIST	0.01671	0.0184	0.0169**
	(1.537)	(1.387)	(2.045)
DRIVACC	−0.00090	−0.00107	−0.0020
	(−0.052)	(−0.054)	(−0.153)
GIR	0.07142**	0.1100***	0.09473***
	(2.479)	(3.595)	(4.670)
SANDSAVE	0.01987*	0.01336	0.01549**
	(1.717)	(1.451)	(2.239)
PUTTPER	−15.6741***	−14.286***	−15.547***
	(−5.753)	(−5.665)	(−8.988)
adjusted R2	0.203	0.439	0.566
n	197	159	356

*, **, *** indicate significance at the .10, .05, .01 levels, respectively.

calculated by the National Committee on Pay Equity. Nevertheless, this figure is unadjusted for skills levels, which have changed, and as such, may be misleadingly irrelevant. Indeed, a positive wage gap by itself can even be consistent with reverse discrimination, as was the case in 1998. Using the method described in equation (3), two sets of terms can be identified to partition the total gap into portions attributable to productivity and discrimination. The 1998 decomposition is listed in Table 3.6.

In the calculations underlying Table 3.6, the separate regressions in Table 3.4 are re-estimated with rescaled skills variables. Each of the skills variables is linearly transformed so that zero represents the worst level of the skill by any golfer and so that all skills are measured positively. This transformation does not affect the coefficients, except for a sign reversal for PUTTPER and except for the constant term, nor does it affect the statistical properties of the regression.

Table 3.6 confirms that women are not discriminated against. A *negative* 29 percent of the earnings gap is due to discrimination, meaning that based on the higher level of skills exhibited by the men, the earnings gap should be even 29

Table 3.6 Decomposition of Earnings Gap 1998
(unadjusted differential = 1.8216)

Variable	% of Gap Due to Differences	
	in Estimated Coefficients	in Average Skill Levels
Constant	−0.272	0
DRIVDIST	0.320	0.689
DRIVACC	0.342	0.020
GIR	−0.463	0.066
SANDSAVE	−0.129	0.029
PUTTPER	−0.088	0.487
Total	−0.290	1.291

Note: The above table weights the percentage of the gap due to differences in estimated coefficients by the women's mean skills and the percentage of the gap due to differences in average skill levels by the men's estimated regression coefficients. When the alternative weighting scheme is used, the totals are −0.057 for discrimination and 1.055 for skills differences.
Source: Shmanske (2000).

percent higher than it is. On a skill by skill basis, there is evidence that women's driving skills are rewarded less than men's by 32 percent for distance and 34 percent for accuracy. However, this deficit is more than made up by the higher payoff on the other skills (especially GIR) and by the 27 percent general favoring of women in the constant term. As indicated in the note to Table 3.6, these figures may overstate the case. With the alternative weighting scheme from equation (3a), the discrimination *against men* is only on the order of 5 or 6 percent. As is usual for an index number of this sort, the truth is bracketed by the two extreme estimates.

Before moving to the discussion of the 2008 decomposition in Table 3.7, one change needs to be explained. In the 1998 comparison, all of the coefficient estimates are the right sign and all but one (SANDSAVE for men) are statistically significant. Therefore, some care should be exercised when interpreting the SANDSAVE portion of the decomposition. Upon examination, SANDSAVE does not seem to be wildly influencing the results. In the 2008 equations, however, the point estimate of the return to DRIVACC is actually negative, although statistically insignificant, and, quantitatively, practically zero. Since negative prices confuse the interpretation of the earnings gap decomposition, and since the coefficients are practically zero anyway, the regressions in Table 3.5 are re-estimated, with rescaled variables as explained above, and excluding DRIVACC. The coefficient estimates and the average skill levels are then used as in equation (3) to decompose the gap, and these measures are normalized by the average gap of 1.5485 log points to derive the percentage estimates in Table 3.7.

Table 3.7 Decomposition of Earnings Gap 2008
(unadjusted differential = 1.5485)

Variable	% of Gap Due to Differences	
	in Estimated Coefficients	in Average Skill Levels
Constant	0.191	0
DRIVDIST	−0.025	0.452
DRIVACC*	0	0
GIR	−0.522	0.084
SANDSAVE	0.161	0.155
PUTTPER	0.103	0.401
Total	−0.092	1.092

Note: The above table weights the percentage of the gap due to differences in estimated coefficients by the women's mean skills and the percentage of the gap due to differences in average skill levels by the men's estimated regression coefficients. When the alternative weighting scheme is used, the totals are −0.097 for discrimination and 1.099 for skills differences.

* DRIVACC is dropped from the regression. The coefficients were negative and the corresponding t-statistics were −0.052 and −0.054 for the men and women, respectively.

The decomposition in Table 3.7 confirms and reinforces the 1998 results. Women are not discriminated against in professional golf. There is a minor amount of discrimination in the returns to putting and SANDSAVE, but this is more than offset in that the women are actually compensated a little more for the skill of driving distance and a great deal more (52 percent) for hitting greens in regulation. Overall, only *negative* 9 percent of the gap between the women's average earnings and the men's average earnings is attributable to discrimination. That is, once the higher level of skills of the men is taken into account, the earnings gap should actually be 9 percent higher.

Summary

High-quality data on the skills required to excel in professional golf allow one to examine gender discrimination in society in a way that controls for productivity. Such is one of the important payoffs to studying economic issues through the lens of sports. Wage or salary gaps between men and women still exist in American society, although they have been narrowing. Nevertheless, such gaps are not evidence of discrimination in and of themselves. The gaps are justified if they are due to productivity differences.

In professional golf, regressions of earnings per tournament on the important skills, as identified by golf production functions, had indicated that there was no discrimination against female golfers in 1998. This chapter updated the analysis to the latest available 2008 data and reached the same conclusion. If anything, point estimates indicate that an even larger gap could be justified once the skills differences are taken into account. This result is reached by including a dummy variable in regressions that pool PGA Tour and LPGA data and by performing a decomposition of the earnings gap by manipulating the coefficients from regressions that segregate the data. The pooled regressions indicate that women earn about $9,000 or 13 percent too much. The decomposition indicates that the wage gap could be about 9 percent higher than it is. However, none of these point estimates is precise enough to reject the null hypothesis that there is no discrimination either way.

The result of no discrimination should not be surprising. The PGA Tour, which is the source of the data for the male golfers in the sample, does not discriminate against women. Women are allowed to play on the PGA Tour and occasionally do so. However, the competition is stiffer on the PGA Tour than it is in the female-only LPGA tournaments. Therefore, female professional golfers find it more lucrative to compete in LPGA events where men are excluded. If the LPGA did not offer at least as good a deal to women as the PGA Tour offers (in fact, the LPGA offers a slightly better deal), then female golfers would leave the LPGA and attempt more often to compete on the open to all genders PGA Tour.

NOTES

1 http://www.pay-equity.org/info-time.html, accessed on August 1, 2009.
2 For example, the skill of putting is measured as the number of putts it takes on average on greens "hit in regulation" (explained below). Since fewer putts are better, the "price" of a putt is negative.
3 See pgatour.com and lpga.com.

REFERENCES

Alexander, D. L., and Kern, W. (2005). Drive for show and putt for dough?: An analysis of the earnings of PGA Tour golfers. *Journal of Sports Economics*, 6(1): 46–60.

Callan, S. J., and Thomas, J. M. (2007). Modeling the determinants of a professional golfer's tournament earnings: A multiequation approach. *Journal of Sports Economics*, 8(4): 394–411.

Kahane, L. H. (2010). Returns to skills in professional golf: A quantile regression approach. *International Journal of Sport Finance*, 5(3): 167–180.

Moy, R. L., and Liaw, T. (1998). Determinants of professional golf tournament earnings. *The American Economist*, 42(1): 65–70.

Nero, P. (2001). Relative salary efficiency of PGA Tour golfers. *The American Economist*, 45(1): 51–56.

Oaxaca, R. (1973). Male-female wage differentials in urban labor markets. *International Economic Review*, 14 (October): 693–709.

Oaxaca, R., and Ransom, M. R. (1999). Identification in detailed wage decompositions. *The Review of Economics and Statistics*, 81 (February): 154–157.

Rishe, P. J. (2001). Differing rates of return to performance: A comparison of the PGA and Senior golf tours. *Journal of Sports Economics*, 2(3): 285–296.

Scully, G. W. (2002). The distribution of performance and earnings in a prize economy. *Journal of Sports Economics*, 3(3): 235–245.

Shmanske, S. (2007). Consistency or Heroics: Skewness, Performance, and Earnings on the PGA TOUR. *Atlantic Economic Journal*, 35(4): 463–471.

Shmanske, S. (2000). Gender, skill, and earnings in professional golf. *Journal of Sports Economics*, 1(4) (November): 400–415.

Shmanske, S. (2004). *Golfonomics*. River Edge, NJ: World Scientific Publishing.

Shmanske, S. (1992). Human capital formation in professional sports: Evidence from the PGA Tour. *Atlantic Economic Journal*, 20(3): 66–80.

Shmanske, S. (2008). Skills, performance, and earnings in the tournament compensation model: Evidence from PGA Tour Microdata. *Journal of Sports Economics*, 9(6): 644–662.

## CHAPTER 4

THE ECONOMICS OF DISCRIMINATION

EVIDENCE FROM HOCKEY

NEIL LONGLEY

1. INTRODUCTION

THE National Hockey League (NHL) is considered one of the four major professional sports leagues in North America. However, when compared to its three counterparts—the National Football League (NFL), Major League Baseball (MLB), and the National Basketball Association (NBA)—the NHL exhibits many differences from these leagues. While these differences exist along numerous dimensions, it is differences in the nature of the labor market, and the corresponding implications for possible discrimination, that are most relevant to this chapter.

The most fundamental difference between the NHL's labor market and that of the other leagues is that the NHL's labor market is characterized by a high degree of international diversity. In fact, it is the only league where Americans do not comprise the majority of players—only about 20 percent of current NHL players are American. Furthermore, there is almost a complete racial homogeneity among these American players, with "white" players comprising nearly 100 percent of players. Unlike the other three leagues, where there is a strong presence of African American players—they comprise, for example, about 80 percent of NBA players and 60 percent of NFL players—African Americans have seemingly never been drawn to the game of hockey, and, with a few exceptions, have essentially been nonexistent within the NHL.[1]

As a result of these differences, the types of discrimination issues studied in hockey are quite unique within the North American setting—discrimination within an NHL context pertains more to issues of national origin and/or ethnicity, rather than race. Thus, in order to study discrimination in the NHL, one needs to have an understanding of the broader social framework within which professional hockey operates in North America. The usual contextual lens through which discrimination in sport is typically studied—that of a racially divided America—is simply not relevant for hockey.

2. BACKGROUND

The NHL

The NHL's existence dates back to 1917, when the league was formed in Montreal, Canada, making the league older than both the NFL (formed in 1920) and the NBA (formed in 1946). In its early years, the league was purely Canadian-based—in its inaugural season of 1917–1918, the NHL was a four-team league, with two franchises in Montreal, and one each in Toronto and Ottawa. It wasn't until 1924 that the first American franchise—the Boston Bruins—was added to the league. By 1926–1927, the league had grown to ten teams, but over the next fifteen years a consolidation of franchises occurred, and by 1942–1943 the league was down to only six teams, two in Canada and the other four in the United States. For the next twenty-five years, these exact same six teams—the Montreal Canadiens, Toronto Maple Leafs, Boston Bruins, New York Rangers, Detroit Red Wings, and Chicago Black Hawks—comprised the NHL, providing the league with a long stretch of uninterrupted franchise stability.

In 1967, the league doubled in size by adding six expansion franchises, all in the United States. With further rounds of expansion over the next several years, the NHL added another six teams, bringing the league's franchise total to eighteen by 1974–1975. The reasons for this rapid expansion by the NHL are traceable, at least in part, to the formation in 1972 of a rival professional hockey league, called the World Hockey Association (WHA)—the NHL sought to enter attractive unserved markets before the WHA. The WHA played its inaugural season in 1972–1973 with twelve franchises, four in Canada and eight in the US. The WHA itself expanded, and by 1974–1975 the league had fourteen franchises. These fourteen franchises, along with the NHL's eighteen franchises, meant there were thirty-two major professional hockey franchises in operation in 1974–1975—compare this with only eight years earlier, when there were just the "original six" NHL franchises in operation. This dramatic and rapid growth in the number of franchises marked a crucial time period for professional hockey, and as will be discussed later, had significant implications for the nature of the labor market, and, ultimately, for issues relating to discrimination.

The WHA eventually folded in 1979, and four teams—the Edmonton Oilers, Quebec Nordiques (now Colorado Avalanche), Winnipeg Jets (now Phoenix Coyotes), and Hartford Whalers (now Carolina Hurricanes)—were absorbed into the NHL, bringing the NHL's franchise total to twenty-one. No new franchises were added during the 1980s, but the 1990s saw the NHL add nine more expansion franchises, bringing the league's franchise total to thirty, the number where it is currently at today. Of these thirty franchises, six are in Canada, and twenty-four are in the United States.

Much of the expansion during the 1990s was into what could be termed "non-traditional" hockey markets—warmer-weather locations, such as Tampa, Miami, Atlanta, and Nashville in the southeastern United States, and Anaheim and San Jose in California. This marked an effort by the league to expand its franchise footprint beyond its more traditional strongholds in Canada and the northern United States.

The Players

Unlike the other three major professional sports leagues in North America—where Americans comprise the great majority of players—American players are a minority group in the NHL, comprising only about 22 percent of all players in the league during 2008–2009. This number is actually at a historical high. Up until the 1970s, there were virtually no American players in the NHL—almost 100 percent of players were from Canada. This dominance by Canadian players for the first half-century of the NHL's existence owes to the league's Canadian origins, and to the immense popularity of the sport in Canada. However, even in the era when virtually all players were from Canada, they were not necessarily a homogenous group. While the majority of Canadian players were of English origin, a significant minority were from the province of Quebec and of French descent. These Francophones possessed a culture and language separate and distinct from the majority group, and, as will be discussed later in the chapter, have been the focus of much of the academic analysis in the area.

During the 1970s, the first non-Canadians began to enter the NHL. With the rapid expansion of the NHL during the late 1960s and early 1970s, and the emergence of the WHA, the demand for players increased dramatically. Some teams, particularly those in the WHA, began to see Europe as a source of untapped talent. The early Europeans in the league were primarily from Sweden, and to a lesser extent, Finland. During the 1970s and through the 1980s, the number of Swedes and Finns in the NHL slowly but steadily grew. During that same era, a small number of players from the former Czechoslovakia also began to enter the league, usually by defecting from the communist country. The 1980s also saw a significant increase in the number of American players in the league. The U.S.

Olympic Hockey team's capturing of the gold medal at the 1980 Winter Olympics is often credited with hastening the interest in the sport in the United States. The U.S. Olympic team—composed of a group of relatively unknown college players—defeated the powerful Soviet Union in the semi-final game, in one of the most memorable moments in American sports. As a result of these broad shifts in the labor market, by 1990 the number of Canadians in the NHL was down to 77 percent of all players, with 15 percent now coming from the United States, and the other 8 percent from Europe.

The demise of the Soviet Union in the early 1990s marked the beginning of unprecedented European migration into the NHL. Players from Soviet-bloc countries were now able to freely leave their country to play in the NHL. The biggest influx was from Russia, but the 1990s also saw increases in the number of Czechs and Slovaks, along with some players from countries like the Ukraine and Belarus. These changes further eroded the dominance of Canadian players in the league, and as of the 2008–2009 season, Canadians comprised 52 percent of NHL players, with Europeans accounting for 26 percent and Americans for 22 percent.

While the United States is now also a major producer of NHL players, it is important to note that the pattern of production is much different from that in the other three major professional leagues. Unlike basketball, baseball, and football, which all have a strong national presence, hockey still has very much a regional element. Thus, while the NHL has expanded to achieve a national footprint in the *output* market, with franchises in 24 U.S. cities, spanning all major geographic regions of the country, the grassroots interest in the game is much more limited. To illustrate, of the American players that have ever played in the NHL, a full 44 percent of them were born in one of two states, Massachusetts and Minnesota, despite the fact that these states comprise only about 4 percent of the U.S. population. If one adds a third state, Michigan, these three states comprise 58 percent of all NHL players born in the United States.[2]

3. Exploring the Roots of Potential Discrimination: Minority Groups in the NHL

The NHL essentially has three minority groups: Americans, Europeans, and French Canadians. However, it has generally been the presumption that if discrimination were to occur, it would most likely involve the latter two, rather than Americans. With the great majority of NHL franchises being located in the United States, and with Americans sharing a similar culture and common language with the league's dominant group (i.e., English Canadians) the possibility of discrimination against American players has not been at the forefront of the discussion. Rather, the focus in the discrimination literature has been on French Canadians, and, to a lesser extent, Europeans.

French Canadians

To better understand the roots of possible discrimination against French Canadians in the NHL, it is imperative to understand key aspects of French Canadian society, and of the relationship between French Canada and English Canada.

Francophones are a minority group within Canada, comprising about 20 percent of the Canadian population. The great majority of Francophones live in the province of Quebec; within Quebec, Francophones are the majority, comprising approximately 80 percent of that province's population. Outside of Quebec, Francophones comprise less than 5 percent of the population.

This geographic segregation, combined with language and cultural differences, has resulted in French Canada being very separate and distinct from the rest of Canada—in some ways, French Canada has elements of being a nation within a nation. French-English relations in Canada have often been referred to as "two solitudes," with each ethnic group coexisting within the same country, but with very little real integration between the two. As an illustration, most of French Canada's film stars, media personalities, and musicians are virtually unknown in the rest of Canada.

With these two distinct founding cultures of Canada, French-English relations, and their corresponding tensions, have occupied much of the political discourse throughout Canada's almost 150-year history. For Francophones, preservation of their distinct language and culture from domination by the majority has always been of great political concern. One manifestation of this concern has been a discomfort with increased "federalism," whereby the power of provinces to exercise control over language, education, immigration, and so on—that is, issues that many Francophones see as particularly important to preserving French culture—are usurped by (Anglophone-dominated) federal governments.

Within Quebec, there have long been political movements that have advocated Quebec's independence from the rest of Canada. However, such sentiments became more starkly visible in 1976, when a political party called the Parti Quebecois won the Quebec provincial election on a platform advocating that the province separate from the rest of Canada. In one of the most dramatic political events in Canadian history, the Parti Quebecois held a provincial referendum on the issue in 1980, seeking to get approval from the Quebec people to begin to negotiate Quebec's exit from Canada. The referendum to seek separation was defeated, but only by a margin of 60 percent to 40 percent, a narrower difference than most observers were predicting. Even more telling was that a majority of Francophones voted in favor of separation.

Fifteen years later, in 1995, another referendum was held on the issue, again organized by a Parti Quebecois government. This referendum was also defeated, but this time by the very narrowest of margins (50.58 percent to 49.42 percent), and in this referendum Francophones overwhelming voted for the separation option (about 60 percent voted in favor of separation)—the referendum was defeated only because the non-Francophone minority in the province voted almost 100 percent against separation. The separatist movement has also had political success at the federal level in Quebec. In 1993, a newly formed party called the Bloc Quebecois won 54 of Quebec's 75 federal seats, the second-highest number for any Canadian party in that election (even though it won no seats outside of Quebec), thus creating the ironic situation in which a party advocating the breakup of Canada was the country's Official Opposition in the House of Commons. The party has continued this success over the past fifteen years, claiming the majority of Quebec seats in each successive federal election since that time.

There has also been a violent element to the history of Quebec independence. In one of the most significant events in Canadian history, the so-called "October Crisis" of 1970 saw a terrorist group known as the Front de Liberation de Quebec (FLQ) kidnap Pierre Laporte, a Quebec provincial politician, and James Cross, the British trade commissioner to Canada; Cross was eventually released, but Laporte was murdered. The FLQ advocated Quebec independence, and had conducted over 200 bombings throughout Quebec during the 1960s. In response to the FLQ kidnappings, Canada's prime minister at the time, Pierre Trudeau, invoked the War Measures Act, which essentially imposed martial law in Canada.

For many English Canadians, events such as the FLQ crisis, along with the rise of the Parti Quebecois and Bloc Quebecois, hardened attitudes over time, and no doubt further increased the gaps between English and French perspectives. Some English Canadians resented what they saw as the desire by some Francophones to break up Canada.

It is within this context, then, that the experiences of French Canadian players in the NHL must be viewed. Although French Canadians have generally comprised only about 10 percent of players throughout the NHL's history, they have impacted the NHL beyond their numbers. Many of the greatest, and most dynamic, players in NHL history have been Francophone—Maurice (Rocket) Richard in the 1950s, Jean Beliveau in the 1960s, Guy Lafleur in the 1970s, and Mario Lemieux in the 1980s and 1990s, to name only a few. In fact, if one examines the top fifty all-time leading goal scorers in NHL history, twelve, or 24 percent, are French Canadians.

In the so-called "original-six" era (prior to 1967), the majority of these French Canadians played for the Montreal Canadiens. In this era, there was no NHL draft, and each team was free to scout and sign whomever it could. However, there was an exception to this general rule—the Montreal Canadiens were given a type of special status, and were essentially given first priority on the top French Canadian amateur players in Quebec. While a few of these French Canadians somehow slipped past the Canadiens—players like Marcel Pronovost, Rod Gilbert, and Jean Ratelle—the Canadiens had an effective monopsony over the best French Canadian talent of that era.

With NHL expansion occurring in 1967, and the corresponding introduction of the player draft, the Canadiens lost their special status. However, their accumulation of talent prior to the introduction of the draft, combined with some shrewd draft strategies in the early years of the draft, meant the Canadiens had a very strong French Canadian presence through most of the 1970s. Since then, French Canadians have been widely dispersed across the league, although the Canadiens often still display a preference for Francophone players, all else equal.

With respect to possible discrimination against French Canadians, those within the game—whether it be league executives, owners, team management, and players—have an obvious interest in denying any existence of discrimination. However, there is anecdotal evidence to suggest that tensions exist. In 2000, Vaclav Prospal, a European player, admitted making an ethnic slur towards Patrice Brisebois, a French Canadian player, and was ordered by the NHL to take sensitivity training.[3] In 2005, Sean Avery, an English Canadian player, was forced to apologize after making disparaging remarks against French Canadians.[4] Long-time Canadian hockey commentator Don Cherry—former coach of the Boston Bruins in the 1970s, and perhaps the most influential media personality in hockey over the past quarter-century—has often been accused of expressing sentiments on Canadian television that could be interpreted as anti-French.[5] Cherry has also used his hockey platform to delve into non-hockey issues, including French-English political issues mentioned earlier.

Joyce's (2007) popular press book on hockey scouts further illustrates these tensions. He reports on an incident he observed at a Quebec Major Junior League game (known in hockey circles as "the Q") in the heavily francophone city of Rimouski, Quebec. He writes that when "O'Canada" (Canada's national anthem) is played, "a good portion of the crowd doesn't stand, a sight you'll see around the Q." This apparent gesture of disrespect by fans toward Canada is reacted to angrily by a (presumably English Canadian) NHL scout, who scolds an elderly fan seated nearby, saying "I guess that means you won't be cashing your *Canada* pension cheque" (emphasis mine).[6]

Europeans

When European players first began arriving in North America in the 1970s, they did not always face a welcoming environment. At the time, the style of play in Europe was very different from that in North America. The European game was faster-paced, and placed more emphasis on such fundamental skills as skating, passing, and stick handling. In contrast, the North American style of game was much more oriented toward physical play and body contact, where skills such as body-checking were highly valued, and where fighting and physical intimidation were both commonplace and an accepted part of the game.

As a result of these differences, the early European players in North America were reported to have been subject to not only constant physical intimidation tactics, but also verbal abuse by their North American opponents—abuse that apparently often involved ethnic slurs. In the (Canadian) media, Europeans were often chided for being "soft" and for taking jobs from "more worthy" North American players. Don Cherry, the aforementioned Canadian hockey commentator, was, and still is, one of the biggest critics of Europeans, and has continued to perpetuate stereotypes of Europeans that were first heard in the 1970s.

However, with the continued migration of Europeans to the NHL over the past four decades, the on-ice differences between Europeans and North Americans has waned, with the two styles of play gradually converging. European leagues now play a more physical style than they did in the 1970s, and, conversely, North American hockey has been heavily influenced by European styles, with relatively more emphasis at the youth level on speed and skill, and somewhat less emphasis on physicality and outright brutality.

Even with this convergence, however, negative perceptions of European players are still sometimes exhibited. Joyce (2007) notes how in major-junior hockey in Canada (the primary amateur feeder system for the NHL, and a league where some high-potential, teenaged European prospects come to play) "some Euros alienate their Canadian teammates within minutes of walking into their dressing rooms," and how "stories of carpetbaggers and prima donnas have given incoming Euros an image problem."[7] On a related note regarding "image," Don Cherry has been particularly critical of the Russian NHL star Alexandre Ovechin for Ovechkin's "excessive" on-ice celebrations after goals, negatively comparing the celebrations to what occurs in soccer, and arguing how players must be taught the "Canadian way."[8]

In summary, it is reasonable to suggest that Canadian fans and media have a much stronger sense of "ownership" of the game of hockey than what is found in the United States. Unlike the United States—where hockey is generally limited to simply being "entertainment," particularly with the NHL's expansion into many nontraditional hockey markets—hockey is part of the cultural fabric of Canada, thus increasing the likelihood that broader social and political issues will impinge on the game.

4. THE LITERATURE

The Economics of Discrimination

The background discussions of the previous section provide a contextual framework within which to analyze the economics literature on the issue. From this background information, it is apparent that the NHL is quite different from the other three major North American sports leagues, particularly in terms of the nature of its workforce—whereas the research question in the other three leagues has largely focused on assessing the extent to which African Americans may have suffered from discrimination, in the NHL the research question revolves more around discrimination based on nationality and ethnicity, rather than race. In this regard, the NHL presents an interesting and complex set of dichotomous relationships— Europeans versus North Americans; Eastern Europeans versus Western Europeans; Americans versus Canadians; English Canadians versus French Canadians, and so on—all of which could, in themselves, provide the necessary conditions and foundations for discriminatory behavior. The question, then, is this: given that there exists in the NHL these potential conditions and foundations for discrimination, does such discrimination actually occur? The question can only be answered through empirical testing, and it has been such empiricism that has characterized most of the work in the area.

The empirical work in the area has its theoretical foundations in the work of Becker (1957), whose seminal work on the economics of discrimination provided the basis for a large volume of literature that followed. While such theoretical foundations will not be reviewed in detail here, it is useful to recall some fundamental principles. First, one can identify three different types of discrimination, based on who is actually doing the discriminating: employer discrimination, coworker discrimination, and customer discrimination. Empirical difficulties often arise, however, in that it is sometimes difficult to discern which one of these three is actually occurring. For example, while it is possible that the source of the discrimination is the employer's own prejudices, it may also be that the employer is simply responding to the prejudices of other employees (i.e., coworkers) in the firm, and/or the prejudices of the firm's customers. Thus, what sometimes appears to be employer discrimination may simply be masking other sources.

It becomes important to identify the source of discrimination, in that different types of discrimination will have different policy remedies. For example, employer discrimination can be reduced or eliminated by increasing the competitiveness of labor markets—with competitive labor markets, employers incur a financial cost to indulging their prejudices, costs that they would not necessarily incur in more monopsonistic labor markets. If, however, the source of the discrimination is coworkers or customers, then employers may actually find it financially advantageous to respond to such prejudices, even in the presence of competitive labor markets.

In addition to differentiating among the different types (sources) of discrimination, one must also recognize that discrimination can take many forms—that is, it can manifest itself in different ways. There are three major forms of discrimination that can occur: salary discrimination, entry discrimination, and segregational discrimination. Salary discrimination exists when a member of the non-preferred group is paid less than others, for a given level of productivity. Entry discrimination occurs when the non-preferred group is underrepresented in an industry, relative to their talent levels. With segregational discrimination, members of the non-preferred group are segregated into certain types of (usually, less important) jobs within the industry, or are segregated into certain geographic regions.

The following discussion is not intended to present an exhaustive list of every article ever written on the subject, but rather provides a sense as to some of the key contributions in the area, and illustrates the way in which the literature has evolved over time.

Early Research

The literature in the area has developed along two separate, yet parallel, streams: one pertaining to entry and segregational discrimination, and the other to salary discrimination.

With entry discrimination, the most significant early work was that of Lavoie, Grenier, and Coloumbe (1987). Focusing on players from the 1982–1983 and 1983–1984 seasons, they first compared the mean performance levels of various groups of players, and found that, for both forwards and defensemen, French Canadians outperformed their Anglophone (Canadian and American) counterparts, This finding suggested that French Canadians were "underrepresented" in the NHL, a result that Lavoie et al. took as evidence of entry discrimination. They then moved beyond this simple comparison of means, and used regression analysis to test specifically for discrimination at the draft, finding that, for a given draft position, French Canadians had superior career performance statistics compared to English Canadians.

In their analyses, Lavoie et al. measured "performance" as a player's points per game. They acknowledged that this measure focused on a player's offensive skills, but they also presented data on two other variables—plus/minus rating, and short-handed goals—that they argued were effective proxies for a player's defensive skills, and found that Anglophones were no more effective in these two categories than were Francophones. Thus, in their view, Francophones were no worse defensively than Anglophones, but were superior offensively, suggesting that Francophones were the *overall* better performers. To the extent this were true, this would then imply that Francophones faced some type of (discriminatory) barrier to entry in the NHL, and that they could reach the NHL only if they were clearly superior performers to Anglophones. Under this view, while the best French Canadian players still reach the NHL, the talents of the more marginal French Canadians are systemically underestimated (relative to marginally talented English Canadians), resulting in most of the marginal players in the NHL being English Canadian, and hence causing the average performance of French Canadians in the NHL to be higher than English Canadians.

Walsh (1992) challenged Lavoie et al.'s findings and conclusions. While acknowledging that French Canadians had superior offensive performance, Walsh argued that they underperformed in the defensive areas of the game, and hence their overall performance was not superior to Anglophones. While Lavoie et al. did provide data to argue that French Canadians were not deficient in defensive areas, Walsh disagreed with their measures of defensive performance. He argued that Lavoie et al.'s measures—plus/minus rating and short-handed goals—were flawed, and instead suggested alternative defensive performance measures, such as voting on the Selke Trophy (awarded to the best defensive forward each year). By this measure of defensive performance, Walsh argued that French Canadians were inferior defensive performers. Walsh also argued that a player's physical size was a positive attribute in the NHL, and that amateur players coming out of the Quebec Major Junior Hockey League (mostly French Canadians at the time) tended to be smaller than players from other parts of the country. He contended that it was this lack of size, and not any discriminatory treatment, that explained the apparent underrepresentation of French Canadians.

Walsh's critique brought a rebuttal from Lavoie, Grenier, and Coulombe (1992), who proposed yet other measures of defensive performance—an "adjusted" plus/minus statistic, and "short-handed participation"—and argued that, with these measures, French Canadians were not inferior performers in defensive areas. They also responded to Walsh's assertion regarding the importance of physical size, noting, for example, that the Selke award winners (for defensive excellence amongst forwards) tended to be physically smaller than the average NHL player.

This debate illustrates a methodological difficulty in testing for discrimination in hockey—specifically, it is difficult to objectively and comprehensively measure "performance." Hockey is a continuous-flow game, where each player on the ice is expected to simultaneously play offense and defense (unlike, say, football and baseball). While offensive performance is relatively easy to measure (by goals and assists) and is generally uncontroversial, defensive performance is much more multidimensional and subtle, and is subject to wider differences of opinion as to what constitutes superior performance. This lack of a widely agreed-upon and comprehensive measure of defensive performance always leaves empirical studies of entry discrimination open to the potential criticism that they are underspecified or mis-specified.

With salary discrimination, the critical early work was that of Jones and Walsh (1988). They examine the 1977–1978 season, and regress player salaries on a series of variables related to player skill and franchise characteristics, and also include a single dummy variable to designate French Canadian players. They run three separate regressions, one each for goaltenders, forwards, and defensemen. While they find no evidence of discrimination against the former two, they do find statistically significant evidence of discrimination against French Canadian defenseman, who were paid about 10 percent less than Anglophones. Jones and Walsh did urge some caution with the results, given the relatively small number (11 players) of Francophone defensemen in their sample.

Lavoie and Grenier (1992) examine data from 1989–1990, the first year for which the NHLPA publicly released official salary data for all players in the League. (Jones and Walsh were forced to rely on unofficial reports of salary figures found in media reports). Lavoie and Grenier found no evidence of discrimination, and argued that the discrimination that had existed in the era examined by Jones and Walsh had apparently disappeared by 1989–1990.

More Recent Directions

Longley (1995) argued that earlier studies of salary discrimination in hockey were flawed in that they tended to treat French Canadians as a single group, and did not consider the possible importance of the *location* of the team for which the player played. He asserted that, since one would not expect French Canadians playing for the Quebec-based teams (the Montreal Canadiens and, at the time, the Quebec Nordiques) to suffer from discriminatory treatment, and since a disproportionate number of French Canadians played for these teams, any possible discrimination elsewhere in the league may be masked by this lack of discrimination in Quebec. Longley examined the 1989–1990 season, and used a series of interaction variables to identify both a player's origin (English Canadian, French Canadian, American, and European), and the location of the team for which he played (English Canada, Quebec, and the United States). He found the only instance of apparent salary discrimination to involve French Canadians playing in English Canada. In his view, the absence of any discrimination against French Canadians playing in the United States invalidated many previous arguments as to why they may be paid less, including the argument that language costs made them less valuable—if this were actually the case, the effects should also be apparent for French Canadians playing in the United States, and not just for those playing in English Canada. Longley hypothesized that the long-standing political and social tensions between English Canadians and French Canadians may be at the root of the issue.

Jones, Nadeau, and Walsh (1999) also examined the 1989–1990 season, but used a more extensive set of performance variables than Longley. They, too, included a series of variables designed to capture the ethnicity-location interaction effects, but concluded that there was no consistent evidence of discrimination against either Europeans or French Canadians. This finding of "no discrimination" is somewhat of an anomaly in the recent literature, and is generally counter to the findings of Longley (1995) that preceded them, and Lavoie (2000) and Curme and Daugherty (2004) that followed them. Curme and Daugherty note how salary models differ widely across authors, ranging from the parsimonious model of Longley, who uses only two performance variables and one franchise-characteristic variable, to Jones and Walsh's dense model that has twenty player-related variables and six city/team measures.

Lavoie (2000) examines the 1993–1994 season, and also focuses on the ethnicity-location interaction. He concludes that French Canadian forwards playing for teams in English Canada are paid about 36 percent less than comparable English Canadians on those teams, a number almost identical to Longley's (1995) results for the 1989–1990 season. However, unlike Longley, he also finds that European and American forwards on English Canadian teams are paid less than English Canadians on those teams. He also finds that European forwards playing for one of the Quebec-based teams earn less than Francophones on those teams, and that Francophone defensemen on U.S.-based teams are paid less than Americans on those teams. Given the relatively large number of ethnicity-location combinations that show salary differentials, Lavoie's general conclusions are that general managers (GMs), particularly those for English Canadian teams, tend to underpay "non-local" players, whatever their ethnicity. With this explanation, it appears to be more the case that fans prefer to see local players, rather than there being overt discrimination against French Canadians.

Curme and Daugherty (2004) advance the analysis in a slightly different direction by considering the role of labor market competitiveness on the likelihood of finding discrimination. Their analysis pertains to the 1999–2000 season, and their various ethnicity-location combinations reveal that the only instance of apparent discrimination in the NHL is again for French Canadians playing in English Canada, who are paid over 30 percent less than English Canadians on those teams. They then extend this base model, and divide their sample into "younger" and "older" players, with those in the older group being of an age where they would have already been eligible for free agency at least once in their career, and hence players who would be subject to less monopsonistic control. Contrary to their expectations, the salary penalty incurred by older French Canadians on English Canadian teams was even larger than for younger French Canadians on those teams. Given these results, Curme and Daugherty speculated that either the salary penalty faced by French Canadians on English Canadian teams was not attributable to discriminatory behavior, or alternatively, that free agency did not necessarily ensure that French Canadians would be able (or willing) to find employment with non-English Canadian teams. Curme and Daugherty did, however, caution that the further subdividing of their data into older and younger players spread the data even thinner.

Turning to the issue of entry discrimination, accounting for the possible effects of team location has also become an important focus in this literature as well. Longley (2000) examined data from 1943 to 1998, and found that French Canadians have consistently been underrepresented on English Canadian teams, relative to their representation on U.S.-based teams. He found that this underrepresentation was greater during periods of particularly high French-English political tensions in Canada. The underrepresentation could not be explained by any "hometown" effect, where English Canadian fans might prefer English Canadian players on their local team, since European players were actually overrepresented on English Canadian teams, relative to their representation on U.S. teams. He also analyzed the NHL draft, and found that in the lower rounds of the draft, where discrimination is most likely to reveal itself, English Canadian teams selected proportionately fewer French Canadians than did their U.S.-based counterparts.

In subsequent work, Longley (2003) sought to explain the source of this under-representation on English Canadian teams. The key to finding an explanation is to uncover differences between English Canadian and U.S.-based teams. One obvious difference is in the ethnicity of the teams' fans—fans of U.S.-based teams are American, and fans of English Canadian-based teams are English Canadian—but another possible difference is in the origins of the coaches and GMs. In this regard, Longley noted that U.S.-based teams had somewhat greater diversity in these positions, being more likely to employ minority (i.e., American or French Canadian) coaches and GMs than were English Canadian teams. If it were the case that some English Canadian coaches and GMs had biases against French Canadians, then the effects of such would be more apparent with English Canadian teams than with U.S.-based teams.

However, Longley's empirical results did not support this hypothesis; during the study period of 1989–1990 to 1999–2000, the ethnicity and/or origin of a team's coach or GM had no impact on the number of French Canadians on the team's roster. For example, English Canadian GMs of U.S.-based teams would be more likely to employ French Canadians than would English Canadian GMs of teams based in English Canada—what mattered was not the ethnicity of the GM, but rather the location of the team. In this way, it appeared as if GMs were responding to local market preferences, and particularly the preferences of fans in English Canada to see fewer French Canadians on their local team—that is, the evidence pointed to customer discrimination, as opposed to employer discrimination, as the source of the underrepresentation. The fact that there was no evidence of discrimination by coaches or GMs should not be surprising. The labor market for these positions is very competitive, and the pressure to win is high; thus, even if a coach or GM had prejudicial views, indulging these views could ultimately reduce the team's chances of winning, and subsequently impact the coach or GM's job security.

Lavoie (2003) took somewhat of a different focus, and updated an approach first developed in Lavoie, Grenier, and Coulombe (1987). Using data from 1993–1994, his regression results showed that, for a given draft position, French Canadians had about 0.12 more points per game than English Canadian players, again suggesting that French Canadians face particular barriers to entering the NHL. In a separate regression, this one including all players—not just French Canadians and English Canadians—and controlling for defensive performance and physical size, he continues to find strong evidence that French Canadians outperform English Canadians. As well, he finds similar evidence of discrimination against Europeans, but no evidence of entry discrimination against Americans.

Lavoie then extended his analysis to examine the effects of team location, still focusing on players active during the 1993–1994 season, and found results somewhat contrary to previous studies. He found that, at the time of the draft, teams in English Canada underestimated the future performance of Europeans, but that no such underestimation occurred with respect to French Canadian players. Instead, he found that it was U.S.-based teams that underestimated the future performance of French Canadians. Lavoie hypothesizes that the apparent discrimination against Europeans on English Canadian teams may be a manifestation of the "Don Cherry" effect. Lavoie urges some caution, however, with his results, in that very few French Canadians in his sample were drafted by English Canadian teams. As Lavoie discusses, this issue raises a broader methodological challenge that faces the literature. To study the interaction effects of player ethnicity and team location, it is inherently necessary to disaggregate the data. However, such disaggregation reduces the sample size, and ultimately leads to more fragile, less robust, statistical results.

Finally, Kahane (2005) takes a very different approach to the issue, and examines (among other things) the effects of French Canadian players on team-level production efficiency. He finds that teams that employ disproportionately (either high or low) numbers of French Canadians are less efficient, implying that these teams incur a cost for their (possibly discriminatory) preferences.

5. SUMMARY AND CONCLUSIONS

This chapter has illustrated that the roots of any potential discrimination in hockey are quite different from those in the other three North American sports leagues. In hockey, the issue is one of nationality and ethnicity, rather than race.

In earlier eras, when Canadians almost exclusively dominated the game at both the player and management level, the primary question was whether French Canadians suffered from discriminatory treatment at the hands of the English Canadian majority. In recent decades, the influx of both Americans and Europeans into the game has broadened the nature of the questions.

The empirical work in the literature has provided less than definitive answers as to the existence and/or extent of discrimination—findings have often varied quite widely across papers. Many factors may contribute to these varying findings: different data sets covering different seasons, different methodological approaches, and so on. One consistent challenge in empirically studying both salary discrimination and entry discrimination is to find a suitable means to measure the defensive performance of players. Without a reliable, objective, and widely agreed-upon measure of defensive performance, any findings of apparent discrimination are open to a criticism that the findings are simply an artifact of a mis-specified model—where the apparent discrimination is simply picking up inferior defensive skills of the player groups in question (usually French Canadians and Europeans). This empirical difficulty is, however, not relevant to the segregational discrimination issue, and is not able, for example, to explain why French Canadians are often found to suffer inferior outcomes on English Canadian teams, as opposed to U.S.-based teams.

Thinking more broadly about the issue, one can ask whether there is reason to suspect that discrimination might be less of a problem now than in eras past. With Europeans players, it has been over three decades since they first began arriving in North America. Much has changed over that time. European players are now more "North Americanized" than in the past—not only in terms of language skills and cultural awareness, but also in terms of their on-ice style of play. Thus, differences between North American and European players are less apparent than in the past. Furthermore, North Americans have now had many decades to adjust to the European presence in the league, and any negative concerns about the European influx (such as, for example, the perception that they are "taking jobs from Canadians"—that is, the Don Cherry effect) have likely been surpassed by the sense that Europeans have added tremendous value to the product produced by the NHL.

With French Canadians, the changes are less clear. Political and social tensions between French Canadians and English Canadians have existed throughout Canada's history, and will undoubtedly continue to exist, occasionally spilling over into the NHL. However, recent years have seen a decrease in tensions, as the threat of Quebec independence has, at least for the time being, subsided. Anecdotal evidence suggests that there has been some modest increase in the number of French Canadians playing for English Canadian teams in recent years. In addition, the Vancouver Canucks currently (as of the 2010–2011 season) have a French Canadian head coach, one of the few Francophone head coaches for an English Canadian team in the entire history of the NHL.

There have also been economic changes that have occurred in recent years that should work to decrease any possible discrimination. While the NHL has historically had the least amount of voluntary player mobility, the most recent collective bargaining agreement signed in 2005 provides for a much more liberalized system of free agency. If it is the case that French Canadians do suffer from discrimination on English Canadian teams—say, due to fan prejudices—more liberal free agency provisions will at least allow French Canadians to more easily leave those teams, even though it will obviously not change those underlying fan preferences.

In terms of future research, there are a number of avenues that are worthy of further exploration. First, replication studies are still needed; the lack of definitive and consistent results across earlier studies provides an opportunity for newer studies using different modeling techniques and/or more recent data.

Second, up to now, studies have generally treated Europeans as a single homogenous group. In fact, however, this group is itself very diverse, with over fifteen European countries represented in the NHL during the 2008–2009 season, and with five of those countries—Russia, the Czech Republic, Slovakia, Sweden and Finland—having what could be termed a critical mass of players in the league. These players come from countries with different languages, cultures, and political systems, and questions naturally arise as to whether any of these subgroups of Europeans may be more or less likely to experience prejudicial treatment in the NHL.

Finally, while the past three decades have seen a great influx of Europeans into the players market, such trends have not applied to coaching and GM positions. In fact, there has never been a European GM in the history of the league, and there have been only two European head coaches, both of whom had very short tenures. More work is certainly needed to determine the causes of such underrepresentation.

Notes

1 While there have been approximately fifty black players throughout the NHL's existence, almost all of these players have been African Canadian, as opposed to African American.
2 Calculated from hockey-reference.com.
3 See http://www.sptimes.com/News/010900/Sports/Slur_not_a_big_deal_t.shtml.
4 See http://sportsillustrated.cnn.com/2008/hockey/nhl/12/03/avery.timeline/.
5 See http://www.cbc.ca/canada/story/2006/11/07/cherry-parliament.html.
6 See page 223.
7 See page 231.
8 See http://www.youtube.com/watch?v=i5ZPa_wmkyI.

References

Becker, Gary (1957). *The economics of discrimination.* Chicago: University of Chicago Press.

Curme, M.A., and Daugherty, G.M. (2004). Competition and pay for National Hockey League players born in Quebec. *Journal of Sports Economics* 5(2): 186–205.

Jones, J. Colin, Serge Nadeau, and William Walsh (1999). Ethnicity, Productivity, and Salary: Player Compensation and Discrimination in the National Hockey League. *Applied Economics* 31(5): 593–608.

Jones, J. C. H., and William Walsh (1988). Salary determination in the National Hockey League: The effects of skills, franchise characteristics, and discrimination. *Industrial and Labor Relations Review* 41(4): 592–604.

Joyce, Gare (2007). *Future greats and heartbreaks.* Toronto: Doubleday Canada.

Kahane, L. H. (2005). Production efficiency and discriminatory hiring practices in the National Hockey League: A stochastic frontier approach. *Review of Industrial Organization* 27: 47–71.

Lavoie, M. (2003). The entry draft in the National Hockey League: Discrimination, style of play, and team location. *American Journal of Economics and Sociology* 62(2): 383–405.

Lavoie, M. (2000). The location of pay discrimination in the NHL. *Journal of Sports Economics* 1(4): 401–411.

Lavoie, M., G. Grenier, and S. Coulombe (1987). Discrimination and performance differentials in the National Hockey League. *Canadian Public Policy* 13(4): 407–422.

Lavoie, M., G. Grenier, and S. Coulombe (1992). Performance differentials in the National Hockey League: Discrimination versus style-of-play thesis. *Canadian Public Policy* 18 (4): 461–469.

Lavoie, Marc, and Gilles Grenier (1992). Discrimination and salary determination in the National Hockey League: 1977 and 1988 compared, in *Advances in the Economics of Sport Volume I* (G. Scully ed.). Greenwich, CT: JAI Press.

Longley, N. (2003). Measuring employer-based discrimination versus customer-based discrimination: The case of French Canadians in the National Hockey League. *American Journal of Economics and Sociology* 62(2): 365–381.

Longley, N. (2000). The underrepresentation of French Canadians on English Canadian NHL Teams: Evidence from 1943 to 1998. *Journal of Sports Economics* 1(3): 236–256.

Longley, N. (1995). Salary discrimination in the National Hockey League: The effects of team location. *Canadian Public Policy* 21(4): 413–422.

Walsh, William (1992). The entry problem of Francophones in the National Hockey League: A systemic interpretation. *Canadian Public Policy* 18(4): 443–460.

PART II

ILLUSTRATIONS
OF PRODUCTION
THEORY

....

## CHAPTER 5

THE PRODUCTION TECHNOLOGY OF MAJOR LEAGUE BASEBALL

....

ANTHONY C. KRAUTMANN

THE production technology is defined as the set of all inputs that produces a particular level of output. McFadden (1978) outlined this input-output relationship in great detail, and pointed out a number of the issues and difficulties that arise when an analyst attempts to empirically estimate the technology. For one, the analysis becomes complicated when one considers a multi-product firm. Separability and cost complementarities make it difficult to estimate such technological features as elasticities of substitution and economies of scale. In addition, the choice of functional form can have important implications as to the degree of restrictiveness asserted on the technology by the analyst. For example, the use of a linear function restricts the estimated technology to constant marginal product, while a Cobb-Douglas functional form restricts the estimated technology to a constant degree of returns to scale.

Estimating the production technology in Major League Baseball (MLB) is greatly simplified by the fact that the team's ultimate and singular output is winning. While Gustafson et al. (1999) did model a team as producing two outputs, winning and attendance, they conclude "that none of the more complicated estimation techniques is clearly superior to using OLS to estimate the separate equations for winning percent and attendance." In this chapter, we take a traditional approach in estimating the production technology by relating winning-output to talent-inputs.

While economists typically use estimates of the production function to shed light on features of the technology, the peculiar nature of sports leagues suggests that we exercise caution in terms of how we interpret such features (Neale, 1964). For example, consider technical change in Major League Baseball. Technical progress is usually defined in terms of the increased output produced from a set amount of inputs. But increasing wins across the entire league is not possible. Winning in a sports league is a zero-sum game, forcing the league-wide winning percent to be equal to 0.500. In this regard, one cannot look for technical progress as implying an overall increase in winning. Technical change could, however, focus on a shift in the means by which teams create wins. For example, a number of analysts have looked at whether the "small ball" strategies discussed in *Moneyball* (Lewis, 2003) might have created an advantage for those teams who initiated this approach. While such an innovation in game strategy might yield the pioneering team(s) an initial advantage, we would not expect this advantage to persist given the speed by which such information is disseminated.

There are a number of reasons that sports economists are interested in the production technology in MLB. For one, winning affects the team's attendance, an important determinant of a team's profits. Estimates of the production technology have also been used to calculate a team's marginal products (MP) for the different talent-inputs. Estimates of the MP can then used to construct the marginal revenue product (MRP) of its players, an important component used to study such topics as the incentive effects of long-term contracts, wage discrimination, and monopsony exploitation.

In this chapter, we empirically estimate the production function in Major League Baseball. We begin by reviewing some of the seminal papers found in the literature pertaining to the production of wins in MLB. These models are then used as the basis for constructing a model that includes a number of the attributes found in these previous papers. We consider a number of different specifications of the talent vector, ranging from a very simple set of performance inputs to a much broader and more complex set of inputs, and finish the analysis by comparing the impact on winning of the different inputs.

ALTERNATIVE MODELS OF PRODUCTION TECHNOLOGY

While much of the literature reviewed below focuses on other topics, they all ultimately involve some specification of a team's production technology. We begin with the hypothetical model given by Fort (2006) that a team's success is a function of the number of "superstars" on its roster. We then move on to the more traditional model introduced by Scully (1974), which formed the basis for the model suggested by Bradbury (2007).

Fort's Model of Superstars

In his textbook, *Sports Economics* (2006), Rod Fort argues that a team's success on the diamond is a function of the number of superstars on its roster. While Fort does not empirically estimate such a model of team wins, his approach does highlight the important relationship that exists between a team's performance and the amount of talent on its roster.

To make this winning-superstar notion operational, one must somehow come up with a measure of the independent variable "number of superstars." Which players deserve superstar status is as tenuous as defining who is rich or who is pretty. But under the assumption of a set roster size, together with a fixed price per unit of talent, one could use the team's relative payroll as a proxy for the relative amount of talent on its roster. In Table 5.1, we see convincing evidence that winning does indeed rise with a team's payroll. From 1999 to 2008, the top 10 teams in terms of relative payroll won (on average) 57 percent of their games, while the bottom 10 teams won just 47 percent of their games.

We begin by looking at a modification of Fort's superstar model that uses the team's relative payroll (RELPAY) as the independent variable.[1] In this model of superstars, we would expect teams with greater amounts of talent, and hence higher payrolls, to win more games. To allow for diminishing returns to talent, Fort suggests that the functional form of the model include a quadratic term in RELPAY. For the ith team in season t, winning is modeled by:

$$WINNING_{it} = \alpha_0 + \alpha_1 RELPAY_{it} + \alpha_2 SQRELPAY_{it} + \epsilon_{it} \qquad (1)$$

Scully/Zimbalist Model of Winning

We now turn to the more traditional model of winning found in the literature, which directly relates different types of talent to the success of the team on the field. The model introduced by Scully (1974) takes the general form that winning is a function of the team's offensive and defensive talent-inputs. In Scully's paper, the offensive talent is measured by the team's slugging percent (SLG) and the defensive talent is measured by the pitching staff's strikeout-to-walk ratio (SO/BB). While Scully's talent inputs are important factors contributing to winning, Zimbalist (1992) argued that an even better set of talent measures would be to use the team's OPS (i.e., the sum of SLG and on-base percent, OBP) and the pitching staff's earned-run average (ERA). It is worth noting that in both models, there is

Table 5.1 Mean Values of Relative Payroll and Winning (1999–2008)

RANK	TEAM	RELPAY*	WPCT	WINS	PAYROLL
1	NYY	2.19	0.593	96.0	174.9
2	BOS	1.59	0.568	91.9	126.5
3	NYM	1.44	0.520	84.2	114.4
4	LAD	1.40	0.521	84.4	110.9
5	ATL	1.32	0.562	90.9	103.7
6	CHC	1.17	0.489	79.1	93.4
7	SEA	1.16	0.513	83.1	93.3
8	ANA/LAA	1.15	0.539	87.3	91.8
9	STL	1.14	0.554	89.7	90.6
10	TEX	1.13	0.484	78.4	88.4
AVERAGE 1–10		**1.37**	**0.573**	**86.5**	**108.8**
11	ARI	1.08	0.515	83.5	84.4
12	SFG	1.07	0.527	85.3	85.4
13	BAL	1.06	0.440	71.2	82.8
14	HOU	1.03	0.528	85.5	81.9
15	PHI	0.99	0.515	83.4	79.8
16	CHW	0.96	0.526	85.3	78.0
17	CLE	0.96	0.524	84.8	74.6
18	DET	0.95	0.440	71.2	76.1
19	TOR	0.92	0.503	81.4	73.3
20	COL	0.87	0.462	74.9	67.8
AVERAGE 11–20		**0.99**	**0.503**	**80.7**	**78.4**
21	CIN	0.79	0.474	76.9	62.5
22	SDP	0.79	0.474	76.8	62.0
23	MIL	0.70	0.454	73.5	55.5
24	OAK	0.68	0.557	90.2	54.3
25	MIN	0.62	0.518	83.9	50.5
26	MON/WSN	0.59	0.444	72.0	47.4
27	PIT	0.59	0.431	69.7	46.7
28	KCR	0.58	0.414	67.1	47.0
29	TBD/TBR	0.57	0.419	67.9	43.6
30	FLA	0.48	0.487	78.8	37.9
AVERAGE 21–30		**0.64**	**0.471**	**75.7**	**58.5**

* The relative payroll variable, RELPAY, is PAYROLL divided by the annual mean payroll. Thus, RELPAY for BOS is 1.59, implying that Boston's payroll was 59% above the mean league payroll; Florida's payroll, on the other hand, was less than one-half the league's average.

only one metric for the offensive input and one metric for the defensive input. The Scully model specification is given by:

$$WINNING_{it} = \alpha_0 + \alpha_1 \left(\frac{SO}{BB}\right)_{it} + \alpha_2 SLG_{it} + \epsilon_{it} \tag{2.s}$$

while the Zimbalist specification is given by:

$$WINNING_{it} = \alpha_0 + \alpha_1 ERA_{it} + \alpha_2 OPS_{it} + \epsilon_{it}. \tag{2.z}$$

Bradbury Model of Production

While Bradbury (2007) agrees that winning is a function of a team's offense and defense, he argues that the production of wins is best modeled by a system of equations. To begin, Bradbury assumes that the offensive side of a team is captured by its runs scored (RS), determined by a team's SLG and OBP. A team's defense, he argues, is captured by its runs allowed (RA), a measure of the number of runs scored against the team. The team's RA is determined by its fielding efficiency (DEFEFF),[2] as well as the pitching staff's strikeout rate (SO/G), walk rate (BB/G), and homerun rate (HR/G). The difference between RS and RA is the team's Runs Differential (RUNDIF), which is assumed to be positively related to winning.

Bradbury's model is then given by the following system of equations:

$$RS_{it} = \alpha_0 + \alpha_1 OBP_{it} + \alpha_2 SLG_{it} + \alpha_3 AL_{it}$$

where $\alpha_1, \alpha_2, \alpha_3 > 0$; and

$$RA_{it} = \beta_0 + \beta_1 \left(\frac{SO}{G}\right)_{it} + \beta_2 \left(\frac{BB}{G}\right)_{it} + \beta_3 \left(\frac{HR}{G}\right)_{it} + \beta_4 (DEFEFF)_{it} + \beta_5 AL_{it}$$

where $\beta_1, \beta_4 < 0$ and $\beta_2, \beta_3, \beta_5 > 0$. Since RUNDIF is the difference between RS and RA:

$$RUNDIF_{it} = RS_{it} - RA_{it},$$
$$= (\alpha_0 - \beta_0) + \alpha_1 OBP_{it} + \alpha_2 SLG_{it} + (-\beta_1)\left(\frac{SO}{G}\right)_{it} + (-\beta_2)\left(\frac{BB}{G}\right)_{it}$$
$$+ (-\beta_3)\left(\frac{HR}{G}\right)_{it} + (-\beta_4)(DEFEFF)_{it} + (\alpha_3 - \beta_5)AL_{it}$$

Finally, Bradbury assumes that winning is an increasing function of RUNDIF:

$$WINNING_{it} = f(RUNDIF_{it}) = \delta_0 + \delta_1 RUNDIF_{it} + \epsilon_{it},$$

where $\delta_1 > 0$. Thus, Bradbury's run-differential model of winning would be estimated by the following reduced-form equation:

$$WINNING_{it} =$$
$$[\delta_0 + \delta_1 (\alpha_0 - \beta_0)] + \delta_1 \alpha_1 OBP_{it} + \delta_1 \alpha_2 SLG_{it} + \delta_1 (-\beta_1)\left(\frac{SO}{G}\right)_{it} + \delta_1 (-\beta_2)\left(\frac{BB}{G}\right)_{it}$$

$$+\delta_1(-\beta_3)\left(\frac{HR}{G}\right)_{it} +\delta_1(-\beta_4)(DEFEFF)_{it} +\delta_1(\alpha_3-\beta_5)AL_{it} +\epsilon_{it}$$

$$= \delta_0^* + \delta_1^* OBP_{it} + \delta_2^* SLG_{it} + \delta_3^*\left(\frac{SO}{G}\right)_{it} + \delta_4^*\left(\frac{BB}{G}\right)_{it}$$

$$+\delta_5^*\left(\frac{HR}{G}\right)_{it} + \delta_6^*(DEFEFF)_{it} + \delta_7^* AL_{it} +\epsilon_{it}$$

(3)

where $\delta_1^*, \delta_2^*, \delta_3^*, \delta_6^* > 0$ and $\delta_4^*, \delta_5^* < 0$.

Estimating These Models of the Production Function

In Tables 5.3, 5.4, and 5.5 we present estimates of equations (1), (2), and (3). Winning is measured here by its most common definition, total wins (WINS). The sample used in this estimation consists of the 300 observations from the 1999 through 2008 seasons. Summary statistics of this sample are presented in Table 5.2.

Table 5.2 Summary Statistics (1999–2008)

	BOTH LEAGUES		AL ONLY		NL ONLY	
	MEAN	STD.ERR.	MEAN	STD.ERR.	MEAN	STD.ERR
ERA	4.48	0.52	4.59	0.52	4.38	0.50
$\widetilde{ERA}$	4.50	0.62	4.61	0.60	4.41	0.63
SAVEFF	0.67	0.07	0.67	0.08	0.67	0.07
DEFEFF	0.69	0.01	0.69	0.01	0.69	0.01
MANWINS	566	551	476	472	644	603
MANWNYR	56	24	52	24	59	23
OBP	0.335	0.01	0.337	0.01	0.334	0.01
$\widetilde{OBP}$	0.336	0.02	0.338	0.02	0.335	0.02
SLG	0.426	0.02	0.431	0.03	0.422	0.02
$\widetilde{SLG}$	0.438	0.09	0.442	0.08	0.435	0.09
OPS	0.760	0.03	0.767	0.04	0.755	0.03
PARK-HR	1.01	0.20	1.01	0.18	1.01	0.21
PARK-RUN	1.00	0.13	1.00	0.10	1.01	0.14
PARK-BA	1.00	0.05	1.00	0.04	1.00	0.06
RELPAY	1.00	0.41	1.04	0.49	0.97	0.33
SO/BB	1.97	0.35	1.96	0.39	1.98	0.31
BB/G	3.37	0.45	3.30	0.49	3.44	0.39
HR/G	1.08	0.15	1.09	0.14	1.08	0.16
SO/G	6.51	0.63	6.30	0.57	6.70	0.63

(Continued)

Table 5.2 (*Continued*)

	BOTH LEAGUES		AL ONLY		NL ONLY	
	MEAN	STD.ERR.	MEAN	STD.ERR.	MEAN	STD.ERR
WPCT	0.500	0.07	0.503	0.08	0.497	0.07
WINS	80.94	11.79	81.41	12.88	80.54	10.77
SBEFF	0.70	0.06	0.70	0.06	0.70	0.06
AL	0.47	0.50	—	—	—	—
# obs.	300		140		160	

Notes: ERA, OBP, and SLG are the raw, unadjusted productivity variables, whereas $\widetilde{ERA}$, $\widetilde{OBP}$, $\widetilde{SLG}$ are these productivity measures, adjusted for park effects.

SAVEFF is Save Efficiency, the percent of save opportunities turned into saves. DEFEFF is Defensive Efficiency, the percent of "balls in play" that are turned into outs. MANWNYR is the average number of wins per year for the manager, up to season (t – 1). PARK – XX are the Bill James's home park indices for HRs, RUNS, and BA. RELPAY is the team's payroll, divided by the league-wide average payroll. SO/BB is the strikeout to walk ratio. BB/G, HR/G, and SO/G are the walks, home runs, and strikeouts per game. WINS is the team's total wins. SBEFF = SB/(SB+CS) AL is a dummy variable equal to 1 if the team is an American League team.

Table 5.3 Fort's Superstar Model of WINS (1999–2008)

Variable	COEF.	*t*-stat.
Constant	65.73	22.5**
RELPAY	17.26	3.4**
SQRELPAY	−1.74	−0.9
F-stat	39.9**	
Adj. R²	0.21	
# obs.	300	

** significant at the 5% level
* significant at the 10% level

Table 5.4 Scully/Zimbalist Single-Input Model of WINS (1999–2008)

	SCULLY		ZIMBALIST	
Variable	Coef.	*t*-stat.	Coef.	*t*-stat.
Constant	−58.6	−7.2**	−10.2	−1.7*
SO/BB	18.6	14.7**	—	—
SLG	241.8	13.1**	—	—
ERA	—	—	−16.4	−32.4**
OPS	—	—	216.3	28.8**

(*Continued*)

Table 5.4 (*Continued*)

Variable	SCULLY		ZIMBALIST	
	Coef.	*t*-stat.	Coef.	*t*-stat.
F-stat		206**		883**
Adj. R²		0.58		0.86
# obs.		300		300

** significant at the 5% level
* significant at the 10% level

Table 5.5 Bradbury's Runs-Differential Model of WINS (1999–2008)

Variable	Coef.	*t*-stat.
Constant	−294.1	−14.4**
SLG	149.1	8.5**
OBP	322.3	10.0**
SO/G	3.14	6.3**
BB/G	−7.22	−10.6**
HR/G	−22.04	−10.9**
DEFEFF	335.7	13.1**
AL	−0.05	−0.1
F-stat	217**	
Adj. R²	0.83	
# obs.	300	

** significant at the 5% level
* significant at the 10% level

Table 5.3 presents the ordinary least squares (OLS) estimates of Fort's Superstar model given in (1). Here we see that a team's relative payroll (a proxy for the amount of talent on its roster) is positively related to winning. Consistent with diminishing returns, the coefficient on SQRELPAY is negative, although it is not significant. Finally, this model has the poorest fit of all four specifications estimated.

Table 5.4 presents the OLS estimates of the Scully/Zimbalist specification given in (2.s) and (2.z). When the model is specified in this manner, we find the not-too-surprising result that teams with better pitching and better hitting win more games. Table 5.4 also shows that Zimbalist's specification of the talent-inputs fits the data better than those specified in the Scully model.

Table 5.5 presents the OLS estimates of Bradbury's model given in (3). All of the coefficients on the inputs are of the expected signs and are significant. Not surprising, the coefficient on the AL dummy variable is insignificant. Consistent with Bradbury's claim, the estimates in Table 5.5 also imply that OBP has a much greater impact on winning than SLG. It is interesting to note that this more extensive specification of the talent inputs fits the data no better than the simple model proposed by Zimbalist.

A Model of the Production Technology in MLB

The four models outlined above provide the foundation for the model of production presented here. We also include a number of additional considerations that should impact the transformation of talent-inputs into winning-output.

Defining the Dependent Variable

We have outlined the general manner by which winning is related to the team's choice of talent-inputs. In Tables 5.3 through 5.5, winning was defined as total games won (WINS). Another common definition seen in the literature is winning percent (WPCT). Since WPCT is simply WINS divided 162, all information about the WPCT-talent relationship is captured by the WINS-talent relationship.[3] The largest value for WINS in the sample is 116, while the smallest value is only 43.[4]

Cross-league Differences

To estimate the production function in MLB, one must assume that all teams play under the same set of rules. But it is possible that the production of wins is fundamentally different between the American and National leagues. The designated-hitter rule, for example, allows a skilled offensive player to bat for the pitcher, thus eliminating an "automatic out" in the ninth hitting position.[5]

The DH rule could have a significant impact on the manner by which teams produce wins. For one, the addition of the DH player alters team rosters directly, which in turn can have a significant effect on the manner by which the game is managed. Further, since there is no automatic out in the pitcher's spot for teams in the American League, this may result in a different emphasis on such skills as sacrifices, base stealing, and other "manufactured runs" attributes. To control for differences between the leagues in terms of how wins are generated, one may need to consider separate regressions for each league.[6]

Park Factors

One of the subtle appeals of MLB arises from the non-uniformity and idiosyncrasies associated with different attributes of a team's home field. For example, the 49 home runs hit by Sammy Sosa in 2002 might be viewed as somewhat less impressive than the 46 homers hit by Barry Bonds in that same season. Sosa, a right-handed hitting outfielder for the Chicago Cubs, played half of his games at Wrigley Field, a park where right-handed batters hit 48 percent more home runs than at the other National League (NL) fields. Bonds, a left-handed hitting outfielder for the San Francisco Giants, played half of his games in Pacific Bell Park, where left-handed batters hit only 50 percent as many home runs than at other NL fields.

To the extent that park factors systematically inflate or deflate a team's performance statistics, our estimates of the relationship between winning and inputs could be affected. To this end, we use Bill James's Home Park Indices (James, various years) to control for these park effects.[7] In a manner similar to how nominal values are deflated using price indices, we "deflate" team inputs by dividing each statistic by a park index. This conversion to "real values" should allow for a more level playing field when comparing inputs across different home parks.

Managerial Input

Field managers play an important role on a professional sports team. Besides managing the egos of highly paid players, the manager must also strategically control the game, as well as prep his players for each opponent. As such, it is important to consider the managerial input in the production process. While previous studies of the role of managers have concentrated primarily on the efficiency of their decisions, we attempt to input the managerial contribution in a more direct manner.[8]

The goal here is to obtain a metric which captures the coaching talent that ultimately contributes to team wins. Unfortunately, there is no direct measure of a manager's input, at least not in the same sense as those associated with offensive and defensive inputs.[9] As such, we are forced to develop a proxy for those coaching skills.

We begin by assuming that a manager's innate and unobservable coaching talent is positively related to his team's success on the field. Moreover, we assume that this talent affects the performance of his past teams in the same manner as it will affect the performance of his present team. For a set endowment of player-inputs, a more-talented manager will have a higher winning percentage than a less-talented manager. Thus, a reasonable proxy for the managerial-input metric would be to divide the manager's cumulative wins up to (but not including) the season in question by the number of years he has managed. That is, we use the manager's average wins-per-season, given by:

$$MANWYR_t = \left(\frac{\sum_{s=1}^{t-1} WINS_s}{EXPERIENCE_{t-1}} \right).$$

Admittedly, this measure is crude in that it proxies the manager's contribution by extrapolating his past contributions; but given that his innate talent is what contributed to his teams' successes in the past, we find it reasonable to believe that these same skills will help contribute to present winnings.

Stealing Bases

Absent in most studies of team winning is the importance of base stealing, which moves runners into scoring position and enhances a team's chances of scoring runs. But total bases stolen may not be the appropriate factor since it only measures the number of successful stolen-base attempts and ignores the opportunity cost of getting caught stealing. That is, a team may lead the league in stolen bases, but if it gets caught stealing 50 percent of the time, then it is giving up a large number of scarce outs. Thus, a better metric that incorporates the team's successes and failures on the base paths is the stolen-base efficiency, *SBEFF*, here defined as the ratio of stolen bases to attempted steals.[10]

Offensive and Defensive Inputs

In the model presented below, we attempt to specify a vector of player-inputs which do a sufficiently good job of capturing the essential elements of the game—but do so in the most parsimonious fashion. While there are many subtle and esoteric aspects of the game that may contribute to a win here or there, our objective is to focus on just those factors that are most important in determining winning.

The goal of any sports team is to score more runs than their opponents. This suggests that the runs-differential model outlined by Bradbury would form a reasonable foundation of team wins. For the offense, we begin by considering two alternatives commonly found in the literature: using SLG and OBP separately, or using them together in terms of OPS (which is the sum of SLG and OBP). The SLG measure, which captures the average number of bases produced per at-bat, is usually thought of as a measure of power. The OBP measure, on the other hand, captures the efficiency of getting on base through any means (e.g., hit, walk, hit-by-pitch). Both aspects of hitting are surely important—the question at hand is whether it is worth separating these two aspects of scoring runs. Since the OPS statistic measures both aspects of hitting, it has the advantage of capturing the offense of either a powerful or efficient hitting team. But using the OPS metric implicitly assumes an equal marginal product to both SLG and OBP. That is, it assumes that a one-point increase in SLG has the same impact on runs scored (RS) as a one-point increase in OBP. If this assumption is true, then there is no harm in using the more compact measure OPS. But if the effect of SLG on RS is different from the effect of OBP on RS, then OPS would not be a legitimate measure of the team's run-scoring capability.

To assist in choosing among these two alternative specification of offense, we ran an auxiliary regression of RS on SLG and OBP. The results of this auxiliary regression showed that the estimated marginal product of OBP was more than ten times that of SLG.[11] This result suggests that it is more appropriate to include the two hitting statistics separately in the model specification.

Finally, as discussed above, these two offensive inputs are deflated by the park indices most closely affecting each component. In particular, we used the park "batting-average" index to deflate OBP, and the park "home run" index to deflate SLG.

To model the defensive side of the game, we begin by recognizing that each team needs to get their opponent out (about) 27 times per game. The objective of the defense is to make these 27 outs while allowing the least number of runs to score. As such, we want to consider both the pitching staff's contribution to avoiding runs, as well as the team's fielding efficiency at getting outs from balls put into play.

Bradbury argued for using the pitching staff's strikeout, home run, and walk rates as the relevant pitching inputs. This assignment arose primarily out of his objective to isolate those performance aspects that are completely under the control of each individual pitcher. But at the team level, we would want a more inclusive measure of the pitching efficiency, one that incorporates the pitcher's performance in conjunction with the complementarities of his teammates. As such, we use the broader and more summative measure of pitching efficiency—the team's ERA. To control for park effects on a pitching staff's ERA, we deflate team ERA by the park "runs scored" index.

Another important aspect of the pitching staff is associated with the team's ability to win close games. The late-September collapse of the 2008 New York Mets is widely attributed to the fact that their bullpen failed to hold the lead in close games. This highlights the importance of converting save opportunities into saves. For the most part, a save opportunity is essentially a condition that a reliever faces when he enters the game and his team is leading by no more than three runs. The team's save opportunities (SAVEOPP) is then the sum of the save opportunities of its pitching staff, and is interpreted as the number of games that its bullpen has an opportunity to save. The bullpen's save efficiency (SAVEFF) is then constructed by dividing the team's actual number of saves (SAVES) by its save opportunities, that is,

$$SAVEFF = \frac{SAVES}{SAVEOPP}.$$

A final component of a team's defense is its efficiency at turning batted balls into outs. One very popular metric of a team's fielding efficiency is its fielding percent (FPCT), which is the percent of fielding chances that are successfully turned into outs. Unfortunately, this metric has so little variation that it would be difficult for the empirical analysis to discern between different team's fielding. An alternative fielding metric with greater variability is a team's defensive efficiency (DEFEFF), defined as the percent of balls in play (excluding home runs) that are turned into outs. While FPCT entails a certain degree of subjectivity by the official scorekeeper as to whether a particular ball in play was or was not a fielding chance, DEFEFF objectively computes the percent of all batted balls turned into outs.

EMPIRICAL ESTIMATION

Utilizing the arguments outlined above, we proceed to construct a model of the production technology where winning is a function of the offensive, defensive and managerial inputs. We consider the following model:

$$WINS_{it} = f\left(OFFENSE_{it}, DEFENSE_{it}, MANWNYR_{it}, SBEFF_{it}\right) \tag{4}$$

where $WINS_{it}$ is team i's total wins in year t; $OFFENSE_{it} = (\widetilde{SLG}_{it}, \widetilde{OBP}_{it})$; $DEFENSE_{it} = (\widetilde{ERA}_{it}, SAVEFF_{it}, DEFEFF_{it})$; $MANWNYR_{it}$ is the manager's average wins per year up to (but not including) season t; and SBEFF is the ratio of stolen bases to steal attempts. As discussed above, the talent inputs $(\widetilde{SLG}_{it}, \widetilde{OBP}_{it}, \widetilde{ERA}_{it})$ have been deflated by the park run, home run, and batting average indices, respectively. The sample used consists of the 300 observations for the 1999 to 2008 seasons. Table 5.1 contains the summary statistics of the sample used in this analysis. None of the productivity metrics are highly correlated (i.e., none have a correlation coefficient greater than 0.37), suggesting a satisfactory level of independence across these inputs.

The estimates of WINS appear in Table 5.6. To allow for diminishing returns, we tested whether the data was consistent with the generalized quadratic functional form, but rejected the significance of the second order own- and cross-terms. We also tested for the significance of just the second order own-terms, and again came to the conclusion that the data was consistent with a simple linear functional form.

Table 5.6 Production Function of WINS (1999–2008)

Variable	BOTH LEAGUES		AL ONLY		NL ONLY	
	Coef.	t-stat	Coef.	t-stat	Coef.	t-stat
Constant	−58.4	−2.4**	0.57	0.02	−127.1	−3.5**
$\widetilde{ERA}$	−10.9	−14.8**	−12.2	−11.8**	−9.7	−9.3**
SAVEFF	36.7	6.4**	41.4	5.6**	28.3	3.3**
$\widetilde{OBP}$	296.8	13.5**	335.2	11.3**	246.9	7.7**
$\widetilde{SLG}$	19.7	4.0**	21.9	3.2**	18.5	2.7**
MANWNYR	0.038	2.4**	0.02	1.1	0.04	1.9*
DEFEFF	60.3	1.6*	−42.5	−0.9	189.7	3.3**
SBEFF	15.7	2.5**	20.7	2.3**	10.9	1.3
AL	2.1	2.8**	—	—	—	—
Adj. R²	0.72		0.79		0.64	
F-stat	96**		76**		42**	
# obs.	300		140		160	

** significant at the 5% level
* significant at the 10% level

Table 5.7 Effect on Wins Going from the 25th to the 75th
Percentile

VARIABLE	AL: 25th percentile (Team) / NL: 25th percentile (Team)	AL: 75th percentile (Team) / NL: 75th percentile (Team)	ΔWINSAL / ΔWINSNL
$\widetilde{OBP}$	0.325 (Texas)	0.348 (Oakland)	+8.1
	0.319 (Arizona)	0.348 (LA Dodgers)	+7.4
$\widetilde{SLG}$	0.379 (Baltimore)	0.497 (Detroit)	+2.2
	0.380 (Ch. Cubs)	0.481 (St. Louis)	+1.8
$\widetilde{ERA}$	4.98 (Baltimore)	4.19 (Ch. White Sox)	+9.7
	4.81 (Florida)	4.01 (Atlanta)	+7.9
SAVEFF	0.607 (Baltimore)	0.731 (Anaheim)	+5.2
	0.622 (Colorado)	0.712 (Dodgers)	+2.5
DEFEFF	0.679 (Kansas City)	0.697 (Angels)	0
	0.683 (Colorado)	0.698 (LA Dodgers)	+3.0
SBEFF	0.662 (Cleveland)	0.741 (NY Yankees)	+1.6
	0.661 (Colorado)	0.739 (NY Mets)	0
MANWNYR	39.25 (Kansas City)	70.96 (NY Yankees)	0
	52.06 (Arizona)	71.21 (Ch. Cubs)	+0.8

Notes: The effect on WINS of a change in the independent variable is evaluated by going from the (league-specific) sample 25th percentile value of the variable to the 75th percentile value of the variable. The team in parenthesis is an example of a team whose mean value in the sample is closest to these quartile values. If a coefficient is insignificant, the effect on WINS is assumed to be zero.

Finally, we tested a fixed-effects model for the managerial input, yet found the data to be consistent with the simple ordinary least squares model.[12] Table 5.7 illustrates the impact on winning by imputing the change in WINS of going from the 25th to 75th quartile for each input.

Tables 5.6 and 5.7 suggest a number of interesting insights about winning in MLB. Most of the coefficients in Table 5.6 are significant and have the correct sign. Table 5.7 uses these coefficient estimates to impute the economic impact of the different independent variables on WINS. The following conclusions can be drawn from Tables 5.6 and 5.7.

- To begin, if the only difference between the two leagues is that the American League won slightly more interleague games (as seen in Table 5.1), then it is possible to aggregate both leagues together and include a simple dummy variable to increase the intercept for American League teams. Table 5.6 includes such an aggregate model. But if the two leagues are systematically different, then such an aggregation may not be appropriate. We tested whether winning is produced by the same process across both leagues by running a Chow test. Given an F-statistic of 3.1, we conclude that there is a significant difference between the two leagues that extends beyond a simple intercept shift. Table 5.6 includes estimates of each league separately, and much of the remaining discussion comparing the two leagues is based on this disaggregated specification.

- Beginning with the offensive inputs, we find strong support for Bradbury's contention that one should model the offense using SLG and OBP separately. The coefficients in Table 5.6 on OBP are much larger than those appearing on SLG.[13] A test of the coefficients on OBP and SLG rejected the null that the two inputs have an equal effect on WINS. Such a conclusion is consistent across both leagues separately, and should be interpreted as strong evidence against the use of OPS in production function estimates.

- To get a feel for how much more sensitive winning is to OBP than SLG, we calculated how WINS is affected by changes in these two hitting statistics. First, consider the impact of a team's OBP increasing from the sample 25th percentile to the 75th percentile—in the AL, this corresponds to a change from 0.325 to 0.348; in the NL, this corresponds to a change from 0.319 to 0.348.[14] Such an increase translates into an increase of about 7 to 8 extra wins. Now, consider the impact of a team's SLG increasing from the 25th percentile to the 75th percentile; such an increase would result in only about 2 extra games won. Thus the greater impact on WINS arising from OBP as compared to SLG surely lends support to the contention made by Billy Beane, general manager of the Oakland Athletics, who has steadfastly pursued an efficient offense over a powerful one.

- Two conclusions can be reached in regards to a team's pitching effectiveness. For one, pitching in general has a greater impact on WINS in the AL than in the NL; and two, ERA has one of the largest effects on winning of all the inputs. To illustrate, consider the impact of a team improving its ERAs from the 25th percentile to the 75th percentiles (in the AL, this corresponds to a change from 4.98 to 4.19, while in the NL it corresponds to a change from 4.81 to 4.01). Such an improvement would result in winning an extra 10 games in the AL versus an extra 8 games in the NL. A similar interleague differential exists in terms of SAVEFF. For the AL, a change from the 25th to 75th percentile would result in winning an extra 5 games; while in the NL it would result in winning about 3 extra games.

- Fielding efficiency appears to have a greater impact in the NL than the AL. For the AL, the point estimate on DEFEFF in Table 5.6 has the wrong sign and is not significant. For the NL, on the other hand, DEFEFF is positive and highly significant; an improvement in fielding going from the 25th to the 75th percentiles, resulting in winning an extra 3 games.

- Neither stolen bases nor the managerial input appear to have much of an impact on winning. Table 5.6 shows that MANWNYR does not significantly affect wins in the AL. For the NL, it is only marginally significant and would result in only a one game improvement for a team going from the 25th to the 75th percentile. Tables 5.6 and 5.7 show that stolen bases do not significantly affect winning in the National League, and only contributes an extra game or so for a team in the American League.

CONCLUSION

Using the results of earlier studies as our guide, we built a model of the production function in Major League Baseball. We begin by focusing on a team's hitting, as measured by slugging and on-base percentages. The defense is captured primarily by a team's pitching input, measured by the earned-run average and the save efficiency. We also considered a team's fielding efficiency, its stolen-base efficiency, and the manager's contribution to winning. Finally, inputs were deflated by Home Park indices to neutralize the variation in stadium dimensions and effects.

Our results suggest that a team's OBP is its most potent offensive input, while a team's ERA is its most important defensive input. The analysis also substantiates Bradbury's claim that OBP and SLG need to be included as separate offensive inputs in the production function. Finally, we find that there are significant differences between the two leagues in the manner by which teams create wins. To the extent that we can generalize, our empirical results suggest that pitching has a greater impact in the AL than the NL, while fielding is more important in the NL.

Given the critical role of the field manager in affecting game outcomes, we are a bit surprised by the weak empirical significance of the managerial input. Perhaps the metric used to proxy this input is simply too crude. Alternatively, perhaps it arises from the fact that the job of the coach is to "manage" the other inputs; thus any contribution coming from the manager may be so intertwined with his players' performances that it is impossible separate out the managerial-input from the other team inputs. This remains an area for further research.

The differences documented here between the leagues are undoubtedly endogeneous to the rules structure in each league. In particular, consider how the designated hitter potentially affects the generation of wins. Without a DH, teams in the NL have essentially an "automatic out" in the ninth-hitting spot. As a result, one might expect a greater premium being placed on fielding in the NL so as to essentially guarantee this out (at least for the first five or six innings when the starting pitcher is still hitting). Without this easy out in the AL, good pitching becomes especially important because of the extra offensive punch coming from the DH.

How important is the DH in terms of the difference between the two leagues? That is difficult to say; however, many sportswriters and bloggers believe that it has been a significant factor in explaining the advantage of AL teams in interleague games. That is, when playing at an AL park (where the DH rule is in effect), the AL team has the advantage of using an experienced hitter-specialist while the NL team is stuck using a utility player as its DH. Even when the games are played in a NL park (where games are played without a DH), the AL teams may still have an advantage because each AL team's roster contains a powerful bench player ready to come in and pinch-hit at critical times of the game. Such speculation about the effect of the DH highlights the importance of how differences in rules affect game strategies, and hence the manner by which wins are produced.

I would like to thank the many participants who gave me useful comments at the 2009 Western Economics Association meetings in Vancouver, B.C. I would like to especially thank Gregory R. Durham for his many helpful and insightful comments.

NOTES

1 A team's relative payroll (RELPAY) in season t is defined as its payroll divided by the average payroll across the league in season t. A relative measure, rather than absolute measure, is used so as to account for differences in talent between opponents.

2 DEFEFF is a measure of a team's fielding proficiency. It is defined as the percentage of the opposing team's balls put into play (excluding home runs) that are turned into outs. A typical team turns about two-thirds of such plays into outs.

3 We would like thank Greg Durham for pointing out to us the redundancy between using WINS and WPCT as the dependent variable. Strictly speaking, this correspondence between the coefficients from WINS and WPCT is true only when there are no missed games due to things like rainouts or other disasters. Even still, the differences in the coefficients is very slight.

4 This 116 wins, achieved by the Seattle Mariners in 2001, tied the major league record set by the Chicago Cubs in 1906. The Detroit Tigers won only 43 games in 2003, the worst showing in the modern 162-game era since the 1962 New York Mets (who won only 40 games).

5 Scully (1989) showed that after the American League added the designated-hitter rule in 1973, the slugging percent of American League teams increased significantly.

6 As discussed above, simply adding a dummy variable to control for the different leagues will only control for the differential between leagues arising from the slight advantage of the AL over the NL in interleague games. A more general approach would consider separate regressions for each league; one could then test for a significant difference across leagues using traditional testing mechanisms (e.g., Chow Test).

7 Bill James has constructed Home Park Indices for a number of statistics, including home runs, batting average, runs scored, and a number of other aspects of the game. These indices are calculated in such a manner as to isolate the effects of the field on these statistics. Essentially, the metric is calculated by comparing what both the home team and visitors accomplished at the park, and comparing that to what the same teams accomplished on the road. An index value of 1.0 indicates a league-average field in regards to that statistic.

8 A separate line of analysis on the production technology of sports teams recognizes the contributions associated with the managerial input, especially as it impacts game outcomes (Porter and Scully, 1982; Lee, 2006). A number of studies look at this from an efficiency perspective, essentially estimating how close a particular manager was to being on the "frontier isoquant" (a hypothetical isocurve that gives the minimum amount of inputs to produce a particular amount of wins). Managerial inefficiency is then measured as the distance from the isoquant to the actual amounts of input each manager employs. The importance of this line of research is that the managerial input is an element of the technology that should not be ignored in the analysis.

9 Sabermetricians have devised a clever measure of the productivity of managers, reported in the *Baseball Encyclopedia* (Gillette and Palmer, 2008). This metric, called the "plus/minus," measures how many games the team actually won compared to how many games the team was expected to win, based on its roster of talent. Positive values indicate that the team won more games than expected, while negative values indicate the team did worse than expected. While this metric would appear to be a worthy candidate for the managerial input, its use in a production function study would be misleading. Assume that whatever model used by these sabermetricians to estimate wins is sufficiently close to that presented here. Because this "plus/minus" statistic is essentially the residual vector from the sabermetric model, it would be essentially the residual vector from our model. As such, including the "plus/minus" metric on the right-hand side of our model would be akin to regressing the dependent variable on a set of independent variables which include the regression residual. We thank Thomas Mondschean for pointing this out to us.

10 We thank Stephen Shmanske for pointing this out to us.

11 These estimated marginal products for OBP and SLG were 1760 and 110, respectively. Given a t-statistic of 6.5, we rejected the null of equal marginal products. (Note that we used the adjusted offensive inputs to conduct this test.)

12 We did not attempt a fixed-effects model for teams, as there were many changes in the managerial regimes across the sample period. Teams tend to fire unsuccessful managers and replace them with (potentially) successful managers. As such, controlling for team effects for a team that switched managers would result in aggregating a sub-par time series with an above-average series—the results of which are unclear. Finally, for those teams that had the same manager across the entire sample, this would be equivalent to controlling for managerial fixed effects.

13 While the coefficients on OBP are larger than those on SLG, one must also keep in mind that the size and variation of SLG is also much larger. For example, the mean value of OBP is about 0.335, while the mean value of SLG is about 0.435. Furthermore, going from the 25th percentile to 75th percentile corresponds to a change in SLG of about 0.110, while an identical comparison of the top quartile to the bottom quartile in OBP corresponds to only a change of 0.030.

14 Note that these examples of moving from the bottom to the top quartiles are based upon the entire 10-year sample period of 1999 to 2008, calculated separately for each league. The teams mentioned are just examples of those that are closest to these sample quartiles (based upon the team-specific averages over the sample period). The first team listed corresponds to the 25th percentile, and the second team listed corresponds to the 75th percentile.

References

Bradbury, J. C. (2007). What is a ballplayer worth? in *The baseball economist: the real game exposed*. New York: Penguin Group, pp. 176–200.

Fort, Rodney (2006). Team cost, profit, and winning, in R. Fort, *Sports economics,* 2nd ed. Upper Saddle River, NJ: Pearson Education, pp. 100–104.

Gillette, Gary, and Pete Palmer (2008). The men in the dugout: The manager register, in *The ESPN baseball encyclopedia*. New York: Sterling, pp.1689–1706.

Gustafson, Elizabeth, Lawrence Hadley, and John Ruggerio (1999). Alternative econometric models of production in Major League Baseball, in *Sports economics: Current research,* edited by John Fizel, Elizabeth Gustafson, and Lawrence Hadley. Westport, CT: Praeger, p. 107.

James, Bill (various years). *The Bill James handbook*. Skokie, IL: ACTA Publications.

Lee, Young Hoon (2006). Team sports efficiency estimation and stochastic frontier models, in *Handbook of sports economic research,* edited by John Fizel. Armonk, NY: M.E. Sharpe, pp. 209–220.

Lewis, Michael (2003). *Moneyball: The art of winning an unfair game*. New York: W.W. Norton & Co.

McFadden, Daniel (1978). Cost, revenue, and profit functions, in *Production theory: a dual approach to theory and applications*. Amsterdam: North Holland, pp. 3–109.

Neale, Walter (1964). The peculiar economics of professional sports. *Quarterly Journal of Economics* 78 (February): 1–14.

Porter, Philip, and Gerald Scully (1982). Measuring managerial efficiency: The case of baseball. *Southern Economic Journal* 48 (January): 642–650.

Scully, Gerald (1974). Pay and performance in Major League Baseball. *American Economic Review* 64 (December): 915–930.

Scully, Gerald (1989). League operating rules and team performance, in *The business of Major League Baseball*. Chicago: University of Chicago Press, pp. 66–68.

Zimbalist, Andrew (1992). Salaries and performance: Beyond the Scully model, in *Diamonds are forever,* Paul Sommers, ed. Washington, DC: Brookings Institute, pp. 109–133.

## CHAPTER 6

MEASURING PERFORMANCE IN THE NATIONAL BASKETBALL ASSOCIATION

DAVID J. BERRI

ECONOMISTS have been known to consider their discipline as the "queen of the social sciences." And when such thoughts come to mind, the emphasis is often on the word "science." With an abundance of data—and extensive training in statistical analysis—economists appear to often think of their work as essentially an objective pursuit of the "truth."

Despite this perspective, though, disagreements about the "truth" abound. We can see such disagreements when we consider the analysis offered by various economists with respect to the most recent economic downturn. Empirical questions such as (1) Should there be a stimulus package, and if so, how big?, or (2) What is the size of the government spending multiplier?, were all given different answers, depending upon the school of thought to which the analyst belonged.

Given the complexity of macroeconomics, one should not be surprised to see such disagreements. After all, macro data is often not sufficient to reach definitive answers to the questions economists are asking. In the world of sports—where the quality of data is much better—disagreements should be less frequent. Alas, this does not appear to be the case.

Consider the issue of how to measure a hitter's performance in baseball. Albert and Bennett (2003) report a variety of measures designed to address this issue. The list of choices included batting average, slugging average, on-base-percentage, OPS,[1] Batter's Run Average,[2] Total Average,[3] least squares linear regression (LSLR) models, and the approach of George Lindsey and Pete Palmer,[4] which focuses on the play-by-play data to generate the value of each state in a baseball game (i.e., runner on first with two outs, runners on second and third with one out, etc.). And this list of measures is incomplete. As Albert and Bennett (2003) report: "The 1999 Big Bad Baseball Annual alone listed over 20 systems for evaluating offensive performance."

Given such diversity in baseball, one should not be surprised to see similar diversity in the sport examined in this chapter. The study of basketball has also yielded a host of different approaches. Within this chapter we cannot touch upon the entire population of these approaches. What we can do, though, is touch upon the primary schools of thought.

Evaluating a Model

This chapter will do more than just present the various approaches. Some effort will also be made to evaluate and ascertain the value of each model. And for this latter objective, evaluation criteria need to be outlined. For our purposes we turn to the work of J. C. Bradbury (2008), who has provided two criteria that should be considered in ascertaining whether or not a performance measure is "good."

For Bradbury there are two issues to consider. First, one needs to consider how the performance measure correlates with outcomes. The outcome we generally consider is team wins. One, though, can also consider the relationship between a performance measure and player salaries. With respect to basketball—as will be detailed below—the ability of a measure to explain wins tends to differ from its ability to explain salaries or other player evaluations (and as we will note, this issue needs to be understood by a researcher utilizing basketball performance data to study an economic issue).

Beyond the issue of how a metric correlates with outcomes is the consistency of the measure over time. Here is how Bradbury explains the importance of consistency:

> One method researchers can use for separating skill from luck is to look at repeat performance of players. If performance is a product of skill, then the athlete in question ought to be able to replicate that skill. If other factors, such as random chance or teammate spillovers are responsible for the performance, then we ought not observe players performing consistently in these areas over time. A common

way to gauge the degree of skill contained in a performance metric is to observe its correlation year to year. If metrics for individual players do not vary much from year to year, then it is likely that players have a skill in that area. If there is no correlation, then it is likely that other factors are heavily influencing the metric. In the latter case, even if a particular metric appears to have a powerful influence on the overall performance of the team, its utility as a measure of quality is quite limited. (Bradbury, 2008, p. 48)

So a "good" measure should be both correlated with outcomes and consistent over time. To specifically address these issues, we will first consider—as illustrated in equation (1)—the link between team winning percentage and the performance measure in question will be ascertained.

$$\textit{Team Winning Percentage} = a_0 + a_1 * \textit{Performance Measure} + e \tag{1}$$

Next we turn to the subject of consistency. This issue will be addressed by looking at how correlated a player's performance in $year_t$ is with the player's performance in $year_{t-1}$.[5]

The Scoring Models

With our criteria outlined, let's first turn to a set of models that will be classified as "scoring models." Scoring totals dominate player evaluation in the NBA. This can be seen when we look at player salaries,[6] the coaches voting for the All-Rookie team,[7] the NBA draft,[8] and the allocation of minutes played.[9] Given how players are evaluated, the simplest evaluation metric is points scored per game. Obviously such a measure, though, leaves out much of what happens on a basketball court. Consequently we should not be surprised that a team's points scored per game only explains 10 percent of a team's winning percentage.[10]

One would expect to do better if other facets of the game were considered. How much better, though, would depend upon how those other facets were incorporated in the performance measure. Perhaps the easiest approach is the NBA Efficiency measure. This measure—as equation (2) illustrates—simply adds together the positive actions a player takes and subtracts the negative.

$$\text{NBA Efficiency} = \text{PTS} + \text{ORB} + \text{DRB} + \text{STL} + \text{BLK} + \text{AST} - \text{TO} - \\ \text{MSFG} - \text{MSFT} \tag{2}$$

where

PTS = Points scored	ORB = Offensive rebounds
DRB = Defensive rebounds	STL = Steals
BLK = Blocked shots	AST = Assists

TO = Turnovers   MSFG = Missed field goals
MSFT = Missed free throws

NBA Efficiency is essentially the same as Robert Bellotti's (1992) Points Created model and Dave Heeren's TENDEX model (1994).[11] According to Heeran (1994), the TENDEX model was developed in the late 1950s. The NBA only came into existence in 1949, so TENDEX could be thought of as the first attempt to capture a player's performance in a single number.

Each of these models is clearly quite simple to calculate. And these measures are quite consistent. The correlation between a player's per-minute NBA Efficiency in successive seasons is 0.82.[12] Similar results are uncovered for Points Created per minute. Unfortunately, when we turn to the issue of explanatory power we see a problem. Estimating equation (1) with a team's NBA Efficiency reveals that this simple model explains only 32 percent of a team's winning percentage. Similar results were uncovered for Points Created. This suggests that the simple scoring models are not well connected to team wins.[13]

Perhaps the problem is that the NBA Efficiency metric is just too simple. For a more complex "efficiency" measure we turn to the work of John Hollinger (2004). The calculation of John Hollinger's Player Efficiency Rating—detailed in equation (3)—is somewhat involved:

Player Efficiency Rating (PER) =

(League Pace/Team Pace) * (15/League Average) *(1/Minutes Played) *
[3FGM + AST*0.67 + (FGM*{2 – [(team AST / team FGM)*0.588]})
+ (FTM*0.5*{1 + [1 + (team AST/team FGM)] + (team AST / team
   FGM)*0.67]})
- (VOP * TO)–(MSFG * VOP * league DRB%)
- {MSFG*VOP*0.44*[0.44 + (0.56*league DRB%)]}
+ [DRB *VOP*(1–league DRB%)] + (ORB *VOP*league DRB%) +
   (STL*VOP)
+ (BLK*VOP*league DRB%)
{PF * [league FTM per PF–(league FTA per PF * 0.44*VOP)]}]   (3)

where

PACE = [(Offensive Pos2osessions + Defensive Possessions) * 48] / (Minutes
       Played/2)
Possession = FGM + 0.44*FTM + TO – ORB
FGM = Field goals made
FTM = Free throws made
League Average = Average PERs value
3FGM = Three point field goals made
VOP = Average points scored per possession for the League
league DRB% = Average defensive rebounds divided by average total
       rebounds

Such complexity can be simplified—as equation (4) illustrates—in Hollinger's Game Score measure:

$$\text{Game Score} = \text{PTS} + 0.4 * \text{FGM} - 0.7 * \text{FGA} - 0.4*\text{MSFT} + 0.7 * \text{ORB} +$$
$$0.3 * \text{DRB} + \text{STL} + 0.7 * \text{AST} + 0.7 * \text{BLK} - 0.4 * \text{PF} - \text{TO} \quad (4)$$

Although PER and Game Score look quite different, Berri and Bradbury (2010) note that these measures are quite similar. PER is a per-minute measure, and Berri and Bradbury (2010) report that there is a 0.99 correlation between a player's PER and his per-minute Game Score.[14]

When we turn back to equation (1) we also see that these measures are quite similar. A team's PER explains 33 percent of the variation in a team's winning percentage, while 31 percent of a team's winning percentage is explained by a team's Game Score.[15]

Such results are quite comparable to what we saw when we looked at the link between NBA Efficiency and winning percentage. In essence, NBA Efficiency, PER, and Game Score—although appearing to be quite different measures—are not tremendously dissimilar.[16] And the most important area where each overlaps is with respect to how each model treats inefficient scoring.

A look back at NBA Efficiency—detailed in equation (2)—reveals the problem. Imagine a player who takes 150 shots from two point range, making 50 and missing 100. According to NBA Efficiency, the 50 made shots will add 100 to his NBA Efficiency value. But the missed shots will reduce his NBA Efficiency value by 100. In sum, making 50 out of 150 shots from two-point range—or shooting 33 percent—allows a player to breakeven on NBA Efficiency. If a player can surpass this threshold—and almost all NBA players can do this[17]—then the more a player shoots, the higher will be his NBA Efficiency value.

A similar story is told for three-point shooting. Again, let's imagine a hypothetical shooter. This time we will have our hypothetical player take 100 shots from three-point range and make 25. According to NBA Efficiency, the 25 made shots increase his value by 75; while the 75 missed shots reduce his value by the same amount. Again, most NBA players who launch three-point shots can hit 25 percent of these attempts.[18] So again, the more a player shoots—even if that player is an inefficient scorer—the higher will be his value.

We see the same problem for Game Score, except that the break-even points are actually lower.[19] Consequently, the scoring models—although different in appearance—all teach the same lesson. The more shots a player takes—as long as he exceeds a minimum threshold—the better the player will look by these metrics. Inefficient scoring, though, can't help a team win games. And having an inefficient scorer take more and more shots cannot improve a team's winning percentage. Hence we should not be surprised that these measures are not highly correlated with team outcomes.

Although the scoring models are not well connected to team wins, these models are quite consistent over time.[20] Furthermore, as noted by Berri and Schmidt (2010), Berri, Brook, and Schmidt (2007), Berri, Schmidt, and Brook (2006), and Berri and Schmidt (2002), these models do a good job of explaining salaries, voting for the All-Rookie team, draft position, and minutes played in the NBA.[21] In other words, if the outcome a researcher wishes to understand is the perception of player performance in the NBA, one of the scoring models may be the preferred choice.[22] If a researcher wishes to examine wins, though, these models appear to come up short.

THE PLUS-MINUS MODEL

The lack of correlation between wins and the "scoring metrics" might have led some to look beyond the box score for a measure of player performance in the NBA. In recent years the plus-minus measure—traditionally employed in the National Hockey League—has been turned to as a measure that might capture even more than the traditional NBA box score. The measure applied to basketball, as John Hollinger (2005) describes, is quite simple:

> Add all the points the team scores when a player is on the court, and subtract all the points the team allows when he is on the court. Subtract the latter from the former, and you end up with the player's "plus-minus"—how many points better or worse (i.e., plus or minus) the team is with that man on the court.

Although simple, the plus-minus measure has some problems. As Hollinger (2005) notes, the quality of a player's teammates will impact his plus-minus measure. In other words, playing with a dominant performer—such as Michael Jordan, LeBron James, or Chris Paul—will cause a player's plus-minus to rise. In essence, the plus-minus statistic runs counter to the very purpose of tracking player statistics in the first place. As Berri (2007) notes, player statistics are tracked to separate a player from his teammates. We know who won the game. Player statistics help us see which players were responsible for that outcome. The plus-minus statistic, though, imbeds a player's evaluation in the performance of his teammates. Consequently this measure does not help a team assign responsibility.

To overcome the problem of plus-minus, researchers have turned to a measure known as adjusted plus-minus. The calculation of this measure involves a regression designed to control for the impact of a player's teammates on his plus-minus value. Although in theory the regression solves the fundamental problem of plus-minus, there is reason to think this approach comes up short.

The first issue is statistical significance. As noted in Berri and Bradbury (2010), many of the player evaluations offered by the adjusted plus-minus would not generally be considered statistically significant. For example, consider the adjusted plus-minus results for the Orlando Magic from the 2008–2009 season. As Table 6.1 reports, for only two players—Rashard Lewis and Anthony Johnson—do we see a coefficient that is at least twice as large as the corresponding standard error. For all

Table 6.1 Adjusted Plus-Minus Values for the Orlando Magic in 2008–2009

Player	One Year Adjusted Plus-Minus	Standard Error
Rashard Lewis	6.82*	3.09
Dwight Howard	4.48	3.56
Hedo Turkoglu	3.73	2.87
Tony Battie	1.09	4.32
Keith Bogans	−0.05	2.65
Courtney Lee	−0.24	3.74
Mickael Pietrus	−1.25	2.81
J.J. Redick	−1.56	3.90
Marcin Gortat	−2.46	5.07
Jameer Nelson	−2.48	3.61
Rafer Alston	−2.68	2.95
Tyronn Lue	−3.45	3.79
Anthony Johnson	−6.79*	3.07

* coefficient is at least twice the value of the standard error.

Source: Basketballvalue.com

other players, the estimated coefficient cannot be statistically differentiated from zero. This would suggest that Dwight Howard—a player who ranks in the top 10 according to all box score based measures considered herein—did not actually impact outcomes for the Orlando Magic in 2008–2009.

The results with respect to the Magic are not unusual. As Berri and Bradbury (2010) report, across a sample of 666 player observations taken from the 2007–2008 and 2008–2009 season, only 10.2 percent of players had an adjusted plus-minus coefficient that was twice the value of the corresponding standard error.[23]

Proponents of this measure note that more data reduces the standard errors; and this does appear to be true. Berri and Bradbury (2010) report that when two years of data are utilized to estimate the adjusted plus-minus coefficients, 14.7 percent of these coefficients are twice the value of the standard error. And if five years of data are employed, 38.9 percent of the estimated coefficients are twice the value of the corresponding standard error. So more data does help, although for most players the estimated coefficients appears to be statistically insignificant.[24]

Beyond statistical significance we also see a problem with consistency. Berri and Bradbury (2010) report that only 7 percent of a player's adjusted plus-minus value in the current season can be explained by what the player did in the prior season. In other words, the correlation coefficient between these two values[25] is only 0.26. When we turn to a sample of players who switched teams, the problem is even worse. For these players, last season's adjusted plus-minus value is not statistically related to what a player does this season. In other words—although adjusted plus-minus supposedly controls for the impact of teammates—if you change all the teammates you dramatically change the evaluation of the player.[26]

Beyond the issues of statistical significance and consistency are two broader critiques leveled by Dean Oliver (2004). First, Oliver notes a problem with looking at different segments of game. Again, plus-minus looks at how teams do with and without a player on the court. So it is essentially breaking down an entire game into segments. But as Oliver notes, teams are trying to win the entire game. Teams are not trying to win each segment of the game. In other words, teams will conserve energy during the course of a contest. Hence, a team playing poorly over a certain stretch of a game may not reflect the true value of the players on the court.

Oliver's second critique focuses on the interpretation of adjusted plus-minus results. Finding that a team appears to do better with a specific player on the court doesn't help decision-makers if you cannot explain how the player is actually helping. This critique points to a fundamental issue in statistical analysis. Analysis can provide us with correlations, but there must be more if we wish to argue causation. And the adjusted plus-minus model—because it does not rely upon any a priori theoretical model—simply doesn't allow a decisionmaker to make the leap from correlation to causation.

So although points scored and points surrendered—or the building blocks of plus-minus—explain 94 percent of team wins;[27] the inconsistency of this measure, coupled with the many other problems discussed, leaves us searching for something more.

THE WIN MODELS

Thus far we have detailed two approaches. The first—the scoring models—do a good job of explaining player salary. And these models are consistent over time. But their ability to explain wins is limited. In contrast, the plus-minus approach can explain wins. This measure, though, is quite inconsistent across time. What is needed is a measure that both explains wins and is more consistent. Such a measure can be found by returning to the box score.

The Win Shares Approach

Dean Oliver (2004) argued that the following four box score factors define wins in the NBA: shooting efficiency from the field, offensive rebounds, turnovers, and free throws. These factors can be measured for the team and the opponent[28] with adjusted field goal percentage,[29] turnover percentage,[30] offensive rebound percentage,[31] and free throws made divided by field goal attempts.[32]

As Table 6.2 reports, these four factors—measured for both the team and the team's opponent—explain 93.6 percent of wins. One can do slightly better with a simpler approach that regresses winning percentage on adjusted field goal percentage, free throw percentage, offensive rebounds per game, and turnovers per game. Either approach, though, reveals that Oliver's four factors do tell us why teams win or lose.

Table 6.2 Evaluating the Four Factors Approach; Dependent Variables: Team Winning Percentage; Ordinary Least Squares Estimation; White Heteroskedasticity-Consistent Standard Errors and Covariance; Sample: NBA Team Data from 1987–1988 to 2008–2009

Variable	Coefficient	t-Statistic	Coefficient	t-Statistic
Adjusted Field Goal Percentage	4.315	47.88	5.083	54.42
Opp. Adjusted Field Goal Percentage	−4.342	−47.26	−5.094	−59.12
Free Throw Ratio	0.899	14.13		
Opp. Free Throw Ratio	−0.970	−12.59		
Offensive Rebound Percentage	1.524	26.85		
Opp. Offensive Rebound Percentage	−1.492	−19.79		
Turnover Percentage	−4.010	−26.47		
Opp. Turnover Percentage	3.553	22.83		
Free Throw Percentage			0.757	12.42
Opp. Free Throw Percentage			−0.789	−7.80
Free Throw Attempts			0.010	14.22
Opp. Free Throw Attempts			−0.011	−14.75
Offensive Rebounds			0.031	25.47
Opp. Offensive Rebounds			−0.030	−18.74
Turnovers			−0.030	−20.41
Opp. Turnovers			0.029	20.62
Constant	0.594	8.93	0.556	6.37
Adjusted R-Squared	0.936		0.942	
Observations	621		621	

Although this approach is enlightening, it does not help us measure the performance of the individual player. Half of the independent variables listed in Table 6.2 come from a team's opponent. And we simply do not know how each individual employed by a team impacted the opponent's accumulation of these statistics.

To move from the team to the individual, Oliver employs what he refers to as "my personal Difficulty Theory for Distributing Credit in Basketball" (2004, p. 145). Essentially, Oliver argues that the more difficult an action is, the greater the action's impact on the measure of a player's value. As argued in Berri, Schmidt, and Brook (2006), though, such an approach shifts the focus away from wins. In other words, just because something is more difficult, it doesn't mean that action has a bigger impact on wins. So although Oliver's work has been employed by Justin Kubatko[33] in developing a metric labeled "Win Shares," the calculation of this metric is somewhat detached from wins.

Despite this critique, Oliver'sapproach does have a certain appeal. In essence, Oliver's focus on "difficulty" is an effort to incorporate scarcity in the evaluation of individual players. In calculating a player's impact on wins, Oliver takes into account the productivity of a player's teammates. For example, consider two players who are equally capable of grabbing rebounds. If one of these players is on a team that is relatively bad on the boards, then that player's rebounds are worth relatively more. So if you do something your team needs, then you are relatively more valuable.

Such an approach is certainly appealing. But the incorporation of the teammates' production in the evaluation of individual players does increase the complexity of this measure. Furthermore, as suspected when one relies on the numbers generated by teammates, consistency is also an issue with Win Shares. If we look at the correlation in per-minute Win Shares across successive seasons we only see a coefficient[34] of 0.67. And if we focus on a sample of players who change teams we only see a correlation coefficient[35] of 0.49.

So Win Shares, relative to the scoring models,does a better job of explaining wins. And it is more consistent than the plus-minus approach. Still, the complexity of Win Shares may limit the usefulness of this measure for academic researchers.

The Wins Produced Approach

For a somewhat less complex approach to measuring performance we turn to the Wins Produced approach. This measure is fully detailed[36] in Berri (2008). It has also been discussed in both Berri, Schmidt, and Brook (2006) and Berri and Schmidt (2010). For our discussion here, we want to focus on how Wins Produced connects to team wins and the consistency of this measure over time.

For the first issue we need to briefly discuss the formulation of this model; and that discussion begins with a measure of soccer created by Gerrard (2007). Gerrard's soccer model is based on the estimation of the following structural equations (SE):

(SE1)   *League Points = f(Goals Scored, Goals Conceded)*

(SE2)   *Goals Scored = Own Conversion Rate × Own Shots at Goal*

(SE3)   *Goals Conceded = (1 – Own Save-Shot Ratio) × Opposition Shots on Target*

(SE4)   *Own Shots At Goal = f(Own General Play)*

(SE5)   *Opposition Shots On Target = f(Own General Play)*

where general play includes number of passes, pass completion rate, crosses, dribbles, tackles won, interceptions, blocks and clearances (Gerrard, 2007).

As one can see, Gerrard (2007) begins with the most basic relationships. Outcomes in soccer are obviously a function of goals scored and goals conceded. Gerrard then moves on to note that goals scored are a function of shots on goal and a team's shooting percentage (i.e., conversion rate). Shots on goal are then a function of what Gerrard refers to as "general play." General play includes most of the actions a soccer player takes on the field. And via regression, each of these actions can be linked to shots.

A similar approach was independently detailed in Berri (2008). Here are the specific steps he employed.

Step One: Wins = f(Points Scored, Points Surrendered)

Step Two: Points Scored = f(Shot Attempts, Shooting Efficiency)
              Points Surrendered = f(Opponent's Shot Attempts, Opponent's Shooting Efficiency)

where   Shot Attempts is defined in terms of field goal attempts and free throw attempts

where   Shooting Efficiency is defined in terms of points-per-shot[37] and free throw percentage.

Step Three: Field Goal Attempts = f(Opponent's Made Field Goals, Opponent's Made Free Throws, Defensive Rebounds, Team Rebounds (TMRB), Opponent's Turnovers, Turnovers, Free Throw Attempts, Offensive Rebounds)
              Opponent's Field Goal Attempts = f(Made Field Goals, Made Free Throws, Opponent's Defensive Rebounds, Opponent's Team Rebounds, Turnovers, Opponent's Turnovers, Opponent's Free Throw Attempts, Opponent's Offensive Rebounds)

Like Gerrard, the first step in Berri (2008) was to link wins to points scored and points surrendered. This simple model is then expanded by noting what determines scoring; and then determining what dictates shot attempts.

Unlike Gerrard, Berri (2008) collapses these steps into a single equation.[38] This is made possible by noting the definition of possessions employed and possessions acquired.[39]

$$Possessions\ Employed\ (PE) = FGA + 0.45{*}FTA + TO - ORB \qquad (5)$$

$$Possessions\ Acquired\ (PA) = Opp.TO + DRB + TMRB + Opp.FGM$$
$$+ 0.45{*}Opp.FTM \qquad (6)$$

Equation (5) describes how a team employs a possession. Once a team acquires the ball, it can take a shot (either a field goal attempt and/or a number of free throw attempts) or commit a turnover. If a shot is missed, additional shot attempts can be gained via an offensive rebound.[40]

The specification of possession employed is quite similar to how both John Hollinger (2002) and Dean Oliver (2004) define a possession. To calculate Wins Produced, a second definition—detailed in equation (6)—is also necessary.

Equation (6) details how a team acquires possession of the ball. Ideally, a team gains possession by forcing a turnover or capturing an errant shot (either a defensive rebound or team rebound). If this doesn't happen though, the opponent will eventually make a shot (either a field goal attempt or a free throw attempt). And by rule, a team also can gain possession when the opponent scores.

As detailed in Berri (2008), the definition of possessions employed and possessions acquired allows one to condense the aforementioned steps into equation (7):

$$\text{Winning Percentage} = b_1 + b_2{}^*\text{PTS/PE} - b_3{}^*\text{Opp.PTS/PA} + e \qquad (7)$$

Equation (7) argues that wins are determined by both offensive efficiency and defensive efficiency, where offensive efficiency is defined as points scored divided by possessions employed, and defensive efficiency is defined as points surrendered divided by possessions acquired. The argument that wins are determined by these two efficiency measures follows the arguments offered by both Hollinger (2002) and Oliver (2005). But by utilizing two definitions of possession, much of what a player does on the court can now be connected to team wins.

Utilizing NBA team data from 1987–1988 to 2008–2009, equation (7)—as reported in Table 6.3—was estimated. The results indicate that 95 percent of the variation in winning percentage can be explained by offensive and defensive efficiency.

As noted in Berri (2008), the coefficients reported in Table 6.3 allow us to determine the impact[41] of points scored, field goal attempts, free throw attempts,

Table 6.3 Estimated Coefficients for Equation (7); Dependent Variable is Regular Season Winning Percentage; Sample: 1987–1988 to 2008–2009

Variable	Coefficient	t-Statistic
Constant*	0.481	8.406
Offensive Efficiency*	3.150	79.147
Defensive Efficiency*	−3.132	−69.889
Adjusted R-Squared	0.95	
Observations	621	

* denotes significance at the 1% level.

turnovers (which includes team turnovers or TMTO), offensive rebounds, opponent's points scored, opponent's turnovers (which includes steals), defensive
rebounds, team rebounds, opponent's field goals made, and opponent's free throws
made. And from the value of the opponent's free throws made—again, as detailed
in Berri (2008)—one can ascertain the impact of a player's personal fouls.

Each of these values is reported in Table 6.4. As one can see, with the exception of factors associated with free throws and personal fouls, most factors listed
in Table 6.4 have the same impact—in absolute terms—on wins.[42] Consequently
the value of anything that gets—or loses—possession of the ball is worth about
one point.

This result returns us to the subject of shooting efficiency. As noted, the
break-even marks with respect to the scoring models reward inefficiency. The
link between offensive and defensive efficiency, though, indicates that players
must score one point per field goal attempt to breakeven.[43] In other words, below-
average scorers actually hurt a team's chances to be successful. And this should
make intuitive sense. Wasting possessions is simply not an action that helps a
team win games.

With the values reported in Table 6.4, we need only two more pieces of information to measure a player's impact on team wins. Of the factors typically reported

Table 6.4 The Impact of Various Player and Team
Factors on Wins in the NBA

Player Factors	Impact on Wins
PTS	0.033
FGA	-0.033
FTA	-0.015
ORB	0.033
TO	-0.033
DRB	0.033
Opp.FTM or PF[47]	-0.017
STL[48]	0.033
Team Factors	**Impact on Wins**
Opp.PTS from Opp.FGA	-0.032
Opp.FGM	0.033
Opp.TO (that are not STL)	0.033
TMTO	-0.033
TMRB	0.033

Source: Berri and Schmidt (2010)

in the box score, only blocked shots and assists are not listed in Table 6.4. As reported in Berri (2008), though, the impact of these two factors can be derived. Such analysis indicates that a blocked shot is worth 0.019 wins, while an assist is worth 0.022 wins.[44]

With values in hand, one can calculate a player's Wins Produced. For the full details of this calculation one is referred to Berri (2008). For here, we will simply note the basic steps.

Step One: Calculate the value of a player's production by multiplying the value of each box score statistic—mostly reported in Table 6.4—by the player's production of each statistic. This calculation is divided by minutes played and multiplied by 48 to give us production per 48 minutes.

Step Two: What we see from Step One needs to be adjusted for the productivity of a player's teammates. This adjustment involves considering the teammate's production of assists and blocked shots. We also need to consider all the team defensive factors listed in Table 6.4. After adjusting for the productivity of a player's teammates we have Adj. P48 (adjusted production per 48 minutes). It is important to emphasize that a team's Adj. P48 explains 95 percent of a team's wins. So this model—as illustrated by equation (7)—is quite consistent with team outcomes. To understand a player's contribution to team success, though, we need to take two more steps.

Step Three: As Berri (2008) notes, player performance in the NBA depends on position played.[45] This is because centers and power forwards tend to get rebounds and tend not to commit turnovers, while guards are the opposite. The nature of basketball is that teams need little men and big men. Given that teams appear to require all five positions, players should be evaluated relative to their position averages. Such a calculation gives us each player's Relative Adj. P48.

Step Four: It is convenient to discuss a player's production of wins, as opposed to his relative production. Such convenience can be achieved by moving from relative wins to absolute wins.

This calculation requires that we simply note that the average team will win half its games, or have 0.500 wins per 48 minutes played. Since a team employs five players per 48 minutes, the average player must produce 0.100 wins per 48 minutes played. Because teams do play overtime games once in awhile, the actual average production of wins per 48 minutes is 0.099.

Given what we know about an average player, equation (8) illustrates how Wins per 48 minutes (WP48) is calculated:

$$\text{WP48} = \text{Relative Adj. P48} + 0.099 \tag{8}$$

One can move from WP48 to each player's Wins Produced. And the summation of each team's Wins Produced—as we saw with the estimation of equation (7)—again explains 95 percent of a team's wins.

So Wins Produced does explain wins. But is it consistent? To address this issue, the correlation between a player's Adj. P48 in successive seasons was calculated.[46] The sample utilized began with the 1977–1978 season and ended in

2007–2008. In all, 6,549 player observations were examined and the correlation uncovered was 0.83. If we only consider players who switched teams, the correlation uncovered is 0.76. In sum, it appears that this latter approach is more consistent than Win Shares and Adjusted Plus-Minus. And Wins Produced explains more of wins than the scoring models. But does this make Wins Produced the best model? The answer to that question depends upon the research question one is addressing.

GUIDE TO RESEARCH: DO YOU NEED TO KNOW PERCEPTIONS OR REALITY?

We began our discussion with various schools of thought and a method for evaluating each approach. Following Bradbury (2008), it was argued that a model should both explain current outcomes and have some consistency overtime. Table 6.5 summarizes how each approach performs with respect to each criterion.

The scoring models appear to be quite consistent over time. But these models simply do not do a very good job of explaining wins. The plus-minus approach appears to be the opposite. This approach may explain current wins, but these measures—for the reasons detailed earlier—are quite inconsistent overtime.

When we turn to the Win approach, we appear to see the best of both worlds. This approach explains both current wins and appears to produce a measure of performance that is consistent over time. Of the two approaches, Wins Produced appears to be more consistent than Win Shares. Nevertheless, both Wins Produced and Win Shares appear to trump the scoring models or the plus-minus models.

If one is interested in explaining a player's impact on wins, it appears that the Wins Model approach should be followed by a researcher. Wins, though, are not the only outcome researchers wish to explain. And here is where research on the NBA becomes difficult.

As explained earlier, player evaluation in the NBA is dominated by scoring.

This feature of the NBA's labor market means that when you shift your focus from explaining wins to explaining decisions, the scoring models suddenly look much better. In fact, these models—as demonstrated in the aforementioned literature—do a better job of explaining perceptions of performance. And again, the scoring models are quite consistent across time.

So which model should a researcher choose? Again, there are different schools of thought. What appears clear is that the specific research question that one is seeking to answer will dictate the choice of models employed.

Table 6.5 Explanatory Power and Consistency of Various Measures of Performance in the NBA; Explanatory power evaluated in terms of team wins; Consistency is the correlation between per-minute performances in successive seasons

Model	Explanatory Power	Consistency	Sample	Observations
The Scoring Models				
NBA Efficiency	0.32	0.82	1977–1978 to 2007–2008	6,549
Points Created	0.34	0.82	1977–1978 to 2007–2008	6,549
Game Score	0.31	0.81	1977–1978 to 2007–2008	6,549
Player Efficiency Rating	0.34	0.80	2005–2006 to 2008–2009	758
The Plus-Minus Models				
Plus-Minus	0.94	0.48	2006–2007 to 2008–2009	364
Net On-Off	0.94	0.35	2006–2007 to 2008–2009	364
Adjusted Plus-Minus	0.94	0.26	2007–2008 to 2008–2009	239
The Oliver-Berri Models				
Win Shares	0.95	0.67	2005–2006 to 2008–2009	758
Wins Produced	0.95	0.83	1977–1978 to 2007–2008	6,549

Regardless of whether one wishes to explain wins or player evaluations in the NBA, though, it does appear that data in basketball is at least as good as what we observe in baseball. As Bradbury (2008) reports, the season-to-season correlation for a metric like OPS is only 0.65. And as Berri and Bradbury (2010) report, OPS only explains 89 percent of the variation in runs scored. Such numbers trail what we see with respect to Wins Produced in basketball. This suggests that although research in basketball is not without its challenges, the performance metrics the researcher can employ in basketball might be the best player data available in the study of professional team sports.

NOTES

The author would like to thank Andrew Walton, Lynn Watson, Arturo Galletti, Dean Oliver, Leo Kahane, and Stephen Shmanske for their assistance.

1 OPS = On-base percentage + slugging average
2 According to Albert and Bennett (2003, p. 170), Batter's Run Average equals on-base percentage multiplied by slugging average. This measure was introduced by Richard Cramer and Pete Palmer.
3 According to Albert and Bennett (2003, p. 166), Total Average was introduced by Thomas Boswell in 1981. This measure is simply the ratio of total bases to total outs.
4 The Lindsey-Palmer approach is discussed in detail in Albert and Bennett (2003).
5 Beyond these two issues, we also should also note that for a researcher, simplicity (i.e., a measure that is easy to explain an academic article) is preferred to something more complex. Academic articles have a finite length and time spent explaining a complex performance measure will take away from the larger story these articles are trying to tell. And of course, researchers have to consider theoretical validity of a measure and a host of econometric issues.
6 See Berri (2006), Berri, Schmidt, and Brook (2006), Berri, Brook, and Schmidt (2007), and Berri and Schmidt (2010).
7 See Berri and Schmidt (2002), Berri, Schmidt, and Brook (2006), and Berri and Schmidt (2010).
8 See Berri, Brook, and Fenn (2010) and Berri and Schmidt (2010).
9 See Berri and Schmidt (2010).
10 This is based on a regression of a team's winning percentage in the NBA on the number of points a team scores per game. Data was taken from the 1987–1988 season to the 2008–2009 season (621 observations).
11 The simple Points Created formula is as follows:
Points Created = PTS + ORB + DRB + STL + AST + BLK – MSFG – MSFT – TO
            – PF/2
Bellotti also presents a more complex measure that adjusts for game pace.
The simple TENDEX formula is quite similar.
TENDEX = PTS + ORB + DRB + STL + AST + BLK – MSFG – MSFT/2 – TO – PF
In evaluating an individual player, one divides TENDEX by minutes played. One then also divides by game pace.
12 The sample used for NBA Efficiency and Points Created included 6,549 player observations from 1977–1978 to 2007–2008. To be included in this sample a player had to play a minimum of 20 minutes per game and 12 minutes per game in consecutive seasons.
13 This regression utilized data from the 1987–88 to 2008–09 NBA seasons (621 observations). Explanatory power of team's Points Created (34%) and a team's TENDEX (34%) are quite similar. If one adds a team's pace as an explanatory variable to equation (1), explanatory power of the NBA Efficiency equation rises to 62%. Similar results are obtained for Points Created (61%) and TENDEX (61%). The specific pace calculation employed is taken from John Hollinger (2004) and is detailed in the discussion of PER.
14 This is based on a sample of 896 players drawn from the 2007–2008 and 2008–2009 season.
15 This regression utilized data from the 1987–88 to 2008–09 NBA seasons (621 observations). If one adds a team's pace as an explanatory variable to equation (1),

explanatory power of the PER equation (which actually is supposed to account for pace as it is originally formulated) rises to 54%. Game Score and pace explains 57% of the variation in a team's winning percentage. One can go one step further and allow the individual components of the team defensive adjustment (detailed in Berri (2008) and employed in the calculation of Wins Produced) to vary. Such a step does raise the explanatory power of PERs to 82%. Wins Produced, though, explains 95% of wins, so even with the team defensive adjustments components added, the more popular measures come up short. On the subject of testing models is the following observation offered by Berri and Bradbury (2010) concerning the unusual approach taken by Lewin and Rosenbaum (2007):

> An alternative testing approach was suggested and originally presented on-line by Lewin and Rosenbaum (2007). Their approach began with a team's efficiency differential, or points scored per possession minus points surrendered per possession. This differential was then regressed on a team's PERs (or whatever metric these authors were examining). Then utilizing the results of this regression, plus the residual from the regression, each player was evaluated. This evaluation was then used to predict the next season's efficiency differential for each team (with a rookies' performance simply taken as given). The results indicated that all the models examined were able to explain between 75% and 77% of future wins. In other words, all models were basically the same. Such a result should not surprise. As Lewin-Rosenbaum (2007) actually argue, any model plus the residual, does an equally good job of explaining current wins. Of course such an argument applies to all models (as any student of econometrics should understand). In sum, it is not clear what the Lewin-Rosenbaum residual approach is designed to tell us. It is certainly well understood that any model plus the residual can explain 100% of a dependent variable. And as we see, when we do not employ the residual in our evaluation, we do see clear differences in the explanatory power of different metrics.

16 Berri and Bradbury (2010) report that there is a 0.99 correlation between NBA Efficiency and Game Score. This is based on a sample of 896 players drawn from the 2007–08 and 2008–09 season.

17 Berri and Bradbury (2010) looked at a sample of 325 players who took at least 100 shots from two-point range during the 2008–2009 season. Of these, only one failed to hit 33% of these shots.

18 Berri and Bradbury (2010) looked at a sample of 158 players who took at least 100 three-point shots during the 2008–2009 season. All of these players converted on at least 25% of their shots from this distance.

19 A player who takes 100 field goal attempts is charged 70 Game Score points. If he makes 29.2 shots from two point range would get 58.4 Game Score points. Plus a player gets 0.4 for each field goal made. So 29.2 made shots increases Game Score by 11.7. Adding 58.4 and 11.7 together and we see that the player who shoots 29.2% from two-point range just breaks even. From three-point range we see a lower break-even point. If he makes 20.6 shots—out of 100 shots—he gets 61.8 Game Score points from his scoring and an additional 8.3 Game Score points from his field goals made. So making 20.6% of shots from three-point range allows a player to breakeven.

20 Previously it was noted that the correlation coefficients for NBA Efficiency and Points Created per minute was 0.82. For Game Score per minute and PER the coefficients are 0.81 and 0.80 respectively. The sample used for to evaluate Game Score included

6,549 player observations from 1977–1978 to 2007–2008. To be included in this sample a player had to play a minimum of 20 minutes per game and 12 minutes per game in consecutive seasons. For PER, the sample included 758 player observations from the 2005–2006 to 2008–2009 seasons. Again, the player had to play a minimum of 20 minutes per game and 12 minutes per game in consecutive seasons.

21 For example, Berri, Brook, and Schmidt (2007) report that a model that employed NBA Efficiency can explain 73% of the variation in the voting for the All-Rookie team (voting done by NBA coaches). A model employing Wins Produced—a metric (described below) that does a better job of explaining wins—only explains 50% of the variation in the coaches' voting. Likewise, 64% of the variation in free agent salaries can be explained by a model that employs NBA Efficiency. A model that employs Wins Produced, though, only explains 41% of the variation in free agent salaries.

22 For example, in a study of monopsony power in MLB, the NFL, and the NBA, Krautmann, Von Allmen, and Berri (2009) utilized NBA Efficiency to study salaries in professional basketball. One should note that NBA Efficiency was chosen over the Player Efficiency Rating. These two models, as noted, are quite similar. NBA Efficiency, though, is far easier to work with and explain.

23 Berri and Bradbury (2010) also note that if we consider players with a coefficient that is 1.5 times the standard error, only 20.4% of observations meet this lower threshold.

24 BasketballValue.com reports coefficients for 292 players who played in both 2007–08 and 2008–09. For this data set—as Berri and Bradbury (2010) report—14.7% of players had a coefficient that was twice the value of a standard error. Looking at the 1.5 threshold, we find that 26.0% of coefficients surpass this mark. An even greater gain is seen if five years of player data is examined. BasketballValue.com reports coefficient for 373 players who played for five seasons. For this sample—again as Berri and Bradbury (2010) report—we see that 38.9% of coefficients are at least twice the value of the standard error. And 50.4% surpass the 1.5 threshold. Again, although more data does increase the level of statistical significance, it is still the case that most players—even when five years of data are employed—are not found by this method to have a statistically significant impact on outcomes. In addition, one should note that increasing sample sizes will depress standard errors and give the impression that results are now more significant. So the power of larger samples in the adjusted plus-minus calculations is probably not as great as proponents of this method claim.

25 Oddly enough, the unadjusted plus-minus measure is actually more consistent. 82games.com reports a player's Net48, which is defined as "the team net points per 48 minutes of playing time for the player." "Net points" is the plus/minus statistic for basketball, or the difference between the points that a team scores and allows when a player is on the court. 82games.com also reports Net On Court/Off Court. A player's off-court performance is the net points a team realizes when the player is not in the game. On court is simply Net48. So Net On Court/Off Court is intended to capture how well a team performs with and without the player. Berri and Bradbury (2010) examined a data set consisting of 364 players from the 2006–2007 to 2008–2009 seasons. The player had to play at least 1,000 minutes in consecutive seasons to be included in the data set. The correlation coefficient for a player's Net On Court/ Off Court in successive seasons is 0.35. Such a mark is higher than what we see with respect to adjusted plus-minus.

26 Lewin and Rosenbaum (2007)—two proponents of adjusted plus-minus—sought to "test" various models (i.e., PERS, Wins Produced, etc.) by looking at the correlation

between player evaluations completed with adjusted plus-minus evaluations and how players were evaluated by other metrics. Such a "test" appears to ignore the problems people have noted with adjusted plus-minus.

27 This result comes from a regression of team winning percentage on points scored and surrendered per game. This regression utilized 621 team observations from the 1987–1988 to 2008–2009 seasons. One should note that the explanatory power reported by adjusted plus-minus may fall short of the explanatory power (i.e. the 94% figure reported) of points scored and points surrendered. As Arturo Galletti (2011) reports, the adjusted plus-minus model employs a model where the margin of each segment in a game where the players are not changed is regressed on dummy variables for each player on the court (and each player not on the court). This regression has an r-squared that is less than 10%. The final results reported at Basketballvalue.com appear to explain more than 10% of team wins. How this result is achieved, though, is not clear.

28 The standard box score data can be found for each team, opponent, and player at Basketball-Reference.com.

29 Adjusted field goal percentage is calculated as follows: (Field Goals Made + 0.5*Three Point Field Goals Made) / Field Goal Attempts. Or one can simply take one-half of points-per-shot (PPS), where PPS = (Points – Free Throws Made) / Field Goals Attempted. Adjusted field goal percentage is also called effective field goal percentage.

30 Turnover percentage is the number of turnovers committed per possession, where possessions are calculated as field goal attempts + 0.44*free throw attempts + turnovers – offensive rebounds.

31 Offensive rebound percentage is calculated by dividing offensive rebounds by the summation of offensive rebounds and the opponent's defensive rebounds.

32 The four factors approach was detailed in Oliver (2004). It is also discussed at Basketball-Reference.com (www.basketball-reference.com/about/factors.html).

33 Win Shares is reported at Basketball-Reference.com. To see the calculation one is referred to the following website: www.basketball-reference.com/about/ws.html

34 The sample included 758 player observations from the 2005–2006 to 2008–2009 seasons. The player had to play a minimum of 20 minutes per game and 12 minutes per game in consecutive seasons.

35 The sample included 249 player observations from the 2005–2006 to 2008–2009 seasons. The player had to play a minimum of 20 minutes per game and 12 minutes per game in consecutive seasons and switch teams sometime during the consecutive seasons examined.

36 As noted in Berri, Schmidt, and Brook (2006) and Berri (2008), an earlier version of this model was reported in Berri (1999).

37 Points-per-shot is simply [PTS-FTM]/FGA. It is also twice a player's adjusted field goal percentage. Both points-per-shot and adjusted field goal percentage take into account a player's three-point shooting.

38 Here is more information on the steps Berri (2008) follows to derive the model.
   Step One: Wins are a function of points scored and points surrendered.
   Step Two: Points scored are a function of how many shots a team takes and how efficiently these shots are turned into points. In other words, points scored are a function of field goal attempts, free throw attempts, points-per-shot, and free throw percentage.
   Step Three: Field goal attempts are a function of a team's ability to acquire the ball and what a team does with the ball upon gaining possession. A team can acquire the ball by the opponent committing a turnover (Opp.TO), by acquiring

a rebound after the opponent misses a shot (DRB, TMRB), or by the opponent making a shot (Opp. FGM, and Opp. FTM). A team loses a shot attempt when it turns the ball over (TO). It can also substitute free throw attempts (FTA) for field goal attempts and garner additional shot attempts by collecting offensive rebounds (ORB).

Step Four: Having noted the factors that explain field goal attempts, we then utilize some substitution to derive the final wins model, reported in model (2). Given all that has been said on the first three steps, we can now see that points scored are functions of points-per-shot, free throw percentage, FTA, TO, ORB, Opp.TO, DRB, TMRB, Opp.FGM, and Opp. FTM. The last five factors in this list are simply possessions acquired, while the first five can be summarized as points scored per possession employed. In other words, one could argue that wins are a function of the following four factors: points scored per possession employed, possession acquired, opponent's points scored per the opponent's possession employed, and the opponent's possession's acquired. Because possessions by the team and the opponent must be approximately equal, possessions acquired and the opponent's possessions acquired must cancelled. And because possessions acquired must approximately equal the opponent' possessions employed, the final model for wins must be what we report in equation (7).

39 One should note that the equations for PE and PA lack an error term. This is because these are essentially identity. Each time a team turns the ball over it loses possession. Each time the opponent commits a turnover the team gains possession. A similar story can be told about rebounds. Kubatko et. al. (2007) actually collected data on possessions and attempted to derive the value of the various factors that comprise possessions via a regression. Their model, though, omitted team rebounds that change possessions and included rebounds from the opponent. One suspects that more rebounds by the opponent would reduce team rebounds that change possession. But the omission of team rebounds that change possession still resulted in a model that was mis-specified. Consequently Kubatko et. al. (2007) erroneously concluded that each rebound was actually worth less than one possession. In other words, grabbing a rebound did not give a team complete possession of the ball. Had it been properly specified the authors would have seen that the only unknown coefficients in possessions are connected to free throws. Consequently, with the exception of ascertaining the value of factors associated with free throws, regression analysis is not necessary for connecting rebounds and turnovers to possessions.

40 The value of a free throw is ascertained in the process of calculating the number of team rebounds that change possession. One should also note that team rebounds are basically an accounting device. The number of missed shots and rebounds should be equal at the end of a game. If a missed shot goes out of bounds, though, a rebound cannot be credited to an individual. Likewise, if a player misses the first of two free throws, no rebound can be recorded for an individual player. Hence, these events are also listed as team rebounds. For the steps one follows to determine the number of team rebounds that change possession one is referred to Berri (2008).

41 To calculate the values listed in Table 6.4 one takes the derivative of winning percentage with respect to points, possessions employed, points surrendered, and possessions acquired. For example, the marginal value of an additional point scored equals b_2 / Possessions Employed. And the marginal value of an additional possession

employed is calculated as [b_2 / Possessions Employed] *[Points Scored / Possessions Employed]. Because one often wishes to compare players across teams, league averages for points scored and possessions employed are used to calculate marginal values. One could also, though, create separate coefficients for each team by using team values. Such an approach would be consistent with how Win Shares is measured, and as noted, make the calculations more difficult and makes comparisons of players across teams somewhat problematic.

42 As Berri and Schmidt (2010) emphasize, from 1987–1988 to 2008–2009, teams averaged 1.02 points per possession. This average illustrates why points and shot attempts have the same impact—in absolute terms—on outcomes.

43 From 1987–1988 to 2008–2009, the average adjusted field goal percentage in the NBA was 48.6%. The average Points-per-Shot (PPS)—which is simply twice the value of adjusted field goal percentage—was 0.97. So on average, players have to score about one point per field goal attempt to be average. Again, below average marks should hurt a team's chances of winning.

44 From Table 6.4 we see that each Opp.FGM costs a team 0.033 wins. To determine the value of a blocked shot one simply regresses Opp.FGM on a team's blocked shots and field goal attempts. The results indicate that each additional blocked shot reduces Opp.FGM by 0.60. Consequently, one can infer that each blocked shot is worth 0.019 wins, or 60% of 0.033 wins. Berri, Schmidt, and Brook (2006) and Berri (2008) detail how the value of an assist is ascertained. The process began by regressing a player's per-minute unassisted Win Score (i.e., Win Score without assists) on a collection of factors (similar to the list employed in the study of coaching discussed in Berri, Leeds, Leeds, and Mondello (2009)that included the number of assists perminute accumulated by teammates. This model suggests that assists do have a positive and significant impact on teammate performance. One should also note that the causality between a player's productivity and the assists of the teammates probably goes both ways, since one only is credited with an assist if a basket is scored after a pass. Hence, this analysis may overstate the value of an assist.

45 For most players it is easy to determine position played. For a few, though, it can be more challenging. Positions in basketball are not like baseball or football. In baseball and football we can tell position by where a player appears on the field. In basketball, though, position designations are more arbitrary. Consequently, two analysts looking at the same team may designate positions differently. Here is the specific process followed: First, it is assumed that minutes are equal at each position. Second, in general, players are allocated across the center and forwards position according to designations noted at on-line website such as ESPN.com and/or Yahoo.com as well as height and weight. Finally, at the guard positions one can also consider number of assists per-minute. The players who get more assists are generally considered point guards.

46 The sample used to evaluate Adj. P48 included 6,549 player observations from 1977–1978 to 2007–2008. To be included in this sample a player had to play a minimum of 20 minutes per game and 12 minutes per game in consecutive seasons. If one looks at WP48 one sees a correlation of 0.75. This lower correlation is a function of the position adjustment, or the technique used to translate a player's production—noted in Adj. P48—into wins. To evaluate the consistency of the Win Produced approach it makes sense to do this before the position adjustment is implemented, since this adjustment does not impact explanatory power. Furthermore—as noted above—the position adjustment is not entirely objective.

47 From Table 6.4 one can see the impact of an opponent making a free throw (Opp. FTM) on team wins. Free throws are taken by the opponent when a player commits a personal foul. It's important to remember that not all personal fouls lead to free throws. Still, one can allocate the percentage of free throws an opponent takes to each player according to the percentage of personal fouls each player commits. For example, Al Horford of the Atlanta Hawks committed 11.8% of the team's personal fouls in 2008–2009. Consequently, of the 1,385 free throws made by Atlanta's opponents, one can assign 11.8% (or 163.4) to Harrington. Since one knows the impact the opponent's free throws have on wins, it is now possible to measure the impact of Horford's propensity to commit personal fouls.

48 A steal counts as a turnover for an opponent. Therefore, the value of the opponent's turnover is the same as the value of a steal. The opponent's turnovers that are not steals will be used to calculate the team defensive adjustment.

References

82games.com

Albert, James, and J. Bennet. (2003). *Curve ball: Baseball, statistics, and the role of chance in the game.* New York: Springer.

Basketball-Reference.com

BasketballValue.com

Bellotti, Robert (1992). *The points created basketball book 1991–92.* New Brunswick, NJ: Night Work Publishing.

Berri, David J. (2008). A simple measure of worker productivity in the National Basketball Association. In *The business of sport*; eds. Brad Humphreys and Dennis Howard, 3 volumes, Westport, CT: Praeger, pp. 1–40.

Berri, David J. (2007). Back to back evaluation on the gridiron. In *Statistical thinking in sport*; eds. James H. Albert and Ruud H. Koning. Chapman & Hall/CRC: 235–256.

Berri, David J. (1999). Who is most valuable? Measuring the player's production of wins in the National Basketball Association." *Managerial and Decision Economics,* 20(8): 411–427.

Berri, David J., and J. C. Bradbury. (2010). Working in the land of metricians. *Journal of Sports Economics,* 11, n1; (February): 29–47.

Berri, David J., Stacey L. Brook, and Aju Fenn (2011). From college to the pros: Predicting the NBA amateur player draft. *Journal of Productivity Analysis,* 35, n1: 25–35, February. On-line citation: DOI 10. 1007/s11123–010–0187-x.

Berri, David J., Stacey L. Brook, and Martin B. Schmidt (2006). *The wages of wins: Taking measure of the many myths in modern sport.* Stanford, CA: Stanford University Press.

Berri, David J., Stacey L. Brook, and Martin B. Schmidt (2007). Does one need to score to score?" *International Journal of Sports Finance,* 2: 190–205.

Berri, David J., Michael Leeds, Eva Marikova Leeds, and Michael Mondello (2009). The role of managers in team performance. *International Journal of Sport Finance,* 4(2): 75–93.

Berri, David J., and Martin B. Schmidt (2010). *Stumbling on wins: Two economists explore the pitfalls on the road to victory in professional sports.* Princeton, NJ: Wharton School Publishing/Financial Times Press.

Berri, David J., and Martin B. Schmidt (2002). Instrumental vs. bounded rationality: The case of Major League Baseball and the National Basketball Association. *Journal of Socio-Economics* (formerly the *Journal of Behavioral Economics*), 31(3): 191–214.

Bradbury, John C. (2008). Statistical performance analysis in sport. In *The business of sport*; eds. Brad Humphreys and Dennis Howard, 3 volumes, Westport, CT: Praeger, pp. 41–56.

Bradbury, John C. (2007) *The baseball economist: The real game exposed.* New York: Dutton.

Galletti, Arturo. (2011). "Deconstructing a Model." arturogalletti.wordpress. com/2011/03/04/deconstructing-a-model/

Gerrard, Bill (2007). Is the moneyball approach transferable to complex invasion team sports? *International Journal of Sports Finance*, 2: 214–228.

Heeren, Dave (1994). *Basketball abstract 1994–95 edition.* Indianapolis: Masters Press.

Hollinger, John (2002). *Pro basketball prospectus 2002.* Washington DC: Brassey's Sports.

Hollinger, John (2005). Hockey stat, with a twist, useful in NBA, too. ESPN.com (March 29).

Jenkins, Jeffery (1996). A reexamination of salary discrimination in professional basketball. *Social Science Quarterly* 77(3): 594–608.

Krautmann, Anthony, Peter Von Allmen, and David J. Berri (2009). The underpayment of restricted players in north american sports leagues. *International Journal of Sport Finance*, 4(3): 155–169.

Kubatko, Justin, Dean Oliver, Kevin Pelton, Dan Rosenbaum (2007). "A Starting Point for Analyzing Basketball Statistics." *Journal of Quantitative Analysis in Sports,* 3(3).

Lee, Young Hoon, and David J. Berri (2008). A re-examination of production functions and efficiency estimates for the National Basketball Association. *Scottish Journal of Political Economy,* 55(1): 51–66.

Lewin, David, and Dan Rosenbaum (2007). The pot calling the kettle black: Are NBA statistical models more irrational than "irrational" decision-makers? Working paper.

Neyer, Rob (1996). Who are the "true" shooters? In *STATS pro basketball handbook, 1995–96,* pp. 322–323. New York: STATS Publishing.

Oliver, Dean (2004). *Basketball on paper: Rules and tools for performance analysis.* Brassey, Inc., Washington, D. C.

Scott, Frank Jr., James Long, and Ken Somppi (1985). Salary vs. marginal revenue product under monopsony and competition: The case of professional basketball. *Atlantic Economic Journal,* 13(3): 50–59.

Winston, Wayne (2009). *Mathletics: How gamblers, managers, and sports enthusiasts use mathematics in baseball, basketball, and football.* Princeton, NJ: Princeton University Press.

## CHAPTER 7

FRONTIER MODELS AND THEIR APPLICATION TO THE SPORTS INDUSTRY

YOUNG HOON LEE

INTRODUCTION

SINCE Scully's groundbreaking empirical analysis of the production function of Major League Baseball (MLB) in 1974, econometric applications to the sporting production process have been disseminated through various team sports industries. This kind of application has now evolved into the study of team efficiency or managerial efficiency. At first, these applications focused on sports that were popular in North America (baseball, basketball, American football, and hockey) (Zak, Huang, and Siegfried, 1979; Porter and Scully, 1982; Ruggiero, Hadley, and Gustafson, 1996; Hoeffler and Payne, 1997; Hadley, Poitras, Ruggiero, and Knowles, 2000; Lee and Berri, 2008), but they were later extended to other team sports popular in other parts of the world. Studies have focused on the English Premier League (Dawson, Dobson, and Gerrard, 2000; Carmichael, Thomas and Ward, 2001), German Bundesliga football (Haas, Kocher, and Sutter, 2001; Frick and Simmons, 2008; Frick and Lee, 2011), the Spanish football league (Barros, del Corral and Garcia-del-Barrio, 2008), English cricket (Schofield, 1988), and Korean baseball (Lee, 2011).

A method for estimating the efficiency of a sports team is important for two main reasons. First, it enables analysis of a coach's ability and of factors that affect team efficiency. The results of these analyses can be used to determine coaching salary and find ways to improve playing performance without increasing input (i.e., without paying higher player salaries). For example, Fort et al. (2008) analyzed empirical evidence and found that given certain playing talent, roster stability is a determinant of team performance. This is important information for team management. Second, by controlling inefficiency factors, this kind of analysis allows more precise estimation of production function. Estimation of production functions is critical to sports economics, because it can be used to derive the marginal product or marginal value product of a player.

In this study, we reviewed previous empirical studies of sports team managerial efficiency and various stochastic frontier models. In particular, we focused extensively on econometrics, and the results should be valuable for sports economists and graduate students interested in empirical studies of managerial efficiency. Lee (2006) already reviewed the relevant literature and discussed the various methodologies for estimating team or managerial efficiency, including the development of stochastic frontier modeling. This chapter overlaps to some degree with the 2006 paper, but it also discusses issues not addressed in that work.

Specifically, this chapter discusses the most recent empirical studies of sports team managerial efficiency as well as recent developments of stochastic frontier models. First, it provides an extensive discussion of stochastic frontier "effects" models, which analyze factors influencing efficiency. All previous sports economics studies on the determinants of efficiency that adopted parametric econometric models have applied the frontier model developed by Battese and Coellie (1995). However, a variety of parametric econometric models are available for this purpose. We will introduce these competing models and discuss their characteristics and the sources of their program codes. Second, we will address an issue related to inference of efficiency estimates, as a lack of inference has been problematic in previous works. For example, Lee and Berri (2008) estimated the average efficiency of National Basketball Association (NBA) teams during the 2000–2001 and 2002–2003 seasons and argued that San Antonio was the most efficient, followed by Dallas, because their relative efficiency measures based on the fixed-effects treatment were 1.00 and 0.965, respectively. This brings up the question of whether a difference of 0.035 is statistically significant, and the answer can only be found through statistical testing. We will introduce various techniques for deriving the confidence interval, with a particular focus on bootstrapping methods. The last addition focuses on time-varying models. Estimation of temporal variations in managerial or team efficiency can be very useful; for example, decisions about firing or retaining a coach may be based on temporal variations in managerial efficiency. However, few studies have addressed variations in efficiency over time. We will discuss stochastic frontier models that include a time-varying efficiency component, which should be very useful for sports team analysis after taking into account the peculiar characteristic of a sports league.

The chapter is structured as follows: section 2 reviews the recent literature on team sports efficiency. It also presents a discussion of the selection of input variables. Section 3 provides an overview of the stochastic frontier model. This overview covers only basic information about stochastic frontiers and notation of general models to enable more in-depth discussion in the following sections, but it includes an extensive discussion of frontier models with time-varying efficiency in the context of sports team analysis. Section 4 compares various models that may be useful in analyses of determinants of efficiency and the effects models. Section 5 addresses methodologies for inference within team efficiency estimation, followed by our concluding remarks.

Managerial Efficiency Estimation in Team Sports and Its Peculiar Characteristic

Early empirical studies of sports team efficiency were limited mainly to estimating managerial efficiency, but more recent studies have addressed other intriguing issues. Kahane (2005) and Fort et al. (2008) tested racial/ethnic discrimination hypotheses. Kahane (2005) found that National Hockey League (NHL) teams with a greater relative presence of French-Canadian players were statistically significantly less efficient and suggested the presence of significant discrimination, in which fans in some regions (such as French-Canadian areas) strongly prefer to see French-Canadian players, so the teams pay a price in terms of lesser output for a given payroll. Fort et al. (2008) assessed racial discrimination in retention of NBA coaches; they found that on average, coaching efficiency did not differ by race, and they found that coaches were retained based on coaching efficiency. Therefore, they found no evidence of racial discrimination with respect to retention of coaches. Stochastic frontier models allowed both studies to control for variation in the level of playing talents across teams or coaches.

Frick and Simmons (2008) used panel data to test the hypothesis that increased expenditure on managerial talent would translate into improved team performance in the German premier football league. Unlike other studies, their study included coaching talent as well as playing talent as an input. They found that extra spending on managerial talent had a positive impact on team production of points, even though it had less elasticity than did spending on playing talent. They also found that, based on career records, better managerial quality or better coaching had greater potential to extract improved performance out of a given playing talent, thereby improving efficiency.

Researchers are intrigued by how different strategies affect winning performance, and this issue has been extensively examined by sabermetricians for baseball. Again, stochastic frontier model estimation can incorporate variations in other factors that influence team performance, and it thereby allows estimation of how a strategy (such as a bunt in baseball) affects winning performance through its effect on team efficiency. Lee (2011) used panel data from Korean baseball to examine this issue, and found that bunting and the substitution of a hitter decreased team efficiency on average, whereas aggressive base running (steal attempt) had a positive impact on winning performance.

Researchers have also compared efficiency between different leagues. Einolf (2004) applied data envelopment analysis to measure efficiency in the NFL and MLB in order to compare efficiency between the two different leagues. Einolf found significance differences in the levels of team efficiency between the two leagues and suggested possible sources for the disparity. Einolf's results indicated that NFL efficiency improved significantly after the salary cap was imposed in 1994, whereas the relatively little revenue sharing and absence of a salary cap in MLB might be a source of inefficiency. McGoldrick and Voeks (2005) applied a stochastic frontier model to the NBA and WNBA for the same purpose. They estimated average team efficiencies in the NBA and WNBA as 0.964 and 0.959, respectively, and this difference was statistically significant. Comparing different leagues is intriguing and can provide valuable information, but it is important to be cautious in the econometric application and the interpretation of the estimation results. Both stochastic frontier models and data envelopment analysis measure team efficiency by calculating the difference between teams' actual output and the best practice in the sample. A low average level of team efficiency in a league implies a wide variation in efficiency across member teams. In other words, an estimated result that average efficiency is higher in the NFL than in the MLB indicates more variation in efficiency across teams in the MLB than in the NFL; it does not imply that the MLB is less efficient on average than the NFL. To compare efficiency between leagues, we can pool data from both leagues to estimate a common production frontier and compare average efficiency scores between leagues. Obviously, it is not reasonable to assume that MLB and NFL have a common production function, so the suggested process would not work in this situation, but the strategy would be legitimate for comparing efficiency between the National League and the American League or between Canadian and American NHL teams.

Previous studies of managerial efficiency can be reviewed from a different perspective: the selection of input variables. Because efficiency estimation requires a production or cost function regression, the specification of production or cost function and then the selection of input variables are critical. In empirical studies of sports team production, the variables that have been used as a proxy for an input factor (playing talent) can be grouped into three main categories: wage bills, productivity measures, and raw playing statistics.

Haas et al. (2001), Haas (2003), Kahane (2005), Frick and Simmons (2008), Frick and Lee (2011) used wage bills as an input. Because the output variable of sporting production (usually winning percentage) is relative, most previous research also used wage bills relative to the league average. As Lee (2009) noted, a team wage bill includes information relevant to both the amount of playing talent and the price of talent. That is, variations in team wage bills depend not only on variation in playing talent, but also on the input price fluctuation. The legitimacy of a team wage bill as a proxy for playing talent requires extracting variations in input price from the wage bill. The "perfect competition" assumption in a player's labor market implies no cross-sectional variation in the unit price of playing talent, whereas the wage bill relative to the league average controls price variation from season to season. Kahane (2005) and Frick and Simmons (2008) deliberately calculated the relative wage bill divided by the league average wage bill to control for salary inflation over the sample period.

Recently, researchers have applied playing talent measures (Dawson, Dobson and Gerrard, 2000; Carmichael, Thomas, and Ward, 2001; Lee and Berri, 2008). Carmichael et al. (2001) used the Opta Index of playing performance statistics for English Premiership football; this process is rarely used due to the scarcity of match play statistics. Lee and Berri (2008) decomposed playing input from basketball teams by position (guards, small forwards, and large forwards) and calculated three different talent measures based on various playing records such as shooting percentage. In contrast, most earlier studies simply used playing records as input and recently McGoldrick and Voeks (2005) also used ratios of two- and three-point shot percentage, free throw percentage, offensive and defensive rebounds, assists, personal fouls, steals, turnovers, and blocked shots as inputs.

To assess which variables are most legitimate as a proxy for playing input, we can apply a selection of input variables used in the manufacturing industry. Basically, a manufacturing firm has labor and capital as inputs; labor can be decomposed into categories of production workers and office workers, or skilled workers and less-skilled workers. This illustrates how an input can be segregated by its role. In a team sport industry, an input is playing talent (coaching talent can be added), and it can also be decomposed based on positions that serve various roles. Lee and Berri (2008) defined three inputs by position (guards, small forwards, and large forwards) in a basketball team. Kahane (2005) identified three main positions (forwards, defenders, and goalies), but Kahane's empirical application used only two positions as inputs because the distinction between the roles of forwards and defenders has diminished over recent decades. The baseball industry can be seen in terms of both offensive and defensive production, which can be separated from each other in the production process. Offensive production has no particular positional distinction, but Lee (2011) argued that in baseball, offensive playing talent includes talent on base, slugging talent, and running talent, even though these three different talents (or roles) are mingled in one player's talent. Lee used on-base percentage, slugging percentage, and the success rate of stealing as proxies for the three distinctive talents.

Based on the reasons outlined above, positional wage bills and positional talent measures are preferable to raw playing statistics as input variables in the team sports industry. Lee (2011) used on-base percentage and slugging percentage even though they are raw statistics, but these were conceptually matched to different playing roles and were not used with other playing records of bases on balls, singles, doubles, triples, home runs, strikeouts, and so on.

This chapter will not go into detail about the *ex ante* versus *ex post* issue because it has already been discussed extensively in Dawson et al. (2000) and Lee (2006). Coaches have both direct and indirect effects on teams' winning performance. The direct effect relates to the coach's ability to convert available player talents into team wins through team selection and choice of strategy. The indirect effect is the coach's ability to train and motivate players to improve their playing talent. That is, coaches are able not only to maximize wins given a certain amount of playing inputs, but also to enhance the amount of inputs. Therefore, if the goal of research is to compare managerial efficiency, *ex ante* input variables should be used; otherwise, both *ex ante* and *ex post* inputs would be acceptable. For example, Lee (2011) was interested in how a manager's aggressive strategy implementation affected team performance. In this case, Lee did not focus on the indirect effect and instead used *ex post* variables.

An Overview of Stochastic Frontier Models

This section briefly presents the basic ideas behind stochastic frontiers and equations for general models, which will be applied in more detail in the following sections. It also presents a more detailed discussion of frontier models with time-varying efficiency.

Cross-section Stochastic Frontier Models

Stochastic production frontier models were proposed by Aigner et al. (1977) and Meeusen and van den Broeck (1977) to make the production frontier stochastic. The model is of the form:

$$y_i = \alpha_0 + x_i' \beta + \varepsilon_i, \quad \varepsilon_i = v_i - u_i, \quad i = 1, 2, \ldots, N \tag{1}$$

Let y and x be output and input in logs, respectively. The error term, $\varepsilon_i = v_i - u_i$, is made up of both a statistical noise term v_i and the technical inefficiency $u_i \geq 0$. The frontier is $\alpha_0 + x_i'\beta + v_i$, which is stochastic because it includes v_i. Estimation of the production function (1) is usually obtained using maximum likelihood estimation, because we can derive the probability density function of ε given distributional assumptions of v and u. Estimation of technical inefficiency can be obtained by separating u_i from ε_i. Jondrow et al. (1982) proposed the conditional expectation of u_i given $\varepsilon_i = v_i - u_i$, evaluated at the fitted values of ε_i (i.e. $\hat{\varepsilon}_i$) and the estimated values of the parameters. With a half-normal assumption for u, the estimate can be expressed as:

$$\hat{u}_i = E(u_i | \varepsilon_i) = \mu_i^* + \sigma_* \left[\frac{\phi(-\mu_i^* / \sigma_*)}{1 - \Phi(-\mu_i^* / \sigma_*)} \right] \tag{2}$$

where $\mu_i^* = -\varepsilon_i (\sigma_u^2 / \sigma^2)$, $\sigma_*^2 = \sigma_u^2 \sigma_v^2 / \sigma^2$, $\sigma^2 = \sigma_u^2 + \sigma_v^2$ and $\phi(\cdot)$ and $\Phi(\cdot)$ are the standard normal density and cumulative distribution functions, respectively; u_i and v_i are distributed as $N^+(0, \sigma_u^2)$ and $N(0, \sigma_v^2)$, respectively, where N^+ denotes a normal distribution truncated from the left at zero. Note that Jondrow et al. demonstrated that u_i conditional on ε_i is distributed as $N^+(\mu_i^*, \sigma_*^2)$. This distributional information can be used to construct confidence intervals for technical inefficiencies, as discussed below.

Panel Data Stochastic Frontier Models with Time-Invariant Inefficiency

Pitt and Lee (1981) and Schmidt and Sickles (1984) were the first to consider stochastic frontier models with panel data. They developed a model with time invariant inefficiencies:

$$y_{it} = \alpha_0 + x_{it}'\beta - u_i + v_{it} = x_{it}'\beta + \alpha_i + v_{it}, \quad i = 1, 2, \ldots, N, \quad t = 1, 2, \ldots, T \tag{3}$$

where $\alpha_i = \alpha_0 - u_i$ and N and T are numbers of observations of cross-section and time series, respectively. Note that $\alpha_i \leq \alpha_0$ and $\alpha_i = \alpha_0$ only when $u_i = 0$. Therefore, a smaller individual-specific intercept implies a lower level of technical efficiency.

Estimation of the model expressed in (3) can be performed by MLE with distributional assumptions as well as a fixed-effects estimation. To estimate technical efficiency for a firm, we can apply the conditional expectation approach proposed by Jondrow et al. (1982). Battese and Coelli (1988) derived the formula $\hat{u}_i = E(u_i | \varepsilon_{i1}, \varepsilon_{i2}, \ldots, \varepsilon_{iT}) = E(u_i | \varepsilon_i) = E(u_i | \bar{\varepsilon}_i)$, where $\varepsilon_i = (\varepsilon_{i1}, \varepsilon_{i2}, \ldots, \varepsilon_{iT})'$ and $\bar{\varepsilon}_i = \frac{1}{T}\Sigma \varepsilon_{it}$. Note that this estimate measures absolute efficiencies because we are measuring the distance of $\hat{u}_i$ from zero, not from the smallest inefficiency level.

With regard to handling fixed effects, Schmidt and Sickles (1984) suggested the following way to estimate technical inefficiency:

$$\hat{\alpha}_0 = \max_j \hat{\alpha}_j, \quad \hat{u}_i = \hat{\alpha}_0 - \hat{\alpha}_i \quad \text{and} \quad T\hat{E}_i = \exp(-\hat{u}_i). \tag{4}$$

If we think of N as fixed, this formula can clearly estimate relative technical inefficiency because it measures the distance of $\hat{u}_i$ from the best practice in a finite sample. Empirically, the fixed-effects approach typically yields lower levels of estimated technical efficiency than the MLE approach does.

Panel Data Stochastic Frontier Models with Time-Varying Inefficiency

Estimation of temporal variations in managerial or team efficiency would be beneficial to many research contexts. For example, in an analysis of regulation changes (such as the adoption of a salary cap), an assessment of fluctuation of team efficiency over seasons would be more useful than a comparison of average managerial efficiency across teams. However, few studies have investigated variations in efficiency over time.

Lee and Berri (2008) and Lee (2006) identified why special care is required to select time-varying frontier models for use in sports team analyses: for sports teams, outputs and inputs are usually relative measures. Winning percentage is one common output variable; it is always relative, because one team always loses when another wins. Wage bills relative to league average or other playing talent measures are also relative input measures. Therefore, average winning percentage is constant over seasons at 0.5. This is a characteristic unique to the sports industry, because the average outputs in other industries fluctuate over time. In addition, this characteristic means that the average efficiency of member teams in a sports league will remain constant over time, even though individual teams could exhibit temporal variations over seasons. Thus, an appropriate frontier model for sports team analysis should allow for different temporal variations in managerial efficiency across member teams. Note that one group of time-varying frontier models (Kumbhakar, 1990; Battese and Coelli, 1992; Lee and Schmidt, 1993) estimates only the temporal pattern of efficiency, thus imposing an identical temporal pattern across different teams on its model. Another group (Cornwell, Schmidt and Sickles, 1990; Cuesta, 2000; Lee, 2006 & 2010; Ahn, Lee and Schmidt, 2007) specifies team-specific temporal variations.

The stochastic frontier production model with time-varying efficiency can be expressed as

$$y_{it} = \alpha_t + x_{it}\beta + v_{it} - u_{it} = x_{it}\beta + \alpha_{it} + v_{it}, \quad i = 1, 2, \ldots, N, \quad t = 1, 2, \ldots, T \tag{5}$$

where $\alpha_{it} = \alpha_t - u_{it}$ is the intercept for firm i in period t. Note that it is not possible to estimate all of the u_{it} (or α_{it}) without some assumptions about their temporal pattern or correlation structure because too many parameters must be estimated. Therefore, various models have emerged as different choices for the form of α_{it} (or, equivalently, u_{it}) with the goal of reducing the number of parameters. Hereafter, the discussion will only include frontier models with different temporal variations.

Cornwell et al. (1990) proposed the following model: $\alpha_{it} = \delta_{i0} + \delta_{i1}t + \delta_{i2}t^2$. Here, the intercept for each firm is quadratic in time, but the form of the quadratic varies over teams because all individual teams have different parameters. Frick and Lee (2011) applied this model to the German premier football league and were able to estimate different temporal movements of managerial efficiency across different teams.

Cuesta (2000) developed the following way to estimate different temporal variations in efficiency: $\alpha_{it} = \theta_{it}\alpha_i$ where $\theta_{it} = \exp[\eta_i(T-t)]$. In this model, η_i depends on i. Note that this model, as well as the model developed by Cornwell et al. (1990), is not legitimate when the sample panel consists of large cross-sectional observations and small time series; this is because both models estimate all team-specific parameters, η_i and $(\delta_{i0}, \delta_{i1}, \delta_{i2})$, respectively, which would result in too many parameters. To date, the Cuesta model has never been applied to sports economics.

Other models that might be useful for the analysis of temporal changes in managerial efficiency include the group-specific models of Lee (2006, 2010) and the multifactor model of Ahn et al. (2007). These models are too technical to discuss here in great detail, but they could be very useful for certain applications. For example, group-specific models could be used to compare how a luxury tax affects efficiency in large- versus small-market teams. Stochastic frontier latent class models, such as those developed by Greene (2005) and Orea and Kumbhakar (2004), may also be helpful. Barros et al. (2008) applied this kind of model to the Spanish football league. Like the group-specific models developed by Lee (2006, 2010), this kind of model uses several classes to control some heterogeneity in the production process of translating inputs into output among teams.

DETERMINANTS OF EFFICIENCY AND THE EFFECTS MODELS

Previous empirical studies have focused not only on estimation of managerial efficiency, but also on the factors that influence managerial efficiency (Kahane, 2005; Fort, Lee, and Berri, 2008; Lee, 2011). For example, a coach's previous win record or experience is a significant determinant of managerial efficiency, and therefore is important data when a team owner hires a coach. Fort et al. (2008) investigated managerial efficiency among NBA teams and found that roster stability and the coach's win record are statistically significant determinants of managerial efficiency, but coaching experience is not.

Interestingly, all these previous studies used the stochastic frontier model developed by Battese and Coelli (1995), even though a variety of econometric models were available. This section discusses and compares stochastic frontier models, particularly with regard to which observable characteristics affect levels of technical inefficiency. For a more detailed discussion of this issue, refer to Wang (2002), Álvarez et al. (2006), and Amsler et al. (2009).

Various "effects" stochastic frontier models have been developed, including those proposed by Kumbhakar et al. (1991) Reifschneider and Stevenson (1991), Caudill and Ford (1993), Huang and Liu (1994), Battese and Coelli (1995), and Caudill et al. (1995). Instead of discussing each model separately, we can categorize them into two groups, using the scaling property set out by Álvarez et al. (2006). Effects models consist of two equations. One is a production function of equations (1) or (3), and the inefficiency equation can be expressed as:

$$u_{it} = u(z_{it}, \delta) \tag{6}$$

where z is a set of variables that affect u. Generally, the variables in z are either functions of inputs or measures of the environment in which the team operates. Thus it is possible for x and z to overlap. Different models use various specifications of $u_{it} = u(z_{it}, \delta)$. In the model developed by Battese and Coelli (1995), equation (6) becomes:

$$u_{it} = z_{it}\delta + w_{it} \tag{7}$$

where w is distributed as $N^+(z_{it}\delta, \sigma_w^2)$.

Álvarez et al. (2006) defined a model as having a *scaling property* if:

$$u(z_{it}, \delta) = s(z_{it}, \delta) \cdot w_{it} \tag{8}$$

where $s(z_{it}, \delta) \geq 0$ is called the *scaling function,* and where $w \geq 0$ has a distribution that does not depend on z. Apparently, the model developed by Battese and Coelli (1995) did not incorporate this scaling property, as equation (7) is a linearly additive form. Of the six models discussed above, the ones developed by Reifschneider and Stevenson (1991), Caudill and Ford (1993), and Caudill et al. (1995) incorporated the scaling property, but those developed by Kumbhakar et al. (1991), Huang and Liu (1994), and Battese and Coelli (1995) did not.

Models with the scaling property are based on the implicit assumption that u is distributed as $N^+(0, \sigma(z, \delta)^2) = \sigma(z, \delta)N^+(0,1)$ where $\sigma(z, \delta)$ corresponds to the scaling function $s(z, \delta)$, above. Specifically, Caudill et al. (1995) assumed that $s(z_{it}, \delta) = \sigma_u \exp(z_{it}'\delta)$. Thus, in models with the scaling property, exogenous factors influence the variance of inefficiency but do not affect the shape of the inefficiency distribution. That is, changes in z affect the scale but not the shape of $u(z, \delta)$. In contrast, models without the scaling property assume that exogenous factors influence the shape of the inefficiency distribution. For example, Battese and Coelli (1995) assumed that the mean of inefficiency depends on z_{it} and δ.

Álvarez et al. (2006) argued that the defining feature of models with the scaling property is an intuitive appeal: firms differ in their mean efficiency, but not in the shape of the distribution of inefficiency. They also discussed the practical advantages of models with the scaling property, one of which is that the interpretation of δ yields simple expressions for the effects of z_{it} on average efficiency. If the exponential scaling function is $s(z_{it}, \delta) = \exp(z'_{it} \delta)$ in equation (8), then $\delta = \partial \ln u_{it} / \partial z_{it}$ implies that δ reflects the percentage in u_{it} with respect to a unit change in z_{it}. In contrast, the expression for the effects of z_{it} on mean efficiency is complicated because it is dependent on the shape of the inefficiency distribution.

One reason that all empirical studies in the sports economics literature have applied the model developed by Battese and Coelli (1995) is the easy access to program code. Coelli (1996) developed the FRONTIER4.1 program, which can yield ML estimation using the panel data model developed by Battese and Coelli (1995). In addition, Wang's web site (http://homepage.ntu.edu.tw/~wangh/) provides STATA program codes, which also include various test methods of the scaling hypothesis based on the most general model developed by Wang (2002). These codes are very useful for the application of the various models mentioned above.

STATISTICAL INFERENCE OF
MANAGERIAL EFFICIENCY

Very few studies have investigated inference of efficiency estimates; this includes not only studies related to sports economics, but also applications of stochastic frontier models to other fields. The reason for this is the recent development of econometric techniques to construct confidence intervals for efficiency estimates. Estimation of managerial efficiency has many more practical uses for the sports team industry than for other industries. For example, estimates of a coach's efficiency in previous seasons would be important information for hiring a new coach or firing an incumbent coach. This kind of managerial decision would be risky if it were made based only on point estimates rather than on inferences about them. Therefore, construction of the confidence interval for managerial efficiency estimates is particularly important to the field of sports economics.

This section discusses econometric methods for deriving distributions of efficiency estimates; the goal is not to provide a complete survey of these methods, but rather to provide a brief introduction to clarify which econometric method would be most useful to various kinds of empirical studies. For a more in-depth analysis, see Kim et al. (2007) and Amsler et al. (2009).

Inference for inefficiency levels can be calculated using several methods: (1) inference with distributional assumptions; (2) multiple comparisons with the best; and (3) bootstrapping. In a cross-sectional stochastic frontier model with a half-normal inefficiency error, the condition expectation of u is the point estimate of u, as proposed by Jondrow et al. (1982). As noted above, Horrace and Schmidt (1996) found that the distribution of u conditional on ε is $N^+(\mu_*,\sigma_*^2)$, where $\mu_* = \varepsilon\sigma_u^2/(\sigma_u^2+\sigma_v^2)$ and $\sigma_*^2 = \sigma_u^2\sigma_v^2/(\sigma_u^2+\sigma_v^2)$. Therefore, we can use the distribution of u, evaluated at $\varepsilon = \hat{\varepsilon}$, to calculate confidence intervals and then to perform inference on u. The same methods can be extended to a panel data situation because the conditional expectation formulas have been derived (for example, Battese and Coelli 1988).

Multiple comparisons with the best (MCB) is a statistical technique that yields confidence intervals for differences in parameter values between all populations and the best population. This method generally yields a wide confidence interval, so it will not be discussed here in detail. For a comprehensive discussion of this method, see Horrace and Schmidt (1996, 2000).

Bootstrapping is the preferred method for deriving distribution of efficiency estimates. In general, when certain conditions are satisfied, the asymptotic distribution of $\sqrt{N}(\hat{\theta}^b - \hat{\theta})$ conditional on the sample is the same as the unknown asymptotic distribution of $\sqrt{N}(\hat{\theta}-\theta)$, where θ is a vector of population parameters, $\hat{\theta}$ is estimates, and $\hat{\theta}^b$ is the bootstrap estimates. Therefore, the asymptotic distribution of $\hat{\theta}$ can be derived from $\sqrt{N}(\hat{\theta}^b - \hat{\theta})$ because both $\hat{\theta}$ and $\hat{\theta}^b$ are observed. The bootstrapping process consists of the following steps: (1) obtain an estimate $\hat{\theta}$ based on sample of $z_1, z_2, ..., z_N$; (2) construct pseudo data $z_1^b, z_2^b, ..., z_N^b$ by random sampling from the original sample $z_1, z_2, ..., z_N$; (3) obtain $\hat{\theta}^b$ from the pseudo sample $z_1^b, z_2^b, ..., z_N^b$; and (4) repeat processes (2) and (3) many times, say B.

In the stochastic frontier model, bootstrapping can be applied to the inefficiency estimates u. This section discusses the fixed-effects estimates in equation (3). Kim et al. (2007) introduced and discussed the characteristics of bootstrapping methods for inefficiency estimates (percentile bootstrap, iterated bootstrap, bias-adjusted bootstrap, bias-adjusted and accelerated bootstrap, bias-corrected percentile, and their own parametric bootstrap). This section focuses on a basic model, the percentile bootstrap, as it will be sufficient to clarify how the bootstrap method operates in efficiency estimation.

The fixed-effects estimates of equation (3) coefficients are denoted as $\hat{\beta}$ and $\hat{\alpha}_i$ and the inefficiency estimates is $\hat{u}_i$ calculated using equation (4). According to the above explanation of bootstrapping, a random sample is required. Here, residuals $\hat{v}_{it} = y_{it} - \hat{\alpha}_i - x_{it}'\hat{\beta}$ $(i=1,...,N, t=1,...,T)$ consist of a random sample. That is, $\hat{v}_1, \hat{v}_2, ..., \hat{v}_N$ are identical to $z_1, z_2, ..., z_N$. The bootstrap samples $\hat{v}_1^b, \hat{v}_2^b, ..., \hat{v}_N^b$ can be drawn by resampling $\hat{v}_1, \hat{v}_2, ..., \hat{v}_N$, and then the same steps are implemented again. The pseudo data $y_{it}^b = \hat{\alpha}_i + x_{it}'\hat{\beta} + \hat{v}_{it}^b$ yield bootstrap estimates $\hat{\beta}^b$, $\hat{\alpha}_i^b$ and $\hat{u}_i^b$, and the bootstrap distribution of these estimates can be used to make inferences about the parameters. The percentile bootstrap is helpful when constructing a confidence interval for u_i. For a certain significance level c, we can obtain lower and upper bounds L_i and U_i such that $P[L_i \leq u_i \leq U_i] = 1-c$ by applying bootstrapping. The percentile bootstrap takes L_i and U_i to be the lower and upper $c/2$ fractiles of the bootstrap distribution of the $\hat{u}_i^b$.

Kim et al. discussed other bootstrap methods and compared their performance with simulation results. They found that the bias-corrected percentile performed better than the percentile bootstrap, especially when a bias problem occurs; a fixed-effects estimate would include upward bias. Equation (4) can be used to estimate an intercept of the frontier and inefficiency by using the *max* operator, but a bias occurs when firm *i* is not actually the best-performing firm. Therefore, the confidence interval from the percentile bootstrap should be precise enough for panel data with sufficiently large time-series observations because a bias problem is less likely. The percentile bootstrap is implemented in the STATA program, but to date, no formal program code is available for performing other bootstrap methods.

Concluding Remarks

This chapter has reviewed previous studies that analyzed various issues related to estimated managerial efficiency in the sports industry. However, the focus was not on the implications of the studies, but on the econometric models and methods used in the studies, as the goal of the research was to provide an extensive econometric discussion for readers who are interested in empirical studies on managerial efficiency.

The chapter included a discussion of econometric models and methods that have not been applied in research about sports economics. In particular, it introduced various stochastic frontier "effects" models and characterized them by the scaling property and its corresponding advantages. It also presented the source of program codes. Another econometric method, bootstrapping, was also discussed in detail. Research about the sports industry has completely neglected to address inference of efficiency estimates, and the bootstrap method can be used to construct confidence intervals as well as estimates of asymptotic distribution of efficiency.

This chapter presented several econometric issues that might occur when stochastic frontier models are applied to sports team efficiency. When selecting a stochastic frontier model for the purpose of estimating managerial efficiency of all individual teams over different seasons, it is important to consider a joint-product characteristic. Because of this characteristic, the average winning ratio of member teams is always 0.5; this is constant over seasons, and the league average efficiency is also constant over time, even though there are temporal variations in the managerial efficiency of an individual team. Therefore, only frontier models that allow for variation in efficiency across teams are legitimate for this research purpose;

this is why these models were introduced here. Other time-varying models that estimate only average temporal changes in efficiency should result in time invariant estimates.

The discussion of the selection of input variables revealed that team playing talents can be decomposed into positional playing talents that have different roles in the process of producing output (producing wins). Therefore, positional wage bills and position talent measures may be preferable to raw playing records, even though almost all studies have used raw playing records as input variables. In fact, raw records (shooting percentage, assists, rebounds, turnovers, etc.) are intermediate goods produced by utilizing the playing talents of inputs.

Another topic that has been treated inappropriately in the literature is the case of multiple outputs. This issue was not analyzed in the text, but a brief discussion will be helpful here. In general, the term "multiple outputs" refers to multiple "final" outputs. For example, the automobile industry produces compact, medium, and luxury cars; the electronics industry produces air conditioners, refrigerators, and televisions. Previous empirical studies of managerial efficiency have tended to use winning percentage, attendance, and revenue as multiple outputs. However, attendance and winning percentage should not be considered as separate final outputs, because winning is closely related to attendance.

Two research directions would be helpful for future studies on managerial efficiency. One is obtaining more accurate estimates of the production function. This would be practically useful because it would allow an owner to evaluate the players precisely. It would require research about the functional forms of production process in team sports as well as measures of input variables. Another intriguing topic would be a further investigation of efficiency determinants, as this could help an owner find ways to improve team performance without increasing costs. For example, the empirical finding that roster stability improves team performance is valuable information for an owner. Various factors might affect team efficiency, for example, the roster mixture, different strategies, racial or national heterogeneity of team players, and so on.

Note

1 This work was supported by the National Research Foundation Grant funded by the Korean Government (MEST)(KRF_2009-220-B00008).

References

Ahn, S. C., Lee, Y. H., and Schmidt, P. (2007). Stochastic frontier models with multiple time-varying individual effects. *Journal of Productivity Analysis,* 27: 1–12.

Aigner, D. J., Lovell, C. A. K., and Schmidt, P. (1977). Formulation and estimation of stochastic frontier production function models. *Journal of Econometrics,* 58: 226–239.

Amsler, C., Lee, Y. H., and Schmidt, P. (2009). A survey of stochastic frontier models and likely future developments. *Seoul Journal of Economics*, 22: 1–23.

Álvarez, A., Amsler, C., Orea, L., and Schmidt, P. (2006). Interpreting and testing the scaling property in models where inefficiency depends on firm characteristics. *Journal of Productivity Analysis*, 25: 201–212.

Barros, C. P., del Corral, J., and Garcia-del-Barrio, P. (2008). Identification of segments of soccer clubs in the spanish league first division with a latent class model. *Journal of Sports Economics*, 9(5):451–469.

Battese, G. E. and Coelli, T. J. (1988). Prediction of firm-level technical efficiency with a generalized frontier production function and panel data. *Journal of Econometrics*, 38: 387–399.

Battese, G., and Coelli, T. (1995). A model for technical inefficiency effects in a stochastic frontier production function for panel data. *Empirical Economics*, 20: 325–332.

Carmichael F., Thomas, D., and Ward, R. (2001). Production and efficiency in association football. *Journal of Sports Economics*, 2 (3): 228–243.

Caudill, S. B., and Ford, J. M. (1993). Biases in frontier estimation due to heteroskedasticity. *Economics Letters*, 41: 17–20.

Caudill, S. B., Ford, J. M., and Gropper, D. M. (1995). Frontier estimation and firm-specific inefficiency measures in the presence of heteroskedasticity. *Journal of Business and Economic Statistics*, 13: 105–111.

Coelli, T. J. (1996). A guide to FRONTIER version 4.1: A computer program for stochastic frontier production and cost function estimation. CEPA Working Paper 96/7, Department of Econometrics, University of New England, Armidale NSW Australia.

Cornwell, C., Schmidt, P., and Sickles, R. (1990). Production frontiers with cross-sectional and time-series variation in efficiency levels. *Journal of Econometrics*, 46: 185–200.

Cuesta, R. A. (2000). A Production model with firm-specific temporal variation in technical inefficiency: with application to spanish dairy farms. *Journal of Productivity Analysis*, 13: 139–149.

Dawson, P., Dobson S., and Gerrard B. (2000a). Stochastic frontiers and the temporal structure of managerial efficiency in English soccer. *Journal of Sports Economics*, 1(4): 341–362.

Dawson, P., Dobson S., and Gerrard B. (2000b). Estimating coaching efficiency in professional team sports: Evidence from English Association football. *Scottish Journal of Political Economy*, 47(4): 399–421.

Einolf, K. W. (2004). Is winning everything? A data envelopment analysis of Major League Baseball and the National Football League. *Journal of Sports Economics*, 5(2): 127–151.

Fort, R., Lee, Y. H., and Berri, D. (2008). Race, technical efficiency, and firing: The case of NBA coaches. *International Journal of Sport Finance*, 3: 84–97.

Frick, B., and Lee, Y. H. (2011). Temporal variations in technical efficiency: Evidence from German soccer. *Journal of Productivity Analysis*, 35: 15–24.

Frick, B., and Simmons, R. (2008). The impact of managerial quality on organizational performance: Evidence from German soccer. *Managerial and Decision Economics*, 29:593–600.

Haas, D. (2003). Technical efficiency in the major league soccer. *Journal of Sports Economics*, 4(3): 203–215.

Haas, D., Kocher, M. G., and Sutter, M. (2001). Measuring efficiency of German football teams by data envelopment analysis. *Central European Journal of Operations Research*, 12: 251–268.

Hadley, L., Poitras, M., Ruggiero, J., and Knowles, S. (2000). Performance evaluation of National Football League teams. *Managerial and Decision Economics*, 21: 63–70.

Hofler, R. A., and Payne, J. E. (1997). Measuring efficiency in the National Basketball Association. *Economic Letters*, 55: 293–299.

Horrace, W. C., and Schmidt, P. (1996). Confidence statements for efficiency estimates from stochastic frontier models. *Journal of Productivity Analysis*, 7: 257–282.

Horrace, W. C., and Schmidt, P. (2000). Multiple comparisons with the best with economic applications. *Journal of Applied Econometrics*, 15: 1–26.

Huang, C. J., and Liu, J.-T. (1994). Estimation of a non-neutral stochastic frontier production function. *Journal of Productivity Analysis*, 5: 171–180.

Jondrow, J., Lovell, C. A. K., Materov, I. S., and Schmidt, P. (1982). On the estimation of technical inefficiency in the stochastic frontier production function model. *Journal of Econometrics*, 19: 233–238.

Kahane, L. H. (2005). Production efficiency and discriminatory hiring practices in the National Hockey League: A stochastic frontier approach. *Review of Industrial Organization* 27, 47–71.

Kim, M., Kim, Y., and Schmidt, P. (2007). On the accuracy of bootstrap confidence intervals for efficiency levels in stochastic frontier models with panel data. *Journal of Productivity Analysis*, 28: 165–181.

Kumbhakar, S. C., Ghosh, S., and McGuckin, J. T. (1991). A generalized production approach for estimating determinants of inefficiency in U.S. dairy farms. *Journal of Business and Economic Statistics*, 9: 279–286.

Lee, Y. H. (2006). A stochastic production frontier model with group-specific temporal variation in technical efficiency. *European Journal of Operational Research*, 174: 1616–1630.

Lee, Y. H. (2009). Identification of segments of soccer clubs in the Spanish League First Division with a latent class model: Comments. *Journal of Sports Economics*, 10: 508–517.

Lee, Y. H. (20010). Group-specific stochastic production frontier models with parametric sspecifications. *European Journal of Operational Research*, 200, 508–517.

Lee, Y. H. (2011). Is the small-ball strategy effective in winning games? A stochastic frontier production approach. *Journal of Productivity Analysis*, 35: 51–59.

Lee, Y. H., and Berri, D. (2008). A re-examination of production functions and efficiency estimates for the NBA. *Scottish Journal of Political Economy*, 55: 51–66.

McGoldrick, K., and Voeks, L. (2005). We got game! An analysis of win/loss probability and efficiency differences between the NBA and WNBA. *Journal of Sports Economics*, 6(1): 5–23.

Meeusen, W., and van den Broeck, J. (1977). Efficiency estimation from Cobb-Douglas production functions with composed error. *International Economic Review*, 18: 435–444.

Pitt, M., and Lee, L-F. (1981). The measurement and sources of technical inefficiency in the Indonesian weaving industry. *Journal of Development Economics*, 9: 43–64.

Porter, P., and Scully, J. W. (1982). Measuring managerial efficiency: The case of baseball. *Southern Economic Journal*, 48: 642–650.

Reifschneider, D., and Stevenson, R. (1991) Systematic Departures from the Frontier: A Framework for the Analysis of Firm Inefficiency. *International Economic Review*, 32: 715–723.

Ruggiero, J., Hadley, L., and Gustafson, E. (1996). Technical efficiency in Major League Baseball, in *Baseball economics: Current research*. ed. J. Fizel, E. Gustafson, and L. Hadley, pp. 191–200. Wesport, CT: Praeger.

Schmidt, P., and Sickles, R.C. (1984). Production frontiers and panel data. *Journal of Business and Economic Statistics*, 2: 367–374.

Schofield, J. A. (1988). Production functions in the sports industry: An empirical analysis of professional cricket. *Applied Economics*, 20: 177–193.

Scully, G. W. (1974). Pay and performance in Major League Baseball. *American Economic Review*, 64: 915–930.

Wang, H. J. (2002). Heteroscedasticity and non-monotonic efficiency effects in a stochastic frontier model. *Journal of Productivity Analysis*, 18: 241–253.

Zak, T. A., Huang, C. J., and Siefried, J. J. (1979). Production efficiency: The case of professional basketball. *Journal of Business*, 52: 379–392.

## CHAPTER 8

AGE AND PERFORMANCE UNDER PRESSURE

GOLFERS ON THE LPGA TOUR

HAROLD O. FRIED AND

LOREN W. TAUER

1. INTRODUCTION

PROFESSIONAL sports spawn statistics to evaluate athletic performance on the team and the individual. These numbers spark debate among enthusiastic fans, provide evidence in negotiations between agents and owners, and constitute the ingredients for sports economists to apply statistical techniques in a labor of love. Golf is a particularly interesting example. There are measures of the fundamental golfing skills: driving accuracy, driving distance, sand saves, and putts. These are individual measures that are not directly contaminated by the performance of other members of a team. Golf is a sport of individuals.[1] There is the golfer, the stationary ball, and the challenge of executing the shot. There are ample statistics to analyze golf performance.

However, every Monday there is an account of the latest weekend tour event that illustrates a critical missing statistic in golf performance: the ability to perform under pressure. For example, the 2009 U.S. Women's Open was played in July at the Saucon Country Club in Bethlehem, Pennsylvania. Christie Kerr was ahead by two over Ji, by four over Lu and Reynolds, and by five over Kim and Kung going into the final round. It was a typical rollercoaster Sunday on the LPGA tour. Kerr was ahead through the turn, only to shoot four over for the day to finish tied for third. Lu and Reynolds shot eight over and finished tied for seventeenth. Kung held it together at two under on Sunday and came in second by a single stroke. Ji struggled with bogeys on holes two, four, and seven and a double bogey on ten, but mitigated that with birdies on six, eight, thirteen, fourteen, and eighteen. At one point Ji, Kerr, Kung, and Kim were all tied. Kerr bogeyed the sixteenth; Kung bogeyed the seventeenth; Kim bogeyed the eighteenth. Ji had a twenty-foot putt for birdie on the eighteenth to win the tournament. "Right before hitting the putt, I was nervous to the point where my hands were shaking, but I told myself to just make sure I saved par." Ji made the putt for birdie, won the $585K prize and the 2009 U.S. Open Championship.[2]

This and other weekend stories illustrate that a critical missing statistic on the LPGA tour is the ability to perform under pressure. It is certainly important to be able to drive the ball accurately and far, to be able get down in few putts, to be able to save par from the sand; but to win tournaments, as Ehrenberg and Bognanno (1990) discuss, it is also essential to shoot four excellent rounds from Thursday through Sunday and to hold it together going down the stretch. Eun-Hee Ji made the birdie putt on the eighteenth hole and won the tournament; Christie Kerr is an excellent golfer, but she lost the Open on Sunday.

In this chapter, we measure the ability to perform under pressure. We embed the golfer into a frontier production function framework and consider the transformation of typical measures of golfing ability (inputs) into earnings per event (output). Observations on the frontier of this production function are dubbed best practice and receive a score of one. Observations below the frontier fail to transform golfing skills into the maximum earnings per event; the difference between actual and frontier performance is a quantitative measure of the ability to perform under pressure. The golfer is not meeting the earnings performance of peers with the same physical golfing skills. We attribute this performance gap to the mental side rather than the physical skill side of the game. The specific method that we use is called order-m FDH. This is a mathematical programming approach that accommodates noise in the data and the influence of outliers. Both are important in the context of golf where luck can matter, and to some extent, players compete in different tournaments. We derive a measure of the ability to perform under pressure for individual golfers, and explore the role of age on this statistic.

The remainder of this chapter is organized as follows. Section 2 reviews the literature. Golf has received the attention of sports economists, although the LPGA has been somewhat neglected. The order-m approach is explained in Section 3. The data and the empirical findings are presented in Section 4, followed by the conclusion.

2. THE LITERATURE

Like many sports where data are readily available, golf attracts the interest of economists. There have been a host of analyses to explain the success of professional golfers. Most of these have concentrated on the men's PGA Tour, but there have been a number of studies analyzing the Ladies Professional Golf Association (LPGA). We review some of those LPGA articles here.

Pfitzner and Rishel (2005) investigate the determinants of player performance as measured by scoring average and earnings on the LPGA tour for the 2004 season. They show that the percentage of greens reached in regulation and putts per round are by far the most important determinants of both scoring average and earnings on the LPGA tour. Driving distance and driving accuracy are found to be equally important factors in success on the LPGA tour. In this chapter, we combine driving distance rank and driving accuracy rank into one variable, drive total. Pfitzner and Rishel (2005) also compute and report the efficiency of individual LPGA golfers by utilizing residuals below a linear regression equation, but do not relate those efficiency scores to age or any other causation factors, nor do they use a nonparametric frontier approach.

Shin and Nam (2004) address the success of Koreans on the LPGA Tour and conclude that at the core of their success are several traits that are consequences of their cultural upbringing: a work ethic that is the envy of the tour, a devotion to the game that is unparalleled, and indomitable mental toughness. Mental toughness is what we attempt to measure in this chapter. We call it the ability to perform under pressure and measure it as the residual after taking into account the innate physical ability of each golfer, using a frontier production function methodology.

Marple (1983) examines recent trends in the earnings of women (compared to men) in professional golf. Data show a convergence in earnings between men and women in golf from the late 1960s to the late 1970s. Women who are in the lower earnings brackets lag behind their male counterparts, although there appears to be convergence. Based on a comparison of performance, women professionals in golf earn less than men for comparable performance. This comparison between men and women professional golfers is relevant because we have previously applied this method of analysis to men professional golfers, and a comparison of results is possible.

Theberge (1980) finds that most players on the LPGA cannot meet their playing and traveling expenses from tournament winnings alone. Supplementary sources of income from sponsorships, endorsements, and fees for teaching golf are often used to meet their Tour expenses. He finds that players are generally satisfied with their careers. We find that there are many women with low earnings per event but who may be golfing to the best of their ability and thus may be measured as efficient, suggesting that there is little upward earning potential given the level of physical golfing skills.

Shmanske (2000) compares the PGA Tour to the LPGA and estimates the impact of skills on earnings using 1998 tournament data. He finds that once skill levels are accounted for, women are not underpaid compared to men. He concludes that the professional golf industry appears to reward the absolute level of skill with no gender bias. This volume contains an update using 2008 data. Interestingly, Matthews, Sommers, and Peschiera (2007) find, unlike the PGA, higher total prize money does not lead to lower scores on the LPGA Tour. The possibilities suggested include unmeasured differences in player ability and/or course difficulty, differences in the responsiveness to financial incentives, the structure of these incentives, the choice of time horizon, the differences in incentives for men and women, and finally, the existence of a "superstar effect." The probabilistic technique we employ in this chapter mitigates the impact of the exceptional or "superstar" golfer in evaluating the ability to perform under pressure. It is like having Lorena Ochoa, counterpart to Tiger Woods, omitted from the Tournament with some probability.

Kalist (2008) examines productivity differences between women with children and women without children on the LPGA tour. Using panel data on women professional golfers, he finds that the productivity of women who eventually become mothers increases in the years before giving birth and then declines thereafter. One further finding is that marriage increases productivity. Although marriage and maternity would be interesting concepts to investigate using our approach, we leave that for a later article. Kalist (2008) also finds that earnings are a concave function of age, which we also find.

Tiruneh (2010) tests the hypothesis that age affects earnings performance of professional golfers and finds that the ages at which golfers on the PGA, European PGA, Champions Tour, and LPGA Tours peak are 35, 30, 52, and 25, respectively. Our regression analysis supports his hypothesis that age affects winning professional golf tournaments.

Fried, Lambrinos, and Tyner (2004) use Data Envelopment Analysis (DEA) to evaluate the performance of golfers on the three tours in the United States: the Professional Golf Association, the Ladies Professional Golf Association, and the Senior Professional Golf Association (SPGA). Two indices are obtained for each golfer: a performance under pressure index and an athletic ability performance index. This chapter continues that approach by estimating performance under pressure, but uses a probabilistic and non-convex production function approach, whereas DEA is deterministic and convex. Convexity implies that linear combinations of golfers can be constructed, which obviously is not the case without team play, and a deterministic model does not allow any performance to be due to luck.

Finally, the analytic technique that we use in this chapter is the technique we used to analyze men golfers on the PGA using earlier data (Fried and Tauer, 2010).

3. The Method

The efficiency of individual golfers is computed using an output-oriented Free Disposal Hull (FDH) routine (Deprins, Simar, and Tulkins, 1984). The output efficiency of a golfer is based upon comparing the output of a golfer to the output of other golfers that use the same or fewer of all the inputs of the golfer being evaluated. The problem with FDH computations is that they are sensitive to outliers. If the output of a golfer is very high, then the efficiency of other golfers are measured relative to the output of that extreme observation, given that the inputs are the same or lower. Our output is earnings per event, which is measured accurately, and the inputs are performance variables that are also carefully measured. Thus we do not expect data measurement error. However, there could be outliers who perform particularly well due to a combination of exceptional ability and luck and noise in the data due to different tournament schedules and injuries. It is not fair to judge the performance of a more typical professional golfer with the exceptional golfer, and it is important to mitigate the impact of noise. As an alternative, a stochastic frontier approach could have been used, which eliminates the deterministic limitation of FDH, but imposes functional structure on the shape of the frontier. FDH does not impose structure on the production frontier. Even better, we employ order-m FDH (Daraio and Simar, 2005), which incorporates a probabilistic specification of the production function.

To implement the order-m approach, the production process is described by the joint probability measure of (X, Y), where X are inputs and Y are outputs. This joint probability completely characterizes the probabilistic production function. Under an output orientation, this joint probability can be written as:

$$F_{Y|X}(y|x) = \text{Prob}(Y \le y \mid X \le x) \tag{1}$$

The expected order-m frontier for a fixed integer value of $m \ge 1$ is the expected value of the maximum of m random variables $Y^1, \dots, Y^m$ drawn from the conditional distribution function of Y, given that $X \le x$. Essentially, a golfer's efficiency is computed in reference to a random sample of m other golfers drawn with replacement who use the same or fewer inputs than the golfer being evaluated. This can be done by Monte-Carlo methods, or more efficiently by numerical integration.

The estimator by integration is given by:

$$\theta_m(x,y) = E[\max(Y^1, \dots, Y^m)|X \le x] = \int_0^\infty (1 - [F_Y \mid x(y \mid x)]^m) dy \tag{2}$$

or:

$$\theta_m(x,y) = \theta(x,y) + \int_0^{\theta(x,y)} (1 - [F_Y \mid x(y \mid x)]^m) dy, \tag{3}$$

where $\theta_m(x,y)$ is the order-m efficiency estimate for each golfer, which is computed from the FDH output efficiency estimate plus the defined integral. These can be computed using nonparametric integration methods, as shown by Daraio and Simar (2005).[3]

To estimate efficiency conditional upon the age of the golfer, the equations are modified so that the output y is not only conditional upon the inputs x, but also conditional upon z, the age of the golfer. Equation (3) is then modified as:

$$\theta_m(x,y|z) = \theta(x,y|z) + \int_0^{\theta(x,y|z)} (1-[F_{Y\,|\,X,z}(y\,|\,x,z)]^m)dy. \tag{4}$$

A nonparametric estimate requires a kernel estimator for z with a bandwidth. A triangle distribution is used as the kernel and a bandwidth of 5.0 is utilized for the age variable z.[4]

4. Results

The Data

The data consist of measures of output and inputs for golfers on the LPGA tour for the years 2006, 2007, and 2008.[5] Output is nominal earnings per event. Inputs are drive total (DT), putts (PUTT), greens in regulation (GIR), and sand saves (SS). DT is an aggregation of driving distance and drives in fairway (accuracy). It is calculated as the sum in the ranks for each variable.[6] The lower is DT, the better is performance. Since DT is an input, and a production function framework assumes that more input is associated with more output, DT is transformed by subtracting it from the highest value plus one. PUTT is the average number of putts for greens hit in regulation. As with DT, a lower value for PUTT is better: it is transformed by subtracting it from the highest value plus 0.01. GIR is the percentage of greens reached in par minus two. SS is the percentage of the time a player gets down in two or better from a green side bunker, regardless of the score for the hole.

The data for the three years are pooled, resulting in 423 golfers. Table 8.1 contains the descriptive statistics. Note that DT and PUTT are untransformed in this table. Mean earnings per event is $12,784, $14,474, and $14,381 over the three years. Although there is a 13 percent increase from 2006 to 2007, thereby increasing the inefficiencies of golfers in 2006, this should not bias our results since it is relative efficiencies that matter. There is little variation in the input data over the three years, suggesting that combining the years is justified. It is interesting to examine the components of drive total. Average driving distance is 252 yards, 249 yards, and 247 yards in 2006, 2007, and 2008, respectively. Drives in fairway is 70 percent, 65 percent, and 68 percent in 2006, 2007, and 2008, respectively. There is no

Table 8.1 Descriptive Statistics

Variable	Definition	2006 (n = 145)		2007 (n = 129)		2008 (n = 149)	
		Mean	SD	Mean	SD	Mean	SD
E ($)	Earnings per event	12,782	17,643	14,474	19,799	14,381	17,168
GIR (%)	Greens in regulation	65	4	61	4	63	4
DT (yards)	Driving total	162	50	145	45	159	47
SS (%)	Sand save percent	38	7	38	8	38	8
PUTT (n)	Average putts for greens reached in regulation	1.82	0.04	1.84	0.03	1.83	0.04
AGE (years)	Age of golfer	32	8	31	7	31	7
EXP (years)	Years on LPGA tour	8	6	8	6	8	6

evidence that "advances" in club technology improved distance and accuracy over this time period for golfers on the professional women's tour.

The Model

The inputs measure fundamental golfing athletic ability. The output measures success on the LPGA tour. All data are annual averages. The unit of observation is an individual golfer for a particular year. The production function for success on the LPGA tour is drive total (lower is better), putts (fewer is better), sand saves, and greens hit in regulation transformed into earnings per event.[7] We envision the process in terms of a frontier production function, which attaches special importance to the outlying observations and identifies best practice. Golfers who perform below best practice transform their golfing athletic ability into lower earnings per event than better golfers. The production function literature dubs the difference in performance between best practice and the practice of a less than best (dominated) observation as inefficiency. We obtain quantitative measures of inefficiency for each of the 423 golfers in our sample. Inefficiency is a measure of the ability to perform under pressure. Our efficiency measures constitute a performance under pressure index (PUPI).

Figure 8.1 illustrates the concept. Earnings per event is measured on the vertical axes. The fundamental measures of athletic ability are measured on the horizontal axes, reduced to one dimension for expository purposes. Each point represents a golfer. A conventional linear or non-linear regression fits a line or curve through the middle of the data and estimates the average relationship between athletic golfing ability and success on the tour. In contrast, a frontier approach, in this case the free disposal hull (FDH), focuses on the outlying observations. The "staircase" FDH frontier reflects the assumptions that inputs are freely disposable and that production can only occur at observed points. Observations on the frontier are efficient;

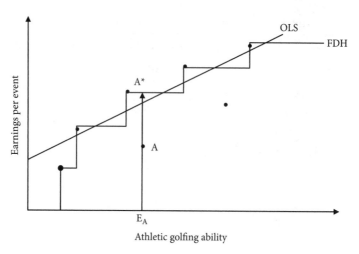

Figure 8.1 The measurement of inefficiency.

observations below the frontier are inefficient. Consider golfer A. She lies below the frontier. Given her athletic golfing ability, the best practice frontier suggests that she should be able to earn A* per event in contrast to A per event. The difference is inefficiency. The measure of efficiency is actual earnings over optimal (best practice) earnings or $E_A A / E_A A^*$. Golfers on the frontier (best practice) have an efficiency score equal to 1. Golfers below the frontier have an efficiency score less than 1. Suppose, a golfer's efficiency score is 0.6. The interpretation is that she is earning 60 percent of best-practice earnings, given her golfing athletic ability. How do we know this? We know this because there is a most dominating golfer in the sample with the same or similar golfing athletic ability who is able to earn 67 percent more.

Consider an example from the 2008 data. Table 8.2 compares the measures of golfing athletic ability and earnings per event for Candie Kung and Ji Young Oh. In terms of the standard measures of golfing performance, Oh appears to be better than Kung; she has a lower DT rank (76 vs. 142), is about the same in greens in regulation and putts (65.7 percent vs. 65.2 percent; 1.83 versus 1.82) and is better out of the sand (38.6 percent versus 31.8 percent). If we disentangle drive total, we find that Oh drives the ball 254 yards on average and is in the fairway 71.4 percent of the time, compared to Kung who drives the ball 247.7 yards on average and is in the fairway 68.7 percent of the time. Oh has more golfing inputs than Kung. According to a traditional production function, Oh would be expected to produce more output than Kung since she has more inputs; any deviation from this would be attributed to statistical noise. In contrast, a frontier production function interprets the difference in performance, given inputs, as a measure of efficiency. If Oh and Kung were the only golfers in the data set, Kung would be best practice and Oh would have an efficiency score equal to 0.78 (23,456/30,214); Oh is producing 78 percent of best-practice output.

We interpret the efficiency score to be a quantitative measure of the ability to perform under pressure, or the mental side of the game. The inputs control for

Table 8.2 Kung and Oh Statistics

Golfer	E($)/Event	DT	GIR	PUTT	SS	DD	DIF	E($)
Ji Young Oh (2008)	23,456	76	65.7	1.83	38.6	254	71.4	680,225
Candie Kung (2008)	30,214	142	65.2	1.82	31.8	248	68.7	876,602

fundamental athletic golfing ability. The output is a measure of success on the professional tour. All data are averages for a golfer over the season. Again, consider Candie Kung and Ji Young Oh. Oh's measures of fundamental golfing ability are the same or better than Kung's, but Oh earned less per event (lower output). In particular, Oh achieved her input averages by perhaps performing well on Thursday, Friday, and Saturday and then falling apart on Sunday, failing to win, failing to earn the big prize. In contrast, even though Kung achieved inferior input *averages*, she was able to put four excellent rounds together on Thursday through Sunday and win the tournament or finish well. Efficiency scores can be interpreted as a quantitative measure of the ability to perform under pressure and are the missing performance statistic for professional women golfers. The mental side of the game drives success.

It is the pressure on a Sunday as the leading golfers battle going down the stretch that captivates fans of the game. There are many golfers who can drive the ball far on average over the season; there are far fewer golfers who can hit the long drive and keep it in the fairway on the eighteenth hole on a Sunday afternoon needing birdie to make a playoff or to win. A typical example is the September 2009 Samsung World Championship at Torrey Pines. At the end of the third round, Na Yeon Choi lead Jiyai Shin by two and Ai Miyazato by three. Choi opened on Sunday with three birdies and an eagle on the first six holes and took a seven shot lead. But golf is all about holding it together under pressure. After three straight bogeys, Choi held a one stroke lead over Miyazato. The drama unfolded. Miyazato, in the group ahead, hit a magnificent tee shot on the 189 yard par three sixteenth, sunk the putt for birdie, and was tied for the lead. Meanwhile, Choi three putted on fifteen for a bogey and fell a stroke behind. Miyazato hit her drive on the 400 yard seventeenth 280 yards, hit her approach shot ten feet from the hole, but missed the birdie putt as it slid three feet past. She converted for par. Miyazata proceeded to the 480 yard par 5 eighteenth with a one shot lead as Choi parred number seventeen. The pressure was huge. Who will crack? Miyazata boomed her drive to the right center of the fairway in perfect position to hit the green in two. She waited for the group in front. She waited. At last, she selected a five wood, hit it short and to the left into the pond that guards the front of the green and ended up with a bogey. Choi and Miyazata were tied. Choi faced the final hole. She hit a perfect drive, leaving 193 yards to the hole. Her second shot was on the fringe in front of the green. She chose the putter. The result was a six foot putt for birdie and the win. The ball rolled—it broke to the left—it fell in the cup. This is performance under pressure. Our efficiency score for Choi for 2008 is 0.90, much higher than the average golfer

Table 8.3 FDH Output Efficiencies and Order-m FDH Output Efficiencies, n = 423

	FDH	m = 200	m = 100	m = 50	m = 25
Average	0.72	0.73	0.75	0.79	0.87
Standard Deviation	0.30	0.31	0.32	0.35	0.41
Minimum	0.01	0.01	0.01	0.00	0.01
Maximum*	1.00	1.54	1.95	2.47	3.11
Number of Efficient Golfers	171	171	177	193	208

* Efficiency can be greater than one, since the reference set may not include the golfer being evaluated. That golfer might lie above the reference set. The value m is the m-order statistic used to trim the number of comparison golfers.

at 0.75 (see Table 8.3). Given her performance discussed above, her score for 2009 could be higher.

Unconditional Efficiency Scores

For each golfer, the order-m efficiency score is calculated by taking the average of a finite number of FDH scores, each based upon a random sample of size m drawn from the sample of LPGA golfers with replacement. Where m equals the sample size, order-m approaches the FDH measure of efficiency.[8] As m decreases, there is a greater likelihood that dominating golfers are not included in some of the samples and each golfer is evaluated relative to a smaller sample; both effects tend to increase efficiency scores. Particularly for small values of m, it is possible that the golfer being evaluated is not included in some of the samples, resulting in an efficiency score greater than one.

Table 8.3 contains descriptive statistics for efficiency scores for various values of m. As expected, large values of m correspond closely to the FDH results. As m equals 50 and 25, there are large increases in the number of measured efficient golfers, the average efficiency scores, and the number of golfers with efficiency scores greater than one. The analysis in this chapter is conducted for m equal to 100.

Table 8.4 contains the efficiency scores for some particularly interesting golfers, illustrating the interpretation of our measure of performance under pressure. Table 8.7 contains the input measures for each golfer discussed. There are golfers who are very successful on the LPGA tour in terms of earnings, have high efficiency scores, and perform under pressure at a best-practice level. They transform their excellent golfing inputs into the maximum (best-practice) earnings per event. Lorena Ochoa, in 2008, is an example. She earns $2.7 million in total and $125,600 per event. She drives the ball 269 yards, in the fairway 66.4 percent of the time, drive total rank is 101, hits the green in regulation 71.6 percent of the time, average putts is 1.78, and saves par from the sand over 50 percent of the time. Her rank in terms of 2008 total earnings is number one. Lorena Ochoa (2008) is an excellent

Table 8.4 Efficiency Scores, Ranking and Earnings, m-order = 100,
          Years 2006–2008

Golfer	2006				2007				2008			
	Rk	Eff	Tot$	E(K)	Rk	Eff	Tot$	E(K)	Rk	Eff	Tot$	E(K)
L. Ochoa	1	1.44	2.6M	104K	1	1.95	4.4M	175K	1	1.64	2.8M	126K
K. Webb	2	1.35	2.1M	100K	22	1.09	630K	30K	18	1.03	854K	43K
A. Sorenstam	3	1.16	2.0M	98K	–	–	–	–	4	1.32	1.7M	79K
P. Creamer	11	0.75	1.1M	40K	3	1.02	1.4M	58K	2	1.19	1.8M	70K
K. Bae	48	0.66	287K	12K	41	1.00	308K	11K	74	1.00	166K	7K
C. Kerr	5	0.76	1.6M	61K	6	1.28	1.1M	50K	10	1.00	1.1M	43K
G. Sergas	78	0.21	122K	6K	62	1.00	184K	8K	43+	0.36	418K	15K

Notes: Rk = rank according to total winnings, Eff = Efficiency sore, Tot$ = total winnings in millions, E(K) = earnings per event in thousands. Annika Sorenstam (2007) is not included because she played in fewer than 14 events.

Table 8.5 Creamer (2006) and Creamer (2007) Statistics

Golfer	E($)/Event	DT	GIR	PUTT	SS	DD	DIF	E($)
P. Creamer (2006)	39,858	103	72.6	1.77	37.5	256.6	72.1	1,076,163
P. Creamer (2007)	57,700	102	68.3	1.78	40.0	246.1	73.7	1,384,798

Table 8.6 Conditional Efficiency, AER, Predicted AER and Age, m = 100,
          h = 5, n = 423

Golfer	2006				2007				2008			
	Age	CEff	AER	PrAER	Age	CEff	AER	PrAER	Age	CEff	AER	PrAER
L. Ochoa	26	0.88	1.26	0.91	27	1.33	1.47	0.91	28	1.23	1.33	0.90
K. Webb	33	0.93	1.26	0.90	34	1.00	1.09	0.90	35	1.00	1.03	0.91
A. Sorenstam	37	1.07	1.08	0.91	–	–	–	–	39	1.05	1.25	0.90
P. Creamer	21	0.62	1.21	0.90	22	0.90	1.13	0.90	23	1.03	1.15	0.90
K. Bae	22	0.90	0.73	0.90	23	1.00	1.00	0.90	24	1.00	1.00	0.90
C. Kerr	30	0.66	1.15	0.90	31	1.05	1.22	0.90	32	1.00	1.00	0.90
G. Sergas	28	0.19	1.12	0.91	29	1.00	1.00	0.90	30	0.34	1.07	0.90

Notes: CEff = Conditional efficiency, AER = Age efficiency ratio, PrAER = Predicted age efficiency ratio.

golfer in terms of the standard golfing performance statistics and in terms of her ability to handle the pressure. She performs up to her full potential. The same story applies to Lorena Ochoa in 2006 and 2007; Karrie Webb in 2006, 2007, and 2008; Annika Sorenstam in 2006 and 2008;[9] Paula Creamer in 2007 and 2008; and others.

Table 8.7 Golfing Performance Inputs of Various Golfers

Golfer	DD	DIF	DT	GIR	PUTT	SS
L. Ochoa (2006)	269	73%	56	76%	1.75	43%
L. Ochoa (2007)	271	68%	54	73%	1.76	47%
L. Ochoa (2008)	269	66%	101	72%	1.78	50%
K. Webb (2006)	260	75%	52	74%	1.75	40%
K. Webb (2007)	258	64%	109	67%	1.83	39%
K. Webb (2008)	257	61%	161	68%	1.80	34%
A. Sorenstam (2006)	261	74%	58	75%	1.76	52%
A. Sorenstam (2008)	251	71%	98	69%	1.79	48%
P. Creamer (2006)	257	72%	103	73%	1.77	38%
P. Creamer (2007)	246	74%	102	68%	1.78	40%
P. Creamer (2008)	246	74%	100	70%	1.77	47%
K. Bae (2006)	250	70%	178	68%	1.81	34%
K. Bae (2007)	247	60%	204	60%	1.82	38%
K. Bae (2008)	244	62%	227	61%	1.80	44%
C. Kerr (2006)	262	73%	72	73%	1.74	51%
G. Sergas (2007)	250	69%	106	62%	1.84	32%
G. Sergas (2008)	256	72%	62	66%	1.78	37%

However, there are also golfers with efficiency scores equal to one or higher who have low earnings. They have relatively poor measures of golfing ability, but transform their athletic inputs into the maximum earnings per event. Kyeong Bae in 2008 is an example. Her DT rank is 227; she drives the ball 244 yards, and hits the fairway 62.4 percent of the time. Greens in regulation is 60.7 percent, average putts is 1.8, and sand save percentage is 43.9. She earns $6,921 per event and $166K for the 2008 season. Her rank in terms of total earnings is 74. Kyeong Bae's efficiency score is one. She transforms her golfing athletic inputs into the maximum (best-practice) earnings because she handles the albeit low pressure well. She is earning up to her full potential.

Some golfers have high earnings and relatively low efficiency scores. In conventional terms, these golfers are very successful, but in fact, they are performing below their potential and could earn more if they were better at handling the pressure. Consider Christie Kerr in 2006: DT is 72 (average drive is 261.9 yards, 72.6 percent in the fairway), GIR is 73 percent, PUTT is 1.74, and SS is 51.3 percent. Kerr earns $60,706 per event and $1.58 million for the season. These are excellent numbers, but Kerr performed below her potential. Her efficiency score is 0.76. Had she been able to handle the pressure at a best-practice level, she would have earned $79,876 per event and $2.08 million for the season, essentially in a tie with Karrie Webb for second on the 2006 money list to the leader Lorena Ochoa who won $2.59 million. Ochoa and Webb are efficient. Kerr's excellent golfing statistics place her in a demanding cohort group. She earns a million and a half dollars, but for her, this is a poor performance. We know this because her performance under pressure statistic is 0.76.

And there are golfers with low earnings and low efficiency scores. These are golfers who are not doing well in conventional terms and have the potential to do much better if they could improve the mental side of the game. Consider Giulia Sergas in 2008. Her fundamental statistics are strong: DT is 62 (average drive is 256 yards, 71.6 percent in the fairway), GIR is 65.9 percent, PUTT is 1.78, and SS is 41.8 percent. However, the strong golfing statistics produce $15,465 earnings per event and $418K for the season. Her performance under pressure index is 0.36. Were she to handle the pressure at best practice, she would earn $42,958 per event and $1.16 million[10] in total for the season. Instead of ranking 43 on the money list, she would rank 8. Sergas has mastered the physical game, but not the mental game. Performance under pressure can make a big difference in the paycheck.

It is also interesting to compare Sergas in 2008 to Sergas in 2007. Sergas is efficient in 2007 and inefficient in 2008: she earns $418K in 2008 with an efficiency score equal to 0.36, compared to $184K in 2007 with an efficiency score equal to1.00. How is this possible? Sergas's golfing inputs increased dramatically in 2008: DT improved from 106 to 62 (DD 256 compared to 250; DIF 71.1 percent compared to 68.6 percent), GIR rose from 61.7 percent to 65.9 percent, PUTT fell from 1.84 to 1.78 and SS went up from 32 percent to 36.5 percent. Sergas in 2008 is a better golfer in the physical sense than Sergas in 2007, so it is not surprising that she earned more in 2008. However, her improved physical inputs raised the bar in terms of the best practice benchmark for managing the mental side of the game. Her golfing inputs placed her in a comparison set that includes the leading money winners on the tour. We know this because if she had transformed her inputs into best-practice earnings, she would have ranked 8 on the money list instead of 43. This clearly illustrates that our concept of efficiency (the PUPI) is conditional on inputs; golfers with high skills can be inefficient and golfers with low skills can be efficient.

Since a golfer in a year is an observation, it is possible to compare the same golfer over different years to isolate the importance of the ability to perform under pressure. Table 8.4 contains the fundamental golfing statistics for Paula Creamer in 2006 and 2007. Creamer had an excellent year in 2007, earning $58K per event and $1.4 million for the season, compared to $40K per event and $1.1 million for the season in 2006. However, according to the standard golfing statistics, Creamer appears to have similar golfing ability in 2006 and 2007: DT is 103 and 102; GIR is 72.6 and 68.3; PUTT is 1.77 and 1.78; SS is 37.5 and 40.0. She hit fewer greens in regulation in 2007, but was a few percentage points better out of the sand. The difference in earnings per event is explained by the performance under pressure index; the PUPI is 0.74 in 2006 and 1.02 in 2007. Creamer did a better job managing the mind and the course to put good scores together over the four days of a tournament in 2007 than she did in 2006.

Conditional Efficiency Scores

The unconditional efficiency score compares a golfer's ability to perform under pressure to all golfers in the data set. The conditional efficiency score restricts the comparison set to a subsample of the golfers based upon an exogenous variable. We consider conditional efficiency scores based upon age. The bandwidth is 5 years. The conditional on age score compares the golfer to other golfers 2.5 years younger and 2.5 years older.

Generally, conditional scores are the same or higher than unconditional scores; the golfer is evaluated relative to a smaller set of golfers.[11] Where conditional and unconditional scores are equal, the golfer is managing the exogenous variable (age) in terms of the mental side of the game at a best practice level. Since the conditional score essentially handicaps for the exogenous variable, equal scores indicate that handicapping is not necessary: a golfer is just as mentally tough compared to the entire sample as to a subsample based upon age. We form the ratio of unconditional to conditional efficiency scores, the age efficiency ratio (AER), plot this ratio against the exogenous variable, and fit a non-parametric regression to the observations. Where the AER tends to rise (fall) with age, golfers manage their age better (worse) as they get older.

The dynamics of the impact of aging on performance under pressure includes physical and experience effects. As golfers age, beyond some point, the physical ability to concentrate and focus fades, but at the same time, the golfer is older, and she has more experience dealing with the pressure. We expect the gains from experience to initially dominate the physical toll, and the AER to rise with age. However, experience gains are subject to diminishing returns; the point is reached at which the physical effects of aging dominate, and the AER is expected to decline with age. Figure 8.2 plots the AER and the non-parametric regression of AER on age using a logistic kernel and bandwidth of 1.98. There is a very subtle rise in efficiency that until around age 36 is barely discernible, and then a decline, with considerable dispersion around the fitted curve.[12] The ability to perform under pressure peaks at 37 years old.

Not only do we identify a systematic relationship between the AER and AGE, but we also generate the AER and the predicted AER for individual golfers. Table 8.6 contains this information for a set of golfers. Ochoa 2007 and Ochoa 2008 have the first and second highest AER. Ochoa in 2007 was 27 years old, her AER is 1.47, and her predicted AER is 0.91. She is managing her age better than predicted. Moreover, she achieves her high AER with a high unconditional efficiency score, high traditional golfing inputs, high earnings per event and total earnings. Ochoa dominated the tour in 2007. The same holds for Ochoa in 2008. If this trend continues, she will remain mentally tough over time and continue to be high on the money list, so long as her shot-making skills do not deteriorate.

Sergas in 2008 was 30 years old and has an AER equal to 1.07, compared to a predicted AER equal to 0.90. Like Ochoa, she is also managing her age better than

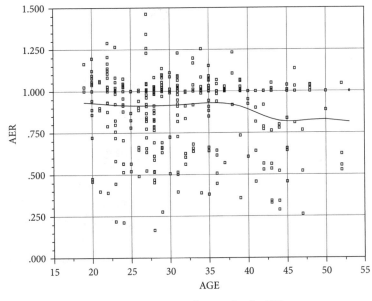

Nonparametric regression for AER

Figure 8.2 Age Efficiency Ratio (AER) as a Function of Age

predicted, but she earns a mere $8K per event and $184K in total. She achieves her AER with unconditional and conditional efficiency scores equal to approximately 0.36. Sergas in 2008 has an equally low PUPI relative to the total sample and relative to her age bracket. Handicapping for age does not help her. As we know from the earlier discussion, Sergas in 2008 is an excellent golfer in terms of shot making; this puts her in the reference set of other excellent golfers in general and around her age bracket who transform their golfing ability into much higher earnings per event. She is doing above average in terms of her age, but this does not translate into success on the tour.

Bae 2006 is another interesting example. She is 22 years old and not managing her age particularly well. Her unconditional score is 0.66, her conditional score is 0.90, her AER is 0.73, and her predicted AER is 0.90. Her performance under pressure is low relative to the total sample, to her age bracket, and to the average benchmark for her age. Her input values are: DT is 178; GIR is 68 percent; PUTT is 1.81; and SS is 34 percent. This constitutes her full statistical profile, including the important measure of performance under pressure. It is consistent with earning $12,000 per event. However, golfing performance changes over time. In 2007 and 2008, her conditional and unconditional scores equal 1, and her AER equals 1, which is greater than predicted in both years; nevertheless, her earnings per event are lower than in 2006. What happened? Bae's golfing inputs deteriorated relative to 2006, putting her in a less demanding reference set. It is important to note that our measure of performance under pressure and the associated AER are relative to the input set.

5. CONCLUSION

The ability to perform under pressure is an important statistic to obtain the full quantitative profile of a golfer on the LPGA tour. It makes a clear contribution over the standard measures of golfing ability that appear in web sites and golf magazines. The mental side of the game matters. However, our measure is fundamentally different from other one-dimensional rankings in that it is inspired by the frontier production function literature and therefore is predicated upon inputs and the stochastic nature of performance. Golfers who do well or poorly in the earnings dimension can have high or low measures of performance under pressure. Golfers with relatively low (high) measures of the traditional golfing inputs are compared to similar golfers and the earnings bar is lower (higher) than it is for golfers with relatively high (low) levels of the traditional golfing inputs. In fact, the correlation coefficient between earnings per event and the ability to perform under pressure is 0.48. This is the same framework that is used for multidimensional benchmarking of firm performance (Fried et al., 2008).

As with all athletes, the careers of golfers occur on the front end of the age distribution. Aging takes a toll on the physical abilities to hit the ball far and accurately, to reach greens in regulation, to putt and to escape from the sand. Aging also affects the mental side of the game: the ability to focus, concentrate, and execute a critical shot late on a Sunday afternoon. There is a classic trade-off between the inevitable deterioration in the mental ability to handle the pressure and experience gained with time. We expect an inverted U-shaped relationship. The AER allows us to explore this question for the impact of age on the ability to perform under pressure. We do obtain a mild inverted U pattern, which was relatively flat in earlier years and fell in later years. The ability to perform under pressure peaks at age 37.

It is late on a Sunday afternoon, the light is fading, and the final pairing is reaching the eighteenth hole. Will the winner be Lorena Ochoa or Ai Miyazato or Christina Kim or ... ? Will a contender sink a long putt or hole out from the bunker for a playoff or the win? Will the leader miss the critical short putt and choke? The tension mounts. On most Sundays, it is not over until the last putt drops.

See you at the nineteenth hole.

Leopold Simar generously provided the Matlab computer code to calculate conditional and unconditional order-m efficiency scores. Cinzia Daraio convinced us of the merits of the order-m approach. Zack Ciesinski worked diligently and meticulously collecting the data. We thank our three coaches. Despite their efforts, our play undoubtedly faltered at times as we caved to the pressure.

NOTES

1 We recognize that the performance of other contending golfers could influence shot selection. Our methodology captures this as the course management component of performance under pressure.

2 See http://www.lpga.com/content_1.aspx?mid=2&pid=20712.

3 We thank Leopold Simar for providing the Matlab code and helping us with implementation.

4 The order-m efficiency of each golfer conditional upon age was also computed from Matlab software code provided by Simar.

5 The data are collected from www.lpga.com.

6 We could include the two components of DT separately, but a more parsimonious specification increases the differentiation in efficiencies. We take advantage of this opportunity to reduce the number of inputs.

7 Scully (2006) and Callan and Thomas (2007) argue that golfing ability maps into score, and score maps into earnings. Scully's argument is based in part on a nonlinear relationship between both ability measures and score and earnings due to a concave prize schedule. We choose to focus on golfing ability measures and earnings because this is a richer specification. Performance under pressure is all about making particular shots under stressful competitive circumstances. Our nonparametric specification accommodates nonlinearities.

8 Where m equals the sample size, the results will not precisely correspond to the FDH results since sampling is with replacement.

9 Annika Sorenstam, 2007, is not in the data set because she played in thirteen events, fewer than our fourteen event cutoff.

10 The hypothetical total is calculated by multiplying the efficient earnings per event by the number of events played.

11 This statement will always hold under standard FDH, but not necessarily under order-m FDH. The reason is that under order-m, samples are drawn with replacement and efficiency scores can be greater than one if the unit of analysis is not included in the sample. This is more likely to occur for unconditional scores than for conditional scores since the unconditional "population" is much larger and m is the same for both cases.

12 As golfers age and their performance deteriorates, they leave the professional tour. The date is sparse beyond 45 years old. Were these older golfers to remain on the tour, the non-parametric regression line would decline more precipitously.

REFERENCES

Daraio, C., Simar, L. (2005). Introducing environmental variables in nonparametric frontier models: A probabilistic approach. *Journal of Productivity Analysis* 24: 93–121.

Deprins, D., L. Simar, and H. Tulkins (1984). Measuring labor efficiency in post offices, in M. Marchant, P. Pestieau, and H. Tulkins. (eds.), *the performance of public enterprises: Concepts and measurement*. Amsterdam: Elsevier Science Publishers, B.V., 243–267.

Ehrenberg, R., and M. Bognanno (1990). Do tournaments have incentive effects? *Journal of Political Economy*, 98(6): 1309–1324.

Fried, H. O., J. Lambrinos, and J. Tyner (2004). Evaluating the performance of professional golfers on the PGA, LPGA, and SPGA Tours. *European Journal of Operational Research*, 154(2): 548–561

Fried, H. O., S. S. Schmidt, and C. A. K. Lovell (2008). *The measurement of productive efficiency and productivity growth*. New York: Oxford University Press.

Fried, H. O., and L. W. Tauer (2011). The impact of age on the ability to perform under pressure: Golfers on the PGA Tour. *Journal of Productivity Analysis*, 35: 75–84,

Gizachew, T. (2009). Age and winning in professional golf tours. Department of Political Science, University of Central Arkansas, http://arxiv.org/abs/0901.0684.

Kalist, D. E. (2008). Does motherhood affect productivity, relative performance, and earnings? *Journal of Labor Research* 29: 219–235.

Marple, D. (1983). Tournament earnings and performance differentials between the sexes in professional golf and tennis. *Journal of Sports and Social Issues*, 7(1):1–14.

Matthews, P. H., P. M. Sommers, and F. J Peschiera (2007). Incentives and superstars on the LPGA Tour. *Applied Economics*, 39(1): 87–94.

Pfitzner, C. B., and T. D. Rishel (2005). Performance and compensation on the LPGA Tour: A statistical analysis. *International Journal of Performance Analysis in Sport*, 5(3): 29–39.

Scully, G. W. (2002). The distribution of performance and earning in a prize economy. *Journal of Sports Economics* 3: 235–245.

Shmanske, S. (2000). Gender, skill, and earnings in professional golf. *Journal of Sports Economics*, 1(4): 400–415.

Shin, E. H., and E. A. Nam (2004). The case of Korean players on the LPGA Tour. *Journal of Sport & Social Issues*, 28(2): 223–244.

Theberge, N. (1980). The system of rewards in women's professional golf. *International Review for the Sociology of Sport*, 15(2): 27–41.

Tiruneh, G. (2010). Age and winning in professional golf tours. *Journal of Quantitative Analysis in Sports*, 6(1): 1–14.

## CHAPTER 9

SALARY DISPERSION AND TEAM PRODUCTION

EVIDENCE FROM THE NATIONAL HOCKEY LEAGUE

LEO H. KAHANE

1. INTRODUCTION

THE issue of salary dispersion and its potential effect on firm production has been a topic of great interest in labor and personnel economics. The early literature on this topic has produced two opposing theoretical predictions. The "tournament model" of Lazear and Rosen (1981), in which worker compensation increases with individual performance, emphasizes the increased worker effort brought about by such a compensation scheme and the potential for increasing firm output. Countering this theory, the work of Akerlof and Yellen (1988, 1990) and Levine (1991) focuses on the issue of "fairness" and how, if cooperation and cohesiveness among workers is important, salary compression may be beneficial to firm efficiency and production. Empirical efforts to sort out which of the two models is supported has produced mixed results. This is partly due to the fact that data on worker skills and salary are hard to come by and that output measurement is often difficult.[1] The goal of this chapter is to empirically test these competing hypotheses using data from the National Hockey League (NHL). The advantages of using data from the NHL are twofold: data on the salary and skills of workers (players in this case) are readily available, and the measurement of output (team winning in this case) is easily obtained.

The remainder of this chapter is organized as follows. The next section discusses the intuition behind the two competing hypotheses and discusses some of the previous literature on this topic (with an emphasis on sports economics examples). Section 3 follows with a discussion of the empirical model and the data used to test the "tournament" versus "fairness" hypotheses. Section 4 presents the empirical results, and section 5 provides some concluding remarks.

2. Salary Dispersion and Firm Production

Competing Theories

The intuition behind the "tournament" model is straightforward. In order to induce maximum effort from workers in a firm, or players on a team, it may be necessary to increase the "prize" associated with their individual accomplishments. This approach to compensation would thus tend to increase the dispersion of salaries within a firm or a team. If this theory is correct, then, *ceteris paribus*, firms with greater salary dispersion should produce greater output in comparison to those with a narrower salary dispersion.

The "fairness" model stresses the point that if workers can easily compare their wages to other workers, and if cooperation and cohesion is important to the production process, then a compressed wage structure may induce greater performance. The basic idea is succinctly expressed by Akerlof and Yellen (1990) as they write, "The motivation for the fair wage-effort hypothesis is a simple observation concerning human behavior: when people do not get what they deserve, they try to get even" (p. 256). Workers may "get even" by withholding effort and, in doing so, reducing firm output or by interfering with the production efforts of coworkers through non-cooperation or sabotage.[2]

Clearly, both of these forces may be at work simultaneously. This possibility is noted by Lazear (1989), who writes:

> Relative comparisons [of wages] imply that individuals can increase their wealth in two ways. Competition encourages increased effort, which has a positive effect on output. This is the idea of Lazear and Rosen (1981). But competition also discourages cooperation among contestants and can lead to outright sabotage.

The larger is the spread between the compensation that the winner and loser receive, the more important is each of these effects. This is much like an arms race: as the value of winning the war increases, each country devotes more resources to fighting. Those additional resources are unproductive. They reduce the other country's output without changing the outcome of the war. If the winning and losing countries fared equally in the postwar situation, fewer resources would be devoted to defense. Similarly, in the labor market, pay equality discourages uncooperative behavior and is one reason why both workers and firms may push for equal treatment. (p. 562)

Thus, according to Lazear, the wider the spread of compensation, the greater the intensity of these two forces. The overall net effect, however, is indeterminate and remains an empirical question.

Previous Empirical Findings

There have been a number of empirical investigations into the effects (if any) of salary dispersion on productivity. For example, Cowherd and Levine (1992) use data on 102 "business units" from 41 corporations to investigate the effects of hourly pay dispersion on perceived product quality, the authors' measure of firm performance. They found a positive, significant relationship between pay equity and product quality, thus supporting the benefits of salary compression. In another study, Pfeffer and Langton (1993) use data from over 17,000 individuals in more than 600 academic departments to assess the effects of salary dispersion on faculty member "performance." They find that " ... the greater the degree of wage dispersion within academic departments, the lower is individual faculty members' satisfaction and research productivity and the less likely it is that faculty members will collaborate on research" (p. 382).

Lazear (1989) notes that while compressed salary structures may enhance the productivity of some, it may not do so for all workers. Specifically, highly productive workers may not respond positively to a compression in salaries. As Lazear writes, "The morale of high quality workers is likely to be adversely affected by pay that regresses toward the mean," (pp. 561–562). Thus Lazear stresses the importance of specifying reference groups. That is, the "fairness" theory is relevant when workers are comparing themselves to others with similar abilities and, as such, empirical analyses of the effects of salary dispersion on productivity should be conditional on observable characteristics and skills. With this idea in mind, Winter-Ebmer and Zweimüller (1999) use panel data for Austrian firms from 1975 to 1991 to estimate the effects of *conditional* wage dispersion (to be discussed in greater detail below) on firm performance. As they are unable to observe firm performance directly, they compute "standardised wages" and use this measure as a proxy for worker productivity. Their results show that for "white-collar" workers there is a non-monotonic relationship between wage dispersion and productivity: greater salary dispersion initially increases worker productivity, but too much dispersion eventually reduces productivity. As for "blue-collar" workers, their productivity generally rose as wage dispersion increased. A similar study by Lallemand, Plasman, and Rycx (2004) uses 1995 survey data from the Belgian private sector to assess the effects of salary dispersion on profits per employee (their measure of firm performance) using both an unconditional and conditional approach.[3] Their findings are similar to those of Winter-Ebmer and Zweimüller (1999).

From the sports economics literature there have been various studies on the effects of salary dispersion on both individual and team sports. When considering the two theories noted above, "tournament" versus "fairness," it would seem that the former would find its greatest support among individual sports, where cooperation and cohesion would not play a central role in performance. There is, indeed, some evidence supporting this view. Research by Ehrenberg and Bognanno (1990a, 1990b), using data from professional golfers, found that they performed better the higher (and more disperse) the purse for winning. Maloney and McCormick (2000) find similar results in the case of foot racing.

As for team sports, the focus has been primarily on the four major North American sports leagues, the National Football League (NFL), the National Basketball Association (NBA), the National Hockey League (NHL) and Major League Baseball (MLB). The results have been mixed. For example, Bloom (1999), Depken (2000), and Frick et al. (2003) find that greater salary dispersion reduces MLB team performance, thus supporting the "fairness" hypothesis. DeBrock et al. (2004), however, find that after conditioning on player characteristics there is little support for the "fairness" hypothesis. Regarding the NBA, Frick et al. (2003) found a positive effect of salary dispersion on team performance, whereas Berri and Jewell (2004) do not find a statistically significant relationship. For the NFL, Mondello and Maxcy (2009) find support for the "fairness" model, as salary dispersion is found to be negatively related to team winning percentage. Frick et al. (2003) also find a negative relationship for the NFL, but their result is not statistically significant. Lastly, regarding the NHL, Gomez (2002) found a positive effect of salary inequality on team performance when employing simple OLS regressions, but this effect disappears when team fixed effects are included. Frick et al. (2003), which estimates a random effects model and employs a larger data set than Gomez (2002), finds no evidence that salary dispersion affects NHL team performance.

3. Modeling Approach and Data

Conditional versus Unconditional Models

The standard approach to exploring the effects of salary dispersion on team productivity is to establish a measure of intra-team salary dispersion and use this measure as a covariate in a regression for team performance. This typical approach is represented in the following equation:

$$P = f(X, Z; \sigma) \tag{1}$$

where P is some measure of team performance[4], X is vector of players' inputs, Z is a vector of team inputs, and σ is a measure of salary dispersion. Controlling for team and players' inputs, a positive relationship between P and σ would lend support to the "tournament" hypothesis whereas a negative relationship would be supportive of the "fairness" hypothesis. The key variable in equation (1) is of course the measure of salary dispersion. Typical measures of intra-team salary dispersion used in previous research include: standard deviations, Gini coefficients, Herfindahl-Hirschman indices, coefficients of variation, the ratio of the maximum to the minimum salaries, and the interquartile range of salaries.

In this typical approach, the bulk of the extant literature implicitly assumes that any perception of "fariness" is derived from the unconditional comparison of players within a team. Thus a player who is paid, say, significantly less than his teammates may feel that he is being unfairly treated and as such may engage in activities that are harmful to team production (e.g., lack of cooperation, or sabotage). This approach, however, may be misleading. Lazear (1989) writes:

> it is far from obvious that a compressed salary structure is morale improving since better workers may feel disenchanted by this scheme. However, when workers' rewards are based on relative comparisons, salary compression reduces uncooperative behavior that is detrimental to the firm. Relative comparisons imply that some reference group must be selected. (p. 561)

The implication of the above quote is that relative wage comparisons should be made within particular groups. Or, put differently, relative wage comparisons should be done, *conditional on worker skills*. For example, in sports, a player may not necessarily feel underpaid relative to a teammate if the former is lesser skilled than the latter and the difference in their salaries is due to these skill differences. If, on the other hand, a player is paid significantly less than another *equally skilled* player, then the former may feel unfairly treated and may take actions that reduce team output. This approach of using conditionally skilled measures of salary dispersion is employed in the work on firm performance by Winter-Ebmer and Zweimüller (1999) and Lallemand et al. (2004) and in the sports economics literature by DeBrock et al. (2000). It is also the approach used in this study of salary dispersion and team production in the NHL.

Player Salaries and Team Production

In order to explore the effects of salary dispersion on team production in the NHL, I follow a similar methodology to Winter-Ebmer and Zweimüller (1999) and Lallemand et al. (2004) and employ a two-step estimation process. In the first step,

I estimate a wage equation for individual players based on various player skills and characteristics, as shown in equation (2):

$$W_{it} = \alpha_o + \alpha_1 X_{it} + \varepsilon_{it} \tag{2}$$

where W_{it} is the reported salary for player i in season t and X_{it} is a vector of player skills and characteristics and α_1 is a vector of coefficients to be estimated.[5] The residual term ε_{it}, representing the difference between the actual salary and the predicted salary based on X_{it}, is then used to construct *conditional* team salary dispersion measures. In this case, two conditional dispersion measures are computed: the within-team standard deviation and the within-team interquartile range.[6]

The second step is to use the above-noted measures of team salary dispersion in team performance regressions. Equation (3) shows the estimated model:

$$P_{jt} = \beta_o + \beta_1 X_{jt} + \beta_2 Z_{jt} + \beta_3 \sigma_{jt} + \gamma_j + v_{jt} \tag{3}$$

where P_{jt} is a measure of team j's performance during season t, X_{jt} is a vector of team player skills, Z_{jt} is a vector of team non-player inputs, σ_{jt} is the conditional team salary dispersions measures computed in step 1, γ_j is a team fixed-effect, and v_{jt} is the stochastic error term.[7]

Team performance, P_{jt}, is measured in two broad ways: regular season performance and post-season achievements. For regular season performance, three dependent variable measures are employed: win percent (*Win %*), points percent (*Points %*), and the difference between goals scored and goals given up during the season (*Goals Difference*).[8] For post-season performance three dummy variables are constructed, indicating whether or not a team advanced to the first, second, or third round in the playoffs. They are: *Playoffs, Conference Semi-Finals,* and *Conference Finals,* where in each case a value of one indicates that a team made it to the given level of playoffs in a season, zero if they did not.

Concerning the measurement of team skill inputs, which are contained in vector X_{jt}, two approaches have been considered in the extant sports economics literature. The most common approach uses career measures of individual players' skills to construct average measures across a team's players. A second approach uses a team's payroll, relative to the average payrolls of all teams in a given season, as a proxy for team talent. There are pros and cons to each approach and as such both will be employed when estimating equation (3).[9] In the former approach, the measures included in X_{jt} (and their expected effects on performance) are described below:[10]

- *Points per Game*, (where points are the sum of goals and assists). A positive coefficient is expected for this variable, as greater offensive skill should increase a team's performance.
- *Penalty Minutes per Game*. The expected sign for this coefficient is ambiguous. On the one hand, more penalty minutes may reduce team performance, as penalties leave the team at a disadvantage on the ice. On the other hand, more penalties may reflect a more aggressive style of play, which could improve a team's performance.

- *Plus/Minus per Game.* This measure is designed to capture "two-way" play. That is, it attempts to measure both the offensive *and* defensive skill of players. A player's plus/minus statistic is computed by awarding a player a +1 if he is on the ice when his team scores an even-strength goal. The player is awarded a -1 if he is on the ice when his team allows an even-strength goal. Other things equal, a positive coefficient is expected for this variable.
- *Save %.* This measure attempts to capture the skill level of goalies and is computed as the percentage of shots faced by the goalie that were stopped from entering the goal. A positive coefficient is expected for this variable.

In computing the above measures, I use beginning of season team rosters and include career measures of players up to, but not including the present season. The team's value for each skill is then computed by a weighted average of the individual players' career measures, where the weights are the players' share of their team's total minutes played in the current season. Further, in order to deal with the fact that some players move up and down between their NHL team and its minor league affiliate, I only include in the weighted calculations the skills of the top 18 skaters (i.e., non-goalies) in terms of total minutes played during a season.

Team inputs that are not specifically player skill measures, (Z_{jt}), include a measure of coaching ability—*Coach Win %*—equal to the head coach's career win percent (excluding the current season). Other things equal, a positive coefficient is expected, as better coaches should be able to increase a team's performance. Also included is a variable equal to the number of top draft picks playing on a team. This variable is used to consider the potential impact on team performance of highly talented younger players for whom careers statistics may not capture their value to the team. A positive coefficient is expected for this variable.[11]

The key explanatory variable for this chapter is the dispersions measure, σ_{jt}. As noted above, two measures are used to capture the conditional dispersion of team salaries. The first is simply the standard deviation (*SD*) of the residuals from step one produced by estimating equation (2) noted above. The second is the interquartile range (*IQR*) of the residuals from step one. A positive coefficient for either of these variables is taken to support the "tournament" hypothesis, a negative coefficient would be in support of the "fairness" hypothesis.[12]

Lastly, one control variable is included to account for some changes that occurred following the lock-out season of 2004–2005. This control variable—*Post-lockout*—takes a value of 1 if the season of the observation is after 2004–2005, zero otherwise.[13]

Data and Estimation Methodology

The data used to estimate equation (3) are from the 2001–2002 through the 2007–2008 NHL seasons for all 30 teams, excluding the 2004–2005 season, which was lost due to the player lockout. The resulting sample size is 180 team-season observations. Table 9.1 presents descriptive statistics and data sources.[14]

Table 9.1 Descriptive Statistics (n = 180)

Variable	Mean	Std. Dev.	Min	Max
Win %	0.468	0.100	0.232	0.707
Points %	0.543	0.091	0.329	0.756
Goals Difference	0	41.976	−113	107
Relative Payroll	1.000	0.281	0.390	1.739
Points Per Game	0.444	0.069	0.243	0.675
Penalty Minutes Per Game	0.778	0.134	0.485	1.223
Plus/Minus Per Game	−0.001	0.064	−0.205	0.169
Save %	0.908	0.008	0.886	0.935
Coach Win %	0.533	0.074	0.302	0.800
SD (salary residuals)	1.054	0.428	0.337	2.686
IQR (salary residuals)	1.009	0.356	0.327	2.064
Top Draft Players	0.261	0.489	0	2

Source: All data are from NHL.com, apart from relative payroll, which were found at usatoday.com.

As can be seen in Table 9.1, the two measures of conditional salary dispersion, *SD* and *IQR*, exhibit significant variation, and this should aid in identifying any salary dispersion effects on team production.

Regular season team performance is estimated with fixed effects and robust standard errors. For each of the three dependent variables described above, (*Win %*, *Points %*, and *Goals Difference*), I alternate between using team-averaged skill vectors and relative payroll (and its square) as team-level inputs. In addition, each regression is estimated using the two measures of conditional salary dispersion described earlier. As for post-season performance, a similar combination of regressions is estimated for the three dummy dependent variables (*Playoffs*, *Conference Semi-Finals*, and *Conference Finals*), described earlier. In this case a random effects probit estimation methodology is employed.

4. RESULTS

Regular season estimation results are presented in Tables 9.2 and 9.3, where *SD* is used as the measure of conditional salary dispersion in the former table, and *IQR* is used in the latter. Overall, these regressions perform fairly well as (within) R-squares range from 0.156 to 0.307, comparable to the results found by Frick et al. (2003) and Gomez (2002). The regressions using team-averaged skill vectors for

Table 9.2 Fixed-Effects Regressions of Regular Season Performance Using the Standard Deviation of Salary Residuals

Variables	(1) Win %	(2) Win %	(3) Points %	(4) Points %	(5) Goals Difference	(6) Goals Difference
Relative Payroll		0.384**		0.328**		179.1**
		(0.177)		(0.160)		(72.83)
Relative Payroll Squared		−0.111		−0.0845		−52.03
		(0.0808)		(0.0741)		(35.25)
Points Per Game	0.349**		0.319**		147.2***	
	(0.146)		(0.123)		(50.08)	
Penalty Minutes Per Game	−0.0304		−0.0182		4.170	
	(0.0691)		(0.0682)		(29.95)	
Plus/Minus Per Game	0.0444		0.121		39.82	
	(0.157)		(0.139)		(61.23)	
Save %	0.124		0.723		228.1	
	(0.846)		(0.714)		(305.3)	
Coach Win %	0.118	0.0597	0.0798	0.0410	44.55	22.36
	(0.104)	(0.101)	(0.103)	(0.0982)	(47.93)	(45.60)
SD (salary residuals)	−0.0138	−0.0481*	−0.0205	−0.0533**	−8.606	−23.83**
	(0.0284)	(0.0276)	(0.0270)	(0.0260)	(11.95)	(10.36)
Post–lockout	0.0585***	0.0406**	0.0183	0.00503	−4.253	−12.87*
	(0.0149)	(0.0177)	(0.0144)	(0.0164)	(6.445)	(7.468)
Top Draft Players	0.0355**	0.0498***	0.0447***	0.0567***	26.11***	32.28***
	(0.0159)	(0.0134)	(0.0135)	(0.0124)	(6.614)	(6.273)
Constant	0.137	0.189***	−0.283	0.323***	−295.0	−111.8***
	(0.772)	(0.0607)	(0.646)	(0.0618)	(279.4)	(31.82)
Observations	180	180	180	180	180	180
Teams	30	30	30	30	30	30
R-squared (within)	0.249	0.283	0.156	0.189	0.157	0.208

***$p<0.01$. **$p<0.05$. *$p<0.1$. Robust standard errors in parentheses.

inputs (see regressions (1), (3), and (5) in Tables 9.2 and 9.3), display very consistent results: team *Points per Game* and *Top Draft Picks* are positive, as expected, and significant in all regressions. At the same time, the measures *Plus/Minus per Game, Save %,* and *Coach Win %* have the predicted signs in all regressions, yet they are not statistically significant. The variable *Penalty Minutes per Game* does not display a consistent pattern of signs, and is not statistically significant in any of the regressions. Concerning the control variable *Post-lockout,* it is positive and

Table 9.3 Fixed-Effects Regressions of Regular Season Performance Using the Iterquartile Range of Salary Residuals

	(1)	(2)	(3)	(4)	(5)	(6)
					Goals	Goals
Variables	Win %	Win %	Points %	Points %	Difference	Difference
Relative Payroll		0.339*		0.277*		156.1**
		(0.173)		(0.162)		(72.49)
Relative Payroll		−0.0911		−0.0655		−44.50
Squared		(0.0832)		(0.0788)		(36.86)
Points Per Game	0.364***		0.320***		146.3***	
	(0.132)		(0.115)		(49.94)	
Penalty Minutes	−0.0291		−0.0180		4.136	
Per Game	(0.0675)		(0.0679)		(30.01)	
Plus/Minus Per	0.0786		0.150		50.27	
Game	(0.154)		(0.135)		(55.25)	
Save %	0.208		0.804		258.8	
	(0.809)		(0.681)		(282.7)	
Coach Win %	0.120	0.0654	0.0813	0.0497	45.17	27.01
	(0.107)	(0.109)	(0.105)	(0.107)	(48.27)	(47.46)
IQR (salary	−0.0366	−0.0625***	−0.0391*	−0.0620***	−15.27*	*25.33***
residuals)	(0.0235)	(0.0205)	(0.0219)	(0.0210)	(8.900)	(7.836)
Post-lockout	0.0568***	0.0422**	0.0169	0.00723	−4.780	−11.77
	(0.0151)	(0.0176)	(0.0147)	(0.0170)	(6.495)	(7.668)
Top Draft	0.0341**	0.0472***	0.0434***	0.0537***	25.65***	30.89***
Players	(0.0159)	(0.0137)	(0.0139)	(0.0127)	(6.714)	(6.061)
Constant	0.0761	0.222***	−0.339	0.355***	−316.1	−99.11***
	(0.737)	(0.661)	(0.612)	(0.0691)	(256.2)	(33.06)
Observations	180	180	180	180	180	180
Teams	30	30	30	30	30	30
R-squared (within)	0.266	0.307	0.178	0.212	0.173	0.223

***$p<0.01$. **$p<0.05$. *$p<0.1$. Robust standard errors in parentheses.

sometimes significant in regressions (1)–(4) in both tables; it is negative and usually not significant in regressions (5) and (6).[15]

The regressions using team relative payroll (and its square) are shown in regressions (2), (4), and (6) in Tables 9.2 and 9.3. These regressions are noticeably consistent with *Relative Payroll* having a positive, significant coefficient in all regressions indicating that relatively larger payrolls lead to greater team performance. The coefficient to *Relative Payroll Squared* is negative in all cases, consistent with a diminishing effect of relative payroll increases, but not statistically significant.

Turning to the key variable of interest, we see that in all twelve regressions for regular season performance, the coefficients to the conditional salary dispersions measures (*SD* and *IQR*) are negative. In the case of *SD*, as shown in Table 9.2, its coefficient is significant in regressions (2), (4), and (6). As for *IQR*, as Table 9.3 shows, its coefficient is significant in all but regression (1). Taken together, the results in Tables 9.2 and 9.3 provide compelling evidence that increased *conditional* salary dispersion has a negative impact on team performance, thus supporting the "fairness" model discussed earlier. Using the estimated results for equation (3) from Table 9.3, a one-unit increase in *IQR* is expected to reduce the team's *Points* % by approximately 3.91 percentage points, all else equal. This difference can be important if we consider the case of the 2007–2008 NHL season. At the end of the regular season, the Nashville Predators made it into the first round of the playoffs with a total of 91 points (or 0.555 percent of total possible points). The Vancouver Canucks, with 88 points (or 0.537 percent of total possible points), missed the playoffs. At the same time, the value for *IQR* was 0.658 for Nashville, while it was almost double the size (1.237) for Vancouver. Other things equal, this difference predicts a 2.26 percentage points disadvantage for Vancouver. In other words, if Vancouver would have had the same *IQR* value as Nashville the model predicts that Vancouver would have had approximately 92 points at the end of the regular season, one point greater than Nashville.[16]

Results for the post-season performance regressions appear in Tables 9.4 and 9.5. Similar to the regular season regressions, a total of twelve regressions were estimated: six using *SD* and six using *IQR*. In regressions using team-averaged skill vectors for player inputs, the results show that estimated coefficients to *Points per Game* and *Plus/Minus per Game* have the predicted (positive) sign and are significant in most regressions. The coefficients to *Penalty Minutes per Game* are consistently negative, indicating that teams that are penalty prone tend to suffer in the playoffs, particularly in the Conference Semi-Finals, when this coefficient achieves its greatest significance. Unlike the results for regular season performance, the coefficients to *Plus/Minus per Game* are positive and significant in all six regressions. This indicates that two-way play is particularly important for teams getting into and advancing in the playoffs. The coefficient to *Top Draft Players* is positive and significant only in the regressions for making it into the first round of playoffs, but not for later rounds. The implication is that teams with a stock of young, talented players stand a better chance of making the playoffs but, once in, these players have little impact on the team's performance (perhaps because most other teams in the playoffs also have a stock of young, talented players).

As for regressions using relative payrolls (and their square) as a proxy for team inputs, Tables 9.4 and 9.5 show similar results. Namely, relative payroll

Table 9.4 Random-Effects Probit Regressions of Playoff Performance Using the Standard Deviation of Salary Residuals

Variables	(1) Playoffs	(2) Playoffs	(3) Conf. Semi-Finals	(4) Conf. Semi-Finals	(5) Conf. Finals	(6) Conf. Finals
Relative Payroll		6.739**		−1.102		1.604
		(2.692)		(2.898)		(2.887)
Relative Payroll Squared		−2.038*		1.311		−0.318
		(1.230)		(1.300)		(1.301)
Points Per Game	3.647*		4.103*		3.257	
	(2.149)		(2.315)		(2.485)	
Penalty Minutes Per Game	−1.319		−1.869**		−1.596	
	(0.819)		(0.895)		(1.024)	
Plus/Minus Per Game	9.743***		5.611**		4.922*	
	(2.503)		(2.378)		(2.529)	
Save %	9.770		6.238		−18.76	
	(14.25)		(15.77)		(17.63)	
Coach Win %	0.585	1.249	−1.151	−0.705	0.266	1.071
	(1.642)	(1.812)	(1.790)	(1.963)	(2.031)	(2.065)
SD (salary residuals)	−0.390	−0.823**	−0.293	−0.710*	−0.656*	−0.738
	(0.297)	(0.397)	(0.315)	(0.428)	(0.368)	(0.467)
Post-lockout	−0.205	−0.388	−0.203	0.0263	−0.0490	−0.0904
	(0.222)	(0.252)	(0.238)	(0.269)	(0.266)	(0.286)
Top Draft Players	0.547**	0.608**	0.113	0.187	−0.196	−0.0540
	(0.233)	(0.270)	(0.257)	(0.296)	(0.297)	(0.286)
Constant	−9.279	−4.215***	−5.790	−0.0433	16.22	−2.181
	(12.87)	(1.486)	(14.26)	(1.679)	(15.92)	(1.693)
Observations	180	180	180	180	180	180
Teams	30	30	30	30	30	30

***$p<0.01$ **$p<0.05$ *$p<0.1$. Standard errors in parentheses.

has a positive, significant (and diminishing) effect on a team's ability to make the first round of playoffs. But beyond the first round, relative payroll has little explanatory power on a team's post-season success. This is likely due to the fact teams making it into the playoffs are already very similar in terms of relative payrolls.[17]

Turning again to the key variable of interest, we see very consistent results: the estimated coefficients for *SD* are all negative and are significant in three of the six

Table 9.5 Random-Effects Probit Regressions of Playoff Performance Using the Interquartile Range of Salary Residuals

Variables	(1) Playoffs	(2) Playoffs	(3) Conf. Semi-Finals	(4) Conf. Semi-Finals	(5) Conf. Finals	(6) Conf. Finals
Relative Payroll		6.640**		−2.057		0.939
		(2.746)		(3.066)		(2.875)
Relative Payroll Squared		−2.110*		1.773		0.0315
		(1.255)		(1.405)		(1.325)
Points Per Game	3.353*		4.143*		2.793	
	(2.014)		(2.164)		(2.384)	
Penalty Minutes Per Game	−1.456*		−1.940**		−1.744	
	(0.818)		(0.900)		(1.064)	
Plus/Minus Per Game	10.33***		6.216**		6.170**	
	(2.559)		(2.431)		(2.687)	
Save %	9.839		7.820		−18.80	
	(14.20)		(15.98)		(18.69)	
Coach Win %	0.720	1.529	−1.123	−0.848	0.290	1.305
	(1.669)	(1.894)	(1.786)	(2.015)	(2.026)	(2.003)
IQR (salary residuals)	−0.704**	−0.950**	−0.690**	−1.100**	−1304***	−1.254***
	(0.324)	(0.372)	(0.343)	(0.428)	(0.447)	(0.468)
Post-lockout	−0.258	−0.419	−0.251	0.0584	−0.103	−0.0687
	(0.226)	(0.258)	(0.242)	(0.276)	(0.274)	(0.287)
Top Draft Players	0.576**	0.605**	0.130	0.174	−0.128	−0.0135
	(0.234)	(0.274)	(0.255)	(0.302)	(0.294)	(0.273)
Constant	−8.862	−4.077***	−6.811	0.793	17.13	−1.582
	(12.82)	(1.561)	(14.43)	(1.813)	(16.90)	(1.694)
Observations	180	180	180	180	180	180
Teams	30	30	30	30	30	30

***p<0.01 **p<0.05 *p<0.1. Standard errors in parentheses.

regressions shown in Table 9.4. In Table 9.5 we see an even stronger result for *IQR* where all six coefficients are negative and highly significant. These results, like those for regular season performance, provide strong support for the "fairness" model over the "tournament" model. Using the results for equation (1) in Table 9.5, the marginal effect for *IQR* is −0.279, thus a one unit increase in *IQR* is expected to reduce a team's probability of making the playoffs by approximately 0.28, other things equal.

5. SUMMARY AND CONCLUSIONS

The topic of how various payment schemes affect production is interesting as it appeals to some very basic human emotions: inspiration and a sense of fairness. The "tournament" model, where greater performance is inspired by greater rewards, suggests that a wider dispersion in compensation schemes will maximize performance. The "fairness" model, on the other hand, argues that a wider spread in compensation may lead workers to feel as though they are not being compensated fairly in comparison to their peers. The expected result in this case is for reduced individual effort and perhaps a compromising of team efforts (if production occurs in a team setting). This chapter has contributed to the extant literature in two primary ways. First, previous studies outside the realm of sports have been hampered by data limitations on output measures and individual worker characteristics. In the context of sports markets, however, detailed, accurate data on firms (teams) and workers (players) are prevalent and this provides for a careful test of the "tournament" versus "fairness" models.

Second, previous efforts to test these two models (both within and outside of sports) have largely focused on *unconditional* measures of salary dispersion where dispersion measures are computed without taking into consideration the differences across workers within a firm. This study joins the very few (and the first for the NHL) that have employed *conditional* salary dispersion measures. The reasoning behind this approach is intuitive: a worker (or player), might not object to a coworker (teammate) earning more money than himself if the co-worker (or teammate) possesses greater skill. However, the same worker (or player) may feel unfairly treated if an equally skilled coworker (or teammate) is paid considerably more.

The empirical results contained in this paper clearly and strongly support the "fairness" model when using conditional salary dispersion measures. In *all* 24 regressions presented in Tables 9.2 through 9.5, the estimated coefficient for the conditional salary dispersion measures are negative; 17 of these 24 estimated coefficients are statistically significant at traditional significance levels. As for whether conditioning on player characteristics is important, regressions using the simple, unconditional standard deviation and interquartile range for player salaries produced highly consistent results as well: *zero* out of 24 estimated coefficients were statistically significant.[18]

As for future research, several ideas come to mind. First, it would be interesting to see if the approach employed in this paper would produce similar results in other sports that have a strong reliance on team play (e.g., basketball). Second, it would be interesting to see if conditional salary dispersion measures can significantly explain *individual* performance differences. In this case one could also explore the possibility of asymmetric effects in which those who are underpaid would react differently to a given conditional salary dispersion from those who are overpaid. These topics are left for future work.

NOTES

1 See Lallemand et al. (2004) for a more detailed discussion of the theory behind the "tournament" and "fairness" models, as well as previous research that tests these hypotheses.

2 Another mechanism that may lead to reduced firm output in the presence of tournament-style compensation schemes is the possibility of rent-seeking activity (Milgrom 1988; Milgrom and Roberts, 1990). That is, workers may employ non-productive activities with an eye toward winning favor from managers in the form of wage increases or promotions. Compressed wage structures may lessen this possibility.

3 They employ two estimation approaches. First they use a simple OLS approach. Second, in an attempt to deal with the likely simultaneity problem that may exist between profits and wage dispersion, they use a two-stage least-squares estimation to instrument firm wage dispersion.

4 In cases where output is difficult to measure various proxies have been used. For example Lallemand et al. (2004) work with data from 397 Belgian firms and use profits per employee as a measure of the firms' performance. As they note using this measure as the dependent variable obviously brings up a simultaneity problems. Specifically, firms with greater dispersion may, say, witness greater profits per employee (supporting the "tournament" model). Yet, greater profits per employee may allow firms to offer even greater salary dispersion. Lallemand et al. (2004) handle this potential problem with a simultaneous equations approach.

5 The variables used to predict player salaries in equation (2) are described in Appendix A.

6 The approach here differs slightly from Winter-Ebmer and Zweimüller (1999) and Lallemand et al. (2004). In their papers the first step is accomplished by estimating separate wage equations by firm. This approach requires a restriction that each firm employ a relatively large number of employees (a restriction of 20 or more employees is used in the former study, and 200 or more in the latter) in order to produce credible by-firm regression results. In the case of the NHL, most teams employ approximately 20 full-time players. Thus, by-team regressions would not be reasonable in this case and as such the pooled data set is used to estimate equation (2). This approach, in fact, may be quite reasonable given that, unlike workers in private industries, player performance and compensation data are publicly available to all players.

7 Year dummies were also included in the regressions. They were, however, dropped as they turned out to be statistically insignificant and the estimated coefficients of the key variable of interest, measures of salary dispersion, were largely unaffected.

8 For the entire period covered by the data set used in this chapter, teams played 82 regular season games. *Win %* is simply computed as the sum of wins/82. Concerning *Points %*, a team is awarded two points for a win, one for a tie, and zero for a loss in regulation time. Thus *Points %* is computed as the sum of regular season points/164.

9 See Kahane, Longley, and Simmons (forthcoming) and Kahane (2005) for brief discussions of the pros and cons of using team-averaged skill vectors versus relative payrolls as proxies for team skill inputs.

10 The estimated model employed here follows that of Kahane, Longley, and Simmons (forthcoming) closely, with the exception of the salary dispersion measure.

11 Top draft picks are computed from the years 1994 to 2000 and for players who have not been traded more than once and who played in at least half the team's games that year. It is this group of players that are likely to be young, high-impact players.

12 An alternative approach for computing the conditional dispersion of salaries was also attempted. In this alternative approach I computed the Gini index for actual and predicted team salaries (using equation (2) to get the predicted results). I then computed the difference of the predicted and the actual Gini measures ("Δ Gini"). A positive coefficient for Δ Gini would be in support of the 'tournament' model, a negative coefficient would be in support of the "fairness" model. In the twelve regressions run, all had negative coefficients supporting the "fairness" model, but only two were statistically significant (the regular season regression for Win % and post-season regression for Playoffs). This alternative model's fit, however, was inferior to one employed in this chapter.

13 See Kahane, Longley, and Simmons (forthcoming) for a greater discussion of the changes that occurred in the NHL following the 2004–2005 season-long lockout.

14 Appendix A contains the description of the model used to estimate equation (2) and to produce the residuals used in computing the conditional dispersion measures for team salaries.

15 While it is not clear that this control variable should necessarily have a positive effect on winning or points percentage, the negative signs for the Goals Difference regressions are not entirely unexpected. Following the 2004–2005 lockout, the NHL implemented a player and team salary cap. The regression results, although statistically weak, seem to indicate that competitive balance in the NHL was increased as the goal differential declined in the post-lockout period.

16 The computation is: $(0.5366 + 0.0226)*164 = 91.709$.

17 A difference in means test for relative payroll rejects the null hypothesis (no difference in means) when comparing teams not in the playoffs to teams in the playoffs (the latter having a significantly greater value than the former). However, a difference in means test for relative payroll for teams making into the playoffs but not advancing versus those that do advance did not reject the null hypothesis. In other words, relative payrolls matter when it comes to making the first round of playoffs, but not beyond that.

18 These results are available upon request from the author.

REFERENCES

Akerlof, George A., and Janet L. Yellen (1988). Fairness and unemployment. American Economic Review, 78: 44–49.

Akerlof, George A. and Janet L. Yellen (1990). The fair wage-effort hypothesis and unemployment. Quarterly Journal of Economics, 105: 255–283.

Berri, David J. and R. Todd Jewell (2004). Wage inequality and firm performance: Professional basketball's natural experiment. Atlantic Economic Journal, 32: 130–139.

Bloom, Matt (1999). The performance effects of pay dispersion on individuals and organizations. Academy of Management Journal, 42: 25–40.

Cowherd, Douglas M., and David I. Levine (1992). Product quality and pay equity between lower-level employees and top management: An investigation of distributive justice theory. Administrative Science Quarterly, 37: 302–320.

DeBrock, Lawrence, Wallace Hendricks, and Roger Koenker (2004). Pay and performance: The impact of salary distribution on firm level outcomes in baseball. *Journal of Sports Economics*, 5: 243–261.

Depken, Craig A. (2000). Wage disparity and team productivity: Evidence from Major League Baseball. *Economic Letters*, 67: 87–92.

Ehrenberg, R., and Bognanno, M. (1990a). Do tournaments have incentive effects? *Journal of Political Economy*, 98: 1307–1324.

Ehrenberg, R., and Bognanno, M. (1990b). The incentive effects of tournaments revisited: Evidence from the European PGA Tour. *Industrial and Labor Relations Review*, 43: 74S–88S.

Frick, Bernd, Joachim Prinz, and Karina Winkelmann (2003). Pay inequalities and team performance: Empirical evidence from the North American Major Leagues. *International Journal of Manpower*, 24: 472–488.

Gomez, Rafael (2002). Salary compression and team performance: Evidence from the National Hockey League. *Zeitschrift für Betriebswirtschaf: Ergänzungsheft 'Sportökonomie,'* 72: 203–220.

Kahane, Leo H. (2005). Production efficiency and discriminatory hiring practices in the National Hockey League: A stochastic frontier approach. *Review of Industrial Organization*, 27: 47–71.

Kahane, Leo, Neil Longley, and Rob Simmons (forthcoming). The effects of coworker heterogeneity on firm-level output: Assessing the impacts of cultural and language diversity in the National Hockey League. *Review of Economics and Statistics*.

Lallemand, Theirry, Robert Plassman, and François Rycx (2004). Intra-firm wage dispersion and firm performance: Evidence from linked employer-employee data. *Kyklos*, 57: 533–558.

Lazear, Edward P. (1989). Pay equality and industrial politics. *Journal of Political Economy*, 97: 561–580.

Lazear, Edward P., and Sherwin Rosen (1981). Rank-order tournaments as optimum labor contracts. *Journal of Political Economy*, 89: 841–864.

Levine, David I. (1991). Cohesiveness, productivity and wage dispersion. *Journal of Economic Behavior and Organization*, 15: 237–255.

Maloney, Michael T., and Robert E. McCormick (2000). The response of workers to wages in tournaments: Evidence from foot races. *Journal of Sports Economics*, 1: 99–123.

Milgrom, Paul R. (1988). Employment contract, influence activities, and efficient organisation design. *Journal of Political Economy*, 96: 42–60.

Milgrom, Paul, and John Roberts (1990). The efficiency of equity in organisational decision processes. *American Economic Review: Papers and Proceedings*, 80: 154–159.

Mondello, Mike, and Joel Maxcy (2009). The impact of salary dispersion and performance bonuses in NFL organziations. *Mangement Decision*, 47: 110–123.

Pfeffer, Jeffrey, and Nancy Langton (1993). The effect of wage dispersion on satisfaction, productivity, and working collaboratively: Evidence from college and university faculty. *Administrative Science Quarterly*, 38: 382–407.

Winter-Ebmer, Rudolf, and Josef Zweimüller (1999). Intra-firm wage dispersion and firm performance. *Kyklos*, 52: 555–572.

Appendix A: Estimation of Equation (2)

The following model was used in step one for estimating individual player salaries and the associated salary residuals:

Salary = f(Right Wing, Left Wing, Defense, Age, Age Squared, Career Games, Career Games Squared, Career Goals per Game, Career Assists per Game, Career Penalty Minutes per Game, Career Plus/Minus per Game, CZE/SVK, SWE, FIN, RUS, OTHER, Draft Pick, Number of Teams, Height, Weight)

where:

Salary is real salary in millions of 2007 dollars.

Right Wing, Left Wing, and *Defense* are dummy variables for a player's position (the omitted case being center).

Age and *Age Squared* is a player's age and its squared value.

Career Games and *Career Games Squared* are a player's career games played (excluding the current season) and its squared value.

Career Goals per Game is a players career, regular season goals scored per game (excluding the current season).

Career Assists per Game is a players career, regular season assists per game (excluding the current season).

Career Penalty Minutes per Game is a players career, regular season penalty minutes per game (excluding the current season).

Career Plus/Minus per Game is a players career, regular season plus/minus value per game (excluding the current season).

CZE/SVK, SWE, FIN, RUS, OTHER are dummy variables for the country of origin of a player. They take a value of one if a player is from the specified country, zero otherwise. The omitted category is USA/Canada.

Draft Pick is the player's draft pick number.

Number of Teams is the number of teams on which the player has played.

Height and *Weight* are the player's height (in inches) and weight (in pounds).

This first step regression was estimated using data for all skaters (i.e., excluding goalies). Rookies were excluded in this regression since there are no career performance measures for them. Furthermore, it seems reasonable to exclude rookie salaries from the dispersion measure since rookies are generally paid less (given their abilities are relatively unknown) and as such they would not serve as a good comparison group for non-rookie salaries. The results of this first step regression are presented in Table A9.1. Overall the regression performs well, as the R-squared is about 64 percent. Most of the estimated coefficients are significant and having the expected signs.

Table A9.1 Estimation of Individual Player Salaries

VARIABLES	Salary (millions of 2007 dollars)
Right Wing	−0.0722 (0.0651)
Left Wing	−0.150** (0.0656)
Defense	0.413*** (0.0621)
Age	0.716*** (0.0703)
Age Squared	−0.0141*** (0.00123)
Career Games	0.00477*** (0.000280)
Career Games Squared	−4.49e-06*** (2344e-07)
Career Goals Per Game	0.00333*** (0.000499)
Career Assists Per Game	0.00839*** (0.000424)
Career Penalty Minutes Per Game	0.000684*** (8.03e-05)
Career Plus/Minus Per Game	0.00441*** (0.000474)
CZE_SVK	0.106 (0.0683)
SWE	0.241*** (0.0877)
FIN	0.137 (0.110)
RUS	0.230** (0.0914)
Other	0.0192 (0.101)
Draft Pick	−0.00112*** (0.000323)
Number of Teams	−0.201*** (0.0192)
Height	0.0125 (0.0162)
Weight	−0.000290 (0.00227)
Constant	−9.529*** (1.388)
Observations	3198
R-squared	0.636
Standard errors in parentheses	***p<0.01 **p<0.05 *p<0.1

## PART III

ILLUSTRATIONS OF ECONOMETRIC METHODS

## CHAPTER 10

TRAVEL AND POPULATION ISSUES IN MODELING ATTENDANCE DEMAND

DAVID FORREST

1. Introduction

It could fairly be argued that matters geographic lie, or should lie, at the heart of sports economics. After all, the most influential and enduring theoretical apparatus in the field, the two-team league model first proposed by El-Hodiri and Quirk (1971), is driven by an assumption that clubs differ in terms of market size. The club with the bigger market has the greater incentive to hire talent because, for it, increased playing success has a larger payoff in terms of marginal box office and other revenue. This greater incentive is the source of the competitive imbalance that is one of the most studied phenomena in the academic study of sports leagues. Of course, this theoretical framework can be neither operationalized nor tested without careful consideration of how to measure market size (which is often identified with population size, though the composition of that population will also play a role). Further, equally careful account should be taken of travel costs because a given population will yield fewer spectators the more costly it is for them to travel to the stadium. Thus it might be expected that population and travel cost issues would play a prominent role in the specification of, in particular, econometric models of attendance demand. However, this has been far from the case until recently, and the author's contention in this chapter is that, even where relevant variables have been included, there has typically been misspecification.

The relative neglect of market size in empirical work is perhaps related to a difficulty in obtaining sensible proxies. For example, the Census population of the metropolitan area in which a club is located has been employed (by, among others, Schmidt and Berri, 2001, in the United States, and Falter and Perignon, 2000, for France) to represent market size in models to account for attendance; but there is a degree of arbitrariness in the definition of an area for Census purposes and, further, if only because different cities have to accommodate different total numbers of people, there will be differences in how far the boundaries reach. A larger population in a physically more extensive city will face higher average costs in reaching any point in the metropolitan area, such as a stadium. To some extent this will weaken correlation between effective market size and metropolitan population.

An underlying theme of this chapter is that the popularization of geographic information systems (GIS) in the last decade has changed the possibilities such that it is now much more feasible than before for attendance modeling to take market size as seriously as it needs to do. For instance, in both the United States and the United Kingdom, it has become routine, thanks to easily available software, to be able to define any shape and size of area around a given point (such as a stadium) and access detailed Census data on its population and socioeconomic characteristics. For example, clubs could be systematically compared in terms of the size of population, and its ethnic makeup, at distances from the stadium of 0–1 mile, 1–2 miles, and so on. This would make for much more precise measurement of market size, allowing more reliable coefficient estimates on both market size itself and on other covariates included in the specification. Again, new possibilities are opened up for more micro-based demand studies since knowledge of the zip or post codes of ticket purchasers allows (through GIS) a picture to be built up of the spatial distribution of attendees at a stadium. This could be used to define catchment areas or, for example, as is done in Feehan et al. (2003), to answer questions related to the social class profile of a club's audience.

This chapter reviews how travel cost and population have been treated in the attendance demand literature and argues that those who have exploited GIS have succeeded in offering new insights in sports economics. It draws freely on work I have done over the last ten years with various combinations of co-authors Babatunde Buraimo, Patrick Feehan and Rob Simmons, who have therefore considerably influenced what appears here (but who of course are not responsible for any errors or eccentricities in the text).

2. THE ROLE OF PRICE: MEASURING THE DEMAND CURVE

Archetypical demand functions in economics specify quantity as dependent on the price of the good and on other factors such as the population size, its income level and tastes, and the prices of substitutes and complements. Particular attention is customarily paid to the relationship between quantity and own-price (with the other elements, termed the conditions of demand, held constant) since this defines the demand curve from which, for example, elasticity may be calculated. Sports studies adopt this broad approach and the structure of the chapter is to examine *first* the role of price in attendance demand (where travel cost merits special attention) and *then* the impact of other factors (including market size and others that might be wrongly assessed if market size is not treated appropriately).

Demand Elasticity

A large number of studies, dating from the earliest days of sports economics as a distinct branch of the discipline, have sought to estimate a demand curve and to use it to estimate elasticity. Noll (1974) proposed that such elasticity estimates could be useful not only for the usual reasons relevant in any market but also to settle a controversy in the emerging subdiscipline of sports economics: was the motivation of clubs better characterized as maximizing profit (as assumed in the model of the two-team league) or as providing a public service? This could potentially be answered by a reliable estimation of elasticity. All clubs enjoy a degree of monopoly power (i.e., they can set price), whether it derives from allocation of exclusive territorial rights (as is typical in American sports) or simply because there are fans the strength of whose affinity with a club makes other sports products highly imperfect substitutes. It is a well-known proposition, taught even to beginning students of microeconomics, that a profit-maximizing monopolist will price on the elastic part of the demand curve (or at the point of unitary elasticity in the case where all costs are fixed). Because, at least in the short run, most of their costs are fixed, and extra patrons to a stadium appear to impose low marginal costs, sports clubs might be expected to select a price-quantity point at which demand is only "slightly" more elastic than –1 (but perhaps a lot more elastic than this if the stadium would sell out at the price where elasticity is unitary). Any other result from estimation of elasticity at current price would be inconsistent with profit maximization (and, it could be added, also with win maximization since extra revenue from raising price to the level corresponding to unitary elasticity could be employed to hire more playing talent).

The literature in fact is remarkably consistent in delivering that other result. Fort (2006, p. 701) tabulated findings from 24 studies (the largest number of which related to Major League Baseball or to football in England) of which twenty reported unambiguously inelastic estimates. Borland and Macdonald (2003) reviewed a slightly different set of twenty studies and likewise reported a consensus (from seventeen of them) that demand (at observed prices) was inelastic. Indeed, across all these studies, the estimate of elasticity was most typically in the range of 0 to −0.5, that is, demand was highly inelastic and sports clubs therefore appeared typically to be very far from (at least short-run) profit (or win) maximization.

That demand was inelastic became one of the best-known stylized facts in sports economics and was regarded in the literature as an anomaly to be resolved. One approach was to suggest alibis that might explain that, after all, inelastic demand could be consistent with profit maximization. For example, Marburger (1997) and Krautmann and Berri (2007) recognized that clubs are multi-product firms that sell not only tickets but also services such as parking, refreshments, and souvenirs. In principle, if persuading additional customers to attend a match affords the club the opportunity to sell them these complementary goods, it could be profit maximizing to price on the inelastic segment of the ticket-demand curve. While the argument is unquestionably valid, it might be noted (Simmons, 2006) that the responsiveness of sales of complements would have to be very high to drive the profit-maximizing ticket price so far into inelastic territory as is typically observed. Further, some of the lowest elasticity estimates, such as −0.08 from Dobson and Goddard (1995), relate to data periods when the sport concerned offered negligible opportunities to spend extra money once beyond the turnstiles.

Feehan (2006) raised the possibility that clubs choose inelastic points on their demand curves because of "queue" and "crowding in" effects. The queue effect is based on the notion that heavily subscribed events (similar to the fully booked restaurants in Becker, 1991) attract attention by virtue of their visible popularity, and this acts as a signal of quality that maintains high demand in the long run. The crowding in effect focuses on the atmosphere in the stadium, which may be enhanced by a large attendance and without which there might be a falling away in interest from both the live and television audiences.

While alibis such as these, though ad hoc, have some degree of plausibility, there is another possible explanation for finding surprisingly low estimates of elasticity and that is that they are wrong and derive from misspecification of the demand function in econometric analysis, whether this employs time series, cross–sectional, or panel data. It is argued here that failure to account properly for travel costs and population size is capable of systematically biasing downward estimates of elasticity and that alternative methodology placing travel cost at center stage might overcome the problems and then generate very different results.

Early studies tended to be based on time series analysis. Three of note were on English football. Bird (1982) modeled aggregate seasonal total attendance for each division for a period of 32 years. Dobson and Goddard (1995) disaggregated to club level, covering 67 seasons of total seasonal attendance at each of 94 clubs. Simmons (1996) analyzed average attendance per match for twenty top tier clubs, employing 44 annual observations. The long data periods chosen for each of these analyses were presumably necessary to obtain sufficient variation in (real) price to permit estimation of demand curves; but they bring problems as it is difficult to control for the multiple changes in tastes that might be expected to have occurred over such lengthy spans of time. Contemporaries will have been able to sense these changes and, in the absence of a measure of tastes, price would then become endogenous if the football industry, for example, raised ticket prices as football improved its popularity and more spectators presented themselves at matches. Such endogeneity would bias elasticity estimates downward.

Another source of potential bias is that, of the three studies, all but the first ignored costs of travel to a match. This leads to a misspecification of the demand function to be estimated because quantity demanded is determined by consumer decisions, which will be influenced by price from the consumer perspective (this will include travel costs to the match, both direct and time costs, as well as the fee for admission), whereas the price on the right-hand side is producer (i.e., ticket) price. Unless the set of regressors is augmented by a measure of travel costs, omitted variable bias will result if there is any correlation between the explanatory variables and travel cost. It is difficult to assess even the direction of change of average travel costs over these periods to the extent that there is no annual (or indeed any) information on, for instance, how far spectators typically traveled and with what modal split in terms of means of transport. But suppose the trend increase in (real) ticket prices had been accompanied by a trend decrease in the (real) cost of travel as transport technology improved and ever greater numbers had access to a car. Such a negative correlation would generate downward bias in the estimate of the responsiveness of attendance to ticket price.

Bird (1982) was the exception in this first generation of demand studies in that he did recognize that travel costs should be treated as part of the total cost, what is now termed the generalized cost, of consuming the product. Accordingly, he defined his price variable as $(P + \gamma Q)$ where P was an index of (real) ticket prices, Q was an index of (real) vehicular running costs, and γ was an additional parameter to be estimated by the model. Unfortunately, this adaptation solved little as γ was constant by design and therefore variations in total travel cost associated with increasing traffic speeds (as roads were improved) and lengthening journey distances (as housing decentralized) could play no role in the estimation.[1]

There are plainly problems with reliance on time series analysis. However, they are not removed by adopting a cross-section methodology or even the recently highly popular panel data approach (where the unit of observation is the match played by home club i at time t and estimation is by a fixed-effects model). Again, endogeneity is the bête noir, since clubs with large markets are likely to be able and likely actually to choose to charge higher prices and still have higher observed attendances, once again masking consumers' sensitivity to changes in ticket price. It is, of course, not possible to control for market size if it is constant (as it will be over short runs of time) and, with the fixed-effect estimator, the influence of market size could not be separated out from that of unobserved heterogeneity across clubs, even if it could be measured with adequate precision. Of course, this particular problem could be addressed by instrumenting ticket price, but it is unclear what variable might plausibly influence price but not (directly) quantity.

Given these problems, Forrest et al. (2002) and Hakes et al. (2011) proposed that it would be useful to apply the Travel Cost Method (TCM) in the context of modeling sports attendance demand and estimating elasticity. The technique had previously been widely employed in the literature on environmental amenities and countryside recreation in order to derive demand curves that could then be used to estimate consumer surplus.[2] It was designed to permit a demand curve to be estimated even where no variation in admission price was observed (for example, use of a country park may be free).

Although an entry fee, zero or positive, may be the same for all attendees, use of a country (or indeed ball) park in fact imposes different generalized costs on different groups of users because they will, depending on residential location, have to spend different amounts of money and time on the journey to reach it. By observing how much propensity to attend falls off as potential users face higher travel costs (i.e., as distance from the site increases), the slope of the demand curve is revealed. If individuals are utility maximizing, they will react in the same way to a unit change in any component of generalized (i.e., total) cost: they should therefore react to a $1 change in ticket price in exactly the same way as they respond to a $1 change in travel cost. Knowledge of the slope of a demand curve in travel cost-attendance or generalized cost-attendance space thus enables calculation of elasticity of demand with respect to ticket price.

The informational requirements of TCM are considerable to the extent that the spatial distribution of attendees and their frequency of attendance need to be ascertained (this is commonly achieved by survey method). There then has to be sufficiently reliable information on the direct and time costs of travel to the park from various distances such that a reliable estimate can be made of the generalized cost faced by potential users at each location in the catchment area.

But, if the method is costly in terms of the amount of information to be collected, its benefits appear particularly strong in the context of estimating attendance demand models. Estimates relate to patterns in attendance at a single point in time such that increases or decreases in the popularity of a sport over time are not able to generate the problems found in time series analysis. Endogeneity of price, acknowledged to be a serious problem in both time series and conventional cross-sectional studies, is avoided since clubs do not determine the travel cost component of the generalized cost faced by each household.[3] Instruments for price are therefore not required.

The Travel Cost Method: Application to English Football

To illustrate the steps required in an application of TCM, and the sports-specific issues that need to be taken into account, the analysis in Forrest et al. (2002) is now reviewed. The authors employed data from a preexisting consumer survey conducted annually on behalf of the FA Premier League. The sample was drawn from box office records at each member club regarding who had purchased a ticket. Questionnaires were administered by mail and a response rate of 35 percent was obtained, making 20,479 returns (across the twenty clubs) available for analysis.

For each of the twenty clubs, a similar procedure was followed. A series of concentric zones was defined around the stadium. Each respondent had been asked his or her postcode, the distance traveled to a home game, and the number of home fixtures attended in the season. With the aid of this information and GIS software, the total of all matches attended by members of the sample could be allocated across the concentric zones. The total number of seats sold in the season for the club (less those purchased for the away supporters' section) was then used to gross up the ticket purchases made by respondents to the survey to construct, for each zone, an estimate of the number of attendances per 1,000 population[4] from that zone. That was the measure of quantity demanded in the attendance model.

The focus explanatory variable was the generalized cost of attendance from the mid-point of the zone. This has three components. The first is the ticket price.[5] The second is the transport cost. The third is the time cost of the journey.

Regarding transport cost, we calculated the round-trip cost of a car journey to the stadium from the zone (assuming car costs were spread across two people) and the round trip cost of going by public transportation. Information was available from the survey on the proportions of attendances by private and public transportation, and these were used to weight the two estimates of journey cost to create a single measure. The calculations were further informed by Department of Transport data on both the running costs of cars and average bus fares for journeys of different lengths. Concessionary fares were taken into account according to the number of children and retirees estimated to attend from each zone. For London, London Transport data on underground railway costs was substituted for that on bus fares. A number of other complexities arose, but this description illustrates that several decisions on valuation have to be made, and thus the methodology calls for a battery of robustness tests to be applied to the results. For our lead results, we consistently adopted conservative assumptions that would tend to lower the estimated degree of elasticity.

The next step was to calculate time costs, which will again vary according to whether a car or public transportation is employed for the journey. The per mile travel time should also be different in the exercise for each different club because of heterogeneity across the country in quality of roads and amount of congestion. The authors made the most appropriate assumptions they could, guided by Department of Transport data on traffic speeds by region and by privately obtained information on bus times. They then converted all estimates of journey times to money terms using the central government's official valuation of non-work time (itself based on results from large-scale stated and revealed preference studies of the amounts that people are willing to pay to save one unit of time).

Following this non-trivial exercise, we had, for each zone, a figure for the generalized cost of one attendance at a match. This is the price term in our specification designed to account for variation between zones in propensity to buy tickets. It is of interest that, for many supporters, the travel cost of attendance easily dominated the ticket cost component. This was true also among Major League Baseball attendees studied in a second TCM study (Hakes et al., 2011) reviewed below. It underlines the potential for serious bias to be present in conventional sports demand studies where travel cost is an omitted variable. Travel cost is actually more relevant than ticket price to determining behavior of potential consumers.

The next step was to select appropriate control variables to be included in the demand model. Demand in most economic analysis is defined as dependent on own price (our generalized cost measure), prices of substitutes (and complements), income, and tastes. Prices of substitutes proved too hard to establish since, as is usual in sports studies, it was not clear what the substitutes were. England is a small country with 92 professional football clubs, so supporters can typically choose between several. Prices of substitutes were therefore omitted from the model, but the authors provided detailed discussion of the likely direction of bias this might impart to their results. Income by zone could not be calculated because the British Census does not ask an income question. However, from Census data, it was possible to include a conventional and plausible proxy in the form of a social class measure derived from the occupation of household heads in the Census.

Particularly in a small and relatively culturally homogenous country, tastes could be safely omitted from many empirical demand functions estimated by cross-sectional analysis where the unit of analysis is defined spatially. But this is not likely to be the case when modeling demand for attendance at a particular football club. Football clubs provide a sense of identity for many supporters and this is bound up with a sense of place. Most fans attach themselves to a club that bears the name of the town where they live and propensity to attend falls off with distance from that town, not only because of steeper travel costs but also partly because the degree of affinity felt with the club becomes typically less and less.[6] If this is not controlled for, the influence of cost on propensity to attend will be overestimated, and consequently elasticity will be overestimated. Fortunately, answers to a question in the survey allowed a measure of enthusiasm for the club in a particular zone to be constructed: the authors used an estimate of the proportion of the zonal population that traveled with the team to away games at least three times per season.

The final specification therefore made attendances per unit of population from zone i a function of the generalized cost of attendance from zone i, the proportion of the population in zone i with heads of household in professional, managerial, or technical jobs and the "affinity" variable just discussed. The last played its expected role, and social class was positive and significant in the results for many clubs. But the focus here is on the price variable. For each club the coefficient estimate on generalized cost was used as an input to calculate ticket price elasticity of demand as measured at the current average ticket price observed at that club.

With a set of very conservative assumptions designed to yield lower bound elasticity values, demand was found to be less elastic than −0.6 at six of twenty clubs. These all shared a common geographic characteristic: four are in London and the other two (whose stadia are almost adjacent) are in Liverpool. Where clubs are close together, it must be the case that, as the distance increases, the cost of attendance at the subject club increases but so too does the cost of attendance at nearby stadia that provide obvious substitute goods. Thus own price will be positively correlated with prices of substitutes. The omission of the latter from the specification of demand will then bias the coefficient estimate on own price downward, leading to understatement of elasticity. There is no obvious solution to this problem. To be sure, GIS permit the measurement of distance to rival stadia but the costs of attending either stadium would be collinear where clubs coexisted near each other. The problem would limit the applicability of the TCM in sports and countries where clubs cluster together. For example, it would be impractical in the context of Australian Rules football because stadium sharing is normal. On the other hand, most American major league franchises have no rivals in the sport in the same region, and there might be no problem at all in omitting a price of substitutes term from the specification.

Among the remaining fourteen clubs, the median elasticity reported by Forrest et al. (2002) was –1.04. Three of the four with highest estimated elasticity were the three in the division that regularly sold out the stadium. Both these findings are highly consistent with profit-maximizing behavior. The TCM avoids important flaws in traditional modeling techniques and appears to resolve the anomaly represented by very low measured elasticity. Of course, it is only one study, but its finding presented a challenge to the truth of a puzzling stylized fact from sports. Fort (2006, p. 703) commented that "it would be interesting to see whether the Forrest et al. results generalise to other leagues." Perhaps because of the high informational requirements of TCM, there has however been only one follow-up study, Hakes et al. (2011), which is now reviewed.

The Travel Cost Method: Application to Major League Baseball

Hakes et al. (2011) followed a similar approach to Forrrest et al. (2002) and with similar results. Rather than provide another detailed account of the methodology, the text below draws attention to points of contrast between the two articles because these highlight some key issues in how TCM may be applied to sport.

(1) Hakes et al. use box office data from one club, the Atlanta Braves, rather than survey data from twenty clubs. Clearly analyzing one rather than twenty cases makes it less convincing that findings can be generalized; but what is feasible is dictated by availability of data. The use of information on the zip codes of those purchasing at the box office avoids risks of response bias inherent in a survey approach. On the other hand, a survey presents the opportunity to ask ancillary

questions, such as the number of attendees who share a car trip to the game, and answers can impart greater precision to estimates of travel cost per mile. A survey may also identify more accurately from where the journey to the stadium begins (zip codes held in box office records sometimes relate to business addresses).

(2) Hakes et al. analyze sales of season tickets rather than number of matches attended. This is legitimate, but any future study could improve on the two already presented by including in the model a consideration of which fans choose season over single tickets. Distance from the stadium will surely play a role in this decision and this introduces an element of endogeneity into the TCM.

(3) Hakes et al. adopt a much smaller unit of observation than Forrest et al., namely an individual zip code. Consequently there are many zones with zero ticket purchases, necessitating estimation by tobit. Smaller units of observation of course generate a larger number of observations, enabling the inclusion of more covariates and a richer understanding of the role of socioeconomic factors driving zonal demand. On the other hand, there are limits to how far this could be taken, as the variation in the number of tickets sold to very small spatial areas would be strongly affected by random noise and the precision of coefficient estimates would suffer.

(4) Hakes et al. analyze a case in which the omission of prices of substitutes from their model is much less likely to bias results than in the case of Forrest et al. The nearest Major League Baseball franchise to Atlanta is 450 miles away and so, across most of the club's catchment area, there are no convincing substitutes.

(5) Hakes et al. have no variable to account for residents at distant zip codes simply feeling less attachment to the team. Forrest et al. have their affinity variable, which aims to address any resulting potential upward bias in the estimation of ticket price elasticity. It could be that this is a less important issue in the United States if teams are perceived as representing regions rather than cities.

(6) Hakes et al. assume that all travel to the game is by car, whereas Forrest et al. calculate a zonal weighted cost of travel, combining separate estimates for private and public transport. This is likely defensible for a car-oriented region of North America. On the other hand, in some countries, application of TCM would have to give detailed consideration to public transport fares and journey times. Burke and Woolcock (2009) show that contemporary stadia in Australia are located and designed in a way that almost compels patrons to use, often especially provided, transit services.

The finding from the case study of Hakes et al. (2011) was of a point elasticity that (for various season ticket packages) was always less elastic than –1 but (in three of four cases) not statistically significantly different from –1. As in Forrest et al. (2002), elasticity was judged to be more elastic than had been claimed in previous literature, and Hakes et al. concluded that there was no need to construct alibis to explain the failure of clubs to maximize profit. The results from TCM were consistent with their already maximizing profit.

To summarize, there is a very large body of work on elasticity of demand for sport. There is a strong consensus that demand is highly inelastic. However, this could be a spurious result generated by repeated failure to take account of travel costs and to deal with the issue of endogeneity. On the other hand, travel costs may not be just part of the problem but also offer a solution. Study of travel cost itself offers a route to an econometric framework that appears to avoid pitfalls encountered in more conventional approaches to modeling attendance demand. However, rather more TCM studies will have to be attempted before it can be said that a new consensus has emerged.

3. Non-price Influences on Demand

Price is a central focus in demand modeling and, accordingly, most of the chapter has addressed the issue of the appropriate estimation of elasticity. However, other elements will be included in the demand function and these will often be focus, and not merely control, variables. In sports economics, a number of important issues have been addressed through demand modeling, including fan preferences over competitive balance and scheduling, effects of recent results, and the impact of televising the game. The influence of market size has been another focus of interest in view of its role in the two-team model, but it proves difficult to capture both because of the problems in defining a market and because of the limitations of the now standard fixed-effects model of attendance demand.

Fixed Effects Modeling

The archetypical study of attendance in recent years takes as its unit of observation the individual match and employs information on all matches played in a league over a season or a small number of seasons. The data are treated as a panel where fixed effects are attributed to the identity of the home club. For most purposes, this is of course an advance on time series modeling as, for example, if uncertainty of outcome is to be included, this varies sharply between games, whereas the average level of uncertainty varies little between seasons even at an individual club.

One travel issue to be controlled for in such modeling relates to the "away fan" component in attendance. Many authors use distance between the home stadia of the two clubs playing the match as a proxy for how costly it is for away supporters to make the trip. For example, Donihue et al. (2007) found distance to be a significant negative determinant in an equation for attendance at baseball. Where distance is entered as a quadratic, as in Forrest and Simmons (2006), it is typically found that attendance still falls with distance between the clubs but at a decreasing rate. This could reflect lower per mile costs on longer journeys or a tendency of the hardest core fans not to be deterred by any distance. Falter and Perignon (2000) substituted a money measure for a physical distance, namely the round-trip rail fare between the two cities represented by the clubs in the match. They also pointed out that the effects of distance could be exaggerated in the estimation because many matches where the distance is short are played between teams where it is primarily historic rivalry that raises interest in attendance, so-called "Derby games." Forrest and Simmons (2006) include a necessarily judgmental "rivalry" dummy, alongside distance, to correct for this effect. Buraimo et al. (2009) refined the consideration of the influence of away fans on the gate by including, in the spirit of the gravity model, not only distance but also indicators of the market size of the away club (the population residing within five miles of its stadium and the degree of competition it faces from other clubs in its region). The two extra elements in their specification were highly significant. Accounting as fully as possible for variation in away support will of course increase the precision of estimates on other variables in the model.

The importance of the market size of the home club is harder to evaluate. It can be entered (for example as the Census population of the urban area) into an ordinary least squares equation used to analyze panel data but usually the measure is time invariant, which then precludes inclusion of other club specific time invariant measures such as ticket price (this is often set for a whole season) or club budget. Consequently, inclusion of market size rules out explicit testing of hypotheses related to, for example, the effect on crowd size of how much the club chooses to spend on players. In this case, the coefficient estimate on market size will collect influences from all these excluded variables.

This is the reason, of course, for using a fixed-effects model instead of ordinary least squares. It avoids the risks of bias but does not remove limitations on the scope of what can be achieved. This is because influence from all of the time invariant club characteristics, whether observed or non-observed, will be subsumed into the fixed effects (which, frustratingly, always account for most of the variation in attendances across the matches in the sample). The impact of all these variables cannot be disentangled from each other. Fixed effects represent a black box and this is clearly a barrier to effective examination of the role of population and other issues in attendance demand.

Alternatives to Fixed Effects Modeling

One way to proceed would be to adopt a two-step model. First, estimate the fixed-effects model. Second, regress the residuals from step one (including fixed-effects) on the exogenous club-specific, time-invariant variables such as population size. The objection to this, raised by Buraimo et al. (2009), is that estimated coefficients on the observed exogenous variables are consistent only if there is no correlation between them and non-observed club specific effects, which is implausible. They therefore advocated employment of the Hausman-Taylor estimator (Hausman and Taylor, 1981; Baltagi, 1991, offers a useful exposition) which had hitherto not been applied in a sports context. This method is robust to correlation between observed and non-observed club specific effects on, in our case, match attendance. This is achieved by creation of instruments within the model. To operationalize it, the researcher must first carefully place each covariate into one of four categories, according to whether it is time varying or time invariant and exogenous or endogenous.

Results on market size are interesting. The estimated elasticity of attendance with respect to the size of the population within five miles of the stadium was only 0.4 (and the size of population at 5–10 miles distance was dropped from the final model because of non-significance). These findings imply that defining city size without regard to how spread out a city is will be inadequate and, of course, that there are sharply decreasing returns to population size for the club. This could be because denser populations bring more opportunities to spend leisure time fruitfully away from football, or perhaps smaller communities promote greater identification with local institutions. In addition, Buraimo et al. (2009) found that the degree of market overlap of the home club has a depressing effect on attendance. This is another measure generated from GIS manipulation of Census data. It represents the proportion of the population within five miles of the stadium which also lies within five miles of another club (the index can far exceed one if there are several neighboring clubs, since the measure of the intersection with catchment areas of other clubs is summed across all such clubs). The result signals that permitting new entry into an urban market, which is a feature of the European model of sport through its promotion and relegation system, will mitigate the advantage in terms of audience size of clubs located in urban areas. In a companion paper, Buraimo et al. (2007) demonstrated that a club's success on the field is similarly positively related to five-mile population and negatively related to the extent to which it shares the market . The two studies together provide support for the two-team model, which can now be more readily tested given the advance in GIS. Further advances in sports economics will doubtless be enabled by the availability of this technology.

NOTes

1 A curiosity is that Bird's estimate of -1.22 refers to elasticity of demand with respect to his representation of generalized cost, i.e. $(P + \gamma Q)$, whereas what is of interest to the industry is elasticity of demand with respect to ticket price P. However, the difference between the two elasticities would probably have been found to be small to the extent that most of the variation in generalized cost in his data was generated by the variation in P. The relatively more serious issue is that per-mile running costs of vehicles constitute an imperfect and inadequate proxy for the total cost associated with a typical trip to a game.

2 Forrest et al. (2000) employed the method outside the countryside to evaluate benefits to consumers from the provision of subsidized live theater in a large British city.

3 An endogeneity issue for TCM would arise if household decisions on where to live were influenced by the location of the stadium. That there is in fact any significant influence appears implausible, as even hardened fans will make many fewer trips to the stadium than to work places, schools, and shops. It is where homes are relative to these facilities that will likely drive the choice of residence.

4 The population count from the Census included only those aged 10–70 years.

5 As is common in other studies of attendance, we abstracted from the complex structure of ticket prices: we took the average self-reported price per match paid by all respondents from the particular club.

6 The correlation between affinity and distance may be strong but is unlikely to be perfect. For example, migrants may typically settle in the inner city and have no sense of affinity with the club despite living in close proximity.

References

Baltagi, Badi H. (1991). *Econometric analysis of panel data*. Chichester UK: Wiley.

Becker, Gary S. (1991). A note on restaurant pricing and other examples of social influence on price. *Journal of Political Economy*, 99: 1109–1116.

Bird, Peter. J. W. N. (1982). The Demand for League Football. *Applied Economics*, 14: 637–649.

Borland, Jeffery, and Robert Macdonald (2003). Demand for sport. *Oxford Review of Economic Policy*, 19: 478–502.

Buraimo, Babatunde, David Forrest, and Robert Simmons (2007). Freedom of entry, market size and compeitive outcome: Evidence from English soccer. *Southern Economic Journal*, 74: 204–213.

Buraimo, Babatunde, David Forrest, and Robert Simmons (2009). Insights for clubs from modelling match attendance in football. *Journal of the Operational Research Society*, 60: 147–155.

Burke, Matthew, and Geoffrey Woolcock (2009). Getting to the game: Travel to sports stadia in the era of transit-oriented development. *Sport And Society*, 12: 890–909.

Dobson, Stephen M., and John A. Goddard (1995). The demand for professional football in England and Wales. *Journal of the Royal Statistical Society, Series D (The Statistician)*, 44: 259–277.

Donahue, Michael R., David W. Findlay, and Peter W. Newberry (2007). An analysis of attendance at Major League Baseball training camps. *Journal of Sports Economics*, 8: 39–61.

El-Hodiri, Mohamed, and James Quirk (1971). An economic analysis of a professional sports league. *Journal of Political Economy*, 79: 1302–1319.

Falter, Jean-Marc, and Christophe Perignon (2000). Demand for football and intramatch winning probability: An essay on the glorious uncertainty of sports. *Applied Economics*, 32: 1757–1765.

Feehan, Patrick (2006). Attendance at sports events. In Andreff, Wladimir, and Stefan Szymanski (eds.) *Handbook on the economics of sport*, pp. 90–99. Cheltenham, UK: Edward Elgar Publishers.

Feehan, Patrick, David Forrest, and Robert Simmons (2003). Premier League soccer: Normal or inferior good? *European Journal of Sport Management*, 3: 41–45.

Forrest, David, and Rob Simmons (2006). New issues in attendance demand: The case of the English Football League. *Journal of Sports Economics*, 7: 247–266.

Forrest, David, Keith Grime, and Robert Woods (2000). Is it worth subsidising regional repertory theatre? *Oxford Economic Papers*, 52: 381–397.

Forrest, David, Robert Simmons, and Patrick Feehan (2002). A spatial cross-sectional analysis of the elasticity of demand for soccer. *Scottish Journal of Political Economy*, 49: 336–355.

Fort, Rodney (2006). Inelsastic sports pricing at the gate? A survey. In Andreff, Wladimir, and Stefan Szymanski (eds.) *Handbook on the economics of sport*, pp. 700–708. Cheltenham, UK: Edward Elgar Publishers.

Hakes, Jahn K., Chad Turner, and Kyle Hutmaker (2011). I don't care if I never get back? Time, travel costs, and the estimation of baseball season-ticket demand. *International Journal of Sport Finance*, 6: 119–137.

Hausman, Jerry A., and William E. Taylor (1981). Panel data and unobservable individual effects. *Econometrica*, 49: 1377–1398.

Krautmann, Anthony C., and David J. Berri (2007). Can we find it at the concessions? Understanding price elasticity in professional sports. *Journal of Sports Economics*, 8: 39–61.

Marburger, Daniel R. (1997). Optimal ticket pricing for performance goods. *Managerial and Decision Economics*, 18: 375–381.

Noll, Roger (1974). Attendance and price setting. In Noll, Roger (ed.) *Government and the sports business*, pp. 115–117. Washington, DC: Brookings Institution.

Schmidt, Martin B., and David J. Berri (2001). Competitive balance and attendance: The case of Major League Baseball. *Journal of Sports Economics*, 2: 145–167.

Simmons, Robert (1996). The demand for league football: A club-level analysis. *Applied Economics*, 28: 139–155.

Simmons, Rob (2006). The demand for spectator sports. In Andreff, Wladimir, and Stefan Szymanski (eds.) *Handbook on the economics of sport*, pp. 77–89. Cheltenham, UK: Edward Elgar Publishers.

CHAPTER 11

......

DEMAND, ATTENDANCE, AND CENSORING

UTILIZATION RATES IN THE NATIONAL FOOTBALL LEAGUE

......

MARTIN B. SCHMIDT

1. INTRODUCTION

......

ALTHOUGH there are some sports, such as professional golf, in which meeting additional demand is relatively costless, most professional sports play in fixed arenas where meeting additional demand beyond capacity is essentially impossible. For example, the National Football League's 2010 season championship, that is, Super Bowl XLV, was played at Cowboys Stadium in Arlington, Texas whose capacity is fixed at 80,000. Allowing the 80,001st fan would, therefore, come at considerable cost to the league and would not likely be met.

Attendance data, in this case, are possibly censored.[1] Essentially, censoring comes about because of the data-gathering process, that is, the data-collection process yields data, which fail to fully capture the data's true values. As an example, suppose a researcher is interested in describing the impact of the number of hours of sleep on academic success. Further suppose that the researcher has individuals' math and reading aptitude scores, which are scaled from, say, 200–800. The problem here is that the data treat observations at either end of the distribution—that is, the 200 and 800—as equal when, in fact, it is unlikely that all students who scored 200 or 800 are truly of equal ability.

In the case of attendance data, the problem exists because a team's true latent demand (the variable of interest) for the game is censored in relation to ticket sales (the attendance data) due to the fact that many games sell out. In other words, the data one has—actual attendance data (Att_i)—does not accurately reflect the variable of interest—latent demand (Att_i^*)—at least not at capacity.

The issues econometrically revolve around the fact that most of the relevant econometric methods are based upon the assumption of normality. In the case of censoring, this assumption is clearly violated, as one or both ends of the distribution are incomplete. The consequences can be significant. For example, consider attendance at FedEx Field, the home stadium for the Washington Redskins. Further suppose that we are interested in estimating the first and second moments of the latent demand for attendance based upon the eight home games played at FedEx Field in 2008. The typical approach, one that treats each data point as yielding equal information on the true distribution, would yield an estimate of 88,600 for the mean and a standard deviation of just over 3,000. However, if the Redskins sold out a quarter of their home games, following Greene (2001), the more accurate estimates would be a mean of 88,864 and a standard deviation of just over 1,680. The increased mean is a reflection that the censored data points yield estimates of the mean that are too low, whereas the lower standard deviation reflects the fact that these data points yield estimates that are too high.[2]

The present paper examines the importance of this issue in terms of estimating a demand function in professional sports. Specifically, we examine the latent demand for National Football League (NFL) game attendance. We present the demand estimates produced when the censoring nature of the data enters the estimation technique unrecognized, that is, OLS, and those that are produced when the censuring nature is recognized, that is, Tobit estimation. In the end, a comparison of these estimates follows the econometric literature in that the OLS estimates produced are downward, in absolute terms, biased. However, as the bias is relatively uniform across variables, the relationship between individual factors is largely unaffected. However, in several cases, statistical relevance does differ across the two sets of estimates.

2. THE MODEL

Although Noll (1974), among others, has examined a cross-section of NFL team total regular-season attendance and its associated determinants over several periods, the present model more closely follows Welki and Zlatoper (1999).[3] Welki and

Zlatoper examine the choice to attend a home game, or, more specifically what factors influence a fan to make use of a purchased ticket.[4] To address this question, Welki and Zlatoper create a dependent variable that is produced from game-day attendance and actual-game ticket sales. Specifically, their dependent variable is the ratio of the number of fans who attended a specific NFL game and the total number of tickets that were sold for that same game.

As we are motivated to explain actual NFL game-day attendance, the dependent variable at hand is theoretically slightly different. In other words, although the measure that Welki and Zlatoper use captures part of this, it fails to capture important aspects. For example, suppose a fan decides at some point during the season to purchase a ticket because of changing interest. To the extent that the fan actually uses the ticket, that is, attends the game, Welki and Zlatoper's measure would remain unchanged.

Our attendance variable then revolves around actual home attendance estimates obtained from NFL.com. Specifically, we incorporate attendance figures for all 256 home games played during the NFL's 2008 regular season.[5] However, as was discussed earlier, capacity constraints exist in most professional sports—perhaps nowhere more so than in the NFL. The simplest way to capture the constraints is to create a utilization rate measure for NFL teams. Furthermore, incorporating a utilization rate allows for each team's censoring to be at the same point, that is, at 100 percent capacity.[6] Specifically, for each team we create a game-stadium utilization rate by dividing actual game-day attendance figures by each team's stadium capacity and constrain these values at (1) to generate each NFL team's utilization rate.[7]

Table 11.1 and Figure 11.1 present average utilization rates for each NFL team over the eight home games played in the 2008 season. Overall, the NFL runs at more than 96 percent capacity and has more than a quarter of the teams running at full capacity. It is these teams, those at capacity, that create the censoring and that explain why estimation requires special care.[8] As was mentioned earlier and will be discussed later, the issues created by censored data revolve around the fact that a portion of the data's distribution, in this case the right tail of the distribution, is missing from the researcher's data.

The general model of interest is highlighted in equation (1).

$$Att_i = f(\text{Cost}, \text{Quality}, \text{Importance}, \text{Time}) \tag{1}$$

Specifically, we estimate the latent demand for game-day NFL attendance as a function of the cost of attendance, the perceived quality of the game, the game's relative importance, and various measures of time.

In terms of cost, we include each team's average ticket price. These figures come from Team Marketing Reports and represent a weighted average of actual ticket prices.[9] In addition, as the true cost of attending a sporting event is much more than just the cost of entrance, that is, parking, food, and so forth, we include a measure of each team's nonticket fan cost.[10] Again these data are available from Team Marketing Reports. As both of these represent out-of-pocket costs for fan

Table 11.1 Average Utilization Rates—National Football League 2008 home games

Team	% of Capacity	Team	% of Capacity
Arizona	0.878	Miami	0.871
Atlanta	0.900	Minneapolis	0.987
Baltimore	**1.000**	**New England**	**1.000**
Buffalo	0.933	**New Orleans**	**1.000**
Carolina	0.995	New York Giants	0.995
Chicago	**1.000**	New York Jets	0.988
Cincinnati	0.986	Oakland	0.916
Cleveland	0.993	**Philadelphia**	**1.000**
Dallas	0.966	Pittsburgh	0.975
Denver	0.992	San Diego	0.974
Detroit	0.839	**Seattle**	**1.000**
Green Bay	0.982	San Francisco	0.968
Houston	**1.000**	Saint Louis	0.981
Indianapolis	**1.000**	Tampa Bay	0.938
Jacksonville	0.893	**Tennessee**	**1.000**
Kansas City	0.932	Washington	0.993

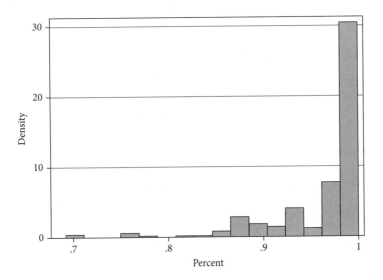

Figure 11.1 Game Utilization Rates, All National Football League 2008 Home Games.

attendance, we would expect these to negatively impact ticket sales and, therefore, decrease a team's utilization rate.[11]

In terms of quality, we begin by including each team's winning percentage prior to each home game. As was mentioned earlier we are interested in estimating the desire to attend a game. One might expect that a fan, given the availability, is more likely to purchase a ticket (either from the team or from an outside outlet) once a team has been revealed to be of higher quality. In addition, fans attending games are not always fans of the home team and, therefore, a similar argument exists for the importance of the away team's winning percentage at the time of the contest.

To the extent that fans enjoy scoring, high-scoring affairs may be preferred to low-scoring ones. We, therefore, include a measure of the amount of scoring a fan might see while attending a game. Given efficient market theory, a game's over/under betting line would capture the average expectation of total point output. More specifically, the higher the betting line the more points that are expected to be scored during the game which, in turn, may lead to an increase in an NFL team's utilization rate. The over/under line was obtained from the individual NFL team pages at Covers.com.[12]

Quality may also be measured by the expected competitiveness of the game. We measure the competitiveness of a particular game by its final betting line, also obtained from the individual NFL team pages at Covers.com. We include the absolute value of the line because it is not clear why a home team being favored by three points would have a separate impact from the home team being the underdog by three points; both would likely represent the expectation of a competitive game.

A final included measure of quality is the individual NFL team's total payroll. If salary is tied to productivity, then one would expect that higher payroll, given efficient markets, should be reflective of higher quality, at least, a priori. In addition, a higher payroll may reflect increased off-season activity and increased optimism for the upcoming season.

We capture the importance of the game by including a dummy variable if the team's home game is against a division rival, and a second variable if the game is played against a competitor in the same conference.[13] Importance here may have two separate interpretations. The first revolves around the fact that, in order to make the playoffs, a team must either win its division or be one of the two best nondivision winners, that is, a wild card entrant. In this case, division and conference games gain in significance because a win directly increases the team's chances of making the playoffs because it leads directly to a loss on the part of one of its competitors for the division title. In addition, competitions against a team's rivals have increased importance. Rivals are most easily found within the division in which an NFL team plays each of its division members twice a year.

A last category of independent variables revolves loosely around the concept of time. In 2008, each NFL begins its season in early September and ends it in late December along the way playing a sixteen-game schedule. We include the week of the season that an NFL team's home game is played to capture changes in the desire to attend a game over this time. Because the NFL is by far the most competitive of the four major professional sports within the United States, this competitiveness may allow fans to be quite excited by their team's chances, at least with incomplete information. However, as a team reveals its true ability over time, the excitement may diminish. In addition, games toward the end of the season may be perceived as more or less important because playoff implications have become clearer.

The remaining variables capture whether the team's home game was played on a day other than Sunday or at night. The typical NFL game is played on Sundays at either 1 P.M. or 4 P.M. (Eastern Standard Time). In fact only roughly 10 percent of games are played on a day other than Sunday, and only about 15 percent are played at night. Because these involve more national interest and less competition from other games, these games may be especially desirable to fans. We, therefore, include dummy variables for whether the game was played at night or on a non-Sunday. Finally, two games were played away from two teams' home stadiums, and these were played in a foreign country.[14] Because of the unique nature of these games, we included a dummy variable for these.

Finally, incorporating stadium-usage rates implicitly assumes that the stadium capacity of each NFL team is somehow comparable or optimal. However, there are several reasons to doubt this. For example a particular city's population may have increased or decreased by more than another city's since its stadium was built, thus (in the case of growth) meaning that the stadium is in a sense *too small* and, therefore, easier to get 100 percent utilization. Or a stadium could be multipurpose or football only, in which case the multipurpose capacity is likely to be some average of optimal capacity for each of its uses as opposed to optimal for football only. In order to control for the unique aspects of the stadium themselves and their associated fans or city, we included city dummy variables.[15]

3. ESTIMATION AND EMPIRICAL RESULTS

Our dependent variable, Att_i, represents the capacity rate for NFL team (i) and is right censored at a value of 1. In that case, Att_i can be defined as follows:

$$Att_i = \begin{cases} Att_i^*, & Att_i^* < 1 \\ 1, & Att_i^* \geq 1 \end{cases} \tag{2}$$

The relationship with the latent variable holds, however, using Att_i (observable capacity) as follows:

$$Att_i = x_i'\beta + \epsilon_i, \quad where \ \epsilon_i \sim N(0,\sigma^2) \tag{3}$$

where the x_i' is capturing the earlier described independent variables. The difficulty that censoring introduces econometrically is that the distribution of the censored dependent variable, Att_i, is made up of two parts. Specifically, the distribution of Att_i follows:

$$f(Att) = f(Att^*)^{d_i} F(1)^{1-d_i} \qquad (4)$$

where d_i is an indicator variable that is equal to 1 if the observation is not censored and 0 otherwise. In this case, the distribution of the censored variables is made up of two parts a discrete part and a continuous part.

Generally, using OLS on the sample or even on just the uncensored data will produce biased estimates of β, that is, assuming that all the data are uncensored forces the distribution of Att_i to be approximated by $f(Att^*)$. In which case, the remaining portion of the distribution of Att_i, that is, $F(1)^{1-d_i}$, would be subsumed in the error term.[16] The error terms' likely correlation with the independent variables would produce the inconsistency.

The obvious desire is to use the full distribution to estimate the βs. The Tobit model does exactly this. The Tobit model uses maximum likelihood to estimate the βs from the following likelihood function:

$$L = \prod_{i}^{N} \left[\frac{1}{\sigma} \phi \left(\frac{Att_i^* - \mu}{\sigma} \right) \right]^{d_i} \left[1 - \Phi \left(\frac{\mu - 1}{\sigma} \right) \right]^{1-d_i} \qquad (5)$$

As before, the first part of the likelihood function uses the data's information, whereas the second iterates out the associated right-hand side of the associated normal distribution.

The results from both OLS and Tobit estimations of equation (1) are reported in Table 11.2. Casual observation of the two columns reveals that the OLS results are consistently lower than those produced from the Tobit estimation. As was mentioned in the introduction, the downward bias, in absolute terms, is the result of treating all data points as yielding similar information and is a result well known in the literature (e.g., Greene 2001).

In terms of estimating the latent demand for game-day attendance in the NFL, the general picture that comes from Table 11.2 is that each season begins with increased interest. However, as the season goes on, each team begins to reveal its true ability and stadium-utilization rates begin to decline. Specifically for each week that goes by, a generic NFL team can expect attendance to decline by nearly 0.2 percent. The declining interest is likely due to overexposure or loss of interest due to lack of competitiveness or due to increased alternatives.[17]

Of the remaining time variables, the only factors that appear to be important are games against a division rival and a game on the Thanksgiving holiday. Specifically, home games that are played against a division rival can expect to increase game-day attendance by over 1.2 percent. Thanksgiving Day games, which are televised nationally, have even more of an impact by increasing attendance by close to 8 percent.

Table 11.2 OLS and Tobit Estimates

Variable	Model 1 OLS Estimates	Model 2 Tobit Estimates
Constant	−0.0458	−0.6381
	(0.0557)	(16.8909)
Week	**−0.0013*****	**−0.0019*****
	(0.0005)	**(0.0006)**
Average ticket price	0.0002	0.0020
	(0.0004)	(0.1855)
Total fan cost index (Non-ticket costs)	−0.0001	−0.0005
	(0.0004)	(0.0635)
Total payroll	0.0001	0.0001
	(0.0010)	(0.0010)
Division game	**0.0076***	**0.0121***
	(0.0046)	**(0.0063)**
Conference game	−0.0016	−0.0001
	(0.0051)	(0.0051)
Winning % $_{-1}$—home team	0.0190	0.0283
	(0.0142)	(0.0206)
Winning % $_{-1}$—away team	0.0151	−0.0001
	(0.0101)	(0.0135)
Betting Line—game	−0.0008	**−0.0018****
	(0.0007)	**(0.0009)**
Over/Under Line—game	0.0006	**0.0014***
	(0.0006)	**(0.0008)**
Monday game	0.0069	0.0098
	(0.0110)	(0.0170)
Thursday game	−0.0036	−0.0027
	(0.0142)	(0.0211)
Saturday game	0.0250	0.0350
	(0.0349)	(0.0407)
Night game	0.0021	0.0076
	(0.0086)	(0.0129)

(continued)

Table 11.2 (*continued*)

Variable	Model 1 OLS Estimates	Model 2 Tobit Estimates
Thanksgiving game	0.0511**	0.0837**
	(0.0237)	(0.0347)
Foreign game	0.0119	−0.0033
	(0.0237)	(0.0306)
(Pseudo) R-squared	0.752	0.444
N	256	256
i	32	32

Notes: The dependent variable is the log of an NFL team's capacity rate for the 2009 season. In addition city dummies were included.

Of the remaining factors, the two betting lines, that is, the betting and over/under lines, are particularly interesting because the OLS results would suggest that these are insignificant, at conventional levels, in terms of game-day demand. In terms of their specific impact, the betting line variable suggests that games that are expected to be more competitive are better attended. Specifically a one-point move downward, in absolute terms, in the betting line would increase an average team's utilization rate by just under 0.2 percent. In which case, the difference between a seven-point spread and a three-point spread is nearly a 1 percent change in usage rates. As the average capacity of an NFL stadium is above 70,000, this movement would mean a change of over 700 fans attending the game.

Along similar lines, the over/under line suggests that NFL fans like increased scoring. Specifically a one-point move upward, in absolute terms, in the betting line would increase an average team's utilization rate by nearly 0.15 percent. In which case, the difference between a relatively low-scoring affair, that is, 31.5 (the lowest in the sample), and a relatively high-scoring affair, that is, 53.5 points (the highest in the sample), is a 3.3 percent change in usage rates. Again as the average capacity of an NFL stadium is above 70,000 this movement would mean a change of over 2,310 fans attending the game.

In terms of the remaining variables, it appears that the game-day demand for NFL football attendance is relatively price insensitive. Specifically, although one of the price variables (nonticket costs) does return the correct sign, neither cost variables are significant. Also, it appears that NFL fans are more concerned with going to an entertaining game (a close or high-scoring game) than they are with the how well their team is doing in terms of winning because neither teams' winning percentage is significant.

Finally, aside from the previously mentioned Thanksgiving Day dummy variable, none of the dummy variables included for the nontraditional game times are significant. In the end, it does not appear that fans care much about whether the game is played at night or during the day or whether the game is played on a Sunday, Monday, Thursday, or Saturday.

4. CONCLUSION

The paper examined the estimation of the latent demand for game-day attendance for NFL games where the dependent variable is likely censored. We provide both OLS and Tobit estimation results when one includes various measures for cost, quality, importance, and time. We find that, although various measures for quality and importance are significant, their estimated impacts do vary across the two estimation techniques. Specifically, the OLS results are almost uniformly lower, in absolute terms, than those produced when the censoring is explicitly recognized. In addition, the marginal significance of several of the variables differs across the two.

In the end we find that game-day attendance in the NFL depends negatively on time and positively on the perceived competitiveness and scoring output of the game. It also increases when the team plays a division rival or when the game is played on Thanksgiving. It is not, however, moved by the cost of attending a game.

NOTES

1 Censoring differs from the concern of truncation. Truncated data are incomplete due the selection of only a subsample of the population, that is, we examine the demand for a public area by examining only those who have visited the area at least once. In this case truncation involves issues of sample size while censuring does not.

2 The first moment is too low because the true data would have observations above capacity. Similarly, the second moment is too high due to the fact that we only capture part of the true data's distribution.

3 Borland and MacDonald (2003) provide a survey the demand literature for both professional and collegiate sport.

4 Along similar lines, Siegfried and Hinshaw (1979) use non-attendance figures to examine the impact of local television blackout rules.

5 Welki and Zlatoper (1999) incorporated two seasons, 1986 and 1987, worth of data. The 1987 season is problematic as the season experienced a labor strike during the season. The twenty-four-day NFL players' strike caused the cancellation of a week's worth of games. In addition, three weeks' worth of games were played with replacement players. Welki and Zlatoper remove these games from their analysis; however it is difficult to know how this strike affected fans post-strike decisions. The 2008 season was not subject to any management-labor strife.

6 The fact that each team's dependent variable is censored at the same point also makes estimation of the Tobit model much simpler.

7 One reason for constraining attendance at capacity is that average ticket prices and
   the fan cost index incorporated in the estimation are computed as "... a weighted
   average of season ticket price for general seating categories, determined by factoring
   the tickets in each price range as a percentage of the total number of seats in each
   ballpark. (www.teammarketing.com)" In which case the cost of standing room and
   other alternative seating, which may be available, is excluded.

8 As our dependent variable, an NFL team's stadium utilization rate, is by construction
   constrained between 0 and 1, we incorporate the log attendance in the actual estimation.

9 http://www.teammarketing.com

10 According to the Team Marketing Reports web site the fan cost index includes: two
   adult average price tickets, two child average price tickets, four small soft drinks, two
   small beers, four hot dogs, two programs, parking, and two adult-size caps. To create
   the nonticket cost measure, we subtracted each team's average cost of two adult tickets
   from the total cost measure.

11 It is unclear how price should impact Welki and Zlatoper's measure. Although higher
   costs should decrease ticket sales, it is unclear why it should impact attendance once
   a ticket is purchased, in which case, a rise in costs should not change usage rates—
   which is the Welki and Zlatoper measure.

12 http://www.covers.com.

13 The NFL consists of thirty-two teams. The teams are split across two conferences
   (National Football Conference (NFC) and American Football Conference (AFC)).
   Additionally each conference is split into four divisions (East, North, South, and
   West). Playoff competitors are the four division winners plus the two teams with the
   best record in the conference as wildcard entrants.

14 The New Orleans Saints hosted the San Diego Chargers on n Oct. 26 at Wembley
   Stadium in London, England and on Dec. 7, the Buffalo Bills hosted the Miami
   Dolphins at the Rogers Centre in Toronto, Canada.

15 We thank one of the editors for raising the issue.

16 Perhaps a more intuitive way of thinking about it is to consider the relationship
   between $x_i' \beta$ and its associated error terms. For relatively low $x_i' \beta$ the expected
   draws of ϵ_i are likely centered around 0. However, for relatively high, those close to or
   at 0, $x_i' \beta$ the expected draws of ϵ_i are likely positive, creating a relationship between
   our independent variables and the estimated error.

17 The NFL season begins as the major league baseball season is ending. However, both
   the NHL and NBA begin play shortly after the NFL season begins.

References

Borland, Jeffery, and Robert MacDonald. 2003. Demand for sport. *Oxford Review of
   Economic Policy* 19(4): 478–502.

Greene, William H. 2000. *Econometric Analysis*. Upper Saddle River, NJ.: Prentice
   Hall Inc.

Seigfield, J. J., and C. E. Hinshaw. 1979. The effect of lifting television blackouts on
   professional football no-shows. *Journal of Economics and Business* 32(1): 1–13.

Welki, Andrew M., and Thomas J. Zlatoper. 1999. US professional football game-day
   attendance. *Atlantic Economic Review* 27(3): 285–298.

## CHAPTER 12

DEMAND FOR ATTENDANCE

PRICE MEASUREMENT

RICHARD C. K. BURDEKIN

INTRODUCTION

IN addition to the role played by ticket prices, attendance in professional sports is influenced by such demographic factors as income and population levels in the team's market area as well as performance variables and the degree of uncertainty about the outcome. Other potentially relevant factors include television broadcasts of the games, the presence of other nearby major sports teams, and the prices of other goods, not to mention idiosyncratic factors like fan preferences. Aside from the possible longer-term option of moving the sports franchise, or seeking public subsidies for a new stadium,[1] the two most obvious ways in which a team owner could encourage more fans to attend games would be by either obtaining higher quality players or by cutting ticket prices. Under profit maximization, the first of these options requires that the marginal cost of the newly-acquired players not exceed their marginal revenue product. The profit maximizing calculation is complicated, however, by the likely increases in other revenue streams, such as television license fees, sponsorship, and concessions, if top players are recruited. Meanwhile, the scope for raising ticket prices as demand shifts up implies that the price-attendance relationship is not just a one-way street.

Table 12.1 Total Revenues and Wage Costs for the English Premier League versus Major League Baseball, NBA, and NFL

League	Revenue	Wages	Wages as Share of Revenue	Net Transfer Costs	Wages plus Transfers as Share of Revenue
English Premier League	1,530	669	44%	284	62%
Major League Baseball	1,781	1,028	55%	N/A	55%
NBA	2,547	1,395	58%	N/A	58%
NFL	3,274	2,001	61%	N/A	61%

Note: English Premier League data for the 2006–2007 season; other data are for 2006. Totals are in millions of pounds sterling.

Source: Deloitte Annual Review of Football Finance, May 2008, p. 42.

On the cost side, comparative data for four top sports leagues actually suggests considerable consistency in the share of revenue accounted for by player compensation. Table 12.1 compares the ratio of wage payments to revenue in the English Premier League over the 2006–2007 season with 2006 data from the top three North American sports leagues: major league baseball, the National Basketball Association (NBA) and the National Football League (NFL). Upon factoring in net payments on transfer fees paid to acquire players in English football, the overall share of wage costs across the four sports leagues is seen to be in quite a tight range.[2] Major league baseball features the lowest ratio at 55 percent and the English Premier League has the highest share at 62 percent, just one percentage point ahead of the NFL. This points to at least one important area of relative commonality of outcome across the top North American and English sports leagues, notwithstanding quite different league structures that, in England as in most European leagues, allow for automatic promotion or relegation. This chapter focuses primarily upon evidence gleaned from these four top sports leagues, although some comparative findings are provided for other sports leagues around the world—including new perspectives on China's football Super League. The question of whether sports teams engage in profit maximization is addressed in detail, along with alternative explanations for many teams seemingly pricing tickets in the inelastic range, whereby price hikes would pull in more gate revenue. The body of this chapter begins with the possible effect of changes in team ownership structures in accounting for departures from profit maximization and ends with the complications to the price-attendance relationship posed by such ancillary factors as customer-based discrimination.

TEAM OWNERSHIP AND ALTERNATIVES
TO PROFIT MAXIMIZATION

Perhaps the most radical changes in team ownership structures in recent years have been those seen in the English Premier League, with Szymanski (2006, p. 461) observing that the "clubs increasingly became the playthings of the rich." The trend toward billionaire ownership began with Blackburn Rovers under Sir Jack Walker in the mid-1990s and accelerated with Russian billionaire Roman Abramovich's 2003 purchase of Chelsea.[3] Initially, only Manchester United, Arsenal, and Liverpool were able to come close to matching the huge funds being spent on Chelsea by Abramovich (whose debt and equity injections totaled £575 million through the 2006–2007 season [*Deloitte Annual Review of Football Finance*, 2008, p. 9]). Table 12.2 depicts the dominance of these "big-four" football clubs over 2003–2007, with their near-monopoly over the top four places in the Premier League seemingly matching their relative expenditure levels off the field. Feddersen and Maennig (2008, p. 163) show that the English Premier League actually had the lowest competitive balance among the five biggest European football leagues from 1999–2000 through 2006–07, after having featured average to higher-than-average competitiveness over the 1980s and 1990s.

In 2006–2007, the wage costs for the big four ranged from £132.8 million for Chelsea to £77.6 million for Liverpool, as compared with a leaguewide average of £48.5 million, which, needless to say, is itself greatly inflated by the huge expenditures of these same top-four clubs.[4] The disparity between wage costs for the big four and the Premier League as a whole is vividly apparent in Figure 12.1, which

Table 12.2 Domination by the English Premier League's Big-Four Clubs, 2003–2004 to 2006–2007

| Club | Wage Cost Rank/ League Rank | | | | Total Wage Costs (in thousands of pounds sterling) for 2006–2007 |
	2003–2004	2004–2005	2005–2006	2006–2007	
Chelsea	1 / 2	1 / 1	1 / 1	1 / 2	132,817
Manchester United	2 / 3	2 / 3	2 / 2	2 / 1	92,310
Arsenal	3 / 1	3 / 2	3 / 4	3 / 4	89,703
Liverpool	4 / 4	4 / 5*	4 / 3	4 / 3	77,589
League average					48,450

Note: * Everton finished in fourth place in this season, despite a 2004–2005 wage cost of £30.84 million that was less than half of Liverpool's £64.23 million and less than a third of Chelsea's £108.89 million.

Source: Deloitte Annual Review of Football Finance, 2005–2008.

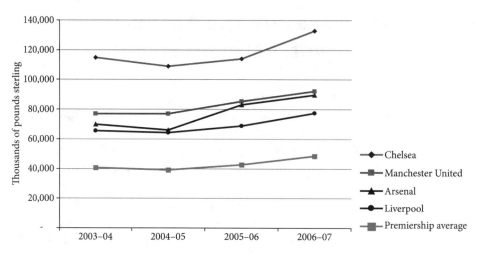

Figure 12.1 Premier League Total Wage Costs, 2003/04–2006/07.

shows a widening gap over the post-Abramovich era. With billionaire owners, or magnates, becoming increasingly prevalent in other European leagues as well, the

> implications for the European soccer system are immense. Since teams with magnates as owners seem to have no budget constraints, the competitive balance can change dramatically ... [and] the attempts by other teams to remain competitive can lead to an arms race. (Feddersen and Maennig, 2008, p. 161)

Could such vast expenditures of sums, with Chelsea's 2006–2007 outlay of £132.8 million representing a further 17 percent year-on-year increase, really be consistent with profit maximization? Or is this just a "sportsman" owner of independent means, who sees the team as a trophy franchise and is motivated more by the celebrity value of team ownership and success on the playing field regardless of any losses entailed by high spending? An apparent U.S. poster child for this phenomenon is Mark Cuban, owner of the Dallas Mavericks NBA franchise, who "clearly views the Mavericks as a consumption good, a chance to have fun and to rub elbows with athletes, celebrities, and fans, rather than as a source of income" (Leeds and von Allmen, 2007, p. 67). Quirk and El Hodiri (1974, p. 42) suggest that the publicity and prestige of team ownership might also attract wealthy owners seeing this as a way to "engender profits in [their] other enterprises." In some cases there may even be specific synergies (or arguably conflicts of interest) with the owner's other business activities, as with Rupert Murdoch's apparent use of his 1998–2004 Los Angeles Dodgers ownership to advance the interests of his regional Fox Sports network (see Leeds and von Allmen, 2007, pp. 99–100). On a more altruistic note, Noll (1974, p. 125) suggests that sportsman owners might not necessarily seek private gain but simply aim to provide a winning team as a public service and engage in "cost-plus pricing," whereby "ticket prices would be set just to cover the operating costs of the team and its player development system."

Sloane's (1971) original utility-maximizing model implies that teams put winning first and are simply concerned with having sufficient revenue to keep going. Under this approach, sports team owners view some minimal level of profit (or maximum level of loss) as a constraint subject to which they simply aim to maximize success on the field. Késenne and Pauwels' (2006) modeling of the win-maximization hypothesis, under the restriction of a fixed-profit rate, predicts higher demand for playing talent but also higher ticket prices than under profit maximization. This casts at least some doubt on the premise that departures from profit maximization can necessarily account for ticket prices being set overly low. After all, if the team acquires higher quality, more expensive players, some positive effect on ticket prices seems inevitable, unless the team owner is able to absorb continually rising losses. The recent trend toward billionaire purchasers of sports teams suggests that this is more than just an academic possibility, however.[5]

DOES INELASTIC TICKET PRICING REFUTE PROFIT MAXIMIZATION?

Ticket pricing behavior certainly seems, at first glance, to support the premise that sports team owners are motivated by something other than profit maximization. Indeed, the widespread empirical evidence of teams pricing in the inelastic region of the demand curve looks to be a rather blatant violation of profit maximization, because it implies that teams are setting ticket prices too low and would boost revenue by raising the price of entry. The initial econometric evidence on this question reviewed by Cairns, Jennett, and Sloane (1986, p. 15) included eight empirical studies testing the effects of price on attendance. This early body of analysis revealed a strong tendency for the estimated price effects to be either insignificant or feature point estimates closer to zero than to the unitary values expected under profit maximization. The sports covered included major league baseball, European football, the NHL, and English cricket. Although one baseball study, Demmert (1973, p. 68), did report a price elasticity close to unity (-0.93), Fort (2006, p. 701) notes that Demmert's reported data and estimated coefficients actually seem to imply an elasticity of just -0.01. Cairns, Jennett, and Sloane (1986, p. 15) suggest, however, that the apparent rejection of profit-maximizing pricing strategies may well simply reflect that fact that "data problems of one form or another have led to the true relationship not being identified." Moreover, Noll (1974, p. 125) notes that, even though his estimated coefficient implies that baseball tickets were being priced in the inelastic range, this estimate is not significantly different from the unitary value and the estimated elasticity is in any event "biased downward because it does not correct for differences among stadiums in the quality of the average seat."

More recent reviews of the empirical literature by Fort (2004a, 2006) and Krautmann and Berri (2007) continue to point to a preponderance of evidence suggesting either inelastic pricing or insignificant effects of ticket prices on attendance.[6] Apparent underpricing of tickets is also suggested by the widespread sell-outs of top-level professional sports events.[7] Fort (2006, p. 702) questions whether findings of inelastic pricing can simply be ascribed to the use of average price data, arguing that the weighted average ticket price should already reasonably reflect underlying variations in the proportion of bad seats across different stadiums. On the other hand, Krautmann and Hadley (2006) note that distortions may arise because the higher priced seats are much more likely to sell out than the cheaper ones, leading to an underestimate of the actual costs paid by patrons entering the stadium. Comparing the weighted average seat price to the alternatives of ticket revenue divided by attendance and a specific common-seat price, Krautmann and Hadley (2006) find that none of these yields any support for an elastic response of attendance to ticket prices over the 1991–1996 major league baseball seasons.[8] Unfortunately, in the absence of complete data on all attendees sorted by seat type, there seems to be little scope for definitively resolving the price measurement issue.

Yet another complication concerns possible variations in price elasticity across season ticket holders vs. daily admission tickets. Here, Simmons (1996) finds that the estimated ticket price elasticity for English football teams changes significantly when correcting for admission of season ticket holders. Using data for nineteen top English football clubs from 1962–1963 through 1991–1992, Simmons (1996) points to substantially higher price elasticities for nine out of seventeen clubs when this correction is made, with five of these ending up with estimated long-run price elasticities above unity (compared to just two based on unadjusted attendance data).[9] Simmons (1996, p. 153) concludes that, insofar as "season ticket holders have lower price elasticity than 'casual' supporters, price discrimination with larger price increases for season ticket holders would appear to be justified."

Given the limitations on the ticket-price data available to most researchers, the consensus favoring inelastic pricing certainly has to be considered suggestive rather than ironclad. Some recent studies of major league baseball attendance (Kahane and Shmanske, 1997; Alexander, 2001; Donihue, Findlay, and Newberry, 2007) and European football (Forrest, Simmons, and Feehan, 2002; García and Rodríguez, 2002) have, in fact, identified price elasticities close to, or even above, unity.[10] Cebula (2009, p. 40) also suggests that increases in ticket-sales revenues arising from discounting "imply that the demand curve for tickets to minor league [baseball] games in the Carolina League may be not only downward sloping but also price elastic." Another important consideration is that, whereas most price-elasticity studies employ data from a single season, or small number of consecutive seasons, long-term price responses over time may be different because of teams' ability to adjust pricing as sellouts become more, or less, frequent. This, in turn, begs the question of ticket price endogeneity (which is addressed in detail further below).

Additional Revenue Sources and Reduced Dependence Upon Gate Attendance

A major innovation in the attendance literature in recent years has been the rationale that has been developed about why inelastic pricing, even if it is the rule in practice, is not necessarily inconsistent with profit maximization at all. A growing number of studies recognize that gate attendance is only part, and often a relatively small part, of total revenue. The widespread decline in the importance of gate receipts in European football since the mid-1990s, for example, is documented in Table 12.3. The importance of gate receipts declined substantially in each of the top English, French, German, Italian, and Spanish football (soccer) leagues at the same time that broadcast revenues were rising (by 40 percent for the German Bundesliga and by 75 percent or more for the other four leagues).[11] Still, great dependence on gate receipts was undoubtedly present before the 1990s. Indeed, Andreff (2006, p. 690) points to a dependence on gate receipts for top-level French football teams of 81 percent in 1970–1971 that subsequently declined to 50 percent in 1985–1986, 29 percent in 1990–1991, and 25 percent in 1993–1994. Meanwhile, in North America, the share of total revenue accounted for by gate receipts across major league baseball, the NBA, and the NFL had, in each case, already fallen below 50 percent by the mid-1990s (see Andreff, 2006, p. 698). The falling reliance on gate receipts has been combined with increased revenue streams from sponsorship as well as television licensing fees.

Building upon Fort and Quirk's (1995) analysis of local and national TV revenue, with gate-revenue sharing, Fort (2004a) suggests that pricing in the inelastic region for gate attendance is consistent with profit maximization so long as local marginal television revenue is sufficiently large relative to average marginal television revenue in the rest of the league. Fort (2004a) finds that this condition was met in practice by all teams in major league baseball over the 1975–1988 seasons.[12] Another source of revenue for teams is the receipt of public subsidies, which may well be inversely related to ticket prices. Based on data from a limited sample of NFL stadiums, Fort (2004b) concludes that, not only were overall subsidies inversely related to ticket prices, but also the elasticity of rent with respect to ticket price was elastic.[13] This gives team owners another possible rationale for trading off gate-revenue gains from ticket

Table 12.3 Declining Dependence Upon Matchday Revenues In Five Top
          European Football Leagues, Mid-1990s versus 2006–2007

League	% of Revenue in mid-1990s / % of Revenue in 2006–07			Total Revenue (in millions of euros) during 2006–07
	Matchday	Broadcast	Commercial (including sponsorship)	
English Premier League	47 / 35	12 / 39	41 / 26	2,273
French League 1	22 / 14	32 / 58	46 / 28	972
German Bundesliga	32 / 22	25 / 35	43 / 43	1,379
Italian Serie A	37 / 13	36 / 63	27 / 24	1,163
Spanish La Liga	46 / 26	20 / 42	34 / 32	1,326

Notes: The comparison year for the English Premier League is 1995–1996 and is 1996–1997 for all other leagues except for Spanish La Liga, for which 1996 data reported in Andreff (2006, p. 691) were used because the Deloitte series commenced only in 2003–2004.

Matchday revenues include season tickets.
Broadcast revenues include television and radio payments from domestic and international competitions.
Commercial revenues include conference and catering, and merchandising fees in addition to sponsorship.

Sources: Deloitte Annual Review of Football Finance, 2004–2008; Andreff (2006).

price hikes against possible lost opportunities in another revenue stream. In short, once gate revenue is seen as just one of many potential team revenue streams, overall profit maximization and inelastic ticket pricing are by no means incompatible.

Tradeoffs with Concession Sales

Concession sales themselves offer a complimentary source of revenue that rises in proportion with the number of fans entering the stadium. Profit-maximizing team business strategy should, in turn, be focused, not on gate revenues alone, but on "gate revenues plus net income from concessions and parking ... [where] the cost of tickets is around only half the cost of attending a game" (Zimbalist, 1992, pp. 53–54). Lowering price into the inelastic portion of the demand-curve pricing will be consistent with profit maximization provided that the gains in concession revenue at least offset the resultant fall in gate revenue (Heilmann and Wendling, 1976). Indeed, ticket sales could end up rather like a supermarket's "loss-leader," designed to attract traffic that will generate profits from accompanying purchases of more expensive (and higher-margin) items. Krautmann and Berri's (2007, pp. 186–187) model incorporating the link between ticket sales and concession revenue yields the following basic first-order condition for profit maximization:

$$MR^T + MR^C = MC \tag{1}$$

where
    MR^T is marginal revenue from ticket sales,
    MR^C is marginal revenue from concessions, and
    MC is marginal cost.
    Rearranging the foregoing, we have:

$$MC - MR^C = MR^T \tag{2}$$

This implies that inelastic ticket pricing, under which MR^T is negative, is consistent with overall profit maximization so long as MC is less than MR^C. Although it is uncertain whether this condition is met in practice, adding in concession revenues, at the very least, makes inelastic ticket pricing more likely. The extra gains from raising the number of patrons has the effect of pushing the profit-maximizing ticket price level downward and profit-maximizing ticket sales upward.[14] Krautmann and Berri's estimates of MR^C, derived from data on the total fan costs of attending major-league baseball games from 1991–2004, suggest that concession revenue gains may have led teams to discount their ticket prices by over 50 percent. That is, prices might have been set approximately twice as high if teams derived revenue from gate entry alone.[15]

Some corroborative evidence on the potential role played by concessions revenue is provided by Coates and Humphreys (2007), who examine data for the NBA and NFL as well as major league baseball. Although their results support ticket pricing in the inelastic range for both major league baseball and the NBA, they find higher elasticities with respect to the fan cost index that includes parking, drinks, and other concession goods.[16] Insofar as the elasticity for the nonticket components of the fan-cost index is likely higher than the ticket-price elasticity, Coates and Humphreys (2007, p. 167) conclude that "revenue maximizing teams price concessions and other goods closer to the revenue maximizing elastic portion of the demand curve and trade off these revenues by pricing tickets in the inelastic portion of the demand curve." Although their findings, like those of Krautmann and Berri (2007), do not actually prove profit maximization, they do offer further evidence that concession sales considerations would lead a profit-maximizing team to set ticket prices lower than would be the case if the franchise depended upon gate receipts alone.

Habit Formation and Short-Run Vs. Long-Run Profit Maximization

Another rationale for pricing tickets in the inelastic range is offered by Ahn and Lee (2007), who distinguish between short-run and long-run maximization. Whereas setting prices at low levels may sacrifice profits today, the authors argue that this strategy leads to higher profits over time if one or both of the following two conditions are met: (1) the intertemporal elasticity of substitution for games is small, meaning that a small increase in the current ticket price will decrease the fan's future attendance in tandem with current attendance, and (2) the games are habit forming, meaning that the attractiveness of attending future games rises with each visit to the ballpark. Ahn and Lee's (2007) empirical analysis using major league baseball data from 1969–1985 plus 1991–2000 supports the premise that attendance is habit forming, in turn offering some justification for teams maximizing long-run profitability by keeping ticket prices at what would otherwise be considered overly low levels.[17] Intriguing as this approach may be, it would be interesting to see the authors extend their work to consider cases in which sellouts are more frequent. The benefits from lower prices would perhaps then depend upon the extent to which this broadens the range of potential customers who get a chance to see the game? Although Ahn and Lee (2007) specifically mention the Chicago Cubs as an exemplar of the fan-loyalty phenomenon, Cubs tickets are notoriously hard to get, and so setting low posted prices may not necessarily make the games more accessible to first-time customers.[18]

On the other hand, recognition of team loyalty effects need not imply that team owners keep prices low forever. Won and Lee's (2008) dynamic habit-forming model points to team owners raising ticket prices in the long run to take advantage of the attendance habit formed when prices were lower. This, in turn, seems to imply that we would observe teams initially keeping ticket prices below the short-run profit-maximizing level but then raising prices as the strategy pays off, after more and more fans are hooked and, presumably, sell outs become more frequent. Such an approach may well be observationally equivalent to reverse causation between ticket prices and attendance, whereby ticket prices rise over time in response to larger attendance levels. Narayan and Smyth (2003) suggest that admission prices set for the Melbourne Cup, Australia's top horseracing event, evince such a tendency for prices to respond to attendance, rather than the other way around. Over 1960–2002 Narayan and Smyth find unidirectional causation running from attendance to the admission price (specified in real terms), and both attendance and the admission price are also responsive to real income levels. Another example of a change in strategy over time is found in the rising prices imposed by English football teams in the 1990s at a time when moves from standing to all-seated arrangements reduced maximum attendance levels and brought stadiums closer to full capacity (Dobson and Goddard, 1998).[19]

The Endogeneity of Ticket Prices in Perspective

Almost all empirical work in sports economics continues to view the price-attendance relationship as a one-way street despite support, both anecdotal and econometric, for exactly the kind of reverse causation running from attendance to ticket pricing in professional sports leagues as that observed by Narayan and Smyth (2003) for the Melbourne Cup. Causation running from attendance to price would, of course, further complicate the inferences derived from standard regressions of attendance on price. Indeed, Narayan and Smyth (2003, p. 1656) argue that, should their findings generalize to other sporting events, "the short run attendance-price results in market demand models of attendance might be biased and … more systematic treatment of endogeneity is required in modelling attendance at sporting events." In the following two subsections, we consider two brief case studies that bear on the attendance-ticket prices relationship plus some econometric analysis highlighting the potential importance of allowing for ticket price endogeneity.

Attendance and Ticket Pricing in the China Super League

Few, if any, professional sports leagues could match the drop in attendance registered by China's Super League, which succeeded the former top division Chinese Football Association Jia (A) league in 2004. Average crowd sizes shrank from 23,000 in 2000 to 10,000 in 2006, with a majority of the teams running at a loss and becoming heavily dependent upon sponsorship, which accounted for 72 percent of total league revenue versus just 4.5 percent from ticket sales (No Quick Fix for China Super League, 2007). Many scandals, including match fixing, had tarnished the league's image, and increased access to broadcasts of European football was likely another factor in the decline. Things got so bad that China's main TV station, CCTV, temporarily pulled the plug on the league in 2008, with Jiang Heping, head of the CCTV sports channel, quoted as saying: "The state of Chinese football at the moment makes everyone bitter" (see Bristow, 2008).

Consistent with the reverse causation view, Chinese football teams responded by cutting ticket prices to historically low levels. Some teams continued to cut prices going into the 2009 season, and single-game ticket prices were as low at RMB 10 (approximately $1.50). With attendance levels partially rebounding to an average of 16,904 through May 18, 2009 (corresponding to 44.89 percent of leaguewide stadium capacity), it remained to be seen if higher prices would be implemented going forward.[20] Meanwhile, Beijing Guoan, featuring both the largest stadium capacity at 62,000 (Beijing's Worker's Stadium), and enjoying the league's largest average crowd size of 35,089, seemed already able to support ticket prices higher than those offered elsewhere, offering seats at prices ranging from RMB 30 to RMB 100 ($4.50–$15) for its August 26, 2009 fixture with Chengdu Sheffield United.[21]

Recent Attendance and Revenue Trends in the English Premier League

Between 1997–1998 and 2006–2007, English Premier League teams increased average stadium capacity by over 15 percent, from 32,386 in 1997–1998 to 37,345 in 2006–2007.[22] Table 12.4 shows that this was accompanied by a more than doubling of average game-day revenue per attendee from £19 in 1997–1998 to £41 in 2006–2007.[23] Rising outlays by fans attending Premier League games were not apparently linked to any difficulties in filling the extra seats generated over this period, however. Attendance remained in excess of 90 percent of overall capacity throughout, and the common uptrend in average revenue per fan and attendance between 1997–1998 and 2006–2007 can be seen in Figure 12.2. Meanwhile, the year-on-year increase in fan-based revenue of over 17 percent between 2005–2006 and 2006–2007, the largest on record, was accompanied by the highest average attendance in the history of the Premier League (and a slight reduction in empty seats). More than half the revenues gains were attributed to stadium development, most notably the opening of Arsenal's new Emirates Stadium and major revamping of

Table 12.4 English Premier League Fan Cost versus Attendance, 1997–98 to 2008–2009

Season	Average Matchday Revenue per Attendee (in pounds sterling)	Average Attendance	Attendance as % of Stadium Capacity
1997–1998	19	29,190	90
1998–1999	21	30,580	91
1999–2000	23	30,707	90
2000–2001	24	32,821	94
2001–2002	25	34,324	93
2002–2003	27	35,445	94
2003–2004	30	35,008	95
2004–2005	34	33,899	94
2005–2006	35	33,873	91
2006–2007	41	34,363	92
2007–2008	—	36,076	—
2008–2009	—	35,600	92

Sources: Deloitte Annual Review of Football Finance, 1998–2008; Sky Sports Football Yearbook 2008–2009 and Sky Sports Football Yearbook 2009–2010.

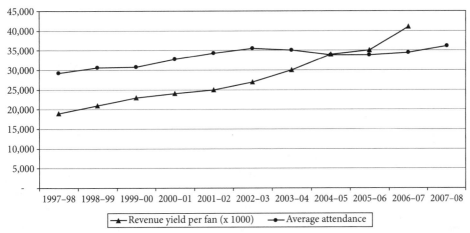

Figure 12.2 Premier League Revenue Yield per Fan vs. Average Attendance, 1997/98–2007/08.

Manchester United's Old Trafford. According to the *Deloitte Annual Review of Football Finance* (2008, p. 53):

> [Arsenal] now generates over £3m per game and matchday revenue has replaced broadcast as the main source of revenue at the club. Arsenal were able to leverage off an arguably unique set of circumstances in terms of the London location, level of previously unfulfilled spectator demand and Highbury's [the old stadium] extremely limited corporate hospitality offering.

The ongoing revenue increases have not, on the surface, been associated with ticket price hikes. Big money has been made from corporate sales and matchday packages, however. Such packages are bundled combinations including premium seating and hospitality services. For example, Arsenal, in addition to far more expensive executive and VIP packages for multiple guests, was offering a "Club Arsenal Package" for its September 19, 2009 fixture with Wigan Athletic priced at £325 per person (plus tax). By comparison, entry-level adult tickets were priced as low as £32.50 (up to a high of £92 for the best general admission seats).[24] Needless to say, even entry-level sales could be expected to draw in significant additional catering and concession sales, as with the major league baseball experience discussed earlier. Indeed, buoyed by a large revenue bump from new media deals coming in at the beginning of the 2007–2008 season, and cognizant of the danger of pricing their traditional fan base out of the market, half of all Premier League teams adopted either cuts in ticket prices or a ticket price freeze for 2007–2008.[25] Of the five clubs (out of a total of 20) that actually implemented price cuts in 2007–2008, three enjoyed increased attendance, one reported no change, and the last (Bolton Wanderers, who had a disappointing season dropping down from seventh place in 2006–2007 to sixteenth place in 2007–2008) faced an 11 percent drop in attendance despite cutting prices more than 10 percent (*Deloitte Annual Review of Football Finance*, 2008, p. 54).

Recent Empirical Evidence from European Football and Major League Baseball

García and Rodríguez (2002) show that allowing for endogeneity of ticket prices via instrumental variables leads to substantially higher elasticity estimates for Spanish First Division football teams over the 1992–1993 through 1995–1996 seasons than those arising under ordinary least squares. This at least raises the possibility that the direction of any bias may be in favor of generating the inelastic pricing pattern seen in most studies of attendance in professional sports. The length of the time series considered may also exert an important influence on the findings. Dobson and Goddard (1996), although finding modest short-run effects of ticket prices on attendance by region across England and Wales over 1955–1992, find no evidence that price changes have long-term effects. Performance on the field and unemployment rates are found to be the significant long-run determinants, with performance also being significant in the short run. Whether this reflects team owners adjusting price to maintain attendance over time remains an open question, however. Given that both the reverse-causation arguments and the habit-forming models of Ahn and Lee (2007) and Won and Lee (2008) point to the effects of price on attendance changing over time, either for strategic reasons or because of evolving levels of fan loyalty, more long-run studies might usefully supplement the existing literature, which tends to focus primarily on relatively short data runs.

One of the longer recent time-series studies of major league baseball attendance is that of Park, Lee, and Miller (2007), who consider over thirty years of data from 1970 to 2003. Park, Lee, and Miller's team-by-team analysis suggests considerable variation across teams, but with most featuring long-run price elasticities significantly below unity. Four teams exhibit elastic demand, however, whereas three have the wrong sign, that is, indicating that higher ticket prices increase attendance. It may not be entirely coincidental that the four teams with elastic pricing are smaller market teams: the Kansas City Royals, Milwaukee Brewers, Oakland Athletics, and San Diego Padres. As such, it is quite possible that, as the authors suggest, these same teams might rely relatively heavily on ticket sales as a source of revenue. Further analysis could usefully examine the extent to which team ticket pricing behavior is tied to the dependence on this revenue source. It would also be interesting to consider possible variations in the concession receipts per fan.

FAN PREFERENCES AND CUSTOMER-BASED DISCRIMINATION

Although a sports team can always look to boost attendance and revenues by acquiring higher quality players on the open market, this obviously raises the cost side of the calculation as well. There is also the danger that high rates of player turnover may alienate fans and backfire by hurting attendance (Kahane and Shmanske, 1997). It is possible, however, that teams could boost attendance by bringing in players who are not necessarily of higher quality or more expensive than their current players, but they may, nevertheless, boost attendance by being more appealing to the team's fan base. At times, such a move may have an entirely idiosyncratic basis, such as the Seattle Mariners' reacquisition of Ken Griffey, Jr. prior to the 2009 baseball season. Mutual expectations of a boost to fan turnout were enshrined in a contract offering a base of $2 million plus an extra $3 million conditional on attendance reaching at least three million for the year (plus Griffey remaining healthy). The Mariners sold 23,000 tickets within two days of the (preseason) February 18, 2009 announcement of the Griffey signing and a sports-apparel shop owner later commented that Griffey shirts were "about the only non-discounted Mariners items selling these days" (see Martinez, 2009).

A potentially more wide-ranging approach to changing the player mix to boost attendance is suggested by the literature on customer-based discrimination. Becker's (1971) concept of racial discrimination by customers is embodied by fan preferences for watching players of their own race or national origin, implying that teams lose revenue and profits when they adopt neutral hiring practices. Accordingly, unlike discrimination by employers and by fellow workers, customer-based discrimination may well persist even in the long run (Nardinelli and Simon, 1990). Burdekin and Idson (1991) and Hoang and Rascher (1999) suggest that NBA teams enjoyed attendance and revenue gains by matching the racial profile of their players with the racial profile of their local market area in the 1980s.[26] Notwithstanding the decline in the number of white players in the NBA since the 1980s, Burdekin, Hossfeld, and Smith (2005) identify a continued tendency for the higher-ranked white players to locate in NBA cities with larger white populations during the 1990s.[27]

Although there is generally less evidence of customer-based discrimination in other major U.S. professional sports, Kahn (1992, p. 308) concludes that, during the 1989 NFL season,

> white players earned significantly more money in metropolitan areas with larger than average percentages of whites in the population than in other areas, and nonwhite players earned significantly more in areas with relatively high proportions of nonwhites in the population. These results are consistent with the presence of customer discrimination ... Evidently, ... fans' prejudice does affect player salaries ...

Elsewhere, there is some evidence of discrimination against black pitchers in major league baseball (Scully, 1974; Rascher, 1999). To the extent that most ticket-buying fans are white, the indicated negative attendance effects associated with black pitchers could be associated with customer-based discrimination. This would not explain Rascher's (1999) additional findings of attendance premiums seemingly associated with Asian and Latino pitchers, however.[28]

Besides customer-based racial discrimination, there is also the possibility of nationality-based discrimination, and a number of studies have tested for both phenomena in European football. Preston and Szymanski (2000) find that English football teams located in areas with a larger black population featured significantly greater ratios of black players over the 1974–1993 seasons but conclude that any discrimination is more likely attributable to the owners than to the fans.[29] Other studies testing for nationality preferences generally report little evidence of fan bias in favor of domestic players (cf, Wilson and Ying, 2003; Pedace, 2008). Pedace (2008, p. 137) does uncover one possible element of customer-based discrimination, however, insofar as preferential labor market treatment identified for South American players can be interpreted as a "perfectly rational reaction by owners who observe increased attendance when there are more appearances by South American players." This again suggests possible gains for teams from better matching the composition of their team to the preferences of their fan base, even though, in this case, these preferences actually appear to favor a different nationality and ethnic group from their own.

Conclusions

The link between price and sports attendance is, to say the least, far from being as straightforward as it may at first appear. First, there are a host of measurement issues on both sides. There are wide varieties of seats that, not only sell for different prices, but also may not sell out in the same proportion, with unfilled seats often concentrated in the less desirable, cheaper sections. Some seats are sold on a one-time basis at the gate, others to season-ticket holders, and others sold packaged with other amenities, likely attracting different types of buyers with different characteristics and varying elasticities of demand. Second, there are complications arising from reverse causation, with the possibility that elasticity estimates may be biased if endogeneity of ticket prices is not taken into account. Third, there is the perennial risk of omitted variable bias given the difficulties of capturing the myriad possible nonprice determinants of fan demand, including possible customer-based discrimination. Finally, even if the widespread finding that sports teams typically price in the inelastic range survives these challenges intact, this may still not allow us to reject profit maximization in favor of alternatives like win maximization. This is because inelastic ticket pricing can itself still be consistent with long-term profit maximization or maximization across other revenue streams, such as television fees or concessions earnings.

Data limitations seem unlikely to allow any irrefutable measures of price and attendance relationships. However, attempts to correct for factors such as season-ticket holders and fans' traveling costs, as in some English football studies, certainly seem like a step in the right direction. There have also been some intriguing and seemingly plausible advances in demonstrating the potential consistency between inelastic ticket pricing and profit maximization that deserve further study. On the other hand, surprisingly few empirical studies have yet taken into account the potential (and likely) endogeneity of ticket prices or examined the evolution of ticket-pricing strategies over the longer term. It is, perhaps, there that future research might have the highest value added, especially if it could be tied to the relatively new applications of habit-formation and lifecycle models to sports demand. Finally, given the burgeoning literature on the demand for sports (almost making one wish for the single-digit total available at the time of Cairns, Jennett, and Sloane's 1986 review!), apologies are due to any studies making advances in these areas that were inadvertently excluded here.

NOTES

....

The author thanks Janet Smith and the editors for helpful comments, Aditya Bindal for research assistance, and the Lowe Institute at Claremont McKenna College for financial support.

1 Rascher and Rascher (2004) assess the merits of specific target cities for NBA relocation along with the importance of the lease agreements with the local authorities. Meanwhile, evidence of strong profit and revenue gains accruing to major league baseball teams moving into publicly subsidized new stadiums seems to be combined with a tendency for these monetary returns to be heavily skewed in favor of the team owner at the expense of the municipality (cf, Depken, 2006; Hakes and Clapp, 2006).

2 These transfer costs represent compensation to the team that formerly had the player under contract and, as the data in Table 12.1 imply, accounted for more than a quarter of total player costs during 2006–2007.

3 This was preceded by another innovation, namely going public on the stock market. Following Tottenham Hotspur's lead in 1983, over 30 clubs obtained stock exchange listings (led by other Premier League teams). Interest in this area seemed to cool after the mid-1990s, however (Feddersen and Maennig, 2008).

4 Although wage cost data were only available through the 2006–2007 season, it may be added that the big-four's monopoly over the top-four league positions continued through the 2007–2008 and 2008–2009 seasons. The post-Abramovich developments do, however, come on the heels of a more generalized increase in competitive imbalance in English football as identified by Dobson and Goddard (2004).

5 The willingness to pay a premium price, and undertake financially losing propositions, likely rises sharply when the potential for winning championships is higher (DeGennaro, 2003). Even clubs without billionaire ownership may be able to sustain ongoing losses, at least up to a point. Buraimo and Simmons (2008) suggest that this may follow from the absence of any scope for forced takeovers of money-losing operations combined with creditors being reluctant to call in the debt because of the bad publicity that may result, with the longstanding overdrafts held by Scottish Premier League clubs with the Bank of Scotland perhaps being a case in point.

6 In addition to newer treatments of the sports covered in the original eight studies, evidence of inelastic pricing has also been found for the NFL (Welki and Zlatoper, 1994; Depken, 2001; Brook, 2006), Australian Rules Football (Borland and Lye, 1992),

and the English Rugby League (Carmichael, Millington and Simmons, 1999). Analysis of the NBA generally finds price effects to be insignificantly different from zero (cf, Burdekin and Idson, 1991; Morse et al., 2008) as does Wilson and Sim's (1995) analysis of the Malaysian Semi-Pro Football League.

7 Although DeSerpa (1994) suggests that this may simply reflect high uncertainty and variance in ticket demand coupled with the infeasibility of changing prices from game to game, variable- ticket-pricing strategies have since been implemented and become quite widespread in major league baseball. Rascher et al. (2007) calculate that variable ticket pricing could have yielded modest revenue gains in 1996, averaging around a 2.8 percent increase but reaching a maximum estimated gain of 6.7 percent. for the San Francisco Giants.

8 Only the common-seat measure (defined based on the published price of a seat in the upper deck in foul territory) was found to yield a significant coefficient at all and the weighted average price is actually associated with a significantly positive coefficient value. The rising variation in seat prices over the years, as teams in newer stadiums derive increasing amounts of revenue from ultra-high-priced luxury boxes, only highlights the potential importance of this definitional issue. Overall, Rascher and Racher (2004) estimate that newer NBA and NHL stadiums increase game-day revenue streams by as much as 50 percent, whereas Hakes and Clapp (2006) estimate that new major league baseball stadiums typically generated present-value revenues of $272 million and Depken (2005) finds an aggregate profit boost that reached $47 million for the average team moving into new facilities during the 1990s.

9 By comparison, the prior long-run study of English football clubs by Bird (1982), using data from 1948–1949 through 1979–1980, suggested an overall price elasticity of just -0.20. The estimated price elasticities were all rendered insignificant when the different divisions within English football were analyzed individually.

10 Both the football studies actually suggest a mix of elastic and inelastic pricing, but with estimated elasticities consistently higher than in most previous work. This may reflect the fact that Forrest, Simmons, and Feehan (2002) control for fans' traveling costs in their econometric work, whereas García and Rodríguez take the endogeneity of prices into account via an instrumental variable technique. A recent study of Brazilian football attendance during 2003–2006 by Madalozzo and Villar (2009) returns the more familiar result of an inelastic pricing regime but does not control for endogeneity of ticket pricing.

11 Meanwhile, the attendance impact of the increased televising of league football continues to be debated. Negative effects on stadium attendance levels (although suggested, for example, by Buraimo's, 2008, analysis of televised second-tier [Championship League] English football matches and Allan and Roy's, 2008, study of the Scottish Premier League) do not seem to have materialized in the English Premier League, which consistently enjoyed better than 90 percent stadium capacity utilization. See Table 12.4 and the discussion that follows.

12 Although Porter (2007) questions Fort's (2004a) focus on the elasticity of revenue with respect to talent rather than ticket prices *per se*, Fort (2007) demonstrates that the original inferences remain valid so long as we accept an underlying relationship between revenue and attendance.

13 Fort (2004b) notes examples of NFL lease agreements in which raising prices above those charged by other teams in comparable facilities would trigger revocation or renegotiation of the lease.

14 See Krautmann and Berri (2007, p. 187) for the formal derivation of this intuitive result.

15 A key empirical issue clearly concerns the actual extent of the complementary boost
    to other revenue streams deriving from ticket sales. In the music business, Krueger
    (2005) links sharp increases in concert prices to a decline in complementarities as
    more and more fans simply downloaded music from the Internet or copied CDs,
    thereby significantly reducing artist royalty levels. By contrast, up until the late 1990s,
    "when greater concert attendance [still] translated into grater artists' record sales,
    artists had an incentive to price their tickets below the profit-maximizing price for
    concerts alone" (Krueger, 2005, p. 25).

16 Results with the NFL data generally showed no significant response of attendance to
    either ticket prices or the fan cost index, a finding that the authors suggest may be
    linked to the much greater prevalence of sellouts.

17 The potential importance of loyalty effects has also been suggested in Kahane and
    Shmanske's (1997) finding that major league baseball attendance was negatively
    affected by higher turnover rates over the 1990–1992 seasons. This is consistent with
    the premise that, if team "rosters change too much, many of the marginal fans may
    give up trying to follow the team" (Kahane and Shmanske, 1997, p. 425). Depken
    (2000, p. 132) actually estimates fan loyalty measures across different major league
    baseball teams, suggesting that teams with lower loyalty levels will feature more elastic
    demand and "stand to lose the most by marginal decreases in quality or increases in
    price." Finally, Depken (2001) provides estimates of relative NFL fan loyalty levels,
    whereas Spenner, Fenn, and Crooker (2010) suggest that NFL attendance is also habit
    forming and consistent with rational addiction models.

18 Indeed, when the Houston Astros' home games against the Chicago Cubs were moved
    to Milwaukee on September 14–15, 2008 after Houston had been hit by Hurricane
    Ike, the stadium was dubbed Wrigley Park North. This phenomenon reflected
    not just Milwaukee's relative proximity to Chicago but also the fact that it offered
    opportunities for Illinois-based Cubs fans to obtain tickets more easily than they
    could at home. For example, one fan was quoted as saying they made the trip because
    "You can't get tickets (to games at Wrigley) anymore unless you're willing to pay
    scalper prices" (see Benson, 2008).

19 Meanwhile, Dobson and Goddard's (1998) empirical work suggests another
    possible reverse causation effect. Specifically, they suggest that, rather than
    higher-performing teams getting higher attendance and revenue because of their
    success on the field, top-performing clubs are able to succeed because they enjoy
    the benefits of stronger fan followings and higher initial revenue. Dobson and
    Goddard's (1998, p. 1641) conclusion that the "natural tendency is for success to
    become concentrated increasingly among a small group of elite, wealthy clubs"
    certainly seems to have borne out in the subsequent dominance in England of the
    big four (see Table 12.2).

20 These attendance data are drawn from http://www.melbournevictory.net/forum/
    showthread.php?t=53318.

21 The ticket prices are as quoted on http://plaocool.com, which is a Chinese equivalent
    of Ticketmaster.

22 Although these data, drawn from the *Deloitte Annual Review of Football
    Finance,* are affected by changes in league composition due to promotion and
    relegation, the primary driver of this increase was clearly stadium expansion and
    new facilities on the part of the top clubs that remained in the league throughout
    this period.

23 There is, unfortunately, no true ticket price series or fan cost index equivalent to those available for the major North American sports leagues. The game day revenue series is itself an approximation calculated by taking total game day revenues for all Premier League teams divided by total attendance at all league matches.

24 The largest difference between premium tickets and regular tickets over the NBA, NFL, and NHL in 2006 was the NBA's 3.50:1 ratio (Mason and Howard, 2008, p. 127). Despite growing prominence of corporate-focused luxury boxes, it is harder to find counterparts to the Premier League's matchday packages for individual fans, however.

25 Interestingly, Premier League teams' 2007–2008 ticket-pricing strategies may actually have reflected sentiments consistent with Ahn and Lee's (2007) emphasis on keeping prices low enough to draw in first-time customers and assure the team's future fan base. That is, a "strategy to attract younger supporters to the matchday experience in order to recruit the season ticket holders of the future" (*Deloitte Annual Review of Football Finance*, 2008, p. 54).

26 On the other hand, Dey (1997), McCormick and Tollison (2001) and Berri, Schmidt, and Brook (2004), using data from the 1980s and/or early 1990s, saw no relationship between the racial match and NBA attendance. (See also the recent in-depth reviews of racial discrimination in the NBA in Berri, 2006, and Kahn, 2011.)

27 Burdekin, Hossfeld, and Smith (2005) further find that white players are significantly more likely to be traded than are black players. Black players are more likely to be traded *from* a team located in a city with a relatively large white population, and are less likely to be traded *to* a team with a high percentage of white players. Relative to black players, white players are significantly less likely to be traded *from* a team located in a city with a relatively large white population, and are less likely to be traded *from* a team that has a large percentage of white players. Taken together, this offers further evidence on the importance of the sorting of players by race in the NBA. (Although Kahn and Shah, 2005, find no significant team composition effects on NBA team attendance during 2000–2001.)

28 There are, of course, myriad other forms of discrimination that may have been important in both major league baseball and the NFL, including asymmetric hiring, retention, and assignment of players (see, for example, Kahn, 2000).

29 Goddard and Wilson (2009), in pointing to a concentration of black players among the upper echelons of English football over the 1986–2001 period, suggest that less elite black players nevertheless found it harder to get into league football than white counterparts with similar skill levels.

References

Ahn, Seung C., and Young H. Lee. 2007. Lifecycle demand for Major League Baseball. *International Journal of Sport Finance* 2: 79–93.

Alexander, Donald L. 2001. Major League Baseball: Monopoly pricing and profit-maximizing behavior. *Journal of Sports Economics* 2: 341–355.

Allan, Grant, and Graeme Roy. 2008. Does television crowd out spectators? New evidence from the Scottish Premier League. *Journal of Sports Economics* 9: 592–605.

Andreff, Wladimir. 2006. Team sports and finance. In *Handbook on the Economics of Sport,* eds. Wladimir Andreff and Stefan Szymanski, 689–699. Northampton, MA: Edward Elgar.

Becker, Gary S. 1971. *The economics of discrimination*, 2nd edition. Chicago: University of Chicago Press.

Benson, Dan. 2008. Chicago fans storm park. *Milwaukee Journal Sentinel*, September 15 http://www.jsonline.com/sports/brewers/32534029.html.

Berri, David J. 2006. National Basketball Association. In *Handbook of Sports Economics Research*, ed. John Fizel, 21–48. Armonk, NY: M.E. Sharpe.

Berri, David J., Martin B Schmidt, and Stacey L. Brook. 2004. Stars at the gate: The impact of star power on NBA gate revenues. *Journal of Sports Economics* 5: 33–50.

Bird, Peter J. W. N. 1982. The demand for league football. *Applied Economics* 14: 637–649.

Borland, Jeff, and Jenny Lye. 1992. Attendance at Australian Rules Football: A panel study. *Applied Economics* 24: 1053–1058.

Bristow, Michael. 2008. China TV bans top football league. *BBC News,* November 17 http://news.bbc.co.uk/2/hi/asia-pacific/7733298.stm.

Buraimo, Babatunde. 2008. Stadium attendance and television audience demand in English league football. *Managerial and Decision Economics* 29: 513–523.

Buraimo, Babatunde, and Rob Simmons. 2008. The profitability of sports teams: International perspectives. In *The business of sports vol. 1*, ed. Brad R. Humphreys and Dennis R. Howard, 33–58. Westport, CT.: Praeger.

Burdekin, Richard C. K., and Todd L. Idson. 1991. Customer preferences, attendance and the racial structure of professional basketball teams. *Applied Economics* 23: 179–186.

Burdekin, Richard C. K., Richard T. Hossfeld, and Janet Kiholm Smith. 2005. Are NBA fans becoming indifferent to race? Evidence from the 1990s. *Journal of Sports Economics* 6: 144–159.

Cairns, J., N. Jennett and P.J. Sloane. 1986. The economics of professional team sports: A survey of theory and evidence. *Journal of Economic Studies* 13: 1–80.

Carmichael, Fiona, Janet Millington, and Robert Simmons. 1999. Elasticity of demand for rugby league attendance and the impact of BSkyB. *Applied Economics Letters* 6: 797–800.

Cebula, Richard J. 2009. The potential role of marketing in promoting free enterprise in the U.S.: A study involving minor league baseball and ticket-sales revenue maximization. *Journal of International and Global Economic Studies* 2: 31–45.

Coates, Dennis, and Brad R. Humphreys. 2007. Ticket prices, concessions and attendance at professional sporting events. *International Journal of Sport Finance* 2: 161–170.

DeGennaro, Ramon P. 2003. The utility of sport and returns to ownership. *Journal of Sports Economics* 4: 145–153.

Deloitte Annual Review of Football Finance (1996–2008). Manchester, England: Sports Business Group at Deloitte.

Demmert, Henry G. 1973. *The economics of professional team sports*. Lexington, MA: D.C. Heath.

Depken, Craig A., II. 2000. Fan loyalty and stadium funding in professional baseball. *Journal of Sports Economics* 1: 124–138.

Depken, Craig A., II. 2001. Fan loyalty in professional sports: An extension to the National Football League. *Journal of Sports Economics* 2: 275–284.

Depken, Craig A., II. 2006. The impact of new stadiums on professional baseball team finances. *Public Finance and Management* 6: 436–474.

DeSerpa, Allan C. 1994. To err is rational: A theory of excess demand for tickets. *Managerial and Decision Economics* 15: 511–518.

Dey, Matthew S. 1997. Racial differences in National Basketball Association players' salaries: A new look. *The American Economist* 41: 84–90.

Dobson, S. M., and J.A. Goddard. 1996. The demand for football in the regions of England and Wales. *Regional Studies* 30: 443–453.

Dobson, S. M., and J.A. Goddard. 1998. Performance and revenue in professional league football: Evidence from Granger causality tests. *Applied Economics* 30: 1641–1651.

Dobson, Stephen, and John Goddard. 2004. Revenue divergence and competitive balance in a professional sports league. *Scottish Journal of Political Economy* 51: 359–376.

Donihue, Michael R., David W. Findlay, and Peter W. Newberry. 2007. An analysis of attendance at Major League Baseball spring training games. *Journal of Sports Economics* 8: 39–61.

Feddersen, Arne, and Wolfgang Maennig. 2008. The European perspective on team ownership, competitive balance, and event impacts. In *The Business of Sports,* vol. 1, ed. Brad R. Humphreys and Dennis R. Howard, 153–185. Westport, CT.: Praeger.

Fort, Rodney. 2004a. Inelastic sports pricing. *Managerial and Decision Economics* 25: 87–94.

Fort, Rodney. 2004b. Subsidies as incentive mechanisms in sports. *Managerial and Decision Economics* 25: 95–102.

Fort, Rodney. 2006. Inelastic sports pricing at the gate? A survey. In *Handbook on the Economics of Sport,* ed. Wladimir Andreff and Stefan Szymanski, 700–708. Northampton, MA: Edward Elgar.

Fort, Rodney. 2007. Reply to The paradox of inelastic sports pricing. *Managerial and Decision Economics* 28: 159–160.

Ford, Rodney, and James Quirk. 1995. Cross-subsidization, incentives, and outcomes in professional team sports. *Journal of Economic Literature* 33: 1265–1299.

Forrest, David, Robert Simmons, and Patrick Feehan. 2002. A spatial cross-sectional analysis of the elasticity of demand for soccer. *Scottish Journal of Political Economy* 49: 336–355.

García, Jaume, and Plácido Rodríguez. 2002. The determinants of football match attendance revisited: Empirical evidence from the Spanish Football League. *Journal of Sports Economics* 3: 18–38.

Goddard, John, and John O.S. Wilson. 2009. Racial discrimination in English professional football: Evidence from an empirical analysis of players' career progression. *Cambridge Journal of Economics* 33: 295–316.

Hakes, Jahn K., and Christopher M. Clapp. 2006. The edifice complex: The economics of public subsidization of Major League Baseball facilities. *International Journal of Sport Finance* 1: 77–95.

Heilmann, Ronald L., and Wayne R. Wendling. 1976. A note on optimum pricing strategies for sports events. In *Management science in sports,* ed. Robert E. Machol, Shaul P. Ladany, and Donald G. Morrison, 91–99. Amsterdam: North-Holland.

Hoang, Ha, and Daniel A. Rascher. 1999. The NBA, exit discrimination, and career earnings. *Industrial Relations* 38: 69–91.

Kahane, Leo, and Stephen Shmanske. 1997. Team roster turnover and attendance in Major League Baseball. *Applied Economics* 29: 425–431.

Kahn, Lawrence M. 1992. The effects of race on professional football players' compensation. *Industrial and Labor Relations Review* 45: 295–310.

Kahn, Lawrence M. 2000. The sports business as a labor market laboratory. *Journal of Economic Perspectives* 14: 75–94.

Kahn, Lawrence M. 2011. The economics of discrimination: Evidence from basketball. (Chapter 2, this volume.)

Kahn. Lawrence M., and Malav Shah. 2005. Race, compensation and contract length in the NBA: 2001–2002. *Industrial Relations* 44: 444–462.

Késenne, Stefan, and Wilfried Pauwels. 2006. Club objectives and ticket pricing in professional sports. *Eastern Economic Journal* 32: 549–560.

Krautmann, Anthony C., and David J. Berri. 2007. Can we find it at the concessions? Understanding price elasticity in professional sports. *Journal of Sports Economics* 8: 183–191.

Krautmann, Anthony, and Lawrence Hadley. 2006. Demand issues: The product market for professional sports. In *Handbook of Sports Economics Research*, ed. John Fizel, 175–189. Armonk, NY: M.E. Sharpe.

Krueger, Alan B. 2005. The economics of real superstars: The market for rock concerts in the material world. *Journal of Labor Economics* 23: 1–30.

Leeds, Michael, and Peter von Allmen. 2007. *The economics of sports,* 3rd edition. Boston: Pearson Addison Wesley.

Madalozzo, Regina, and Rodrigo Berber Villar. 2009. Brazilian football: What brings fans to the game? *Journal of Sports Economics* 10: 639–650.

Martinez, Amy. 2009. What does Griffey's return mean for local businesses? *The Seattle Times*, March 13 http://seattletimes.nwsource.com/html/businesstechnology/2008851456_griffey13.html.

Mason, Daniel S., and Dennis R. Howard. 2008. New revenue streams in professional sports. In *The Business of Sports,* vol. 1, eds. Brad R. Humphreys and Dennis R. Howard, 125–151. Westport, CT: Praeger.

McCormick, Robert E., and Robert D. Tollison. 2001. Why do black basketball players work more for less money? *Journal of Economic Behavior & Organization* 44: 201–219.

Morse, Alan L., Stephen L. Shapiro, Chad D. McEvoy, and Daniel A. Rascher. 2008. The effects of roster turnover on demand in the National Basketball Association. *International Journal of Sport Finance* 3: 8–18.

Narayan, Paresh Kumar, and Russell Smyth. 2003. Attendance and pricing at sporting events: Empirical results from Granger causality tests for the Melbourne Cup. *Applied Economics* 35: 1649–1657.

Nardinelli, Clark, and Curtis Simon. 1990. Customer racial discrimination in the market for memorabilia: The case of baseball. *Quarterly Journal of Economics* 105: 575–595.

No quick fix for China super league, June 8, 2007. http://news.oneindia.in/2007/06/08/no-quick-fix-for-china-super-league-1181299677.html.

Noll, Roger G. 1974. Attendance and price setting. In *Government and the Sports Business*, ed. Roger G. Noll, 115–157. Washington, DC: Brookings Institution.

Park, Kwang Woo (Ken), Soonhwan Lee, and Phillip Miller. 2007. *Ticket pricing per team: The case of Major League Baseball (MLB).* Mankato, MN: Mimeo, Minnesota State University. http://krypton.mnsu.edu/~millep1/papers/JSM-Elasticity-Nov-2007.pdf.

Pedace, Roberto. 2008. Earnings, performance, and nationality discrimination in a highly competitive labor market as an analysis of the English Professional Soccer League. *Journal of Sports Economics* 9: 115–140.

Porter, Philip K. 2007. The paradox of inelastic sports pricing. *Managerial and Decision Economics* 28: 157–158.

Preston, Ian, and Stefan Szymanski. 2000. Racial discrimination in English football. *Scottish Journal of Political Economy* 47: 342–363.

Quirk, James, and Mohamed El Hodiri. 1974. The economic theory of a professional sports league. In *Government and the Sports Business*, ed. Roger G. Noll, 33–80. Washington, DC: Brookings Institution.

Rascher, Daniel. 1999. A test of the optimal positive production network externality in Major League Baseball. In *Sports Economics: Current Research*, eds. John Fizel, Elizabeth Gustafson, and Lawrence Hadley, 27–45. Westport, CT: Praeger.

Rascher, Daniel, and Heather Rascher. 2004. NBA expansion and relocation: A viability study of various cities. *Journal of Sport Management* 18: 274–295.

Rascher, Daniel, Chad D. McEvoy, Mark S. Nagel, and Matthew T. Brown. 2007. Variable ticket pricing in Major League Baseball. *Journal of Sport Management* 21: 407–437.

Scully, Gerald W. 1974. Discrimination: The case of baseball. In *Government and the Sports Business*, ed. Roger G. Noll, 221–273. Washington, DC: Brookings Institution.

Simmons, Robert. 1996. The demand for English league football: A club-level analysis. *Applied Economics* 28: 139–155.

Sky Sports Football Yearbook 2008–2009. 2008. Ed. Glenda Rollin and Jack Rollin. London: Headline.

Sky Sports Football Yearbook 2009–2010. 2009. Ed. Glenda Rollin and Jack Rollin. London: Headline.

Sloane, Peter. 1971. The economics of professional football: The football club as a utility maximizer. *Scottish Journal of Political Economy* 18: 121–146.

Spenner, Erin LeAnne, Aju J. Fenn, and John R. Crooker. 2010. The demand for NFL attendance: A rational addiction model. *Journal of Business & Economics Research* 8, No. 12 http://journals.cluteonline.com/index.php/JBER/article/view/777.

Stacey L. Brook. 2006. Evaluating inelastic ticket pricing models. *International Journal of Sport Finance* 1: 140–150.

Szymanski, Stefan. 2006. Football in England. In *Handbook on the Economics of Sport*, ed. Wladimir Andreff and Stefan Szymanski, 459–462. Northampton, MA: Edward Elgar.

Welki, Andrew M., and Thomas J. Zlatoper. 1994. US professional football: The demand for game-day attendance in 1991. *Managerial and Decision Economics* 15: 489–495.

Wilson, Dennis P, and Yung-Hsiang Ying. 2003. Nationality preferences for labour in the international football industry. *Applied Economics* 35: 1551–1559.

Wilson, Peter, and Benson Sim. 1995. The demand for semi-pro league football in Malaysia 1989–91: A panel data approach. *Applied Economics* 27: 131–138.

Won, Dong C., and Young H. Lee. 2008. Optimal dynamic pricing for sports games with habitual attendance. *Managerial and Decision Economics* 29: 639–655.

Zimbalist, Andrew. 1992. *Baseball and billions: A probing look inside the big business of our national pastime*. New York: Basic Books.

PART IV

ILLUSTRATIONS
OF INDUSTRIAL
ORGANIZATION

CHAPTER 13

....

MAJOR LEAGUE BASEBALL IS JUST LIKE MCDONALD'S?

LESSONS FROM UNRECOGNIZED RIVAL LEAGUES

....

RODNEY FORT

1. INTRODUCTION

....

COMPETITION among sports leagues illustrates interesting components of industrial organization. Leagues are quite interesting organizations because, once a league structure is chosen, they are cooperative ventures by definition. Thus, competition between rival sports leagues is actually competition between rival cooperative ventures. Ultimately, the result in North America has always been the return to a dominant league outcome. This chapter concerns the impact on fans, the ultimate concern in antitrust, due to the return to dominant leagues over the history of Major League Baseball (MLB).

In MLB, there has been a distinct path in these cases. Through 1915, covering the National League (NL), American Association (AA), Union Association (UA), Players League (PL), and Federal League (FL), it appears there was economic competition. Thus, the calmer times in this period (equilibrium?) should have teams in each location where a team can be viable as well as something approximating marginal cost pricing. The dominant league (the NL prior to 1901 and the NL and AL, what we now know as MLB, from 1903–1915) typically allowed a few owners from the rival league to join and absorbed intercity competitive franchises into single new units. Because this happened through the usual forces of competition, there would be little suspicion that there was a social problem in these earliest cases.

However, MLB's behavior toward rival leagues from the 1940s through the 1960s is a cause for concern—for example, African American Leagues (AALs) in the late 1940s, the Pacific Coast League (PCL) in the late 1950s, and finally on to the Continental League (CL) in the early 1960s. In these cases of rival leagues, the actions of individual owners through their MLB organization led to the reduction in both the quantity and quality of baseball enjoyed by vast numbers of fans. Owners in rival leagues were not asked to join MLB and, rather than absorption of competing intercity rival franchises, typically the number of teams was reduced. It is these later rival league cases that are the focus of this chapter. Since MLB has faced no serious challenge for well over forty years, the note here is one of eternal antitrust vigilance.

The exercise in this chapter also generates insights into current debate over the "single-entity" status of sports leagues (see Fort, 2007). Once the league is chosen as an organizational form, cooperation is required to define the league product. One important question: Which actions by owners through their league simply create higher profit through the exercise of market power rather than just defining league output and creating league play? In turn, an important element in this question is the extent to which competition dominates in their franchising activity. Are sports league franchises subject to the vigorous competition faced in other industries, for example, fast service? The suggestion from the examples of rival leagues from the 1940s on is clearly that they are not. First, their original formation was entirely different. McDonald's was a small restaurant chain owned by a single individual. Baseball leagues were originally formed among teams owned and managed by separate individuals. Second, placement of McDonald's franchises does not eliminate competition so that only McDonald's franchises remain! But the examples of rival leagues after the 1940s make it clear that this is exactly what can happen with MLB franchising.

The examples after the 1940s are, indeed, rival leagues just as surely as any of the more famous earlier rivals. AALs were viable and eliminated by the racial integration of MLB. The PCL was more than a minor league by MLB's own admission. Here, rather than skimming the best talent (as in the AAL case), MLB simply took over the most important territories in this budding rival league. Finally, the CL was a rival in the planning stage when done in by MLB relocation and expansion choices. This illustrates the ongoing societal problem associated with sports league market power—the elimination of rival leagues is the elimination of competition. Even though MLB eventually made it to some of the cities that lost teams, the result appears to have been harmful to consumers.

The chapter proceeds as follows. The early history in the next section shows the rough and tumble competition outcomes for the AA, UA, PL, and FL. Section 3 shows the decidedly different outcome that reduced competition in the case of the AALs, the PCL, and the CL. Observations and conclusions round out the chapter.

2. EARLY HISTORY: THE REIGN OF ECONOMIC COMPETITION

Many histories exist on the early rival leagues. My recent favorites are Pietrusza (2005), and Jozsa (2006). To begin, so-called organized baseball was governed from the outset by the National Agreement. The National Agreement was first signed in 1883 by the two competing major leagues, the NL and AA, along with the minor Northwest League. It has been in force, in one form or another, ever since. By 1900, fourteen different leagues had signed the National Agreement. Teams that have tried to form rival major leagues outside of the National Agreement are often referred to as "outlaw" leagues and there remain a few so-called independent minor leagues that are not signatories.

The NL (originally christened the National League of Professional Baseball Clubs) grew out of the weaker forerunner, the National Association of Professional Base Ball Players. Table 13.1 shows the cities served during the first phase of competitive leagues in baseball, involving the NL, AA, and UA, 1881–1885. By 1881, the NL had settled to an eight-team league in eight different cities. The AA began play in 1882 with six teams in six different cities so that major league baseball was enjoyed in fourteen different cities. The following year, the AA added teams in Columbus and New York, but the NL lost its Troy and Worcester teams, replaced by teams in New York and Philadelphia. This put sixteen major league teams in fourteen different cities between the two. From the fan's perspective, adding a second major league almost doubled the number of cities with major league teams.

The UA appeared on the scene for only the 1884 season with twelve teams. The NL stayed the same at eight teams but the AA added five teams. As a result, thirty-three major league teams served twenty-three different cities. What a difference competition makes, but it seems unlikely that all these locations could support teams; many were simply "filler" as leagues sorted out team location based on economic competitiveness.

When the UA folded, its St. Louis and Boston teams folded into their NL counterparts, but the NL's Cleveland franchise closed. The AA cut to eight teams and the UA teams in Baltimore, Cincinnati, and Philadelphia folded into their AA counterparts. The resulting end-of-the-UA saw sixteen NL and AA teams serving thirteen different cities by 1885. This was one less team but the same number of cities served compared to 1883, the year before the UA attempted to join the major

Table 13.1 National League—American Association—Union
Association, 1881–1885

City	1881	1882	1883	1884	1885
Altoona Mountain City				UA	
Baltimore		AA	AA	AA/UA	AA
Boston	NL	NL	NL	NL/UA	NL
Brooklyn				AA	AA
Buffalo	NL	NL	NL	NL	NL
Chicago	NL	NL	NL	NL/UA	NL
Cincinnati		AA	AA	AA/UA	AA
Cleveland	NL	NL	NL	NL	
Columbus			AA	AA	
Detroit	NL	NL	NL	NL	NL
Indianapolis				AA	
Kansas City				UA	
Louisville		AA	AA	AA	AA
Milwaukee				UA	
New York			NL/AA	NL/AA	NL/AA
Philadelphia		AA	AA/NL	NL/AA/UA	NL/AA
Pittsburgh		AA	AA	AA	AA
Providence	NL	NL	NL	NL	NL
Richmond				AA	
St. Louis		AA	AA	AA/UA	NL/AA
St. Paul				UA	
Toledo				AA	
Troy	NL	NL			
Washington				AA/UA(2)	
Worcester	NL	NL			
NL	8	8	8	8	8
AA		6	8	13	8
UA				12	
Teams	8	14	16	33	16
Cities	8	14	14	23	13

Source: Compiled from league membership reports at baseball-reference.com

league ranks. It is tempting to cry foul on this reduction relative to the presence of the UA from the perspective of fan welfare, but the remaining leagues were both still fiercely economically competitive. For the next four years, the two leagues maintained their same size of eight teams each but then expanded to cover two more cities by 1889.

The next league to try its hand at major league status was the PL for just the 1890 season. In addition, the AA ended the year after in 1891. Table 13.2 detail teams and locations for this episode, 1889–1892. By 1889, the year prior to the PL entry, the NL and AA had come to serve fifteen different cities with sixteen teams in total between them, two more cities than five years earlier. In the NL, Buffalo, Detroit, Providence, and St. Louis were gone, but now there were teams in Indianapolis, Pittsburgh, and Washington. In the AA, New York was gone, Pittsburgh had joined the NL, and new teams now played in Columbus and Kansas City. The PL entered in 1890 with eight teams covering eight different cities. In the same year, the NL dropped Indianapolis and Washington, replacing them with Brooklyn and Cincinnati. In the AA, the Cincinnati team had jumped to the NL, Kansas City folded, and Rochester, Syracuse, and Toledo joined the league. Between the three major leagues, twenty-five teams served sixteen different cities. The attempted entry of a third major league added only one additional city served! Since competition was in action, it is pretty clear that the number of true major league cities was in the neighborhood of sixteen.

In 1891, with the PL gone, the NL remained in the same cities as in 1890. The AA dropped Brooklyn, Rochester, Syracuse, and Toledo, added the PL's Boston team, folded the PL's Philadelphia team into its AA counterpart, and began play in Washington for the second time. Thus, at the end of the PL, the NL and AA served fourteen cities with seventeen teams. The number of cities served fell by one relative to the year before the PL tried its hand, even though these cities were served by one additional team relative to 1889.

The AA closed up shop just one year after the PL had done so, after the end of the 1891 season. In addition to the eight teams already in the NL, AA teams in Baltimore, Louisville, St. Louis, and Washington joined the NL. The NL ended up serving twelve different cities without any repetition. Overall, from the year before, this was five fewer teams in the remaining major league and two fewer cities served (Columbus and Milwaukee were now without any major league baseball). Given that three-league competition had generated sixteen teams, it's pretty safe to say that dropping to twelve was a noncompetitive result.

The NL stayed the same size, in the same cities, until it tried to reduce its offerings after the 1899 season. For the 1900 season, presumably to take advantage of its newfound market power, the NL dropped Baltimore, Cleveland, Louisville, and Washington. Enter the AL, depicted in Table 13.3. Formerly a minor league under the National Agreement, the AL turned "outlaw" major league, offering eight teams starting in 1901 (three AL teams were in NL cities—Boston, Chicago, and Philadelphia). Combined, the two leagues had sixteen major league teams serving thirteen different cities. In the next season (1902), the AL replaced Milwaukee with

Table 13.2 National League—American Association—Players
League, 1889–1892

City	1889	1890	1891	1892–1899
Baltimore	AA	AA	AA	NL
Boston	NL	NL/PL	NL/AA	NL
Brooklyn	AA	NL/AA/PL	NL	NL
Buffalo		PL		
Chicago	NL	NL/PL	NL	NL
Cincinnati	AA	NL	NL/AA	NL
Cleveland	NL	NL/PL	NL	NL
Columbus	AA	AA	AA	
Indianapolis	NL			
Kansas City	AA			
Louisville	AA	AA	AA	NL
Milwaukee			AA	
New York	NL	NL/PL	NL	NL
Philadelphia	NL/AA	NL/AA/PL	NL/AA	NL
Pittsburgh	NL	NL/PL	NL	NL
Rochester		AA		
St. Louis	AA	AA	AA	NL
Syracuse		AA		
Toledo		AA		
Washington	NL		AA	NL
NL	8	8	8	12
AA	8	9	9	
PL		8		
Teams	16	25	17	12
Cities	15	16	14	12

Source: Compiled from league membership reports at baseball-reference.com

St. Louis, dropping the number of cities served to twelve. In 1903, a new National
Agreement was written that made peace between the NL and the AL but, at the
same time, the AL's Baltimore team moved to New York, further reducing the
number of cities served again to eleven. All-in-all, AL and NL economic peace left
the number of cities served at one less than at the end of the war between the NL
and the AA, ten years earlier in 1892.

Table 13.3 National League—American League, 1899–1903

City	1899	1900	1901	1902	1903–1913
Baltimore	NL		AL	AL	
Boston	NL	NL	NL/AL	NL/AL	NL/AL
Brooklyn	NL	NL	NL	NL	NL
Chicago	NL	NL	NL/AL	NL/AL	NL/AL
Cincinnati	NL	NL	NL	NL	NL
Cleveland	NL		AL	AL	AL
Detroit			AL	AL	AL
Louisville	NL				
Milwaukee			AL		
New York	NL	NL	NL	NL	NL/AL
Philadelphia	NL	NL	NL/AL	NL/AL	NL/AL
Pittsburgh	NL	NL	NL	NL	NL
St. Louis	NL	NL	NL	NL/AL	NL/AL
Washington	NL		AL	AL	AL
NL	12	8	8	8	8
AL			8	8	8
Teams	12	8	16	16	16
Cities	12	8	13	12	11

Source: Compiled from league membership reports at baseball-reference.com

The FL announced its major league presence for the 1914 and 1915 seasons. This episode is portrayed in Table 13.4. The NL and AL refused to recognize this bid and labeled the PL "outlaw." This was an incorrect use of the term because the FL had grown out of an independent minor league not subject to the National Agreement in the first place. Just prior to the FL bid (1913), the AL and NL still served the same eleven cities with sixteen teams that it did in 1903. Neither league changed at all in the two-year stint of the FL (or after its demise for that matter). The FL entered in 1914 with eight teams, four in cities served by one of the other leagues (Brooklyn, Chicago, Pittsburgh, and St. Louis). Thus, as competition should make happen, the twenty-four major league teams served fifteen different cities. In 1915, Newark replaced Indianapolis and the coverage of the three leagues remained at fifteen cities.

At the end of the 1915 season, players from the Pittsburgh, Newark, Buffalo, and Brooklyn teams were assimilated into AL or NL teams. Two FL owners were allowed to buy into struggling teams, merging their St. Louis Terriers with the

Table 13.4 National League—American League—Federal League, 1913–1916

City	1913	1914	1915	1916–1953
Baltimore		FL	FL	
Boston	NL/AL	NL/AL	NL/AL	NL/AL
Brooklyn	NL	NL/FL	NL/FL	NL
Buffalo		FL	FL	
Chicago	NL/AL	NL/AL/FL	NL/AL/FL	NL
Cincinnati	NL	NL	NL	NL
Cleveland	AL	AL	AL	AL
Detroit	AL	AL	AL	AL
Indianapolis		FL		
Kansas City		FL	FL	
New York	NL/AL	NL/AL	NL/AL	NL/AL
Newark			FL	
Philadelphia	NL/AL	NL/AL	NL/AL	NL/AL
Pittsburgh	NL	NL/FL	NL/FL	NL
St. Louis	NL/AL	NL/AL/FL	NL/AL/FL	NL/AL
Washington	AL	AL	AL	AL
NL	8	8	8	8
AL	8	8	8	8
FL		8	8	
Teams	16	24	24	16
Cities	11	15	15	11

Source: Compiled from league membership reports at baseball-reference.com

St. Louis Browns of the AL and their Chicago Whales with the Chicago Cubs in the NL. The FL's Kansas City franchise went bankrupt. The FL's Baltimore owners rejected a similar offer to join MLB. The Baltimore owners had sought to buy and move an existing MLB franchise to their city, but were rebuffed. Their lawsuit, referred to in short as the *Federal Baseball* case, eventually was lost in 1922 when the U.S. Supreme Court created the "antitrust exemption" that held in MLB labor relations until the passage of the Curt Flood Act in 1998.

The upshot of all of this for fans is that rough-and-tumble economic competition ruled major league baseball until 1915. This suggests that during the calmer periods, some sort of equilibrium ruled. Teams existed in all viable locations and were driven close to marginal cost pricing and zero economic profit by the threat of entry by rivals. Thus, it is difficult to argue that behavior of dominant leagues toward rival leagues represented much, if any, of a social problem in terms of dominant leagues with market power.

But as we turn to the period after 1915, especially on through the 1940s and 1960s, it's a different story. Despite population growth and movement west, MLB served the same eleven cities until the move of the NL's Boston Braves to Milwaukee for the 1953 season, followed by the move of the AL's St. Louis Browns to Baltimore for the 1954 season. Thus, the number of cities was constant for thirty-eight and thirty-nine years in the NL and AL, respectively. During this period, all increases in fan willingness to pay were collected by the owners of the same sixteen AL and NL teams. In doing so, MLB did have to contend with additional rivals. However, they reacted to these more recent rivals entirely differently, arguably with quite different consequences for fan welfare.

3. LATER HISTORY: PRECLUSION OF COMPETITION

This abruptly different treatment of rival leagues began with the AALs and the integration of MLB in 1947. It followed with the PCL and the move of the Dodgers and Giants to California for the 1958 season. Finally, MLB expansion and relocation in 1961 and 1962 ended the planned CL. No longer did competition determine the number and location of teams and leagues. Instead, talent was hired away in the AAL case, and territories were simply taken over in the PCL and CL cases. Therein lies the possibility of a social problem—re-establishing a single dominant league *by reduced opportunities for fans* may reduce social welfare.

African American Leagues

This presentation on AALs draws entirely from my earlier work with Joel Maxcy (Fort and Maxcy, 2000, 2001), and the reader is referred there for all references, not restated here. The AALs rose to full rival status with MLB by the early 1930s. The Negro National League (NNL) and the Negro American League (NAL) were two full-fledged, economically viable sports leagues. Circa 1945, the two AALs grossed almost $2 million. The Kansas City Monarchs routinely cleared $100,000 annually and most teams at least broke even. Indeed, with twelve to fifteen teams in the two leagues, the $2 million figure yields a minimum of $133,000 per team in total revenues. AAL crowds of 12,000 to 15,000 were common in 1946 compared to 15,600 in the AL and 14,500 in the NL.

As an additional indicator of economic success, AAL team owners were able to cover steep rental fees for MLB ballparks in the major cities. As a general principle, rent at major stadiums was typically 20 percent of gate. The Cuban Stars leased off time at the Cincinnati Red's ballpark for $4,000. Yankee stadium rented for $3,500 per game in 1939 but that rose dramatically to $100,000 annually by 1942. Griffith Stadium in Washington went for about the same amount.

The annual crowning glory of the AALs was their East-West All-Star series rather than their World Series, which was also played occasionally. The AAL All-Star series, sometimes as long as a best-of-five series, was fabulously successful, filling MLB's ballparks in Chicago and Washington over a span of days. The AALs' All-Star series twice drew more than 50,000 spectators in Chicago and averaged 34,276 compared to the MLB all-star game average of 40,342. On a per-game basis, the AAL version outdrew its MLB counterpart seven times from 1933 to 1950 and for three straight years, 1942–1944.

In addition, AAL players were adequately compensated in all cases and handsomely in some cases. In the late 1940s, typical salaries were in the $400 per month range. The average MLB salary was $1,100 in 1943. AAL *stars* made considerably more. Pressured by competition from the Mexican League, Josh Gibson's salary hit $6,000 in the 1940s. At his peak, Satchel Paige's $30,000 to $40,000 was comparable to MLB star players of the time.

The AALs were also economic competitors with MLB—rivals for some of the same attendance sought by professional white baseball teams. MLB attendance per team per capita in all cities with AAL competition showed the same pattern— attendance fell at about the time that the AALs caught on in the 1920s and 1930s. As a nearly perfect natural experiment, only Boston had no AAL competition and its attendance rose throughout these comparison decades. In all cities with competition, except Pittsburgh, MLB and AAL attendance are negatively correlated, especially in the 1930s but also on into the 1940s. AAL strongholds like Chicago, New York, and St. Louis showed the strongest negative relationship.

As with all previous rival league episodes, the most observable characteristic of competition was talent raiding. However, in racially segregated America of that time, the raiding was decidedly one-sided, and MLB's raiding of AAL talent really was shameless. Most of the big league clubs didn't pay the AAL owners by buying up the players' contracts, as they did when they hired a player away from owners in organized white major or minor league baseball. Branch Rickey, who signed up to sixteen AAL players for the Brooklyn organization, excused talent raiding without compensation claiming that many of the AAL owners were numbers runners. These claims painted the AALs as a "racket" to be prosecuted, not compensated. Effa Manley, the female manager of the Newark Eagles, put a different spin on Rickey's "racket" angle: "He took players from the Negro leagues and didn't even pay for them. I'd call that a racket." Manley also saw a "bigger picture" behind Rickey's claims:

> Gullible Negro fans who think white owners take on colored players through
> any altruistic pangs of democracy had better quit kidding themselves. There's a

potential two million Negro fans to draw from. Any baseball businessman would be looney (*sic*) not to see that.

In the end, Rickey never paid the Kansas City Monarchs a penny for Jackie Robinson. At a time when future major league star contracts went for as much as $100,000, those owners that did buy out AAL contracts typically did so for around $5,000 (Monte Ervin went from the Newark Eagles to the New York Giants at this price). A few players generated $15,000 (Dan Bankhead, Piper Davis, Larry Doby, and Willie Mays).

Nowhere can I find any documents showing an overt, concerted effort by MLB to eliminate the AALs, but the integration of MLB had precisely that result, brutally and quickly. Table 13.5 shows team locations for these various leagues as of 1947, the year Rickey integrated the NL. As they had since 1915, sixteen MLB teams covered eleven different cities. The AALs had twelve teams also covering eleven cities. They shared five MLB cities—Chicago, Cleveland, Philadelphia, Pittsburgh, and New York. Thus, between the four leagues (the NL, AL, NNL, and NAL), twelve different cities enjoyed the highest level of baseball (white and African American). New

Table 13.5 Major League Baseball and AAL Team Locations, 1947

City	NL	AL	NNL	NAL
Baltimore			Elite Giants	
Birmingham				Black Barons
Boston	Braves	Red Sox		
Brooklyn	Dodgers			
Chicago	Cubs	White Sox		American Giants
Cincinnati	Reds			
Cleveland		Indians		Buckeyes
Detroit		Tigers		
Indianapolis				Clowns
Kansas City				Monarchs
Memphis				Red Sox
New York	Giants	Yankees	Cubans; Black Yankees	
Newark			Eagles	
Philadelphia	Phillies	Athletics	Stars	
Pittsburgh	Pirates		Homestead Grays	
St. Louis	Cardinals	Browns		
Washington		Senators		

Source: baseball-reference.com for the NL and AL; Wikipedia for the AALs

York had an incredible four teams and Chicago and Philadelphia each had three. Competition did its job and, unlike previous rival league episodes, this actually was a long-term equilibrium. Major league baseball and the AALs had coexisted peacefully, from the economic perspective, since the 1920s.

After the 1948 season, just two years after integration, thirty-six former AAL stars were in MLB. The NNL, with four of its six teams competing in MLB cities, folded never to form again. All of its teams, except the New York Black Yankees, joined the NAL, which managed to play recorded baseball to the end of the 1950 season. The reorganization of the NAL saw Cleveland move to Louisville and Newark to Houston, so, for two seasons, thirteen different cities were covered by three major leagues (the AL, NL, and NAL). Even though the NAL managed exhibition ball and recorded championships to the end of the 1950s, fans never again enjoyed steady, predictable AAL play after 1950. Thus, it was back to the ten cities covered by MLB. A few years later, in 1953, the Boston Braves moved to Milwaukee, and, in 1954, the St. Louis Browns moved to Baltimore, increasing coverage to twelve cities even though Baltimore was partly covered by the NAL (NNL prior to 1948) Elite Giants prior.

African American fans suffered costs as well as benefits as a result of integration since attendance opportunities were dramatically reduced with the demise of the AALs. Countless thousands of fans lost out from decreased live attendance opportunities. For example, Newark Eagles' home attendance dropped from 120,923 in 1946 to 57,000 in 1947 and was down to 35,000 in 1948, a 71 percent decline in two years. Indeed, the team moved to Houston hoping to increase attendance when it joined the NAL for the 1949 season. The offset from the fan-welfare perspective was from African American fans now switching attendance to MLB games or listening on the radio to follow previous AAL stars with their new MLB teams.

MLB missed no tricks. The actual extinction of the AALs was facilitated by the lock-hold that MLB had over minor league baseball, the only other possible avenue AAL team owners might have used to escape from the MLB onslaught. As AAL franchises were weakened, with no other organized baseball option, the Browns' move to Baltimore (1954) and the Athletics' move to Kansas City (1955) were both into previous AAL strongholds. The Elite Giants had ruled Baltimore and the powerhouse Monarchs had the same hold over Kansas City. Despite this previous only-game-in-town status, Monarchs owner Tom Baird immediately sold the Monarchs with the arrival of MLB's Athletics in Kansas City.

The result was dramatic profit increases for both MLB teams (*The Sporting News*, January 3 and 14, 1959). From 1950 to 1953, the Browns lost hundreds of thousands of dollars per year but, from 1954–1958, reincarnated as the Orioles in a previously AAL-only city, the team only showed losses in one year after the move and averaged $258,000 in the other four years. Similarly, the Athletics lost money every year from 1950–1954 in Philadelphia, typically in the hundreds of thousands of dollars, but showed modest profits in 1955–1956 after the move to Kansas City.

This treatment of the AALs is quite a departure from the type of outcomes observed to the end of the FL in 1915. Anticompetitive outcomes by purposeful action replaced rough and tumble competition that ruled in baseball previously. The impact of this type of change on baseball fans, African American in this case, was unmistakable. Although integration captured the attention of many fans in the stadium and on the radio, and represented an important turning point for American society, countless thousands of other African American fans were denied live major league-level play.

Pacific Coast League

I find Zingg and Medeiros (1994) a definitive history of the PCL up to the arrival of the Dodgers and Giants for the 1958 season, and D'Antonio (2009) is a truly impressive review of the process of the Dodger-Giant move to California. Originally, truly a minor league, the PCL was producing plenty of major league talent by the 1940s. For example, Hall of Famers Earl Averill, Bobby Doerr, Joe DiMaggio, Tony Lazzeri, Ernie Lombardi, Ted Williams, and Paul Waner all moved to MLB from the PCL. Indeed, major league caliber talent often chose to stay in the PCL because life was pretty swell, especially in sunny southern California, and the pay was competitive enough.

In addition, dramatic population increases in California resulted in lucrative baseball. Data provided by the PCL to the U.S. House of Representatives (1951, p. 1629) summarized in Table 13.6 show that the league generated average profits from 1946–1950 totaling just over $1.8 million ($2009). This swamped the other two AAA minor leagues. Over this same five-year period, average profits in the American Association (now a minor league) totaled about $2,300 ($2009) and in the International League about $216,800 ($2009). The PCL average attendance was almost 3.7 million in each of these five years, nearly twice that of the other two AAA leagues. The PCL was clearly distinguished from the rest of the highest-classification minor leagues.

Table 13.6 PCL Average Profit/Loss, 1946–1950

Year	Profit/loss	CPI	$2009
1946	$77,451	10.93	$846,539
1947	$72,020	9.56	$688,511
1948	$36,238	8.85	$320,706
1949	$54,024	8.96	$484,055
1950	-$55,317	8.85	-$489,555
Total	$184,416		$1,850,257

Source: Inflation-adjustments to data in U.S. House of Representatives (1951)

Attendance was much higher in MLB, of course. For example in 1950, attendance was 9.1 million and 8.3 million in the AL and NL, respectively. Limited financial data (*The Sporting News,* January 3 and 14, 1959), on the other hand, show profits for the St. Louis Browns of $43,000, whereas the Philadelphia Athletics lost $316,000 and the Boston Braves lost $317,000. Although clearly not a general statement, *some* PCL teams were doing as well or better than *some* MLB teams financially.

The PCL pursued classification as the third major league through its affiliation under the National Agreement beginning in 1945. In 1948, PCL leaders insisted that all they needed in order to achieve major league status was exemption from the (then) annual minor league draft. Once quality rose a bit, added revenues would allow the PCL to bring its parks up to major league caliber. A re-concerted effort for major league status came again in 1951. MLB responded by inventing AAAA special status for the PCL (the only minor league ever designated in this way) and detailed the requirements to actually achieve major league status:

- The proposed league shall show an aggregate of 15,000,000 in its eight cities.
- Each club shall have a minimum of 25,000 capacity in any single park.
- They shall have had an average paid attendance of 3,500,000 over a three-year period, next preceding the application.
- They will adopt the major league minimum salary agreement with no maximum salary limitations.

Many of MLB's own teams could not meet the aggregate 3.5 million attendance requirement. As Hamlet's mother observed, "The lady doth protest too much, methinks"; the belief that the PCL was a rival league is apparent in the barriers that MLB tried to erect. Eventually, this led to the PCL being classified as open in 1952, almost entirely sheltered from the minor league draft. At least the owners in the league could begin building the overall level of talent in the league without losing it to MLB.

A confluence of occurrences in MLB led to the move of the Dodgers and Giants to California, knocking the PCL from its lofty perch. First, in the face of MLB's reluctance to go west, hearings were held in 1951 with the clear Congressional message to either relocate teams west or grant the PCL request or face formal antitrust scrutiny. Second, Walter O'Malley was fighting a losing battle with New York Park Commissioner Robert Moses over land for a new Dodger stadium. O'Malley felt financially cramped in Ebbets Field, the sixth largest of the eight NL venues. Third, Horace Stonheham's New York Giants were wallowing in fan apathy in the expansive (and dangerously located) Polo Grounds. Fourth, despite fan support for the PCL, city leaders in Los Angeles and San Francisco were hungry for the MLB version of baseball. The move of the Dodgers and Giants west served MLB's need to brush off Congressional meddling, O'Malley's desires for a better stadium situation, Stoneham's need for any glimmer of financial hope, and demands for MLB by California politicians.

O'Malley convinced Phillip Wrigley to swap (with some cash) his Los Angeles territory for O'Malley's Dallas territory. O'Malley also convinced Horace Stoneham to join him in a move west. Stoneham worked out a strict territory swap (Minnesota for San Francisco) with Red Sox (and Oakland Seals) owner Tom Yawkey. In addition, lucrative stadium deals, including land and infrastructure support, were struck for both teams. The NL voted unanimously to allow the move.

What MLB wanted, the PCL was made to give under the rules of the National Agreement. The rules required a higher-level organization to announce its intentions and then simply compensate the lower-level league for territory takeovers. The Dodgers and Giants already had acquired the team territories, so compensation to only the remaining six teams was required. The amount was $450,000 from each of the Dodgers and Giants (Wolff, 1984, p. 293) and the deed was done.

Again, I find no evidence of concerted collusive effort to end the PCL's chance as a rival major league. However, any chances surely went to zero after the Dodgers and Giants occupied the anchor territories in Los Angeles and San Francisco. Rather than adding a perfectly (economically) happy third league, MLB moved the long-standing rivalry between the Dodgers and Giants west. The impact on baseball fans served by the PCL, like their AAL counterparts a decade earlier, was brutal and quick.

By 1957, the PCL thrived with teams in Los Angeles, San Francisco, Vancouver (B.C., replacing Oakland in 1956), San Diego, Hollywood, Seattle, Portland, and Sacramento. There are no financial data for comparison purposes at this time (the data just mentioned cover this period but only for the three MLB teams), but AL and NL attendance in 1957 was 8.2 million and 8.8 million, respectively, compared to PCL attendance of 1.7 million (most blame TV for the decline in minor league attendance to this date). All three leagues had eight teams and the PCL teams played a 168-game season to major league baseball's 154 so the PCL pales still further on a per-game basis. Combined PCL attendance in the Los Angeles area was about 419,000 and in San Francisco about 285,000. Their eventual major league occupants drew just over 1 million in Brooklyn and about 654,000 in New York in 1957.

With this ready-made historical MLB rivalry now in their area, some baseball fans shifted loyalty away from their old PCL teams and toward MLB's new Los Angeles Dodgers and San Francisco Giants. Shortly after the Dodgers and Giants appeared, the PCL was almost entirely out of California, with only the Padres remaining in San Diego. The other California teams moved to Phoenix, Salt Lake City, and Spokane. After losing their anchor cities, the PCL was relegated to AAA minor league status. Indeed, most of the remaining teams in the AAA version of the PCL were either purchased by MLB teams or entered into close contractual "player development" relations with MLB teams. Clearly, the relocation of the Dodgers and Giants ended all chances for the PCL to obtain major league stature.

Even worse, from the antitrust perspective, although Los Angeles and San Francisco fans now had major league talent, and attendance in these two areas grew to 1.8 million and 1.3 million in their first MLB year 1958, attendance in the re-shuffled PCL fell to 1.5 million. Now, the actual welfare loss depends on the net impacts on Los Angeles area and San Francisco minor league fans and on the rest of the fans in new PCL cities. Phoenix, Salt Lake, and Spokane all saw initial enthusiasm wane so that attendance fell in these three cities from 610,000 in 1958 to 519,000 in 1959 (about 15 percent). PCL attendance after displacement went as follows:

> 1959—1.5 million; 1960–1.3 million (Tacoma replaces Phoenix)
> 1961—1.4 million (Hawaii replaces Sacramento)
> 1962—1.1 million

Thus, PCL attendance fell 21 percent from 1959 to 1960, held almost steady for 1961, and fell 21 percent from 1961 to 1962. Overall, this is a 27 percent decline from 1959. Comparisons beyond 1963 are clouded because the PCL instituted two 5-team divisions, dropping Vancouver and adding Oklahoma City, Dallas-Ft. Worth, and Denver.

On April 15 the Giants and Dodgers opened up the 1958 season in front of 23,192 fans at Seals Stadium in San Francisco. Three days later, the same two teams met in the Los Angeles Coliseum in front of a record NL crowd to that date of 78,682. Although five of the eight 1957 PCL territories would eventually be home to MLB teams (Oakland-1968, San Diego-1969, and Seattle-1977, in addition to Los Angeles and San Francisco), MLB had successfully ended the PCL's hopes to become a third major league, and they had done it without the talent bidding wars that occurred with prior outlaw leagues. The result was the end of another MLB rival and, arguably, damage to many minor league fans that may not have been completely offset by increased satisfaction for fans that turned to the Dodgers and Giants. Indeed, in the limiting extreme of Seattle in 1977, major league enjoyment in previous PCL cities was postponed for nearly twenty years. A similar approach would end the last attempt at a third major league, the Continental League (CL).

Continental League

The best presentation I have read of the rapid appearance and elimination of the CL is in Lowenfish's (2007) extensive biography of Branch Rickey. The portrayal of locations and team numbers is in Table 13.7. William Shea and Branch Rickey, perhaps the most famous baseball businessman in history, formulated the CL. In 1959, the two announced that the CL would begin play in 1961. They obtained ownership commitments in the still gaping holes in MLB territory coverage, starting with Dallas-Ft. Worth, Houston (recall the previous move by the NAL's Eagles), Minneapolis, New York City, and St. Paul. Shortly after that it was announced that Atlanta, Buffalo, Denver, and Toronto would round out the eight-team CL offering. Had the league actually gotten off the ground, this would have made twenty-four teams covering twenty-two cities, increasing major league offerings by 47 percent! Like the PCL's attempt at major league status, Rickey and Shea

Table 13.7 National League—American League—Continental League,
         1958–1962

City	1958	1959	1961–1962
Atlanta		CL	
Baltimore	AL	AL	AL
Boston	AL	AL	AL
Buffalo		CL	
Chicago	NL/AL	NL/AL	NL/AL
Cincinnati	NL	NL	NL
Cleveland	AL	AL	AL
Dallas/Ft. Worth		CL	
Denver		CL	
Detroit	AL	AL	AL
Houston		CL	NL
Kansas City	AL	AL	AL
Los Angeles	NL	NL	NL/AL
Milwaukee Braves	NL	NL	NL
Minneapolis/St. Paul		CL	AL
New York	AL	AL/CL	NL/AL
Philadelphia	NL	NL	NL
Pittsburgh	NL	NL	NL
San Francisco	NL	NL	NL
St. Louis	NL	NL	NL
Toronto		CL	
Washington	AL	AL	AL
AL	8	8	10
NL	8	8	10
CL		8	
Teams	16	24	20
Cities	15	22	17

Source: Compiled from league membership reports at baseball-reference.com

refused to go "outlaw" and, instead, approached MLB with the idea of creating a third major league.

Paying lip-service to Rickey and Shea, MLB owners took two steps that eliminated any chances for CL success. First, the new league would be forced to stock its shelves entirely with free-agent players; there would be no expansion draft. This practically guaranteed that the CL could only be a weak third major league at best for many years. Another set of Congressional hearings started in 1959, focused specifically on this issue of player availability. They discovered that some teams controlled as many as 400 players in their minor league systems.

Second, MLB owners asked Shea and Rickey if they would be willing to dissolve if four of their teams were included in a re-organization and expansion plan. The Senators would move to claim not just Minneapolis, but the entire state of Minnesota (the first team to claim more than a city affiliation), and an expansion Senators II would replace them. In addition, the AL would also expand to Los Angeles. Finally, the National League would expand to New York (the Metropolitans) and Houston (the Colt .45s). It is fair to say that MLB simply engineered a take-over of the choicest territories identified by the CL. On August 2, 1960 the CL owners agreed to dissolve after modest indemnity payments had been paid a couple of weeks earlier (Koppett, 1998, p. 277).

So, prior to the CL plans, in 1959, the AL and NL had sixteen teams covering fifteen cities (again, see Table 13.7). The CL would have covered an additional seven cities with its eight teams (the only duplication was in New York). MLB's plan then put it with twenty teams in seventeen different cities. This plan also preempted three of the eight CL planned locations. Eventually, MLB teams would occupy all but one of the remaining proposed CL locations. Milwaukee would move Atlanta (1966), Washington II would move to Dallas-Ft. Worth (1972), and expansion would put teams in Toronto (1977) and Denver (1993).

Although the CL episode did dramatically increase the number of teams from sixteen to twenty, and city coverage increased by two, issues remain for fan welfare. Technically, Buffalo is the only city that remains without major league baseball that it would have enjoyed under the CL plan. However, from the fan perspective, it is important to note that this would all have happened years earlier if the CL had been admitted as a third major league. In the limiting extreme of Denver, fans would have enjoyed major league-level play thirty years earlier! The CL is the last serious rival to face MLB.

4. Observations and Conclusions

To the end of the FL in 1915, forces of economic competition dictated major league baseball rival league outcomes. In intervening equilibrium periods, teams probably were pretty much in all locations where one could survive and prices were driven to the vicinity of marginal cost. After that, with "harmony" collusively guaranteed for the AL and NL by the revised 1903 National Agreement, sixteen MLB owners in ten different cities collected all increased profits from major league output for about forty years. After that, actions toward rival leagues took a decidedly different turn. The AALs, PCL, and CL all were precluded from meaningful economic competition with MLB by direct actions taken by the individual team owners comprising this dominant league.

Arguably, in each of these three cases, the welfare of fans at the major-league level was reduced, on net. The case seems clearest for the AAL and CL episodes, because each of these rival leagues (at least planned for the CL) served many more additional cities than MLB. The case is less clear for the PCL episode. It might be argued that minor league-level play was replaced by major league level play and then AAA baseball spread to cities that previously had enjoyed even lower-level classifications. However, even this last is really an empirical issue. First, the conclusion depends on whether major league-level play already was occurring in Los Angeles and San Francisco! What would have happened to attendance if the existing PCL had been granted major-league status, drawing MLB teams as opponents? Second, although Dodger and Giant attendance increased in California, the enjoyment of the teams was lost to New Yorkers. Finally, attendance at the re-organized PCL was much lower than it had been prior to 1958.

As a final observation let's return to the single entity distinction and franchising decisions by MLB in the face of rivals from the 1940s through the 1960s (extending observations in Fort, 2007). Nothing about territory preservation that precludes competition completely in the defined market of major league-level play has anything to do with making play happen. Team owners undertook these actions as joint ventures, through their MLB definition, with obvious economic consequences. MLB territories were preserved for their new occupants, new territories were occupied by MLB teams, and three competitive leagues were eliminated.

This could not be farther from the usual results of competitive franchising. First, although McDonald's can close franchises, it does not take the entire operation of an existing franchise and move it somewhere else in order to (1) make the franchisee better off and (2) preclude competition by rival fast service franchisors. Second, if McDonald's opens a new franchise, minimum efficient scale is not such that it precludes meaningful competition. Typically, competitive franchising does not end the chances for a rival to survive nearby.

The note of caution suggested by these three MLB cases is easy to extend to other leagues. Most recently, the merger between the National Basketball Association and American Basketball Association ended the latter after the 1975–1976 season. Four teams entered, extending the number of cities enjoying top level of basketball by three (Denver, Indianapolis, and San Antonio; New York was already served). However, fans in Kentucky, San Diego, Utah, and Virginia were now denied the same. The merger between the National Hockey League and the World Hockey Association was approved in 1979 and the latter ceased operations. Four teams from the rival league (Edmonton, New England, Quebec, and Winnipeg) joined the NHL for the 1979–1980 season, but fans in Birmingham, Cincinnati, and Indianapolis lost out. Only the merger between the National Football League and the fourth version of the American Football League, ending the latter after its 1969 season (the 1970 Super Bowl was the last between the two rival leagues), saw all teams in the rival league join the dominant league (Boston, Buffalo, Cincinnati, Denver, Houston, Kansas City, Miami, New York, Oakland, San Diego).

Because these most recent cases in other leagues happened, literally, under the scrutiny of antitrust officials, there was clearly concern over the type of issues raised by the AALs, PCL, and CL in baseball. Apparently, however, in the eyes of our political overseers, all ended well from the perspective of fans, and these recent mergers were allowed. The historical lessons from MLB treatment of its most recent rivals—the African American leagues, the Pacific Coast League, and the Continental League—suggest that this close scrutiny is well deserved and should be exercised into the future.

REFERENCES

D'Antonio, M. 2009. *Forever blue: The true story of Walter O'Malley, baseball's most controversial owner, and the Dodgers of Brooklyn and Los Angeles.* NY: Riverhead Hardcover.

Fort, R. 2007. Antitrust and the sports industry. In *Industry and Firm Studies,* eds. V.J. Tremblay and C.H. Tremblay, 245–266. Armonk, N.Y.: M.E. Sharpe, Inc.

Fort, R., and J. Maxcy. 2000. The economic demise of African American baseball leagues. *Unpublished* manuscript, Baseball Hall of Fame Library, Cooperstown, NY.

Fort, R., and J. Maxcy. 2001. The demise of African American baseball leagues: A rival league explanation. *Journal of Sports Economics* 2: 35–49.

Jozsa, F.P. 2006. *Big sports, big business: A century of league expansions, mergers, and reorganizations.* Westport, CT: Praeger Publishers.

Koppett, L. 1998. *Koppett's concise history of Major League Baseball.* Philadelphia: Temple University Press.

Lowenfish, L. 2007. *Branch Rickey: Baseball's ferocious gentleman.* Lincoln, NB: University of Nebraska Press.

Pietrusza, D. 2005. *Major Leagues: The formation, sometimes absorption and mostly inevitable demise of 18 professional baseball organizations, 1871 to present.* Jefferson, NC: McFarland and Company, Inc.

U.S. House of Representatives. 1951. Hearings before the subcommittee on market power, committee on the judiciary, 82nd Congress, 1st session, part 6, serial no. 1, various dates in July, August, and October, 1951.

Wolff, R. ed. 1984. *The Baseball Encyclopedia,* 8th edition. New York: Macmillan.

Zingg, P.J., and M.D. Medeiros. 1994. *Runs, hits, and an era: The Pacific Coast League, 1903–58.* Champaign-Urbana: University of Illinois Press.

## CHAPTER 14

THE MARKET STRUCTURE OF PROFESSIONAL SPORTS AND THE IMPLICATIONS FOR STADIUM CONSTRUCTION AND TEAM MOVEMENTS

ROBERT A. BAADE

ECONOMISTS, under the rubric industrial organization, have long studied the question of how market structure influences social well-being. Industrial organization theory has been applied to the market for professional sport, and scholars have written extensively about the negative social welfare implications commonly ascribed to monopoly in the commercial sports sector. Aspects of market structure, even in those industries that appear to have a "textbook" construct, are nuanced in ways that have social welfare implications that compel further study. The structure of the professional sports industry displays characteristics that distinguish it from other monopolistic industries. The purpose of this chapter is to identify the character of the commercial sports market, and to analyze how that unique structure affects the financing of sports facilities and the movement of teams.

The chapter is organized as follows. The market structure of professional sports is identified and analyzed in the introduction. This first section includes a review of the literature with emphasis on those works that best identify the peculiarities of professional sport that account for its structural uniqueness. The second part of the chapter identifies and analyzes the extent to which individual team and league interests conflict, and the implications of such incompatibilities for league policy as it relates to the questions of facility financing and team relocation. The third portion argues that league policy as it relates to team movement and facility construction can be better understood through the application of game theory. A primitive game theoretic construct is defined and the matrix of outcomes are discussed and analyzed. Conclusions and policy implications are discussed in the final section of the chapter.

1. INTRODUCTION

Competition in the realm of sports requires at least two participants, which means that the entertainment that sports provides is jointly produced.[1] Joint production requires some degree of coordination of the activities and behavior between and among competitors, and leagues provide the necessary administration. Leagues define the rules of the game, develop schedules, and settle disputes. Professional sports leagues are much more than administrative bodies, however, and they exist in equal part to advance the economic interests of the teams that comprise the professional/commercial sports leagues. Not every decision made by the league is Pareto optimal. It may be that the economic interests of some teams, at least in the short term, are compromised to advance the economic interests of other clubs, arguably toward the end of maximizing profit for teams collectively. Teams arguably seek to maximize wins and profits in the short run, and the league may have to moderate that urge in favor of the long-term profitability and viability of all teams.[2] The fundamental incompatibility of short-term interests between teams during the contest is tautological—one team wins and the other loses. Success is defined by wins, but wins by definition equal losses. League actions relating to influencing the outcome of contests in large part defines and distinguishes the structure of professional sports markets. Leagues arguably are motivated to create a structure that maximizes the unpredictability of a contest's outcome since that uncertainty is generally thought to heighten consumer interest and team revenues. The intent of policies promoting *competitive balance* is to prevent a team or a few teams from dominating play through time, and to spread the winners around the league over time.

While professional sports leagues have adopted policies that promote competition through sharing revenues among member teams, league policies serve
to restrict competition regionally. The motivation for geographic monopolies for
individual teams is transparent; all else equal, the larger the area that a team serves,
the greater the fan base and revenue potential. When the Washington Nationals of
Major League Baseball (MLB) encroached on the Baltimore Orioles turf beginning
with the 2005 season when they moved from Montreal, the Orioles were compensated by MLB for the reduction in their potential drawing power.[3] Professional
sports leagues thus represent a collection of teams that enjoy geographic monopolies. The teams, in turn, agree to a league structure to include the selection of a
commissioner and staff to oversee, to a degree acceptable to teams, their activities.
The commissioner exists by the grace of the teams, and his or her ability is limited
to some extent by owners. Teams are inherently different due to regional variations, and this reality sets the stage for disagreements among teams on a variety
of issues, not the least of which relate to revenue sharing, team relocation, facility
construction, and salary caps.

League policies in the United States ordain and protect team geographic
monopolies. Generally speaking, no matter how large the city, few cities in the
United States have more than one team competing within a particular league.
As noted previously in the case of the Nationals, when a franchise does invade
a league-defined exclusive territory, the league facilitates negotiations to ensure
that the incumbent team is adequately compensated for sharing its revenue
potential with a rival. Even in the case of New York, the largest city in the United
States, the New York Mets had to pay the New York Yankees $10 million to share
the New York MLB market.[4] Given the profitability of the Yankees and Mets,
the Yankees, the oldest team in the New York market, cannot be thought of as
a natural monopoly. The same would be true for the original teams in the largest metropolitan areas in the United States—markets that are sufficiently large
to profitably support multiple teams within a particular league.[5] It follows then,
that league policies sustain extra-normal profits for their members and may well
support teams that operate inefficiently or at least less efficiently than a potential
rival. The "promotion and relegation" system in European football/soccer (open
as opposed to closed leagues) offers far less support for inefficiency, but even
the "open" European leagues do encourage less than optimal efficiency to some
extent through limiting the number of teams that compete at the highest levels.
Consumers are victimized both when geographic monopolies are imposed and
when the number of teams in leagues is limited.

Team allocation, therefore, is severely limited by geographic monopolies, and if
there is no "natural" defense for geographic monopolization, there are fewer options
with regard to team movement, and that impairs social well-being. Even though
cities as large as New York, Chicago, and Los Angeles likely can support more than
their present roster of teams, leagues will not expand to those metropolises unless
pushed through social institutions operating independently of the leagues. On a
practical level, that pressure generally can come only from government, and that

introduces an additional actor into this analysis, which brings the total number of actors to three in determining team location: leagues, teams, and government. Most often the leverage that government uses to induce league expansion takes the form of threats to remove the antitrust exemption that professional sports leagues enjoy through the 1922 Supreme Court ruling that opined that baseball "exhibitions" did not qualify as interstate commerce, and were, therefore, exempt from the Sherman Antitrust Act.[6] Congressional legislation is the only recourse available to consumers to address the social welfare losses that emanate from league policies restricting the supply of teams.[7]

The inaccessibility of the largest markets in the United States to expansion or to teams who wish to relocate limits the number of viable markets to which teams can move. The demographics required to support major league teams are such that few cities remain that have the capability of supporting a team over the long term. Team movements that do occur in recent times, therefore, generally involve relocations from one small market to another as teams search for greater profits at least in the short term. Table 14.1 records all movements in the four major professional sports leagues in North America in the last twenty-five years.

There are several things worth noting from the information recorded in Table 14.1. First, aside from the three team relocations from Los Angeles and Houston, all of which were moves within the NFL, the remaining fourteen moves involved relocations from smaller markets. Second, NFL teams abandoned Los Angeles and Houston due to an inability to secure satisfactory public subsidies to finance new stadiums. Third, all cities that were abandoned by NFL teams have received replacement franchises, except for Los Angeles. Los Angeles has been without an NFL team since 1995. Only one of the cities deserted by the NBA or NHL has received a replacement franchise. It is clear, by way of summary, that within the last twenty-five years the majority of franchise relocations within the four major professional sports leagues within North America involve moves from one smaller market to another.

The pattern of relocations follows that identified by James Quirk.[8] Quirk's analysis of why teams relocate followed the logic of profit maximization; teams moved to enhance profits, and the movements largely involved small markets. Large-market teams generally could not expect to benefit through relocating to a smaller market. The movements of NFL teams to smaller markets were exceptions because of more lucrative stadium contracts offered the Raiders and Rams by Oakland and St. Louis, respectively, and that was not a development Quirk could have foreseen in his 1974 paper.

A watershed event in terms of stadium financing occurred in 1987. Joe Robbie, the owner of the NFL Miami Dolphins at that time, tired of failed referenda to publicly finance a renovation of the Orange Bowl where the Dolphins played. Robbie decided to build his own stadium, and he parlayed the upfront money he received from the sale and lease of luxury seating to privately finance the construction of what is now called Land Shark Stadium (previously known as Pro Player Park). The incremental revenue from luxury seating was substantial enough that

Table 14.1 Team Movements in the Four Major Professional Sports Leagues in North America, 1984–2009

Year/League	NFL	MLB	NBA	NHL
1984	Baltimore Colts to Indianapolis		San Diego Clippers moved to Los Angeles	
1985			Kansas City Kings to Sacramento	
1986				
1987				
1988	St. Louis Cardinals to Phoenix			
1993				Minnesota North Stars to Dallas[e]
1994				
1995	Los Angeles Raiders to Oakland[a]			Quebec Nordiques to Denver
1996	Cleveland Browns moved to Baltimore[b]			Winnipeg Jets to Phoenix
1997	Houston Oilers to Memphis[c]			Hartford Whalers to Raleigh, N.C.
2001			Vancouver Grizzlies to Memphis	
2002			Charlotte Hornets to New Orleans	
2005		Montreal Expos to Washington	New Orleans Hornets to Oklahoma City[d]	
2008			Seattle Supersonics to Oklahoma City	
Total	6	1	6	4

Sources: Team historical information from the team web sites.

[a] The Oakland Raiders became the Los Angeles Raiders in 1982, and this move reverses that relocation. The Raiders' move back to Oakland resulted from the unwillingness of Los Angeles to subsidize the construction of a new stadium to the extent demanded by the Raiders and the Rams.

[b] The City of Cleveland was awarded an expansion franchise in 1999 to replace the one the City lost in 1996.

[c] The City of Houston was awarded an expansion franchise in 2002.

[d] This relocation was temporary as it followed the incapacitation of the New Orleans Arena following the devastation wrought by Hurricane Katrina. The Hornets moved back to New Orleans for all games in 2006.

[e] Minnesota was awarded a replacement franchise in 2000 (Wild).

it ushered in an unprecedented period of stadium and arena construction in the four major sports leagues. Much of the luxury seating revenue had the further advantage of being exempt from revenue sharing arrangements, and in the case of the NFL that implied avoidance of a 40 percent "tax," the portion of gate that went to the visiting team in the NFL's revenue-sharing arrangement. Given the vastly superior revenue-generating potential in large markets, prior to 1987, it made little sense for large-market clubs to move to smaller cities. The move of both the Los Angeles Rams and Raiders to St. Louis and Oakland can be explained in terms of greater revenue potentials in these smaller markets due to the luxury-seating phenomenon.

Facility revenues exempt from revenue sharing, "local stadium revenues" by name, coupled with generous public subsidies to attract teams, changed the stadium construction and team relocation dynamic significantly. Small markets could compete for teams as long as they could convince citizens or civic leaders in a potential host city to partner in financing the team's activities. Cities that seized the new stadium-subsidy initiative had an advantage over other suitor cities and established professional sports host cities as long as their rivals for the scarce supply of professional sports teams did not offer similar largesse. Subsidies could increase the profitability of marginal franchises in the same way that "the reverse order of the draft" and the "reserve clause" allowed small markets to appropriate player rents through the sale of exceptional talent to large market clubs. Clubs from larger markets, of course, could alter the dynamic by building their own new stadiums, complete with luxury seating and other luxury amenities. Baseball teams in New York as of 2009 were playing in new stadiums, and the New York Giants and Jets will do so as well beginning in 2010. Los Angeles remains on the sidelines, and will continue to do so until a stadium is built for an NFL franchise with significant public financial support. The subsidy will have to be substantial enough to improve the profit potential for some existing franchise. The Minnesota Vikings appear to be a good candidate for relocation to Los Angeles if the citizens of Minnesota continue to balk at subsidizing the construction of a new stadium there.

It should be noted, by way of summary, that leagues are motivated to promote competitive balance, which heightens interest in games between teams through increasing the uncertainty of outcome. League policies such as reserve clauses and drafts of amateur players in reverse order of team standings in the previous season theoretically can resolve the fundamental imbalance problem. These policies, however, have proved inadequate to the task of inducing competitive balance. The reason is clear. In the absence of meaningful revenue sharing, particularly in the free-agency era, the wealthiest teams are best positioned to sign the best players. Quirk observed:

> Even the reserve clause, however, unrestricted bidding for new talent has the effect
> of unbalancing the league in the direction of the big-city franchises, since higher

bids for new talent will be forthcoming from these teams, where the revenue potential of the player is higher ...

The extent to which an imbalance in revenue potential and consequent imbalance in playing strengths will exist in a professional sports league depends crucially on the gate-sharing rules of the league.[9]

Following the virtually complete overhaul of sports facility infrastructure in the four major professional sports leagues in North America during the past two decades, the problem confronting leagues is convincing member clubs to agree to more comprehensive revenue sharing, one that includes local facility revenues emanating from luxury seating and amenities. Given that host cities exhibit markedly different local revenue-generation potential, in a very real sense leagues have found themselves at square one in terms of legislating competitive balance. Zimbalist in a recent article has provided statistics that capture the extent of the imbalance.

> Today, between the national television money and the DirecTV contract the NFL pays out approximately $140 million to each team annually. National licensing money from NFL properties is also distributed equally to each team and amounts to around $4 million per team. Ticket sales and club seat revenues are subject to the 60/40 distribution, after 15 per cent is deducted for day-of-game costs. All this sharing means that there is a modest range from top to bottom team revenues, with the top-revenue team earning only 1.6 to 1.7 times more than the bottom team revenue team. In contrast, for pre-revenue sharing in baseball this ratio is almost 10 to 1, while post-sharing revenue is around 3.5 to 1. In the National Basketball Association (NBA), where there is salary cap and sharing only out of national TV and licensing money (around $30 million per team), the to-to-bottom revenue ration is around 3 to 1. In the National Hockey League (NHL), where there is no salary cap and no sharing beyond the relatively diminutive national TV contracts (around $3 million per team and falling), the top-to-bottom revenue ratio is approximately 2.5 to 1.[10]

Zimbalist's article was published in 2006, and the previously mentioned new stadiums in New York for their football and baseball teams and for the NFL Dallas Cowboys promise to expand the imbalance, given the revenues generated from luxury seating and personal seat licenses in those facilities. The salary cap in the NFL and the luxury tax imposed on team salaries beyond a certain level in baseball have not deterred the bidding for free-agent talent permitted by the financial advantage enjoyed by the big-market clubs. If both the Cincinnati Bengals and the New York Giants face the same salary cap, the Giants potentially are far more profitable than are the Bengals because of their local stadium revenue advantage. The challenge for the NFL and all professional sports leagues is to make their revenue-sharing policies more comprehensive in the pursuit of competitive balance. The next portion of this chapter identifies conflicts in the motivations of teams and leagues as it relates to facility construction and team relocation. The process through which the conflicts are resolved or allowed to persist are discussed.

2. League and Team Conflicts
and Their Consequences

Few would dispute that professional sports leagues in North America operate as unregulated monopolies as a practical matter. Leagues are not-for-profit entities in the United States, but their economic function is to enhance the profitability of the teams that comprise the league. Teams, on the other hand, are welfare maximizers. Teams are not equals, and that inequality largely reflects the economic makeup of their host communities and the objectives of their owners. Some owners could be characterized as utility maximizers,[11] while others are profit and/or wealth maximizers. League administrative officers serve at the grace of the collection of team owners as noted previously, and they must be mindful of operating the league in a way that serves the interests of the owners. Given that team owners are not equal and pursue incompatible interests, at least in the short term, policies promulgated by the league will conform to the interests of the extraordinary majority of team owners.[12]

Consistent with well-understood monopoly practice, league cartels act to maintain an excess demand for teams (supply of teams is less than what would be considered socially optimal), which compels a price for franchises above that which would exist in a more competitive environment. Teams, of course, endorse the league's actions as it relates to fostering excess demand for franchises both locally (geographic monopolies or limiting the number of teams within a community) and nationally (limitation of the number of teams in the major leagues). Leagues, as previously noted, understand that fan interest and revenues depend on uncertain outcomes for games. Uncertainty requires competitive balance, which, in turn, necessitates equal distributions of playing talent. Equalizing playing talent in the free-agent era requires financial equality. Given that teams are profit or win (utility) maximers, the fundamental conflict between leagues and teams revolves around the question of how much competitive balance, and by extension, financial equality, is necessary to maximize fan interest and revenues. The very nature of championship play necessitates that a single team prevails at the conclusion of a season, but the abiding belief is that profit maximization for the collective is achieved if each team has an equal chance to emerge as a champion in any one season. This requires, in the final analysis, that leagues appropriate revenues from the more financially successful teams and share them with those teams that are less endowed financially. It is hardly revelatory to note that taxation by a central authority is generally abhorred by those who pay.

Leagues represent team interests in negotiating TV contracts, bargaining with player associations, and appeasing government concerns as it relates to the behavior of the leagues and its members as it affects the public. The judicial branch of government can interpret league practice as anti-competitive. The legislative branch of government has the power to regulate professional sport or at least take away the antitrust exemption that MLB, and the other leagues by extension, currently enjoy. Leagues are conscious of the fact that government involvement is more likely the more league policy and practice come to loggerheads with the well-being of citizens. Frequent team relocations and the use of public funds for subsidizing team activities and infrastructure invite greater public concern and scrutiny, even though such actions in the short term may well serve league and team interests. Leagues, as is true of any federal authority, should take a collective and long-term view. Table 14.2 provides a summary of league, team, and

Table 14.2 Summary of Dispositions for Leagues, Teams, and Government Toward Team Relocation, Stadium Subsidies, and Revenue Sharing

Issue/Entity	League	Teams	Government
Relocation	Ambiguous: Pro: Insures greater profitability for individual teams. Increases size of shared revenue pool. Con: Harms fans in abandoned communities inviting government scrutiny, and potential regulation. Encourages rival league development. Overall: Guardedly for	Unambiguously for since it allows freedom to maximize profit. Overall: Strongly favor	Local and Regional Government: Against since well-being of at least some citizens declines. Federal Government: Against unless it can be demonstrated that a relocation enhances consumer well-being. Overall: Strongly oppose
Public Subsidies for facilities	Ambiguous: Subsidies increase profitability of teams, but invite public scrutiny and criticism if not adequately rationalized. Overall: Strongly favor	Unambiguously for since it allows for greater profitability. Overall: Strongly favor	Local and Regional Government: All else equal, would oppose, but excess demand for franchises compels subsidization. Federal Government: Against as the operation of an unregulated monopoly compels the subsidies. Overall: Strongly oppose
Revenue Sharing	For: Helps to achieve competitive balance and maximizes revenue. Overall: > Strongly favor	Large Markets: Against: Tax imposed on operations and potentially encourages team inefficiency. Small Markets: Promotes competitive balance. Overall: Favor with reservations	Ambiguous: Pro: Allows small market clubs to compete. Con: Encourages inefficiency. Overall: Favor

government stances as it relates to questions of stadium subsidies, team relocation, and revenue sharing.

Revenue sharing is seen by all three actors identified in Table 14.2 as necessary and desirable; all perceive their well-being served by supporting revenue
sharing except for possibly the large-market clubs. Government does not object
to revenue sharing, despite its blatant cartel-revealing character, presumably
because government perceives that the social benefits derived from it exceed the
social costs incurred. Just as revenue sharing provides the financial wherewithal
for small markets to compete, fan interest and well-being in each major league
community are bolstered by the prospect that their teams can contend. The more
comprehensive the revenue sharing, all else equal, the more likely that hope can be
realized. Relocation and public subsidies for facilities enjoy no broad consensus,
and to understand developments relating to relocation and subsidies, additional
analysis is necessary. The next section of the paper provides outcome matrices for
government regulation and the absence of it, and a Nash equilibrium is identified
and discussed.

3. Conflict Resolution and Nash Equilibrium

The potential conflict between the league and member clubs on the issues identified in Table 14.2 requires resolution. Practically speaking, resolution does occur
when an extraordinary majority vote of teams approves league legislation or action
regarding a particular issue, but that approval rests on convincing teams that it is
in their interest to support league initiatives. Teams, it is safe to say, will act in their
own interest, and an outcomes matrix can be used to help understand where the
interests of the league and an extraordinary majority of teams coincide and determine an outcome, or a Nash equilibrium.

The team-relocation issue is complex. Government at the federal level in theory
would not support team relocation motivated simply by a club's desire to increase
its profitability in the short term. The lack of franchise stability would jeopardize
fan and social well-being, and leagues apparently recognize that a sport's financial
interests would not be served by franchise moves designed to improve the short-
term bottom line. This is true for a variety of reasons, not the least of which has
to do with the finite number of communities that have the capacity to support a
major league team. Eventually the league may well have to return to cities that
they abandoned, and rebuilding a fan base is a difficult undertaking. Leagues also
recognize that abandoning markets that supported teams for a prolonged period
creates opportunities for rival leagues. If a sufficient number of vibrant markets

exist, a rival league's prospects for competing with an incumbent league would be enhanced. The major sports leagues in North America, as a consequence, have a list of conditions that have to be met before they will support team relocation or expansion. Such a list of conditions makes it easier for a league to justify a move in the face of public criticism that invariably follows such an action. If such a justification cannot be identified, for example, a demonstrated lack of fan support, then a negative government response to the move is sure to follow, and the outcome of government scrutiny could lead to a legislative outcome that is detrimental to league interests. The NFL's willingness to challenge the Los Angeles Raiders' move back to Oakland in 1995 corroborates the contention that leagues must be sensitive to the public antipathy that results from team moves inspired by a transparent pursuit of team short-term economic interests at the expense of the well-being of a host city's citizens.

The Raiders lawsuit and the move of the Cleveland Browns to Baltimore compelled the NFL to more aggressively push for a formal antitrust immunity. Paul Tagliabue, the commissioner of the NFL at the time when the Raiders and Browns abandoned Los Angeles and Cleveland, respectively, rationalized that the League needed such an exemption to enable it to enforce league rules relating to relocation. Such enforcement could not occur in the absence of an explicit league exemption from the Sherman Antitrust Act, Tagliabue argued.[13] Government recognized that an exemption had far-reaching implications, not the least of which was the loss of a credible government threat to legislate away the de facto antitrust immunity under which the four major professional sports leagues currently operate. It is not surprising in light of this that government consistently has opted to avoid legislation on the issue. One can only conclude that the government threat to legislate better serves society than does an explicit position one way or another on the question of whether sports leagues warrant an antitrust exemption.

Understanding the government action/inaction as it relates to the question of antitrust immunity for professional sports leagues can be better understood through a simple matrix of outcomes for a game theoretic construct. Table 14.3 depicts the matrix of outcomes under the assumption the government does not regulate.

There is a Nash equilibrium that can be identified, and Figure 14.1 illustrates the behavioral dynamics that bring it about.

Table 14.3 Matrix of Outcomes for a Two-Actor Game, Team and League Assuming No Government Regulation

Team/League	For Team Relocation	Against Team Relocation
Move	Team Outcome: > 0 League Outcome: > 0	Team Outcome: < 0 League Outcome: > 0
No Move	Team Outcome: < 0 League Outcome: > 0	Team Outcome: = 0 League Outcome: = 0

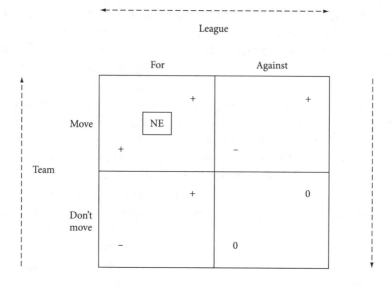

Figure 14.1 Nash Equilibrium for a Team and League Game
Assuming No Government Intervention.
Notes: (1) Cell payoffs: Bottom left for teams; top right for league,
(2) Horizontal arrows show league preferred moves, (3) Vertical arrows
show team preferred moves, (4) Nash Equilibrium (NE) is located
in the northwest quadrant.

If both the league and the team understand that there will be no government regulation, then the Nash equilibrium is for the team and league to agree on relocation. A team move would presumably be financially beneficial to the team or it would not be considered, and league revenues would increase as a consequence of a team commercially inspired move. The increase in pooled revenues would benefit all clubs.

If the government response to proposed franchise relocation is unclear, the league's stance in response to a team's proposed relocation is complicated. The league would have to consider how the government response would influence revenue-generating potential for the league in making a decision to support the move. A government decision to regulate the league in response to a socially indefensible move potentially would have dramatic and disastrous consequences for the profitability of all teams in the league for a variety of reasons. Among those reasons, perhaps most prominent among them, would be the inability of teams to "encourage" host cities to subsidize team activities, for example, funding playing and practice facilities, as an alternative to losing the franchise. The only reasons that a league would consider opposing relocation if it would increase a team's revenue, aside from potential government intervention, would relate to the ready markets provided a competitive league, and the perception among potential small-market host cities that an investment in a professional sports team is a high-risk venture.

Leagues have to take seriously the willingness of communities to invest in professional sports infrastructure. The Oakland Raiders versus NFL trial revealed how significantly individual teams and the NFL have benefited from new stadium construction. The NFL has to consider how its actions relating to relocation affect the decisions of cities to fund new stadium construction. Communities are far less likely to assume a substantial financial burden if there are fewer impediments to quelling the exercise of teams' nomadic urges.[14] If a league has a clear signal from government on its position as it relates to regulation, the league's understanding of the implications of its policies as it relates to team relocation and the encouragement of public subsidies is vastly improved. It may well be the case that government inaction in the policy arena as it relates to the question of sports and antitrust is intentionally left ambiguous.

4. Conclusions and Policy Implications

The purpose of this chapter was to analyze how the character of the market for professional sports in the United States has affected the financing of sports infrastructure and the movement of franchises. This issue has been analyzed previously, but there have been significant developments in the professional sports industry that have compelled further study. It is particularly noteworthy, for example, that the issues of stadium construction and team relocation have become so much more entwined in the past two decades. New or significantly renovated playing facilities have substantially increased team revenues, and have provided impetus for franchise relocations from cities unwilling to subsidize the construction of the new generation of stadiums to communities that will. The structure of the professional sports industry has played a substantial role in determining the extent of stadium construction/renovation and team relocation.

Other articles have concentrated on the particulars of stadium construction and team movements. This chapter sought to focus on how the structure of the market for professional sports and the relationship of professional sports to government have influenced decisions relating to stadium construction and team relocation. There is nothing novel about the conclusion that the four major professional sports leagues in the United States operate as unregulated monopolies and that teams enjoy the benefits of their status as geographic monopolies—a condition that leagues have developed and maintained. This chapter makes two contributions. First, explicit attention is devoted to a discussion of how new stadium construction has changed the relationship between leagues, member clubs, and government in nontrivial ways. The substantial increase in local stadium revenues has compelled leagues to pressure all member clubs to build new infrastructure. The ability of leagues to develop more comprehensive revenue-sharing programs requires that each team contribute as much as it can to league coffers. The failure of individual teams to do so undermines the willingness of any team to contribute their local revenues to a league pool. Even in the NFL, with its history of comprehensive revenue sharing, tensions have surfaced about salary caps and the now depleted G-3 program for funding new stadium construction.[15] New stadiums and their substantial local revenue streams may undermine competitive balance.

Second, some discussion and analysis have been devoted to how the ambiguous government position on league antitrust immunity may serve the public interest through creating uncertainty in league offices as it relates to government responses to team moves and the public financing of stadium construction. Leagues need to be mindful of the potential threat posed by government regulation of the industry. There is reason to suspect that league policies and actions as they relate to the public funding of stadiums and team relocation have been moderated somewhat by the prospect of government regulating the professional sports industry at least in theory. The government's ambiguous stance may in the final analysis provide something of a de facto regulatory structure.

Financial innovation in professional sports has been substantial during the past twenty-five years, and the nature of the interaction among various actors within the professional sports industry, not surprisingly, changed as a consequence. Team motivations may not have changed all that much, but clearly leagues and governments have struggled to maintain competitive in an industry where the construction of new, more lucrative facilities have changed team operating income and wealth significantly. That revenue, which teams are not required to share presently, may lead to an era of substantial competitive imbalance—exactly that which leagues understand could undermine the financial viability of their sport.

NOTES

1 See, for example, Stefan Kessene (2007), *The Economic Theory of Team Sports: An Analytical Treatment* (Cheltenham, UK: Edward Elgar Publishing). Chapter 1 provides a particularly useful rendering of the peculiarities of professional team sports and insight into the objective utility functions of owners.
2 For an insightful discussion of the impact league revenue sharing has on the incentive for teams to win, see: Andrew Zimbalist (2006), "Organizational Models of Profession Team Sports Leagues," in *Handbook on the Economics of Sport,*" edited by Wladimir Andreff and Stefan Szymanski (Cheltenham, UK: Edward Elgar Publishing), 443–446.
3 The most important features of the deal worked out between MLB and Peter Angelos, the Orioles owner, is that the Nationals and Orioles shared revenues from a new, jointly owned cable sports network and MLB has guaranteed that Angelos will garner

at least $365 million when he sells the Orioles. See http://www.fieldofschemes.com/news/archives/2005/04/2256_angelos_payoff.html. Accessed on August 20, 2009.

4 Roger Noll (2003), "The Organization of Sports Leagues," *Oxford Review of Economic Policy,* Vol. 19, No. 4, 530–551.

5 This assumes that a test for natural monopoly is that if the first team in an area generates extra normal profit, additional teams cannot do so. See Roger Noll, op. cit., p. 538.

6 *Federal Baseball Club v. National League,* 259 U.S. 200 (1922). Both *Toolson v. New York Yankees,* 346 U.S. 356 (1952), and *Flood v. Kuhn,* 407 U.S. 258 (1972) reaffirmed the 1922 decision. It is fair to say that the National Football League, the National Basketball Association, and National Hockey League, the three other major sports leagues in the United States, have ridden the coattails of MLB's explicit antitrust exemption.

7 In 1992 San Francisco Giants owner Bob Lurie agreed to sell the team to a group in Tampa Bay, and MLB did not approve the sale. That decision prompted Senator Connie Mack of Florida to threaten to take steps to remove MLB's antitrust exemption. Senator Mack's actions prompted MLB to expand to both Miami and Tampa Bay.

8 James P. Quirk, (1973–1974), "An Economic Analysis of Team Movements in Professional Sports," *Journal of Law and Contemporary Problems,* Winter-Spring, 42–66.

9 Ibid., p. 45.

10 Op. cit., p. 443.

11 Stefan Kesenne would note this, for example. See Kesenne (2007).

12 This would be true because to be approved, changes in league policy require an extraordinary vote of team owners in most cases in particular as it relates to league expansion, team relocation, collective contract (single entity) negotiations, and revenue sharing and salary cap arrangements.

13 See *Antitrust Issues in Relocation of Professional Sports Franchises: Hearing Before the Senate Subcommittee on Antitrust, Business Rights, and Competition of the Committee of the Judiciary, United States Senate,* November 1996.

14 The saga of the NHL's Phoenix Coyotes is particularly instructive in this regard. It is highly unlikely that the City of Glendale, Arizona would have provided substantial financial support in constructing a new arena for the Coyotes if it had been aware of the team owner's willingness to use bankruptcy laws in the U.S. to help him in his attempt to relocate the team to Hamilton, Ontario, Canada.

15 The G-3 program involved the NFL providing low-cost loans to teams for the purpose of constructing or renovating stadiums. The funds for the program were provided through each team contributing $1 million of their national television money to the league office over the duration of the program. The G-3 fund was depleted through the loan extended the New York Giants and Jets to construct their new stadium ($300 million loan) and a loan to the Kansas City Chiefs for the renovation of Arrowhead Stadium. No provision has been made for replacing the G-3 program because some small market clubs have opined that the program contributes to the financial gap between large- and small-market clubs.

References

http://www.fieldofschemes.com/news/archives/2005/04/2256_angelos_payoff.html. Accessed on August 20, 2009.

Kessene, Stefan (2007). *The economic theory of team sports: An analytical treatment,* Cheltenham, UK: Edward Elgar Publishing.

Noll, Roger (2003). The organization of sports leagues. *Oxford Review of Economic Policy,* 19(4): 530–551.

Quirk, James (1973–1974). An economic analysis of team movements in professional sports. *Journal of Law and Contemporary Problems* (Winter–Spring): 42–46.

Zimbalist, Andrew (2006). Organizational models of profession team sports leagues. in *Handbook on the economics of sport,* eds. Wladimir Andreff and Stefan Szymanski. Cheltenham, UK: Edward Elgar Publishing, pp. 443–446.

....

## CHAPTER 15

LOCATION, LOCATION, LOCATION?

SPORTS FRANCHISE PLACEMENT IN THE FOUR MAJOR U.S. SPORTS LEAGUES

....

KARL W. EINOLF

THE study of the economics of sports is appealing because of the extensive data available to prove or disprove theoretical assertions about the nature of the sports industry. The examination of sports also allows economists to better understand economic relationships in general. In other industries and economic disciplines, data are not as available as in the sports industry. Extreme popularity, combined with government scrutiny, places most of the private sports enterprise's business practices and data into the public domain. The sports industry serves as a learning laboratory in which broader economic concepts and theories are examined. In addition to explaining the workings of the sports industry, research in sports economics enhances the knowledge base of the field of economics as a whole.

This chapter is an example of how using available sports industry data to study an economic problem leads to a better understanding of similar situations in other industries. Specifically, this chapter examines the location of franchises in sports leagues. One would expect a league to place its franchises in a network of cities to maximize exposure to its customers' disposable income. This chapter shows, however, that the four major sports leagues in the continental United States do not all locate franchises in this manner. In fact, the less the franchises in a league are dependent on local income, the less likely the franchises are placed in locations with the highest income available. While the facility location problem has been thoroughly studied in other industries, the availability of data in the sports industry provides a unique look into why an organization in any industry may *not* place its business units in a set of locations that maximizes access to local income.

This chapter uses a facility location model from the industrial engineering and management science literature to determine an optimal assignment of sports franchises to metropolitan locations within the continental United States. The model indicates how a league should optimally locate its franchises, and it also shows how a league's existing franchise placement compares with the model's optimal design.

The chapter specifically examines the location of franchises within the four major sports leagues in the continental United States: Major League Baseball (MLB), the National Football League (NFL), the National Hockey League (NHL), and the National Basketball Association (NBA). Each league's franchise locations are compared to the facility location model's best possible design for the league. The architects of these leagues conceivably placed franchises in locations with the greatest potential for franchise and league profitability. The chapter considers the relationship among revenue-sharing arrangements, franchise dependence on local income, and how far franchises are located from their optimal placement. This chapter also uses the facility location model to identify the best expansion prospects for each league.

The facility location model is used in industrial engineering and management science to solve various location problems: locating water treatment facilities throughout cities to maximize coverage while minimizing costs; locating warehouses to maximize product distribution at the lowest possible cost; and locating store franchise sites to maximize profits and market share while minimizing costs and customer travel time. Brandeau and Chiu (1989) provide a nice history of the academic research in this area, and Snyder (2006) presents a comprehensive review of recent facility location research.

Most of the research on franchise location in the sports economics literature examines the benefits and costs of locating a sports franchise in a particular city. Baade and Dye (1988), Siegfried and Zimbalist (2000), and Coates and Humphreys (2003) have written seminal papers in this area. This line of research focuses on the economic impact, both tangible and intangible, that sports franchises and their stadia have on a local metropolitan area. Baade and Dye (1988) examine the specific issue of building a new stadium, and they characterize the conditions under which local governments should subsidize the costs. Siegfried and Zimbalist (2000) describe the economic environment under which sports leagues abuse their monopoly power to force cities to subsidize sports franchises. They make a number of policy recommendations to adjust the inefficiency and inequity in the market of franchise location. Coates and Humphreys (2003) find that a professional sports franchise has a negative net effect on both earnings and employment in a metropolitan area.

Other research has yielded similar results. Shropshire (1995) describes the tactics that cities employ to capture a sports franchise and the fierce bidding wars that often take place, and Johnson (1983) warns that city officials must be careful yielding to the pressures of sports entrepreneurs. Johnson states that the benefits of hosting a franchise are significantly outweighed by the subsidies demanded by the sports team. Rappaport and Wilkerson (2001) find that there is no benefit to a city hosting a sports franchise if one considers economic activity and tax benefits. However, they point out that "quality-of-life" benefits could justify public expenditures on sports franchises. Nunn and Rosentraub (2003) concur with this point; however, they also point out that a metropolitan region—a city and its suburbs—must act as a collective unit to avoid falling into the trap of a bidding war for a sports facility.

At the macro level for a league, however, is the question of which metropolitan areas to locate in. As a league expands into a new market, leagues must select between potential cities and choose one that is most profitable for the league and the new franchise. Fort and Quirk (1995) examine optimal financial structures of sports leagues, and they recognize that a major problem for leagues is keeping franchises in weak-drawing markets viable.

Bale provides a comprehensive study of sports and location in his book *Sports Geography* (2003). Bale examines the cultural, geographical, and economic influences on the location of sports leagues and their franchises. He points out that while leagues should locate franchises in the highest population centers to gain access to the most income available, it is often history, inertia, and physical landscapes that determine location. Bale recognizes that a more detailed quantitative analysis is necessary to explain the economic geography of sports. This chapter attempts to do this by examining how similar existing league franchise locations are to optimal income-generating locations. This chapter is the first paper to use a facility location model to examine the optimal placement of sports franchises in a league and to identify the best expansion prospects for a sports league.

THE p-MEDIAN FACILITY LOCATION MODEL

The *p*-median facility location model finds the location of an exogenous number of facilities, denoted by *p*, on a network so that the total cost of serving the network is minimized. Hakimi (1965) first defined the *p*-median problem using a network of nodes and arcs. He described each node as a source of demand, and the arcs represented transportation connections between the nodes. Facilities could be located at any node or at any point on the arcs. Hakimi proved that at least one optimal solution to the p-median problem existed such that facilities were located entirely on the nodes in the network. This was an important result because many location applications require that facilities be built on existing nodes within a network. Without Hakimi's result, the problem would also be significantly more difficult to solve, as the model would have to consider a set of infinite location possibilities within the arcs on the network. ReVelle and Swain (1970) were the first to formulate the p-median problem as an integer programming model, and Daskin (1995) provides an excellent description of the model used in contemporary research.

In the context of this chapter, the p-median model locates a predetermined number, p, of sports franchises on a network that has three hundred nodes. The nodes are the 300 highest personal income–earning metropolitan statistical areas (MSA) in the United States as reported by the U.S. Department of Commerce's Bureau of Economic Analysis for 2006.[1] The distances between nodes are calculated using "as the crow flies" measurements, using the latitude and longitude of the primary city in the MSA.

The p-median model assigns p sports franchises to p unique nodes within the 300-node network. Each sports franchise has exclusive access to the income at its home node. The model then assigns the income at each of the remaining nodes that did not receive a franchise to one of the p franchises. The model calculates the total income-weighted distance in the network by multiplying the income at each node by the distance to its assigned franchise and then summing these products. This is referred to as *distanced income* throughout the remainder of the chapter. The p-median model locates the franchises optimally by minimizing the distanced income in the network. By minimizing the network's distanced income, accessibility to income is maximized.

The model in this chapter is similar to ReVelle and Swain (1970), although Daskin's (1995) notation is used. One small change is made to these models: this chapter adds a factor, α, to control how sensitive the model is to distances between the nodes. This addition is important because it facilitates a consideration of the amount of income that will actually travel to a nearby franchise in the network. The model follows:

Inputs

h_i = income at node i where $i \in [1,300]$ and each node is an MSA
d_{ij} = distance between node i and candidate site j where $i, j \in [1,300]$
p = number of sports franchises to locate
α = level of sensitivity of the distance between node i and candidate site j

Decision Variables

$$X_j = \begin{cases} 1 & \text{if a sports franchise is located at candidate site } j \\ 0 & \text{if not} \end{cases}$$

$$Y_{ij} = \begin{cases} 1 & \text{if node } i \text{ is served by a sports franchise at node } j \\ 0 & \text{if not} \end{cases}$$

Using this notation, the p-median problem is formulated as follows:

$$\text{Minimize} \quad \sum_i \sum_j h_i (d_{ij})^\alpha Y_{ij} \tag{1a}$$

$$\text{Subject to} \quad \sum_j Y_{ij} = 1 \qquad \forall i \tag{1b}$$

$$\sum_j X_j = p \tag{1c}$$

$$Y_{ij} - X_j \leq 0 \qquad \forall i, j \tag{1d}$$

$$X_j = 0, 1 \qquad \forall j \tag{1e}$$

$$Y_{ij} = 0, 1 \qquad \forall i, j \tag{1f}$$

The objective function (1a) minimizes the total distanced income in the network. While the ReVelle/Swain and the Daskin models only consider the case when α is equal to one, the objective function (1a) is more robust as it uses α to examine the model's sensitivity to distances between the nodes.

Constraint (1b) requires each demand node i to be assigned to exactly one sports franchise j, and constraint (1c) allows only p sports franchises to be located. Constraint (1d) links the nodes where sports franchises are located (X_j) and the demand nodes (Y_{ij}). The constraint only allows demands at node i to be assigned to a sports franchise at location j ($Y_{ij} = 1$) if a sports franchise is located at node j ($X_j = 1$). Constraints (1e) and (1f) simply require that X_j and Y_{ij} have a value of either zero or one.

To illustrate how the p-median model works, Figure 15.1 exhibits a simple four node network of cities A, B, C, and D with incomes of 4, 5, 5, and 10 respectively. The distances between the cities are indicated on the figure. Suppose that two sports franchises are to be located at two of the cities in the network. The p-median model considers each of the six possibilities in which the franchises may be placed: AB, AC, AD, BC, BD, and CD.

If the sports franchises are placed at cities A and B, then D's income would go to franchise A (because A is the closest franchise to D) and C's income would go to B. Using a value of 0.5 for α, the distanced income for a placement at A and B is 204.67 ($10{*}200^{0.5} + 5{*}160^{0.5}$). Table 15.1 lists the distanced income for each of the six possible placements. The p-median model would determine that the optimal

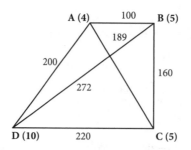

Figure 15.1 A Four-Node Network.
Note: Miles between the nodes are indicated on the line segment and income
at each node is noted in parentheses.

Table 15.1 Distanced Income on a Four Node Network

Franchise Placement	Distanced Income
AB	204.67
AC	191.42
AD	118.74
BC	188.32
BD	103.25
CD	118.24

placement of the two sports franchises is at cities B and D, which have the lowest distanced income. It is intuitive that the sports franchises would be placed at B and D or at C and D because these cities have the highest income. The optimal placement turns out to be B and D, because the income at city A is closer to B than it is to C.

SELECTING ALPHA: HOW FAR WILL INCOME TRAVEL TO SUPPORT A SPORTS FRANCHISE?

The *p*-median model in this chapter includes the factor, α, to control how sensitive the model is to distances between the nodes and the income at selected nodes. The greater α is, the greater the distance factor is relative to the income at a node. When a higher α used in the *p*-median model, the less sensitive the model is to the income at the node where a franchise is placed. A lower α forces the model to place franchises at the highest income nodes.

To illustrate the effect of selecting α, the p-median model was used to optimally locate eight franchises across the continental United States using three different α values: 1.0, 0.5, and 0.1.[2] The choice of α affects how sensitive the model is to the distance between nodes when minimizing distanced income in the network. Table 15.2 exhibits the different optimal placements of the eight franchises based on the values of α that are used.

When α is equal to one, the model selects Lakeland, Florida, as one of the eight optimal locations for a sports franchise in the continental United States, even though Lakeland is the ninety-ninth largest MSA. The model does this because Lakeland is located near three large income nodes: Tampa Bay, Orlando, and Miami. With alpha equal to one, the model is not sensitive to the lower income at Lakeland. The model considers that the income from Tampa Bay, Orlando, and Miami will travel to Lakeland to support the franchise.

When a very small value of α is used, the model is extremely sensitive to the income at each node, and income from nearby cities is not used to support a sports franchise at another node. When α was set to 0.1, the model simply placed the sports franchises in the eight highest-income MSAs in the continental United States.

When α was set to 0.5, the model finds an appropriate optimal location for the eight franchises. This alpha establishes a balance between placing franchises in high-income MSAs and allowing nearby income to support a sports franchise. The model selects Miami, instead of Lakeland, which seems appropriate given that Miami has the highest income of MSAs in Florida. The model also does not locate a franchise in Seattle, and instead places a franchise in Washington, D.C. Figure 15.2 and Figure 15.3 show the differences in locations selected when different alphas are used in the model. An α of 0.5 is used to determine the optimal locations of franchises for the remainder of the chapter.

Table 15.2 Optimal Franchise Locations of 8-Team League

alpha = 1.0		alpha = 0.5		alpha = 0.1	
MSARank	MSA	MSA Rank	MSA	MSA Rank	MSA
1	New York	1	New York	1	New York
2	Los Angeles	2	Los Angeles	2	Los Angeles
3	Chicago	3	Chicago	3	Chicago
6	San Francisco	4	Washington D.C.	4	Washington D.C.
7	Dallas	6	San Francisco	5	Philadelphia
11	Atlanta	7	Dallas	6	San Francisco
13	Seattle	10	Miami	7	Dallas
99	Lakeland, FL	11	Atlanta	8	Boston

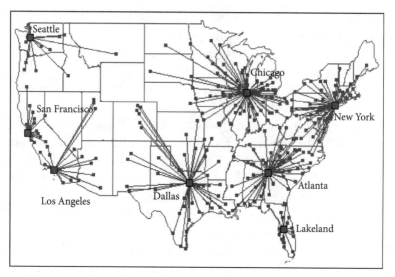

Figure 15.2 Optimal Franchise Placement in an Eight Team League
When Alpha is 1.0: The Lakeland Result.

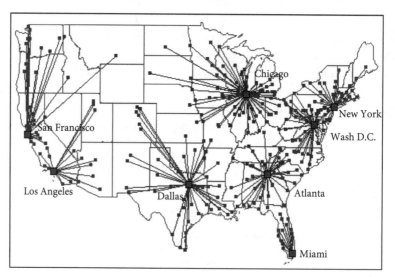

Figure 15.3 Optimal Franchise Placement in an Eight Team League
When Alpha is 0.5.

OPTIMAL FRANCHISE LOCATION IN THE FOUR MAJOR SPORTS

The p-median model is used to examine how each of the four major United States sports leagues has located franchises in comparison to the p-median model's optimal franchise placement. The analysis only considers MSAs in the continental

United States and does not address the issue of the optimal number of franchises within one MSA.

Major League Baseball (MLB) currently has thirty teams, including a franchise in Toronto, Canada, and two franchises in each of the Chicago, Los Angeles, New York, and San Francisco MSAs. Thus, MLB has franchises in twenty-five MSAs in the continental United States. The *p*-median model identified the twenty-five optimal franchise locations for MLB. Table 15.3 compares the actual and the optimal locations of franchises for MLB. There are only three cities where MLB should not be located, according to the model: Baltimore, Cleveland, and

Table 15.3 Actual vs. Optimal Franchise Locations for the MLB

Actual Location		Optimal Location	
MSA Rank	MSA	MSA Rank	MSA
1	New York	1	New York
2	Los Angeles	2	Los Angeles
3	Chicago	3	Chicago
4	Washington D.C.	4	Washington D.C.
5	Philadelphia	5	Philadelphia
6	San Francisco	6	San Francisco
7	Dallas	7	Dallas
8	Boston	8	Boston
9	Houston	9	Houston
10	Miami	10	Miami
11	Atlanta	11	Atlanta
12	Detroit	12	Detroit
13	Seattle	13	Seattle
14	Minneapolis	14	Minneapolis
15	Phoenix	15	Phoenix
16	San Diego	16	San Diego
17	*Baltimore*	19	Denver
19	Denver	20	St. Louis
20	St. Louis	22	Tampa Bay
22	Tampa Bay	23	Pittsburgh
23	Pittsburgh	*25*	*Portland*
24	*Cleveland*	26	Cincinnati
26	Cincinnati	28	Kansas City
28	Kansas City	*35*	*San Antonio*
34	*Milwaukee*	*37*	*Charlotte*

Milwaukee. The three cities where MLB should instead be located are Portland, San Antonio, and Charlotte.

The p-median model can also indicate how close a league's actual franchise placement is to the optimal franchise assignment. The model's objective function (1a) minimizes the distanced income from each of the model's 300 MSAs to their assigned sports franchises. A comparison is made between the distanced incomes of the leagues' actual and optimal franchise locations. MLB's actual distanced income is 43,576,898 while its optimal distanced income is 41,925,259.[3] The ratio of the actual distanced income to the optimal distanced income measures the level of inefficiency of the actual franchise location system. In the case of the MLB, the franchise location inefficiency ratio is 1.039. (MLB's actual franchise location is 3.9 percent inefficient.)

The National Football League (NFL) currently has thirty-two franchises in thirty different MSAs in the continental United States. There are only two MSAs in which the NFL has multiple franchises: New York and San Francisco. The p-median model identified the thirty optimal franchise locations for the NFL. Table 15.4 compares the actual and the optimal locations of franchises for the NFL. There are six cities where the NFL should not be located according to the model: Baltimore, Buffalo, Green Bay, Indianapolis, Jacksonville, and Nashville. The six cities where the NFL should instead be located are Las Vegas, Los Angeles, Portland, Rochester, Salt Lake City, and San Antonio. Figure 15.4 is a map with the thirty optimal NFL locations. The NFL's franchise location inefficiency ratio is 1.185.

The National Basketball Association (NBA) currently has thirty franchises, including one in Toronto, Canada and two in both the New York and Los Angeles markets. The NBA has franchises in twenty-seven different MSAs in the continental United States. The p-median model identified the twenty-seven optimal franchise locations for the NBA. Table 15.5 compares the actual and the optimal locations of franchises for the NBA. There are seven cities where the NBA should not be located according to the model: Cleveland, Indianapolis, Milwaukee, Memphis, Oklahoma City, Orlando, and Sacramento. The seven cities where the NBA should instead be located are Cincinnati, Kansas City, Pittsburgh, San Diego, Seattle, St. Louis, and Tampa Bay. The NBA's franchise location inefficiency ratio is 1.095.

The National Hockey League (NHL) currently has thirty franchises, and only twenty-four of these are located in the United States. The NHL is represented in twenty-one different MSAs in the continental United States. The NHL has a large presence in Canada, and six of its franchises are located there. The NHL also has multiple franchises in New York and Los Angeles. The p-median model identified the twenty-one optimal franchise locations for the NHL in the continental United States. Table 15.6 compares the actual and the optimal locations of franchises for the NHL. There are five cities where the NHL should not be located according to the model: Buffalo, Columbus, Nashville, Pittsburgh, and San Jose. The five cities where the NHL should instead be located are Cincinnati, Houston, Kansas City, Seattle, and San Francisco. The NHL's franchise location inefficiency ratio is 1.187. Table 15.7 summarizes the distanced incomes and the inefficiency ratios for the four leagues.

Table 15.4 Actual vs. Optimal Franchise Locations for the NFL

Actual Location		Optimal Location	
MSA Rank	MSA	MSA Rank	MSA
1	New York	1	New York
3	Chicago	2	*Los Angeles*
4	Washington D.C.	3	Chicago
5	Philadelphia	4	Washington D.C.
6	San Francisco	5	Philadelphia
7	Dallas	6	San Francisco
8	Boston	7	Dallas
9	Houston	8	Boston
10	Miami	9	Houston
11	Atlanta	10	Miami
12	Detroit	11	Atlanta
13	Seattle	12	Detroit
14	Minneapolis	13	Seattle
15	Phoenix	14	Minneapolis
16	San Diego	15	Phoenix
17	*Baltimore*	16	San Diego
19	Denver	19	Denver
20	St. Louis	20	St. Louis
22	Tampa Bay	22	Tampa Bay
23	Pittsburgh	23	Pittsburgh
24	Cleveland	24	Cleveland
26	Cincinnati	25	*Portland*
28	Kansas City	26	Cincinnati
32	*Indianapolis*	28	Kansas City
37	Charlotte	*31*	*Las Vegas*
39	*Nashville*	*35*	*San Antonio*
44	*Jacksonville*	37	Charlotte
49	*Buffalo*	*50*	*Rochester*
62	New Orleans	*51*	*Salt Lake City*
145	*Green Bay*	62	New Orleans

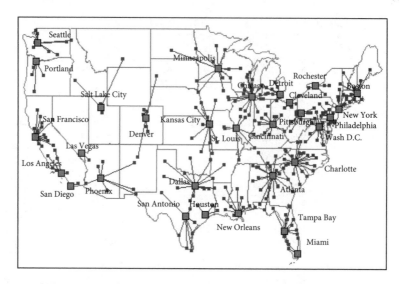

Figure 15.4 The Optimal Franchise Locations for the NFL.

Table 15.5 Actual vs. Optimal Franchise Locations for the NBA

Actual Location		Optimal Location	
MSA Rank	MSA	MSA Rank	MSA
1	New York	1	New York
2	Los Angeles	2	Los Angeles
3	Chicago	3	Chicago
4	Washington D.C.	4	Washington D.C.
5	Philadelphia	5	Philadelphia
6	San Francisco	6	San Francisco
7	Dallas	7	Dallas
8	Boston	8	Boston
9	Houston	9	Houston
10	Miami	10	Miami
11	Atlanta	11	Atlanta
12	Detroit	12	Detroit
14	Minneapolis	*13*	*Seattle*
15	Phoenix	14	Minneapolis
19	Denver	15	Phoenix
24	*Cleveland*	*16*	*San Diego*
25	Portland	19	Denver
27	*Sacramento*	*20*	*St. Louis*
29	*Orlando*	*22*	*Tampa Bay*

(Continued)

Table 15.5 (*Continued*)

Actual Location		Optimal Location	
MSA Rank	MSA	MSA Rank	MSA
32	*Indianapolis*	23	*Pittsburgh*
34	*Milwaukee*	25	Portland
35	San Antonio	26	*Cincinnati*
37	Charlotte	28	*Kansas City*
45	*Memphis*	35	San Antonio
48	*Oklahoma City*	37	Charlotte
51	Salt Lake City	51	Salt Lake City
62	New Orleans	62	New Orleans

Table 15.6 Actual vs. Optimal Franchise Locations for the NHL

Actual Location		Optimal Location	
MSA Rank	MSA	MSA Rank	MSA
1	New York	1	New York
2	Los Angeles	2	Los Angeles
3	Chicago	3	Chicago
4	Washington D.C.	4	Washington D.C.
5	Philadelphia	5	Philadelphia
7	Dallas	6	*San Francisco*
8	Boston	7	Dallas
10	Miami	8	Boston
11	Atlanta	9	*Houston*
12	Detroit	10	Miami
14	Minneapolis	11	Atlanta
15	Phoenix	12	Detroit
19	Denver	13	*Seattle*
20	St. Louis	14	Minneapolis
21	*San Jose*	15	Phoenix
22	Tampa Bay	19	Denver
23	*Pittsburgh*	20	St. Louis
33	*Columbus*	22	Tampa Bay
37	Charlotte	26	*Cincinnati*
39	*Nashville*	28	*Kansas City*
49	*Buffalo*	37	Charlotte

Table 15.7 Distanced Income and Inefficiency Ratios

| League | U.S. Locations | Distanced Income | | Inefficiency Ratio |
		Optimal	Actual	
MLB	25	41,925,259	43,576,898	1.039
NBA	27	39,870,214	43,672,274	1.095
NFL	30	37,101,601	43,949,728	1.185
NHL	21	46,929,814	55,702,822	1.187

Why Are the Leagues Not Located Optimally?

The p-median model is useful, in the sports industry and elsewhere, because it identifies an optimal placement of an organization's facilities to maximize exposure to customers and their income. With the data that is available in the sports industry, however, further analysis can be done to examine why it may not be prudent for an organization to use the optimal p-median model solution. It is also possible to characterize the organization that is more or less likely to use the optimal placement. This analysis and discussion serves as an example of how sports economics can be used to guide policy makers in other industries.

Of the four major U.S. sports, Major League Baseball is the closest to an optimal franchise location design. Individual MLB franchise revenue also has the highest correlation with local income among the four leagues. The coefficient of determination (R-squared) between 2006 MLB franchise revenue and personal income in a franchise's home city was 0.797. Because an MLB franchise has many home games (81 per season) and because MLB franchise television revenue comes mostly from local media outlets, it is not surprising that MLB franchises are so dependent on the city in which they are located.

When compared to MLB, the National Football League's franchise location design is much farther from an optimal placement, with a location inefficiency ratio of 1.185. The NFL has an extensive league-wide revenue-sharing arrangement and individual franchises are much less dependent on local income. Most of the NFL's revenue comes from a national broadcast rights agreement, and individual franchises only have 8 home games per season. Table 15.8 shows that the NFL's coefficient of variation of 2006 revenue is considerably lower than all of the other leagues. The NFL also has the lowest coefficient of determination (R-squared) between 2006 NFL franchise revenue and personal income in a franchise's home city at 0.548. Because NFL franchises are not as dependent on income from their individual franchise location, they are not located as optimally as franchises in the other leagues.

The National Basketball Association falls in the middle of MLB and the NFL with a franchise location inefficiency ratio of 1.095. The NBA is also between MLB and the NFL in terms of its dependence on local markets. NBA franchises have 41 home games each season, limited revenue sharing, and broadcast revenue that

Table 15.8 Comparison of Franchise Location and Revenue among the Four
Major Sports

League	Home Games	Franchise Location Inefficiency Ratio	Franchise Revenue Coefficient of Variation	Franchise Revenue and MSA Income R-Squared
MLB	81	1.039	0.220	0.797
NBA	41	1.095	0.238	0.748
NFL	8	1.185	0.126	0.548
NHL	41	1.187	0.229	0.785

comes from both local and national media outlets. The coefficient of determination (R-squared) between 2006 NBA franchise revenue and personal income in a franchise's home city was 0.748.

With greater revenue sharing, fewer home games, and a lucrative national television rights contract, a league has less pressure to locate a franchise in a city with the highest income available. The local market is not essential to ensure that a new franchise is profitable. A league can capitalize on other incentives from smaller cities—tax breaks, publicly funded stadiums, and other government subsidies—to replace the income lost by not locating in a larger market. As MLB, the NBA, and the NFL demonstrated, the less an organization's franchises are dependent on local income, the less likely the franchises will be placed in the p-median model's optimal solution.

On the surface, the National Hockey League appears to throw a wrench in the argument that sub-optimal franchise location occurs when a league is not dependent on local income. The NHL has the worst franchise location inefficiency ratio of 1.187, even though NHL franchise revenue is strongly correlated with the income available in local markets. The coefficient of determination (R-squared) between 2006 NHL franchise revenue and personal income in a franchise's home city was 0.785. Larger markets do generate more revenue for NHL franchises, yet the p-median model indicates that the NHL places its franchises in too many smaller markets. For example, the model suggests that the NHL should move its franchise from Buffalo and place it in Houston. What the p-median model does not consider is that the percentage of income spent on hockey most likely varies more from market to market than in any other sport. Buffalo is a "hockey town"; Houston is not. While the NHL may not be placing its franchises optimally according to the p-median model, the NHL's current placement could be optimal if consumer "disposable hockey income" was available to be used in the model instead of personal income.

When the p-median model is used in other industries to identify an optimal facility placement, additional factors that affect a facility's profitability must also be taken into account. The income available at a node may not be the only factor. The model should be adjusted to consider subsidies and externalities at each node if it is to properly identify an optimal facility placement. As the analysis of the four major sports organizations in the U.S. demonstrates, the *p*-median model's optimal solution is less likely to be the best option for an organization if its facilities are less dependent on the income available at a node on the network.

EXPANSION

Since 1990, all of the four major U.S. sports created new franchises and expanded into new markets. Table 15.9 details these changes. According to the *p*-median model, Major League Baseball did the best job in expanding to optimal locations. Major League Baseball added five new teams, and, considering where the other MLB franchises were already located, four were placed in optimal locations: Miami, Phoenix, Denver, and Tampa Bay. Because of its existing Baltimore franchise, the p-median model would have placed a new MLB franchise in Charlotte instead of in Washington, D.C.

According to the *p*-median model, the NBA did poorly by moving from Seattle to Oklahoma City. Before this move, the NBA also located two new franchises in Memphis and New Orleans, instead of in St. Louis and Kansas City. The NFL also did not fare well by moving two franchises out of Los Angeles. The NFL optimally placed franchises in St. Louis and Charlotte, but it did not do well by placing teams in Baltimore, Nashville, and Jacksonville, instead of in Los Angeles, Portland, and San Antonio.

Since 1990 the National Hockey League expanded into nine new markets in the continental United States. The *p*-median model agreed with six of the moves: Dallas, Miami, Atlanta, Phoenix, Denver, and Tampa Bay. The model did not concur with the moves into Columbus, Charlotte, and Nashville. Instead it would have placed franchises in Houston, Seattle, and Cincinnati.

Table 15.9 Actual vs. Optimal Expansions since 1990

Actual Expansion		Optimal Expansion	
MSA Rank	MSA	MSA Rank	MSA
Major League Baseball			
10	Miami	10	Miami
15	Phoenix	15	Phoenix
19	Denver	19	Denver
22	Tampa Bay	22	Tampa Bay
4	*Washington D.C.*	*37*	*Charlotte*

(Continued)

Table 15.9 (*Continued*)

MSA Rank	MSA	MSA Rank	MSA
	Actual Expansion		**Optimal Expansion**
National Basketball Association			
45	*Memphis*	20	*St. Louis*
62	*New Orleans*	28	*Kansas City*
13	*Left Seattle*	13	*Stay in Seattle*
48	*Oklahoma City*		
National Hockey League			
40	Left Hartford	40	Left Hartford
7	Dallas	7	Dallas
10	Miami	10	Miami
11	Atlanta	11	Atlanta
15	Phoenix	15	Phoenix
19	Denver	19	Denver
22	Tampa Bay	22	Tampa Bay
9	*Houston*	33	*Columbus*
13	*Seattle*	37	*Charlotte*
26	*Cincinnati*	39	*Nashville*
National Football League			
20	St. Louis	20	St. Louis
37	Charlotte	37	Charlotte
2	*Left Los Angeles*	2	*Stay in Los Angeles*
17	*Baltimore*	25	*Portland*
39	*Nashville*	35	*San Antonio*
44	*Jacksonville*		

The *p*-median model also identified two expansion prospects for each of the leagues. Using each league's existing franchise locations, the model is able to find the best locations for two new franchises if the league were to expand into two new markets. Table 15.10 indicates where p-median model suggests the four leagues should locate their next two franchises if they decided to expand.

Table 15.10 Future Optimal Expansions for Each of the
Four Major Sports Leagues

	MLB	NBA	NFL	NHL
Expansion Prospect 1	Charlotte	Seattle	Los Angeles	Seattle
Expansion Prospect 2	Portland	St. Louis	Portland	Houston

CONCLUSION

The analysis presented in this chapter has a few limitations. The first is that the model does not consider the possibility of placing multiple franchises in a single location. Certainly, there are markets—New York, Los Angeles, and Chicago—that easily support multiple franchises. In its current form, the model is unable to determine whether it would be better to place a third MLB franchise in New York or a new franchise in Charlotte.

A second limitation with this application of the p-median model is that the percentage of income that a sports league captures may vary from market to market. This limitation was discussed previously with respect to the NHL. Although Houston may have more total income available than Buffalo, the income spent on hockey may be greater in Buffalo than in Houston. This limitation can be dealt with by surveying residents in cities to determine their willingness to spend on particular sports, but these data are difficult to accurately acquire.

A third limitation is that the p-median model assigns income from cities that do not receive franchises entirely to the closest franchise. There are fans, however, who do travel farther than the closest franchise to another franchise with which they identify more closely. Allowing income from nearby nodes to go to franchises that are farther away can change the optimal placement of franchises. For example in the NFL, the Harrisburg, Pennsylvania, MSA is closest to the Baltimore Ravens franchise, and Harrisburg is officially assigned to Baltimore in the NFL broadcast rights contract. However, the Pittsburgh Steelers are the most popular franchise in the Harrisburg area, according to the local CBS television affiliate.[4] Making an adjustment to account for this limitation would also require acquiring data that is difficult to obtain.

Even with these limitations, the p-median model provided a unique look into how and why a sports league places its franchises in a set of locations that may or may not maximize the league's access to local income. This chapter showed that the four major sports leagues in the continental United States do not all locate franchises optimally, according to the model. When a league has more revenue sharing, fewer home games, and a shared national television rights contract, the league has less pressure to locate where the highest local income is. The league looks for other incentives—typically in the form of tax incentives from local governments—and places franchises in smaller markets.

NOTES

1 See http://www.bea.gov/bea/regional/reis/.
2 Mark Daskin's Sitation software (version 5.7.0.26) was used to obtain the results.
3 Distanced income is in millions of dollars. The specific value has no useful interpretation. What matters for the study is the comparison between the actual and optimal values of distanced income.
4 See http://www.eveningsun.com/localnews/ci_11481650?source=rss.

REFERENCES

Baade, R., and Dye, R. (1988). Sports stadiums and area development: A critical review. *Economic Development Quarterly*, 2 (3): 265–275.

Bale, J. (2003). *Sports geography*. New York: Routledge.

Brandeau, M. L., and Chiu, S. S. (1989). An overview of representative problems in location research. *Management Science* 35(6): 645–674.

Coates, D., and Humphreys, B. (2003). The effect of professional sports on earnings and employment in the services and retail sectors in US cities. *Regional Science and Urban Economics*, 33(2): 175–198.

Daskin, M. (1995). *Network and discrete location: Models, algorithms, and applications*. New York: Wiley.

Fort, R., and Quirk, J. (1995). Cross-subsidization, incentives, and outcomes in professional team sports leagues. *Journal of Economic Literature*, 33(3): 1265–1299.

Hakimi, S. L. (1965). Optimum distribution of switching centers in a communication network and some related graph theoretic problems. *Operations Research* 13(3): 462–475.

Johnson, A. (1983). Municipal administration and the sports franchise relocation issue. *Public Administration Review*, 43(6): 519–528.

Nunn, S., and Rosentraub, M. (2003). Sports wars: Suburbs and center cities in a zero-sum game. In J. Lewis and T. Miller (eds.), *Critical cultural policy studies: A reader*. Malden: Blackwell, pp. 211–224.

Rappaport, J., and Wilkerson, C. (2001). What are the benefits of hosting a major league sports franchise? *Federal Review Bank of Kansas City Economic Review*, pp. 55–86.

ReVelle, C., and Swain, R. (1970). Central facility location. *Geographical Analysis*, 2: 30–42.

Shropshire, K. L. (1995). *The sports franchise game: Cities in pursuit of sports franchises, events, and stadiums*. Philadelphia: University of Pennsylvania Press.

Siegfried, J., and Zimbalist, A. (2000). The economics of sports facilities and their communities. *Journal of Economic Perspectives*, 14(3): 95–114.

Snyder, L. (2006). Facility location under uncertainty: A review. *IIE Transactions* 38 (7): 537–554.

## PART V

ILLUSTRATIONS
OF FINANCE

CHAPTER 16

EVENT ANALYSIS

EVA MARIKOVA LEEDS AND
MICHAEL A. LEEDS

INTRODUCTION

SINCE the seminal work by Ball and Brown (1968) and Fama et al. (1969), event analysis has been a valuable tool for researchers in economics, finance, and marketing. Event analysis is valuable because it allows researchers to evaluate the impact of an exogenous event or a firm's own actions on its profitability, even when researchers do not have access to internal firm data. Event analysis uses stock price movements to gauge the impact of incidents ranging from stock splits to tragic plane crashes on the value of publicly held corporations.

If financial markets operate efficiently, stock returns react immediately to new information about the firm. These movements allow researchers to estimate the impact of policies or exogenous events *ex ante,* before the occurrence has affected the firm's profits. Such studies do not have to wait months or years to observe earnings, which would be required for *ex post* studies. During this period, outside factors that would offset or reinforce the incident are likely to occur. Identifying and accounting for these outside factors could be very difficult. Event analysis avoids such complications by looking at what happens on the day of the occurrence and the period immediately surrounding it.

In the next part of this chapter, we briefly explain what event analysis is, when it is appropriate, and what it does. We also provide a brief history of event analysis in the finance literature. In the third section, we show how to perform an event analysis. We present both the standard methodology from the finance literature as well as an approach that sports economists are likely to find more intuitively appealing. In the fourth section, we review many papers that have applied event analysis to the realm of sports. These studies appear in the economics, finance, and marketing literatures.

What Is Event Analysis?

As the term suggests, event analysis measures the impact of a specific event or incident on the value of an enterprise. An event can take many different forms. Announcements of impending actions, changes in regulations, and natural disasters have all been the subject of event analysis. The analysis takes the form of estimating how the value of the firm responded to the surprise. In effect, it measures the difference between the actual value of the company and the value that would have prevailed in the absence of the event. In perhaps the earliest attempt at an event analysis, Dolley (1933) postulated that stock splits affect the value of a corporation and that one could measure this impact by looking at stock prices. Event analysis has also been used to measure the impact of government regulations, such as the impact of anti-smoking regulations on the cigarette industry (Mitchell and Mulherin, 1988) and on the hospitality industry (Tomlin, 2009). It has also been used to evaluate the impact of truly exogenous occurrences, such as the impact of the ValuJet Airline crash on the profitability of ValuJet (Nethercutt and Pruitt, 1997).

Event analysis has also been applied on the macro level. Elmendorf (1996), for example, analyzes the impact of several attempts by Congress to limit deficit spending (the Gramm-Rudman-Hollings law of 1985 and the Budget Enforcement Act of 1990) on real interest rates. In the sports literature, macro-level studies focus on how an event affects the behavior of overall stock market indices. These studies provide *ex ante* analyses of how the announcement of such mega-events as hosting the Olympics or smaller-scale events, like a national team's performance in international competition, affect a nation's economy.

Ball and Brown (1968) and Fama et al. (1969) created the theoretical framework and the empirical methodology that still underlie event studies. Like Dolley (1933), Fama et al. analyzed the impact of a stock split on a firm's value. The key theoretical contribution was to apply Fama's efficient markets hypothesis to this problem. According to the efficient markets hypothesis, investors respond immediately to new information. In the case of good news, the stock becomes more attractive to investors, and its price rises. If the news is bad, investors anticipate lower profits and drive the stock's price down. The stock price of a corporation is thus the best estimate of the company's value. For example, when a firm announces that its profits rose more than expected, investors expect the firm to be more profitable, the demand for the company's stock rises, and the price of the company's stock increases. Assuming for simplicity that a company's stock price is initially constant, Figure 16.1a shows that the announcement of a split causes investors to reevaluate the value of the company and immediately bid the stock's price to a new, higher level.[1]

The increase in price can also be thought of as a one-time, positive holding period return. The Center for Research in Security Prices (CRSP) defines a holding period return as "the change in the total value of an investment in a common stock over some period of time per dollar of initial investment" (CRSP, 2009). The length of the holding period can vary but is most commonly a day. CRSP, for example, uses the return extending from the previous close of the market to the close on the current day. If the price is constant, the holding period return is zero. The rise in price causes the holding period return to increase. The holding period return goes back to zero if the price settles at its new level. The one-time increase in value on date t_0 shown in Figure 16.1a can therefore be viewed as the brief increase in the firm's holding period return on t_0 shown in Figure 16.1b. Similarly, the announcement of bad news, such as lower-than-expected earnings, immediately reduces the value of the company and causes negative holding period returns.

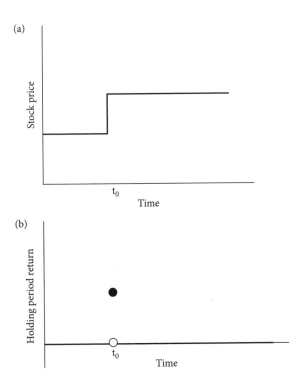

Figure 16.1 The Impact of an Event on a Stock's
Price and Its Holding Period Return.

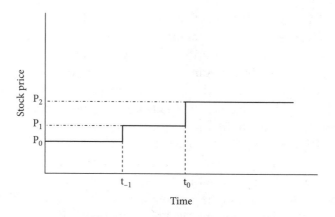

Figure 16.2 The Impact of an Event When Information Leaks Out in Advance.

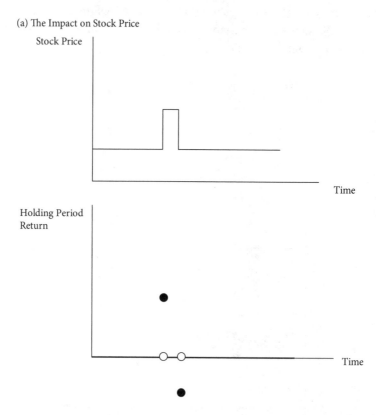

Figure 16.3 An Event That Has a Short-lived Impact.

The impact of an event is not always as clear as in Figure 16.1. This is particularly true when the event is an announcement of an action that has already occurred (such as corporate earnings) or that will take place (such as the imposition of a tariff). In these cases, a limited number of people might anticipate the event before it is announced. If these people act on their prior knowledge by buying (selling) stock in the company, they could cause the value of the company to rise (fall) prior to the announcement, as shown in Figure 16.2. If the announcement made at time t_0 came as a surprise, then the stock price would jump from P_0 to P_2 at that time. If some people learned of the announcement at time t_{-1}, some of the increase, say from P_0 to P_1, would occur then. We illustrate this as a discrete jump at time t_{-1}, though it could be a gradual increase starting at t_{-1}. The impact of the event will therefore appear be smaller because some people have already acted on the new information.

Finally, an event could result in a brief outburst of "irrational exuberance" (or panic) that quickly dissipates. Agents might buy stock upon first hearing the announcement, only to sell their stock soon after. In that case, the event could cause an immediate rise in the stock price and a positive holding period return. That rise, however, is quickly offset by a decline in price, perhaps back to its original level. We illustrate one such possibility, in which the price immediately returns to its original level, in Figure 16.3.

How to Perform an Event Analysis

The first step in performing an event analysis is to determine whether such a study is feasible. As our discussion above suggests, an event analysis requires a clearly identified incident that takes place at a well-identified moment in time.

After specifying the event and the date, one must identify the firm or firms that are affected by the event. Not all companies are suitable for an event analysis. Because event analysis is based on movements in a company's stock price, one cannot perform it on a privately-held company. In addition, one must sometimes play detective to find out which firm is affected by an event. For example, an event study would not be able to measure the impact of an event (such as a sponsorship deal or a celebrity endorsement) on the Miller Brewing Company because Miller is no longer a stand-alone company. Instead, the purchase would affect the value of Phillip Morris, Miller's parent company.

After determining that an event analysis is feasible, one must collect the appropriate data. A standard source of data for event analyses is the Center for Research on Security Prices (CRSP), which provides holding period returns for companies on NYSE, AMEX, and NASDAQ. CRSP data are available online through Wharton Research Data Services (WRDS). One can also compute the holding period return directly from stock prices. However, when using stock prices, one must be careful to account for stock splits and dividends, which affect stock prices and hence holding period returns.

Second, one must construct a baseline holding period return and compute the abnormal rate of return. Unlike the simple example described above, holding period returns are not always stable. Event analyses therefore use a stock's *abnormal return,* the difference between the actual holding period return and the expected return had the event not taken place. Using MacKinlay's (1997) notation, the abnormal return to asset i on date t is given by:

$$AR_{it} = R_{it} - E(R_{it}|X_t)$$ (1)

AR_{it} is the abnormal return, R_{it} is the observed return on asset i in period t, and $E(R_{it}|X_t)$ is the expected return of the asset conditional on the information, X, available at time t. The expectation $E(R_{it}|X_t)$ forms a baseline holding period return against which one measures the impact of a shock. The baseline depends on one's view of financial markets.

Most estimates create a baseline using the *market model.*[2] The market model, which was proposed by Fama et al. (1969), assumes that the holding period return to a specific asset is a linear function of the holding period return to an overall market index. According to the market model, one can generate the predicted holding period return for company i by regressing it on the market rate of return:

$$R_{it} = \beta_0 + \beta_1 R_{Mt} + \varepsilon_{it}$$ (2)

R_{it} is the holding period return for company i at time t, R_{Mt} is the holding period return for an appropriate market index at time t, and ε_{it} is a random error term that has a mean value of zero and is invariant over time ($Var(\varepsilon_{it}) = \sigma_i^2$).

One computes the baseline return over the *estimation window.* While there is no universally accepted value for the length of the estimation window, many studies use a period that begins 170 business days before the event and ends 20 business days before the event. The estimation window typically ends far in advance to prevent the baseline from being corrupted by the actions of people who anticipate the event. In general, this is a concern only when the event is an announcement or action about which some people might have foreknowledge. In the case of a truly exogenous event, such as a natural disaster, one need not take such precautions.

To compute the abnormal return, one first estimates equation (2) over the estimation window. One then uses the estimated parameters $\hat{\beta}_0$ and $\hat{\beta}_1$ and the observations of the market index (typically the Standard and Poor's 500) to generate the predicted values of the holding period return for company i over the *event window.* The event window generally extends from 20 days before the event to 20 days after the event. The 20 days prior to the event account for possible abnormal returns due to the leakage of inside information. The 20 days after the event are included to determine whether the event has only a transitory impact.

The abnormal return on the day of the event (or any other day in the event window) is the difference between the observed and predicted returns as noted in equation (1). One must then test whether the abnormal return is statistically significant.[3]

When estimating abnormal returns for many firms, one can evaluate the over-all impact of the event by computing the *mean abnormal return*, which is the arith-metic mean of the individual abnormal returns. One can also use the results of the event analysis to estimate what causes different firms to respond differently to the same event. The second stage estimation takes the form:

$$AR_i = \beta_0 + \sum_j \beta_{ij} x_{ij} + \varepsilon_i \qquad (3)$$

where x_{ij} are a series of characteristics of firm i, and ε_i is a firm-specific error term.

Third, if the impact of the event is the result of brief excitement and not of any change in the underlying profitability of the firm, any positive abnormal returns on or immediately following the event date are offset by negative abnormal returns in the days that follow. For that reason, one typically also computes the *cumulative abnormal return* (CAR). The CAR is the sum of abnormal returns from day τ to date $\tau + N$:

$$CAR_{i\tau} = \sum_{t=\tau}^{\tau+N} AR_{it} \qquad (4)$$

$CAR_{i\tau}$ is the cumulative abnormal return for firm i starting at date τ, and continu-ing for N days. τ is often the date of the event, but, if one believes that investors have anticipated the event, it can be several weeks before the event. If $CAR_{i\tau}$ is not statistically significant, then the event does not add to the firm's value even if the immediate impact is significant, as illustrated in Figure 16.3.

MacKinlay (1997) points out an important limitation of computing CARs in this manner. The standard error of the CAR is based on the implicit assumption that the covariances of the abnormal returns are zero. Because there is no reason to assume this is the case, particularly if the impact is temporary, the standard errors—and hypothesis tests—might not be valid.

The Dummy Variable Approach

Salkever (1976) and Karafiath (1988) provide a more intuitively appealing approach to event analysis, which also avoids the problem with standard errors. This method uses dummy variables to measure the impact of an event. The dummy variable method amends equation (2) by adding a series of dummy variables to form the following equation:

$$R_{it} = \beta_0 + \beta_1 R_{Mt} + \sum_{s=\tau-20}^{\tau+20} \delta_s D_s + \varepsilon_{Mt} \qquad (5)$$

D_s is a dummy variable equal to 1 for the sth day before or after the event. The coefficient δ_s is the abnormal holding period return for day s. The event generates a statistically significant abnormal return on day o if $\hat{\delta}_0$ is significantly different from zero.

One can easily extend this methodology to determine whether the immediate impact is only transitory. To do this, one computes the CAR by adding the coefficients for all the days in the event window:

$$CAR_{i\tau} = \sum_{s=\tau}^{s=\tau+20} \hat{\delta}_s \qquad (6)$$

The CAR is statistically significant if the sum in equation (6) is statistically significant. Post-estimation commands to perform such a test are now available in several statistical packages. Alternatively, one can compute the relevant standard error using the covariance matrix of the regression.

Event Analysis on a Macro Level

The preceding analysis pertains to the impact of an event on the value of a single company. As noted earlier, however, several studies look at how a sports-related event affects an entire economy. Typically, these studies measure macroeconomic effects by the movement in a nation's stock market. Estimating how an event affects a broad market index means that one cannot use the standard market model, as equation (1) uses the market index as an explanatory variable.

Some studies resolve this difficulty by identifying a still broader index. For example, Edmans et al. (2007) use an international index of national exchanges to explain movements in national indices. Studies of small economies can choose an index from a larger nation as an explanatory variable. For example, Boyle and Walter (2003) use an index from the United States in their study of New Zealand.

Still other studies forgo outside indices and instead use lagged values of the holding period return of the index, turning equation (1) into an autoregressive model. Berman et al. (2000), Veraros et al. (2004), and Leeds et al. (2009) all conclude that the rate of return follows an AR(1) process:

$$r_t = \beta_0 + \beta_1 r_{t-1} + \sum_{s=\tau-20}^{\tau+20} \delta_s D_s + \varepsilon_t \qquad (7)$$

where r_t is the holding period return for a national index, r_{t-1} is the lagged return, and D_s is a dummy variable that equals 1 on day s and equals zero otherwise. As before, we interpret δ_s as the abnormal return on day s.

The dummy variable method has two important advantages. First, the estimation is easier to perform, and its interpretation is simpler than the standard approach. Second, its underlying assumptions are less restrictive than those of the standard method. The hypothesis tests of the CAR do not rely on the assumption that the error terms are uncorrelated, as the dummy variable approach uses the covariance matrix of the regression.

A Review of Event Studies in Sports Economics

Event studies in sports have taken both the micro approach and the macro approach. Micro studies have focused largely on how a variety of sponsorship and advertising initiatives affect the firms that undertake them. Macro studies have examined the impact of two events: securing the Olympics and the performance of a national team in international competition. We review both types of studies and events.

Micro Studies

From the beginning of professional and intercollegiate sport in the nineteenth century, firms have recognized the value of sponsorships. By associating their products with a team, league, facility, or event, firms hope to generate name recognition and goodwill among fans and the public at large. The sponsoring companies hope that publicity and positive feelings will translate into increased sales and profits.

Event analysis has been used to measure the value of a variety of sports sponsorship deals. An early study by Mishra et al. (1997) examines the impact of a variety of sponsorships, including the Olympics, tennis tournaments, concert tours, and stadium naming rights. Their event window extends from five days before the sponsorship was announced to five days after the announcement. They find a mean abnormal return of 0.556 percentage points on the day of the announcement but no impact on any other day in their event window. Since they do not construct a CAR, one cannot say whether they find a permanent or transitory effect.

Farrell and Frame (1997) study the impact of becoming an official sponsor of the 1996 Atlanta Olympics. They acknowledge the possibility that investors anticipate the announcement and attempt to capture this effect by regarding t_0 as the day *before* the announcement appeared in *The Wall Street Journal*. They compute standardized abnormal returns to reduce the impact of firms with unusually large variation in returns.[4] The mean abnormal return is statistically significant at the 10 percent level for dates $t_0 + 1$ and $t_0 + 2$, but the mean CAR for dates running from $t_0 - 5$ to $t_0 + 5$ is insignificant. They run second-stage regressions of the individual abnormal returns for dates t_0, $t_0 + 1$, and $t_0 + 2$ on several firm-specific variables. However, there is little reason for running this regression for individual dates, and the window for their second stage CAR is too short (t_0 to $t_0 + 2$) to have any meaning.

Miyazaki and Morgan (2001) also look at sponsors of the Atlanta Summer Olympics of 1996. They do not find a statistically significant impact for any one day. Miyazaki and Morgan compute two CARs, one extending from four days before the event to the day of the event and the other running from three days before the event to the day of the event. Because they do not extend beyond the day of the announcement, the CARs do not provide any information as to the permanence of the effect.

Two studies examine the value of corporate sponsorships in the form of facility naming rights. Clark et al. (2002) find a statistically significant mean abnormal rate of return of 0.73 percent on the day the purchase was announced. Using a 3-day event window that extends from one day before the announcement to one day after the announcement, they find a statistically significant CAR of 1.65 percent. This event window is also too short to support the claim that sponsorship has a permanent effect.

Leeds et al. (2007) come to a very different conclusion from Clark et al. They use the dummy variable approach and an event window that extends from 20 days before the announcement to 20 days afterward. They find that only three companies showed positive and statistically significant abnormal returns on the day of the event, while two companies had negative and significant abnormal returns. Leeds et al. report only two statistically significant effects for the CAR, both of which are negative. The difference between this result and Clark et al. stems from one company's having such a high abnormal return on the day of the announcement that the mean abnormal return for the entire sample was positive.

Motorsports provide a highly visible form of sponsorship, particularly for firms in the automotive industry. So many sponsors have placed their names on the cars that the cars have become mobile billboards for their underwriters. Cornwell et al. (2001) examine the impact of sponsoring a winning entry in the Indianapolis 500 on a company's value, while Pruitt et al. (2004) study the impact of a company's announcement that it will be sponsoring an entrant in the NASCAR circuit.

Cornwell et al. find no statistically significant impact on the mean stock price—which they use instead of the holding period return—on the day of the race. Nor do they find a statistically significant mean CAR. They then regress individual values of the CAR for the period extending from two days before the event to two days after the event on a series of variables related to the winning car and the company that sponsored it. They find evidence that surprise winners (as measured by a relatively slow qualifying speed and a first-time victory) have a greater impact on stock prices than do winners whose success was more easily predicted. They also find a statistically significant positive effect for a dummy variable that indicated whether the sponsor was in an industry related to cars (e.g., Ford or Pennzoil) or unrelated to them (e.g., Anheuser-Busch). Again, though, the event window is too short to permit any real conclusions to be drawn.

In contrast to the results for the Indianapolis 500, Pruitt et al. find that NASCAR sponsorship announcements have a strong, positive impact on the value of the sponsoring firms. For the date of the announcement, they find a statistically significant mean abnormal return of 1.29 percent, though, as noted for the naming rights study, the use of a mean abnormal return might obscure individual returns. Rather than compute the CAR for the date of the announcement and several days afterward, they compute the mean cumulative abnormal return for the 100 days following the announcement. When they find that this is insignificant, they claim that this shows that the announcement had a significant permanent effect when, in fact, the results do not support this conclusion. They then compute individual CARs for a much shorter window—from the day before the announcement to the day of the announcement—and regress the CARs on a series of characteristics of the race teams and sponsoring companies. The extremely short CAR that they use cannot represent a permanent impact on company value, so little weight can be placed on these second-stage regressions.

Leeds (2009) uses the dummy variable method to measure the impact of the 2006 Tour de France on the value of Phonak, which sponsored the team led by Floyd Landis. Landis won Stage 17 of the 2006 Tour by an unheard-of six minutes to take the overall lead, winning the Tour a few days later. Shortly afterward, a drug test revealed an unusual mount of testosterone in Landis's system, and Landis was eventually stripped of his victory and banned from racing. Leeds estimates the impact of both the good and bad news on the holding period return for Phonak on the Swiss stock exchange. He finds that none of these events had an immediate impact on the holding period return to Phonak stock. However, the CAR for the 21-day period starting with Stage 17 (the Tour ended on Day 3 of this period, and the drug test was announced on Day 6) was positive and significant. This result suggests that being associated with a disgraced cyclist was still good publicity for Phonak.

By associating the name of the company with a team, event, or setting, sports sponsorship is a passive form of advertising in that a viewer is exposed to the sponsor by following the coverage of the sport. Advertising, such as commercials and celebrity endorsements, can appeal more directly to the public at large. The difference between the two is illustrated by Buick's sponsorship of the Buick Open Golf tournament and an ad in *The New Yorker* showing Tiger Woods driving a Buick.

Agrawal and Kamakura (1995) were among the first to apply event analysis to advertising. They find that the announcement of a contract or a pending contract with a celebrity to endorse a product results in a 0.44 percent abnormal rate of return. Using an event window that extends from 10 days before the announcement to 10 days afterward, they do not find a statistically significant CAR.[5] They do not say anything about the celebrities in their sample, so it is not clear whether there were any sports figures present.

Farrell et al. (2000) estimate the impact made by a single celebrity—Tiger Woods. They attempt to measure the impact that Tiger Woods's performance in golf tournaments had on the profitability of companies with which he had signed endorsement contracts. Unfortunately, the estimation procedure is generally opaque and, where transparent, problematic. The authors effectively start with the second stage, having somehow already computed abnormal returns for the firms. They then regress these abnormal returns on industry-wide abnormal returns (which they do not define) and measures of Tiger Woods's performance. Apparently, the data set consists only of dates surrounding 48 golf tournaments in which Woods appeared, though again this is not completely clear. They find that Tiger Woods's performance had a positive and statistically significant impact on the value of firms for which he had endorsement contracts. However, the extremely short window and the lack of clarity in how the underlying data were calculated make it impossible to draw any firm conclusions from the findings.

Fizel et al. (2008) estimate the impact of a company's announcement that a star athlete will endorse its products. Their analysis uses very large estimation and event windows. The estimation window begins 255 days before the announcement, and the event window begins 40 days before it. They find no statistically significant CAR for companies receiving athlete endorsements. The only statistically significant impact occurs two days prior to the announcement. They attribute this negative effect to news leakage. This suggests that athlete endorsements negatively affect company value. They then run separate analyses for individual sports. The only sport to yield statistically significant mean abnormal returns is golf, which shows a positive impact, which might relate less to the sport as a whole than to a "Tiger Woods effect."

Macro Studies

Three papers claim to provide an event analysis of the impact of successive Olympics on the host nation's economy. Berman et al. focus on the 2000 Sydney Games, Veraros et al. on the 2004 Athens Games, and Leeds et al. on the 2008 Beijing Games. Each study examines the impact of the announcement of the city's selection as Olympic host city on a broad stock market index. If the selection is a surprise and if investors expect the Olympics to have a positive impact on the nation's economy, the index should rise. All three studies use variants of the autoregressive approach described above, and all three come to similar conclusions.

Berman et al. (2000) and Veraros et al. (2004) use techniques common to event studies, but neither is truly a complete event study. Berman et al. compute abnormal daily returns for the Australian Stock Exchange as well as for indices for specific sectors of the Australian economy. They find no overall impact and highly limited sectoral impacts on the day of the announcement. This could imply that there was no exuberance regarding the future of the Australian economy, though the construction, contracting, and engineering sectors do seem to have shown some initial enthusiasm. Because they do not calculate any CARs, there is no way to make a definitive statement about the long-term effect of the announcement.

Veraros et al. (2004) use weekly stock exchange data from both the winning city, Athens, and one of the losing cities, Milan. They find that the announcement had a positive, significant impact on the overall Athens exchange index and on the industrial and construction sectors, both of which create the infrastructure for the Games, but they do not find a negative effect on the Milan exchange index. The use of weekly returns data for a day-specific event and the lack of any analysis of a CAR mean that Veraros et al., like Berman et al., do not perform a standard event analysis.

Because they use daily data and compute CARs, Leeds et al. (2009) provide the first full event analysis of the macro effects of the Olympics. They find that the announcement that Beijing would host the Olympics had an immediate impact on the Shanghai exchange index that was positive and statistically significant. The positive impact, however, was short-lived. The immediate impact was wiped out by the ninth day after the announcement. Neither of Beijing's two major contenders was affected by losing the 2008 Games. The four major industrial indices on the Shanghai exchange—Commercial, Industrial, Properties, and Utilities—were significantly impacted by the announcement. Unlike the other sectors in this study, and contrary to previous studies, the CAR for the Industrial index was negative.

Another set of event studies estimates the impact of a national team's performance on the return to an overall stock index. Because winning a soccer or rugby match does not affect anything "real" in the economy, there is no *a priori* reason for overall economic activity to rise. Instead, the studies focus largely on "irrational investor responses to sporting contest results [that are] transitory at best" (Boyle and Walter, 2203, p. 225) and do not bother to compute CARs. Used in this way, event analysis can be an important tool for the emerging field of behavioral economics.

Ashton et al. (2003) estimate whether the performance of England's national soccer team affects the FTSE index. Rather than using an AR(1) process or an outside index, they regress the return on the FTSE on a dummy variable equal to one if England won the day before. They find positive abnormal returns following a win by England and negative abonornal returns following a loss, suggesting mood swings by investors. However, because their estimation technique is an ANOVA, the study is not a pure event analysis.

In contrast to Ashton et al., Boyle and Walter (2003) find that the performance of New Zealand's national rugby team (the "All Blacks") does not affect its national stock market. As noted earlier, Boyle and Walter do not appeal to an auto-regressive process. Instead, they use the NYSE as a determinant of the movements of the New Zealand stock market. Their use of monthly index values in an attempt to explain a day-specific event, however, is questionable.

Edmans et al. (2007) analyze the impact of a nation's performance in international soccer, cricket, rugby, and basketball matches on its stock market. They use a world market index from Datastream to estimate a variant of equation (5). They perform an event analysis using the specific contest as the event and then regress the abnormal returns on two dummy variables, one equal to one if the national team won and the other equal to one if the national team lost. In some sports, such as soccer, a draw is the default variable. In other sports, such as basketball, this specification is more problematic. Nonetheless, their results are compelling, particularly for soccer. Using data from World Cup and continental championships, they find that stock markets respond negatively to losses but do not respond to wins. The negative impact is particularly acute for losses in important matches (e.g., losses that result in elimination) and for "major" soccer countries (Argentina, Brazil, England, France, Germany, Italy, and Spain). Other sports show a similar pattern, though the impact is much smaller—perhaps reflecting the lesser importance of these sports.

CONCLUSION

Event analysis can be a valuable econometric tool. It allows researchers and policy makers to see how an incident or announcement affects the profitability of a firm before the profits ever accrue. Moreover, it can provide a clearer picture of those profits than retrospective studies can. When used inappropriately or incorrectly, however, an event analysis can lead to improper conclusions and misguided policy. A good event analysis should follow a few simple rules.

The first rule is to choose an appropriate event. An incident that has only a marginal impact on a firm's profitability is unlikely to generate a statistically significant abnormal return. Even if the incident does have an effect, there is no guarantee that an event analysis will detect it. Abnormal returns reflect surprises. If the event is widely expected by the time it occurs, it can be extremely difficult to find its impact.

The second rule is to use data that are appropriate to the task. In most cases, that means using daily holding period returns. Using weekly or monthly returns to measure the impact of an occurrence at a moment in time fails to control for outside factors that could reinforce or offset the impact of the event. The analyses by Boyle and Walter (2003) and Veraros et al. (2004) suffer from using inappropriately long time units.

The third and final rule is to include—where appropriate—the days preceding and following the event. Many studies content themselves with measuring the impact of an incident on the day that it occurs. Others look only one or two days beyond the incident. Such analyses might pick up transitory moments of exhilaration or despair. They do not necessarily reflect a lasting impact. MacKinlay's including the 20 days after the event in the CAR is a good standard. In addition, except when the event cannot be foretold, as in the case of such disasters as plane crashes, some investors might have advance knowledge of the incident or announcement. In that case, one must look for abnormal returns in the days lead-ing up to the incident. Again, MacKinlay's inclusion of 20 days prior to the event provides a useful guide.

The above rules do not guarantee successful research. They will, however, help prevent errors of analysis that have plagued previous studies. The studies by Farrell and Frame (1997), Farrell et al. (2000), Miyazaki and Morgan (2001), Cornwell et al. (2001), Clark et al. (2002), and Pruitt et al. all attempt to test for a permanent effect but do not use a sufficiently long CAR. Mishra et al. (1997) do not use a CAR at all. Thus, the results of these studies do not support the conclusions that they draw. In contrast, the studies by Ashton et al., Boyle and Morgan, and Edmans et al. test for excess variability in stock returns, not for permanent changes in value. Those studies correctly do not look far beyond the date of the event. While it is usually impossible to have foreknowledge of the outcome of a sporting event, some outcomes are bigger surprises than others. The studies cited here do not account for that possibility.

This review has shown that event analysis is a potentially valuable econometric tool. It has, however, not been extensively employed in sports settings and, when used, it has often been imperfectly applied. There is therefore much room for stud-ies that use event analysis in the future.

Notes

1 For a for a more complete set of such figures and a good intuitive treatment of event analysis, see Schweitzer (1989).
2 For information on the alternative *constant mean model,* see MacKinlay (1997).
3 For details regarding the standard error of the abnormal return, see MacKinlay (1997).
4 They define the standardized abnormal return for firm i on the kth day following an announcement as $SAR_{i,t+k} = AR_{i,t+k} / \hat{\sigma}_i$, where $\hat{\sigma}_i$ is the standard deviation of the error term in equation (2).
5 They find a significant CAR for the event window extending from the day before the announcement to the day of the announcement, but this is not enough of a window to establish a permanent effect.

References

Agrawal, Jagdish, and W. Kamakura (1995). The economic worth of celebrity endorsers: An event study analysis. *Journal of Marketing,*59(3): 56–62.

Ashton, J. K., B. Gerrard, and R. Hudson (2003). Economic impact of national sporting success: Evidence from the London Stock Exchange. *Applied Economics Letters,* 10(12): 783–785.

Associated Press (2009). Manchester United signs up Aon as New Jersey sponsor," *USA Today,* June 3, 2009, online at http://www.usatoday.com/sports/soccer/europe/2009–06–03-manchester-united-aon-sponsorship_N.htm.

Ball, Ray, and Phillip Brown (1968). An empirical evaluation of accounting income numbers. *Journal of Accounting Research,* 6(2): 159–178.

Barros, Carlos Pestana, Catarina de Barros, Abel Santos, and Simon Chadwick (2007). Sponsorship brand recall at the Euro 2004 Soccer Tournament. *Sport Marketing Quarterly,* 16(3): 161–170.

Berman, Gabrielle, Robert Brooks, and Sinclair Davidson (2000). The Sydney Olympic Games announcement and Australian Stock Market reaction. *Applied EconomicsLetters,* 7(12): 781–784.

Boyle, Glenn, and Brett Walter (2003). Reflected glory and failure: international sporting success and the stock market," *Applied Financial Economics,* 13(3): 225–235.

Clark, John M., T. Bettina Cornwell, and Stephen W. Pruitt (2002). Corporate stadium sponsorships, signaling theory, agency conflicts, and shareholder wealth. *Journal of Advertising Research,* 42(6): 16–32.

Cornwell, T. Bettina, Stephen W. Pruitt, and Robert van Ness (2001). The value of winning in motorsports: Sponsorship-linked marketing. *Journal of Advertising Research,* 4(1): 17–31.

CRSP//The Center for Research in Security Prices (2009). *WRDS,* online at http://wrds.wharton.upenn.edu/ds/crsp/dstk/dsf/, viewed November 3, 2009.

Dolley, James C. (1933). Characteristics and procedures of common stock split-ups. *Harvard Business Review,* 11(3): 316–326.

Edmans, Alex, Diego Garcia, Oyvind Norli (2007). Sports Sentiment and Stock Returns. *Journal of Finance,* 62(4): 1967–1998.

Elmendorf, Douglas W. (1996). The effects of deficit reduction laws on real interest rates. *Federal Reserve Board Finance and Economics Discussion Series,* 1996–44.

Fahy, John, Francis Farell, and Pascale Quester (2004). Competitive advantage through sponsorship. *European Journal of Marketing,* 38(8): 1010–1030.

Fama, Eugene F., Lawrence Fisher, Michael C. Jensen, and Richard Roll (1969). The adjustment of stock prices to new information. *International Economic Review,* 10(1): 1–21.

Farrell, Kathleen A., and W. Scott Frame (1997). The value of Olympic sponsorships: Who is capturing the gold? *Journal of Market Focused Management,* 2(2): 171–182.

Farrell, Kathleen A., Gordon V. Karels, Kenneth W. Monfort, and Christine A. McClatchey (2000). Celebrity performance and endorsement value: The case of Tiger Woods. *Managerial Finance,* 26(7): 1–15.

Fizel, John, Chris R. McNeil, and Timothy Smaby (2008). Athlete endorsement contracts: The impact of conventional stars. *International Advances in Economic Research,* 14(2): 247–256.

Hotchkiss, Julie L., Robert E. Moore, and Stephanie Zobay (2003). Impact of the 1996 Summer Olympic Games on employment and wages in Georgia. *Southern Economic Journal,* 69(3): 691–704.

Karafiath, Imre (1988). "Using dummy variables in the event methodology. *Financial Review,* 23(3): 351–357.

Leeds, Eva Marikova, Michael A. Leeds, and Irina Pistolet (2007). A stadium by any other name: the value of naming rights. *Journal of Sports Economics,* 8(6): 581–595.

Leeds, Michael A. (2010). Is bad news always bad? The impact of Floyd Landis's rise and fall on Phonak. *Applied Economics Letters,* 17(8): 805–808.

Leeds, Michael A., John M. Mirikitani, and Danna Tang (2009). Rational exuberance? An event analysis of the 2008 Olympic announcement. *International Journal of Sport Finance*, 4(1): 5–15.

MacKinlay, A. Craig (1997). Event studies in economics and finance. *Journal of Economic Literature*, 35(1): 13–39.

Mitchell, Mark L., and J. Harold Mulherin (1988). Finessing the political system: The cigarette advertising ban. *Southern Economic Journal*, 54(4): 855–862.

Mishra, Debi P., George Bobinski, and Harjeet S. Bhabra (1997). Assessing the economic worth of corporate event sponsorships: A stock market perspective. *Journal of Market Focused Management*, 2(2): 149–169.

Miyazaki, Anthony D., and Angela G. Morgan (2001). Assessing market value of event sponsoring: Corporate Olympic sponsorships. *Journal of Advertising Research*, 41(1): 9–15.

Naming rights online (2009). http://www.namingrightsonline.com/basics.htm, viewed September 3, 2009; Evan Buxbaum, Mets and the Citi, *CNN.com/US*, April 13, 2009, online at http://www.cnn.com/2009/US/04/13/mets.ballpark/.

Nethercutt, Leonard L. and Stephen W. Pruitt (1997). Touched by tragedy: Capital market lessons from the crash of ValuJet Flight 592. *Economics Letters*, 56(3): 351–358.

Pruitt, Stephen W., T. Bettina Cornwell, and John M. Clark (2004). The NASCAR phenomenon: Auto racing sponsorships and shareholder wealth. *Journal of Advertising Research*, 44(3): 281–296.

Salkever, David (1976). The use of dummy variables to compute predictions, prediction errors, and confidence intervals. *Journal of Econometrics*, 4(4): 393–397.

Schweitzer, Robert (1989). How do stock returns react to special events? *Business Review—Federal Reserve Bank of Philadelphia*, (July–August): 17–29.

Tomlin, Jonathan T. (2009). The impact of smoking bans on the hospitality industry: New evidence from stock market returns. *The B.E. Journal of Economic Analysis & Policy*, 9(1).

Veraros, Nikolaos, Evangelia Kasimati, and Peter Dawson (2004). The 2004 Olympic Games announcement and its effect on the Athens and Milan stock exchanges. *Applied Economics Letters*, 11(12): 749753.

CHAPTER 17

BEHAVIORAL BIASES AND SPORTSBOOK PRICING IN MAJOR LEAGUE BASEBALL

RODNEY J. PAUL

ANDREW P. WEINBACH

1. INTRODUCTION

MORE detailed data on gambling markets have recently become available to researchers, allowing for a more thorough investigation of how sportsbooks truly set prices. In addition, this data has deepened our understanding of efficient markets, or lack thereof, within this market. Under the traditional models of sportsbook behavior, such as Pankoff (1968), Zuber et al. (1985), and Sauer et al. (1988), sportsbooks were assumed to set a market-clearing price by balancing the book. This price would split the betting action between both sides of the wagering proposition. Setting prices that balance the book allows sportsbooks to earn risk-free returns when wagering balance is achieved, with sportsbooks earning their commission (under an 11-to-win-10 betting rule) on losing bets. Given that the observed price was assumed to be a result of the actions of bettors, sports betting markets became a natural place to test the efficient markets hypothesis. Findings in support of the efficient markets hypothesis within these wagering markets, where public sentiment is likely to run extremely high, served as a significant stamp of approval of this theory and supported the notion of the general "wisdom of crowds."

Levitt (2004) challenged the traditional models of sportsbook behavior. His hypothesis assumes that sportsbooks set prices to maximize profits, rather than setting prices to balance the book. Through the use of data from a betting tournament for the NFL, Levitt showed that bettors tend to prefer certain wagers, such as road favorites, and sportsbooks incorporate these known bettor biases into prices. With biased prices, sportsbooks earn higher profits by becoming an active participant in the wager, effectively wagering on the less-popular side of the proposition. Under the Levitt hypothesis, sportsbooks are not only good at forecasting game outcomes, but also know the likely biases of bettors, and are able to exploit these advantages through their pricing.

One problem with the study of Levitt (2004) was the use of a betting tournament rather than data from an actual sportsbook. Given the betting tournament participants were a small group and paid only an entry fee to participate, marginal incentives (the outlay of money per bet and the actual payoff or losses occurring with each game bet) normally present in sports gambling markets were absent in the data from the betting tournament. Given the small number of participants and the lack of marginal incentives, doubts of the validity of these results were expressed.

In recent articles in the *Journal of Prediction Markets* and the *International Journal of Sports Finance*, Paul and Weinbach tested the Levitt model of sportsbook behavior using actual betting data from real sportsbooks. Through the use of actual sportsbook data from www.sportsbook.com and data from multiple sportsbooks collected by www.sportsinsights.com, Paul and Weinbach showed that betting dollars are not balanced evenly between favorites and underdogs (or overs and unders in the totals markets) in the National Football League (NFL) (Paul and Weinbach, 2007) and in the National Basketball Association (NBA) (Paul and Weinbach, 2008). Unlike the assumptions of the traditional models, favorites receive a disproportionate share of the betting dollars. In each sport, as the point spread on the favorite increased, the percentage of dollars bet on the favorite also increased. In addition, there was an additional increase in percentage of dollars bet on road favorites as opposed to home favorites.

These results cast doubt on the traditional models of sportsbook behavior, as the betting dollars definitely do not appear balanced. Although the findings of these papers allow for a rejection of the null hypothesis that sportsbooks attempt to balance betting dollars evenly, the alternative hypothesis is not necessarily the hypothesis noted by Levitt (2004). The notion that sportsbooks price to maximize profits, using common bettor biases to their advantage, requires a much stronger result. This result would require sportsbooks to earn greater profits by pricing where bettors will be wrong more often than they are correct.

To determine if sportsbooks are earning greater profits through their choice to set prices other than prices that would balance the betting dollars, Paul and

Weinbach (2007, 2008) tested and reported results where the sportsbook became active participants in the wagers. Specifically, returns were calculated and tested for significance in situations where betting dollars were significantly imbalanced. When the percentage bet on the favorite exceeded a certain threshold, such as 60 percent or 70 percent, returns to betting the favorite (the same side as the public) and returns to betting the underdog (the side the sportsbook is "betting" by not balancing the dollars) were calculated. If sportsbooks are truly pricing to maximize profits, the betting public should lose disproportionately more of their bets on the favorites and the sportsbook should win with bets on the underdog.

In the case of the NFL (Paul and Weinbach, 2007), pricing to exploit bettor biases was found to be successful. A strategy of wagering against the betting public was found to generate positive profits. Therefore, sportsbooks were winning often enough to earn higher profits by taking a position on the underdog. In the NBA, however, this was not the case. Favorites and underdogs were found to evenly split wins and losses against the point spread, independent of how large of a betting imbalance toward the favorite was seen. Therefore, it was concluded for the NBA, sportsbooks are pricing more as a forecast of actual game outcomes, rather than to maximize individual game profits. Pricing as a forecast may still be a long-run profit-maximizing strategy, however, even in the presence of imbalanced betting dollars, due to the likely repeated game nature of sports wagering. In setting a price as a forecast where each side of the proposition wins in proportion to set odds, sportsbooks still earn their commission on losing bets in the long run, without the transactions costs necessary to attempt to balance the book or price to exploit biases on a game-by-game basis. This strategy also lessens the incentive for informed bettors to enter the market, possibly taking away profits from sportsbooks in the long run.

This chapter expands the study of actual sportsbook behavior, comparing the traditional models to the Levitt hypothesis and considering alternative theories, by examining the betting market for Major League Baseball. The study of betting percentages in Major League Baseball is different from the NFL, as prices are set in the form of odds, rather than a point spread. The nature of the market allows for examination of whether sportsbooks are pricing to exploit known bettor biases (as the Levitt, 2004, suggests), if they are pricing to balance the book (as suggested in the traditional models), or pricing as a forecast (as suggested by Paul and Weinbach, 2008). In addition, given odds rather than a point spread, the favorite-longshot bias can be investigated.

In professional sports that use odds in the betting market, such as Major League Baseball and the National Hockey League, a so-called "reverse favorite-longshot bias" was found. This reverse bias implies that favorites are over-bet and underdogs are underbet, meaning that bets on the underdog will win more often than implied by efficiency and could lead to profits, which is the opposite of results found in horse racing (the traditional favorite-longshot bias). These results were found by Woodland and Woodland (1994, 2001). Both sports were found to have a significant reverse favorite-longshot bias. Woodland and Woodland did not equate a unit bet on the favorite and the underdog in the proper manner, so their tests were corrected by Gandar, Zuber, Johnson, and Dare (2002) and by Gandar, Zuber, and Johnson (2004). After the corrections were implemented, the baseball betting market was shown not to exhibit the bias for all underdogs, but the bias remained significant for the subgroups of slight underdogs and home underdogs. Similarly, after the corrections, the bias was still found in the hockey betting market, although to a slightly lesser extent than originally estimated.

This study uses actual betting market data from four sportsbooks reported by www.sportsinsights.com for Major League Baseball (MLB). Tests of whether the sportsbook proportionally balances the betting action compared to odds are performed. In addition, sportsbooks using a strategy of setting prices to maximize profits is investigated through simple betting simulations. The reverse favorite-longshot bias (likely the overbetting of good teams) and home/road biases are also explored.

2. Sports Insights Betting Data: Major League Baseball, 2003–2008

The Major League Baseball betting data contains information from six seasons of play. Baseball uses an odds betting format, where the bettor may lay more than $1 on the favorite to win $1 and lay less than $1 to win $1 on underdogs. Sports Insights presents combined data from online sportsbooks to show the percentage of bets on the favorite and underdog for its subscribers. The eight online sportsbooks are 5Dimes.com, BetUS.com, CaribSports.com, Skybook.com, Sportsinteraction.com, SportBet.com, Sportsbook.com, and Wagerweb.com. Data was available for each game played in the six seasons, where odds were posted. The raw data set includes information on playoff games, all-star games, preseason games, and so on. For the purposes of this study, however, only regular season games were included.

Given the importance of the home/road distinction found in studies of sports that use odds betting (specifically baseball and hockey) in Gandar et al. (2002) and Gandar et al. (2004), we decided to break the data into home favorites (road underdogs) and road favorites (home underdogs) to examine the actions of bettors and observe results of various betting strategies. The easiest place to begin with this detailed data is to plot the results. To illustrate the possible preferences of bettors and betting strategy results, we have arranged the data from the biggest favorites to the smallest favorites for the groupings of home favorites and road favorites. Given the availability of the game odds set by the sportsbook, the percentages bet on favorites and underdogs, and actual game results, we decided to plot all data side by side in terms of betting percentages.

If sportsbooks were basing odds off of the flow of dollars bet and setting prices to clear the market, under the assumptions of the traditional models of sportsbook behavior, the odds should reflect the percentage of dollar bets received on the favorite and the underdog. The percentage bet on the favorite and the underdog based on actual odds is obtained by taking the absolute value of the midpoint of the odds (between the absolute value of the favorite odds and the underdog odds) and dividing this value by the midpoint of the odds plus 100. The midpoint of odds is necessary due to the commission charged on bets by sportsbooks. For instance, if favorite odds were −210 and underdog odds were +190 (favorite bettors would need to lay $2.10 to win $1 for winning wagers and underdog bettors would receive $1.90 plus their original $1 bet on winning wagers[1]), the midpoint of the odds is −200. With these odds, the favorite should have attracted two-thirds of the betting action, and the underdog should have attracted one-third of the betting dollars.[2]

In terms of the favorite, the percentage of bets that the favorite should have attracted to clear the market (based on odds), the actual percentage bet on the favorite, and the actual win percentage of a strategy of betting the favorite are presented in Figure 17.1. The data are arranged in terms of the percentage of bets that should have been received on the favorite, based on actual sportsbook odds, organized from highest percentage (biggest favorites) to lowest percentage (smallest favorites)

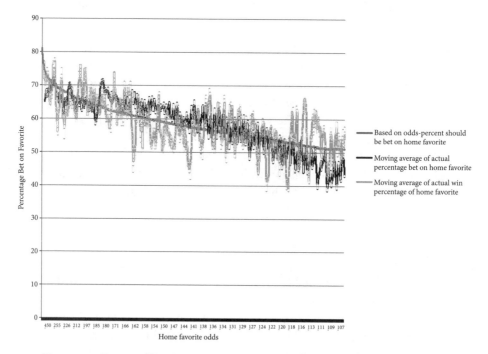

Figure 17.1 Expected Betting Percentages, Actual Betting Percentages, and Win Percentage for Home Favorites in Major League Baseball 2003–2008.

from left to right. To clearly illustrate the tendencies and results, the actual betting percentages on favorites received by the sportsbook and the winning percentage of the favorite are shown as 200-game and 100-game moving averages, respectively. This plot allows an easy visual of this market.

In the sample of home favorites, all three plots appear to move somewhat closely together. The expected percentage bet on the favorite (based on the odds), the actual percentage bet on the favorite, and the favorite win percentage appear to be closely related. Closer inspection shows the actual percentage bet generally lies slightly higher than the expected percentage bet based on the odds in the middle of the odds range and slightly below at the ends of the distribution. This could imply a possible reverse favorite-longshot bias, which is further explored later.

Although the home favorite data appears rather closely mapped, the road favorites show a much different story. In Figure 17.2, the expected percentage bet on the favorite based on the odds, the actual percentage bet on the favorite, and the favorite win percentages are plotted side by side for all Major League Baseball road favorites.

Figure 17.2 shows that the actual percentage bet on road favorites clearly exceeds the expected percentage bet based upon the odds. Sportsbooks seem to attract a much higher percentage of the betting dollars on road favorites, as opposed to the odds they actually set. The actual game outcomes (winning percentage of road favorites) tend to map much more closely to the odds set by the sportsbook, rather than the percentages bet by the wagering public.

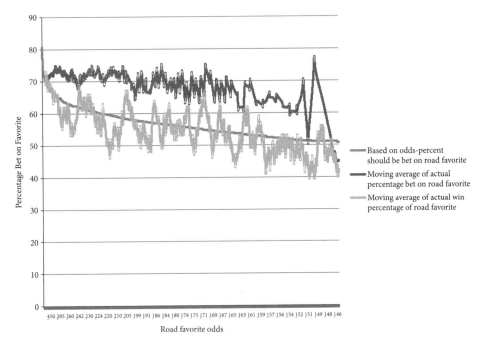

Figure 17.2 Expected Betting Percentages, Actual Betting Percentages, and Win Percentage for Road Favorites in Major League Baseball 2003–2008.

Visual evidence suggests that odds are not set by the sportsbook based on the percentage wagered by bettors, as bettors seem to overestimate the odds of road favorites winning. It appears that bettors prefer road favorites by a large margin, but this is not captured by the sportsbook odds, which, likely not coincidently, tend to map closer to actual favorite win percentages. The following sections present formal tests to explore the notion of bettor preferences, sportsbook pricing, and returns to various betting strategies.

3. Testing the Balanced Book Assumption Using Simple Regressions

The premise of the traditional models of sportsbook behavior, in terms of point spreads, was that sportsbooks were attempting to attract even betting dollars on both sides of the proposition. If achieved, this position would clear the market and would allow the sportsbook to capture its commission on losing bets without risk. Extending this idea into odds wagering, such as hockey and baseball, sportsbooks were assumed to be attracting betting dollars proportionally with respect to odds (i.e., with a midpoint in odds of –200, favorite bettors would attract two-thirds of the action; with a midpoint in odds of –300, favorite bettors would attract three-quarters of the action; etc.).[3]

If sportsbooks are not setting odds based on the betting percentages received on favorites and underdogs, they are not pricing to balance the book. If this is not true, claims of market efficiency driven by the actions of bettors in gambling markets are suspect. Bettors in the aggregate may not be revealing the "wisdom of crowds," but may actually be quite biased, while the sportsbook may be setting the price (odds) for other purposes.

To test the null hypothesis sportsbooks set odds to clear the market, we test the following simple regression model:

$$(\text{Actual \% Bet on Favorite}) = \beta_0 + \beta_1 (\text{Expected \% Bet on Favorite Based on Odds}) + \varepsilon_i.$$

The dependent variable is the actual percentage bet on the favorite by bettors from the Sports Insights data. The independent variable is the percentage that should have been bet on the favorite based on the posted sportsbook odds. If sportsbooks are setting prices to clear the market, $\beta_0 = 0$ and $\beta_1 = 1$. Therefore, a simple F-test for this null hypothesis is tested for the groups of home favorites and road favorites. Coefficients and t-statistics for the intercept and independent variable are presented along with the F-statistic for the null hypothesis of market clearing behavior by sportsbook in tables 17.1 (home favorites) and 17.2 (road favorites).

Table 17.1 Balanced Book Regression Tests: Home Favorites

Variable	Dependent Variable: Actual Percentage of Dollars Bet on the Home Favorite	Observations: 8378
	Coefficient	T-Statistic
Intercept	−8.6703	−5.1365
Percent Bet on Home Favorites Based on Market Odds	1.1447	39.8994
F-Statistic on Test of Null Hypothesis	Intercept = 0 and Slope Coeff. = 1 (Probability Value in Parentheses)	13.4421 (0.0000)

Table 17.2 Balanced Book Regression Tests: Road Favorites

Variable	Dependent Variable: Actual Percentage of Dollars Bet on the Road Favorite	Observations: 3866
	Coefficient	T-Statistic
Intercept	29.1206	10.8428
Percent Bet on Road Favorites Based on Market Odds	0.6787	14.2836
F-Statistic on Test of Null Hypothesis	Intercept = 0 and Slope Coeff. = 1 (Probability Value in Parentheses)	1264.865 (0.0000)

The null hypothesis that sportsbooks set prices to clear the market is rejected for both samples. The actual percentage of bets on the favorite is not one-to-one with the odds set by the sportsbook. Sportsbooks do not appear to set odds based solely on the actions of market participants. The alternative hypothesis here is not that sportsbooks set prices to maximize profits based on bettor mis-perceptions (as seen in Levitt, 2004), simply that prices are not being set to balance the book. How and why sportsbooks are pricing the Major League Baseball betting market requires additional tests to determine if they are exploiting known bettor biases or pricing in an alternative manner, such as pricing as a forecast.

4. RETURNS TO SIMPLE
BETTING STRATEGIES

To determine if sportsbooks are truly pricing to maximize profits, as suggested by Levitt (2004), we examine returns to simple betting strategies. Examination of returns to simple betting strategies allows us to determine if the pricing by sports-books is efficient and if the sportsbook earns higher returns by pricing through some mechanism other than clearing the market. To begin, we simply calculate returns to betting strategies based on simple rules of wagering on all favorites or all underdogs for the entire sample and at various thresholds. As in the previous section, the sample is split into home favorites and road favorites. Table 17.3 presents the results for home favorites (road underdogs) and table 17.4 presents the results for road favorites (home underdogs). In each table, the relevant odds range, number of observations in the range, expected return to betting underdogs, actual returns to betting on underdogs, and Z-statistics for the null hypothesis of a fair bet (actual earnings are equal to expected earnings) and the null hypothesis of no profitability are presented.

There is a reverse favorite-longshot bias in the Major League Baseball bet-ting market. For both samples of favorites, a strategy of wagering on underdogs loses less than a strategy of wagering on favorites. Betting on road underdogs earn negative returns overall, but in the subset of games where there are underdogs of greater than or equal to 200, positive returns were earned (statistically significant compared to a fair bet). Wagering on home underdogs earns positive returns, with statistical significance compared to a fair bet (compared to expected returns) at

Table 17.3 Home Favorites: Returns to Strategies of Betting Road Underdogs Overall and at Certain Thresholds, Assuming $1 Bet

Odds	Observations	Expected Returns to Betting Underdogs	Actual Returns to Betting Underdogs	Z-Statistic Null Hypothesis of Fair Bet	Z-Statistic Null Hypothesis of No Profits
≥300	54	−0.0157	0.3133	1.1075	1.0545
≥250	210	−0.0164	0.0890	0.8110	0.6848
≥200	888	−0.0161	0.0865	1.8754*	1.5807
≥150	3137	−0.0140	−0.0066	0.2960	−0.2616
≥140	3994	−0.0140	−0.0003	0.6332	−0.0127
≥130	5073	−0.0142	0.0137	1.4919	0.7315
≥120	6248	−0.0146	−0.0030	0.7058	−0.1826
All	8378	−0.0156	−0.0067	0.6544	−0.4920

Significance at 10% is denoted by *.

Table 17.4 Road Favorites: Returns to Strategies of Betting Home Underdogs Overall and at Certain Thresholds, Assuming $1 Bet

Odds	Observations	Expected Returns to Betting Underdogs	Actual Returns to Betting Underdogs	Z-Statistic Null Hypothesis of Fair Bet	Z-Statistic Null Hypothesis of No Profits
≥300	9	−0.0160	0.3889	0.6472	0.6216
≥250	20	−0.0153	0.0025	0.0432	0.0061
≥200	126	−0.0155	−0.0040	0.0805	−0.0285
≥150	777	−0.0137	0.0199	0.6847	0.4062
≥140	1104	−0.0139	0.0494	1.5815	1.2348
≥130	1587	−0.0143	0.0452	1.8389*	1.3972
≥120	2214	−0.0149	0.0227	1.4138	0.8542
All	3866	−0.0164	0.0160	1.7085	0.8443

Significance at 10% is denoted by *.

the 10 percent level for the subsample of all home underdogs greater or equal to 130, but the overall returns for all groupings are not great enough to earn statistically significant profits. In summary, for both the overall samples of home favorites and road favorites, statistically significant profits are not found.

What has been somewhat awkwardly termed "the reverse favorite-longshot bias" has been identified in baseball before (Woodland and Woodland, 1994; Gandar, Zuber, Johnson, and Dare, 2002), which postulates that baseball bettors prefer wagering on favorites. We do not believe that this bias is the opposite of the bias originally found in horse racing, where bettors were found to overbet longshots (Griffith, 1949; McGlothlin, 1956; Ali, 1977; Asch et al., 1986). We believe the overbetting of longshots more likely reflects the opportunity for high potential returns if the longshot horse were to win the race, as suggested by Golec and Tamarkin (1998). Longshots in baseball betting are of a magnitude more similar to favorites in horse racing; therefore we believe the source of the bias is not based upon preference for skewness of returns, but a reflection of fans' desires to bet on the best baseball teams, as suggested by Vaughan Williams and Paton (1998). This is similar to biases found in pointspread markets, where the best teams are overbet, leading to big underdogs winning more than implied by efficiency (Vergin and Scriabin, 1978; Tryfos et al., 1984; Paul et al., 2003).

Tables 17.5 and 17.6 illustrate the returns to simple betting strategies when more bets occur on favorites (or underdogs) than implied by the sportsbook odds. These situations represent cases where the public is backing one team more heavily than implied by the odds paid by favorite bettors (or odds offered to underdog bettors). Table 17.5 presents the results for home favorites and table 17.6 presents the results for road favorites. Each table is separated into two parts, the top portion being where a higher percentage of bets (compared to the odds) is on the favorite, while

Table 17.5 Home Favorite: Difference between Actual Percentage Bet on Favorite and Expected Percentage Bet Based on Odds—Strategy of Betting With or Against the Betting Public

Difference— (Actual— Expected)	Observations	Expected Returns to Betting Underdogs	Actual Returns to Betting Underdogs	Z-Statistic Null Hypothesis of Fair Bet	Z-Statistic Null Hypothesis of No Profits
≥30	303	−0.0173	0.0462	0.9017	0.6559
≥20	777	−0.0163	0.0155	0.7011	0.3421
≥10	2260	−0.0152	−0.0063	0.3336	−0.2327
≥0	4493	−0.0152	0.0016	0.8792	0.0853
≤−30	317	−0.0163	0.0656	1.0730	0.8592
≤−20	814	−0.0165	−0.0289	−0.2660	−0.6203
≤−10	1949	−0.0164	−0.0096	0.2314	−0.3254
≤0	3889	−0.0161	−0.0143	0.0831	−0.6930

the bottom portion presents cases where a higher percentage of bets (compared to the odds) is on the underdog.

From Table 17.5, when more of the bets are on the home favorite than the odds imply, betting the road underdog wins often enough to earn positive returns per dollar bet. Results, however, are not statistically significant. When a greater percentage of the bets are on the road underdog than implied by the odds, negative returns are generated for betting strategies of wagering on underdogs (and favorites). For the sample of home favorites, there does not appear to be much shading of the odds toward the favorite, even though bettors clearly prefer to wager on favorites compared to underdogs (from Figures 17.1 and 17.2 above). Although some slight shading of the odds may exist toward the favorite, bettors who bet the contrarian strategy of wagering on the underdog (and the sportsbook itself which has an active position in this wager) are not earning statistically significant profits.

In the sample of road favorites (Table 17.6), a simple of strategy of betting the home underdog when a greater percentage of bets are on the road favorite earns positive returns overall. Although positive, these returns are not great enough to reject the null hypotheses of a fair bet or no profitability. When more money is on the home underdog, betting the underdog in samples where the percentage is 10 percent or greater and 20 percent or greater is found to generate positive returns. For the sample of games where the percentage bet is 10 percent greater on the underdog, the null hypothesis of a fair bet can be rejected, but the null of no profitability cannot. In the other cases, the null hypotheses cannot be rejected.

Table 17.6 Road Favorite: Difference between Actual Percentage Bet on Favorite and Expected Percentage Bet Based on Odds—Strategy of Betting With or Against the Betting Public

Difference— (Actual— Expected)	Observations	Expected Returns to Betting Underdogs	Actual Returns to Betting Underdogs	Z-Statistic Null Hypothesis of Fair Bet	Z-Statistic Null Hypothesis of No Profits
≥30	267	−0.0175	−0.0271	−0.1358	−0.3819
≥20	984	−0.0165	0.0081	0.6596	0.2182
≥10	2213	−0.0162	0.0198	1.4239	0.7826
≥0	3062	−0.0163	0.0128	1.3410	0.5897
≤−30	49	−0.0175	−0.2602	−1.4143	−1.5165
≤−20	112	−0.0173	0.0236	0.3446	0.1988
≤−10	299	−0.0170	0.1228	1.9112*	1.6787
≤0	720	−0.0170	−0.0008	0.3475	−0.0180

Overall, the key conclusion drawn from the results in this section is that there are no statistically significant returns to betting against the public. For example, although the betting public clearly has a strong preference for road favorites, this bias is not fully priced into the odds. If the odds did reflect this preference of bettors, we would expect that home underdogs would win more than implied by efficiency. Although strategies of wagering on home underdogs generate positive returns, these returns are not statistically significant compared to expected losses (a fair bet), let alone profitable (compared to the null of no profitability). Some slight shading of the odds appears to be occurring toward the road favorite, but sportsbooks (and contrarian bettors) are not earning significant profits by setting prices (odds) to exploit these easily identifiable biases. Instead, odds appear to reflect more of a forecast of game outcomes, rather than the biased preferences of the betting public.

5. CONCLUSIONS AND DISCUSSION OF SPORTSBOOK BEHAVIOR

The availability of actual betting percentages from online sportsbooks allows for a more detailed study of the betting market for Major League Baseball. The traditional sportsbook models were based on the assumption of a balanced book, where equal amounts of money were attracted on each side of the proposition. This allowed for the testing of the efficient markets hypothesis, where the point spread was tested as an optimal and unbiased predictor of the outcome of the game. Findings in support of the efficient markets hypothesis were deemed a result of market participants and contributed to the notion that bettors on the whole displayed the "wisdom of crowds" as point spreads and totals generally appeared to represent reasonable, if not perfect, forecasts of outcomes of games.

Levitt (2004) challenged the view that sportsbooks set prices to balance the book (based on the actions of market participants) and showed, using a betting tournament, that sportsbooks will exploit clear bettor biases to maximize profits. The betting tournament data, however, did not perfectly mimic a true sportsbook, as it was a relatively small sample of bettors and did not include the marginal costs and benefits normally seen in these markets.

The availability of actual betting data from real sportsbooks, through www.sportsinsights.com, allows for a deeper understanding of sportsbook behavior and actions of participants within this market. In the odds-based market for Major League Baseball, a few results are immediately observable. First, sportsbooks do not set prices to balance the book. There are significant systematic imbalances of actual bets compared to expected bets proportional to the odds set by the sportsbook. This was seen through a simple plotting of the data for home and road favorites and also through F-tests based on simple regression results. Bettors definitely prefer road favorites, as percentages bet on these teams generally exceed the percentage of bets that would be expected based on the odds set by the sportsbook.

When sportsbooks do not price to balance the book, they do not necessarily price to exploit known biases to maximize profits. In some cases, odds (prices) are set slightly too high and the sportsbook earns greater profits given more of the betting dollars are on the losing side of the proposition. In most cases, however, it appears that sportsbooks price as a forecast of the actual game outcome. This results in win frequencies for favorites and underdogs that are in line with the posted odds on the game. Therefore, in the long run, simple wagering strategies do not win enough to earn statistically significant profits, despite the presence of bettor biases.

This long-run strategy of setting the odds as a forecast of actual game outcomes may occur for a variety of reasons, which could lead to greater profits for the sportsbook over time. One reason for this strategy by the sportsbook is that betting is not generally a one-shot game, but a repeated game over a season or many seasons for the majority of bettors. When sportsbooks price as a forecast, and favorites and underdogs have win percentages in line with posted odds, bettors are expected to lose the sportsbook commission (on losing bets) over time. If sportsbooks did price in line with bettor preferences (higher odds [prices] for road favorites, for instance), bettors may lose a greater sum more quickly, but may not continue their activity of betting over time. Therefore, a long-run strategy of pricing as a forecast may earn greater profits over time for the sportsbook, rather than pricing to exploit well-known biases for each game.

Another potential reason that sportsbooks may price as a forecast is to discourage entry into this market by informed bettors. If sportsbooks were to "shade" the odds toward road favorites (for example), informed bettors may enter the market and capture some of the potential profits of the sportsbook for themselves. Pricing as an optimal and unbiased forecast discourages entry, as informed bettors are expected to lose the sportsbook commission on losing bets, and may allow the sportsbook to keep more of the profits for themselves, rather than simply transferring money from the uninformed public to informed bettors.

A third reason that sportsbooks may price as a forecast, as opposed to attempting to exploit known bettor biases, is that the active management of the sportsbook in setting biased odds may be quite costly. The transactions costs involved in attempting to limit or deny the betting actions of informed traders (to prevent them from exploiting the biased odds) may be more costly than the long-run profits that could be earned by setting biased odds. It may simply not be worth it for the sportsbook to try to actively exploit bettor biases to earn higher profits.[4] Given that baseball gamblers may also wager on other sports or place bets in online casinos (or play slots or table games in actual casinos, which also offer sports wagering in Nevada), pricing to exploit the biases of these bettors may lead to these recreational gamblers to lose enough money in a short period of time to quit gambling altogether or drive them to bet at competing sportsbooks that tend to offer more attractive odds on favorites. This may ultimately lead to fewer long-run profits for sportsbooks and the gambling business in general, if they chose to actively pursue this pricing strategy.

The findings that sportsbooks do not set prices to balance the book calls into question the source of some of the earlier findings of market efficiency in sports wagering markets and its underlying support for the forecasting power of prediction markets. Under the balanced book assumption, findings of market efficiency were deemed a result of the actions of bettors. When sportsbooks do not desire a balanced book, due to pricing as a forecast of game outcomes, findings where the null hypothesis of efficient markets could not be rejected may be the result of excellent forecasting on the part of the sportsbook, rather than the collective actions of biased bettors.

NOTES

1 Some betting outlets use fractional odds for baseball. Many of these books (often illegal bookies) will quote game odds as a team is 6/5 favorites. These odds imply a 20-cent vigorish compared to the normal 10-cent vigorish in Las Vegas. 6/5 favorite implies that favorite bettors would lay $1.20 to win $1 (on winning bets) and underdog bettors would be receiving even money odds—lay $1 to win $1. Other fractions follow similar logic.

2 This example is an approximation used for ease of illustration. As Gandar et al. (2002) demonstrate mathematically, and in great detail, if a book were truly setting prices to become indifferent between a win by the favorite and a win by the underdog, a posted odds of −210, +190 would reflect a game where the probability of an underdog win was 0.3373

3 Again, this is a close approximation used for ease of illustration. See Gandar et al. (2002) for a detailed explanation.

4 For sports with extremely large betting volume, such as the NFL, it may become worth the transactions costs to actively price to exploit known bettor biases, which could be why betting on home underdogs (against road favorites) were found to earn profits in the professional football betting market (Levitt, 2004).

REFERENCES

Ali, Mukhtar M. (1977). Probability and utility estimates for racetrack bettors. *Journal of Political Economy*, 85(4): 803–815. Reprinted in Hausch, Donald, Lo, Victor, S. Y., and Ziemba, William, T. (eds.), *Efficiency of racetrack betting markets.* San Diego CA: Academic Press, 1994.

Asch, Peter, Malkiel, Burton G., and Quandt, Richard E. (1986). Market efficiency in racetrack betting. *Journal of Business*, 59(1): 157–160.

Gandar, J. M., Zuber, Richard, Johnson, R. S., and Dare, W. (2002). Re-examining the betting market on Major League Baseball Games: Is there a reverse favorite-longshot bias? *Applied Economics*, 34: 1309–1317.

Gandar, John M., Zuber, Richard A., and Johnson, R.Stafford (2004). A reexamination of the efficiency of the betting market on National Hockey League games. *Journal of Sports Economics*, 5(2): 152–168.

Golec, Joseph, and Tamarkin, Maury. (1998). Bettors love skewness, not risk, at the horse track. *Journal of Political Economy*, 106(1): 202–225.

Griffith, R. M. (1949). Odds adjustments by American horse race bettors. *American Journal of Psychology*, 62: 290–294. Reprinted in Hausch, D., Lo, V., and Ziemba, W. (eds), *Efficiency of racetrack betting markets.* San Diego CA: Academic Press, 1994.

Levitt, Steven D. (2004). Why are gambling markets organized so differently from financial markets? *The Economic Journal*, 114: 223–246.

McGlothlin, William H. (1956). Stability of choices among uncertain alternatives. *American Journal of Psychology*, 69: 604–615. Reprinted in Hausch, D., Lo, V., and Ziemba, W. (eds), *Efficiency of racetrack betting markets.* San Diego CA: Academic Press, 1994.

Pankoff, Lyn D. (1968). Market efficiency and football betting. *Journal of Business*, 41: 203–214.

Paul, Rodney J., Weinbach, Andrew P., and Weinbach, Chris J. (2003). Fair bets and profitability in college football gambling. *Journal of Economics and Finance*, 27(2): 236–242.

Paul, Rodney J. and Weinbach, Andrew P. (2008). Price setting in the NBA gambling market: Tests of the Levitt model of sportsbook behavior. *International Journal of Sports Finance*, 3(3): 2–18.

Paul, Rodney J., and Weinbach, Andrew P. (2007). Does Sportsbook.com Set pointspreads to maximize profits? Tests of the Levitt model of sportsbook behavior. *Journal of Prediction Markets*, 1(3): 209–218.

Sauer, Raymond D., Brajer, Vic, Ferris, Stephen P. and Marr, M. Wayne (1988). Hold your bets: Another look at the efficiency of the gambling market for National Football League games. *Journal of Political Economy*, 96: 206–213.

Tryfos, P., Casey, S., Cook, S., Leger, G., and Pylypiak, B. (1984). The profitability of wagering on NFL games. *Management Science*, 30: 123–132.

Vaughn Williams, Leighton, and Paton, David (1998). Why are some favourite-longshot biases positive and others negative? *Applied Economics*, 30: 1505–1510.

Vergin, Roger C., and Scriabin, Michael (1978). Winning strategies for wagering on National Football League games. *Management Science*, 24, 809–818.

Woodland, Linda M., and Woodland, Bill M. (1994). Market efficiency and the favorite-longshot bias: The baseball betting market. *Journal of Finance* 49(1): 269–280.

Woodland, Linda M., and Woodland, Bill M. (2001). Market efficiency and profitable wagering in the National Hockey League: Can bettors score on longshots? *Southern Economic Journal*, 67(4): 983–995.

Zuber, Richard A., Gandar, John M., and Bowers, Benny D. (1985). Beating the spread: Testing the efficiency of the gambling market for National Football League games. *Journal of Political Economy*, 93: 800–806.

PART VI

ILLUSTRATIONS OF PUBLIC FINANCE

CHAPTER 18

....

MULTIPLIER
EFFECTS AND LOCAL
ECONOMIC IMPACT

....

PETER VON ALLMEN

FUNDAMENTAL to the prosperity of local economies is the presence of sufficient employment opportunities to provide consumption dollars in the form of wages earned. Income earned and re-spent in the local economy generates economic growth. Thus, when it comes to economic development, projects that promise to generate substantial increases in income and employment effects are likely to garner widespread public support.

The economic impact of hosting a professional sports team (and constructing the stadium that serves as the venue for play) represents one of the most persistent chasms between the findings of economic research and policy decisions of local politicians. As Siegfried and Zimbalist (2000), Coates and Humphries (2008), and others have noted, in study after study economists have found that the economic development benefits of professional sports are either zero or so modest that they should be considered negligible.[1] Yet, teams, public officials, and even local development authorities continue to espouse their value in this regard. To bolster their arguments, these latter groups often rely on economic impact studies funded by interested parties (pro-subsidy groups) that (mis)use economic tools and terminology—most notably the multiplier effect,—to explain why investment in facilities to obtain and maintain a local franchise is a good idea.

In keeping with the theme of this volume, the purpose of this chapter is to describe how the sports industry might serve as a model for the evaluation of local economic impact study and multiplier effects. As the title of this chapter indicates, the focus here is on multiplier effects and local economic development. There are, of course, consumption benefits as well. Teams may generate large positive externalities, and consumers may derive substantial consumer surplus from the existence of teams in their local areas. In chapter 19 of this volume, Bruce Johnson and John Whitehead discuss contingent valuation methods by which one might determine if the consumption benefits merit public funding and so they are not reviewed here. Nor is the purpose here to provide a comprehensive review of the existing literature or to advocate or criticize a specific political decision. Instead, the goal is to show how, given an initial expenditure, local multipliers might contribute to economic growth, and the reasons that sports venues tend to serve as counterexamples of this phenomenon. Given the recession of 2008–2009, specific attention is paid to the impact of the economic downturn on stadium construction and hosting teams as an economic development strategy.

Overview

Multiplier effects are the increased economic impact following an initial net new expenditure in an economy. The initial spending could be the income generated from the presence of a new employer, school, or as discussed here, a new sports stadium. When a local government pays for the construction of a new stadium, as in the case of the new baseball stadium built in Washington, DC for the Nationals, there are two sets of expenditures to consider: the impact on incomes from the initial construction spending, and the annual increase in local income from the ongoing operations of the team playing in the stadium. Beyond the direct expenditure, an added benefit to the economy is that there are, at least theoretically, multiplier effects associated with each. Offsetting these benefits are the costs. Costs include the initial expenditure, ongoing maintenance and operating costs (and implicitly the opportunity costs of allocating funds to the project), and externalities.

Crompton (1995) and Hudson (2001) and others note that the actual stadium construction of the venue is likely to generate little or no economic net benefit, as the funds raised from the local economy are actually taken from local residents in the form of taxes to fund bond payments and so actually represent reductions in other spendable income.[2] Even if the local government still collected the taxes to fund the construction, it could have spent those funds on any number of projects. As such, the focus here is on the ongoing net benefits (economic impact) of hosting a team, rather than the initial construction of a stadium. An accurate accounting of the benefits requires that the correct local multiplier be applied to the appropriate base (initial direct expenditure).

As Coates (2007) notes, studies of economic impact can be divided into two categories: *ex ante* economic impact studies and *ex post* econometric analysis. It is common to see *ex ante* economic impact studies that offer impressive claims of impact in the hundreds of millions of dollars and employment generation that claims new jobs numbering in the thousands. A recent paper by Baade, Baumann, and Matheson (2008) lists five *ex ante* studies (3 MLB, 1 NFL, 1 NBA) that claim an average benefit of over $290 million from hosting a team (regular season only). Equally, perhaps even more impressive, are claims of benefits from mega-events such as the Super Bowl, the World Cup, and the Olympics. Such work tends to be done through consulting arrangements and used as evidence on behalf of stadium proponents. However, most economists, using *ex post* econometric based research, believe that the impact is much less (see, for example, Baade and Matheson, 2004). As noted above, the large majority of empirical studies offer evidence that hosting a professional sports team generates little or no positive economic impact on a local economy. Arguments for meaningful positive economic impacts are the exception rather than the rule.

There are two fundamental reasons for the lack of empirical evidence of large multiplier effects: inflated estimates of the direct effects, or the "base" increase in spending; and leakage from the local economy that diminishes the multiplier. First, consider the determination of the correct base amount.

THE INITIAL EXPENDITURE

To get an accurate estimate of the total effects, it is important to incorporate the correct base increase (direct effect) in spending to which subsequent multiplier effects apply. One possibility is to simply use team revenues plus all increases in revenues of ancillary businesses, such as hotels, restaurants, and souvenir shops, generated by visitors from outside the economy. There are several problems with such an approach. First, as Crompton (1995) points out, the goal of economic development policy is to increase income, not sales. To use revenues to measure economic impact assumes that all revenues are spent in the local economy such that they end up as income for employees of the team, the stadium authority, or other local businesses. While no data on profits are available for individual teams, it is widely assumed that most teams in most leagues earn profits (as do the ancillary businesses). To the extent that profits are retained or exported from the local economy, the base is reduced. Further, it is only reasonable to assume that all firms, including the teams, make significant expenditures outside the local economy for items such as travel and transportation, hotel and meals, scouting, and materials (bats, uniforms, etc.). Finally, to include revenue increases of ancillary firms implicitly assumes that such increases are driven by consumers from outside the region (discussed in more detail below). As Baade and Dye (1990) point out, "[T]he new restaurant across from the stadium may be offset by putting an old restaurant

out of business in another neighborhood" (p. 6). Thus, to use revenues significantly overstates the base. The portion of team revenues that might enter the local
economy as income is thus made up primarily of salaries paid to workers, taxes
paid within the local economy, plus purchases from local vendors (Crompton,
1995). Although elements of the base expenditure increase are certainly made up of
consumption expenditures by fans, by no means should the entirety of fan expenditures be loaded into the base increase in spending. Further, as discussed below,
there are several double counting issues to be addressed.

From the consumer spending perspective, there are three types of spending
increases that impact the base: increases in consumption spending, changes in
imports, and changes in exports. Thus, there are three important questions to ask
regarding consumer expenditures at the stadium: To what extent do team revenues
represent a true increase in spending rather than a substitution of one form of
spending for another? To what extent does spending that creates team revenue represent an increase in exports? And, does the presence of a team create a meaningful
decrease in imports?

Substitution Spending

When presented with a new entertainment option for spending in a local economy,
consumers will, to the extent of demand at given prices, generate revenue for the
team in the form of attendance and related expenditures. To determine total economic impact (i.e., including multiplier effects) it is only appropriate to include
new spending in the initial round of expenditures. This value should include only
expenses that would not have occurred had the team not been present.

Consider the actions of a local resident of Washington, D.C., who spends $80
to attend a Wizards game. To include this $80 in the base expenditure carries the
implicit assumption in the economic impact calculation that if the individual were
not to attend the game, he would leave that money tucked under his mattress. Yet,
if the Wizards were not located in Washington, and that individual had instead
spent $50 going to see a college game, only $30 of the spending on the Wizards
game represents net new spending. Thus, when local residents patronize professional sporting teams, the magnitude of the initial round of spending is limited by
the extent to which they increase their entertainment spending from savings plus
entertainment spending that was previously allocated outside the local economy
that is moved inside as a result of the presence of the team.[3] The former represents
an increase in the average propensity to consume; the latter represents a decrease in
imports as fewer citizens purchase their entertainment from elsewhere (discussed
below). Substitution spending, spending on professional sports by local residents
that replaces other forms of local spending, merely moves the effects around in the
local economy—akin to taking money out of one pocket and putting it in the other.
Baade and Dye (1990) note that such calculations are very difficult to make and so

are typically assumed (set exogenously) as all new spending in economic impact studies. As they point out, the results of the model are then driven by assumptions that have little behind them in the way of facts.

Decreases in Imports

Consider the NFL Houston Oilers' move to Nashville, where they were renamed the Tennessee Titans. If, prior to the arrival of the Titans in 1999, Nashville football fans traveled outside the Nashville area to watch professional football, the arrival of the Titans caused a decrease in imports. Given that the nearest existing team is in St. Louis, Missouri, approximately 300 miles away, this seems unlikely. However, prior to the Nationals' arrival in Washington, D.C., residents of that city could have made a relatively short drive to see the Baltimore Orioles play, as their stadium is just 37 miles from downtown Washington. As these examples show, changes in import spending are likely to be highly idiosyncratic and dependent on the availability of substitutes. Yet even under the best of circumstances, as in the case of Baltimore and Washington, Siegfried and Zimbalist (2002) report a study by the Virginia Baseball Stadium Authority that found that only 13 percent of fans at Camden Yards (the Orioles' home venue in Baltimore) were from the Washington area.[4] More comprehensive, league-wide empirical estimates of these changes in imports would be difficult to quantify for at least two reasons. First, the combined number of expansion teams and teams that move to new locations across the four major sports leagues is small, providing few chances to measure discrete changes in the form of a natural experiment. Second, it would be difficult to objectively measure the spending patterns of fans who leave markets that might be large enough to support a major league team to see games in another (i.e., *before* a team comes to town, what is the leakage from a local economy that represents spending on sports elsewhere?) One potential topic of interest in this area is whether families may substitute local spending on sports events for out-of-town non-sports related leisure spending, such as vacations, over the course of the business cycle. To the extent that this occurs during recessionary periods such as 2008–2009, having local entertainment options could be stabilizing.

Increases in Exports

Spending may also increase in the local economy by non-residents as a result of hosting a team. The extent to which attendance and related expenditures that become team revenue are generated by visitors, such activity counts as an export. This could be a powerful source of increased income, as it is by definition new spending injected into the economy. That said, it may not contribute to growth in the larger (regional, national) sense in that it may merely redistribute spending from one local economy to another.

Continuing with our example of the Washington Wizards, if the visitor traveled to Washington for the primary purpose of seeing a game, and would not otherwise have made the trip, then this spending does count as all net new. As an added benefit, the expenditures of out-of-town attendees may be higher if they utilize other city services, such as hotels, restaurants, and rental vehicles. It is these types of expenditures that local travel and tourism officials often tout when lobbying for subsidies to professional teams. However, as many scholars who have studied local economic impacts have pointed out (Crompton, 1995; Hudson, 2001; Noll and Zimbalist, 1997; and others) such spending is easy to over-count. If visitors to a city for some other primary purpose attend a game as a secondary activity (and would have visited the city anyway), the money spent on a game would likely have been spent on some other activity (a play, a tour, shopping) if no game were available. Siegfried and Zimbalist (2002) report that the portion of fans who attend sports events who do not live in the local economy is less than 20 percent. Given that at least some portion of these fans are visitors for some other primary purpose and would have spent their discretionary income on some other activity, the percentage of total expenditures on any given team that is actually attributable to net new export spending is surely quite small.

In summary, the appropriate base expenditure (the direct effect) of hosting a team in a city is the net new spending on local incomes and businesses plus local taxes paid. This total should not include: receipts of the team and other local businesses that are not re-spent in the local economy (such as profits and imports), and substitution spending by locals. Any net exports included in direct expenditures as new must be adjusted for exports that would have occurred anyway.

THE MULTIPLIER EFFECT IN
A LOCAL ECONOMY

While economic development can mean naturally occurring increases in economic activity that generate increased income through private markets, economic development in this chapter refers to active policy making with the intent of increasing economic activity within a certain area,—i.e government intervention into professional sports markets through the subsidization of team expenses. Local development policy can take many specific forms, including direct expenditure (e.g., the new Washington Nationals ballpark was 100 percent financed through a public bond issue), tax advantages (such as the tax-exempt bonds used by the Yankees and Mets to fund their new venues), and land grants (such as Dodger Stadium in Los

Angeles). Whether the government makes a direct investment of expenditures, or induces increased expenditure through financing subsidies, or an overall reduction in the firms' cost of capital through land grants, the result is an increase in spending in the local economy. Increased spending (i.e., sales), however, does not necessarily mean increases in income. Crompton (1995) argues that the confusion between sales and income increases is a critical source of error in economic impact studies that claim extraordinary benefits from hosting a franchise. Economic development increases incomes. While spending occurs as part of the process, it is not the end in and of itself.

Multiplier effects are localized versions of the familiar macroeconomic multiplier, in which the final size of the stimulus to the economy is some multiple (presumably greater than 1) of the original expenditure. The multiplier effect results from re-spending of the original stimulus dollars by the first recipients.

Equation (1) shows the basic expenditure multiplier. The multiplier, m, is determined by the marginal propensity to consume, MPC, and the tax rate t. Equation (2) shows the total impact on the local economy (ΔI) from the initial increase in spending (S).

$$m = \frac{1}{(1 - MPC[1-t])} \tag{1}$$

$$\Delta I = m(\Delta S) \tag{2}$$

For example, the median NBA team generated revenues of $117.5 million in 2008.[5] If none of the revenues are retained as profits (i.e., saved) or spent outside the local economy, the entire revenue stream is re-spent in the form of wages and other operating costs (with local firms) and would be subject to the multiplier. In the absence of other forces, the total impact is unreasonably large. For example, a MPC of 0.9 with a tax rate of .2 generates a multiplier of 3.57, implying that the median NBA team contributes over $419 million of net new activity into the local economy each year that would otherwise be $0.

As numerous authors have pointed out (see Siegfried and Zimbalist, 2002; Noll and Zimbalist, 1997; and Crompton, 1995, for example), the basic multiplier shown in Equation 1 must be adjusted to account for spending leakages in the first round of spending. These are expenditures made by the team for which the payments leave the local economy, and other reductions in local spending, such as increased savings rates of those who receive wages.

At the local economy level, payments made outside the local economy are likely to be very substantial, given that the source may be as close as another nearby local economy.[6] For example, when the Wizards purchase their uniforms, supplies, and equipment, some of these dollars flow outside the DC area. Thus, the payment made to that supplier leaks out of the local economy. The same is true for payments to labor. Although it may be reasonable to assume that most of the wages of stadium workers remain in the local economy, this is not the case for most

NBA players. For example, according to the NBA's official web site, Wizards for-ward Antawn Jamison divides his time between Washington, D.C., and Charlotte, North Carolina.[7] Thus, assuming that he divides his expenditures as well, when the Wizards paid Jamison his salary of $9.9 million for 2008–2009, only about half of this salary could be subject to local multiplier effects. The example of Jamison is not merely an anecdote. Siegfried and Zimbalist (2002) found that for the 1999–2000 season, only 29 percent of NBA players lived in the cities in which they played, compared to 93 percent for other workers. Thus, given that the vast majority of salaries paid by all professional teams are paid to players (which represent a little over half of team revenue), and that those players are likely to live only part-time in the city for which they play, a large fraction of the wages paid by the team represent imports and are not subject to multiplier effects.

Taxes, the Marginal Propensity to Consume, and the Multiplier

The multiplier is further reduced when the marginal propensity to consume of wage earners falls, or marginal tax rates rise. Such a reduction in the *MPC* would be particularly severe if the *MPC* of the initial recipient of the wages is smaller than in the overall economy. There are two reasons that we would expect professional athletes to have higher savings rates: their level of income, and the relatively short expected career length. As incomes rise, for example, we expect that expenditures on daily living expenses will fall as a proportion of total income, and the mar-ginal utility of additional consumption spending will fall as consumption rises, leading to higher savings rates. Second, if athletes expect to earn an extraordinary income for only a few years, they would have an incentive to save more for future consumption.

It is worth noting that while such reasoning appears sound, there is ample anecdotal evidence that many players do in fact spend all of their incomes (and more). Pablo Torre (2009) reported that a significant majority of former NFL and NBA players are bankrupt or under financial stress within just a few years of retire-ment.[8] Thus, we have theoretical predictions about savings rates that predict one outcome and at least some evidence to the contrary. In the absence of a complete data set on savings rates, we can only leave this issue as an open question for future research and say that if most players do spend all of their incomes, and those expen-ditures are in the local economy, multiplier effects will increase. If instead most income is saved or spent outside the local economy, multiplier effects are reduced.

The effect of tax rates on the multiplier is less ambiguous. Much of what play-ers earn is taxed at the highest marginal rate of 35 percent. For example, based on

2009 federal tax rates, ignoring deductions for a moment, an individual earning $75,000 would be taxed at an average rate of 18.42 percent. A professional athlete earning $10 million, however, would be taxed at an average rate of 34.75 percent (not including local taxes). Even if the professional athlete is more able to reduce his or her taxable income through investment and tax planning strategies, a marked difference in average tax rates will persist.

Using equation (1) we can see what the impact of part-time residence and higher taxes mean for the local multiplier. First, if we assume a *MPC* of 0.9, all of the income stays in the local economy and the average tax rate is 20 percent, the impact of the $10 million paid to the player is $10(3.57) = $37.5 million. If the *MPC* stays the same and the tax rate rises to 0.35, the multiplier is reduced to 2.41. If, in fact players do save more of their income and savings rates are higher, the multiplier is further reduced. For example, if players save 25 percent of their income and the marginal tax rate remains at .35, the multiplier falls to 1.95. If we apply this multiplier to the player's share of income likely to be spent locally (given the leakages discussed above), we get an approximation of the impact of this distribution of team revenues into the local economy. If the player spends 50 percent of his income, or $5 million in the local economy, the economic impact of that $10 million salary is just $9.75 million, which, of course, is *less* than the player's salary rather than some multiple greater than one. Using similar logic, Noll and Zimbalist (1997) estimate the sports multiplier to be 1.2. In the above example, if savings rates of players are no better than the broader population and the appropriate multiplier is 2.41 on a base of $5 million, the total impact on the economy is $12.05 million, which also implies a multiplier of 1.2. Thus, it seems highly unlikely that the actual multiplier that should be applied to player salaries is much above 1.0, if at all.

Job Creation: Non-athlete Jobs and Salaries

To the extent that non-athlete employment increases in the local economy when teams locate in a given city, the argument for increased economic impact is strengthened. If, for example, moving the Montreal Expos to Washington, D.C., or moving the Houston Oilers to Tennessee (to become the Titans) created a large number of full-time positions at the stadium and in the team offices that are hired from the local labor force, these new positions and the salaries that come with them stimulate the economy. Moreover, a greater portion of the expenditures by these workers are more likely to remain in the local economy than athletes who are free to take up part-time residence elsewhere in the off-season.

Unfortunately, the record of job creation is not good. Most of the employment generated by locating a stadium in a given local economy is part-time by nature—vendors and other game-day stadium employees. Given that teams in the NFL, NHL, NBA, and MLB play a maximum of 81 home games, and as few as eight (plus pre-season), game-day employment is decidedly part-time. In the minor leagues, the same is true. For example, Johnson (1995) reports city officials claim that bringing minor league AA baseball to Harrisburg, Pennsylvania, resulted in approximately eight full-time positions and 70 part-time jobs. At the major league level, Siegfried and Zimbalist (2000) state that sports teams employ between 70 and 120 people in their front offices, and that beyond the front office staff and the athletes, teams hire roughly 1,000 to 1,500 part-time workers. Clearly, the full-time employment benefits are small, as the ratio of part-time to full-time employment is roughly ten to one. The imbalance of employment between high paying full-time jobs and low paying part-time jobs is such that Baade and Dye (1990) suggest that stadium-based development actually hinders economic development rather than promoting it.

Government, Growth, and Recession

The role of government in stimulating economic growth has always been the subject of debate in macroeconomics. At the federal level, the wisdom of short-term fiscal and monetary policy ebbs and flows with the emergence of events that cannot be explained with existing models and political fortunes. In the arena of short-run stabilization, Republicans have typically favored a smaller role for government and a more *laissez faire* policy perspective, while Democrats tend toward an active role for government in stabilization. As for growth, while long-run increases in economic activity are certainly linked to increases in productive capacity, political differences also exist regarding the role of government in fostering or even partnering with private industry. Ironically, as the Bush presidency drew to a close and the economy sagged badly in 2008, with high unemployment and negative growth, it was a Republican president who signed a major stimulus package designed to stabilize the economy in October 2008. With no end of the recession in sight and continued crises in the financial and housing sector, President Obama signed an additional $787 billion stimulus package in February 2009. The passage of this bill was highly contentious, with extensive debate over the balance between tax cuts and spending increases. Economists and politicians alike also disagreed fervently not only on whether the stimulus package was a good idea, but also which subgroups within the population would be net "winners."

Such spending clearly rests on the long debated Keynesian notion that governments should pursue active fiscal policy. Some of the criticism of these recent stimulus packages is aimed directly at the claim of large multiplier effects. Barro (2009), for example, argues that even the use of a multiplier of one presumes that the goods and services generated are essentially free to society, and requires the assumption that the government is better able to employ resources than private markets. In his view, it is best to presume a multiplier of zero for peacetime government purchases.

When it comes to local economic development, issues such as stadium construction projects are often just as contentious for similar reasons. Will public spending lead to (local) economic development? And, is funding stadium construction the best use of limited funding capacity of local governments? As noted in this chapter, the vast majority of the economics literature indicates that it is not. Yet, if local officials believe that stadium construction for the purpose of hosting a professional franchise is such a good idea from a development standpoint (or is politically expedient given the pressure to create local jobs), stadium funding may increase rather than decrease in times of recession. An interesting example is the Marlins' new stadium in Miami, Florida. After several years of delays, the Miami-Dade commissioners agreed to a $409 million bond package that will fund much of the construction, in part based on the Marlins President David Sampson's claim that it would lead to increased employment. In an interesting attempt to localize the benefits, the agreement includes a stipulation that 50 percent of the workers who build the facility must be from Miami-Dade County and 20 percent must be from the city of Miami.[9] Interestingly, the availability of credit could hinder efforts in other cities even if they have the will to proceed. The Marlins stadium deal was only finalized after the team agreed to cover a $6.2 million shortfall in revenue from bond sales.[10]

While the Marlins moved ahead, in Minnesota, Vikings officials' suggestion that a new stadium would create an economic stimulus was met with skepticism from local officials. The Vikings have long sought public funding to build a new facility, and principal owner Zygi Wilf suggested that it would be an economic boost to the area. If so, the project would almost certainly be welcomed, as the state faces a $4.6 billion budget deficit. Yet, top state officials, including Speaker of the House Margaret Kelliher and Senate Majority Leader Larry Pogemiller, spoke out against the idea.[11]

In the case of Tampa Bay, Florida, and their baseball team, the Rays, it appears that a combination of lack of voter will and the recession have derailed efforts to complete a new stadium deal, despite urgings from MLB commissioner Bud Selig. The Rays would like to build a retractable roof stadium but withdrew a public funding proposal in 2008. Public support has not materialized for the project, as revealed by a news poll that indicated 68 percent of voters were opposed to the new stadium.[12] Interestingly, in acknowledging that garnering approval for stadium projects is difficult in the current economic climate, he focused on the Rays' need for additional revenue to compete in the American League East rather than economic development.[13]

As local officials and (perhaps more importantly) voters become more aware of the consistent conclusions of academic economists regarding the lack of development effects, the importance of consumption benefits is likely to increase over time. If so, research on consumer surplus generated by the presence of local teams becomes all the more important.

Conclusion

Local economic impact studies, often funded by stadium proponents, argue that stadium projects and playing host to a professional sports team are legitimate engines of economic growth. In contrast, public finding of professional stadium projects has been called into question by the majority of academic research in the field. At issue are the value of the initial base expenditure injected into the economy by the team and leakages from the multiplier. There now exists a wide-ranging set of empirical research on teams and cities of all sorts that reach essentially the same conclusion. That is, hosting a major league professional team does not dramatically increase local income or employment. Effective local economic development is best served by projects that: (1) generate a large number of full-time jobs using labor drawn from full time residents of the local market; and (2) generate significant exports by drawing expenditures from outside the region. Yet, most spending on professional sports is merely a substitution for other forms of entertainment spending by existing residents; increases in exports are relatively small; most jobs that are created are part-time; and leakages from the multiplier process (which would be high in any case when considered at the local level) are extraordinary in the case of sports. In times of recession, while teams and leagues may argue more strenuously for projects to move forward on the grounds that they will boost recovery, garnering financing will be more difficult if voters and financial markets become increasingly wary.

Notes

1 For two excellent examples of discussion and critique of the existing literature, interested readers should see *Sports, Jobs and Taxes*, edited by Noll and Zimbalist (1997), and Coates and Humphries (2008), which provides a well-organized survey of the literature.
2 Barro (2009) notes that the same problem occurs with attempts to stimulate the economy at the national level, a point I return to later in the chapter.
3 It has been argued by many authors that consumer entertainment expenditures are income inelastic. That is, they tend to have a specific entertainment budget, which may

be spent on tickets to a game, but could also be spent on movie tickets, museums, etc. (see Coates and Humphries, 2008 for example and discussion).

4 Siegfried and Zimbalist (2002).

5 "NBA Team Valuations," *Forbes.com*. The Washington Wizards had revenues of $118 million and the Sacramento Kings had revenues of $117 million.

6 As Crompton (1995) and Hudson (2001) explain, the choice of what counts as "in" and what counts as "out" of a local economy drive results in two important ways. First, the smaller the geographic boundary set as the local economy, the greater the portion of spending that will count as exports. On the other hand, the larger the boundary, the greater will be the multiplier, as less economic activity will leak out in each round if the area under consideration includes other counties and towns.

7 Antawn Jamison. At http://www.nba.com/playerfile/antawn_jamison/bio.html.

8 Torre, *Sports Illustrated* (2009).

9 Haggman and Palgliery, *Miami Herald online,* July 9, 2009.

10 Firas, *PalmBeachPost.com*, July 1, 2009.

11 Marquez Estrada, *Startribune.com*, January 2, 2009.

12 Sharokman, *St. Petersburg Times*, June 4, 2008.

13 Goodall, *Floridatoday.com*, July 14, 2009.

References

Antawn Jamison. At http://www.nba.com/playerfile/antawn_jamison/bio.html. Accessed March 28, 2011.

Baade. R. A., R. Baumann, and V. A. Matheson (2008). Selling the game: Estimating the economic impact of professional sports through taxable sales. *Southern Economic Journal,* 74(3): 794–810.

Baade R. A., and R. F. Dye (1990). The impact of stadiums and professional sports on metropolitan area development. *Growth and Change,* 2: 1–14.

Baade R.A., and V.A. Matheson (2004). The quest for the cup: Assessing the economic impact of the World Cup. *Regional Studies,* 38(4): 343–354.

Barro, Robert J. (2009). Demand side voodoo economics. *The Economists' Voice,* 6(2): Article 5.

Coates, D. (2007). Stadiums and arenas: Economic development or redistribution? *Contemporary Economic Policy,* 25(4): 565–577.

Coates, D., and B. R. Humphries (2008). Do economists reach a conclusion on subsidies for sports franchises, stadiums, and mega-events? *Econ Journal Watch,* 5(3): 294–315.

Crompton, J. L. (1995). Economic impact analysis of sports facilities and events: Eleven sources of misapplication. *Journal of Sport Management,* 9: 14–35.

Firas, Carlos. (2009). Done deal: Work begins on construction site of Florida Marlins' new stadium. *PalmBeashPost.com,* July 1, 2009. At http://www.palmbeachpost.com/marlins/ content/sports/epaper/2009/07/01/0701marlins_stadium.html. Accessed July 14, 2009.

Goodall, Fred (2009). Tampa Bay exploring options for new stadium. *Floridatoday. com,* July 14, 2009. At http://www.floridatoday.com/article/20090714/ BREAKINGNEWS/90714053/ 1002/SPORTS/Tampa+Bay+exploring+options+for+ new+stadium. Accessed July 22, 2009.

Haggman, Matthew, and Jose Palgliery (2009). Florida Marlins stadium a hot ticket for job seekers. *Miami Herald online,* July 9, 2009. At http://www.miamiherald. com/news/miami-dade/story/1133636.html?asset_id=Thousands%20apply%20 for%20jobs%20at%20new%20Marlins%20stadium&asset_type=html_module. Accessed July 14, 2009.

Hudson, I. (2001). The use and misuse of economic impact analysis. *Journal of Sport and Social Issues.* 25(1): 20–39.

Johnson, Arthur T. (1995). *Minor league baseball and local economic development.* Urbana: University of Illinois Press.

Marquez Estrada, Heron (2009). Wilf pushes vikings stadium—as economic stimulus. *Startribune.com,* January 2, 2009. At http://www.startribune.com/local/ west/36983709.html. Accessed July 14, 2009.

NBA Team Valuations (2008). *Forbes.com* at http://www.forbes.com/lists/2008/32/ nba08_NBA-Team-Valuations_Revenue.html. Accessed March 28 2011.

Noll, R. G., and A. Zimbalist, eds. (1997). *Sports, jobs and taxes.* Washington, DC, Brookings Institution Press.

Sharokman, Aaron (2008). Baseball commissioner says Rays must have new ballpark. *St. Petersburg Times,* June 4, 2008. Online at http://www.tampabay.com/news/ localgovernment/article605708.ece. Accessed July 22, 2009.

Siegfried, J., and A. Zimbalist (2000). The economics of sports facilities and their communities. *Journal of Economic Perspectives,* 14(3): 95–114.

Siegfried, J., and A. Zimbalist (2002). a note on the local economic impact of sports expenditures. *Journal of Sports Economics,* 3(4): 361–366.

Torre, Pablo S. (2009). How (and why) athletes go broke. *Sports Illustrated.* March 23, 2009. Online at http://vault.sportsillustrated.cnn.com/vault/article/magazine/ MAG1153364/ index.htm. Accessed July 13, 2009.

## CHAPTER 19

CONTINGENT VALUATION OF SPORTS

BRUCE K. JOHNSON AND
JOHN C. WHITEHEAD

INTRODUCTION

ALL across the world, from Canada to Argentina, from California to the United Kingdom, from Norway to South Africa, local, state and provincial, and national governments subsidize amateur and professional sports. Governments spend billions of dollars to pay for stadiums and arenas, provide tax incentives to teams and leagues, identify and train elite athletes, and sponsor the hosting of mega-events such as the soccer World Cup and the Olympic Games.

Sports, in turn, provide a wide array of benefits. People buy tickets to games, of course, to experience the excitement of attending a match, whether they enjoy it in the wind and rain lashing the nosebleed seats in the end zone, or from the luxurious comfort of a private suite at the 50-yard line. They may subscribe to a team's cable television network or may pay to watch individual games through pay-per-view services. For each of these benefits, people pay the team.

But many people enjoy benefits from sports without ever paying the team or event organizer. They participate in fantasy baseball and football leagues, attend or host game-day parties, read about and discuss players, teams, and games. They bask in civic pride because they live in a major league city or national pride when their nation's athletes win Olympic medals. They line the streets of Manhattan for tickertape parades when the Yankees win the World Series, or pack Trafalgar Square in London and the beaches of Rio de Janeiro to celebrate their cities' being awarded the Olympic Games.

This complicates benefit-cost analysis of government policies supporting sports. In principle, measuring the benefits from ticket purchases and cable subscriptions is easy. Market data on ticket prices and sales, for instance, allow estimation of demand functions, and consumer and producer surplus. Such methods use revealed preference data, so called because peoples' purchases reveal their preferences for sports over alternative goods and services.

But no markets exist for tickertape parades and office conversations about last night's game. No league or team collects statistics measuring national pride or the value fans place on checking the highlights at ESPN.com or the league standings in their local newspapers. Crompton (2004) calls such benefits "psychic income" and says they are perhaps the greatest intangible benefits produced by sports.

No market activity reveals fans' preferences for these public goods. We do not know the quantities consumed, nor do we observe how those quantities change when prices change, because there are no prices to change. A benefit-cost analysis using only revealed preference data for sports would therefore underestimate, perhaps by a large amount, the benefits from sports.

In this respect, sport resembles the environment. Both produce important benefits in the nature of non-rival and non-excludable public goods. No one disputes that many people value public goods such as scenic vistas, survival of endangered species, and clean air. But no one has to go to the corner shop or to an online seller to buy them. In other words, as in sport, many of the benefits are difficult to value because there are no revealed preference data with which to estimate demand and consumer surplus.

Fortunately for sports economists, environmental economists have developed a method to measure the benefits of non-traded public goods. Because consumers do not reveal their preferences through market transactions, we ask them to state their preferences in carefully designed surveys. This chapter describes the use of the Contingent Valuation Method (CVM) to conduct such surveys and to analyze the data to measure the benefits produced by sports public goods (Mitchell and Carson, 1989; Alberini and Kahn, 2006).

WHAT IS THE CVM?

There's an old joke about an economist and an engineer stranded on a desert island with nothing to eat but canned peas, and no way to open the cans. The engineer proposes a complicated scheme involving an explosion and calculating the subsequent trajectory of the flying peas. The economist says, "Let's assume we have a can opener." In the same spirit, economists who want to measure the value of public goods have said, "Let's assume we have a market." Fortunately, if properly conceived, imaginary markets are more useful than imaginary can openers. Imaginary markets are the key to CVM surveys. The idea is straightforward. Respondents are presented with a hypothetical scenario in which they can pay for a specified improvement in a public good or pay to avoid a specified loss of a public good. Their willingness-to-pay is contingent upon the hypothetical scenarios described to them.

To illustrate the economic theory behind CVM analysis, consider the following example. Imagine that Jane spends her income to achieve a certain target level of utility from her consumption of goods and services, including the goods produced by her local sports team. If the team should leave, Jane's utility will fall. To return to her target utility level, she must increase her consumption of other goods and services. She may have to spend, for instance, $30 more per year on other things to replace the utility she got from the team. If so, her annual willingness-to-pay to keep the team is $30.

CVM surveys also ask about consumption of private goods, such as attending games, and public goods, such as civic pride. By correlating willingness-to-pay with responses about private and public goods consumption, household willingness-to-pay can be broken into two components: the willingness-to-pay for private goods, sometimes called use value, and the willingness-to-pay for public goods, or non-use value. Willingness-to-pay can also be correlated to such personal and demographic characteristics as sex, age, race, income, and education.

Because CVM surveys ask about consumption and willingness-to-pay for goods with which people may have little direct experience, the surveys must be carefully designed (Whitehead, 2006). Just as a pitcher performs better if he warms up before entering the game, respondents answer more accurately if they think about the topic a bit before answering the important valuation questions. The CVM survey should start with a brief warm-up section. For instance, a survey designed to elicit willingness-to-pay for the national pride of seeing one more compatriot win an Olympic gold medal should begin with general questions about the Olympics. Do you watch the Games? Do you pay attention to the medal standings? Are gold medals important to a nation's world standing?

Once respondents are warmed up, bring them into the game by presenting them with the hypothetical scenario. It must be short, realistic, and simple. The components of a CVM scenario include a description of the resource or policy context, the policy or change in resource allocation that will be valued, a payment vehicle, and a policy implementation rule.

The description should be done in a paragraph or two while describing exactly what is being discussed. A concrete scenario allows each respondent to understand what, exactly, they are paying for. It also allows for different versions of the scenario. Each version can become an independent variable in the model of willingness-to-pay.

Respondents must have a way to pay for the change in resource allocation. The payment vehicle should be realistic, believable, and neutral. Typical payment vehicles suitable for sports applications include increases in ticket prices and taxes. The payment rule can be explicit or implicit, but it must be enforceable. Otherwise, the contingent valuation question will not be incentive compatible. If payment is through taxes, for instance, respondents know the government can raise taxes and enforce their payment. The payment rule in this case is: if enough people are willing to pay, then the government will raise taxes. Respondents have at least a weak incentive to tell the truth.

Here's a sports scenario from a survey in Jacksonville, Florida, in the spring of 2002 (Johnson et al. 2007).

> Professional football teams often move to new cities. Since 1984, National Football League teams have left Baltimore, St. Louis, Oakland, Houston, Cleveland, and Los Angeles (twice). Consider the following situation. Within the next 10 years the owners of the Jaguars decide to sell the team. The new owners want to move the team to another city, such as Los Angeles, where they could make higher profits. Suppose the city of Jacksonville was able to buy a majority of the team. If the city owned a majority of the team the Jaguars would never leave Jacksonville. Large sums of money from Duval County taxpayers would be needed to buy a majority of the team. It has been estimated that it would take annual tax payments of $40 for the next 20 years from all Duval County households to buy a majority of the team. Your total payment would be $800.

The tax payments mentioned will vary from respondent to respondent, as may the number of years over which the payments will be required.

After the hypothetical scenario, the survey asks whether respondents would be willing to pay for the hypothetical benefit. There are two types of valuation questions: open-ended and closed-ended. Open-ended questions, such as, "What is the maximum amount of money that you would be willing to pay for a football team?" are difficult to answer. They are also incentive-incompatible, that is, easy to "free ride" on. Respondents might answer "zero" or "$1" even if they place a much higher value on the team.

A better open-ended format is the payment card. It is easier to answer because it provides dollar interval response categories. Respondents could be given the following response categories: "between $1 and $15," "between $16 and $35," "between $36 and $60," and "more than $60." Respondents indicate the interval containing their maximum willingness-to-pay. This produces an almost continuous dependent variable if the data are coded at the midpoint of the intervals. But payment card questions are prone to "range bias" since many people are open to suggestion when answering unfamiliar questions. In this example, the average willingness-to-pay would likely be between $1 and $60. But if the response category "between $61 and $100" were added, the average willingness-to-pay might rise.

The closed-ended dichotomous choice question has become the dominant CVM question format. Its major advantage is that it is easy to answer. Each respondent is asked a single valuation question such as, "Would you be willing to pay $40 per year in higher taxes for 5 years to keep the football team in town?" However, for statistical purposes, larger samples are necessary to implement the dichotomous choice approach. Hence, dichotomous choice surveys can be expensive to conduct.

Various types of valuation questions have been used in the sports economics literature. Several studies have used a dichotomous choice question with a payment card follow-up (e.g., Johnson and Whitehead, 2000; Johnson, Groothuis, and Whitehead, 2001; Johnson, Mondello, and Whitehead, 2006). The payment card results are presented as a result of the low sample sizes and statistical inefficiency of the dichotomous choice data. Johnson et al. (2007) and Fenn and Crooker (2009) use dichotomous choice data. All of these studies use tax payments as the payment vehicle. The dichotomous choice studies use a referendum vote payment rule.

Methodological Challenges

While the CVM allows estimation of benefits when revealed preference methods cannot, some potential pitfalls can undermine its value for benefit-cost analysis. See Whitehead and Blomquist (2006) for more detail on the issues in this section.

Hypothetical Bias

Hypothetical bias is the tendency for hypothetical willingness-to-pay values to exceed actual willingness-to-pay. People in field surveys and laboratory markets tend to say they will pay more than they actually do pay when given an opportunity to purchase the good. One simple cause of hypothetical bias is failure of the *ceteris paribus* condition to hold between the actual and hypothetical scenarios. Income and time constraints limit respondents' consumption and willingness-to-pay in the present. But if respondents think the hypothetical scenario applies to the future, and if they think they will have more money and time in the future, they may overstate their hypothetical willingness-to-pay. The CVM willingness-to-pay estimates must be considered upper bounds of benefits in the context of benefit-cost analysis unless steps are taken to mitigate hypothetical bias.

Research to discover question formats that minimize hypothetical bias finds that hypothetical willingness-to-pay is similar to actual willingness-to-pay when adjusted by respondent certainty about payment. Applying this method, Johnson et al. (2007) asked respondents who said they would vote for higher taxes to expand amateur sports programs in Alberta to rate, on a 10-point scale, how certain they were of their "yes" votes. Recoding uncertain "yes" votes as "no" votes had a big effect. For instance, 51 percent of those asked if they would pay $10 per year said yes. But only 36 percent said they were sure to vote yes. Of those asked to pay $50 per year, 36 percent said yes, but only 26 percent were certain. Recoding the uncertain responses reduced estimated willingness-to-pay substantially, possibly mitigating hypothetical bias and providing a more accurate estimate of benefits from expanded sports programs.

Making the payment vehicle a tax rather than a voluntary contribution also helps mitigate hypothetical bias because tax questions are less prone to free-riding behavior. Atkinson et al. (2008), in estimating willingness-to-pay for the 2012 Summer Olympics in London, used higher taxes as the payment vehicle for London respondents. However, since the Olympic bid was an initiative of the London government, there was no credible tax mechanism to require non-Londoners to pay. A voluntary contribution payment vehicle was used for respondents in Manchester and Glasgow. This raises the possibility of hypothetical bias in non-Londoners' estimated willingness-to-pay for the Olympics.

Temporal Bias

The CVM researcher must decide whether to ask respondents for their willingness-to-pay in perpetuity (Johnson and Whitehead, 2000), for a finite period of years (Johnson, Mondello, and Whitehead, 2007), or a one-time lump sum (Fenn and Crooker, 2009). Theoretically, the present value of the annual payments should equal the lump sum. But people sometimes have a hard time responding like the fully informed, rational actor in economic theory. As a result, the annual willingness-to-pay question often yields larger estimates of the present value of willingness-to-pay than the lump-sum question. The result is temporal bias, defined as the upward bias in willingness-to-pay if the annual payment format is used when the lump-sum format is more appropriate.

Most CVM surveys elicit annual payments under the assumption that the annual budget constrains willingness-to-pay. If the project being valued is a stadium with an expected useful life of 30 years, the present value of willingness-to-pay is the discounted sum of 30 years of annual payments. But this overstates willingness-to-pay if respondents mistakenly expect to pay for less than 30 years. To avoid this pitfall, elicitation questions should explicitly state the time period.

Some surveys avoid this problem by assuming that respondents are constrained not by their annual budget but by their lifetime wealth. They elicit a lump-sum payment: "Would you be willing to pay $400 this year as a one-time payment for a new football stadium?" Respondents apply their own rate of time preference to the project and state the present value of their willingness-to-pay. But this approach will tend to underestimate willingness-to-pay if respondents have difficulty with discounting or if they cannot borrow in perfect capital markets.

The empirical evidence suggests that respondents have a difficult time discounting. However, in a sports example, Johnson et al. (2006) found realistic implicit discount rates in a Jacksonville, Florida, survey to determine willingness-to-pay for professional football and basketball teams. The discount rates were comparable to the interest rates charged by credit card lenders.

Multi-Part Policy

Many government policies involve substitute or complementary relationships with other policies. For example, some cities subsidize separate baseball and football stadiums, treating the sports as substitutes, while other cities treat them as complements by subsidizing a single stadium to house both. This complicates the application of the CVM. The resulting problems have been called embedding, part-whole bias, and sequencing and nesting.

In theory, the sum of the individual willingness-to-pay values for two projects will be greater than willingness-to-pay for both together if the projects are substitutes, and less if the projects are complements. A related issue occurs when the same survey asks respondents their willingness-to-pay separately for two different policies. The order in which they are asked may affect the valuation. Willingness-to-pay for a basketball team, for instance, may be higher if respondents are asked to value it before being asked to value a football team. Independent valuation, or valuing at the beginning of a sequence, will always lead to the largest of the possible willingness-to-pay estimates with the CVM due to substitution and income effects.

The best approach is to randomly vary the order in which the policies are presented to respondents and to test whether ordering affects the results. Johnson, Mondello, and Whitehead (2006) randomly vary the ordering of football and basketball scenarios and find only limited evidence that multi-part policy plays a role in willingness-to-pay estimates.

Standing

In benefit-cost analysis, the researcher must decide who has standing, that is, whose benefits count. Should average willingness-to-pay be aggregated over a city's entire population or over the state's population? And how should the researcher extrapolate the sample average willingness-to-pay to non-respondents? The answers to these questions can have a significant impact on estimated benefits.

Many CVM studies choose to sample a narrow geographic or political region (e.g., Johnson, Mondello, and Whitehead, 2007). The implicit assumption is that households located on the other side of the border are willing to pay nothing. But if the project's benefits spill over regional boundaries, this will lead to an underestimate of benefits.

An alternative assumption is that willingness-to-pay declines with distance from the site, but does not vanish at, say, the city line. This is plausible if exposure to the team and its fans generates utility and if the exposure is more costly to obtain farther from the stadium. The geographical extent of the market reaches to the distance at which the willingness-to-pay drops to zero, which may be quite far for teams with strong regional identities. Owen (2006) found that Minnesotans' willingness-to-pay for professional football, basketball, and baseball in Minneapolis fell as their distance from Minneapolis increased. Atkinson et al. (2008) found that people in Manchester and Glasgow were less willing to pay for the 2012 London Olympics than were Londoners. Nevertheless, in both Minnesota and Britain, people far away from Minneapolis and London received large benefits from sports, and failure to account for them would result in underestimation of sports benefits.

Survey Response Rates

The response rate for most CVM surveys is too low to allow aggregation across the population without major adjustments. The percentage of people who participate in surveys is low, and has fallen in recent years with the rise of telemarketing. Mail survey response rates tend to be even lower than telephone rates. Furthermore, telephone survey samples routinely exclude people without land lines, a percentage that is rapidly growing in the age of the mobile phone. People who cannot afford phones usually have lower willingness-to-pay for public goods. Those who choose cell phones alone may differ significantly from those with land lines.

The relevant question for benefit-cost analysis is: "Do survey non-respondents have standing?" Assigning full standing and aggregating over the entire population sampled when only, say, 30 percent responded to the survey will lead to an overestimate of benefits if respondents are more willing to pay than are non-respondents. Denying standing to non-respondents surely underestimates aggregate benefits.

Several approaches for adjustment of sample average willingness-to-pay to non-respondents are available. If the sample suffers from non-response bias, the sample average willingness-to-pay can be weighted on those observable characteristics for which the bias occurs. If demographic and other preference information is available on non-respondents, willingness-to-pay estimates can be econometrically adjusted to be representative of the population.

Unfortunately, information on non-respondents is typically not available, and benefit-cost analysts are usually left with ad-hoc adjustment procedures. An extreme adjustment procedure, most recently illustrated by Johnson, Mondello, and Whitehead (2007), is to alternatively assign non-respondents values of zero and one hundred percent of sample average willingness-to-pay to provide lower and upper bounds for aggregate willingness-to-pay. This approach can lead to wide bounds of aggregate willingness-to-pay.

APPLICATIONS

Contingent valuation method surveys covering sports from American football to the Olympics have been conducted. In most cases, the estimates of willingness-to-pay for sports public goods fall far short of the public subsidies given to sports, suggesting that costs usually exceed benefits for government policies promoting sports. See Johnson (2008) for more detailed summaries of some of the cases discussed below.

Lexington, Kentucky

The seminal application of CVM to sports estimated willingness-to-pay for two projects in Lexington, Kentucky (Johnson and Whitehead, 2000). A mail survey in 1997 asked respondents their willingness-to-pay for two hypothetical scenarios, the building of a new arena for the University of Kentucky (UK) basketball team and the building of a stadium to attract and host a minor league baseball team. The UK basketball team is extremely popular, with an excess demand for tickets at every home game. The hypothetical scenario proposed a larger arena that would generate more income, enhance practice facilities, and make UK more competitive.

The estimated cost of a new arena at the time was $100 million. Based on the CVM responses to the valuation questions, the aggregate net present value of Lexingtonians' willingness-to-pay for a new arena was just $7.28 million, about $5 million of which was because people thought it would be easier to get UK tickets. The remainder was willingness-to-pay for public goods, including a more competitive UK team. Not surprisingly, since UK had won the national championship in 1996 and narrowly lost the 1997 title game in overtime a few weeks before the survey, most respondents did not think a new arena would make UK more competitive.

The minor league baseball scenario elicited willingness-to-pay for a stadium to attract a team to Lexington, at the time one of the largest metro areas in the nation without a professional baseball team. The aggregate discounted value of willingness-to-pay was less than $7.1 million, of which just 10 percent was for public goods.

Pittsburgh

The Lexington survey demonstrated the feasibility of using the CVM to estimate willingness-to-pay for sports public goods, but left unanswered the question of how much major league sports public goods are worth. The first application of CVM to major league sports estimated willingness-to-pay to keep the National Hockey League Penguins from moving out of Pittsburgh (Johnson, Groothuis, and Whitehead, 2001). A survey of people throughout metropolitan Pittsburgh presented a hypothetical scenario in which the city of Pittsburgh would buy the Penguins to keep them from leaving.

Although 72 percent identified themselves as fans, only 52 percent favored higher taxes to keep the Penguins. The average Pittsburgh household in 2000 was willing to pay a total of $5.57 per year to keep the Penguins in town, including $4.08 for public goods such as reading about the Penguins and discussing them with friends. The aggregate metropolitan annual willingness-to-pay to keep the Penguins ranged between about $1.9 million, if all non-respondents are assumed willing to pay zero, to about $5.3 million, assuming no difference between respondent and non-respondent willingness-to-pay. At an interest rate of 8 percent, that could finance a lump sum payment of $23.5 million to $66 million. The latter figure is the maximum estimate for both use and non-use benefits, far less than the cost of Pittsburgh's new arena opening in 2010 at a cost of $290 million.

Jacksonville, Florida

The low willingness-to-pay for the Penguins may result from hockey's status as the least popular major league sport. Pittsburgh's civic pride in its major league status would be intact if the Penguins left, since the city also hosts baseball's Pirates and football's Steelers (Rappaport and Wilkerson, 2001). Johnson, Mondello, and Whitehead (2007) estimate the value of public goods produced by the National Football League (NFL) Jaguars, the only major league team in Jacksonville, Florida. As the 46th largest metropolitan area in the United States, and the second-smallest city among those represented in major league football, basketball, or baseball, few would call Jacksonville without the Jaguars a major league city. Certainly that was the case when the NFL awarded the Jaguars to Jacksonville, prompting pundits to dismiss Jacksonville as "small," "dumpy," and a "joke" (*USA Today*, 1993).

As in Pittsburgh, the Jacksonville survey asked how much people would be willing to pay in higher taxes to keep their team in town. It also asked two questions about public goods that benefit fans and non-fans alike: "Do you think having the Jaguars in town puts Jacksonville 'on the map,' just like other 'major league' cities?" "Do you think having the Jaguars in town helps improve relations among whites, African-Americans, Hispanics, and other groups?" About three-fourths believed the Jaguars put Jacksonville on the map, while 43 percent said they improved racial and ethnic relations.

The net present value of aggregate willingness-to-pay to keep the Jaguars ranged between $13.3 million and $35.8 million. This is much lower than Pittsburgh's willingness-to-pay for the Penguins, largely because Jacksonville is only half the size of Pittsburgh. The NFL required Jacksonville to upgrade Municipal Stadium as a condition to get a franchise. Through 2001, Jacksonville spent $207 million on stadium renovations and upgrades (Long, 2005, p. 122), far above the use and non-use benefits from the Jaguars. It appears that Jacksonville made a lousy bargain with the NFL.

To test the hypothesis that additional teams have declining marginal value to a city, the Jacksonville survey also contained a hypothetical scenario about upgrading an arena to attract an NBA team. Jacksonville area households were willing to pay between about $9.7 million and $26.1 million for the NBA. This is less than the figure for the Jaguars, consistent with the hypothesis of declining marginal value of teams. But maybe it just means they prefer football, since respondents overwhelmingly named football as their favorite sport.

Minnesota

In 2003 the NFL's Minnesota Vikings were threatening to move unless taxpayers built them a new stadium. A statewide survey asked Minnesotans if they would be willing to pay a one-time, lump-sum amount for a new stadium (Fenn and Crooker, 2009). The survey covered the entire state to test whether non-residents of the Twin Cities value the Vikings. Apparently they do, since rural Minnesotans value the Vikings the same as residents of the Twin Cities, even though economic theory suggests that willingness-to-pay should drop as distance increases. The aggregate willingness-to-pay of all Minnesota households was about $700 million, close to the estimated $750 to $954 million cost of the new stadium planned for the Vikings. However, it is unclear how non-respondents were treated when aggregating willingness-to-pay. The response rate was 42 percent, but there appears to have been no attempt to grapple with the issue of non-response or sample-selection bias—the estimate may therefore be too high, if non-respondents care about football much less than do respondents.

Owen (2006) also conducted a statewide survey asking Minnesotans about their willingness-to-pay for the Vikings. Owen found that Minnesotans living outside the Twin Cities value the Vikings but that their willingness-to-pay for the Vikings declines as distance from Minneapolis increases. Owen estimated aggregate willingness-to-pay for the Vikings of $218 million to $544 million, which, at the upper end of the range, approaches Fenn and Crooker's estimate.

Owen also asked Minnesotans about their willingness-to-pay for baseball's Twins and basketball's Timberwolves. He surveyed Michiganders about their willingness-to-pay for Detroit's baseball Tigers, football Lions, basketball Pistons, and hockey Red Wings. He found that willingness-to-pay, while large, typically falls short of the cost of a new stadium or arena, and that most respondents were unwilling to pay anything at all.

Portland, Oregon

Before the Montreal Expos decided to move to Washington, D.C., in 2005, Major League Baseball (MLB) considered several new homes, including Portland, Oregon. Before Washington was chosen, a CVM survey asked people in the Portland metropolitan area about their willingness-to-pay higher taxes for 30 years to finance a stadium to attract a baseball team (Santo, 2008).

The survey asked if a baseball stadium would improve Portland's economy. Sixty-nine percent thought so, and were willing to pay $7 more per year than those who thought otherwise. Though a huge literature shows that stadiums have minimal effects on employment and income (Coates, 2007), most Portlanders seem unaware of this, suffering a phenomenon that has been called "stadium illusion," (Johnson and Whitehead, 2000, p. 52). Despite Portlanders' willingness-to-pay for a nonexistent economic boost, their 30-year aggregate discounted willingness-to-pay for a stadium was only about $74 million, far below a stadium's cost.

London

In 2005, the International Olympic Committee (IOC) awarded the 2012 Olympic Games to London, after several years of intense competition between London, Paris, New York, Madrid, and Moscow. The IOC prefers that host governments underwrite the cost of staging the games, requiring a sizable public subsidy. In 2004, a CVM survey asked people in London, Manchester, and Glasgow about their willingness-to-pay to attract the Olympics to London (Atkinson et al., 2008). It asked about intangible benefits including national pride and unity, inspiring children to exercise, building new facilities that would be useful after the games, and improving the environment while converting brown field sites into Olympic venues. They also asked about intangible costs including crowding and congestion, increased risk of petty theft, increased risk of terrorism, and transport delays during the games.

Taking intangible costs and benefits into consideration, London households on average were willing to pay £22 per year for 10 years beginning in 2006. Manchester households were willing to pay £12 per year and Glasgow households £11 per year. Another survey in Bath and Southwest England also found that non-Londoners valued the Games in London (Walton et al., 2008). Aggregating over all London households and discounting at 5 percent yields a total willingness-to-pay in London of £480 million. Extrapolating the Manchester and Glasgow estimates to the rest of the United Kingdom yields an aggregate discounted willingness-to-pay of £1.47 billion outside London, for a U.K. total of £1.95 billion (Atkinson et al.), about $3.2 billion at early 2011 exchange rates.

British willingness-to-pay for the Olympics dwarfs estimated willingness-to-pay for American professional sports. There are several reasons. First and most important is standing. Major league sports teams produce their public goods on a local or state level. Jacksonville has 426,000 households. The United Kingdom has more than 24 million. A second reason is the lack of substitutes for the Olympics, which dominate the sporting world's attention in a way no single team or league can. Third, the Olympic host gains a status far more rarified than that of a major league city. An Olympic city is one of a handful in any given generation, whereas 47 North American cities have a team in one or more of the four major sports leagues.

Even though British willingness-to-pay is high, it falls short of the Olympian levels needed to justify the subsidies British taxpayers will likely end up providing for the 2012 Olympics. The projected cost of hosting the 2012 Olympics had reached £9.3 billion in 2007 (Carlin and Bond), more than 4.5 times the CVM estimates of benefits.

Alberta, Canada

Most sports CVM surveys have focused on spectator sports. But participatory sports often receive public subsidies, too. The province of Alberta, Canada, subsidizes scores of amateur sport and recreation programs, from Alpine skiing to hockey to water polo. Amateur sports provide use value for participants and may provide non-use value for others. For instance, organized sports may keep adolescents under adult supervision and off the street.

A random telephone survey of households throughout Alberta was conducted to determine willingness-to-pay for expanding participation rates of 2 to 10 percent in these programs (Johnson et al., 2007). The hypothetical scenario said the expansion would be funded by increases in the provincial income tax of $10, $25, or $50 CDN per year. Because the three tax and two expansion rates were mixed and matched, six different combinations were presented to respondents. Respondents were asked whether they would vote for a referendum to raise income taxes.

Albertans were willing to pay $18 CDN per household per year to expand sport and recreation participation rates. Aggregated over all Alberta households, the present discounted willingness-to-pay for a small increase in participation rates is $214 million CDN, or about $218 million US at early 2011 exchange rates, far exceeding most CVM estimates for professional sports in the United States.

How could willingness-to-pay to avoid total loss of a major league team be so far below that for a small increase in the provision of amateur, participatory sport and recreation programs? Several possible explanations exist. First, the Alberta programs directly involve many more people than does a major league team. Nearly two-thirds of respondents said they participated in the previous 12 months as a player, official, volunteer, or parent of a player. Second, the experience of playing, coaching, or organizing a sport may be more intense and satisfying than passively watching professional sports played by strangers. Third, pro sports may not match the preferences of many fans. If you aren't a football fan in Jacksonville, too bad—it's the only major league game in town. With more than 100 organized sport and recreation activities, Albertans have a good chance of finding one that closely matches their preferences.

Conclusions

The contingent valuation method has yielded important insights in sports economics. The notion that the value of public goods for sports teams, arenas, stadiums, and mega-events are larger than the costs of these events has been largely dispelled, suggesting that public subsidies are too large. Additional insights about the demand for sports have been attained. Yet, there remains more to be accomplished. Few sports CVM studies have considered the key issues of validity and reliability of the estimates. Validity tests for hypothetical bias, scope, and other factors could be explored in future research in order to better understand the structure of demand for sports public goods. Considering the reliability of willingness-to-pay in the sports area, a test-retest of a CVM instrument before and after mega-events or a championship season could be pursued to understand the permanence of willingness-to-pay. Comparisons between willingness-to-pay and life satisfaction (i.e., happiness) values could be used to assess the alternative form reliability of the two measures of welfare.

Conducting a CVM survey offers an opportunity, if the budget permits, to ask questions to allow stated preference methods other than CVM to be employed to inform public policy related to sports. Choice experiments could be implemented to provide an alternative method for estimating non-use value. For instance, people could be asked how much more they would be willing to pay for tickets with the addition of various amenities to the local stadium. Another method, contingent behavior, can be used to understand changes in behavior in response to changes in sports opportunities. For example, an understanding of ticket demand in a new arena could be elicited by asking people how many tickets they would purchase at various prices. Finally, combination of stated preference data with revealed preference data, such as that obtained from the travel cost method or hedonic price method, could be used to validate and improve the estimates of benefits obtained from both.

References

Alberini, Anna, and James R. Kahn (2006). *Handbook on contingent valuation.* Cheltenham, UK: Edward Elgar Publishing.

Atkinson, Giles, Susana Mourato, Stefan Szymanski and Ece Ozdemiroglu (2008). Are we willing to pay enough to 'back the bid'?: Valuing the intangible impacts of London's bid to host the 2012 Summer Olympic Games. *Urban Studies* 45(2): 419–444.

Carlin, Brendan, and David Bond (2007). Olympics budget trebles to £9.3 billion. *Daily Telegraph,* March 16, 2007, http://www.telegraph.co.uk/news/main. jhtml?xml=/news/2007/03/16/nolym16.xml (accessed March 16, 2007).

Crompton, John (2004). Beyond economic impact: An alternative rationale for the public subsidy of major league sports facilities. *Journal of Sport Management,* 18: 40–58.

Fenn, Aju J., and John R. Crooker (2009). Estimating local welfare generated by an NFL team under credible threat of relocation. *Southern Economic Journal* 76(1): 198–223.

Groothuis, Peter A., Bruce K. Johnson, and John C. Whitehead (2004). Public funding of professional sports stadiums: Public choice or civic pride? *Eastern Economic Journal* 30(4): 515–526.

Johnson, Bruce K. (2008). The valuation of nonmarket benefits in sports, in Brad R. Humphreys and Dennis R. Howard, eds., *The Business of Sports*, v. 2, Economic Perspectives on Sport, Westport, CT: Praeger Publishers, pp. 207–233.

Johnson, Bruce K., and John C. Whitehead (2000). Value of public goods from sports stadiums: The CVM approach. *Contemporary Economic Policy* 18(1): 48–58.

Johnson, Bruce K., Peter A. Groothuis, and John C. Whitehead (2001). The value of public goods generated by a major league sports team. *Journal of Sports Economics* 2(1): 6–21.

Johnson, Bruce K., Michael J. Mondello, and John C. Whitehead (2006). Contingent valuation of sports: Temporal embedding and ordering effects. *Journal of Sports Economics* 7(3): 267–288.

Johnson, Bruce K., Michael J. Mondello, and John C. Whitehead (2007). The value of public goods generated by a National Football League team. *Journal of Sports Management* 21(1): 123–136.

Johnson, Bruce K., John C. Whitehead, Daniel S. Mason, and Gordon J. Walker (2007). Willingness-to-pay for amateur sport and recreation programs. *Contemporary Economic Policy*, 25(4): 553–564.

Long, Judith Grant (2005). Full count: The real cost of public funding for major league sports facilities. *Journal of Sports Economics*, 6(2): 119–143.

Owen, Jeffrey (2006). The intangible benefits of sports teams. *Public Finance and Management* 6(3): 321–345.

Mitchell, Robert Cameron, and Richard T. Carson (1989). *Using surveys to value public goods: The contingent valuation method*. Washington, DC: Resources for the Future.

Rappaport, J., and Wilkerson, C. (2001). What are the benefits of hosting a major league sports franchise? *Economic Review, Federal Reserve Bank of Kansas City* (First Quarter): 55–86.

Santo, Charles (2007). Beyond the economic catalyst debate: Can public consumption benefits justify a municipal stadium investment? *Journal of Urban Affairs* 29(5): 455–479.

Walton, Harry, Alberto Longo, and Peter Dawson (2008). A contingent valuation of the 2012 London Olympic Games. *Journal of Sports Economics* 9(3): 304–317.

Whitehead, John C. (2006). A practitioner's primer on contingent valuation. Chapter 4 in *Handbook on contingent valuation*, eds. Anna Alberini and James R. Kahn. Cheltenham, UK: Edward Elgar Publishing, pp. 92–115.

Whitehead, John C., and Glenn C. Blomquist (2006). Contingent valuation and benefit-cost analysis," Chapter 3 in *Handbook on contingent valuation*, eds. Anna Alberini and James R. Kahn. Cheltenham, UK: Edward Elgar Publishing, pp. 66–91.

PART VII

MISCELLANY

## CHAPTER 20

THE ECONOMICS OF CRIME RECONSIDERED

A GAME THEORETIC APPROACH WITH AN EMPIRICAL TEST FROM MAJOR LEAGUE BASEBALL

JOSEPH P. MCGARRITY

We didn't wear an iron helmet. We wore a felt hat. I saw many a ball coming right at my head. When I pitched for San Francisco in 1921 I hit 19 men. On purpose. No way to say how many I missed.

Lefty O'Doul[1]

1. INTRODUCTION

IN the economic analysis of crime, researchers assume that police effort does not change when the legislature increases criminal penalties. However, if the relationship between the police and the potential crook is modeled as a game, and the government spends resources to catch criminals, a surprising result occurs. The government will spend fewer resources trying to catch the crook when the

penalty is increased, and the potential crook will attempt the crime the same percentage of the time. The game theoretic results make the counterintuitive prediction that increasing the criminal's punishment will lead to more successful crime.

Major League Baseball serves as a useful analogy for the game between a criminal and the police. A batter can be thought of as a potential criminal in this story.
He can stand in the middle of the batter's box (this is akin to the decision to be law
abiding), or he can "cheat" and lean into a pitch, allowing him to better reach the
outside portion of the plate. The pitcher plays the role of the police in this analogy.
He wants the batter to stand in the middle of the batter's box. The pitcher can try
to catch the batter who leans into a pitch by throwing inside. An inside pitch is like
a police force expending its effort to try to catch criminals. The pitcher bears a cost
to try to enforce a normal stance by the batter. If the batter does not lean in, the
batter may be able to avoid the pitch, and a ball will be called, leaving the pitcher
with a worse count. A pitcher must decide how often to throw inside, and a batter
must decide how often to lean into a pitch.

When a pitcher can throw with greater velocity, the batter will face a larger cost
from getting hit with the pitch, simply because it hurts more. This is much like a criminal facing a bigger fine if he gets caught. The game theoretic result is that the high-
velocity pitcher will throw inside less, because he doesn't need to do so as often.[2]

The baseball analogy is convenient because Major League Baseball generates a
wealth of statistics that can readily be used to test economic theories. These theories
would be harder to test using actual social statistics. In analyzing crime, the society-
level data suffers from several problems; for example, many crimes are not reported.
Baseball data has many advantages. Because so many people follow the game, and
gamble on the outcome, the statistics that are generated are very accurate. Because
so much of baseball is recorded in statistical format, it provides a useful starting
ground to test theories before trying to see if the results hold outside of baseball.

This paper uses a data set of all pitchers from the 2007 season. It finds that a
National League pitcher whose average fastball velocity increases from 91.77 to 96.43
miles an hour will throw inside 8.01 percent fewer times. Batters will lean into these
96-mile-an-hour pitches just as often, but, while leaning in, these batters are intentionally hit 0.054 percent less often. This is very counterintuitive, and runs against the
standard economics of crime story. This paper's result implies that an increase in a batter's (criminal's) penalty led to the same amount of leaning in, and to more instances
of leaning in without getting hit by the pitch (that is, more successful crime).

2. THEORETICAL DISCUSSION

In the plate appearance game, the hitter and pitcher are adversaries. The pitcher
would like to throw to a batter who stands in the middle of the batter's box. The
batter would like to lean into the pitch to try to be able to get a better swing at

outside pitches. The pitcher can throw the ball inside to brush back a player. If the batter leans in when the pitcher tries to brush him back, the batter is hit by the pitch, and it will hurt. The pitcher must decide whether to pitch normally or throw a brush-back pitch. The pitcher uses the brush-back pitch to discourage the batter from leaning into his pitches. The batter must decide whether to lean into the pitch, or stand up straight in the batter's box.

The game is characterized in Table 20.1. Instead of giving the players specific cardinal utilities for each outcome, Table 20.1 presents the pay-offs in general form. The pitcher's utility for each outcome is given by the capital letters (A, B, C, D), and the batter's pay-offs are represented by the lower case letters (m, n, o, p)

Consider the four outcomes. A,m are the pay-offs for the normal state of affairs. The pitcher throws normally and the batter stands up straight in the box. B,n are the pay-offs when the batter leans in, and the pitcher pitches normally. In this outcome, the batter is much more likely to get a hit than he was in the previous outcome because now he can reach the low outside pitch. C,o are the pay-offs when the pitcher throws inside, but the batter does not lean inside. This will result in a ball taken inside. The final box, with the pay-offs of D,p, represent what happens when the batter leans in and the pitcher throws inside. In this case, the pitch hits the batter. The pitcher's preference ordering is: (A,D,C,B). That is, he prefers normalcy, followed by a hit batter, a ball, and the batter getting away with leaning in on a normal pitch.[3]

This preference ordering takes into account that a pitcher wants to establish a reputation for throwing inside. If the game were only going to be played once, the pitcher would never throw at a batter. The pitcher would not want to hit a batter and allow a sure base runner (D). He would rather pitch normally to a hitter and face the increased risk that the batter gets a hit (B). However, this same game is played many times. The pay-off to the pitcher in box D includes both the loss from allowing a batter to reach first base and the gain from establishing a reputation for being willing to throw inside. A pitcher's willingness to throw inside occasionally ensures that future batters will not lean in all of the time. The pitchers concern for the likelihood that future batters will lean into a pitch ensures that $D>B$. The batter's preference ordering is: (n,o,m,p). In order, these indicate: when the batter is most likely to get a hit, when he takes a ball, the normal situation, and finally when he gets beaned.[4]

Although there is a dynamic element to the pitcher's pay-offs, the game is best modeled as a one-shot game. The dynamic element is incorporated in the pay-off D.

Table 20.1 Plate Appearance Game Hitter

		Normal Stance (y)	Lean-in (1–y)
Pitcher	Pitch Normally (a)	A, m	B, n
	Throw Inside (1–a)	C, o	D, p

pay-offs: pitcher, batters.

The game is not a repeated play between the same two players. The pitcher faces many different batters. Because the batters keep changing, the pitcher and batter will not find a cooperative equilibrium that is often the result when there is a repeated game between the same two players. This one-shot game is played repeatedly with the same pitcher but different batters.

The pitcher does not have a dominant pure strategy. His best strategy depends upon what he believes the batter will do. Because $A>C$, the pitcher will pitch normally when he thinks the hitter will take a normal stance. However, because $D>B$, the pitcher will throw inside when he thinks the batter will lean in. The batter also does not have a dominant pure strategy. Because $n>m$, the batter will lean in when he thinks the pitcher will throw normally. However, since $o>p$ the batter will stand in a normal position when he believes the pitcher will throw inside.

In any given box, one player will want to move clockwise to the next box, so there is no stable Nash equilibrium among the pure strategies. However, there is a mixed strategy Nash equilibrium. Suppose the pitcher pitches normally with a probability of a, and the hitter takes a normal stance with a probability of y. One can use the pay-off equating method to solve for both probabilities. First, consider the pitcher's pay-off function. In the mixed strategy equilibrium, the pitcher will be indifferent between his two options. That is, the pitcher's pay-offs from pitching normally and his pay-offs from throwing inside must be identical. The pay-off equating method exploits this equality to solve for the unknown probabilities. The pitcher's pay-off from his two strategies are:

$$\text{Pay-off}_{\text{(pitch normally)}} = Ay + (B(1-y))$$

$$\text{Pay-off}_{\text{(throw inside)}} = Cy + D(1-y)]$$

Next, set both pay-offs equal to get:

$$Ay + (B(1-y)) = [Cy + D(1-y)]$$

This can be simplified to:

$$Ay + B - By = Cy + D - Dy$$

$$Ay - By - Cy + Dy = D - B$$

$$y(A - B - C + D) = D - B$$

$$y = D - B / [(D-B) + (A-C)] \tag{1}$$

Therefore, the probability that a batter will stand upright in the box, is solved for using the pay-offs from the pitcher. By similar logic, the probability that a pitcher will pitch normally, (a), can be solved by referring to the batter's pay-offs for (1) standing up straight and (2) leaning in. The pay-offs from each action are:

$$\text{Pay-offs}_{\text{(normal stance)}} = am + (1-a)o$$

Pay-offs $_{\text{(leaning-in)}}$ = $an + (1-a)p$

Because the batter is indifferent between the two strategies in equilibrium, one can set the pay-offs equal.

$$am + (1-a)o = an + (1-a)p$$

This can be simplified to:

$$am + o - ao = an + p - ap$$

$$am - ao - an + ap = p - o$$

$$a(m - o - n + p) = (p - o)$$

$$a = p - o / [(p - o) + (m - n)] \qquad (2)$$

The probability that a pitcher will throw normally is expressed in terms of the pay-offs of the batter.

Equations (1) and (2) give the general results for the probability that a batter will stand up straight (y), and the probability that a pitcher will pitch normally (a). As a way of illustrating these results, let the general parameters found in Table 20.1 be replaced by the specific cardinal utilities found in Table 20.2. The utility values keep the same preference orderings for both the pitcher and the batter. Also, the pay-offs in the northwest box, the normal case, are zero for both players. When a player does better than this baseline case, he gets a positive utility value. If he does worse he gets a negative value.

Next, plug in these values into equation (1) to get:

$$y = (-1.86 - (-6))/[(-1.86 - (-6)) + (0 - (-3)] = 0.580$$

Doing the same for equation (2) yields:

$$a = (-850 - (3))/[(-850 - (3)) + (0 - (6)) = 0.993$$

This example suggests that the batter will take a normal stance in the box 58 percent of the time, and lean in 42 percent of the time. The pitcher will pitch normally, 99.3 percent of the time, and throw inside 0.7 percent of the time. The joint probabilities are found by multiplying either a or (1−a) by either y or (1−y). This gives the probability of the occurrence of each outcome, as shown in Table 20.3.

In this case, 57.6 percent of the time the pitcher throws normally to a batter in a normal stance. The batter leans in on normal pitches 41.7 percent of the time. The

Table 20.2 Plate Appearance Game Hitter

		Normal Stance (y)	Lean-in (1-y)
Pitcher	Pitch Normally (a)	0, 0	−6, +6
	Throw Inside (1-a)	−3, 3	−1.86, −850

pay-offs: pitcher, batters.

Table 20.3 Plate Appearance Game Hitter

		Normal Stance (y = 0.58)	Lean-in (1−y) = 0.42
Pitcher	Pitch Normally (a = 0.993)	0.57594	0.41706
	Throw Inside (1−a) = 0.007	0.00406	0.00294

pitcher throws inside when the batter takes a normal stance 0.4 percent of the time, and throws inside when the batter leans in 0.29 percent of the time.

The cardinal utility values given in the previous example were arbitrary. However, they were created to produce values of a and y found in the later empirical work. This exercise produces results that provide a useful benchmark that can be used to analyze the effect of changing one of the pay-offs. Suppose a pitcher can throw the ball faster, and that this only affects how much a beanball hurts. Only pay-off p, from the general pay-offs given in Table 20.1, will be changed. Remember that pay-off p does not influence the equilibrium probability that a batter will lean in (y). It only influences the probability that a pitcher will throw normally (a). Consider the specific example from Table 20.2's pay-offs. When pay-off p changes from −850 to −1,000, a becomes:

$$a = (-1,000 - (3))/[(-1,000 - (3)) + (0 - (6))] = 0.994$$

The pitcher will pitch normally 99.4 percent of the time, or 0.1 percentage point more often. This is a counterintuitive result. A batter who faces more punishment when he is caught leaning in does not alter his behavior. Instead, the pitcher can get away with throwing fewer inside pitches. The new joint probabilities for the example with specific cardinal utilities appear below in Table 20.4.

Consider how the outcomes in Table 20.4 compare with the outcomes of Table 20.3. The probability of an outcome occurring on the top row increased, while the chance of an outcome on the bottom row decreased. Interestingly, the pitcher's best outcome (pay-off A), and his worse outcome (pay-off B) occurred more often. The criminal activity, leaning in, still occurred 42 percent of the time. Only now, the breakup of that 42 percent changed. The criminal activity occurred more often when there were normal pitches, and occurred less often when the pitcher was throwing a pitch inside. Also, the fast pitcher will bean fewer batters and waste fewer throws to try to keep a batter honest. He will throw inside 0.6 percent of the time, instead of 0.7 percent of the time.

Table 20.4 Plate Appearance Game Hitter

		Normal Stance (y = 0.58)	Lean-in (1−y) = 0.42
Pitcher	Pitch Normally (a=0.994)	0.57652	0.41748
	Throw Inside (1−a)=0.006	0.00348	0.00252

This result from the specific example holds in the general case. Equation 2 appears again below.

$$a = p - o / [(p - o) + (m - n)] \tag{2}$$

In equation (2), $(p\text{-}o)$ will be negative; p is negative since it represents the batter receiving the punishment of being hit by the pitch; o is a good outcome for the batter since he gets a ball and thus a more favorable count, so when o is subtracted from p, the result is a number less than the negative number represented by p. If m is normalized to zero, then $(m - n)$ will be negative since n is a positive utility (and the batter's best outcome), so subtracting n from m leaves a negative number. Therefore, the terms in each of the three parentheses will be a negative value. Note that as the punishment p becomes greater, $(p - o)$ will become a larger negative number. Since $(p - o)$ appears in the numerator and denominator, a (the probability that a pitcher will throw normally) will approach one as p increases.

3. EMPIRICAL ISSUES

In order to empirically test the game theoretic model, several issues need to be addressed. First, the theoretical model assumed that every batter who leaned into a pitch would be hit if the pitcher threw inside. The model also assumed that a brush-back pitch would occur when the pitcher threw inside but the batter did not lean into the pitch, but rather took a normal stance. However, as a practical matter, it is very likely that a pitcher's velocity will determine, at least in part, how often a batter, who is leaning into the pitch, will be hit. A pitcher who throws 88 miles an hour (mph) may throw inside. However, a batter who is leaning in has a pretty good chance of getting out of the way, since an 88 mph pitch is slow enough that he has time to dodge it. This situation will be counted as a brush-back pitch, even though the batter was leaning in when the pitcher threw inside. In contrast, a pitcher who can throw the ball 95 miles an hour is likely to hit a batter who is leaning in because the batter probably will not have a chance to get out of the way. Continue, for a moment, to consider inside pitches to batters who lean in. As a pitcher's velocity increases, more pitches will be counted as hit batsmen, and fewer will be counted as brush-back pitches. Although the model predicts that brush-back pitches will decline when velocity increases, I cannot meaningfully look at this relationship. I cannot, because additional velocity may just be capturing a transfer from brush-backs to hit batsmen. The way out of this problem is to look, instead, at the theoretical model's prediction that a pitcher with more velocity will throw at a batter less often. That is, I can measure throw-ats instead of brush-backs and have a meaningful theoretical prediction. Let throw-ats equal brush-backs plus hit batsmen. The game theoretic model predicts that the pitcher will throw at fewer batters as velocity increases, while the standard crime model would assume that the pitcher's throw-ats would remain unchanged and the batter would respond by leaning in less often.

Second, velocity also influences throw-ats in a way not captured by the theoretical model. There is a trade-off between control and pitch speed. When compared to a pitcher who throws the ball at 88 miles an hour, a pitcher who can throw 96 miles an hour is more likely to have a pitch get away from him. This errant pitch may be counted as a hit batsman or a brush-back, even though the intent to throw inside was not there. This effect is illustrated in Figure 20.1 by the upward sloping line labeled Wild. The Wild curve measures the total throw-ats tossed due to lack of control. The y axis measures throw-ats and the x axis measures velocity. As velocity increases, a pitcher will have more errant pitches, and thus more throw-ats, so the curve slopes upward.

The other effect of velocity on throw-ats is the important effect in this discussion. As the theoretical model shows, a pitcher who can throw a ball faster will want to waste fewer pitches by throwing inside. This effect is represented by the downward sloping line labeled "Saved Policing Effort." This line represents the number of throw-ats a pitcher decides against throwing at each velocity. Note that the downward sloping "Saved Policing Effort" line gets steeper as velocity increases. To see why, consider Figure 20.2, which, for each pitcher in the 2007 season, shows the scatter plot of: (1) the percentage of a season's pitches that are throw-ats, and (2) the average velocity of the pitcher's fastball during the season. This data has the largest concentration of observations near the mean, which implies that many

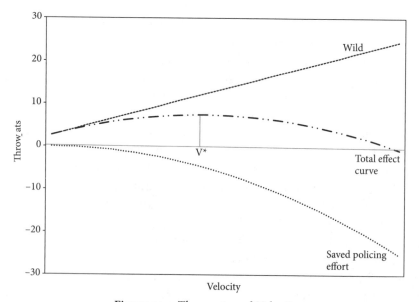

Figure 20.1 Throw-ats and Velocity.

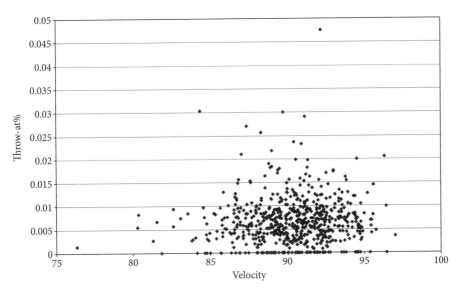

Figure 20.2 Scatterplot of Throw-at %.

pitchers can add one more mile an hour to their velocity if mean velocity is taken as the starting point. However, fewer and fewer pitchers can add a mile to their velocity as the starting point increases past the mean. This suggests that batters see few very fast pitchers, and so they have less practice getting away from their inside pitches. These very fast pitchers should be able to get away with throwing fewer inside pitches.

In Figure 20.1, the total effect of velocity on throw-ats can be found by adding the "Saved Policing Effort" and the "Wildness" curves to form the "Total Effect" curve. This is a concave curve. It also matches the shape found in Figure 20.2. In Figure 20.1, after the velocity V*, the Total Effect curve is downward sloping, which is the relationship predicted by the theoretical model. After V*, the "Saved Policing Effort" relationship is strong enough to overcome the Wildness factor that obscures the relationship that I am interested in.

My model accounts for the difference in throw-ats between the leagues in Figure 20.3. There is a downward sloping "Saved Policing Effort" for each league. The American League curve is above the National League curve to capture the increased number of beanballs that the literature suggests will occur in the American League. The two "Saved Policing Effort" curves also have different slopes. The National League curve is steeper, suggesting that a National League pitcher is more likely to avoid wasting a pitch when his velocity increases. The National League pitcher will want to avoid pitching inside because of the retribution that pitchers face in this league. Articles by Goff et al. (1997, 1998), Bradbury and Drinen (2007), and Bradbury (2006) suggest that pitchers in the American League are more likely to try to hit batters than a similar pitcher in the National League. They attribute this difference to the designated hitter rule in the American League. A pitcher in

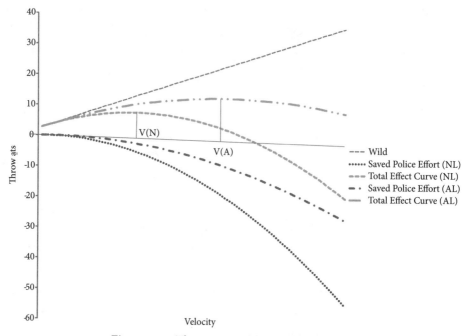

Figure 20.3 Throw-ats and Velocity by League.

the National League who hits a batter must come up to bat and face possible retribution from the other team's pitcher. In contrast, the American League pitcher never has to take a turn at bat, so he will not be the player facing the retribution.[5] Because the National League pitcher faces the full cost of throwing a beanball, he is more likely to avoid throwing inside pitches when extra velocity allows.

The Total Effect curves suggest that there will be more throw-ats in the American League for any level of velocity. They also suggest that velocity will start to have a negative impact on throw-ats at a lower velocity in the National League. The upcoming results section will present estimates of the two concave functions for Total Effects.

4. Model and Data

I estimate the model below[6] on data from the 2007 Major League Baseball season. The data[7] is reported by season totals for each pitcher. There are 642 observations.[8] Summary statistics appear in Table 20.5.

$$\text{Throw-ats}_i = f(\# \text{Pitches}_i, \text{Velocity}_i, \text{Pitcher Quality}_i, \text{Situation}_i)$$

The dependent variable is throw-ats by pitcher i in the 2007 season. Throw-ats are brush-back pitches plus hit batsman. Previous research has only considered hit batsmen because brush-back data did not exist until the 2007 season. Stats LLC, the company that collects data for ESPN, collects certain variables for a single year. For instance, they collected the number of broken bats one year. In 2007, at my suggestion, they collected brush-back data. Because previous

Table 20.5 Summary Statistics

Variables	Statistic	MLB	NL	AL
Throw-ats	Mean	7.43	6.997	7.96
	Min	0	0	0
	Max	54	38	54
Throw-at %	Mean	0.00659	0.00611	0.00719
	Min	0	0	0
	Max	0.0476	0.0303	0.04762
H.B.	Mean	2.72	2.70	2.755
	Min	0	0	0
	Max	19	16	19
(H.B. / Pitches)	Mean	.00265	0.00255	0.00281
	Min	0	0	0
	Max	0.0303	0.0303	0.01818
Brush-backs	Mean	4.7087	4.29	5.20
	Min	0	0	0
	Max	42	30	42
(Brush-back / Pitches)	Mean	0.00394	0.00356	0.004386
	Min	0	0	0
	Max	0.0476	0.02	0.047619
Pitches	Mean	1,108.04	1,092.55	1,127.21
	Min	22	22	25
	Max	3,691	3,691	3,635
Velocity	Mean	90.29	90.097	90.54
	Min	76.34	81.31	76.34
	Max	96.99	96.43	96.99
(Starts / Games)	Mean	0.365	0.3700	0.3713
	Min	0	0	0
	Max	1.0	1.0	1.0
(Saves / Games)	Mean	0.03296	0.0315	0.03558
	Min	0	0	0
	Max	0.7231	0.7231	0.6522

(continued.)

Table 20.5 (*Continued.*)

(SO/ OATBAT)	Mean	0.1919	0.1944	0.1891
	Min	0.0208	0.05263	0.0208
	Max	0.5556	0.5556	0.4098
(BB / OATBAT)	Mean	0.1032	0.1008	0.1044
	Min	0	0	0.0216
	Max	0.625	0.6250	0.3571
/Run Difference/	Mean	0.2674	0.2867	0.2553
	Min	0	0	0
	Max	2.5	2.5	1.5038
# observations		642	336	282

Variable definitions appear in a data appendix. In this table the abbreviations are as follows: HB is hit batsmen, SO is strikeouts, BB is base on balls, OATBAT is opponent at bats.

researchers only had access to data on hit batsmen, these scholars were able to observe less than half of the intentionally thrown inside pitches. Pitchers throw at batters 6.59 times for each thousand throws; 2.65 of these inside pitches are hit batsmen, and 3.94 are brush-backs. Therefore, pitchers throw brush-backs 48.7 percent more often than they hit a batter. During the course of the season, on average, each pitcher throws at 7.43 batters. The data is count data, so the model is estimated with a Poisson regression, as well as other techniques designed for count data.

Throw-ats cannot be meaningfully compared across pitchers because the number of throws to the plate varies between 22 and 3,691. For instance, a pitcher who hurls 7 throw-ats out of 22 throws is behaving very differently from a pitcher who hurls 7 throw-ats out of over 3,000 throws. In order to facilitate a comparison, this paper will analyze the rate of throw-ats, instead of the actual number. To do this, I take the log of number of throws by a pitcher. When I estimate the model, the coefficient should close to one.

Velocity is the main independent variable that can test my theory. It captures the punishment a batter receives if he is hit by a pitch. A faster pitch hurts more. The variable is the average velocity of a pitcher's fastball during the course of a season. The estimated model includes velocity, and velocity squared, in the equation, so it will be possible to estimate the concave relationship discussed in the previous section.

Velocity may have another influence on the number of inside pitches thrown. A fast pitcher may not have to worry about keeping the batter from leaning into the pitch, since the batter may have difficulty hitting his pitch no matter where it is thrown. Therefore, the fast pitcher will not have to throw as many inside pitches to keep the batter from leaning in. The empirical model accounts for this with *Pitcher Quality*, a vector of two variables, which serve as control variables. Collectively, these variables will hold constant the variation in throw-ats that is due to the ability of the pitcher. The estimate of the influence of velocity on the number of throw-ats will be made holding constant the effect of *Pitcher Quality*.

The first *Pitcher Quality* variable is the percentage of opponent batters that the pitcher struck out. The second variable is the percentage of opponent batters that the pitcher walked.[9] One can assume that high-quality pitchers will throw more strikeouts, and give up fewer walks.

Situation represents a vector of three variables that measure a pitcher's cost from throwing inside. A pitcher will be more likely to throw inside when the cost is low. The first variable is /Run Difference/. This is the absolute value of the average run support a pitcher receives per inning minus the average earned runs the pitcher gives up per inning. When /Run Difference/ is large, the cost of throwing inside is low. The second variable is the percentage of games pitched in which a pitcher has a save. The final variable is the percentage of games in which he played that he started. A starter will be very interested in enforcing that the batter does not lean in because he pitches so regularly. Also, because he pitches in the beginning of the game, the team often has plenty of time to catch up if the wasted pitch has a bad result for the pitcher. Contrastingly, pitchers who come in save situations usually pitch in the last inning of close games. Wasted pitches thrown inside are very costly here because a single base runner could be instrumental in a defeat.

Table 20.5 also lists the summary statistics for pitchers who played exclusively in the National League, as well as those pitchers who played exclusively in the American League. It is interesting to note that the rate of throw-ats, the rate of hit batsmen, and the rate of brush-backs are all higher in the American League. The rate of hit batsmen in 2007 is 10.2 percent higher in the American League. This is in line with data from earlier years. Goff, Shughart, and Tollison (1997) report that between 1973 and 1990, American League batters were between 10 percent and 15 percent more likely to be hit than National League batters. Goff et al. (1997, 1998), Bradbury and Drinen (2007), and Bradbury (2006) attribute the higher rate of hit batsmen in the American League to the low cost that American League pitchers face when they hit a batter. Because American League pitchers do not bat, they do not face retaliation after hitting a batter with a pitch. One pitcher cannot hit another pitcher with the ball in this league. This lower cost makes American League pitchers more willing to hit batters with a pitch.

5. RESULTS

As a starting point, I estimate the model with a Poisson regression on (1) the data set of National League pitchers, and (2) the data set of American League pitchers. Column 1 of Table 20.6 presents the results from the National League data,

Table 20.6 Throw-at Equation for National League

	National League		American League	
	Poisson	Poisson Hurdle	Poisson	Poisson Hurdle
Count Model				
Constant	−33.42 (−1.94)	−38.029 (−3.23)	−24.13 (−2.00)	−26.11 (−3.09)
% Games Started	−0.0264 (−0.40)	−0.0174 (−0.31)	0.180 (2.41)	0.215 (3.52)
% Strikeouts	−1.045 (−2.33)	−1.05 (−3.47)	−0.648 (−1.44)	−0.411 (−1.29)
% Base on Balls	0.725 (1.09)	0.734 (1.35)	1.409 (2.12)	1.263 (2.54)
Log (# Pitches)	1.111 (24.02)	1.10 (28.84)	0.958 (19.75)	0.916 (20.90)
% Saves	−0.581 (−2.28)	−0.257 (−1.15)	−0.182 (−0.75)	−0.124 (−0.69)
Velocity	0.597 (1.55)	0.707 (2.67)	0.389 (1.45)	0.440 (2.33)
Velocity2	−.0032 (−1.48)	−0.0039 (−2.59)	−0.0019 (−1.29)	−0.0022 (−2.10)
/Run Difference/	0.183 (1.24)	0.217 (1.67)	0.210 (1.43)	0.264 (2.32)
Probit Equation				
Constant	−5.12 (−6.81)	−4.032 (−4.63)		
Log(# Pitches)	1.069 (7.81)	0.989 (5.68)		
% Saves	−2.34 (−2.63)			
% Strikeouts		−3.01 (−1.69)		
L.L.F	−844.72	−839.23	−746.35	−742.62

Numbers in parenthesis are t-statistics. The National League data set has 336 observations and the American League data set has 282 observations.

and column 3 presents the results from the American League data. The separate estimates seem to be the appropriate approach. Using the log-likelihoods from the separate estimates, as well as one from an estimate on the combined data set,[10] one can reject, at conventional levels, the hypothesis that the data set should be combined.[11]

The Poisson model assumes that the conditional variance and conditional mean are equal. However, even when this assumption is violated, this estimation technique is often still worth reporting since it produces consistent results, as long as the model is correctly specified. In practice, the conditional variance is often larger than the conditional mean, in which case the Poisson model has over-dispersion. Indeed, a test proposed by Cameron and Trivedi (1998) suggests that there is over-dispersion in both reported Poisson estimates.[12]

Cameron and Trivardi (1998) note that over-dispersion will cause extra zeros in a data set. Figure 20.4 shows a histogram for each league of the percentage of pitches that are throw-ats for each pitcher. The distribution tails off on either side of the averages (.007 in the American League, and .006 in the National League), then it spikes at zero. Cameron and Trivedi (1998) argue that a large mass of zeros may be due to the data being generated from two-step decision processes. In this case, a pitcher may first make a decision of whether or not to try to keep the batter

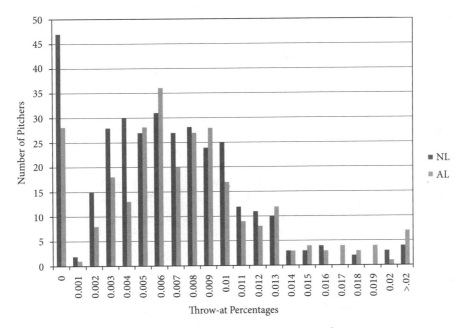

Figure 20.4 Histogram of Throw-at Percentage by League.

from crowding the plate. A pitcher who will make only 50 pitches in a season may not worry about trying to stop a batter from leaning into pitches. The pitcher will not be facing this batter again (or even enough other batters) to reap the gains from his enforcement activity. In contrast, a pitcher who throws 1,000 pitches in a season is willing to risk hitting a batter today, allowing a runner to reach first, so that batters do not lean into his pitches in the future. In the second step, those pitchers who decide that they are willing to throw inside have to decide whether they actually will throw inside. Therefore, the zeros in the data set are a mixture of zeros generated by pitchers who would never throw inside, and zeros generated by pitchers who would throw inside, but decided against it.

This two-step process can be estimated with a Hurdle Poisson model.[13] Two equations are estimated. A Probit model estimates the probability of a non-zero outcome. In this case, it estimates the probability that a pitcher throws inside even once. Next, a truncated Poisson model is estimated to explain the non-zero outcomes. As a starting point, I estimate the two steps of the Poisson Hurdle model. In both equations I use all of the right-hand side variables from the simple Poisson estimation in column one. Next, I removed the insignificant variables from the probit equation, and re-estimate the model. The results are reported in columns 2 and 4 of Table 20.6. Vuong statistics, which allow us to test the Poisson model against the Hurdle Poisson, are indeterminate. Positive values suggest the hurdle specification and negative values favor the Poisson specification. The values are 1.09 in the American League and 1.04 in the National League. However, these statistics are evaluated against a standard normal distribution, so neither specification is supported by a statistic that reaches a conventional level of significance. The positive numbers favor the hurdle specification more than the Poisson specification. However, there is another approach available to test for hurdle effects. A complementary log log hurdle model, with the same regressors in both the binary and count equations, can also be used to compare the Poisson and the Poisson hurdle estimates. A likelihood ratio test easily rejects, at the .01 level, the Poisson estimate in favor of the Poisson hurdle estimate in both the National (chi squared statistic = 12.20) and American League (chi squared statistics = 11.30) estimates.

The coefficients of primary interest are the velocity terms. Likelihood Ratio tests easily reject the hypothesis that the two velocity terms are jointly insignificant in explaining throw-ats.[14] In all four estimates, the velocity coefficient is positive and the squared term is negative. This specification can capture the two opposing effects of velocity on throw-ats. To gauge separate marginal effects of velocity, I consider a representative pitcher and use the estimated coefficients from the two hurdle models. This pitcher's attributes are considered at the means of the National League data set. Table 20.7 summarizes these marginal effects. First consider the influence of velocity on wildness. In either league, wildness causes a pitcher to throw between 1.5 to 2 more inside pitches for each extra mile an hour on the velocity of his throws.[15]

The negative coefficient on the velocity squared term represents a pitcher choosing not to waste as many inside pitches as his velocity increases. The theoretical model predicted that the sign on this term would be negative. The estimates suggest that the number of purposeful inside pitches will decrease at an increasing rate as velocity increases. However, some of this decrease in inside pitches may occur because the pitcher threw additional inside pitches by mistake due to wildness, so he does not need to throw as many inside pitches on purpose. Generally, this reduction in purposeful inside pitches offsets the increased inside pitches that come with wildness. However, eventually the reduction in purposeful inside pitches becomes a greater effect than the increase in such pitches due to wildness. In the National League, once a pitcher can throw 91.77 miles an hour, an increase in velocity decreases the number of inside pitches he throws on purpose by more than it increases the number of inside pitches he throws due to wildness. In the National League, 97 out of 336 (29 percent) pitchers throw faster than 91.77 miles an hour.

The net effect of velocity on throw-ats in the National League also appears in Table 20.7. If a pitcher can throw 92 miles an hour, he will reduce his throw-ats by 0.56 percent if his velocity increases to 93 mph. The effect becomes progressively larger. A pitcher who can throw the ball 95.43 mph will throw inside 3.14 percent less often if he can add one mile per hour to his pitches. This would represent an increase in speed to match the fastest pitcher in the National League, who throws 96.43 miles an hour.

Interestingly, velocity causes throw-ats to increase in the American League until the speed of 98.84 miles an hour is reached. However, since the top speed in this league is 96.99 mph, no pitchers in this league will reduce throw-ats as velocity

Table 20.7 Marginal Effects of Velocity

Vel	Throw-ats	1)	2)	3)
National League				
90	7.287	0.99%	2.027	−2.007
91	7.359	0.20%	2.027	−2.023
92	7.374	−0.56%	2.027	−2.039
93	7.333	−1.32%	2.027	−2.054
94	7.236	−2.07%	2.027	−2.070
95	7.086	−2.83%	2.027	−2.086
96	6.885	−3.57%	2.027	−2.102
97	6.639			
95.43	7.005	−3.14%	2.027	−2.093
96.43	6.785			
91.77 maximum number of throw-ats				
American League				
90	7.825		1.552	−1.496
91	8.121		1.552	−1.502
92	8.390		1.552	−1.509
93	8.630		1.552	−1.516
94	8.838		1.552	−1.523
95	9.010		1.552	−1.529
96	9.145		1.552	−1.536
97	9.241			
98.84 maximum number of throw-ats				

Throw-ats calculated at mean of variables for National League Players, as well as the indicated velocity. Each variable mean is multiplied by the coefficient from the Hurdle equation. These products are summed, and then an exponential is taken of the sum.

1) The percentage change in throw-ats when a pitcher can throw one mile an hour faster.
2) Extra throw-ats due to wildness when a pitcher can throw one mile an hour faster. This is found by taking the exponential of the coefficient for velocity.
3) Extra throw-ats due to "Saved Policing Effort" when a pitcher can throw one mile an hour faster. This is found by multiplying the coefficient for velocity squared by velocity squared, in time period one and in time period two, then difference the first product and the second product, then take the exponential of this difference.

decreases. That is, the influence of wildness is greater than the influence of the pitcher trying to avoid wasting pitches. However, velocity still has a negative influence on the number of purposeful inside pitches thrown; it is just that this effect is not as great as the wildness effect.[16]

The estimates suggest that there are important differences between the leagues. As pitch speed increases one mile an hour, a pitcher in the National League throws about 0.5 fewer inside pitches on purpose than his American League counterpart. The fear of retribution makes National League pitchers more eager to take advantage of better velocity by throwing fewer inside pitches. The coefficients in the model also suggest that pitchers respond to the cost of wasting pitches. American League starters are more likely to throw inside because they pitch early in the game, when there is plenty of time to make up for the damage done by hitting a batter and putting him on base. On the other side of the spectrum, in the National League, as a pitcher has more saves, he is less willing to waste a pitch. These pitchers usually come into the game when the game is close and in the last inning. These pitchers have little margin for error and are not as willing to bear the cost of wasting a pitch.

6. Calibration of Model

Next, consider the largest possible influence that velocity has on the number of throw-ats in the data set examined. Consider a representative National League pitcher whose values for the independent variables are taken at the means. Let his velocity be 91.77 miles an hour. Remember that at a lesser speed, velocity added to throw-ats, and at a greater speed, velocity reduced the number of these inside pitches. At 91.77 miles an hour, the predicted number of throw-ats is 7.376. The mean number of pitches is 1092.55, so the pitcher will throw inside with a probability $(1-a)$ of 0.006751 (7.36/1,092.55). Therefore, a will equal 0.993249. Suppose that one can use the average rate of throw-ats, of brush-backs, and of hit batsmen to determine what happened to inside pitches. Table 20.5 suggests that 41.7 percent of the inside pitches are hit batsmen (0.00255/.00611), and 58.3 percent of inside pitches are brush-backs. If all batters who lean into a pitch are hit when there is an inside pitch, and all those who take a normal stance take a ball on an inside pitch, we know that y must equal .58 and $(1-y)$ must equal .42. Table 20.8 presents the probability of each outcome occurring for these values of a and y.

Next, suppose the representative pitcher's velocity increased to 96.43, to match the speed of the fastest pitcher in the National League. I find the predicted number of throw-ats and calculate the rate of inside pitches. $(1-a)$ drops from 0.6751 percent to 0.6210 percent (6.785/1092.55). The batter's probability of leaning in will not change. The numbers in brackets represent the probabilities of each outcome occurring. It is still 41.7 percent. The chance of a batter getting beaned with the ball dropped 8.01 percent, and the chance of a pitcher throwing a brush-back pitch also dropped by 8.01 percent. The chance that the batter could lean in without getting hit increased by 0.054 percent. Also, a normal stance and normal pitch occurred 0.054 percent more often as well.

In sum, the greater penalty allowed by an increased velocity caused no change in a batter's (criminal's) decision to lean in (commit a crime). The batter leans into the

Table 20.8 Plate Appearance Game Hitter

		Normal Stance (y = 0.582629)	Lean-in (1 − y) = 0.417371
Pitcher	Pitch Normally (a=0.993249)	0.578696	0.414553
	(When a=0.99379)	[0.579011]	[0.414779]
	Throw Inside (1 − a)=0.006751	0.003933	0.002818
	(When (1 − a) = 0.006210)	[0.003618]	[0.002592]

pitch 41.7 percent of the time, regardless of pitch velocity. Counterintuitively, increased velocity led to leaning in (crime) being successful more often. Velocity also allowed fewer resources (inside pitches) to be used to prevent leaning in (criminal activity).

7. DISCUSSION

While many people care about sports, the results in this paper are important if they generalize to criminal decisions outside of baseball. Baseball was simply the natural laboratory that I used to test the theory. The availability of reliable data in baseball makes it well suited as a testing ground for economic theories. The findings in this paper apply most directly to cases when there is private policing. The empirical test in this paper was conducted in a situation where there was no central authority. The punishment and the policing were done privately by the pitcher. The umpire does not throw a batter out of the game for leaning into a pitch.

Next consider how well the results generalize to crime and public policing. Interestingly, pitchers threw 0.611 percent of their pitches inside in the National League and 0.719 percent of their pitches inside in the American League. Consider the analogy to crime again. Each pitch is productive activity, and each inside pitch is police activity meant to deter crime. Baseball pitchers and the different levels of government each devote about the same level of resources to policing criminals and batters. In the United States during 2005, $94 billion dollars were spent on police.[17] and GDP was $12.4 trillion, so a 0.76 percent share of GDP was spent on police in the United States. Because the allocation of police effort and inside pitches is so similar, exogenous changes in baseball may give some insight into how our police force will react to changes in policy.

This chapter can make a contribution to the scholarly debate on the effectiveness of criminal punishments in deterring crime. To date, most empirical research has failed to find a link between the severity of punishment and crime rates.[18, 19, 20] Gogger (1991) finds that increasing the severity of the punishment does not have a significant deterrent effect; rather, he finds that increasing the certainty of the penalty is a more effective way to deter crime. In reviews of the literature, Dobb and Webster (2003) and Bushway and Reuter (2008) both note that the overwhelming empirical evidence suggests that the severity of a criminal sentence does not have a deterrent effect. Dobb and Webster (2003) suggest that some researchers, particularly economists (as opposed to criminologists), have clung to a belief in deterrence, despite the evidence, because deterrence is intuitively appealing, and because it is a prediction derived from a rational choice framework. The model in this chapter provides an alternate model that is written in the rational choice framework. However, this model explains why deterrence may not be effective—namely, because an increase in criminal punishment may lead to an offsetting decline in police effort.[21] The model in this chapter has the advantage of being a rational choice model, as well as being consistent with the findings in the literature.[22]

Second, the empirical work in this paper, if applicable to a wider scope of policing activities, suggests that the drop-off in police efforts should get more pronounced as the punishments continue to increase. An extremely harsh penalty, like capital punishment, may cause a large drop-off in policing effort. This approach offers another explanation of why capital punishment, a very severe penalty, may not effectively reduce the crime rate.[23]

There are policy implications to my work. In order to obtain a drop in criminal activity, a larger punishment may have to be accompanied by steps to reduce police shirking. For instance, the police often have Special Forces to deal with mobsters and gang members. These are steps to prevent a reduction in policing effort, and may allow the tough penalties to be effective.

While this chapter provides an interesting first step in exploring the implications of game theoretic analysis on the deterrent effects of punishments, it is only a first step. Further research needs to examine these insights outside of the realm of baseball. The next step is to capture the responsiveness of police effort to penalties for various different types of criminal activities. My results will be most relevant for crimes where police would like to, or would be able to, save policing effort or shirk their policing duty. Police shirking may mean different things for different types of crimes, or in different environments. In developing countries a shirking policeman may take a nap. In the war on drugs, a policeman may shirk by taking bribes. Shirking may just entail working slower than normal, or avoiding more risk than usual. For private policing, saving policing effort just allows a person to go about his business and spend less time trying to prevent a crime from occurring.

8. SOCIAL WELFARE CONSIDERATIONS

Economists have an unusual way of looking at the costs of robbery. They do not believe the actual amount taken is important, since the theft just reallocates wealth, resulting in no net loss to society.[24] An economist is unwilling to make the value judgment that it is better for the victim to have the stolen property, instead of the thief. To economists, the important costs of theft results from criminals and victims engaging in unproductive behavior. First, there is an opportunity cost of the criminal's time. He could have been making something new, instead of trying to steal something that has already been produced. Second, there are costs that law-abiding citizens take to protect themselves from theft. These efforts include buying locks, paying for police, and so on. These resources could have been redirected to productive activities.

A standard approach of the economics of crime is to assume that if the government increases the punishment of the bad behavior, some potential criminals will decide against committing a crime. The result is less crime (which is not a big concern for economists) and less unproductive behavior by criminals and victims (which is a big concern for economists). With less crime, the potential crooks will spend less time thieving, and the victims will feel that they need to use fewer resources to protect their wealth. Both groups are now free to substitute time or resources toward productive pursuits. The increase in punishment led to a decrease in the important and unimportant economic costs.

The game theoretic results suggest the following impact of increased penalties. In the case of crime that must overcome private policing efforts, fewer resources may be spent on private policing. However, in the case of crimes that must avoid detection by public police, citizens may need to spend additional resources to prevent crime, because successful crime has increased. On the other hand, there is a gain in social welfare because the police will have to spend fewer resources once the criminal penalty increases.

9. CONCLUSION

The baseball analogy is convenient because Major League Baseball generates a wealth of statistics that can readily be used to test economic theories. These theories would be harder to test using actual social statistics. These statistics have many problems; for example, crime statistics are often too low since many victims do not report crimes. Because so much of baseball is recorded in statistical format, it provides a useful starting ground to test theories before trying to see if the results hold outside of baseball.

The game theory approach has not been applied to a game where (1) policing effort and criminal effort are the choice variables, and (2) the increase in criminal penalties is an exogenous shock. The existing literature follows Becker (1968), who assumes that police enforcement efforts stay constant when a legislature or executive decides to increase the penalty.[25] This chapter uses the batter-pitcher competition in baseball as an analogy for crime. The batter, who leans into the pitch to better reach the outside portion of the plate, is the criminal in this analogy. The pitcher wants the batter to stand up straight in the batter's box. The pitcher throws an inside pitch to try to catch the batter if he leans into the pitch. Inside pitches are the policing effort expended by pitchers. The batter is punished if caught leaning into a pitch by the pain he feels when hit by the pitch.

Using this analogy, this chapter develops a mixed-strategy game theoretic model. The model uses a pitcher's average fastball velocity to measure the cost to the batter of being hit by a pitch. The game theoretic model predicts that a pitcher who can throw with greater velocity will have to waste fewer inside pitches to keep a batter from leaning into a pitch. It also predicts that the batter will not respond to the greater punishment he faces from being hit by the ball. Using a unique data set of all inside pitches (both brush-back pitches and hit batsmen) thrown by each pitcher during the 2007 Major League Baseball season, I find that when a National League pitcher increases his average fastball velocity in a season from 92 to 96 miles an hour, he will throw inside 8.01 percent fewer times. These results are consistent with the predictions derived from the mixed-strategy game theory model.

If the results in this chapter apply to other environments with both punishment and policing, the results have some policy implications. If the larger fine does not alter criminal behavior, but instead allows the police to reduce their policing effort, then it may be bad policy to increase criminal penalties. Hiring more effective or more dedicated police, changing the incentives for police, or coupling safeguards against police shirking with increased criminal penalties may all be better options than simply increasing criminal penalties.

This chapter serves another purpose as well. Most tests of a mixed-strategy equilibrium are performed in a laboratory. Chiappori, Levitt, and Groseclose (2002) note that "tests of mixed strategies in non-experimental data are quite scarce" (p. 1138). The papers that do exist have used sports to test whether decision makers play mixed strategies. Chiappori, Levitt, and Groseclose (2002), Palacios-Huerta (2003), and Coloma (2007) examine soccer penalty kicks, and all find evidence of mixed-strategy play. Walker and Wooders (2001), Hsu et al. (2007), and Klaussen and Magnus (2008) consider tennis serves, but do not reach a consensus about whether mixed strategies are played. McGarrity and Linnen (2010) use the pass / run decision in football to generate data for a test of mixed strategies outside the laboratory. These papers have a modest goal of using real-world data to test whether mixed strategy equilibriums exist in the decisions made during sporting events. However, these papers do not try to generalize the results to a policy question. My study tries to reformulate the approach of the economic study of crime by using a comparative static analysis of mixed-strategy equilibriums.[26]

NOTES

I would like to thank the following people for helpful comments: Tim Bisping, J. C. Bradbury, Mike Casey, Craig Depken, Ling He, Jac Heckelman, Bruce Johnson,

Courtney LaFountain, Ed Lopez, Marc Poitras, Bill Shughart, John Solow, Dan Sutter, and Bob Tollison.

1 Ritter, Lawrence S. The Glory of Their Times, New York: Perennial, 2002, p.274.

2 This result probably goes against conventional wisdom. The most feared brush-back pitchers, such as Bob Gibson, and Don Drysdale, all had good overpowering fastballs. However, the conventional wisdom may have been the result of a few exceptions to the rule, or simply because their bean balls hurt more and thus generated more discussion.

3 The preference ordering A,C,D,B provides the same result.

4 The batter will prefer to get a ball over the normal pitching / batting situation, since he will have a more favorable count for the next pitch. However, the ordering of o and m does not change the results of the model.

5 Trandel et al. (1998) and Levitt (1998) present another argument. They contend that the Designated Hitter Rule in the American League adds a good hitter to the lineup of American League teams, while the National League teams still have a weak hitting pitchers take their turn at bat. The cost of hitting a pitcher with the ball is high because the pitcher was an easy out. The cost of plunking a designated hitter is comparatively low since he was likely one of the best hitters on the team. They argue that the difference in the cost of hitting batters between leagues explains why there are more hit batsmen in the American League.

6 The independent variables in this model are based on, and draw heavily from, work by Bradbury and Drinen (2007).

7 All the data used to estimate the model was purchased with a research grant from Stats L.L.C. The data is proprietary and was purchased with a research grant for $2,500. Craig Wolf is the contact person at Stats L.L.C.

8 The data came in two files. The first file had pitcher's average velocity by pitch type. The second file had the remaining pitcher statistics. The first file had statistics for 664 pitchers. The second file had all of these pitchers plus Jeff Cirillo and Aaron Rakers. These two players are position players and are not included in the sample. Pitchers were also dropped from the sample unless they had at least one inning pitched, one strike out, and one base on balls. This left 642 pitchers.

9 I also estimated the model after adding an independent variable for opponent batting average. However, this variable was insignificant at conventional levels in the estimates, and these results are not reported.

10 In the Poisson estimate on the combined data set, the coefficients and t statistics for the velocity terms were as follows: velocity: 0.395 (1.85), and velocity squared: -0.0020 (-1.68). The t statistics appear in parenthesis.

11 The log likelihood from the Poisson estimate on the combined data set is 1,600.53. The log likelihood from the separate regressions is reported in Table 20.6. Equal coefficients in both estimates can be rejected at the .05 level with a likelihood ratio statistic of 18.94.

12 Cameron and Trivedi (1998) suggest two test statistics to test for over dispersion. Both are t-statistics. In the National League estimates, these statistics are 6.56, and 8.35, while in the American League these statistics are 4.89 and 6.02. See Greene (2003, p743) for a discussion.

13 I also tried to estimate the model with a Negative Binomial Hurdle model. However, in Limdep, this model failed to converge.

14 The Likelihood Ratio statistics are found from comparing the log likelihood functions when the estimates are made without the velocity terms with the log likelihood functions when the estimates are made as reported in Table 20.6. From left to right,

the likelihood ratio statistics are 9.96, 8.20, 26.84, and 25.62. The critical chi-squared value for two degrees of freedom is 5.99 for the .95 level.

15 The marginal effects were found by taking the exponential of: the coefficient of the velocity variable times one.

16 The data are season aggregates of each pitcher's performance, so there is no available data on opponent batting quality for each pitcher. However, as a way to try and remove the influence of variation of opponent batter quality, I estimate the model using data from pitchers who have started 10 or more games. Starting pitchers have to face the whole line up, so they have to face both the good and poor hitters. The number of weak batters a starting pitcher faces should average out over the course of a season. In the National League, there were 91 pitchers who started at least 10 games. I used a Poisson estimation since these pitchers throw enough pitches that there should not be hurdle effects (although hurdle estimates produces similar results). The velocity coefficients suggest a concave shaped relationship between velocity and the rate of throw-ats, just like the relationship found in Table 20.6. The peak of the function was 91.44 miles an hour. This is very similar to peak of the function (91.77 miles an hour) when the full data set is used in the National League. In the American League, there were 83 starters with 10 or more starts. Again, the Poisson estimates produced the predicted concave function. The function peaked at 95.07 miles an hour. This is less than the peak of 98.84 miles per hour found when the model is estimated on the full dataset from the American League. Therefore, when the model is estimated using only starting pitchers, in an effort to minimize the effect of variation in batter quality on the results, the estimates in the National League are very similar to those reported in Table 20.6. Also, the estimates in the American League allow the Saved Policing Effort Effect to overcome the Wildness Effect at a lower mile per hour.

17 See Expenditure National Estimates from The U.S. Bureau of Justice Statistics.

18 Previous research has had several hurdles to overcome in its attempt to isolate the deterrence effect of punishments. Currently, much of the literature has examined the link between the length of prison sentences and crime rates. However, this is really a joint test of the influence of incapacitation and deterrence on crime. Incapacitation is when a prisoner cannot commit a crime if he is in prison. See Kessler and Levitt (1999) on this point. In this article, the authors use sentence enhancements to isolate the influence of deterrence. The idea is that because enhancements are tacked on to the regular penalty, the incapacitation effect will not occur for several years and the short run effect on crime by enhancements will be exclusively due to deterrence. Also, see Erlich (1996) for a review of the deterrence literature. In baseball there is no incapacitation effect. A batter who is hit by a pitch can lean into the pitch when it is his turn to bat, and the next batter who comes to the plate can lean in if he wishes. These batters are not removed from the game for leaning into a pitch.

19 Another issue in the literature centers on questions of causation (see Levitt, 1996; Nagin, 1998). Do states have stiff punishments because of high crime rates? Or, do large penalties reduce the crime rate? Each of these variables is influenced by and influences the other variable. The debate has degenerated into arguments about statistical specification. The test in this paper has an advantage that average velocity of a pitcher's fastball can be considered an exogenous variable. A hurler's average pitch speed depends mostly on innate ability as well as training, and does not depend upon the number of times a pitcher plans to hit a batter.

20 Levitt and his coauthors are a notable exception. They have found evidence of deterrence (see articles already cited). Levitt's empirical work has sought to overcome

the causation problem, as well as overcome the problem of separating deterrence from incapacitation.

21 Other explanations exist for why an increase in penalties may lead to a high crime rate, rather than a lower crime rate. Kuziemko and Levitt (2004) suggest that an increase in penalties for drug crimes may disrupt a drug lord's property rights, leading to more competition among drug lords and potential drug lords and thus more violence. They also note that if drug sellers face larger penalties, the price of the drug will increase. A drug user with an inelastic demand for drugs may commit more crimes to pay the higher price.

22 Besides considering the deterrent effect of punishments in sports, several papers have used sports settings to test whether policing effort impacts crime. McCormick and Tollison (1984) and Depken and Wilson (2004) find an extra referee deters bad behavior by players in College Basketball and in the National Hockey League. Heckelman and Yates (2003) report that an extra referee in hockey did not deter a player from committing an infraction, but instead allowed a greater portion of infractions to be observed, and thus called, by the referee.

23 Further, the work on baseball may explain why stiff penalties have not reduced crime in many developing countries. Again, the harsh criminal penalties may cause more police shirking.

24 This statement should be tempered. There is a long run and short run distinction here. Economists recognize that in the long run an increase in robbery will diminish property rights, which in turn will lower economic growth.

25 Becker (1968) sought to examine the optimal policies to deter crime. In his model, the public had two choice variables which influenced the number of offenses committed. The society could 1) choose the probability that a criminal was caught and convicted (through expenditures on police and the court system), as well as 2) choose the punishment for those convicted. Becker was mostly concerned with the optimal mix of these choice variables. In my model, punishment is exogenously determined, and the optimization takes place in a two player game, not as a one player optimization exercise performed by Becker. In Becker's model, the partial derivative of offenses with respect to a change in the penalty is negative (equation 13, page 177). In my model, a chain rule type derivative will occur. An increase in penalties will decrease the chance of getting caught. This decreased chance of getting caught will increase the number of offenses by exactly enough to offset the decrease in offenses caused directly by an increase in the penalty.

26 After completing this study, I stumbled across Tsebelis (1989). This article presents the theoretical framework for a game between a person who may speed in his car and the police who have to decide enforcement effort. While I am used to seeing other social sciences borrow from economics, this is a case where economics can benefit from the political science literature. Economists have recently renewed their interest in the analysis of crime. Levitt's work, which is cited in this paper, has been an important reason for the renewed interest in crime among economists. However, the recent literature has not used the game theoretic model of Tsebelis (1989), or the one found in this chapter. Instead, the literature has focused on econometric specification issues. This study does differ from Tsebelis (1989) in that it provides an empirical test of the game theoretic model. There is a great need for future research that provides empirical tests of mixed-strategy play outside of a laboratory. There is also a need for empirical scrutiny of whether the game theoretic model of crime holds outside of the laboratory, as well as outside of the baseball diamond.

References

Becker, Gary (1968). Crime and punishment: An economic approach. *Journal of Political Economy*, 76: 169–217.

Bradbury, John Charles (2006). The designated hitter, moral hazard, and hit batters: New evidence from game level data. *Journal of Sports Economics*, 7: 319–329.

Bradbury, John Charles, and Douglas Drinen (2007). Crime and punishment in major league baseball: The case of the designated hitter and hit batters. *Economic Inquiry*, 45: 131–144.

Bushway, Shawn, and Peter Reuter (2008). Economists' contribution to the study of crime and the criminal justice system. Working paper.

Cameron, A. Colin, and Pravin Trivedi (1998). *Regression analysis of count data*. Cambridge, UK: Cambridge University Press.

Chiappori, P. A., S. Levitt, and T. Groseclose (2002). Testing mixed strategy equilibria when players are heterogeneous: The case of penalty kicks in soccer. *American Economic Review*, 92: 1138–1151.

Coloma, German (2007). Penalty kicks in soccer: An alternative methodology for testing mixed strategy equilibria. *Journal of Sports Economics*, 8: 530–545.

Depken, Craig, and Dennis Wilson (2004). Wherein lies the benefit of the second referee in the NHL? *Review of Industrial Organization*, 24: 51–72.

Doob, Anthony, and Cheryl Webster (2003). Sentence severity and crime: Accepting the null hypothesis. *Crime and Justice*, 30: 143–195.

Ehrlich, Isaac (1996). Crime punishment, and the market for offenses. *Journal of Economic Perspectives*, 10: 43–67.

Goff, Brian, William Shughart, and Robert D. Tollison (1997). Batter up! Moral hazard and the effects of the designated hitter rule on hit batsmen. *Economic Inquiry*, 35: 555–561.

Goff, Brian, William Shughart, and Robert D. Tollison (1998). Moral hazard and the effects of the designated hitter rule revisited. *Economic Inquiry*, 36: 688–692.

Heckelman, Jac, and Andrew Yates (2003). And a hockey game broke out: Crime and punishment in the NHL. *Economic Inquiry*, 41: 705–712.

Hsu, Shih-Hsun, Chen-Yin Huang, and Cheng-Tao Tang (2007). Minimax play at Wimbledon: Comment. *The American Economic Review*, 97: 517–523.

Kessler, Daniel, and Steven Levitt (1999). Using sentence enhancements to distinguish between deterrence and incapacitation. *Journal of Law and Economics*, 42: 343–363.

Klaassen, Franc, and Jan Magnus (2009). The efficiency of top agents: An analysis through service strategy in tennis. *Journal of Econometrics*, 148: 72–85.

Kuziemko, Iiyana, and Steven Levitt (2004). An empirical analysis of imprisoning drug offenders. *Journal of Public Economics*, 88: 2043–2066.

Levitt, Steven (1996). The effect of prison population size on crime rates: Evidence from prison overcrowding litigation. *The Quarterly Journal of Economics*, 111: 319–351.

Levitt, Steven (1998). The hazards of moral hazard: Comment on Goff, Shughart, and Tollison. *Economic Inquiry*, 36: 685–687.

McCormick, Robert E., and Robert D. Tollison (1984). Crime on the court. *The Journal of Political Economy*, 92: 223–235.

McGarrity, Joseph P., and Brian Linnen (2010). Pass or run: An empirical test of the matching pennies game using data from the National Football League. *Southern Economic Journal*. 76: 791–810.

Nagin, Daniel (1998). Criminal deterrence research at the outset of the twenty-first century. *Crime and Justice*, 23:1–42.

Palacios-Huerta, Ignacio (2003). Professionals play Minimax. *Review of Economic Studies*, 70: 395–415.

Ritter, Lawrence S. *The glory of their times*. New York: Perennial, 2002.

Trandel, Gregory, Lawrence White, and Peter Klein (1998). The effect of the designated hitter rule on hit batsmen: pitcher's moral hazard or team's cost benefit calculation? A comment. *Economic Inquiry*, 36: 679–684.

Tsebelis, George (1989). The abuse of probability in political analysis: The Robinson Crusoe fallacy. *American Political Science Review*, 83: 77–92.

Walker, Mark, and John Wooders (2001). Minimax play at Wimbledon. *American Economic Review*, 91: 1521–1538.

Appendix I: Variable Definitions

Velocity = Average velocity of a pitcher's fastball over the course of the 2007 season

brush-backs = Number of pitches thrown at batters that do not hit the batters

hit by pitches = Number of pitches thrown that hit the batter

Throw-ats = Hit by pitches + brush-backs

% Game Started = Games Started / Games Played

% Strikeouts = Strikeouts / Opponent at Bats

% Base on Balls = (Base on Balls—Intentional Base on Balls) / Opponent at Bats

pitches = Number of pitches thrown by a pitcher in a season

/Run Difference/ = The absolute value of (run support per inning—earned runs given up per inning)

## CHAPTER 21

ILLUSTRATIONS OF PRICE DISCRIMINATION IN BASEBALL

DANIEL A. RASCHER AND ANDREW D. SCHWARZ

1. INTRODUCTION

AFTER many years of overly simplistic pricing, pricing strategy in Major League Baseball has now evolved to recognize the complexity of the supply and demand factors for baseball tickets. Most important among these factors is the demand uncertainty that teams experience from game to game, often with a high degree of variation. There are many causes of this variation, such as the quality of the opponent or the day of the week. Perhaps the least understood factor is competition for fans' discretionary spending, yet in other industries this is of paramount concern when setting price. If an owner is lucky, there are capacity constraints (i.e., limited stadium seating) that prevent the team from satisfying total demand. Calling such a constraint lucky is ironic; owners of teams playing in smaller stadiums used to complain that they couldn't compete financially because they had fewer seats to sell, but times have changed, along with the economic model of a sports team. Now, team owners pine for smaller facilities with more amenities where they can charge higher prices for regular seats, club seats, and luxury suites, taking advantage of the excess demand that a small, high-quality venue can generate. For example, the new Yankee Stadium has a reduced seating capacity of 52,325 (including standing room) compared to the old stadium's capacity of 56,886.[1]

In general in a sports facility, the quality of each seat varies to such an extent that the best seat in the stadium can sell for twenty times the price of the worst seat. "Scaling the house" or pricing integrity (where prices are set with the goal of filling the stadium from the bottom up) is achieved by trial and error. This need for experimentation is especially strong when a team moves into a new stadium, where demand for each quality level of seat is more difficult to predict and where no history exists upon which to base a pricing decision. Such a situation arose in 2009 when the Yankees opened the new Yankee Stadium and found they had priced the first nine rows of seats substantially above the sell-out level, some as high as $2,625 for a single game! Games after opening day saw the first nine rows of some sections entirely empty. The team quickly cut many of the seat prices in half. This learning-by-doing aspect of pricing is typical in sports; baseball, with many games to learn from, can quickly reach equilibrium.

Adding to the complexity is the notion that fans are purchasing an array of products and services, not just a ticket. Fans pay for parking, concessions, and merchandise. All MLB teams generate additional revenues from some or all of these sources. Pricing a ticket involves understanding not only the attendance decisions of fans, but also how that ticket price might impact the purchase decisions of fans upon entering the stadium. It is typically in the franchise's interest to charge a lower ticket price if the club shares in these ancillary revenue streams than would be the case if the club cared only about ticket revenues (or was paid a fixed fee from a concessionaire for pouring rights).[2] This follows from the standard economics of multi-product firm pricing.

In fact, Krautmann and Berri (2007) find that a typical MLB team charges a price that is 56 percent lower than it would be otherwise, in order to bring more fans to the game and thus make more money at the concessions stand. Teams with large facilities face added pressure to discount (or even give away tickets for free) in order to fill the house. A full stadium adds to the fan experience, helps create future fans, adds to ancillary revenues, and helps satisfy sponsors (who want as many eyeballs noticing their sponsorship as possible, which in turn allows the team to charge the sponsor more). Moreover, an unsold ticket "expires" with the event itself and cannot be saved for sale at a later date, unlike the situation facing a durable goods company that can hold the product and sell it later. In this sense, a baseball franchise has similar economics to a hotel or airline in that the inventory is perishable. However, the short-run profit-maximizing decision to sell tickets cheaply (or give them away) can influence future demand because customers may become accustomed to giveaways or price discounts. This in turn may lower long-term profits, as in the vacation cruise and hotel industries, where last-minute discounting has become expected and price-sensitive consumers may delay their purchase decisions hoping for a discount.[3] Franchises fight this urge to discount, but it is much easier to resist if the team's stadium is smaller, lowering, or eliminating entirely the need to give away free tickets to ensure a sellout.

Recently, secondary (or resale) markets have grown in importance with StubHub and eBay leading the way. These online markets allow a fan or broker to sell a ticket (below, at, or even above face value) to a final purchaser who attends the game. Less formal secondary market sales, commonly called "scalping," have existed for baseball tickets for decades, and MLB has traditionally disapproved of ticket reselling. Team owners felt that the scalper was making money on a product from which only the franchise should benefit. They also feared being blamed if fans purchased counterfeit tickets through the secondary market. Nevertheless, when the Chicago Cubs saw how much money ticket brokers were making from Cubs tickets (whose games routinely sell out), the team experimented with the secondary market. The Cubs created its own broker and sold high-quality tickets directly to the secondary market rather than offering these for sale to the public at face value (essentially via an informal auction). While the Cubs suffered negative public relations and media coverage when it was revealed that the team was "scalping" its own tickets, nevertheless the experiment proved how lucrative the secondary market can be to a team with excess demand for its tickets. This may have contributed to MLB's new attitude toward resellers—MLB recently signed a deal with StubHub to formalize Baseball's relationship with the secondary market and make it easy for fans to resell their tickets online through the MLB web site.

At the same time that teams have embraced the secondary market, clubs have also begun to shift some of the secondary market revenues into their primary markets by introducing variable ticket pricing (VTP). Under VTP, a franchise charges a different price for the same seat at different games throughout the season, depending on an estimate of demand for each game, made prior to the start of the season. Usually, teams selected higher price levels for a key rivalry game, for the traditional popular days of the week or month, or for special events like July 4th, and lower prices for less popular games. As teams have become more comfortable with VTP, they have created as many as five different price levels throughout the season for a single seat (Rascher, McEvoy, Nagel, and Brown, 2007). An even more robust version of VTP is known as "dynamic pricing," in which teams use an auction mechanism or a daily calculation of demand to allow the price of all unsold tickets to rise and fall with demand, right up to the day of the game (as opposed to VTP, where prices are locked in at the start of the season based on estimated demand). The San Francisco Giants began this process for all of their tickets for the 2010 season (after experimenting with selected seats in 2009).

Essentially, the law of one price does not apply to baseball. Creative pricing strategies that have been in place in other industries, including second- and third-degree price discrimination, two-part tariffs, and dynamic pricing, are now being adopted by baseball franchise owners after many years of more simplistic pricing strategies. Indeed, much of the current wave of sophisticated baseball pricing is essentially what, for nearly a century, economists have been calling second-degree price discrimination.

2. PRICE DISCRIMINATION

Arthur Pigou is generally credited with first explaining in detail the economics of price discrimination and creating the commonly used taxonomy of first-, second-, and third-degree price discrimination.[4] Although to "discriminate" simply means to separate or differentiate, the term now carries a more common negative meaning related to the unfair treatment of a person based on the group or class to which that person belongs, rather than on merit. Economists, though, still use the word "discrimination" in the term "price discrimination" to mean charging a different price for the same or similar product to different market segments or customers, without any negative undertones.

Stigler (1987) defined price discrimination as occurring "when two or more similar goods are sold at prices that are different ratios to marginal costs." This helped handle the issue of the inclusion of transport costs leading to two different prices (because of different transport costs). It also creates a definition more suitable to the sort of price discrimination seen in sports, where every ticket sold differs from every other ticket on some dimension (e.g., different opponent; different day of the week; different section, row, or seat), or so two identical products are never sold. Traditional examples of price discrimination include first-, second-, and third-class tickets on trains,[5] senior or youth discounts for movies or food, matinee movie pricing, lunch pricing at restaurants, and the difference in pricing of hardcover versus paperback books.

Stigler's definition makes an important point: price discrimination, as practiced, typically does not involve identical goods, but rather goods or services that may be identical on many core dimensions, but which differ with respect to ancillary features. A narrow definition of price discrimination implies that different prices for any two *different* seats at a game does not constitute price discrimination because the quality of the seat location varies across the two seats. However, focusing on highly similar goods (rather than identical ones) creates a definition of price discrimination that is consistent with what is seen in sports, different prices for different seats.

Indeed, the need for price discrimination to go hand-in-glove with some form of product differentiation has been recognized from the start in economics (Phlips, 1981). The classic examples of price discrimination listed above do not involve identical goods. Seeing a movie during the day is a different product from seeing it at night (because of the time difference). The decision to buy a hardcover or paperback book involves products with different quality covers, but more importantly, involves a question of timing, since paperback books are typically only sold months after the release of the hardback. Clearly lunch and dinner differ in terms of timing, but also potential ambience and import (hence some of the success of the dating service "It's Just Lunch"). Yet, in all of these examples (including the example of two different tickets to see the same Red Sox game), while the products may differ on many dimensions, the core product is sufficiently similar, and the differentials in pricing are not purely related to the marginal cost of providing the ancillary dimensions. Indeed, in many cases, the cost of providing two differently priced sports ticket is identical.

Rosen and Rosenfeld (1997) show that any industry where marginal cost is less than average cost (as occurs in baseball) will tend to price discriminate. Also, Dana (2001) shows that demand uncertainty and price setting in advance (both occurring in baseball) under monopoly lead to price dispersion and price discrimination. As economic theory predicts, price discrimination is common in sports. For example, Shmanske (2004) comprehensively studies pricing at golf courses and finds that there are different prices based on the age of the golfer, the day of the week, time of day (twilight rates), whether the golfer is a resident of the local community (or resides outside of the area), and volume discounts. He shows that greater variability in prices results in increased profits.

Baseball, in particular, is filled with examples of price discrimination and, as Baade and Matheson (2006) point out, the growth in new baseball stadiums has provided more opportunities to price discriminate. For instance, the differences in regular and premium seating are magnified in new stadiums by providing premium ticket holders with access to clubs and restaurants and larger seats. Additionally, new stadiums tend to sell out more often, which may indicate that fans received higher consumer surplus attending games in these new facilities (as evidenced by the excess demand and prevailing prices leading to sellouts).

3. First-Degree Price Discrimination

Perfect or first-degree price discrimination is when a firm is able to charge each customer her willingness-to-pay (WTP). For many reasons, this type of pricing is not relevant to baseball (or any other industry), not the least of which is that a customer has no incentive to reveal her WTP to the seller. Theoretically, perfect price discrimination is actually welfare maximizing because the team would continue to sell tickets right up to the point where its incremental or marginal costs are equal to the price of the ticket. Indeed, as Phlips wrote in 1981, "generally, discriminatory prices will be required for an optimal allocation of resources in real life situations" (p. 1). Given the relatively low costs of selling an additional ticket, this would effectively sell out almost any stadium (given sufficient demand). In other words, because perfect price discrimination results in more of the product being sold, total welfare ends up higher, even though welfare is captured by the seller and none by the consumers. See Table 21.1 for a general taxonomy of price discrimination and examples in baseball.

Table 21.1 Taxonomy of Price Discrimination in Baseball

Level of Discrimination	Concept	Examples
First-Degree Price Discrimination	Charging each consumer his/her true reservation price	Mostly theoretical. Well-designed auctions can approximate first-degree price discrimination
Second-Degree Price Discrimination	Offering a menu of options and letting consumers self-select based on their preferences	Volume Discounts
		Family Plans
		Group Plans
		Bundled Pricing
		Season Tickets
		Mini-Plans
		All-You-Can-Eat
		Non-Price Promotions (e.g., Bat Day)
		Two-Part Tariffs
		Purchasing a Ticket then Concessions
		PSLs
		Quality Discrimination
		Multi-tier Pricing
		Variable Pricing
		Dynamic Pricing
		*Secondary (Resale) Markets**
Third-Degree Price Discrimination	Offering a menu of options but requiring proof of membership to access desirable pricing	Discounts to identifiable groups
		Senior Discounts
		Youth & Student Discounts
		Military Discounts

*Note that Secondary Markets are a form of second-degree price discrimination, where fans who value certainty will tend to pay face value in advance in the primary market, and fans who are willing to be flexible can often get discounted seats close to game time. Secondary markets can also distinguish consumers willing to give up time (to wait in line in a primary market) vs. those willing to spend more money (for popular tickets sold above face value in a secondary market.

However, secondary markets also work to make other forms of second-degree price discrimination work more effectively. For example, season tickets will tend to sell more quikcly when fans who value the bundle also know they can dispose of lower-value tickets within the bundle in a secondary market or can choose to sell one or two high-value tickets and consume the bulk of the bundle.

4. SECOND-DEGREE PRICE DISCRIMINATION

A more practical approach to price discrimination comes in the form of second-degree price discrimination. Second-degree price discrimination occurs when a seller offers consumers a menu of consumption options, each priced differently, and asks consumers to self-select their preferred categories. One common example of second-degree price discrimination is a volume discount, where a firm will offer one unit of a product for $5, but three units for $10. Consumers who value a lower price (even if they have to store excess units) will pay less per unit if they buy three at a time; consumers who prefer not to store the product will pay $5. The seller doesn't need to police who is given access to the discount; instead, the seller lets consumers sort themselves.

Second-degree price discrimination is well suited to many of the questions of baseball pricing because it is so flexible. One form of second-degree price discrimination that has been with baseball from its early days is the idea of multi-tiered pricing. Fans are well conditioned to pay one price for upper reserved tickets to a game and to pay more for box seats, and fans sort themselves out into categories based on their willingness to pay more for higher quality seats. This is the essence of second-degree price discrimination—the team offers a pricing menu and fans self-select their preferred combination of quality and price.

This example shows how useful it is to be flexible in recognizing that while a box seat to a game is not an identical product to an upper reserved seat at the same game, the two tickets sufficiently share the core product (in this case, attendance at a particular baseball game) that the price discrimination framework is useful for analyzing pricing, even if the products are clearly not identical on every dimension of quality.

Volume Discounts

Price discrimination in many industries involves discounts for volume purchases. These can often be tied to cost differentials, but when they are not, it is a form of price discrimination. Baseball teams typically will offer lower prices and an enhanced experience to a group willing to purchase tickets in bulk.[6] Teams may also create special events at their games, where respected members of the community (such as teachers or firefighters) are honored or where cultural groups are encouraged to attend and a group discount is offered.[7] Similarly, teams offer family plans that which provide a discount for two adults and two or more children from the same family. For example, the Arizona Diamondbacks offer "Family Fridays at Chase Field,"[8] and the St. Louis Cardinals offer an "Albert Pujols Family Pack."[9]

Bundled Pricing

Product bundling is the practice of offering multiple products for sale as one combined product. In baseball, season tickets are a bundled product because each ticket could be sold separately. Season tickets have been available for decades in MLB. Historically, season tickets were the same price (per ticket) as individual tickets for the same seat. The purchaser was guaranteeing a ticket for each game in the same seat as well as a guaranteed option to buy tickets to playoff games, should the team reach the post-season. Also, season ticket holders were guaranteed the same seat (or better) the following season. More recently, MLB season tickets often come with a per-game discount. For instance, the San Diego Padres in 2010 offered up to 35 percent off the single game ticket price when buying a full-season ticket in some seating locations.[10]

A more recent development is the partial season ticket, or mini-plan. For example, in 1993, the Milwaukee Brewers began selling 16- and 13-game ticket packages with themes such as Sunday games only or day games only. The franchise increased its full-season equivalent ticket package sales by 43 percent compared to the previous season (Howard and Crompton, 2003).

"Loaded" Ticket

There are a number of reasons to bundle two different products. These include leveraging one product in order to sell another product, realizing economies of scope that may exist across products, the provision of products that work together more seamlessly, or capturing more of the existing value in the marketplace that is lost from separately pricing two products. In professional baseball, the last of the above-listed reasons seems to be the impetus for offering an "all-you-can-eat" (AYCE) or "loaded" ticket that includes a seat to the game, all-you-can-eat concessions, and a parking pass.

If the willingness-to-pay (WTP) for tickets and food varies widely across consumers to the point at which some value the "experience" that includes concessions more than the game, and others value the game itself more than the concessions, then bundling for that reason alone can be more profitable. Bundling allows more of this joint value to be captured by the seller than if the items were sold separately. An optimal pricing strategy, called mixed bundling, accounts for this diversity of preferences by having some seats with a bundled ticket and other seats (the rest of the stadium) priced for the game alone with concessions sold separately. In total, this will capture more of the WTP of the entire fan base (which, it is assumed, has fans who are distributed across the spectrum between mostly preferring the game and mostly preferring the food and experience). Adams and Yellen (1976) show that mixed bundling will always dominate pure bundling.

Specifically, it turns out that bundling is most effective when there is a negative correlation between the values that the different customer types have for each item, for instance, if there is a group of pure baseball fans and a group who like to eat at the game. Both groups value both products within a "loaded" ticket, but each one has a different ranking of the importance of them. Bundling effectively lessens the degree of variation of the individuals' valuation of the product, thus allowing a better price to be chosen for the bundled product. This is why bundling works (Varian, 1989).

The St. Louis Cardinals (MLB) have offered these bundled tickets for over a decade, and recently increased the number of seats with the all-you-can-eat (AYCE) option to over 2,000. Most other teams limit their use of this pricing tactic to premium and club seats. However, clubs have recently begun offering these AYCE deals to lower-priced seats that typically have gone unsold. In 2007, the Los Angeles Dodgers (MLB) segregated a section of their $6–$8 bleacher seats and added AYCE concessions, raising the total ticket price to $35. This section, sponsored by convenience store retailer *am/pm* to emphasize the food and beverage aspect of the bundle, has resulted in the largest price increase of those analyzed in Table 21.2 (DeSchriver and Rascher, 2008).

The Atlanta Braves (MLB) recently offered two different AYCE packages. One, called "Ballpark Favorites," charges an additional $30 for all-you-can-eat from a limited menu that includes hot dogs, popcorn, soft drinks, chips, and so on, and another option called "Barbecue and More" offers barbecued food along with beer for an additional $60.

Non-price promotions, aimed at getting fans out to the ballpark, have a long tradition in baseball. Bat day and other non-price promotions are a form of bundled pricing where the customer (or just the first 15,000 customers, for instance) receive special merchandise, like a cap, bat, bag, or bobble head, along with their seat at the game. McDonald and Rascher (2000) showed that these types of promotions increased attendance by 14 percent, more than outweighing the cost of

Table 21.2 All-You-Can-Eat Tickets in MLB

Team	Seats	Ticket Price	Package Price	Difference (in $)	Difference (in %)
Atlanta Braves	1,000	$12	$30	$18	150%
Atlanta Braves	200	$32	$60	$28	88%
St. Louis Cardinals	2,010	N/A	N/A	N/A	N/A
Kansas City Royals	400	$22	$35	$13	59%
Los Angeles Dodgers	N/A	$7	$35	$28	400%
Baltimore Orioles	800	$25	$40	$15	60%
Texas Rangers	450	$23	$29	$6	26%
Average	810	$20	$38	$18	130%
Weighted Average					76%
Median	625	$23	$35	$17	74%

Note: The weighted average is weighted by the number of seats, so it does not include the Cardinals or Dodgers.

providing the promotions. In this case, product bundling worked quite easily. In fact, the Beanie Babies promotions in the late 1990s and early 2000s drew thousands of additional fans to each MLB game that offered special, limited edition, Beanie Babies stuffed toys.[11]

Two-Part Tariff

If the ticket and concessions purchases are unbundled (as opposed to the bundled "loaded" ticket described above), then this is more akin to a two-part tariff (Depken and Grant, 2011), where in order to purchases concessions, one must first purchase a ticket. In this view, an MLB team is a multi-product firm selling concessions, but only to customers who first purchase a ticket. Using data from 1991–2003, Depken et al. show that MLB teams engage in price discrimination that involves the trade-off between ticket and concessions pricing.

Personal Seat Licenses

A pure example of a two-part tariff is the personal seat license (PSL). PSLs are a fairly recent development, typically used by teams and municipalities as a way to help finance a new sports facility. High-demand fans (with enough income or wealth) are targeted and are sold a PSL, allowing them the right to then purchase season tickets each year, typically for as long as the stadium is used by the team. This is a form of a two-part tariff because in order to buy a season ticket, one must first purchase a PSL. It is a mechanism to help finance a facility's construction by capturing some of the additional consumer surplus up front (see Fort, 2003; and Leeds and von Allmen, 2002).

For example, if a fan values a season ticket at $2,000 per year, but is only charged $1,500 per year, then the net present value of the additional $500 going out 20 years (the expected useful life of the stadium) can be charged to the consumer up front. Of course, a franchise is not going to know each customer's exact WTP, but can come up with estimates. Leeds et al. suggest that PSLs allow the club to charge a competitive (or more competitive) price for the season tickets. This sells more tickets and removes some of the deadweight loss associated with monopoly power pricing. However, the club captures some of the consumer surplus via the PSL.

Quality Discrimination

As described by Tirole (1988), quality discrimination is the common means of putting price discrimination into practice. The formal economic analysis of quantity discrimination is the same for quality discrimination (i.e., the math laying out the benefits of pricing discounts based on volume different volume levels works identically for pricing which varies based on quality differences). Consumers have varying tastes for quality. The quality of the seat is used as a market segmentation device (similar to how BMW segments buyers with the 525, 535, and 545 series or how The Gap, Inc., uses Banana Republic, The Gap, and Old Navy as channels to target three different segments).

Multi-tiered Pricing

There are different schools of thought as to the breadth of the definition of price discrimination, and how price discrimination compares to price dispersion and multi-tiered pricing. For example, Fort (2003) explains that charging different prices by the time of day, day of week, and age of fans is price discrimination, but charging different prices for different seats at the same game or for different opponents over the season (VTP) is not price discrimination, because in his view, the latter products are sufficiently different to constitute distinct products. Moreover, because a fan can generally resell his or her ticket, true price discrimination is rarely possible, argues Fort, because effective price discrimination requires the ability to prevent arbitrage. To Fort, pricing baseball tickets based on quality differences is simply multi-tiered pricing (charging different prices for different goods from the same seller).

Yet, as Dupuit explained over a hundred and fifty years ago, offering different levels of quality is typically the mechanism that allows second-degree price discrimination to work, even with the possibility of arbitrage. Building the second-class train car with a roof and nicer amenities compared with the third-class train car helped nudge the higher income (or higher demand) passengers into the better seats. Certainly, the higher income passenger could purchase the less expensive ticket (directly or from a reseller), but the variation in quality of travel was used to encourage self-selection and thus sell tickets in each train car. Nineteenth-century trains were similar to a modern baseball stadium with more expensive, more comfortable seating closer to the action, with access to special clubs and/or food service at one's seat. While the product is different in a strict sense, nevertheless, the quality difference causes consumers on a different part of the demand curve to identify themselves by which level of quality they select. Fort's assertion is more relevant to third-degree price discrimination, where the exact same product is sold at different prices and reselling must be prevented to make discrimination effective. Second-degree price discrimination is much less vulnerable to arbitrage concerns.[12]

In addition to simply selling tickets, baseball teams also try to make sure the best seats, those nearest to the field, sell out even if the upper deck is not full, a process known as "pricing integrity." In order to achieve this, the team needs to "scale the house" to ensure that the differences in price between the lower- and upper-section seats result in high demand for the lower sections. In other words, the best seats need to feel like the better deal to enough fans that they prefer to spend more and get the high-quality seat, if given the chance. If too few fans see the good seats as the comparative bargain, the upper deck will fill up and the prime seats will go unsold.

Humphreys and Soebbing (2008) discuss how new baseball stadiums tend to show greater price dispersion. Price dispersion is simply the situation in which more than one price exists in the marketplace for the same product. This usually occurs when multiple sellers are selling a common product, but because it can also arise with a single seller, the concept of price dispersion overlaps with the concept of price discrimination. Using data from MLB, Humphreys et al. show that teams with more price dispersion (more price options on their menu) have higher attendances, all else equal. This raises total welfare because more seats are sold for a given demand. Newer facilities tend to have more prices available because new stadium designs accentuate differences among seating sections and also because historical precedent has made teams in older stadiums reluctant to completely revamp their prices.

Variable Ticket Pricing

Variable ticket pricing is a form of second-degree price discrimination, where games for which demand is expected to be higher have higher prices than low-demand games. Variable ticket pricing has been used in college athletics for years, much earlier than its adoption in professional sports. For instance, tickets to the "Big Game" between the University of California at Berkeley and Stanford have had higher prices (often twice as high) for that event than for the other football games of either team throughout the season for at least two decades. The phenomenon came much later to baseball. Starting in the early 2000s, a few MLB teams (e.g., Giants and Rockies) first implemented variable ticket pricing. The Rockies charged four different prices for the same seat based on the time of year, day of the week, holiday, or the quality of the opponent (as determined prior to the season). In 2004, a seat in the outfield pavilion ranged from $11 for a value game to $21 for a marquee game. In 2010, the outfield pavilion prices ranged from $18 to $50.

Technically, one could describe this as "intertemporal price discrimination" because while the core product (attendance at a given team's games) is the same, on the important dimension of time the products differ and consumers are asked to self-select. Instead, economists reserve the term "intertemporal price discrimination" for the phenomenon (common in durable goods like electronics), where prices to "early adopters" tend to be high, and prices are lower for less enthusiastic buyers who are willing to wait to purchase the product. Moreover, VTP doesn't just offer a choice between times; the opponent varies as well, which pushes right to the edge of the question of what is the core product and what is an ancillary dimension.

The theory of variable ticket pricing is straightforward, as described by Rascher et al. (2007). The revenue-maximizing price for any product varies as the demand for that product rises and declines. As shown in Figure 21.1, the solid line represents the average demand for an Atlanta Braves game in 1996. The price $13.06 (Point A, with an elasticity of –1.0) maximizes revenue and draws almost 36,000 fans. However, the dashed line shows the demand for opening day, which drew nearly 49,000 fans (Point B, with an elasticity of –0.73). If the same price of $13.06 was charged for opening day, then ticket revenues would have been about $640,000 for the game. If instead the price were raised to maximize revenues for this specific game, revenues would have been $655,000 at a price of $15.46 (Point C, with an elasticity of –1.0). The 18 percent price rise would increase ticket revenue by 2.5 percent.

Carrying this exercise out for all 30 MLB teams across their 81 home games would have resulted in an increase in ticket revenues of about 2.6 percent. While this is not a large increase in revenues, the increase in revenues translate almost directly to profit because there are virtually no additional costs associated with the adoption of variable ticket pricing. In a business like MLB, where profit margins are typically reported to be less than 10 percent (and often are negative), this strategy can result in double-digit increases in income for an MLB club. Rascher et al. expand their analysis to incorporate games that are sold out (where the true demand at the given prices is not known) as well as the impact of lower attendance (at a higher priced VTP game) on complementary concessions and merchandise revenues.

In two case studies of individual MLB clubs, Mondello and Rishe (2004) and Cabral (2010) each focus on the variable ticket pricing of the St. Louis Cardinals and New York Mets, respectively. Mondello et al. shows that between

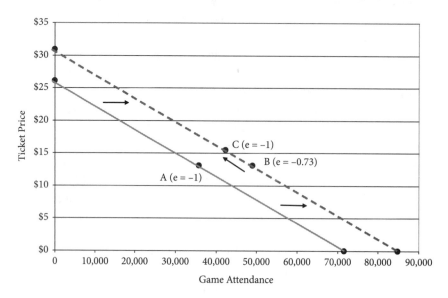

Figure 21.1 An Example of Variable Ticket Pricing.

30–50 percent of Cardinals' fans would be willing to pay higher ticket prices for higher quality opponents and weekend games. Cabral notes that the Mets sold out most of their seating sections (1994–2004), but not the Upper Reserved section, which had a lot of game-by-game variability. He also finds that VTP ought to lower the variability in attendance from game to game by lowering attendance at high-demand games, *ceteris paribus*, and raising it at low-demand games. The Mets converted to VTP during 2003, but the resulting ticket sales did not comport with Cabral's original hypothesis (indeed, Mets ticket revenue dropped in their first season using VTP). In addition, attendance variance was constant pre- and post-VTP. Cabral found a price elasticity of demand of –0.35 for that Upper Reserved section alone, consistent with other findings in baseball. A confounding factor is that the team played worse during 2003 compared with 2002, their last season without variable ticket pricing. Thus Cabral concludes that the 2003 results did not adequately test the hypothesis in question, because the lower revenues might have been caused by lower game quality, not the switch to VTP.

Dynamic Pricing

In 2009, the San Francisco Giants (one of the first teams to adopt VTP) experimented with more dynamic pricing. Specifically, the ticket price for 2000 seats in certain sections in the bleachers and upper deck that had not been selling well was changed each day (until it sold) based on sales conditions, pitching matchups, the weather, opponent, recent team performance, promotions, and day of the week. In one example, during a series against the Mets, some bleacher seats regularly priced at $17 sold for between $15 and $33, depending on the pitching matchups, and other factors. The Giants claim that revenue earned on those seats increased by 17 percent in 2009. Beginning in 2010, the Giants began selling all of the seats for all 81 home games this way. Such dynamic pricing is essentially the extreme version of VTP. With VTP, ticket prices vary by game, but are pre-set prior to the start of the season based on estimates of demand for each game. In dynamic pricing the fluctuations in demand during the season are captured in the selling price by the market, because the team allows ticket prices to move with demand.

Secondary (Resale) Markets

The same economic analysis that demonstrated the benefits of variable and dynamic ticket pricing also supports the conclusion that secondary markets lead to more efficient (higher total welfare) outcomes and generally results in fans who most value attendance attending any given game. As with dynamic pricing (as well as VTP), secondary markets result in higher prices for seats/games in high demand

and lower prices for seats/games with low demand. However, with dynamic (and variable) ticket pricing, the gains in efficiency are typically captured by the team in the form of higher profits. In a secondary market, the same efficiency gains are typically shared among consumers (who are able to find other consumers with higher valuations and make a mutually beneficial trades) and firms engaged in resale (ticket resellers, often disparaged as "scalpers").

Secondary markets allow for an additional form of second-degree price discrimination, where fans who value price certainty will tend to pay face value in advance in the primary market (but give up flexibility), and fans who are flexible can often get discounted seats close to game time. Sweeting (2008) explains that baseball ticket prices typically decline as the game approaches (a ticket is a perishable good and as the event draws closer there is an increased probability of not selling the ticket at all), for many of the same reasons that hotels and cruises will offer last-minute discounts. On the other hand, Courty (2003) shows that some fans are uncertain as to their own valuation of attendance at an event and thus are willing to pay a premium to attend a desirable game without an advance commitment. These distinct pricing options are similar to the sort of second-degree pricing seen in air travel, where late-paying consumers may either get a bargain on a flight with low demand or may pay a very high price for the flexibility of purchasing a last-minute, unrestricted ticket.

Secondary markets also play an efficiency role, making other forms of price discrimination function more smoothly. For example, secondary markets reduce the risk to early (first-sale) purchasers in a market, by providing a form of insurance to fans who purchase in advance, who thus know that if their plans change, the ticket can be sold, mitigating any losses and potentially providing for a profit. This is in stark contrast with the less efficient market for airlines tickets, where resale is highly restricted (purportedly because of security concerns) and, as a result, advance-sale tickets can go unused, and where demand in the primary market may be reduced for fear of purchasing a non-refundable ticket that goes unused.

The benefits to consumers and teams from the existence of a robust secondary market are many.

For example, demand for season tickets will generally be higher when season ticket holders know that for the subset of their purchase for which they hold a low personal valuation, it will be possible to offer those tickets up to fans with higher valuations. This can result in higher first-sale prices and higher sales. For teams that value sellouts and high attendance, secondary markets provide an efficient way to sell tickets in advance (especially through season tickets) without risking too many "no shows," who fail to purchase ancillary services like parking, concessions, and team merchandise.

Nevertheless, ticket resellers are typically denigrated by teams as "scalpers" and middlemen, who profit from the value created by others. This is an economically naïve critique that ignores the fact that in many industries, distribution channels are often a source of value and economic efficiency and as a result are often profitable lines of business. Instead, the historical animosity to ticket resale appears to have stemmed, in part, from teams' inability to capture the profits from resale, and thus, as discussed above, once MLB teams found a way to participate in the revenue streams generated from resale (through deals with firms like StubHub), this resistance to ticket resale has subsided.

Other concerns, such as the legitimate concern that re-sold tickets open the opportunity for counterfeiting, appear to have diminished as the ticket resellers have become more corporate—with web sites such as StubHub and TicketExchange offering money-back guarantees replacing a "scalper" standing on a street corner with no possible recourse for a dodgy deal.

As discussed throughout this chapter, much of the history of sports ticketing has involved fairly simplistic strategies for pricing, which led to large gaps between ticket price and consumers' (high) valuation of the best seats and the best games. See, for example, Courty (2003), who discusses the traditional view that underpricing in the primary markets is the primary driver of the economic efficiency gains from secondary markets. However, even as first-sale ticket pricing has become more sophisticated, secondary markets continue to provide efficiency gains. Some of these gains have come from technology—as Internet resale has helped make secondary markets much less spotty than street-corner sales. Other gains come from the fact that even the most dynamic of ticket pricing strategies cannot diversify away all fan risk to changed circumstances, and so secondary markets continue to provide demand-enhancing "insurance" to fans purchasing in the primary market.

One potential downside to secondary markets is the extent to which these markets distort pricing in the primary market. Because secondary markets grow demand for tickets (by lowering the risk of a first-sale purchase), they can increase prices, but generally this sort of increase is associated with increased welfare (though increased demand). However, some argue that vibrant secondary markets encourage profit-seeking ticket brokers to come into the primary market and to capture profits that teams should have earned (with dynamic pricing) or to capture surplus that fans should have captured (by getting an underpriced ticket through effort, like waiting in line, or through good luck). In some sense, these arguments are less about economics and more about societal attitudes towards resellers— regardless of whether a team, a broker, or another fan ultimately makes the final sale to the fan who attends, the economics of matching tickets with those who value them the highest is fundamental to maximizing total welfare.

5. THIRD-DEGREE PRICE DISCRIMINATION

Third-degree price discrimination is the form easily understood because it includes the classic examples like senior or youth discounts. This type of price discrimination requires the seller to segment the market and price to each group according to their price elasticity of demand, but unlike second-degree discrimination, third-degree discrimination requires that the seller prevent one group from purchasing at the other group's price. For example, this is done by requiring identification for age-related discounts or for military discounts. The San Diego Padres offer a military discount whereby a member of the military gets $6 off any ticket regularly priced at or above $14.[13]

The key to successfully implementing third-degree price discrimination is to prevent resale of the good by the low-priced purchaser to the high-priced purchaser (creating an arbitrage opportunity). This contrasts with second-degree discrimination where the seller simply provides a menu and lets the heterogeneity inherent in demand sort out who wants and gets what. With third-degree price discrimination, one purchase option is usually unambiguously preferred by all consumers, but the seller only lets certain identifiable buyers purchase at the favored price. This is easy to implement for goods that are hard to resell (like electricity or other services like food at a restaurant or personal exercise training services). In other cases, a seller may use a contract with a customer that says the product cannot be resold (like when students get educational discounts on software but agree not to resell their software).

Third-degree price discrimination works best when groups with distinct demand can be separately identified. For example, assume a minor league baseball game has the following inverse demand function for non-students: $P = 20-Q/80$, and the marginal cost of selling a ticket is $0. Similarly, the inverse demand function for students (who can be identified via a student ID card) is $P = 10-Q/40$. The revenue-maximizing single price is $8.33, leading to $8,333 in ticket revenue. This is represented by the horizontal and vertical dotted lines in Figure 21.2 at $8.33. If the team instead offered a discount to students who can show a student ID, and everyone else paid the full price, the results change substantially. The two-tiered

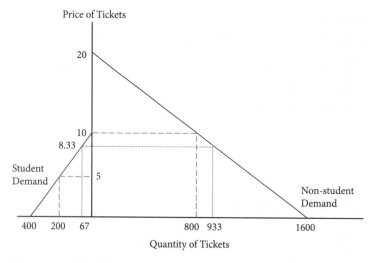

Figure 21.2 Third-Degree Price Discrimination—Student Discounts.

optimal pricing is at $5 for students and $10 for non-students (shown by the dashed lines in the figure). This results in the same 1,000 seats being sold, but with total ticket revenue at $9,000, an increase of 8 percent.

6. CONCLUSION

Leaving aside the questions of terminology—whether price discrimination requires the exact same product be sold at different prices by the same seller, or whether one follows the traditional, broader definition as originally posited by Dupuit (1849) and Pigou (1912 and 1920), which allows for price discrimination in conjunction with product differentiation—it is clear that Major League Baseball teams engage in pricing practices that are consistent with many of the teachings of the price discrimination literature. In particular, baseball teams commonly offer a large menu of options for customers that vary by seat location, day of week, opponent quality, group size, number of games purchased, age, military status, and so on, all of which mirror the teachings on second- and third-degree price discrimination. These economic theories can be understood and their impacts can be observed by viewing the actual outcomes that take place in baseball. It is one of the few industries in which we can observe demand at prevailing prices (notwithstanding sellout games). This allows economists to test empirically the economic theories of pricing.

As just one such example, baseball pricing proves the welfare benefits of price discrimination. Bradbury (2007) notes that regardless of whether MLB has monopoly power, it is a price-discriminating organization. A single price is not charged, but instead many prices across the thirty teams and within each franchise. Given the wide-ranging menu of prices, there is not a restriction of output and thus there is not the usual welfare loss or deadweight loss associated with single-price monopoly pricing. In fact, welfare is increased by price discrimination.

Price discrimination is an attempt to capture consumer surplus, but also to satisfy demand by those whose willingness to pay is less than the "one-price" optimal level. Teams utilize and accentuate the notion that sitting closer to the field provides a higher quality experience, by charging different prices. Part of the price difference is the quality difference and part of it is price discrimination (or as Tirole labeled it, quality discrimination).

Price discrimination of this nature, focused on differing degrees of quality, bundled goods, volume discounts, and other forms of second-degree price discrimination, is commonplace in MLB. Indeed, it is safe to say that every single MLB ticket is sold under some form of price discrimination. As teams grow increasingly sophisticated in their pricing strategies, price discrimination is becoming more precise, more widespread, and more profitable, while at the same time providing more opportunities for more fans to find tickets at a price they are willing to pay.

Unlike a baseball game, where one team must lose and one must win, price discrimination allows for win-win economic outcomes for teams and fans alike.

NOTES

We would like to thank Ronald Park for his excellent research assistance.

1 http://newyork.yankees.mlb.com/nyy/ballpark/new_stadium_comparison.jsp

2 See Krautmann and Berri (2007), Marburger (1997), Fort (2003), and Rascher, McEvoy, Nagel and Brown (2007) for discussions of the complementarity of tickets and concessions.

3 See for example, "Travelers Find It Pays to Wait for Late Deals," at http://online.wsj.com/article/SB123854405756676003.html

4 See Pigou (1912) and Pigou (1920).

5 In 1849, Dupuit analyzed the phenomenon of third-class trains being intentionally shabby (to discourage well-off travelers from purchasing the inexpensive tickets). So questions related to the pricing of different quality seats at the same event are nothing new to economists.

6 http://sandiego.padres.mlb.com/sd/ticketing/groups/benefits_pricing.jsp and http://oakland.athletics.mlb.com/oak/ticketing/group_info.jsp

7 http://oakland.athletics.mlb.com/oak/ticketing/group_events.jsp

8 http://arizona.diamondbacks.mlb.com/ari/ticketing/familyfridays.jsp

9 http://stlouis.cardinals.mlb.com/news/press_releases/press_release.jsp?ymd=20080214&content_id=2373636&vkey=pr_stl&fext=.jsp&c_id=stl ("To allow fans an opportunity to be a part of some of these great promotional dates, a Pujols Family Pack ... [has] been created and contain[s] seven games for the price of five. The Pujols Family Pack includes the Fredbird Bobble Belly, the Albert Pujols bobblehead as well as the Build-a-Bear Workshop Bear, Coca-Cola/Wal-Mart lunch box, Yadier Molina pennant, Six Flags tickets and more.")

10 http://sandiego.padres.mlb.com/sd/ticketing/season.jsp

11 Sandomir, Richard. "Baseball: And Now Batting Cleanup...; Maybe Valentino the Beanie Baby Can't Hit, but Who Cares?" The New York Times. 11 August 1998, p. C1.

12 Arbitrage would be a problem for second-degree discrimination based on quality if fans could purchase inexpensive upper reserved seats and then, once inside the stadium, move into better seating. This would be the equivalent, in Dupuit's train example, of riding first class on a third-class ticket. In very low-attendance situations, this can be a problem, but generally teams use ushers, and seat information printed on the tickets, just as trains have and continue to use conductors to prevent this sort of arbitrage.

13 http://mlb.mlb.com/sd/ticketing/military.jsp

REFERENCES

Adams, W., and Yellen, J. (1976). Commodity bundling and the burden of monopoly. *Quarterly Journal of Economics*, 90: 475–498.

Baade, R., and Matheson, V. (2006). Have public finance principles been shut out in financing new stadiums for the NFL? *Public Finance and Management*, 6(3): 284–320.

Bradbury, J. C. (2007). *The baseball economist: The real game exposed*. New York: Penguin Group.

Cabral, L. (2010). Variable pricing at the New York Mets. Unpublished manuscript.

Courty, P. (2003). Ticket pricing under demand uncertainty. *Journal of Law and Economics*, 46: 627–652.

Dana, J. (2001). Monopoly price dispersion under demand uncertainty. *International Economic Review*, 42(3): 649–670.

Depken, C. ,and Grant, D. (2011). Multiproduct pricing in Major League Baseball: A principal components analysis. *Economic Inquiry,* 49(2): 474–488.

DeSchriver, T., and Rascher, D. (2008). An analysis of luxury suite/club seat pricing at Red Bull Park. Report prepared for New York Red Bulls.

Dupuit, J. (1849). On tolls and transport charges. Translated in *International economic papers*. London: Macmillan (1952).

Flynn, M., and Gilbert, R. (2001). The analysis of professional sports leagues as joint ventures. *The Economic Journal*, 111: 233–252.

Fort, R. (2003). *Sports economics*. Upper Saddle River, NJ: Prentice Hall.

Howard, D., and Crompton, J. (2003). *Financing sport*. Morgantown, WV: Fitness Information Technology.

Humphreys, B., and Soebbing, B. (2008). Price dispersion and attendance in Major League Baseball. Unpublished manuscript.

Krautmann, A., and Berri, D. (2007). Can we find it at the concessions? Understanding price elasticity in professional sports. *Journal of Sports Economics*, 8(2): 183–191.

Leeds, M., and von Allmen, P. (2002). *The economics of sports*. Boston: Addison Wesley.

Marburger, D. (1997). Optimal ticket pricing for performance goods. *Managerial and Decision Economics*, 18: 375–381.

McDonald, M., and Rascher, D. (2000). Does bat day make cents? The effect of promotions on the demand for Major League Baseball. *Journal of Sport Management*, 14: 8–27.

Mondello, M., and Rishe, P. (2005). Variable ticket pricing in Major League Baseball: A case study of the St. Louis Cardinals. *International Journal of Sport Management*, 6(3): 214–232.

Phlips, L. (1981). *The economics of price discrimination*. Cambridge: Cambridge University Press.

Pigou, A. C. (1912). *Wealth and welfare*. London: Macmillan.

Pigou, A. C. (1920). *The economics of welfare*. London: Macmillan.

Rascher, D., McEvoy, C., Nagel, M., and Brown, M. (2007). Variable ticket pricing in Major League Baseball, *Journal of Sport Management*, 21: 407–437.

Rosen, S., and Rosenfeld, A. (1997). Ticket pricing. *Journal of Law and Economics*, 40: 351–375.

Shmanske, S. (2004). *Golfonomics*. Hackensack, NJ: World Scientific Publishing Company.

Stigler, G. (1987). *The Theory of Price*. New York: Macmillan.

Sweeting, A. (2008). Equilibrium price dynamics in perishable goods markets: The case of secondary markets for Major League Baseball Tickets. NBER Working Paper 14505.

Tirole, J. (1988). *The theory of industrial organization*. Cambridge, MA: MIT Press.

Varian, H. (1989). Price discrimination. In R. Schmalensee and R. D. Willig, eds., *Handbook of industrial organization*, volume I, pp. 597–654. Amsterdam: Elsevier.

CHAPTER 22

....

CONTEST THEORY AND ITS APPLICATIONS IN SPORTS

HELMUT DIETL,

EGON FRANCK,

MARTIN GROSSMANN, AND

MARKUS LANG

1. INTRODUCTION

....

THE purpose of this chapter is to outline how the theory of contests is applied to professional team sports leagues. In the first part, we present the traditional Tullock contest and explain some basic properties of the equilibrium. We will then extend this static contest to a two-period model in order to analyze dynamic aspects of contests. In the second part of this chapter, we will present applications of contest theory in sports. In particular, we will show how the Tullock framework is applied to models of team sports leagues. For this purpose, we will first explain the value creation process in team sports leagues and show how club revenues are related to the contest success function. Then, we present some basic modeling issues; for instance, we show how the assumption of flexible vs. fixed talent supply depends on the league under consideration and how it influences the equilibria. Furthermore, we explicate the effect of revenue sharing on competitive balance in the different models. Then we address the relationship between competitive balance and social welfare. Finally, we illustrate why many clubs tend to "overinvest" in playing talent in many team sports leagues. The chapter ends with a short conclusion.

2. A SIMPLE CONTEST MODEL

The Basic Tullock Contest

We consider a contest in which two risk-neutral and expected profit-maximizing contestants are competing to win a prize. The contestants differ with respect to the valuation of the prize, where v_i denotes contestant i's valuation of the contest prize.[1] Each contestant $i = 1,2$ independently expends irreversible and costly effort $e_i \geq 0$. These efforts determine via the contest success function (CSF) which contestant will receive the prize. Formally, the CSF maps efforts (e_1, e_2) into probabilities of winning the prize for the different contestants. We will only consider the logit formulation, which is one of the most widely used functional forms in contests. Its general form was introduced by Tullock (1980) and subsequently axiomatized by Skaperdas (1996) and Clark and Riis (1998).[2] The probability of success for contestant $i = 1,2$ in a Tullock contest is defined as:

$$p_i(e_1, e_2) = \begin{cases} \frac{e_i^\gamma}{e_1^\gamma + e_2^\gamma} & \text{if max} \{e_1, e_2\} > 0 \\ 1/2 & \text{otherwise} \end{cases} \tag{1}$$

Note that (1) incorporates an adding-up constraint such that the probabilities must sum up to unity, i.e., $p_1 + p_2 = 1$. The probability of success p_i increases in i's own effort and decreases in the effort of the other contestants. Moreover, the parameter $\gamma > 0$, the so-called "discriminatory power" of the CSF, measures the sensitivity of success to effort. As γ increases, the winning probability for the contestant with higher efforts increases and the differences in efforts affect the winning probability in a stronger way. For all $\gamma \in (0, \infty)$, the contest under consideration is a so-called "non-discriminatory" contest.

In the limiting case where γ approaches infinity, we would have a so-called "fully discriminatory" contest in which the contestant with the highest effort wins the prize with certainty.[3] This form of contest is equivalent to an "all-pay auction" in which all bidders must pay regardless of whether they win the prize, which is then awarded to the bidder with the highest bid.[4] An all-pay auction type of contest is an appropriate approach whenever contestants compete, for example, in footraces, in which an objective standard like "time" measures success. In contrast, team sports leagues are usually modeled via the "non-discriminatory" Tullock contest.

Efforts generate costs according to a cost function $c_i(e_i)$, which in the classic contest literature is often assumed to be linear such that[5]

$$c_i(e_i) = c \cdot e_i,$$

where $c > 0$ is the (constant) marginal cost of efforts.

The expected pay-off of contestant i is given by the probability of success p_i multiplied by the value of the contest prize, v_i, less the cost of effort:

$$\pi_i = p_i v_i - c(e_i) = \frac{e_i^\gamma}{e_1^\gamma + e_2^\gamma} v_i - c e_i.$$

The reaction function of contestant i, which describes the best response to any possible effort choice of the other contestant, can be computed from the following first-order conditions:

$$\frac{\gamma e_i^{\gamma-1} e_j^\gamma}{(e_1^\gamma + e_2^\gamma)^2} v_i = c,$$

with $i, j = 1,2$, $i \neq j$. The Nash equilibrium (e_1^*, e_2^*) in pure strategies is then characterized by the intersection of the two reaction functions and is given by:

$$(e_1^*, e_2^*) = \left(\frac{\gamma v_1^{\gamma+1} v_2^\gamma}{c \left(v_1^\gamma + v_2^\gamma \right)^2}, \frac{\gamma v_1^\gamma v_2^{\gamma+1}}{c \left(v_1^\gamma + v_2^\gamma \right)^2} \right),$$

$$(p_1^*, p_2^*) = \left(\frac{v_1^\gamma}{v_1^\gamma + v_2^\gamma}, \frac{v_2^\gamma}{v_1^\gamma + v_2^\gamma} \right).$$

The contestant with the higher valuation of the contest prize expends more effort and wins with a higher probability. Moreover, individual and aggregate efforts are increasing in the valuation of the prize and in the discriminatory power of the CSF.

Transitional Dynamics in the Tullock Contest

Contests frequently occur dynamically in several periods and therefore effort decisions are often intertemporarily connected. The effort that a contestant exerts in today's contest may affect the probability of winning tomorrow's contest. Examples are numerous: many military conflicts endure for long periods of time, and duopolists compete for customers not only once but every day, much like lobbyists who repeatedly campaign for a political rent. Furthermore, if a political party campaigns for electoral votes, it builds a political reputation that may affect not only this but also subsequent elections.

Grossmann and Dietl (2009) extend the basic model with two contestants by introducing two periods in order to account for these dynamic aspects of contests.[6]

As in the previous section, the contestants differ with respect to the valuation of the prize, where v_i denotes contestant i's valuation of the contest prize. Contestant $i=1,2$ contributes effort $e_{i,t}$ in period $t=1,2$. In period 1, contestant i exerts effort $e_{i,1}$ and builds up an asset stock $E_{i,1} = e_{i,1}$. The asset stocks $E_{1,1}$ and $E_{2,1}$ determine the probability of success $p_{i,1}$ of contestant i in period 1 according to the Tullock CSF given by (1). To simplify matters, the authors set the discriminatory power parameter γ of the CSF to $\gamma=1$. Moreover, they assume that part of the asset stock depreciates according to a depreciation factor $\delta \in (0, 1)$. Contestant i, however, is able to increase the remaining asset stock by additionally exerting effort $e_{i,2}$ in period 2. Contestant i's second-period probability of success $p_{i,2}$ depends on the resulting asset stocks $E_{1,2}$ and $E_{2,2}$ in period 2. Expected second-period profits are discounted by the factor $\beta \in (0, 1)$. In both periods, efforts $e_{i,t}$ generate costs according to a weakly convex cost function given by $c(e_{i,t})$ with $c'(e_{i,t}) > 0$, for $e_{i,t} > 0$, $c'(0) = 0$, and $c''(e_{i,t}) \geq 0$.[7]

Contestant $i=1,2$ maximizes expected profits π_i, given by:

$$\pi_i = \frac{E_{i,1}}{E_{1,1} + E_{2,1}} v_i - c(e_{i,1}) + \beta \left(\frac{E_{i,2}}{E_{1,2} + E_{2,2}} v_i - c(e_{i,2}) \right),$$

with $E_{i,1} = e_{i,1}$ and $E_{i,2} = (1-\delta)E_{i,1} + e_{i,2}$. In order to solve the maximization problem, one has to think about the information structure in this model. Whether contestants are able to observe the opponent's effort choice after period 1 may influence contestants' optimal strategies. In the economics literature, two different concepts have been elaborated in order to solve this kind of maximization problem. If effort choices are (not) revealed after the first period and before exerting second-period effort, then contestants optimally apply closed-loop (open-loop) strategies.[8]

According to the model, if the contestants apply closed-loop (open-loop) strategies, then the term $\partial E_{i,2} / \partial E_{j,1}$ for $i, j=1,2$ and $i \neq j$ can differ from zero (equals zero). Grossmann and Dietl (2009) show that in the case of constant marginal costs c, closed-loop and open-loop equilibria coincide. In this case, the optimal asset stocks $E_{i,t}^*$ of contestant $i=1,2$ in period $t=1,2$ are given by:

$$\left(E_{1,1}^*, E_{2,1}^* \right) = \left(\frac{v_1^2 v_2}{c[1 - \beta(1-\delta)](v_1 + v_2)^2}, \frac{v_1 v_2^2}{c[1 - \beta(1-\delta)](v_1 + v_2)^2} \right),$$

$$\left(E_{1,2}^*, E_{2,2}^* \right) = \left(\frac{v_1^2 v_2}{c(v_1 + v_2)^2}, \frac{v_1 v_2^2}{c(v_1 + v_2)^2} \right).$$

In equilibrium, the probability of success is then given by:

$$p_{i,t}^* = \frac{v_i}{v_i + v_j},$$

with $i, j=1,2$, $i \neq j$, $t=1,2$. It is easy to see that the contestant with the higher prize valuation has a higher asset stock and achieves a higher probability of success in each period if marginal costs are constant. In comparison to the basic one-period model with $\gamma = 1$, contestants increase their efforts in period 1 because the marginal revenues of effort contribution increase due to the transitional effects on second-period assets. However, the extension of the basic model does not alter the final asset stocks in period 2 as compared to the basic model.

On the other hand, the optimal behavior of the contestants changes considerably by assuming strictly convex costs.[9] In the case of a closed-loop concept, two equilibria are possible. In each period, either the contestant with the lower prize valuation has a higher asset stock *or* the contestant with the higher prize valuation has a higher asset stock.[10]

The latter equilibrium is intuitive because the contestant with the higher prize valuation and therefore (*ceteris paribus*) higher marginal revenues exerts more effort. The former equilibrium, however, is the counterintuitive outcome and differs from the results in the basic model. In this equilibrium, both contestants assume that the contestant with the lower prize valuation contributes more effort in both periods. It should be noted that marginal revenues depend not only on the prize valuation but also on the effort contribution of both contestants. The contestant with the lower prize valuation anticipates that a higher effort contribution in period 1 decreases the opponent's second-period efforts.[11] Therefore, marginal revenues increase for the contestant with the lower prize valuation due to this strategic effect. Otherwise, the contestant with the higher prize valuation anticipates that a higher effort contribution in period 1 increases the opponent's second-period efforts.[12] Thus, marginal revenues decrease for the contestant with the higher prize valuation. Due to this interaction, it is possible that the contestant with the lower prize valuation has higher asset stocks in equilibrium.

The extension of the basic model suggests that dynamic aspects may modify contestants' optimal behavior. Moreover, due to the result of multiple equilibria, it is not possible to predict which equilibrium will actually be reached.

In the following sections, we narrow the context of general contests and introduce peculiarities that are typically inherent in sports contests. We show how these peculiarities are embedded in the sports contest models, and we discuss their implications on the optimal behavior of the contestants.

3. APPLICATIONS OF CONTEST THEORY IN SPORTS

The research in the application of contest-theoretical concepts to sporting activities is primarily focused on professional *team* sports to the comparative neglect of *individual* (non-team) sports such as golf, boxing, athletics, auto sports, and the like.[13] Although individual sports are sometimes organized on a team basis, the teams are not generally organized in leagues ranked in line with their success over the season. The main reason that sports economists are interested in team sports is that "professional team sports leagues are classic, even textbook, examples of business cartels" (Fort and Quirk, 1995). The important difference between sports leagues and other cartels, however, is the special nature of the former. Neale (1964) referred to this as "the peculiar economics of professional sports." The essence of sports leagues is the associative character of competition. No club can improve its position in the ranks without worsening the position of other teams.[14]

An important issue to do with sports leagues is the suspense associated with a close contest and its influence on fan demand. The "uncertainty of outcome" hypothesis, which goes back to Rottenberg (1956), claims that spectators prefer close rather than less balanced contests. In this respect, a certain degree of (competitive) balance within the league is assumed to be necessary in order to maintain fan interest and with it the revenue stream from the sale of the product (the joint game). Thus, in order to guarantee a successful competition, teams have a strong interest in the economic viability of other teams. Unlike Toyota, Microsoft, and Wal-Mart, who benefit from weak competitors in their respective industries, Real Madrid and the New York Yankees need strong competitors to maximize their revenues. In sports, a weak team produces a negative externality on its stronger competitors.

Due to its peculiarities and perhaps its popularity, the professional team sports industry enjoys several exemptions from common antitrust regulations. For example, salary caps (Késenne, 2000b; Dietl, Lang, and Rathke, 2009, 2011), transfer restrictions (Dietl, Franck, and Lang, 2008b) and centralized marketing by league monopolies (Falconieri, Palomino, Sakovics, 2004; Gurtler, 2007) would not be tolerated in other industries. These exceptions result in very interesting labor market peculiarities within professional team sports. These peculiarities make the industry of professional team sports an interesting research field for economists. Because the industry is organized differently across the world, and because we even can often observe different institutional arrangements within a given country, professional team sports is an interesting source of natural experiments.

Value Creation in Team Sports Leagues

The club-specific revenues of professional sports clubs are largely compiled from five sources: Match-day revenue and broadcasting rights combined account for one-half to three-fourths of total league revenue; the rest is made up by merchandising, advertising, and sponsoring (Deloitte and Touche, 2009). At first sight, any single game and the attention generated by it are relevant for match-day and broadcasting revenue. However, when comparing revenues from exhibition games to those from championship games, it becomes evident that the value of the latter significantly exceeds the value of the former. The value of any game depends on the participating teams' playing strengths. But a larger contribution to the game's value is made by the relevance of the game for the championship. Seen from this viewpoint, value creation in professional team sports occurs in two distinct stages (Franck, 2003). In the first stage, the stage of the individual clubs, club owners invest into the playing strength of their respective teams. No single team, however, is able to produce a marketable product: any team is in need of at least one opponent. In the second stage of the production process, the stage of the league, single games act as inputs for the production of the final meta-product, the championship itself.[15]

Club Revenues and the Contest Success Function

In this section, we show how club revenues are related to the contest success function. By concentrating on match-day and broadcasting revenue and by neglecting the other sources of club revenues, Dietl and Lang (2008) and Dietl, Lang, and Werner (2009, 2010) derive club-specific revenues from a general fan utility function by assuming that a fan's willingness to pay depends on the fan type, on the preferred team's win percentage, and on the suspense associated with a close competition (competitive balance).[16]

The authors consider a continuum of fans who differ in their willingness to pay for a match between club i and club j with quality q_i, $i, j = 1, 2$, $i \neq j$.[17] Every fan l has a certain preference for match quality that is measured by θ_l. For simplicity, they assume that these preferences are uniformly distributed in $[0,1]$, that is, the measure of potential fans is one. Furthermore, they assume a constant marginal utility of quality and define the net utility of fan l as $\max\{\theta_l q_i - p_i, 0\}$. At price p_i, the fan who is indifferent to the consumption of the product is given by $\theta^* = \frac{p_i}{q_i}$.[18] Hence, the measure of fans who purchase at p_i is given by $1 - \theta^* = \frac{q_i - p_i}{q_i}$. The fan demand function of club $i = 1, 2$ therefore yields:

$$d(m_i, p_i, q_i) = m_i \frac{q_i - p_i}{q_i},$$

where $m_i \in R^+$ represents the market size parameter of club i. Note that fan demand increases in quality, albeit with a decreasing rate, i.e., $\frac{\partial d}{\partial q_i} > 0$ and $\frac{\partial^2 d}{\partial q_i^2} < 0$.

Clubs are assumed to be heterogeneous with respect to their market size. For a given set of parameters (p_i, q_i), the club with a higher drawing potential ("large-market" club) generates higher demand than the club with lower drawing potential ("small-market" club).

By normalizing all other costs (e.g., stadium and broadcasting costs) to zero, club i's revenue is simply $R_i = p_i \cdot d(m_i, p_i, q_i)$. Then, the club will choose the profit-maximizing price $p_i^* = \frac{q_i}{2}$. Given this profit-maximizing price, club i's revenue depends solely on the quality of the match and is derived as $R_i = \frac{m_i}{4} q_i$.

The authors further assume that match quality q_i depends on two factors: the probability of club i's success, and the suspense associated with a close competition. The probability of club i's success is measured by the win percentage of this club, denoted by w_i.

As standard in the sports economic literature, the relationship between talent investments and win percentage/probability of winning, denoted by w_i, is characterized by the Tullock CSF (1) presented in Section 2:

$$w_i(t_1,t_2) = \frac{t_i^\gamma}{t_1^\gamma + t_2^\gamma},\tag{2}$$

where t_i represents the talent investment of club i.[19]

The suspense associated with a close competition is measured by the competitive balance CB in the league and can be specified by the product of the win percentages $w_i w_j$.[20] Competitive balance attains its maximum of ¼ for a completely balanced league in which both clubs invest the same amount in talent such that $w_1 = w_2 = 1/2$. A less balanced league is then characterized by a lower value of CB.

With the specification of the win percentage and competitive balance, the quality function is then derived as:

$$q_i = \mu w_i + (1-\mu)w_i w_j,$$

with $i,j = 1,2$, $i \neq j$. The parameter $\mu \in [0,1]$ represents the relative weight that fans put on their own team winning and competitive balance, respectively.

The revenue function of club $i = 1,2$ is thus given by:[21]

$$R_i = \frac{m_i}{4}q_i = \frac{m_i}{4}\left(w_i - (1-\mu)w_i^2\right).\tag{3}$$

Note that club i's revenue initially increases with winning until the maximum is reached for w_i' with $w_i' \equiv \frac{1}{2(1-\mu)}$. By increasing the win percentage above w_i', club i's revenue starts to decrease because excessive dominance by one team is detrimental to match quality. This reflects the uncertainty of outcome hypothesis: the lower the value of μ, that is, the higher the fans' preference for competitive balance, the lower the threshold value w_i' and the sooner revenues start to decrease due to dominance by one team.

If fans only care for their own team winning, that is, by setting $\mu = 1$, the revenue function (3) is linear in w_i and is then equivalent to the revenue function derived in the basic Tullock contest. The difference, however, is the interpretation of the parameter m_i. In the sports context, m_i is interpreted as the market size of club i, whereas m_i is interpreted as the valuation of the contest prize of contestant i in the Tullock contest.

Flexible and Fixed Supply of Talent

In the traditional contest literature, the "supply" of effort e_i of contestant i is perfectly elastic and does not influence the supply of contestant j. In contest models of team sports leagues, however, the assumption regarding the supply of talent depends on the league under consideration. In the European sports leagues, talent supply is often assumed to be flexible, especially after the Bosman verdict in 1995, which has established an international player market. In contrast, in the U.S. major leagues, the supply of talent is usually considered as being fixed because all talent wants to play in the major leagues. Under the assumption of a flexible supply of talent, the number of talent hired by club i has no influence on the talent pool that is available to the other club j. That is, a club can sign additional talent without decreasing the number of talent in other clubs that compete in the same league. Under the assumption of fixed supply, aggregate talent within the league is constant, and the race for talent is a zero-sum game between owners.

We will see that the assumption regarding the supply of talent crucially affects the modeling of team sports leagues, in particular the derivative of the CSF. By setting the discriminatory power γ equal to one, the derivative of the CSF (2) is computed as:

$$\frac{\partial w_i}{\partial t_i} = \frac{t_1 + t_2 - t_i(1 + \frac{dt_j}{dt_i})}{(t_1 + t_2)^2}, \tag{4}$$

where the term $\frac{dt_j}{dt_i}$ is called a "conjectural variation." The crucial point regarding this conjecture is whether the supply of talent in the league is assumed to be fixed or flexible. As Szymanski (2004) has shown, the assumption of a fixed talent supply is often used to justify the so-called "Walrasian fixed-supply" conjectures given by $\frac{dt_j}{dt_i} = -1$, which means that a one-unit increase in talent hired at team i leads to a one-unit reduction of talent at the other team j. In this case, equation (4) becomes:

$$\frac{\partial w_i}{\partial t_i} = \frac{1}{t_1 + t_2}.$$

In a two-club league, the Walrasian fixed-supply conjecture collapses the non-cooperative choice of talents into a choice of winning percentages by only one club owner. Under the Walrasian fixed-supply conjectures, the game between profit-maximizing owners loses its non-cooperative character and leads to results that are more in line with joint profit-maximization (Szymanski, 2004).

In contrast, in a league with a flexible supply of talent, a one-unit increase in talent hired at one team does not influence the amount available to the other team. In such a setting, the so-called "Contest-Nash" conjectures are given by $\frac{dt_j}{dt_i} = 0$, leading to:

$$\frac{\partial w_i}{\partial t_i} = \frac{t_j}{(t_1 + t_2)^2}.$$

Szymanski (2004) argues that the "Nash solution to the non-cooperative game of talent choice in a professional sports league [...] is inconsistent with the standard representation of the competitive equilibrium." According to Szymanski, the so-called "Walrasian fixed-supply conjecture model" is not meaningful. This model does not fulfill the conditions of a Nash equilibrium, as the incorporation of the constant supply conjectures leaves one team without a choice of strategy. Szymanski and Késenne (2004) agree with Szymanski (2004), stating that "when the choice of one team automatically constrains the other in a two-team model, every possible choice of talent is a Nash equilibrium because the other team has only one feasible response, which is therefore the 'best.' However, this clearly makes little sense as an economic model."

Fort (2006b), however, has replied to Szymanski's criticism of the "Walrasian conjectures" and concludes that the appropriate concept depends on the analyzed league. Moreover, Fort and Quirk (2007) show that the competitive talent market model generates a unique rational expectations equilibrium. Thus, the disagreement regarding the Contest-Nash conjectures versus Walrasian conjectures still remains an open area for research in the sports economic literature.[22]

We will see in the next section how assumptions about the supply of talent and the corresponding conjectural variations lead to different results, for example, those regarding the effect of revenue sharing on competitive balance.

The Effect of Revenue Sharing on Competitive Balance

Based on the uncertainty of outcome hypothesis, professional team sports leagues have introduced a variety of measures to increase competitive balance. Two of the most prominent measures are reserve clauses and revenue-sharing arrangements. Whether these measures actually increase competitive balance is the most disputed question in the sports economics literature. According to Rottenberg's "invariance proposition,"[23] the distribution of playing talent between clubs in professional sports leagues does not depend on the allocation of property rights to players' services. In particular, changes in property rights, such as the introduction of a reserve clause, will not alter the allocation of players and will therefore have no impact on competitive balance. El-Hodiri and Quirk (1971), Quirk and El-Hodiri (1974), Fort and Quirk (1995), and Vrooman (1995) extend this invariance proposition to gate revenue sharing.

Traditionally in the sports literature, gate revenue sharing is modeled as follows. The share of revenues that is assigned to the home team is given by the parameter $\alpha \in (\frac{1}{2}, 1]$, while $(1 - \alpha)$ is assumed to be the share of revenues received by the away team. The after-sharing revenues of club i, denoted by R_i^*, are then given by:

$$R_i^* = \alpha R_i + (1 - \alpha) R_j$$

with $i, j = 1, 2$, $i \neq j$ and the revenues R_i are given, for example, by equation (3). Note that a high parameter α represents a league with a low degree of redistribution. That is, $\alpha = 1$ characterizes a league without revenue sharing, while the limiting case of $\alpha = 1/2$ would characterize a league with full-revenue sharing. Another popular form of revenue sharing in sports leagues is pool revenue sharing. Under a pool-sharing arrangement, each club receives an α-share of its revenue and an equal $(1 - \alpha)$-share of a league revenue pool, where $\alpha \in (0, 1]$. In this case, the after-sharing revenues of club i are given by:

$$R_i^* = \alpha R_i + \frac{(1-\alpha)}{2}(R_i + R_j).$$

The theoretical analyses regarding the effect of revenue sharing on competitive balance can be grouped along two dimensions of assumptions: profit- versus win-maximization and fixed versus flexible supply of talent. Along the first dimension, club owners may be modeled as either profit- or win-maximizers. Profit-maximizers do not care about winning percentages unless they affect profits. Win-maximizers invest as much as they can into playing talent and are only constrained by zero profit.[24] The second dimension concerns the elasticity of talent supply as discussed in the previous section.

According to this categorization, the invariance proposition with regard to revenue sharing is derived under the assumptions of profit maximization and fixed supply. There is wide agreement that the invariance proposition does not hold in leagues with either win-maximizing owners or a flexible talent supply (see Atkinson, Stanley, Tschirhart, 1988; Rascher, 1997; Késenne, 2000a, 2005; Vrooman, 2008). There is disagreement, however, over whether the invariance proposition holds in a league with profit-maximizing owners and a fixed talent supply. For example, Szymanski and Késenne (2004) use the Contest-Nash conjectures and argue that increased gate revenue sharing results in a more uneven distribution of talent between large- and small-market clubs, even in a league with profit-maximizing clubs and a fixed supply of talent.

Competitive Balance and Social Welfare

Even though the relevance of competitive balance for demand is intuitively plausible, there is mixed evidence on its empirical significance. First of all, it is unclear which dimension of competitive balance affects demand the most. Sanderson (2002) as well as Sanderson and Siegfried (2003) differentiate three notions of competitive balance: (1) uncertain match outcome, (2) uncertain championship outcome and (3) long-term uncertainty of outcome, that is, the absence of so-called dynasties. Apart from these problems of proxying competitive balance, the empirical evidence on the effects of the different notions of competitive balance on demand remains ambiguous. Szymanski (2003) surveys twenty-two empirical studies and concludes that "ten offer clear support for the uncertainty of outcome hypothesis, seven offer weak support, and five contradict it." A similar conclusion is drawn by Downward and Dawson (2000), who state that "the evidence suggests that uncertainty of outcome has been an overworked hypothesis in explaining the demand for professional sports."[25] Note that there is not only mixed empirical evidence on the relevance of competitive balance for attendance but also the specifications used to examine competitive balance and attendance vary significantly across the studies (e.g., the specification of consumer demand and the relevant elements of outcome uncertainty, handling the time series characteristics of attendance data beyond a correction for serial correlation, etc.).[26]

In our opinion, the invariance proposition and the related literature on competitive balance miss the point by raising the wrong question. We believe that it is much more important to analyze the welfare effects of different assumptions and issues of league design, such as club owner objectives and revenue sharing, than their effect on competitive balance. If consumers' utility and thus their willingness to pay are increasing in the winning percentage of their supported team, then the clubs' individual potential fan bases, their market sizes, must be considered when deriving the optimal degree of competitive balance. An additional win of a large-market team will generate higher aggregate marginal utility than that of some small-market team, due to the larger number of fans deriving utility from that additional win. Therefore, a fully balanced league might not maximize social welfare because social welfare does not monotonically increase as competitive balance increases. It follows that an exclusive focus on the effects of different assumptions and measures on competitive balance may result in inefficient policy conclusions.

Dietl and Lang (2008) develop a contest model of a team sports league to study the effect of alternative gate revenue-sharing arrangements on social welfare and confirm this finding. By using the Contest-Nash conjectures, they show that the non-cooperative league equilibrium is too balanced. A lower degree of competitive balance would yield a higher level of social welfare. Moreover, they challenge the invariance proposition by showing that gate revenue-sharing decreases competitive balance. Combining both results, they conclude that in order to increase social welfare, arrangements that decrease, not increase, competitive balance should be implemented.

In another contest model, Dietl, Lang, and Werner (2009) analyze the effects of heterogeneous club objectives on club profits, consumer surplus, and player salaries. The authors also apply the Contest-Nash conjectures and show that the social efficiency of measures that increase the competitiveness of small-market clubs depends on the league type. If the large-market clubs are profit maximizers, for example, small-market clubs should win fewer rather than more games in order to increase social welfare. In such leagues, all measures in favor of small-market clubs, such as transfer restrictions and reverse-order drafts, are dangerous because they will lead to a decrease instead of an increase in social welfare. Moreover, in profit-maximizing leagues, revenue sharing decreases and in win-maximizing leagues it increases competitive balance. In both cases, the effect on social welfare is positive because profit-maximizing leagues have too much and win-maximizing leagues too little competitive balance without revenue sharing. In mixed leagues, on the other hand, revenue-sharing arrangements decrease competitive balance and social welfare.

The Overinvestment Problem in Team Sports Leagues

In this section, we will apply the basic contest model from Section 2 to explain the tendency to "over-invest" in playing talent in many team sports leagues.

In the past decade, many football clubs in Europe were able to increase total revenues due to higher broadcasting receipts, bigger crowds, sponsorship and a more professional approach to merchandising. According to Deloitte and Touch (2009), the combined revenues generated by the top divisions of Europe's "Big Five" leagues[27] increased by more than 300 percent, from approximately €1.9 billion in the season 1995–1996 to €7.7 billion in the season 2007–2008. Manchester United, the world's second-richest club, even augmented its turnover from €25 million in

1990 to about €325 million in 2008, an increase by 1,200 percent (*Economist*, 2002; Deloitte and Touche, 2009).

At the same time, however, there is growing evidence of a financial crisis spreading throughout the European football leagues. Many European clubs face serious financial difficulties. Some have even gone bankrupt. Examples illustrating this general tendency are numerous. In Spain's Primera Division, the total amount of debt in 2008 amounted to €3.2 billion. Of the top forty teams, eight sought protection from creditors to stave off bankruptcy in the last two seasons. In particular, FC Valencia is seriously in debt with €502 million.[28] In England, the twenty Premier League clubs actually owe a total of €2.5 billion in bank overdrafts, loans, and other borrowings; Manchester United and Chelsea are the most indebted clubs, each owing about €810 million.[29] In Italy, the Serie A clubs accumulated total losses of €1.2 billion in the period from 1995–1996 up to 2002–2003, with 84 percent of theses losses sustained from 2000–2001 to 2002–2003 (Deloitte and Touche, 2004). In particular, AC Fiorentina went bankrupt in 2002 and was relegated to the third Italian league. A court declared AC Parma insolvent in April 2004 with €310 million in debt. In Switzerland, Servette Genf was declared insolvent in February 2005; following FC Lugano and Lausanne Sports in 2002, this was the third club to go bankrupt.[30]

How can this "paradox of rising revenues and declining profits" be explained? A first explanation stresses inadequate club constitutions. As organizations without residual claimants, traditional clubs are more likely to behave as win maximizers. Having no ownership stakes in the operation and, at the same time, lacking genuine owners as monitors, club managers have the discretion to maximize individual utility through sportive success. The chance to privatize a part of the fame and glamour derived from sporting success while socializing the inherent financial risks creates strong incentives to invest too much in playing talent. However, a closer look at the real situation in professional team sports shows the limitation of this constitutional explanation. The paradox of raising revenues and declining profits persists even in leagues where clubs have been transformed into capitalistic corporations with profit-maximizing owners. Obviously, the problem must have deeper roots.

Based on a contest model of a team sports league with profit-maximizing clubs, Dietl, Franck, and Lang (2008a) deal with these roots. They show that the tendency to "over-invest" in playing talent leading to the dissipation of the league's revenue is a direct consequence of the ruinous competition between the clubs. In the following, we will briefly explain their model for a league with two clubs.[31]

The authors assume that total league revenue is a concave function of aggregate investments in playing talent, given by:[32]

$$LR(t_1,t_2) = (t_1 + t_2)^{\frac{1}{2}}.$$

This function reflects the fact that with raising investments in playing talent, for example, better players, the league becomes more attractive for fans or TV broadcasters. Therefore, the league income increases but does so with decreasing returns to scale. The authors consider a league with a revenue-sharing arrangement in which the defeated club also receives a certain amount of the league revenue. The share of the endogenously determined league prize $LR(t_1,t_2)$ which is awarded to the winner of the championship, is given by the parameter $\alpha \in (\frac{1}{2},1]$, while $(1-\alpha)$ is assumed to be the share of the endogenous league prize received by the defeated club. Furthermore, in order to concentrate on the overinvestment problem, the authors consider a symmetric league in which both clubs have the same marginal cost of talent investment, that is, $c_1 = c_2 = c$.

The league's optimal level $(\bar{t}_1,\bar{t}_2)$ of talent investments maximizes the social surplus of the clubs and is defined as:

$$(\bar{t}_1,\bar{t}_2) = \arg\max_{(t_1,t_2)} \left(LR(t_1,t_2) - c \cdot (t_1 + t_2) \right).$$

By considering the symmetric league optimum only, the solution to the maximization problem is given by $\bar{t}_i = \frac{1}{8c^2}$. The terms "over-invest" and "under-invest" are defined as situations in which a club invests more and less, respectively, in equilibrium than in the league optimum.

The expected profit of club $i = 1,2$ is given by:

$$\pi_i(t_1,t_2) = w_i \alpha LR(t_1,t_2) + (1-w_i)(1-\alpha)LR(t_1,t_2) - ct_i. \tag{5}$$

The expected pay-off of club i depends on the probability of winning w_i multiplied by the share α of the endogenous league prize $LR(t_1,t_2)$ awarded to the winner, plus the probability of losing $(1-w_i)$ multiplied by the share $(1-\alpha)$ of the endogenous league prize $LR(t_1,t_2)$ awarded to the defeated club, minus the investment costs in playing talent ct_i. Note that the probability of winning w_i is again given by the CSF (2).

Each club chooses an investment level of playing talent such that expected profits (5) are maximized, that is, club i solves $\max_{t_i \geq 0} \pi_i$. The equilibrium investments, win percentage and profits for club $i = 1,2$ are then given by:

$$t_i^* = \frac{(1+2\gamma(2\alpha-1))^2}{32c^2}, \quad w_i^* = \frac{1}{2},$$

$$\pi_i^* = \frac{(1+2\gamma(2\alpha-1))(3-2\gamma(2\alpha-1))}{32c}.$$

Note that both clubs realize identical, strictly positive investment levels and obtain with an equal probability of ½ the endogenously determined league revenue of size $R(t_1^*,t_2^*) = \frac{1+2\gamma(2\alpha-1)}{4c}$. Expected pay-offs are non-negative in equilibrium and thus clubs decide to participate in the league competition if either the discriminatory power γ is restricted to $\gamma \in [0,\bar{\gamma}(\alpha)]$ with $\bar{\gamma}(\alpha) \equiv \frac{3}{2(2\alpha-1)}$ or the parameter α is restricted $\alpha \in \left[\frac{1}{2},\bar{\alpha}(\gamma)\right]$ to with $\bar{\alpha}(\gamma) \equiv \frac{2\gamma+3}{4\gamma}$. Otherwise, the competition does not take place because clubs prefer to abstain.[33]

The "ratio of dissipation," which measures the degree of dissipation of the league revenue, is defined as:[34]

$$D(\alpha,\gamma) = \frac{\bar{T} - T^*}{\bar{T}} = \frac{(-1+2\gamma(2\alpha-1))^2}{4} \in [0,1],$$

where $\bar{T} = R(\bar{t}_1,\bar{t}_2)-c\cdot(\bar{t}_1+\bar{t}_2)$ and $T^* = R(t_1^*,t_2^*)-c\cdot(t_1^*+t_2^*)$ characterize the net surplus at the first-best allocation and the Nash equilibrium, respectively. Note that a higher value of $D(\alpha,\gamma)$, implies a higher degree of dissipation of the league revenue.

Dietl, Franck, and Lang (2008a) show that if (1) the discriminatory power γ of the CSF is within the interval $(\gamma^*,\bar{\gamma}] = \left(\frac{1}{2(2\alpha-1)}, \frac{3}{2(2\alpha-1)}\right]$, or (2) the revenue-sharing parameter α is within the interval $(\alpha^*,\bar{\alpha}] = \left(\frac{2\gamma+1}{4\gamma}, \frac{2\gamma+3}{4\gamma}\right]$, there is a guaranteed existence of a Nash equilibrium in which each club invests more than in the league optimum and therefore dissipates parts of the league revenue.

As a consequence, both a higher discriminatory power and a lower degree of revenue sharing contribute to aggravate the over-investment problem in team sports leagues. Intuitively, this is clear; if smaller differences in talent investments have a stronger impact on the probability of success, then the clubs have stronger incentives for higher talent investments. The same holds true for a lower degree of revenue sharing. Moreover, if the discriminatory power γ or the revenue sharing parameter α equals $\bar{\gamma}(\alpha)$ or $\bar{\alpha}(\gamma)$, then the net surplus T^* at the Nash equilibrium equals zero, and $D(\alpha,\gamma)$ reaches its maximum of one. In this case, the clubs dissipate the whole league's revenue. Note that even though marginal costs influence the equilibrium efforts, they have no influence on the over-investment problem because altering marginal costs does not affect the ratio of dissipation.[35]

However, the increase of the talent investments in the Nash equilibrium compared to the league optimum does not affect the probability of success in equilibrium because clubs simultaneously increase their efforts and end up with exactly the same relative performance as in the league optimum, i.e., $w_i^*(t_1^*,t_2^*) = w_i(\bar{t}_1,\bar{t}_2) = 1/2$. Even though the clubs would be better off if they agreed upon the investment level at the league optimum, this solution does not characterize a feasible equilibrium strategy due to strategic interaction, that is, it cannot be sustained without cooperation. Starting at the league optimum $\bar{t}_i$, club i has an incentive to increase its talent investments because this behavior raises the probability of success to win the share of league revenue awarded to the winner. However, because the other club has the same incentives, both clubs are caught in a typical prisoners' dilemma type of equilibrium. As a result, each club will enter in a ruinous competition leading to the symmetric Nash equilibrium where clubs overinvest and achieve no relative gain in performance compared to the league optimum.

4. CONCLUSION

Many types of competitions take the form of contests in which competitors make efforts by investing tangible and intangible resources and are rewarded based on their relative efforts. In business, for example, employees compete in promotion contests (Rosen, 1986; Bognanno, 2001), firms compete in market share contests (Schmalensee, 1976; Piga, 1998), and research and development labs compete in patent race contests (Loury, 1979; Nalebuff and Stiglitz, 1983; Taylor, 1995). Competition in the form of contests, however, is not limited to the world of business. Contests can be observed in all fields of social life. Litigation (Baye, Kovenock, and Casper 2005; Wärneryd, 2000; Gurtler and Krakel, 2008), rent seeking (Nitzan, 1994; Farmer and Pecorino, 1999; Lockard and Tullock, 2001; Baye and Hoppe, 2003), art competitions, beauty pageants, political campaigns (Glazer and Gradstein, 2005; Klumpp and Polborn, 2006), military conflicts (Garfinkel and Skaperdas, 2007), and many other forms of competitions take the form of contests. A further, and perhaps the most obvious, application of contests is sports. Not surprisingly, the contest aspect of sport has attracted considerable attention in the recent sports economics literature.

This chapter presented some basic applications of the theory of contest in team sports leagues. After a short outline of the traditional Tullock contest in both a static and a dynamic setting, we explained the relationship between club revenues and the contest success function (CSF). Then, we analyzed the effect of revenue sharing on competitive balance depending on the assumptions regarding the derivative of the CSF. We further concluded that an exclusive focus on competitive balance may result in inefficient policy conclusions. Finally, due to the contest structure, team sports leagues carry the risk of over-investing in playing talent.

The chapter has shown that contest theory is a suitable instrument to analyze team sports leagues from a theoretical point of view. However, one has to take into account that the team sports industry is characterized by some important peculiarities (Neale, 1964).

NOTES

The authors gratefully acknowledge the financial support provided by the Swiss National Science Foundation (Grant No. 100014–120503).

1 See also Nti (1999). Another possibility to model an asymmetric contest is via different marginal costs with respect to effort (see Szymanski and Valletti, 2005) or via different abilities in the CSF (see Dixit, 1987).

2 For surveys of this CSF in a rent-seeking contest, see Nitzan (1994) and Lockard and Tullock (2001). For general properties of this CSF, see Nti (1997). An alternative functional form would be the probit CSF (Lazear and Rosen, 1981; Dixit, 1987) and the difference-form CSF (Hirshleifer, 1989).

3 For existence conditions of Nash equilibria, see Konrad (2007).

4 See, e.g., Baye, Kovenock, de Vries (1996). Note that in such a framework with complete information, only Nash equilibria in mixed strategies exist (see, e.g., Dasgupta and Maskin 1986a,b).

5 Exceptions are Moldovanu and Sela (2001), who analyze the optimal allocation of prizes in an all-pay auction type of contest in which contestants can have linear,

concave or convex effort costs. For a dynamic Tullock contest with convex costs, see, e.g., Grossmann and Dietl (2009) and Grossmann, Dietl, and Lang (2010).

6 In the following, we present a simplified version of their model without revenue sharing.

7 In the case of linear costs, $c'(0)$ is positive.

8 See Fudenberg and Tirole (1991) for a detailed discussion of open-loop and closed-loop strategies.

9 If costs are strictly convex, then marginal costs in period 2 depend on first-period effort, whereas if costs are linear, then first-period effort has no influence on marginal costs in the second period. Therefore, intertemporal dynamics are more complex with strictly convex costs.

10 Note that in the case of an open-loop concept with strictly convex costs, there is only one equilibrium in which the contestant with the higher prize valuation has a higher asset stock in each period.

11 The contestant's first-period effort is a strategic substitute for the opponent's second-period effort contribution in this equilibrium due to the cross-derivative of the logit CSF.

12 First-period effort of this contestant is a strategic complement for the opponent's second-period effort contribution in this equilibrium.

13 Some research has been conducted into individual sports. For instance, see Scully (2000) (athletics); Tenorio (2000) (boxing); Shaw and Jakus (1996) (climbing); Ehrenberg and Bognanno (1990a,b), Orszag (1994) (golf); Fernie and Metcalf (1999) (horse-racing); Maloney and Terkun (2002) (motorcycle-racing); Szymanski (2000) (Olympics); Lynch and Zax (2000), Maloney and Terkun (2000) (running).

14 Note that this rank order contest can lead to a rat race, which induces clubs to "overinvest" in playing talent (Dietl, Franck, and Lang, 2008a).

15 In some leagues such as the European soccer leagues, there exists a third stage, in which the output of the second stage, the national champions, represent inputs for a higher-order championship of national champions, the UEFA Champions League.

16 Note that Dietl and Lang (2008) and Dietl, Lang, and Werner (2009) implicitly assume that there is decentralized broadcasting such that each club generates its own revenues. For an analysis of centralized versus decentralized broadcasting, see Falconieri, Palomino, Sakovics (2004) and Gurtler (2007).

17 See also Falconieri, Palomino, Sakovics (2004).

18 The price p_i can, for example, be interpreted as the gate price or the subscription fee for TV coverage of the match.

19 Note that the decision variable in sports contest models is not effort but "playing talent," which is often denoted by t_i and is measured in perfectly divisible units.

20 See also Szymanski (2003) and Vrooman (2008).

21 This quadratic club-specific revenue function is consistent with the revenue functions used, e.g., in Hoehn and Szymanski (1999); Szymanski (2003); Szymanski and Késenne (2004); Késenne (2006, 2007), and Vrooman (2007, 2008).

22 For further discussions, see Eckard (2006) and Szymanski (2006).

23 Rottenberg's invariance proposition is often regarded as a predecessor of the famous Coase Theorem (see Fort, 2005).

24 For a discussion of the clubs' objective function, see Sloane (1971); Hoehn and Szymanski (1999); Késenne (2000a); Fort and Quirk (2004); Késenne (2006); Garcia-del Barrio and Szymanski (2009).

25 See also Borland and MacDonald (2003).

26 See Fort (2006a) who reviews all of the different ways in which game uncertainty, playoff uncertainty and consecutive season uncertainty have been measured. Moreover, he shows how the specification error of not including all of the different measures of outcome uncertainty can lead to bias in coefficient estimates in demand analyses.

27 The "Big Five" leagues in Europe are: *Premier League* (England, 20 clubs), *Ligue 1* (France, 20 clubs), *Bundesliga* (Germany, 18 clubs), *Primera Division* (Spain, 20 clubs) and the *Serie A* (Italy, 18 clubs).

28 http://www.football-industry.com

29 Guardian, 2nd of June 2009.

30 Kicker, 12th of January 2004.

31 Note that Dietl, Franck, Lang (2008a) consider a league with n clubs. Moreover, they assume a flexible supply of talent and therefore use the Contest-Nash conjectures.

32 See also Dietl et al. (2009). In terms of a contest model, the total league revenue can be interpreted as an endogenously given contest prize (see, e.g., Chung, 1996).

33 Note that comparative statics regarding the equilibrium investments yield the same results as in standard contest models.

34 The ratio D is called "ratio of rent dissipation" in the rent-seeking literature.

35 Note that $D(\alpha, \gamma)$ is independent of marginal costs c because also the league optimum proportionally decreases with c.

References

Atkinson, S., Stanley, L., and Tschirhart, J. (1988). Revenue sharing as an incentive in an agency problem: An example from the National Football League. *The RAND Journal of Economics*, 19: 27–43.

Baye, M., and Hoppe, H. (2003). The strategic equivalence of rent-seeking, innovation, and patent-race games. *Games and Economic Behavior*, 44: 217–226.

Baye, M., Kovenock, D., and Casper, G. (2005). Comparative analysis of litigation systems: An auction-theoretic approach. *Economic Journal*, 115: 583–601.

Baye, M., Kovenock, D., and De Vries, C. (1996). The all-pay auction with complete information. *Economic Theory*, 8: 291–305.

Bognanno, M. (2001). Corporate tournaments. *Journal of Labor Economics*, 19: 290–315.

Borland, J., and MacDonald, R. (2003). The demand for sports. *Oxford Review of Economic Policy*, 19: 478–502.

Chung, T. (1996). Rent-seeking contest when the prize increases with aggregate efforts. *Public Choice*, 87: 55–66.

Clark, D., and Riis, C. (1998). Contest success functions: An extension. *Economic Theory*, 11: 201–204.

Dasgupta, P., and Maskin, E. (1986a). The existence of equilibrium in discontinuous games. *Review of Economic Studies*, 53: 1–26.

Dasgupta, P., and Maskin, E. (1986b). The existence of equilibrium in discontinuous economic games, I: Theory. *The Review of Economic Studies*, 53: 1–26.

Deloitte and Touche (2009). *Annual review of football finance.*

Dietl, H., Franck, E., Hasan, T., and Lang, M. (2009). Governance of professional sports leagues—Cooperatives versus contracts. *International Review of Law and Economics*, 29: 127–137.

Dietl, H., Franck, E., and Lang, M. (2008a). Overinvestment in team sports leagues: A contest theory model. *Scottish Journal of Political Economy*, 55: 353–368.

Dietl, H., Franck, E., and Lang, M. (2008b). Why football players may benefit from the "shadow of the transfer system." *European Journal of Law and Economics*, 26: 129–151.

Dietl, H., and Lang, M. (2008). The effect of gate revenue sharing on social welfare. *Contemporary Economic Policy*, 26: 448–459.

Dietl, H., Lang, M., and Rathke, A. (2009). The effect of salary caps in professional team sports on social welfare. *The B.E. Journal of Economic Analysis and Policy*, 9: Article 17.

Dietl, H., Lang, M., and Rathke, A. (2011). The combined effect of salary restrictions and revenue sharing in sports leagues. *Economic Inquiry*, 49: 447–463.

Dietl, H., Lang, M., and Werner, S. (2009). Social welfare in sports leagues with profit-maximizing and/or win-maximizing clubs. *Southern Economic Journal*, 76: 375–396.

Dietl, H., Lang, M., and Werner, S. (2010). The effect of luxury taxes on competitive balance, club profits, and social welfare in sports leagues, *International Journal of Sport Finance*, 5: 41–51.

Dixit, A. (1987). Strategic behavior in contests. *American Economic Review*, 77: 891–898.

Downward, P., and Dawson, A. (2000). *The Economics of Professional Team Sports*. London: Routledge.

Eckard, E. (2006). Comment: "Professional team sports are only a game: The Walrasian fixed-supply conjecture model, contest-Nash equilibrium, and the invariance principle." *Journal of Sports Economics*, 7: 234–239.

Economist (2002). For love or money. *Economist*, 363: 7.

Ehrenberg, R., and Bognanno, M. (1990a). Do tournaments have incentive effects? *Journal of Political Economy*, 13: 1307–1324.

Ehrenberg, R., and Bognanno, M. (1990b). The incentive effect of tournaments revisited: Evidence from the European PGA tour. *Industrial and Labor Relations Review*, 43: 74S–88S.

El-Hodiri, M., and Quirk, J. (1971). An economic model of a professional sports league. *Journal of Political Economy*, 79: 1302–1319.

Falconieri, S., Palomino, F., and Sakovics, J. (2004). Collective versus individual sale of television rights in league sports. *Journal of the European Economic Association*, 5: 833–862.

Farmer, A., and Pecorino, P. (1999). Legal expenditure as a rent-seeking game. *Public Choice*, 100: 271–288.

Fernie, S. and Metcalf, D. (1999). It's not what you pay, it's the way that you pay it, and that's what gets results: Jockeys' pay and performance. *Labour*, 13: 385–411.

Fort, R. (2005). The golden anniversary of 'the baseball players labor market.' *Journal of Sports Economics*, 6: 347–358.

Fort, R. (2006a). Competitive balance in North American professional sports, in J. Fizel, ed., *Handbook of sports economics research*. Armonk, NY: ME Sharpe, pp. 190–206.

Fort, R. (2006b). Talent market models in north American and world leagues, in R. Placido, S. Kesenne, and J. Garcia, eds, *Sports economics after fifty years: Essays in honour of Simon Rottenberg*, Oviedo: Oviedo University Press, pp. 83–106.

Fort, R., and Quirk, J. (1995). Cross-subsidization, incentives, and outcomes in professional team sports leagues. *Journal of Economic Literature*, 33: 1265–1299.

Fort, R., and Quirk, J. (2004). Owner objectives and competitive balance. *Journal of Sports Economics*, 5: 20–32.

Fort, R., and Quirk, J. (2007). Rational expectations and pro sports leagues. *Scottish Journal of Political Economy*, 54: 374–387.

Franck, E. (2003). Beyond market power: Efficiency explanations for the basic structures of north American major league organizations. *European Sport Management Quarterly*, 3: 221–239.

Fudenberg, D., and Tirole, J. (1991). *Game theory*. Cambridge, MA: MIT Press.

Garcia-del Barrio, P., and Szymanski, S. (2009). Goal! Profit maximization and win maximization in football leagues. *Review of Industrial Organization*, 34: 45–68.

Garfinkel, M., and Skaperdas, S. (2007). Economics of conflict: An overview, in T. Sandler and K. Hartley, eds, *Handbook of defense economics*. Amsterdam: Elsevier, pp. 649–709.

Glazer, A., and Gradstein, M. (2005). Elections with contribution-maximizing candidates. *Public Choice*, 122: 467–482.

Grossmann, M., and Dietl, H. (2009). Investment behaviour in a two period contest model. *The Journal of Institutional and Theoretical Economics*, 165: 401–417.

Grossmann, M., Dietl, H., and Lang, M. (2010). Revenue sharing and competitive balance in a dynamic contest model. *Review of Industrial Organization*, 36: 17–36.

Gurtler, O. (2007). A rationale for the coexistence of central and decentral marketing in team sports. *German Economic Review*, 8: 89–106.

Gurtler, O., and Krakel, M. (2010). Double-sided moral hazard, efficiency wages, and litigation. *Journal of Law, Economics, and Organization*, 26: 337–364.

Hirshleifer, J. (1989). Conflict and rent-seeking success functions: Ratio vs. difference models of relative success. *Public Choice*, 63: 101–112.

Hoehn, T., and Szymanski, S. (1999). The Americanization of European football. *Economic Policy*, 14: 204–240.

Késenne, S. (2000a). Revenue sharing and competitive balance in professional team sports. *Journal of Sports Economics*, 1: 56–65.

Késenne, S. (2000b). The impact of salary caps in professional team sports. *Scottish Journal of Political Economy*, 47: 422–430.

Késenne, S. (2005). Revenue sharing and competitive balance: Does the invariance proposition hold? *Journal of Sports Economics*, 6: 98–106.

Késenne, S. (2006). The win maximization model reconsidered: Flexible talent supply and efficiency wages. *Journal of Sports Economics*, 7: 416–427.

Késenne, S. (2007). *The Economic theory of professional team sports: An analytical treatment*. Cheltenham, UK: Edward Elgar.

Klumpp, T., and Polborn, M. (2006). Primaries and the New Hampshire effect. *Journal of Public Economics*, 90: 1073–1114.

Konrad, K. (2007). Strategy in contests: An introduction. *WZB-Markets and Politics Working Paper* No. SP II 1, 2007.

Lazear, E. and Rosen, S. (1981). Rank-order tournaments as optimum labor contracts. *Journal of Political Economy*, 89: 841–864.

Lockard, A., and Tullock, G. E. (2001). *Efficient rent-seeking: Chronicle of an intellectual quagmire*. Boston: Kluwer Academic Publisher.

Loury, G. (1979). Market structure and innovation. *The Quarterly Journal of Economics*, 13: 395–410.

Lynch, J., and Zax, J. (2000). The rewards to running: Prize structure and performance in professional road racing. *Journal of Sports Economics*, 1: 323–340.

Maloney, M., and Terkun, K. (2000). The response of workers to wages in tournaments: Evidence from foot races. *Journal of Sports Economics*, 1: 99–123.

Maloney, M., and Terkun, K. (2002). Road warrior booty: Prize structures in motorcycle racing. *Contributions to Economic Analysis and Policy*, 1: 1–18.

Moldovanu, B., and Sela, A. (2001). The optimal allocation of prizes in contests. *American Economic Review*, 91: 542–558.

Nalebuff, B., and Stiglitz, J. (1983). Prizes and incentives: Towards a general theory of compensation and competition. *The Bell Journal of Economics*, 14: 21–43.

Neale, W. (1964). The peculiar economics of professional sports: A contribution to the theory of the firm in sporting competition and in market competition. *Quarterly Journal of Economics*, 78: 1–14.

Nitzan, S. (1994). Modelling rent-seeking contests. *European Journal of Political Economy*, 10: 41–60.

Nti, K. (1997). Comparative statics of contests and rent-seeking games. *International Economic Review*, 38: 43–59.

Nti, K. (1999). Rent-seeking with asymmetric valuations. *Public Choice*, 98: 415–430.

Orszag, J. (1994): A new look at incentive effects and tournaments. *Economics Letters*, 46: 77–88.

Piga, C. (1998). A dynamic model of advertising and product differentiation. *Review of Industrial Organization*, 13: 509–522.

Quirk, J., and El-Hodiri, M. (1974). The economic theory of a professional sports league, in R. G. Noll, ed., *Government and the sports business*, Washington, DC: Brooking Institution: 33–80.

Rascher, D. (1997). A model of a professional sports league, in W. Hendricks, ed., *Advances in economics of sport*, Vol. 2, Greenwich: JAI Press: 27–76.

Rosen, S. (1986). Prizes and incentives in elimination tournaments. *American Economic Review*, 76: 701–715.

Rottenberg, S. (1956). The baseball players' labor market.' *Journal of Political Economy*, 64: 242–258.

Sanderson, A. (2002). The many dimensions of competitive balance. *Journal of Sports Economics*, 3: 204–228.

Sanderson, A., and Siegfried, J. (2003). Thinking about competitive balance. *Journal of Sports Economics*, 4: 255.

Schmalensee, R. (1976). A model of promotional competition in oligopoly. *The Review of Economic Studies*, 43: 493–507.

Scully, G. (2000). Diminishing returns and the limit of athletic performance. *Scottish Journal of Political Economy*, 47: 456–470.

Shaw, W., and Jakus, P. (1996). Travel cost models of the demand for rock climbing. *Agricultural and Resource Economics Review*, 25: 133–142.

Skaperdas, S. (1996). Contest success functions. *Economic Theory*, 7: 283–290.

Sloane, P. (1971). The economics of professional football: The football club as a utility maximizer. *Scottish Journal of Political Economy*, 17: 121–146.

Szymanski, S. (2000). The market for Olympic gold medals. *World Economics*, 1: 1–8.

Szymanski, S. (2003). The economic design of sporting contests. *Journal of Economic Literature*, 41: 1137–1187.

Szymanski, S. (2004). Professional team sports are only a game: The Walrasian fixed supply conjecture model, contest-Nash equilibrium and the invariance principle. *Journal of Sports Economics*, 5: 111–126.

Szymanski, S. (2006). Reply: "Professional team sports are only a game: The Walrasian fixed-supply conjecture model, contest-Nash equilibrium, and the invariance principle." *Journal of Sports Economics*, 7: 240–243.

Szymanski, S., and Késenne, S. (2004). Competitive balance and gate revenue sharing in team sports. *The Journal of Industrial Economics*, 52: 165–177.

Szymanski, S., and Valletti, T. (2005). Incentive effects of second prizes. *European Journal of Political Economy*, 21: 467–481.

Taylor, C. (1995). Digging for golden carrots: An analysis of research tournaments. *American Economic Review*, 85: 872–890.

Tenorio, R. (2000). The economics of professional boxing contracts. *Journal of Sports Economics*, 1: 363–384.

Tullock, G. (1980). Efficient rent-seeking, in J. Buchanan, R. Tollison and G. Tullock, eds., *Toward a theory of rent seeking society*. College Station: Texas A & M University Press, pp. 97–112.

Vrooman, J. (1995). A general theory of professional sports leagues. *Southern Economic Journal*, 61: 971–990.

Vrooman, J. (2007). Theory of the beautiful game: The unification of European football. *Scottish Journal of Political Economy*, 54: 314–354.

Vrooman, J. (2008). Theory of the perfect game: Competitive balance in monopoly sports leagues. *Review of Industrial Organization*, 31: 1–30.

Wärneryd, K. (2000). In defense of lawyers: moral hazard as an aid to cooperation. *Games and Economic Behavior*, 33: 145–158.

CHAPTER 23

....

TOURNAMENT INCENTIVES IN PROFESSIONAL BOWLING

MICHAEL L. BOGNANNO

....

1. INTRODUCTION

....

SEVERAL early theoretical articles concerned with contracting presented models that base pay on relative performance.[1] In tournament models, pay is based solely on rank order. Under certain conditions, tournaments have been shown to dominate wage schemes that base pay upon measures of individual output. Tournament theory provides for a basis for skewness in pay structures in multi-round competitions with elimination. The skewed pay structures provide incentives for all those in the tournament with aspirations for the top and are necessary to maintain the incentives of those nearing the top.[2] It is not, however, a theoretical implication of tournament theory that overall effort rises with pay structure skewness in tournaments when those not in contention for top prizes continue to participate in a multi-round framework.

This chapter uses panel data from professional bowling tournaments to test for prize structure incentives. Given a hypothesized relationship between effort and bowling scores, bowling tournaments provide a good setting for this task. The criterion for advancement in bowling tournaments is based on a known and objective measure of output. Rewards are based on a rank ordering of player output. The prize structures differ across tournaments in level and skewness. Furthermore, players compete in many tournaments and data exist to control for nonmonetary influences on scores. Thus, the incentive effects of different aspects of tournament prize structures can be directly examined.

This chapter is closely related to many others testing aspects of tournament theory with professional sports data. The brief review of the literature provided here is not intended to be comprehensive but rather focuses on a subset of papers that were particularly interesting or novel. In the first paper to find of evidence tournament incentives in a non-experimental setting, Ehrenberg and Bognanno (1990a) found strong support for the proposition that the level and structure of prizes on the U.S. Men's Professional Golf Association Tour influenced players' performance. Higher prize money tournaments, with correspondingly higher dispersion between prizes, elicited more effort from golfers in the tournament overall, as evidenced by lower scores. In addition, players with larger marginal returns to effort, those near the top of the leader list at the end of the third round, facing larger gaps between prizes due to the highly skewed prize structure, had lower scores in the last round. These findings were replicated using data from the European Men's Professional Golf Association Tour in Ehrenberg and Bognanno (1990b).

Two other papers employing professional golf data are quite interesting. First, Bronars and Oettinger (2008) examine hole-by-hole performance in the final round of PGA Tour events to examine how players respond to the incentives created by the convex rank-order prize structure employed in the tournaments. They consider effort incentives deriving from the local slope of the prize-score relationship and risk-taking incentives deriving from the convexity of the local prize-score relationship. The prize money consequences of gaining or losing a stroke on the field depend on the player's rank at that point in the final round, the distribution of competing players, and the prize structure in the specific tournament. In confirmation of incentive effects, they find that golfers have better scores on holes when winnings are more strongly influenced by marginal score changes. They also find evidence of risk-taking when the relationship between prize winnings and score changes is more convex. Risk-taking increased the score variance and was found to be harmful to performance on average. Given this, it follows that risk-taking was primarily exhibited in the final holes of the tournament rather than during the entire round of play.

A second recent paper utilizing professional golf data considers the impact of competing against a superstar. The incentive to compete is not only a function of the prize money at stake but also of the player's ability to influence the probability of winning through the exertion of effort. When ability differences are large, the impact of effort on the probability of winning diminishes and the incentive to exert effort is reduced. Brown (2008) found that higher skilled golfers played worse by almost one stroke a tournament when Tiger Woods was in the field and on top of his game. Lesser players were not affected and better players were not affected when Woods was off his game.

Sunde (2009) also tests the idea that heterogeneity among contestants reduces effort as large differences in ability make effort less influential in determining the winner. The novel aspect of this paper is that it derives testable implications for tennis matches, an environment without an observable measure of absolute output, such as scores in golf. There are two hypothesized effects of increasing the ability difference between players in a tennis match. First, both players exert less effort as the incentive to exert effort is diminished. Second, the better player increases in dominance over the lesser player by virtue of the expanding ability gap. This capability effect leads to more games being won by the better player and fewer by the lesser player, regardless of incentive effects. For lesser players, the incentive effect and the capability effect work in the same direction, both reduce relative performance. For the better players, the capability effect, increasing relative performance, is mitigated by the incentive effect, reducing performance. If the incentive effect doesn't exist, ability differences lead to only a capability effect of equal but opposite signs for the two players. If the incentive effect exists and works in the theorized direction, better players will be affected by heterogeneity to a smaller extent than their lesser opponents. These predictions are confirmed. Not surprisingly, lesser tennis players win fewer games per set in matches with larger ability differences. More significantly, better tennis players were less affected by the ability gap than lesser players providing evidence that increased heterogeneity reduced the incentive to exert effort.

Garicano and Palacios-Huerta (2005) looked for evidence of the stronger incentives to win professional soccer matches created by a rule change that increased the points allocated to a winning a match from two to three. The intent of the rule change was to encourage an attacking style of play and more goal scoring. Aside from exploiting this rule change, following from the theoretical underpinnings provided by Lazear (1989), they analyzed indicators of both productive and destructive effort in response to the increased reward for winning matches. Lazear pointed out that when the incentives to win are strong, the probability of winning can be increased both by exerting productive effort to increase one's own performance and by exerting destructive effort to hinder the performance of one's competition. Garicano and Palacios-Huerta found that net scoring did not change due to the stronger incentives to win because of increases in both productive and destructive effort. One direct measure of the increases in destructive effort or sabotage was that after the rule change the fouls committed during matches increased. This was the first finding that stronger incentives to win can bring about destructive effort.

Maloney and Terkun's (2002) study of motorcycle racing is novel in that it tests implications of tournament theory, not related to participant incentive effects, but in how sponsors vary prize structures. Because the effort exerted by participants due to strong incentives in the prize structure (from large prize gaps) is costly, sponsors in competition with one another should raise overall prize levels in compensation for strong incentives. As well, one way for a sponsor to remain competitive against a rival sponsor offering high overall prize levels is to reduce the incentives in their prize structure (by reducing prize gaps) and thereby eliciting less costly effort from participants. Support for the notion that sponsors recognize the cost of effort imposed on participants from strong prize structure incentives and compensate participants with higher prize levels is found.

This chapter contributes to the empirical work on tournaments primarily by studying the influence of skewness on performance. The research on golf tournaments explored the incentive effects of tournament prize structures by examining how the prize level (which was a measure of the difference between prizes) and the prize money at stake for individual golfers given their rank in the tournament influenced scores, but did not consider the effects of differing prize structure skewness on total scores over the course of the tournament. This was because the percentage of the total prize purse paid to each finishing place varied little though the purse itself varied considerably. On PBA Tour events, however, enough variation exists in the percentage of the total prize allocated to various finishing places across tournaments to allow the effects of skewness to be studied independently of the effects of changes in the prize level.

The following section discusses the data and the format of bowling tournaments. Section 3 draws implications from tournament theory regarding the influence of dispersion and skewness in the prize structure on effort. The empirical model and results are reported in Section 4. The two most distinct portions of bowling tournaments are analyzed separately. Estimations are first performed on the qualifying and match play rounds and then on the televised match play, elimination championship round. Concluding remarks are made in Section 5.

2. A Description of the Data

The data used in this study for estimations on the qualifying and match play rounds come from most of the Professional Bowling Association Tour events held from 1985 through 1991. Data were unavailable for 1988, and specific tournaments were excluded because the participants were not regular touring players or because of a nontraditional format. A total of 185 tournaments are used. The information available for each tournament includes, in part, the name of the tournament, the name of the site, the date, all prize money awarded and, for the top twenty-four finishers, individual total scores. The data used for estimations on the championship round come from tournaments held in 1989, 1990, and 1991. To better understand the data, a description of the tournament format is necessary. Bowling tournaments are composed of four parts: the pro tour qualifier, the qualifying round, the match play round, and the championship round. In the pro tour qualifier, nonexempt players compete over ten games for entry into the tournament. The nonexempt players with the top total scores in the pro tour qualifier advance into the qualifying round to fill slots not taken by exempt players. Exempt players are exempt from participation in the pro tour qualifier; they have automatic entry into the qualifying round field of 160. The twenty-four bowlers with the highest total scores over the typical eighteen-game qualifying round advance to the match play round of the tournament.

In the match play round, each bowler completes twenty-four games. In each of these games, a player competes against one of the other qualifying players.[3] In addition to his game score, a player adds to his point total by beating his opponent in match play. Points begin accumulating in the qualifying round, where they consist of the sum of the bowler's scores, and carry over into match play, where, in addition to the bowler's game score, a bonus of thirty points is added for each match play victory. The name of the match play round is somewhat misleading since the players, though paired against one another in competition for the thirty bonus points, remain in competition with the entire field with respect to total points. Players losing a game in the match play round are not eliminated from the tournament. At the end of the match play round, the five players with the most total points advance into the championship round with their rank determining their entry position in it. Players not finishing in the top five at the end of the match play round are done in the tournament and receive a prize based on their rank. The measure of player output used in this study in the qualifying and match play round estimations is the average game score of the player during the qualifying and match play rounds of the tournament.

The championship round consists of four matches following a step ladder format. It begins with the fourth- and fifth-ranked players meeting in the bottom match. The winner advances to face the third-ranked player, and the winner of that match goes on to compete against the player ranked second. The semi-finals winner faces the top-ranked player in the finals to decide first place. The individual game scores serve as the dependent variable in the championship round estimations. Each tournament yields eight individual championship-round game scores.

3. Hypotheses to be Tested

Tournament theory provides a basis to draw implications about how two aspects of the prize structure, dispersion and skewness, should affect the effort of competitors and, hence, their scores.[4] Tournament theory is premised on the notion that increasing the gap between the winning and losing prizes increases effort. This basic implication of the theory suggests that increases in the gaps between prizes, or in the dispersion of prizes, should lead to higher average scores in bowling tournaments. Regardless of a player's rank at any point in the qualifying and match play rounds, the reward to better performance will be greater when the inter-rank spreads in the tournament prize structure are greater.

Rosen (1986) establishes the incentive effects of prize structure skewness in a sequential match play elimination tournament (such as a tennis tournament). In tournaments of this type, assuming risk aversion, increasingly large prizes are necessary to maintain the incentives of those advancing in the tournament. If the differences between the higher ranking prizes do not increase, contestants will exert less effort as they advance because the value of further success in the tournament diminishes. This result implies that contestants should exert more effort in tournaments with more skewed prize structures because the survival value is greater. Allocating more of the prize pool to top prizes yields incentives throughout the course of the tournament, whereas bottom prizes cease to be motivating early in the tournament after their recipients have been decided.

If bowlers make a single decision on the exertion of effort, perhaps in the form of pre-tournament preparation, then the implication for skewness is clear. Skewness should increase effort and scores. However, if bowlers vary their effort from game to game within the tournament, then the effects of skewness should differ between players performing well and those performing poorly relative to others in the field. This difference results because the qualifying and match play round bowling data are not in an elimination format. All of the bowlers finishing the qualifying round ranked among the top twenty-four competitors complete the entire match play round. One would expect that, over the course of the twenty-four games played in the match play round, middle- and low-ranking bowlers would become discouraged by more of the total prize money being allocated to the top finishing places. They would recognize the slight chance they had of a high finish and would face the smaller differences between prizes in the lower ranks because of the larger share of the total prize money allocated to top prizes. It is not inconsistent then, with these tournament data, for skewness to have a negative influence on scores overall if the demoralizing effect on those not expecting a top finish exceeds the motivation provided to those with better expectations. If skewness has a negative overall effect, it should be less so for bowlers with higher expectations of a top finish. Furthermore, in a sample of bowlers who are in contention for top prizes, skewness should have a positive influence on scores.

In addition to the incentives created by the prize structure, in the championship round the possible effect of the difference between players in ability is examined. As noted in the literature review, increased player heterogeneity should reduce the scores of both players competing head to head because the influence of effort on the probability of winning is reduced.

Skewness is marked in bowling prize structures and results in a very uneven distribution of rewards across players both within a single tournament and over the course of a season. Considering that 160 players participate in the qualifying round and the top third collect prize money, allocating 17 percent of the total prize level on average to first place and nearly 40 percent to the top five places constitutes a highly skewed distribution of pay.

The pay that players accumulate over the season is also distributed unevenly, especially in comparison to the differences between players in ability. For instance, in 1985 the bowler ranking 50th in average score over the course of the season had an average score that was 97 percent of the top-ranked average score, while the 50th ranked player by earnings that season earned only 14 percent of the $201,200 earned by the top player. A similar contrast can be made between players within a single tournament where prize differences are proportionately much larger than differences in total pins. While small differences in player average scores will be evidenced over forty-two games, it is payment based on rank order together with a highly skewed prize structure that creates the large earnings disparities.

4. EMPIRICAL MODEL AND RESULTS

Models of the form below were estimated on the group of players appearing in the match play round of each tournament. The model assumes that a player's output depends on his effort, the prize structure, his ability, the ability of competitors, the tournament characteristics and random influences.

$$s_{ji} = a_0 + a_1 Dispersion_i + a_2 Skewness_i + a_3 Ability_j + a_4 y_i + a_5 z_i + v_{ji}$$

Player j's output in tournament i, s_{ji}, is represented by the player's average score over all games played in the qualifying and match play rounds. Dispersion is represented by the sum of all prizes awarded in tournament i and, as an alternative, by the standard deviation of prizes within the tournament. The total of prizes awarded serves as a measure of dispersion because additional prize money affords much larger top prizes, stretching out the prize distribution and creating large prize gaps in the structure. The total prize variable is used to allow comparison with the professional golf studies and because it is easy to interpret. It should be noted that the prize level and the standard deviation of prizes in a tournament have a correlation coefficient of .97. It is not possible in these data to separate the effects of the dispersion in prizes from the total prize level. All prize variables are stated in 1985 dollars.

Skewness is also measured in two ways. First, the coefficient of skewness is computed on the distribution of prizes within a tournament. The coefficient of skewness measures the departure from symmetry in a distribution. A value of zero for the coefficient of skewness indicates a symmetric distribution, which in this case would require that the first and last place prizes were equal. Since all bowling prize distributions award the most to first place and a lesser or equal amount to each successive prize, the prize distributions are skewed to the right. Tournaments with the largest coefficients of skewness are the most skewed. The second index of skewness, one well suited to use on bowling prize structures, is the percentage of the total prize allocated to first place. Tournaments awarding a greater percentage of the total prize to first place have more skewed distributions because less is available for the other places. Additionally, most of the variation across tournaments in the percentage of the total prize money awarded to a given finishing rank occurs among the top few places. The percentage going to first place is positively correlated with the percentage of the total prize allocated to the second through fifth place prizes and the gaps between the first through fifth place prizes. It is negatively correlated with the percentage going to finishing prizes beneath fifth. Controlling for the total prize level, the share allocated to first place is positively correlated with eight of the top ten prize gaps and negatively correlated with all forty or so beneath. Thus, after controlling for the prize level, for the majority of players who are not ranked among the leaders late in the tournament, a higher share for first place should reduce the effort that they exert late in the tournament.

The control for the ability of player j is constructed as the player's average pins per game over all tournaments in which he was a top twenty-four finisher, excluding the player's performance in the given tournament. This construction ensures that current observations of the dependent variable are not reflected on the right-hand side. The vector y_i includes controls for the ability of the tournament field and the dispersion of ability in the tournament field. The controls for field ability and the dispersion of ability in the tournament field were computed by taking the average of the player ability measure for all players in the field and the standard deviation of the player ability measure. Besides these variables created using the information on all twenty-four finalists, an additional field quality measure was constructed as the mean ability of the top five players in the field. These measures were included because it has been shown that the difference in ability between players in two player tournament models influences effort.

The vector z_i includes controls for tournament characteristics and v_{ji} is a random error term. The tournament characteristics controlled for are the number of prizes awarded, tournament importance, the number of games played and the date of play. The number of prizes awarded is often linked to the number of entrants and could affect the initial odds of a top finish. Victory in a major tournament may carry greater commercial rewards and, thus, have value beyond the prize money awarded. Major tournaments may also elicit additional effort because of their greater prestige. On the other hand, major tournaments often have many more entrants, resulting in greater lane use. This causes lane conditions to change more rapidly as the oil on the surface of the lanes is altered and may result in reduced scores. In either case, whether a tournament is a "major" may influence scores. Some tournaments require more qualifying games, perhaps introducing a fatigue factor and reducing scores. Therefore, the number of games played is included as an explanatory variable. As equipment and technique advance, athletes are generally surpassing the achievements of their predecessors. A trend variable is used to capture this effect. Bowlers as a group show improving scores over the seven year sample period.

Table 23.1 presents the results of the four models estimated on all of the qualifying round and match play data. The first two columns include the full set of explanatory variables discussed and are without any fixed effects. The construction of the ability variable reduces the number of observations by 149, the difference in observations between this model and the models estimated with player fixed-effects rather than the player ability variable. Columns 3 and 4 contain both site and player fixed-effects. Site effects are included should there be any site-specific influences on output that might correlate with the prize level biasing the key parameter estimates and player effects to overcome possible deficiencies in the constructed measure of player ability. The variables major and games are omitted from this model because they do not vary across years at a given site and thus cannot be identified given the site fixed effects. The data contain 59 different sites and 444 different players.

In looking at the explanatory power of the model in Table 23.1, one notices that the variation in scores explained by the models is low. This was expected for two reasons. The setting is nearly uniform across tournaments, and players are very close in ability. Therefore, tournament controls and player ability controls would be unlikely to explain much of the variation in scores. Additionally, the perhaps small changes in pretournament preparation and concentration during the tournament that are hypothesized to result from differing prize structures across tournaments would be expected to result in even smaller changes in scores for professional bowlers. Presumably the ability of professional bowlers to increase their scores in response to strong incentives in the prize structure is limited and subject to diminishing marginal returns. Similarly, weak incentives in the prize structure are unlikely to result in careless bowling and much lower scores because the players are professionals with at least their reputations at stake. Players also pay an entry fee in order to compete.

Turning to the results in Table 23.1, when significant, the number of prizes awarded in the tournament leads to higher scores.[5] The measure of player ability is positive as expected across specifications, showing that better players have higher average scores. Controlling for a player's own ability, increasing the ability of the field decreases the player's average score. This is evidenced by the signs on mean field ability and the mean ability of the top five players. Facing a better field is likely to reduce the probability of a high finish. Increasing the standard deviation of the field's ability increases average scores. This result is unexpected because players in a field very close in ability should have more influence over their final rank than players in tournaments where ability differences are marked. However, the measure is somewhat crude and reflects only the dispersion of ability before the tournament, taking no account of how close players are in performance as the tournament proceeds. Major tournaments had a negative influence on output. This might result from more difficult lane conditions in major tournaments. The trend coefficient indicates that players' scores were generally rising during the sample period. Increases in the number of games in a tournament reduce average scores, perhaps because of player fatigue.

Table 23.1 Dependant Variable: Average Score per Game in the Qualifying and Matchplay Rounds Data Pooled Across Tournaments and Players (absolute value t statistics)

	(1)	(2)	(3)	(4)
CONSTANT	553.461 (9.8)	544.545 (9.6)		
TPRIZE	2.713 (5.3)		1.644 (2.9)	
SD		0.001 (4.3)		0.0003 (2.4)
FIRSTSHR	−49.273 (5.7)		−33.273 (3.0)	
CS		−3.065 (5.6)		−2.548 (3.7)
NPRIZES	−0.005 (0.3)	0.180 (5.4)	−0.057 (1.8)	0.088 (2.1)
ABILITY	0.384 (8.9)	0.384 (8.9)		
TOPABIL	−1.008 (3.2)	−0.946 (3.0)	−1.013 (2.6)	−0.909 (2.4)
MABILITY	−0.940 (2.4)	−0.973 (2.4)	−1.236 (2.8)	−1.314 (3.0)
SDABILTY	1.385 (4.5)	1.400 (4.6)	0.567 (1.6)	0.470 (1.4)
MAJOR	−1.267 (2.2)	−1.563 (2.6)		
TREND	0.069 (11.2)	0.060 (10.4)	0.054 (7.1)	0.049 (7.0)
GAMES	0.003 (0.1)	−0.014 (0.6)		
R-Square	0.06	0.06	0.35	0.35
N	4274	4274	4423	4423

Notes: Columns 3 and 4 contain player and site fixed-effects.

Variable Definitions:

TPRIZE	Inflation adjusted total tournament prize money awarded (in 100,000's)
SD	Inflation adjusted standard deviation of prizes within a tournament
FIRSTSHR	Percentage of the total prize allocated to first place
CS	Coefficient of skewness in prizes within a tournament
NPRIZES	The number of prizes awarded in the tournament
ABILITY	Player's average pins per game over all tournaments in which he was a top 24 finisher in the data excluding the given tournament
TOPABIL	Mean of the top five values of ABILITY in the tournament
MABILITY	Mean of all values of ABILITY in the tournament
SDABILTY	Standard deviation of the values of ABILITY in the tournament
MAJOR	1 = U.S. Open, Tournament of Champions or PBA National Championship, 0 = other
TREND	Counts months from the date of first tournament to the date of the last
GAMES	Number of games played in a tournament prior to the championship round and not including pre-tournament qualifying games played
RANK	Player's rank by prior year earnings for the top fifty players. (50 = top earner)

The two most noteworthy findings in Table 23.1 relate, first, to the total prize level and the standard deviation and, second, to the percentage of the prize allocated to first place and the coefficient of skewness. Both of the alternative measures of dispersion, the prize level and the standard deviation of prizes, have a positive and statistically significant influence on scores. In accord with theory, higher prize levels and, hence, dispersion among prizes leads to higher output. A $100,000 increase in the total prize level increases an average game score by 2.7 pins according to column 1 and would raise a player's total score over the course of a 42-game tournament by 113.4 pins.[6] Column 2 suggests that a $1,000 increase in the standard deviation increases average scores by 1 pin. Importantly, however, across specifications both of the alternative measures skewness, the percentage of prize money allocated to first place and the coefficient of skewness, have significantly negative coefficients. Increasing the share of the total purse allocated to first place by 10 percent reduces average scores by 4.9. This result is contrary to theory when the tournament is viewed as a one shot event.

Tables 23.2 and 23.3 were estimated to further explore the influence of skewness in the prize structure on scores. Table 23.2 presents a set of regressions identical to those in Table 23.1 except that an interaction between the measure of skewness employed and the player's rank in terms of prior year earnings is included. Including rank reduces the sample to the top fifty ranking players by prior year earnings because only their year-end total earnings are available. Total earnings in the prior year is the most direct measure of expected future earnings apparent in the data. The top-ranked players are multiple tournament winners who benefited

Table 23.2 Dependant Variable: Average Score per Game in the Qualifying and Matchplay Rounds Data Pooled Across Tournaments and Players (absolute value t statistics)

	(1)	(2)	(3)	(4)
CONSTANT	754.087 (7.8)	758.392 (7.9)		
TPRIZE	3.564 (4.0)		9.287 (5.9)	
SD		0.001 (4.0)		0.002 (5.0)
FIRSTSHR	−41.270 (2.7)		−82.200 (3.3)	
FIRSTSHR×RANK	0.054 (0.8)		0.042 (0.5)	
CS		−3.036 (3.2)		−3.321 (2.0)
CS×RANK		0.002 (0.8)		0.002 (0.5)
NPRIZES	−0.097 (4.0)	0.090 (1.5)	−0.315 (4.5)	−0.052 (0.6)
ABILITY	0.539 (4.5)	0.542 (4.5)		
TOPABIL	−2.245 (3.9)	−2.170 (3.8)	−1.996 (2.8)	−1.733 (2.4)
MABILITY	−0.760 (1.1)	−0.866 (1.3)	−0.852 (1.0)	−1.363 (1.7)
SDABILTY	1.183 (2.1)	1.197 (2.1)	0.741 (1.1)	0.536 (0.8)
MAJOR	0.854 (0.9)	0.420 (0.4)		
TREND	0.059 (5.5)	0.050 (5.1)	0.063 (4.0)	0.031 (2.3)
GAMES	0.004 (0.1)	−0.005 (0.1)		
R-Square	0.08	0.08	0.36	0.36
N	1348	1348	1348	1348

Notes: Columns 3 and 4 contain player and site fixed-effects.

Table 23.3 Dependant Variable: Average Score per Game in the Qualifying and Matchplay Rounds Data Pooled Across Tournaments and Different Samples of Players (absolute value t statistics)

	(1)	(2)	(3)	(4)
CONSTANT	758.253 (4.5)	752.503 (4.4)	393.621 (3.7)	389.467 (3.7)
TPRIZE	3.635 (2.3)		1.933 (2.0)	
SD		0.001 (2.5)		−0.0003 (1.3)
FIRSTSHR	−42.418 (1.6)		−37.618 (2.4)	
CS		−3.614 (2.2)		−1.718 (1.7)
NPRIZES	−0.140 (3.0)	0.079 (0.8)	−0.003 (0.1)	0.102 (1.7)
ABILITY	0.491 (2.6)	0.504 (2.7)	0.028 (0.3)	0.029 (0.3)
TOPABIL	-2.346 (2.2)	-2.298 (2.2)	-1.327 (2.2)	−1.262 (2.1)
MABILITY	−0.628 (0.5)	−0.669 (0.5)	0.513 (0.7)	0.454 (0.6)
SDABILTY	1.680 (1.6)	1.719 (1.6)	2.084 (3.7)	2.076 (3.6)
MAJOR	−0.268 (0.2)	−1.027 (0.6)	−1.626 (1.5)	−1.516 (1.3)
TREND	0.050 (2.7)	0.042 (2.5)	0.053 (4.6)	0.045 (4.1)
GAMES	0.049 (0.6)	0.038 (0.5)	−0.061 (1.3)	−0.079 (1.7)
R-Square	0.08	0.09	0.06	0.05
N	424	424	881	881

Notes: Columns 1 and 2 are estimated on players who ranked are among the top 20 in prior year earnings. Columns 3 and 4 are estimated on the top five finishers in the given tournament.

in the prior year by high first-place prizes. The purpose of including this interaction is to test whether better players respond more favorably to increased skewness than do lesser players. Or stated differently, in light of Table 23.1, whether better players are at least less averse to increased skewness.

As seen in Table 23.2, the interaction of rank and the share allocated to first, as well as, between rank and the coefficient of skewness is positive but insignificant. Had the estimates been significant, they would have shown that the share of prize money going to first place exerts a greater negative influence on the performance of poorer players than on the performance of players highly ranked in terms of prior year earnings. Players with better expectations of a high finish based on past performance should react more favorably to increased skewness than poorer players. However, since the interaction is insignificant, no support for this result can be claimed.

Table 23.3 presents regressions identical to the first two columns of Table 23.1 but with two different samples. The first two columns of Table 23.3 are estimated on the sample of players finishing in the top twenty by prior year earnings. Columns 3 and 4 are estimated on the top five players in the given tournament, all of whom end the qualifying and match play round with an opportunity to win first place in the championship round. These estimates are done to determine if increased skewness has a positive influence on the scores of those few players facing increased prize gaps because of it. The results show that skewness reduces the scores of even the top twenty players by earnings in columns 1 and 2. Columns 3 and 4 show that even players who remain in contention for first place throughout the tournament do not exhibit higher scores in response to increased skewness. We are unable to find significant evidence of skewness increasing scores among any sample of players, even those who would benefit the most from it.

It was initially hypothesized that if players view the tournament as a whole and make one decision with respect to effort, then scores should increase with skewness. The results here suggest that the opposite is true. Players in aggregate had reduced scores due to increased skewness in Table 23.1 and better players could not definitively be said to act differently from poorer players based on the interaction terms in Table 23.2, nor based on the results in columns 1 and 2 of Table 23.3. It was also hypothesized that, if players are making multiple effort decisions as the tournament proceeds, then increased skewness should positively influence the scores of those in contention for the very top prizes. This implication is rejected based on columns 3 and 4 in Table 23.3. The results of the three tables support none of the hypotheses with respect to the influence of skewness on player scores. Summary statistics for the qualifying and match play rounds appear in Appendix Table 23.A1.

The last estimations conducted concern only the championship round data. Since these data are in a match play elimination format, it is exactly the structure modeled by Lazear and Rosen. The estimations in Table 23.4 explore the incentive effects from the prize gaps facing players and the incentive effects from differences in player ability. Two alternative measures of the prize gap are examined. The first is the simple prize gap between fourth and fifth place in the first match of the championship round, between third and fourth place in the second match, between second and third place in the third match, and between first and second place in the finals. The second measure is a weighted prize gap reflecting the difference between winning and losing the given match assuming a 0.5 probability of winning each subsequent match. Two alternative measures of the ability gap between players are also used. The first is the difference in the total prize money earned in the prior year and the second is the difference in the prize money rankings from the prior year.

Whereas in the previous tables, each observation was the average game score over the 42 games of the qualifying and match play rounds, in Table 23.4 the score variable is simply the score in a single game. Hence, the amount of information in an observation in Table 23.4 is much less and coefficients are largely statistically insignificant. The simple prize gap measure is the closest to significance and is positive, indicating evidence in favor of prize structure incentives. No other coefficients in the table approach statistical significance. The weighted prize gap did not outperform the simple prize gap, as would be expected if players consider the larger prizes awarded with potential subsequent wins in deciding their effort level. Summary statistics for the championship round are found in the Appendix Table 23.A2.

Table 23.4 Dependant variable: Score Data Pooled Across Tournaments and Different Samples of Players Championship Round Results—Match Play Elimination (absolute value t statistics)

	(1)	(2)	(3)	(4)	(5)	(6)
CONSTANT	210.6 (163.4)	211.1 (117.2)	211.9 (114.0)	214.0 (80.4)	211.9 (114.0)	214.0 (80.4)
PGAP	0.0004 (1.8)		0.0003 (1.1)		0.0003 (1.1)	
WPGAP		0.0001 (0.7)		−0.0001 (0.3)		−0.0001 (0.3)
CASHDIFF			0.000004 (0.2)	0.000004 (0.2)		
RANKDIFF					0.0138 (0.2)	0.0137 (0.2)
R-SQUARE	0.00	0.00	0.00	0.00	0.00	0.00
N	784.00	784.00	392.00	392.00	392.00	392.00

Variable Definitions:

SCORE	The score of the given player in a championship round match
RPRIZE1	Real prize for the finals winner (1985$)
RPRIZE2	Real prize for the finals loser (1985$)
RPRIZE3	Real prize for the second round loser (1985$)
RPRIZE4	Real prize for the third round loser (1985$)
RPRIZE5	Real prize for the fourth round loser (1985$)
PGAP	Immediate real prize gap assuming loss in subsequent round when the current round is not the finals
WPGAP	Weighted value of winning in the current round based on the current round's prizes and subsequent round prizes, assuming 50% probability of winning in each round.

Finals round: wpgap = rprize1 – rprize2

2nd Round: wpgap = 0.5 (rprize1 + rprize2) – rprize3

3rd Round: wpgap = 0.25 (rprize1 + rprize2) + 0.5 rprize3 – rprize4

4th Round: wpgap = 0.125 (rprize1 + rprize2) + 0.25 rprize3 + 0.5 rprize4 – rprize5

CASHX	The total prize money earned in prior year by the given player
CASHO	The total prize money earned in prior year by the given player's match play opponent
CASHDIFF	The difference in prior year earnings (CASHX – CASHO)
RANKX	Player's rank by prior year earnings for the top fifty players (50 = top earner)
RANKO	Rank of the opponent on the list of prior year money winners
RANKDIFF	The difference in prior year earnings rank (RANKX – RANKO)

5. CONCLUDING REMARKS

Tournament theory is premised on the notion that increased differences between prizes lead to increased effort and, hence, output. This implication was strongly upheld in professional bowling and adds to several articles in the literature finding evidence of prize structure incentive effects. However, no evidence was found to show that increases in the percentage of the total prize money going to first place or in the coefficient of skewness increased player scores as was hypothesized. Skewness decreased the scores of even those players in contention for top prizes. In bowling, it is likely that the pressure for skewed prize structures comes from tournament sponsors favoring large top prizes to create more spectator interest in the televised championship round portion of the tournament. Further exploration in different venues may shed some light on contradictory findings found here, particularly if more effort is focused on how different properties of the prize distribution affect incentives.

NOTES

1 See, e.g., Lazear and Rosen 1981; Holmstrom 1982; Carmichael 1983; Green and Stokey 1983; Nalebuff and Stiglitz 1983; O'Keefe, Viscusi and Zeckhauser 1986.
2 See Rosen 1986.
3 In the last game of the match play round, after a player has met each of his twenty-three opponents, a twenty-fourth game serves as a positional round that pairs the first- and second-place players, the third- and fourth-place players, and so forth.
4 Effort in tournament theory as originally modeled by Lazear and Rosen (1981) is not affected by the prize level but only by the differences between prizes.
5 The variable names in Tables 23.1 to 23.4 are defined at the bottom of Table 23.1.
6 This compares with a 1.1 stroke improvement for the same increase in the total prize over the entire tournament for professional golfers (Ehrenberg and Bognanno 1990).

REFERENCES

Bronars, Stephen, and Gerald Oettinger (2008). Giving 110 percent and going for broke: The effort and risk-taking responses of professional golfers to tournament incentives. Unpublished.

Brown, Jennifer (2008). Quitters never win: The (adverse) incentive effects of competing with superstars. Unpublished.

Carmichael, H. Lorne (1983). The agent-agents problem: Payment by relative output. *Journal of Labor Economics*, 1: 50–65.

Ehrenberg, Ronald, and Bognanno, Michael (1990a). Do tournaments have incentive effects? *Journal of Political Economy*, 98: 1307–1324.

Ehrenberg, Ronald, and Bognanno, Michael (1990b). The incentive effects of tournaments revisited: Evidence from the European PGA. *Industrial and Labor Relations Review*, 43: 74–88.

Garicano, Luis, and Palacios-Huerta, Ignacio (2005). Sabotage in tournaments: Making the beautiful game a bit less beautiful. Unpublished.

Green, Jerry, and Stokey, Nancy (1983). A comparison of tournaments and contracts. *Journal of Political Economy*, 91: 349–364.

Holmstrom, Bengt (1982). Moral hazard in teams. *Bell Journal of Economics*, 13: 324–340.

Lazear, Edward (1989). Pay equality and industrial politics. *Journal of Political Economy*, 97: 561–580.

Lazear, Edward and Rosen, Sherwin (1981). Rank order tournaments as an optimum labor contracts. *Journal of Political Economy*, 89: 841–864.

Maloney, Michael, and Terkun, Kristina (2002). Road warrior booty: Prize structures in motorcycle racing. *Contributions to Economic Analysis & Policy*, 1(1): article 3.

Nalebuff, Barry, and Stiglitz, Joseph (1983). Prizes and incentives: Towards a general theory of compensation and competition. *Bell Journal of Economics*, 14: 21–43.

O'Keefe, Mary, Viscusi, W. Kip, and Zeckhauser, Richard (1984). Economic contests: Comparative reward schemes. *Journal of Labor Economics*, 2: 27–56.

Rosen, Sherwin (1986). Prizes and incentives in elimination tournaments. *American Economic Review*, 76: 701–716.

Sunde, Uwe (2009). Heterogeneity and performance in tournaments: A test for incentive effects using professional tennis data. *Applied Economics*, 41: 3199–3208.

APPENDIX TABLES

Table 23.A1 Summary Statistics for the Qualifying and Match Play Round Data

Variable	N	Mean	Std. Dev.
MEANPINS	4423	214.66	6.82
TPRIZE (100,000s)	4423	1.26	0.43
SD	4423	3598.38	1511.4
FIRSTSHR	4423	0.19	0.02
COEFSKEW	4423	4.48	0.5
NPRIZES	4423	53.38	8.33
ABILITY	4274	214.8	2.43
TOPABIL	4423	217.53	0.57
MABILITY	4423	214.8	0.63
SDABILTY	4423	2.33	0.59
MAJOR	4423	0.1	0.3
TREND	4423	41.77	26.04
GAMES	4423	44.58	5.26
CASHRANK	1348	28.9	14.57

Table 23.A2 Summary Statistics: Championship Round Data

Variable	N	Mean	Std. Dev.
ROUND	800	2.5	1.12
SCORE	800	212	26.4
RPRIZE1	883	22914	10504
RPRIZE 2	883	12123	5702
RPRIZE 3	883	7372	3181
RPRIZE 4	883	5671	2077
RPRIZE 5	883	4627	1428
PGAP	784	4566	4798
WPGAP	784	8025	4875
CASHX	565	95753	48599
CASHDIFF	404	−63.9	69586
RANKX	565	32	13.4
RANKDIFF	404	−0.06	18.5

Index